The Garden
Plant Selector

THE ROYAL HORTICULTURAL SOCIETY

The Garden Plant Selector

DAVID JOYCE

photography by JERRY HARPUR

additional photography by MARCUS HARPUR

TED SMART

DEDICATION

This book is lovingly dedicated to
Anna, my family and my friends,
all of whom have been neglected
on its account.

First published in Great Britain in 1998
by Ryland Peters & Small
Cavendish House
51-55 Mortimer Street
London W1N 7TD

Text ©1998 David Joyce
Design and illustration © 1998
Ryland Peters & Small

This edition produced for
The Book People Ltd,
Hall Wood Avenue,
Haydock,
St Helens WA11 9UL

Printed and bound in China

ISBN 1-85613-610-8

A catalogue record for this book is
available from the British Library

Project Editor Caroline Davison

Art Editor Paul Tilby

Editors Polly Boyd, Jane Chapman,
    Mary Lambert, Helen Ridge,
    Lesley Riley, Stella Vayne

Editorial Assistant Maddalena Bastianelli

Designers Michael Whitehead,
    John Grain, Richard Scott,
    Alison Shackleton

Art Assistant Sailesh Patel

Picture Research Emily Hedges

Production Manager Kate Mackillop

Production Consultant
    Norman de Brackinghe

Art Director Jacqui Small

Publishing Director Anne Ryland

**Jacket photography by
Jerry and Marcus Harpur**

Front jacket:
Inset: RHS Rosemoor in Great Torrington,
Devon. In the foreground are red
Crocosmia 'Lucifer', yellow *Achillea
filipendulina* 'Gold Plate', yellow day
lilies (*Hemerocallis*), golden rod
(*Solidago*) and rudbeckias. In the
background are *Buddleja globosa* and
Robinia pseudoacacia 'Frisia'.

Back jacket:
Top left *Lobelia* 'Bees' Flame' and
    Crocosmia masoniorum
Top right *Taxus baccata* 'Standishii'
Bottom left *Tulipa kaiserkroon*
Bottom right *Ribes speciosum*

Page 1 *Bletilla striata*
Page 2 *Lobelia* 'Bees' Flame' and
    Crocosmia masoniorum
Page 3 *Iris* 'Cantab'
Page 45 *Molinia caerulea* subsp.
    arundinacea 'Windspiel', *Sedum*
    'Herbstfreude' and *Rudbeckia
    fulgida* var. *sullivantii* 'Goldsturm'
Endpapers *Helenium* 'Moerheim
    Beauty'

Contents

Introduction

Without an agricultural prelude, beginning with the early cultivation of grain crops in about 7000BC, the making of gardens is inconceivable. The history of gardens has, however, its own long course, with evidence of sophisticated gardens in ancient civilizations such as those of Assyria, China and Egypt. Along the way very large numbers of plants have been brought into cultivation, with a climax of introductions in the 19th and early 20th centuries. Miraculously, even now when it might be thought that the remotest regions of the world had long ago been scoured for plants of garden value, a small stream of introductions, usually made judiciously by specialists who are aware of the vulnerability of plant populations in the wild, adds to the number of plants in cultivation.

It is exhilarating to scan the vast armies of plants from the wild that are worth a place in gardens and also the countless auxiliaries ranked behind them that are the result of selection and breeding. It is, however, daunting to make choices from this vast array that will be relevant to a particular garden. A major purpose of this book is to provide gardeners with a "Plant Directory" (pp. 106–336) that represents a manageable selection of good garden plants suitable for growing in temperate regions. Although reflecting personal preferences, the comprehensive range takes account of the wisdom and experience of other gardeners. A high proportion of the plants described have received the Royal Horticultural Society's Award of Garden Merit (AGM), an accolade which the society reserves for plants that have proved to be of outstanding garden value. The "Plant Index" (pp. 342–51) shows which plants have received the award and also highlights a personal selection of 250 plants that would provide material for a delectable paradise garden, admittedly one with an astonishing range of growing conditions.

The plants in the "Plant Directory" are organized by major categories ("Trees"; "Shrubs"; "Conifers"; "Climbers"; "Roses; "Perennials"; "Bulbs, Corms and Tubers"; "Annuals and Biennials"; "Bamboos, Grasses and Grass-like Plants"; and "Ferns"). The plants are arranged alphabetically by the current internationally accepted botanical name. Common names with wide currency are given in

Opposite **This well-drained garden contains ornamental grasses mixed with flowering perennials. Orange-flowered red hot pokers (*Kniphofia*) contrast with small purple-flowered *Verbena bonariensis*, steely blue sea hollies (*Eryngium*), alliums and globe thistles (*Echinops*).**

Above A wide range of ornamentals can be grown in sunny borders with moist soil. Here, pure white *Phlox* grows alongside knotweed (*Persicaria*) and the yellow daisy-like flowers of *Ligularia dentata*.

Opposite The long summer display of this sunny garden results from bringing together plants from different regions of the world with others of garden origin. A hybrid lily, *Lilium* 'Fire King', and hybrid roses mingle with hollyhocks (*Alcea rosea*) from western Asia and *Lychnis coronaria* Alba Group and lavender (*Lavandula*) which are plants of southern Europe. The frilly edging is of lady's mantle (*Alchemilla mollis*), a plant tolerant of a wide range of conditions that is native to Turkey and the Caucasus.

Right The foliage of moisture-loving plants is often as important ornamentally as their flowers. Here, the strap-like leaves of *Iris sibirica* contrast with the rounded leaves of *Ligularia dentata* and the graceful stems of Solomon's seal (*Polygonatum hybridum*).

the entries and these, as well as genus synonyms, are listed in the "Plant Index". For those with an initial reluctance to come to grips with botanical names, the reality is they provide the only systematic and accurate way of writing and talking about plants. At bottom, the problem with botanical names often turns out to be pronunciation. The best advice is to use the bluffing techniques to which the experts sometimes resort.

To make the best use of the selection in the "Plant Directory" gardeners need to take on board the theme running through the first two sections, "Plants in the Wild" (pp. 16–47) and "Plants in Gardens" (pp. 50–101). Stated simply it is that plants differ in their adaptations and requirements and that the conditions in which they thrive in the wild give a clue to the conditions in which they and, in many cases, the plants derived from them, are most likely to succeed in gardens. The boundaries of the temperate world are too confining for this discussion, in which plants have been set in a worldwide context that includes tropical and arid conditions. Some of the plants used as illustrations in these two sections are well known but do not have entries in the "Plant Directory", usually because they are not suitable for outdoor cultivation in temperate regions.

In a book of this scope the relationships that exist between different natural environments and the plants adapted to them must be treated as broad patterns, although with illustrations from specific habitats and plant associations. The impact of climate, drainage, exposure to sun and shade, soil chemistry, in fact a very broad range of environmental factors, on what grows where has its own intrinsic interest, and prepares us for a fundamental truth of gardening, sometimes wilfully or ignorantly neglected: a successful garden is made by matching plants to the conditions available.

By definition a garden is an environment that has been meddled with, more or less artfully, even when it it has the semblance of natural woodland or a boggy streamside. A garden has, however, an underlying character, more frequently a mixture of characters, which is defined by the climate of the region, and by factors such as orientation, the chemistry of the soil and drainage. Cultivation can undoubtedly modify the character of a garden to some extent, improved drainage and the addition of organic matter, such as well-rotted compost, broadening the range of plants that can be brought together in a particular garden. Nonetheless, the principle remains that plants have optimum growing conditions and we make our gardening easier, less demanding of limited water resources and more of a piece when we are serious about choosing plants that are appropriate to the particular conditions to be found in our gardens.

Above There is growing recognition of the ornamental value of grasses such as *Miscanthus sinensis* and *Stipa tenuissima*, both of which prefer well-drained soil in full sun. They are useful for landscape planting but are also suitable for mixing with sun-loving perennials.

Opposite Several perennials have been naturalized in grass to create a meadow-like garden. They include thick swathes of purple-flowered *Verbena bonariensis*, which thrives in moist but well-drained soil in full sun.

Below Most bulbs that grow under the canopy of deciduous trees flower before the leaf cover develops. The American trout lily (*Erythronium revolutum*) naturalizes readily in conditions matching the moist dappled shade of its native habitat.

This applies to the vast number of selections and hybrids of horticulturally important groups, such as annuals and roses, as it does to species, although it is generally true to say that plants of garden origin tolerate a broader range of conditions than plants from the wild. If you are looking for plants for specific growing conditions, consult the section on "Plants for Special Conditions" (pp. 337–40) which contains lists of plants for a range of "problem" conditions such as dry shade or acid and alkaline soils.

An inescapable and alarming conclusion from any survey of plants in the wild is that human activity has had and continues to have a devastating and sinister impact on communities of living organisms in many areas of the world. Even if gardeners are not actively involved in promoting measures to safeguard the planet's threatened environments, they can help to conserve plants and their habitats by being vigilant consumers. Some plants, especially bulbs and orchids, are still collected indiscriminately from the wild, timber is harvested with no thought to the renewal of the forest and peat is greedily extracted from fragile habitats for use as a soil conditioner and planting medium. Buying plants only from reputable sources, selecting timber that has been certified as harvested from plants that are managed on a renewal basis and choosing to use substitutes for peat are the sort of measures consumers can take in order to redress the balance in favour of conservation.

Above Italian cypresses (*Cupressus sempervirens*) and lavender (*Lavandula*) suggest long dry Mediterranean summers but here they thrive in sun and well-drained soil in the famous gardens of Tresco Abbey on the Isles of Scilly.

Right The ornamental onions from Central Asia such as the purple-flowered *Allium hollandicum* are adapted to low rainfall and long hot summers. In gardens a good match for them is the perennial wallflower *Erysimum* 'Bowles' Mauve', which thrives in well-drained positions in full sun and flowers over a long season.

Far left The yellow-spired mullein (*Verbascum*) and the frothy white *Crambe cordifolia* do well in full sun on alkaline soils, even those that are poor.

PLANTS IN THE WILD

The Making of Plant Communities

Plants are a major component of forests and other natural environments but they are only part of a complex self-perpetuating community of living things in a distinctive landscape. The term "ecosystem" refers to an environment and all the life forms particular to it. The interrelationships of life forms are complex enough in, say, temperate deciduous woodland but much more so in tropical rainforests where ecosystems fizz with the interplay of countless living things (see p. 27). The forces giving ecosystems their essential character and marking their boundaries are environmental. This quickens our interest as gardeners because the broad factors, particularly climatic, that influence plant communities in nature also affect the conditions in our gardens.

To be fully relevant to gardeners the broad brushstroke approach that follows needs qualification. Within any environment a specific set of conditions, or habitat, is required for a community of species to exist. Trees such as the silver birch (*Betula pendula*) and many conifers can be found over very wide areas. But there are other plants and life forms that are much more specific in their requirements. Their habitats are determined by a wide range of variables within the broad environment. Of these variables among the most important are microclimates, the atmospheric conditions modified by factors such as slope, orientation to the sun and shelter from wind. In any natural environment, as in a garden, microclimates create a patchwork of conditions that often allow a wide range of plants to grow within a small area.

TEMPERATURE

An ascent in 1802 of Mount Chimborazo in Ecuador, rising to a height of 20,000ft (6,100m), led the great Prussian naturalist Alexander von Humboldt to the conclusion that zonation of vegetation on mountains paralleled latitudinal zonation from the equator to the poles. The exactitude of his vegetation zones was oversimplified but the connection he made is not surprising. In fact many factors make it difficult to relate precisely the distribution of plants to isotherms, the lines on a map linking the same temperature readings (calculated, say, as averages). Yet for all plants there is a range of tolerance and an optimum temperature at which, all other factors being equal, they will grow best.

Very high temperatures, 104°F (40°C) or more, cause an increase in transpiration and difficulties for the proper function of enzymes that play a key role in biochemical reactions. Even so there are plants, such as date palms (*Phoenix dactylifera*) in Saharan oases, that survive scorching temperatures. Cold as a limitation to plant growth is more familiar to most gardeners. In temperate regions where the climate is seasonal, many plants lose their leaves in autumn, shutting down until favourable growing conditions return in spring. Frost, a killer in the garden because we often try to grow plants outside their natural range,

Top The vegetation of Japan reflects varying climatic influences over its four main mountainous islands. The rainfall is generally high, the south-east monsoon bringing heavy summer rains but, due to the north-west monsoon, the centre has cold winters. Much of the original vegetation was deciduous forest with a rich layer of herbaceous plants.

Above The coastal plain on the Caribbean side of Costa Rica has a hot humid climate and a tropical vegetation to match. The flowering plant is a species of *Heliconia*, many species of which are found in tropical forest in Central and South America. Some species, however, are adapted to the drier conditions of open scrub.

requires an adaptation of the cells to prevent them being ruptured by the formation of ice. The plant-less polar regions of today are a reminder that the present distribution of plants has been profoundly influenced by climatic changes of the distant past, the ice ages accounting for many characteristic features of the vegetation in Europe and North America.

The temperature at which the seed of a plant germinates best has much to do with the climatic conditions in which it is found growing naturally. The seed of most plants from cold regions only germinates if subjected to a cold period. Many Mediterranean plants germinate at relatively low temperatures, about 50°F (10°C). In a Mediterranean climate germination in winter, the wet season, gives seedlings the best chance of becoming established before the long dry summer. In habitats where the rainfall is irregular, as in the grassland of steppes, plants can germinate over a broader range of temperatures, the key to successful establishment being an adequate but unpredictable water supply.

RAINFALL, HUMIDITY AND MOISTURE IN THE SOIL

Water is vital for plants, as it is for all living creatures. It provides the hydrogen for photosynthesis, the chain of chemical reactions in which plants, using the green pigment chlorophyll, convert solar energy into sugars. Water carries in solution the nutrients that are essential for healthy growth. For non-woody plants it plays yet another role, acting as a filling that gives the structure rigidity. Plants take up water through fine root hairs, situated near the root tip, but lose it in the process known as transpiration through their pores (stomata), the openings on the leaves through which gases pass in and out. To survive, plants must strike a balance between intake and loss. In a stable environment where there is a regular and generous supply of moisture, plants maintain this balance without special adaptations, although they do have guard cells that can close the pores and reduce transpiration.

Different regions of the world show great variations in rainfall and in many the balancing act that plants perform can only be sustained because of special adaptations. Some areas of desert may go without measurable precipitation for years. Persistent low temperatures that lock water in the form of snow and ice, as in the polar regions, create

Top Alaska is a region of mountainous topography and harsh climate, a large part of it lying inside the Arctic Circle. The main vegetation is coniferous forest and, in the north, vast expanses of tundra, a treeless region that usually has an underlying permafrost (see pp. 36–37).

Above centre (left) The saguaro cactus (*Carnegia gigantea*) epitomizes desert Arizona where it may live, despite low rainfall, for more than 200 years, reaching a height of up to 60ft (18m). Water is stored in the plant's succulent stems and a highly efficient and wide-spreading root system gathers available moisture.

Above centre (right) In desert and semi-desert regions, as here in South Africa, rain triggers a dramatic but usually short flowering season, in which annuals rapidly complete their whole life cycle.

Above High humidity, as in this temperate Japanese forest, encourages the rich growth of mosses. Bacteria, fungi, lichens, mosses and ferns may not have the glamour of flowering plants but are no less important ecologically.

17

"frozen deserts". In some regions of the world rainfall is very unevenly distributed throughout the year, drought following flood in a regular pattern. In others rain is a daily saturating event. Rainfall itself is not the only source of moisture. In mountainous regions precipitation is in the form of snow, providing a protective cover in winter and melt water in spring. In some areas condensation from mist and fog is a critically important source of moisture. The strip of California where the coastal redwoods (*Sequoia sempervirens*) are found would have a summer as long and dry as the rest of the region without mist and fog.

In general, there is a marked correlation between distribution of rainfall and types of vegetation, the gradation from forest to grassland and desert reflecting a general reduction in the amount of moisture for plants. Among the most remarkable of all adaptations in plants are those to drought. In seasonally dry areas of the tropics many plants are deciduous but more radical adaptations, such as succulence in the case of cacti, are found in almost waterless deserts where alternation of searing heat and icy cold add to the harshness of the environment. At the other extreme are plants in the zone where land and water meet and these too require adaptations for a life in poorly aerated soils. Among the most striking adaptations are the knobby upright growths from the roots of the swamp cypress (*Taxodium distichum*).

SUN AND SHADE

The prime biological process, photosynthesis, relies on light as its energy source. All green plants must have light but different plants have different requirements. Differences in light demand and shade tolerance, part of the genetic constitution of plants, are major factors in the composition and ordering of plant communities. Among the plants most hungry for light are quick-growing annuals, rapidly producing numerous seeds in their short lives. The germination of their seed is often triggered by light of a certain intensity. Slower growing are pioneer trees, such as the pines (*Pinus*), which colonize open ground, whether disturbed by natural forces such as fire or clearing by human activity. Plants that are adapted to shade are often slow growing and in many instances do not rely exclusively on flowering and seed production to maintain their populations. Shade tolerance, however, is not necessarily fixed for life. Tree seedlings, for example, generally show much greater shade tolerance than adults of the same species.

The light regime created by the canopy of a forest has a marked effect on the growth of plants beneath it and even in low scrub there is a shady understorey. Dense coniferous forests usually have very little undergrowth and few herbaceous plants grow under the light-trapping canopy of beech (*Fagus sylvatica*). In temperate deciduous forests some plants of the understorey avoid the periods of lowest light

Top left Heath and moorland, which are dominated by heather or ling (*Calluna vulgaris*) and species of *Erica*, are found on acid soils in many parts of Europe, often merging with bog and tundra.

Top The European beech (*Fagus sylvatica*) does well on chalk and limestone soils, beech "hangers" being a feature of the chalk downs in southern Britain.

Above Ericaceous plants – that is, members of the heath family – are generally intolerant of alkaline soils. Attractive representatives from California include the pink-flowered *Phyllodoce breweri* and *Cassiope mertensiana*.

intensity, when trees are in leaf, by growing, flowering and setting seed before the foliage of the canopy develops. In coppiced woodland timber is regularly harvested without trees being felled. In these conditions a mixture of herbaceous plants and bulbs benefits from periodic exposure to relatively high levels of light. The floor of a tropical rainforest is usually heavily shaded. Lianas grow quickly towards the light but the herbaceous layer has to make do with sun flecks, spots of light that get through gaps in the canopy. There is strong evidence that much of the photosynthesis carried out by plants of the relatively thin herbaceous layer occurs during the brief periods when light is most intense.

SOIL

The detailed processes of soil formation have to be set against the large-scale geological processes that, like the ice ages, have played a role in the distribution of plants. Among the most intriguing relationships in the plant world are those that suggest how the continents drifted into their present positions after the breakup of a single large land mass.

The raw material of soil is bare rock, which is broken down by various weathering processes such as frost. Soils provide an anchor for plants and hold the water, inorganic nutrients and air that plants need to make satisfactory growth. However, they vary enormously in their composition, their chemistry, their structure, and their nutrient and organic content. Several broad soil types are strongly associated with particular types of climate and vegetation. Among the poorest soils are those of the tundra, north of the tree line in the Northern Hemisphere. It consists of partially decomposed peat and a sticky clay (gley) sitting over permanently frozen subsoil (permafrost). Coniferous forest and heath in the cold north have podzols, the Russian name referring to the ash-grey colour of the soil. The brown earths are typical of temperate

Below Shade from the forest canopy inhibits the growth of many tree seedlings. Their chance of getting established may come when the canopy is removed by fire or with the timely collapse of a forest giant. Other trees show a tolerance of shade when they are seedlings but not as adults.

Bottom In this Californian landscape, which is momentarily brilliant with flowers, low rainfall and fast-draining soil limit the growth of trees and shrubs, while openness allows light-demanding plants such as annuals to flourish when the conditions are favourable.

deciduous forest, the black chernozems, rich and valuable as agricultural land, of humid grasslands. Heavy rains leach the soils of tropical forests. These lateritic soils, consisting of red clay coloured by iron and aluminium oxides and low in nutrients, are most common where there are alternating wet and dry seasons.

There are also local soils, usually reflecting topography or the character of the underlying rock. Although they may present problems to many plants, others are specially adapted to them. In poorly drained soils, for example, the pores are filled with water and there is little air containing the oxygen needed for respiration. Saline conditions near the sea complicate the taking up of water and comparable problems are found, as well as the lack of water, in desert areas where there are accumulations of salt. Deficiencies in or toxic levels of certain minerals can also pose limits to plant growth. Even when the minerals necessary for successful growth and reproduction are present in the soil, marked acidity or alkalinity may prevent them being available to plants. The degree of acidity or alkalinity is measured on a pH scale from 0 to 14. Most plants have the best chance of taking up the available nutrients when the soil has a pH of 6.5; that is, nearly neutral. Marked acidity or alkalinity also affects bacterial and fungal activity in the soil, which is responsible for the breakdown of organic matter.

WIND

Large-scale wind movements cause the circulation of water vapour and form an integral part of worldwide weather patterns that result from the interraction of atmosphere and oceans powered by the heat of the sun. In areas of the world where there is a reasonably uniform distribution of rainfall the scale of global circulatory systems may hardly be evident except when there appears to be an aberration in the pattern, as happens periodically with the El Niño effect, originating in the eastern Pacific. The case is different in South-east Asia, where the monsoon is a seasonal wind that blows from the north-east in winter and from the south-east from about April to October, sweeping in from the Indian Ocean with heavy rains that are life-giving but also potentially destructive. Elsewhere, wind can be an important factor in the making and moulding of landscape, as in the formation of the loess plateau of north-west China, composed of wind-blown particles from the desert interior. Drought, overgrazing, the cultivation of marginal lands and combinations of these allow wind the upper hand with consequences on the scale of the sheet erosion in America's Great Plains in the 1930s.

Apart from its role in pollination and in the distribution of seeds, the main direct influence of wind on plants is to increase the rate at which leaves lose water. Wind can also cause a sand blasting effect or more moderate abrasion from the particles it carries and violent gusts can break branches and wrench off leaves. In coastal areas salt carried by fierce winds can affect plants well beyond the normal spray zone.

Above At high altitudes the force of prevailing winds, as in the Selkirk Mountains of British Columbia which are shown here, can strongly modify the growth of plants. Above the tree line – the limit at which trees grow to approximately their normal size – trees are dwarfed and shaped by the wind so that the branches only develop on the side away from the wind.

Few plants seem to be adapted to irregular violent winds but some palms can survive typhoons and other tropical storms, probably because their leaves are held loosely and the divisions of the leaves offer little resistance to wind. The large undivided leaves of bananas (*Musa*) have regular strips of weak tissue running at right angles to the rib, strong winds causing these to tear but leaving the shredded leaf able to function. The most marked adaptations to winds, however, are found near the sea and in deserts. The leaves are often leathery, hairy or waxy and greatly reduced in size. The pores may be reduced in number and recessed. In alpine and tundra regions plants are compact and often huddled in close mats and cushions for mutual protection.

HUMAN INFLUENCE

Over thousands of years human exploitation has modified natural vegetation in many parts of the earth. Forests have been felled, grasslands ploughed, hillsides grazed, minerals extracted, and vast areas built over with factories, housing and roads or contaminated with waste. Humans have also intentionally and accidentally introduced plants and other life forms to areas where they were not native. Some of these are now weeds, pests and diseases of major significance.

The scale of environmental devastation, with the loss of habitats and species, has undermined our confidence in the resilience of the natural world. But prompt action is needed. Although gardens can play a role as refuges for endangered plants, this is a last-ditch solution and not a substitute for protecting self-sustaining communities in the wild.

Far left The combination of wind, salt spray and negligible soil limits the range of plants that can grow on rocky coastlines. Sea thrift (*Armeria maritima*) is widely distributed as a coastal plant in the Northern Hemisphere and is also found in mountainous regions.

Below left Cultivation has extended the range of many plants. The olive (*Olea europaea*), one of the classic plants of the Mediterranean, is now widely cultivated in regions with hot dry summers and mild moist winters. The field poppy (*Papaver rhoeas*), an annual that almost certainly originated in the eastern Mediterranean, has been widely distributed in the world along with the seed of the cereals among which it grows as a weed.

Below Tropical rainforest is the most seriously threatened of all natural ecosystems. Burning and clearing, as here in Brazil, produces land with very short-lived fertility.

Major Plant Communities

FORESTS, WOODS AND WOODLAND

The dedication of sacred groves and the veneration of individual trees are an indication of the reverence and awe that since ancient times humankind has felt towards the largest members of the plant world. The survival in China of the maidenhair tree (*Ginkgo biloba*), a unique living representative of an order of seed-bearing trees earlier than conifers in the geological record and unknown in the wild, is most probably due to its cultivation in the grounds of palaces and temples.

Forests, woods (usually smaller in extent than forests) and woodland (either a wood or a habitat where the trees do not form a continuous canopy) have been greatly modified by human activity almost everywhere. Changes in climate may have contributed to the transformation of the pre-classical vegetation that covered the Mediterranean region but, centuries ago, land clearance, felling for timber and firewood, heavy grazing (especially by goats) and soil erosion also reduced the original evergreen forest to a form of scrub (see "Scrubland", pp. 30-31). Elsewhere in the world what seem like vast areas of untouched forest are in most cases greatly reduced from their original extent and very often modified by human activity. In some parts of the world, the level of human influence has been stabilized and special reserves and national parks provide some protection for what survives. Elsewhere, particularly in the tropics (see "Tropical Forests", pp. 26-29), there is reckless exploitation that has implications for us all.

In temperate regions with moderate annual rainfall – about 30-60in (750-1,500mm) – the natural plant cover is deciduous woodland. During the cold winters that are a feature of much of the temperate zone, the movement of sap slows down and eventually stops as the temperature falls. Dropping leaves is a way of minimizing water loss when water cannot be replaced from the ground, particularly at a time of year when photosynthesis is at its most inefficient in any case because of low light levels. Deciduous woodland is uncommon in the Southern Hemisphere: in Tierra del Fuego at the tip of Argentina, forests of Antarctic beech (*Nothofagus antarctica*) drop their leaves in autumn, but members of the same genus in other parts of the hemisphere are evergreen. In the Northern Hemisphere, however, deciduous forest once covered much of western Europe, eastern North America and parts of Asia, including Japan. One consequence of the ice ages is that western Europe has a relatively small range of tree species. Furthermore, the forests that survive have been influenced by

Below The woodland of Britain has been greatly modified by human activity over many centuries. Oaks (*Quercus robur* and *Q. petraea*) have been favoured at the expense of other deciduous trees. Here, oak is the main constituent of Padley Wood in the Peak District.

Bottom left Shade-tolerant ferns and mosses provide a lush floor to a moist mixed woodland of deciduous trees and conifers in New York State.

Bottom centre Even the grandest forest trees succumb to death and decay, bacteria and fungi eventually breaking down the woody carcasses. In the cool woods and forests of Sweden, as here, the process is slow.

human activity. Traditional methods of woodland management have, however, helped to maintain some plant communities. Coppicing and pollarding of trees such as common or English oak (*Quercus robur*) and hornbeam (*Carpinus betulus*) let light onto the woodland floor, a periodic exposure that favours a number of bulbs and herbaceous perennials such as bluebells (*Hyacinthoides non-scripta*) and primulas (*Primula vulgaris*). The deciduous forest of north-east North America and Asia is much richer in tree species and in the plants of the shrub and herbaceous layers. In Japan, as well as in New England, many maples (*Acer*) give the forest its autumn brilliance.

The deciduous forest contains relatively few climbers and the main epiphytic, or perching, plants are ferns. The shrubs and herbaceous plants vary according to soil moisture and chemistry, root competition from trees as well as the microclimate, which is influenced by the density of the tree canopy and other factors. In woods of common beech (*Fagus sylvatica*), the foliage is very efficient at trapping light but it prevents rain reaching the forest floor and casts dense shade with the result that there is little undergrowth. Even where the canopy is lighter, as in mixed woodland containing ash (*Fraxinus excelsior*) and hornbeam, most plants of the woodland floor have to make growth and flower before the tree foliage is fully developed. In heavy shade, the main plants of the woodland floor are ferns.

Below and bottom right Sugar maple (*Acer saccharum*) and silver maple (*Acer saccharinum*) are among the trees that give the deciduous forest which survives in Vermont in north-east USA its exceptionally rich colouring in the autumn. Other species found growing with these maples in the forests include American beech (*Fagus grandifolia*), white ash (*Fraxinus americana*) as well as red oak (*Quercus rubra*).

Many broad-leaved trees and shrubs of tropical and subtropical regions are evergreen, that is, although the leaves are replaced on a regular basis, they are not all lost at the same time. Most conifers are evergreen. In evolutionary terms, it is approximately 80 to 90 million years since conifers were overtaken by flowering plants. The key advance of the flowering plants was the enclosure of the ovules, which develop into seeds when fertilized. Despite the apparently evolutionary handicap of having naked seeds, which are in fact protected in woody cones, conifers remain highly successful plants in many parts of the world. Although low in the number of species represented, some of the vast coniferous stands in the Northern Hemisphere are among the largest forests in the world. Big trees or giant redwoods (*Sequoiadendron giganteum*), which can reach 265ft (80m) tall with a diameter at the base of 33ft (10m), form groves at altitudes of 5,000–8,000ft (1,524–2,438m) in a belt about 250 miles (400km) long on the western slopes of the Californian Sierra Nevada. It is estimated that some have lived to more than 4000 years. Even longer lived by several hundred years are specimens of the bristlecone pine (*Pinus aristata*), found at over 10,000ft (3,000m) in eastern California and Nevada.

Conifers are fast-growing "pioneer" plants that produce valuable timber and pulpwood. Pioneer plants, usually at a disadvantage because their seedlings are intolerant of shade, are quick off the mark when trees fall or fire clears the ground as part of the natural cycle. In fact, some pines need fire for the cones to release seed. It is not surprising that the Scots pine (*Pinus sylvestris*) and other conifers can be successfully planted on exposed sites, stabilizing sandy soils, forming shelter belts and protecting slower growing and more vulnerable trees. The success of *Pinus radiata* as a timber tree is astonishing when the scale of its plantations on poor soils in many parts of the world is set against its distribution in the wild, where it is confined almost entirely to a few small areas on the Monterey Peninsula of California.

The boreal forest forms a broad belt, as much as 500 miles (800 km) wide, across North America, Europe and Siberia. At its northern extreme, before it peters out in the tundra, the forest becomes more open. In the taiga, as this chilly parkland is called, stunted conifers such as black spruce (*Picea mariana*) tip drunkenly in shallow soils above permafrost. The narrow, conical form with its drooping branches furnished with needles helps shed snow and reduces the risk of injury. The small needles are adapted to conserving moisture and, because they are evergreen, photosynthesis can take place when conditions are favourable. Larches (*Larix*), among the few deciduous conifers, are among the hardiest survivors; the northernmost forest in the world in eastern Siberia is dominated by *L. gmelinii*. One of the few plants on the floor of these dark forests is dwarf cornel (*Cornus canadensis*).

To the south of this belt coniferous forests commonly form a conspicuous zone on mountain slopes between broad-leaved forest and alpine tundra. In an area of North America known as the cordillera, coniferous forests of trees such as Douglas fir (*Pseudotsuga menziesii*) sweep up from the lowlands to a sharply marked tree line and form some of the most magnificent stands of trees in the world, the species varying with altitude and latitude. Where the summers are not too dry, as is the case on the west side of the Olympic Mountains in Washington, the dominant trees are sitka spruce (*Picea sitchensis*) and western hemlock (*Tsuga heterophylla*). The mossy floor of these forests is thick with ferns. Along a narrow strip at the south-west margin of the cordillera, frequent fog modifies what would otherwise be a dry Mediterranean climate. Thanks to this climatic quirk, the world's tallest tree, the coastal redwood (*Sequoia sempervirens*) forms dense stands in which individual specimens regularly reach a height of 330ft (100m).

The distinctive conifers from the Southern Hemisphere include the spiny-leaved monkey puzzle (*Araucaria araucana*) as well as its relatives. These conifers are often plants of mixed forest, the New Zealand kauri (*Agathis australis*) usually towering massively among evergreen broad-leaved trees. The evergreen rainforests of warm temperate areas have a distinct annual rhythm, but their high rainfall, about 60–120in (1,500–3,000mm), is distributed quite evenly throughout the year. There are many similarities between these temperate areas and tropical and subtropical rainforest, especially that found at higher altitudes. Climbers, such as species of *Clematis* and *Rubus* that are familiar in temperate regions, and epiphytes, including orchids, are common. The numerous ferns include some, such as species of *Dicksonia*, that have tree-like proportions.

(For plants in gardens, see pp. 66–67; pp. 70–71; pp. 72–73).

Top left A Pacific dogwood (*Cornus nuttallii*) here frames a stand of the big tree or giant redwood (*Sequoiadendron giganteum*) in the Sequoia National Forest, California. No other tree can match the giant redwood for bulk. It is remarkably resistant to fire and there is a healthy population of young trees in the groves but these are, nonetheless, limited to a small area of the Sierra Nevada.

Left Although conifers can be found in many regions of the world, their key territory is the cold north and the mountain ranges of the Northern Hemisphere. Their evergreen foliage, adapted to conserve moisture, allows them to make growth when conditions are favourable without having to put energy into the formation of leaves.

Below The warm temperate rainforests of Tasmania have many similarities with tropical and subtropical rainforest. A striking feature is the wealth of tree ferns.

TROPICAL FORESTS

To those whose view of the plant kingdom has been formed by the woods, hedgerows, fields and meadows of temperate regions, a first encounter with the luxuriance of a tropical rainforest is startling and even disorienting. The space-grabbing energy of tropical plants makes their temperate relatives seem prissily decorous. Their curious flowers imply ingenious sexual habits. The variety is so overwhelming that by comparison the temperate flora can seem impoverished. Perhaps most bewildering of all is the apparent abandonment of seasonal rhythms. Instead of a synchronized burst in spring heralding a season of growth followed by autumnal decline and winter dormancy, there seems to be random flowering, fruiting and leaf fall throughout the year. If the impression left by tropical forests is one of biological chaos, this is misleading. Their rhythms, far from fully understood, are interdependent

Below Palms can be found in a wide range of habitats. Although these trees are mainly native to tropical areas, there is also a European species, *Chamaerops europaeus,* which grows on sandy or rocky slopes as well as in scrub in the western Mediterranean. The fan palms, such as species of *Licuala,* a genus which is strongly represented in South-east Asia, are well adapted with their large grooved leaves to catch the light penetrating the canopy of the rainforest and to shed heavy falls of water. The species illustrated here is growing in lowland rainforest in Queensland, Australia.

Right The canopy of this tropical rainforest in Belize in Central America is composed of a large number of species through which isolated taller palms emerge.

Below Even where water courses run though tropical rainforest, light penetrates the dense canopy only as fleeting patches and flecks.

Bottom left and right Many of the tropical trees familiar as ornamentals come from areas with a marked wet and dry season (see p. 29). This is so for jacaranda (*Jacaranda mimosifolia*) from savanna country in Brazil, deciduous in the dry season and with violet-blue flowers before the leaves open. The pink poui or rosy trumpet tree (*Tabebuia rosea*), the national plant of El Salvador, is seasonally deciduous and usually flowers when leafless.

in a number of complex and fragile ways: there are trees loaded with epiphytes, birds and bats acting as agents of pollination, fruit-eating monkeys helping disperse seed, and creatures and organisms, including fungi and microscopic bacteria, recycling the forest's detritus.

Tropical rainforest is found in a number of areas near the equator, on a large scale in the Amazon basin of South America, in western Africa and in South-east Asia. These regions have a very high annual rainfall: over 78in (2,000mm) is normal and in some areas it exceeds 395in (10,000mm). In the tropical heartlands the sluicing of torrential rains can be expected throughout the year, the temperature remains fairly constant, with a yearly mean of about 79–81°F (26–27°C), and the humidity (near saturation most of the time) is exhausting for those unaccustomed to it. The phenomenal growth creates a misleading impression of soil fertility. As rain water leaches through the soil, it removes nutrients and what is returned through decomposition is not

retained. The forest is its own powerhouse and once the tree cover is felled, as is happening at a staggering rate, the future of the land is very bleak. Successful farming is short-lived, the nutrients being quickly exhausted, and heavy erosion leads to permanent degradation of the land. Tropical habitats and species are being lost irrevocably with no compensating long-term benefits.

The distinctive hierarchical structure of the trees in a tropical forest has no parallel in deciduous broadleaf and coniferous forests. Very tall trees, 150–200ft (45–60m) high and only branching near the crown, stand above the general level of the forest. Like most of the vegetation in the rainforest these exposed trees or "emergents" are shallow-rooted but buttress roots help to stabilize them. The layer of trees below them, usually without buttress roots, forms a canopy at a height of about 100–130ft (30–39m). Beneath this, there is usually a third layer of narrow-crowned trees and what might be thought of as a shrub layer, in which palms are often a conspicuous feature. Many plants in the lower layers have leaves with elongated tips or "drip-tips",

Far left The rainforests of South-east Asia, dominated by tall buttressed trees covered with trailing lianas and supporting numerous epiphytes, are the most complex in the tropics. In Sumatra, where this photograph was taken, there is high rainfall throughout the year, which is brought by both the south-east and north-east monsoons. Forests that are rich in trees of commercial value have, however, suffered from heavy exploitation.

Top left The emerald creeper or jade vine (*Strongylodon macrobotrys*) gets its name from the spectacular trail of blue-green flowers that hang from the twining stems. In its vigour this native of the Philippines is like many tropical climbers, growing from the shady floor of the forest to a height of 70ft (22m) or more.

Centre left (top) Orchids are found in almost every region of the world and in a wide range of habitats. It is in the tropics, however, that they achieve their fullest development. Many tropical species, such as this *Cymbidium*, are epiphytic, with grey or white tangled aerial roots. The green tip of these roots absorbs moisture and nutrients.

Centre left (bottom) A large number of tropical ferns are epiphytic, including the widely distributed bird's-nest fern (*Asplenium nidus*).

Bottom left A large number of the bromeliads, such as this species of *Nidularium*, are plants of tropical rainforest and many of them are epiphytic.

Below On the floor of this Costa Rican forest, ferns compete with various shade-tolerant herbaceous plants, including a species of *Aphelandra* that is in flower.

which allow water to run off freely. As well as being very rich in species, the composition of the rainforest is extraordinarily diverse even in quite small areas and it is rare for a single species to dominate.

From ground level it is very difficult to get an idea of what is going on in the tropical forest. The place to be is in the canopy, where insects, birds, mammals (including pollinating bats), reptiles and amphibians are busy in a way that can scarcely be guessed at from below. Some fresh insights into the complex life of the tropical forest have been made possible by specialized climbing techniques that have given scientists access to the canopy. It is possible, as a poor second best, to get an idea from the channel of a river of the activity taking place high up. When the forest is looked at from such a vantage point two other categories of plants stand out: lianas and epiphytes. The criss-crossing stems of lianas occur almost everywhere but are very thick along watercourses. These nimble vines, rooted in the floor of the forest but desperate for the light of the canopy, make up the tangle that is the principal obstacle to those penetrating the forest.

Light is also important for a large number of epiphytes. These are perching plants that shun the dark forest floor for a better position higher up in the trees. The great variety of these flowering plants and ferns, staged at various levels, make the upper levels of the forest look like hanging gardens. Many epiphytes have special roots which help secure the plant and absorb moisture from the air. This is so for the large numbers of epiphytic tropical orchids (see pp. 100–101). The epiphytic bromeliads, mainly from Central and South America, include a number that have become popular ornamentally for their curious flowers. These are cupped in a colourful "leaf-vase" at the centre of the leaf rosette, forming a reservoir for the plant. Not all the plants lodged in the canopy are as innocent as they seem. Some of the figs, including the weeping fig (*Ficus benjamina*), widely grown as a houseplant, turn stranglers if their seed germinates in the crook of a branch. For a while the fig seems like a simple epiphyte, but with a criss-cross of roots around its host. Eventually it sends down vertical roots and once it gets its feet in the ground it forms a strangling network of roots, although shade cast by its top growth is probably the real killer. When the host dies and decays the fig is left as a self-supporting cylinder.

Far from all tropical areas have the rainfall to support true rainforest. Where there is a distinct dry season, as in areas affected by the monsoon, the forest is less varied and many of the trees are semi-deciduous or deciduous, losing their leaves during the dry season and most coming into flower with the rains. Some widely planted ornamentals in tropical and subtropical regions, such as the flamboyant tree (*Delonix regia*) of Madagascar, come from regions in the tropics with a seasonal rhythm. In areas with a long dry season the forest does not form a continuous cover and is reduced to trees such as thorny acacias scattered in grassland (see p. 33).

(For plants in gardens, see pp. 98–101).

Left In Greece the low scrub that covers hot dry slopes is known as phrygana. Garrigue, its name in France, and to a lesser extent the taller scrub called maquis, are surprisingly rich in species. There are many aromatic shrubs such as rosemary (*Rosmarinus*) and numerous bulbs. Species of rock or sun rose (*Cistus*), some of which are flowering here, are found in both kinds of scrub.

Below The Cape Peninsula of South Africa has a unique and very rich flora. Most of the region has evergreen scrub, Mediterranean in character but with a different range of shrubs, including proteas and numerous species of *Erica*. In spring and summer annuals, bulbs and perennials flower in profusion.

SCRUBLAND

Of all the words describing scrub none are more evocative than maquis and Corsican macchia, with their romantic associations of banditry and resistance in trackless wildnesses. Scrub has many names, describing the plant associations found in a range of similar habitats: chaparral in California, fynbos in South Africa, garrigue as well as maquis in France, mallee scrub in Australia, matorral in Chile, phrygana in Greece, and tomillares in Spain. These represent variants of a vegetation found in the Mediterranean or in regions with a similar climate characterized by hot dry summers and relatively mild winters. The moderate annual rainfall, in the range of 12–36in (300–900mm), is concentrated in the winter months.

In addition to the vegetation of these regions, there are large tracts of continental interiors with semi-desert scrub. South of the Sahara, for example, in areas where the rainfall may be as little as 5in (130mm) a year, acacias and other thorny plants, which are sometimes mixed with succulents such as some of the shrubby euphorbias, form open scrubland that reaches a height of about 6ft (1.8m) with an understorey of thorny herbs. Scrub also occupies various marginal zones where climatic and environmental factors limit the growth of trees. For instance, there is often a shrub zone above the tree line in mountains.

The influence of the classical world on western culture permeates even our attitude to plants, many from the Mediterranean region holding a privileged place in gardens. The maquis itself, of which many of these plants are a constituent, is composed largely of hard-leaved evergreen shrubs or small trees that make more or less dense cover to a height of about 10ft (3m). The maquis may be the natural plant community in some parts of the Mediterranean but elsewhere it is certainly the result of modifications to evergreen forest, including the clearing of holm oak (*Quercus ilex*), that once covered large areas. Characteristic plants of the maquis include: strawberry trees (*Arbutus*), rock or sun roses (*Cistus*), myrtle (*Myrtus communis*), olive (*Olea europaea*), Jerusalem sage (*Phlomis fruticosa*), lentisc (*Pistacia lentiscus*) and Spanish broom (*Spartium junceum*).

Right In the vast, ancient island of Australia, the genus *Eucalyptus* holds a dominant position. Among the 500 or so species in the genus some are forest trees but many are found in scrub and semi-desert. Like the eucalypts of scrubland, the curious grass trees (*Xanthorrhoea*), which are known as blackboys, are fire-resistant.

Bottom There is rarely a sharp divide between scrubland and desert. Here, the merging of scrub and desert vegetation can be seen in the Saguaro National Monument, in Arizona. Cacti, including the columnar saguaro (*Carnegia gigantea*), grow with various other drought-resistant shrubs including the yellow-flowered brittle bush or incienso (*Encelia farinosa*).

Heavy grazing, fires and cutting are responsible for the relatively stable dwarfer shrub communities described as garrigue, phrygana and tomillares. However, the vegetation can be so degraded that it consists of no more than a few spiny shrubs thinly scattered over stony ground with a vestige of soil. Many maquis plants, such as rock or sun roses and Spanish broom, are also found in garrigue and comparable communities. Characteristic adaptations that help conserve moisture include thick and hairy leaves while prickliness discourages browsing. A high proportion of the shrubs are familiar aromatic garden plants and include lavenders (*Lavandula*), rosemary (*Rosmarinus officinalis*), savories (*Satureja*) and thymes (*Thymus*). As with maquis shrubs, growth is made in late winter and the main flowering season is spring, before the long, parching and bleaching summer. In late winter and spring and to a lesser degree in autumn, the shrubs are overshadowed by bulbous plants like onions (*Allium*), anemones, autumn crocus (*Colchicum*), true crocuses, sternbergias and terrestrial orchids.

Many parallels can be drawn between Mediterranean communities and the chaparral of southern California, where the dominant plants are also hard-leaved evergreen shrubs. On some of the driest slopes chamise (*Adenostoma fasciculatum*) forms almost pure stands. More mixed scrub includes manzanitas (*Arctostaphylos*), Californian lilac (*Ceanothus*) and scrub oak (*Quercus dumosa*) – the word chaparral is derived from *chaparra*, a Spanish word for evergreen oak. An aspect of chaparral, and of scrubland in general, that is difficult to reconcile with building development is the part fire plays in its renewal. Chaparral produces shrub litter that is cleared every 20 to 35 years, as is most of the top growth, by fire caused by lightning. During a temporary phase, grasses, annuals and perennials, such as lobelias, phacelias and Californian poppies (*Romneya*), flourish. Many shrubs shoot from ground level after a few months while fire triggers others, including *Ceanothus*, to germinate. Within a few years shrubs dominate again, some chemically inhibiting the germination and growth of herbs.

The plant communities of the Mediterranean and regions with similar climates are of intrinsic interest and a valuable source of ideas for gardeners facing long hot summers and reduced water supplies. **(For plants in gardens, see pp. 88–91).**

GRASSLANDS

In hunter-gatherer communities, 10,000 to 20,000 years ago, humans were already dipping in to the cereal bowl. They fed omniverously, opportunistically gathering ripening grain on the stem before the heads shattered or feasting on meat after the lucky kill of a grazing animal. From this, a world economy has developed that is based on grasses (Poaceae) to a remarkable degree. A major advance made in South-west Asia and the Middle East was the development, from wild *Triticum* and *Hordeum* species, of wheat and rye that did not shatter before the grain could be harvested. In tropical Asia the principal cereal was rice (*Oryza sativa*). In America it was maize (*Zea mays*). Africa has several indigenous cereals, including sorghum (*Sorghum*

bicolor) and pearl millet (*Pennisetum glaucum*), which were brought into cultivation early. Vast areas of the earth's surface are now under cultivation to raise annual grasses that provide grain crops and a few perennial grasses, the most important of which is sugar cane (*Saccharum officinarum*), originally from South-east Asia. Large areas are also maintained with a perennial grass cover to feed flocks and herds of domesticated grazing animals. All of this is on such a scale that it can give a misleading impression of the earth's natural grass cover.

It seems that grasses, late developers among the flowering plants, started off in forests. Some grasses, such as the European wood millet (*Milium effusum*), are still found under a tree canopy. The best move that grasses made, however, was to move into the open. Many grasses can grow well enough in a forest climate; the farmland of western Europe, once wooded, is testimony to this. It is shade that puts them at a disadvantage. Grasses have succeeded where the climate does not favour trees or where other factors, including human intervention, prevent the development of forest. Rainfall, rather than temperature, is the key factor. As a broad generalization, the great natural grasslands are found in a climatic zone that is too dry for forest but not as dry as desert. The majority of grasses do show some degree of adaption to or tolerance of drought. The annuals avoid the problem by moving quickly through their life cycle in what may be a very short rainy season. Perennial grasses have also adapted to drought, the breathing pores

Top left The bond that has always existed between nomadic tribes and their horses was originally forged in the grasslands of Central Asia. Although nomadism as a way of life has declined, horse raising continues to this day, even here at the western edge of the Tibetan plateau.

Above The pressure of growing populations threatens even the vast grasslands of Africa. Here, in Tanzania's plateau, the rainy season that takes place in the summer brings new growth to the savanna and more open expanses on which herds of wildebeest and buffalo depend.

(stomata) of some being protected inside furled leaves. They have dormant winter buds, often below the surface of the soil, and the litter of the previous season's leaves helps reduce the loss of moisture.

The tall grasslands that still cover large areas of Africa, providing pasture for the last remaining large herds of wild grazing animals, represent a type found throughout tropical regions where there are marked wet and dry seasons. The term "savanna" that is applied to these grasslands is a broad category covering almost pure grassland, a more park-like landscape in which open areas of grassland are more or less sparsely dotted with thorny trees and bushes, and country where trees grow more closely but where the canopy is still well broken up. These variations reflect differences in the length of the dry season, which usually lasts 3 to 5 months, and in an annual rainfall range of

Top right There are three broad zones of North American prairie, broadly related to the height of the grass: tall in the east, short in the west and mixed in between. Short-grass prairie used to support large bison herds. In areas like Montana and South Dakota, as here, ponderosa pine (*Pinus ponderosa*) grows in short-grass prairie.

Above right Tussock grasses are the dominant plants among the treeless vegetation of the islands in the southern oceans (see p. 34). On Campbell Island, which lies south of New Zealand, the herbaceous perennial *Bulbinella rossii*, shelters among the tussocks.

8–39in (200–1,000mm). The higher the rainfall, the denser the tree cover. Nutrients tend to be washed out of the soil when heavy rains fall in a relatively short season and these soils often drain poorly because of the formation of a hardpan. Where they are used for ranching, as in the llanos of northern Columbia, Argentina and Venezuela, the original grasses have been largely replaced by introduced species and fire is used to lift nutrient levels and prevent the growth of scrub or trees.

Since pioneer days the vast grasslands of central North America have had their boundaries obscured and their character altered by agriculture, forest clearing and urban development. But the broad outlines are clear. The prairies, bordered by the coniferous forests of Canada in the north and the deserts of Mexico in the south, are brought to a halt in the west by the Rocky Mountains and by forest in the east. The divide was never sharp, accidents of topography and microclimates (local climates that differ from the surroundings) ensuring a complex mixture of grassland and forest. The broad frontier has moved backwards and forwards. For example, the fires used by hunting Indians checked the growth of trees and the prairie moved east.

The variation in the composition of the prairie grasslands from east to west is also an indication of the effect of climate. In the east, in a zone now mainly devoted to the cultivation of corn and soya bean, there was tall-grass prairie, in which grasses such as big bluestem (*Andropogon gerardii*) formed a dense sward that reached a height of

Below Hybrid Texas bluebonnets (*Lupinus texensis*) grow here with other annuals and perennials.

Below In New Zealand's South Island natural sub-alpine tussock grassland, including species of *Chionochloa*, is affected by grazing.

Bottom The poet's narcissus (*Narcissus poeticus*) is widely distributed in the moist alpine meadows of southern Europe.

6–10ft (1.8–3m) in summer. Numerous herbaceous plants, including species of *Aster*, *Baptisia*, *Lupinus*, *Monarda* and *Solidago*, are native to this zone. Reflecting a much lower rainfall of 10–15in (25–38mm) a year, the Great Plains east of the Rocky Mountains had a short-grass prairie, usually under 10in (25cm) high, which included buffalo grass (*Buchloe dactyloides*) and blue grama or mosquito grass (*Bouteloua gracilis*). This prairie supported great herds of bison but they have now gone and heavy grazing, managed by humans, has taken its toll on the natural vegetation. In the Great Drought of the 1930s, the blowing of topsoil was worse where cropping, especially of wheat, had been pushed into short-grass prairie. The transitional character of the zone between these two prairies, now more or less occupied by the wheat belt, was reflected in the mixture of grasses.

Rainfall too low or sporadic for trees has favoured the development of grasslands in the pampas of Argentina and the steppes that extend from central Hungary eastwards through the former USSR and on to northern Mongolia and north-east China. From the Russian *chernaya zemlya*, which means black earth, has come the word chernozem (see p. 20), used to describe the characteristically rich black soil that develops in grassland in cool or temperate regions. There are enormous variations in this region of cold steppe, where for at least 4 months of the year temperatures are often well below freezing and where the fierce heat of summer leads to drought. Where the rainfall is low, grassland becomes desert. Many other areas that are less bleak in winter, including the South African veld, have a dense grass cover but where the winter rains are uncertain, as in the Sahel steppe south of the Sahara, semi-desert scrub develops. A tundra-like vegetation dominated by tussock grasses is found in the islands of the southern ocean and also in sub-alpine zones in the Southern Hemisphere.

Many grasses are native to regions of the temperate world such as western Europe and the eastern United States where rainfall favours the growth of trees but natural expanses of grassland are limited. The pastures and meadows of Europe owe much of their character to human interference over the centuries. The Romans are said to have been the first to use hay on a large scale as winter fodder for livestock. In sub-alpine regions of Europe, a combination of mowing and grazing

Below These sub-alpine meadows in the Alps fill with flowers in late spring and early summer.

regimes has favoured the development of meadows rich in bulbs and herbaceous perennials. The timing of the mowing is critical; if it is too early plants do not have a chance to flower and set seed. In some areas winter sports and water developments pose a threat to sub-alpine vegetation. Ancient management of grassland in Britain has resulted in one of the floral highlights of a country where the devastation of the ice ages has left the natural flora impoverished. Sheep and rabbit grazing on chalk downs allows several attractive flowers to compete with the grasses. Small scabious (*Scabiosa columbaria*), rampion (*Phyteuma orbiculare*), horeshoe vetch (*Hippocrepis comosa*) and a number of terrestrial orchids are found on the thin soils. Species of *Ophrys* take pollination to bizarre extremes by relying on the copulatory motions of bees and wasps that they resemble. Grazing also prevents the establishment of shrub and tree seedlings that might lead to the reclothing of chalk downland with woods of beech (*Fagus sylvaticus*). A fall in the rabbit population, dramatic when myxomatosis was first prevalent, combined with reduced sheep grazing, has shown what a fragile hold these small flowers have on downland. For those who find lawn dull, chalk downland, old meadows and ancient churchyards sometimes serve as models for ornamental mixtures of grasses and flowers. The painfully slow recovery of downland after ploughing, which may leave discernible effects for hundreds of years, is a reminder that rich and stable plant communities cannot be created at a stroke.

Due to a superficial resemblance to grasses, several other groups of plants are often lumped together with them. These include the reeds and sedges (Cyperaceae) that are major components of wetland and marshy vegetation (see p. 38). One of the largest of the sedges is papyrus (*Cyperus papyrus*). Extensive papyrus swamps on the Nile Delta, graphically depicted in reliefs and murals of the pharaonic period as the haunt of wildfowl, have largely been eliminated as a result of drainage and irrigation schemes. In the Northern Hemisphere the cotton grasses (*Eriophorum*) animate vast areas of bog and tundra with the rabbit-tail bobbing of their tufts. The species of two other families, the rushes (Juncaceae) and reedmaces (Typhaceae), are also mainly plants of swampland and often form very large colonies.

(For plants in gardens, see pp. 64–65).

Above left Sub-alpine meadows in the Pyrenees are full of perennials including clover (*Trifolium*) hawkweeds (*Hieraceum*) and yellow rattle (*Rhinanthus minor*).

Bottom Cotton grasses (*Eriophorum*) are sedges, found in bog and tundra in the Northern Hemisphere.

HEATH, MOORLAND AND TUNDRA

Some of the emptiest landscapes of western Europe, which are exhilarating and monotonous in equal measure, are stained purple with the flowers of heather or ling (*Calluna vulgaris*) in late summer. This is a wide-spread member of the heath family (Ericaceae), which includes the rhododendrons as well as many dwarf evergreen shrubs with bell- or urn-shaped flowers. Most are intolerant of alkaline soils and, like all members of their family, are dependent to some degree on fungi that live in association with the roots (mycrorrhizal fungi) for the take-up of nutrients, a problem for many other plants on highly acidic soils. They have the foliage of plants adapted to exposed and sometimes dry conditions, the tough leaves being scale- or needle-like. Like heather, various heaths (*Erica*) and species of *Daboecia* are major constituents of the low shrub cover that is often found on the poor soils of sandy heaths or on moorland over peat. They frequently form a low canopy 3–4ft (90–120cm) high, beneath which there is a layer of a few herbs and grasses growing in a mosaic of mosses and lichens. Other dwarf shrubs of the heath family that are sometimes found with them include berrying species such as the bilberry (*Vaccinium myrtillus*) and shrubs that resemble heaths, among them the crowberries (*Empetrum*). In peat bog the main plants of the wet hollows are sphagnum mosses and sedges but typical heath plants are conspicuous in the drier parts.

In North America similar communities of plants but with slightly different species are found on acid soils where there is a moist maritime climate. The concentration of *Erica* species in South Africa gives a different complexion to heaths found in the area known as "mountain fynbos" in the southern part of Cape Province. Here "Cape heaths" make a low scrub with related plants like species of Cape myrtle (*Phylica*). Australia has virtually no members of the heath family but heath-like communities exist in which the dominant plants are members of a mainly Australian family, Epacridaceae. In South America, even on the remote island of Tristan da Cunha, crowberries make a reappearance in communities that have similarities to Northern European heaths.

There is debate about the role humans have played in the formation of heath and moorland of western Europe but there is no doubt that human interference maintains many of these landscapes in their present state. In Britain much heath on poor sandy soils is degraded woodland, the exercise of commoners' rights to grazing and the gathering of fuel playing a major role in keeping the vegetation to a low cover of heather, gorse (*Ulex europaeus*), bracken (*Pteridium aquilinum*) and grasses. In the medieval period and later heath was often used for the managed grazing of rabbits in established warrens. It is clear from old legislation against burning that fires on these heaths were often intentionally lit. Burning continues to be the major method of managing grazed moorland and grouse moor. Left to itself heather (*Calluna vulgaris*) degenerates after 30 or 40 years, the plant finally dying. A cycle in which the heather is fired every 10 to 12 years keeps plants dense and encourages the growth of soft young shoots. When burning and grazing stop, pioneer trees quickly become established.

At their northern-most limits heath communities merge imperceptibly with the vegetation of the tundra, a vast circumpolar region beyond the tree line. Although low in rainfall, usually less than 8in (200mm) a year, this area is poorly drained in its brief summer, when only a shallow layer of soil is thawed above permafrost. There are parallels to make between the vegetation of this harsh environment and that above the tree line in mountains (see pp. 40–43) but the striking feature is the small number of species: sedges, mosses and lichens, like the reindeer moss (*Claydonia rangiferina*), a lichen not a moss, are the most characteristic. The shrubby component, less conspicuous as the tundra extends northwards, consists of heath plants, dwarf willows (*Salix*) and birches (*Betula*). Adaptations include reduced reliance on

Top left Grasses, bracken (*Pteridium aquilinum*) and brambles (*Rubus*) are often subordinate parts of a vegetation dominated by members of the heath family.

Centre left Moorland, coniferous forest and tundra meet in the harsh climatic conditions of the far north.

Below left When grazing pressure on the open sandy heathlands of Britain is reduced, trees such as birch (*Betula pendula*) and pine (*Pinus sylvestris*) invade.

Right It has been widely believed that a vast pine forest stretched across the central Highlands of Scotland even in historical times. The evidence is not persuasive but pine (*Pinus sylvestris*) certainly occurs widely in the moorland of the Highlands that is dominated by heather (*Calluna vulgaris*).

Below The tundra-like vegetation of mountainous regions in the sub-arctic, as in Norway, includes mosses and lichens, members of the heath family such as species of *Vaccinium*, low-growing conifers and stunted birches (*Betula*).

seed for maintaining populations, most plants spreading from rhizomes or stems, and an ability to take advantage almost at once of favourable conditions. Dense growth in close communities also traps snow, recycles nutrients and creates a microclimate less harsh than that in fully exposed tundra. In Antarctica the ice and snow cover is nearly complete and there is no vegetation comparable to that of the tundra, only limited patches of slow-growing mosses, a grass and a cushion-like herb. **(For plants in gardens, see pp. 80–81).**

WATER AND WET PLACES

Over-zealous owners of houseplants unwittingly execute a kind of water torture. The idea that plants can have too much water is difficult to grasp but the plants that can live in water or in waterlogged soils are specially adapted to these conditions. The most common structural solution that allows the free movement of oxygen, the great problem facing these plants, is a system of air channels that run from the roots to the shoots. In watery and boggy places, plants that are adequately adapted to these conditions are easy to recognize because they produce some of the lushest growth found in the plant world.

The term "bog garden" is misleading. It defines a permanently wet area of the garden that is normally richly planted with giant-leaved perennials, such as gunneras, and brightly coloured flowers like astilbes and primulas. Natural bog is, in fact, wet peatland. In temperate regions the main plants are sphagnum mosses (several species interestingly have their own zonation according to preferences for wet or dry conditions) and sedges such as cotton grass (*Eriophorum angustifolium*). Only in drier parts of bog is there a heath-like vegetation and even this in no way provides a model for exuberant planting. A broader range of plants is found on fens, where the plants also grow on peat but the water supply is rich in minerals. Familiar fen plants include the common reed (*Phragmites australis*), a plant of wide distribution throughout the world, and bulrushes or reedmaces (*Typha*). Fen sometimes develops into a kind of damp woodland called carr. In Europe the most common trees of carr are alders (*Alnus*).

For the gardener considering the range of plants that can be grown in water or watery places, a more useful model than bog, fen or carr is provided by natural ponds or lakes and their margins. Open bodies of water tend to be converted to land, with a sequence of plant communities succeeding one another in textbook order as the water becomes more shallow. The reduction of the water depth, perhaps with the build up of planktonic debris, allows enough light to reach the bottom of the pond or lake for submerged weeds such as the pondweeds (*Elodea*) to become established. These are followed by water lilies (*Nymphaea*) and similar floating plants rooted in the mud. It is not until the water is about 3ft (90cm) deep or less that plants with leaves standing above the water, the emergents, can become rooted.

Above Yellow skunk cabbage (*Lysichiton americanus*), a member of the arum family, is widespread in western North America where the margins and streams as well as the bogs are permanently moist. The paddle-shaped leaves develop as the yellow spathes – modifed bracts around a flower cluster – wither.

Below The bog arum (*Calla palustris*) is found throughout the cool Northern Hemisphere, growing in shallow water, where the soils are peaty and acid, and even thriving in the shade cast by trees at the water's edge. The small flowers with a white spathe are followed by red berries.

Above left Carnivorous plants tend to live in nitrogen-deficient soils. *Sarracenia flava* and other pitcher plants of eastern North America are found in acid bogs that are low in nutrients.

Above right In their adaptation to a watery environment, the water lilies (*Nymphaea*) seem highly developed, but it is clear from the fossil record that they are among the most primitive of flowering plants. Water lily stems have conduits for the movement of air that may help to give the leaves buoyancy.

Below left Fenland that is covered with stable woodland composed of trees such as these alders (*Alnus*) is known as carr.

Below right The regal fern (*Osmunda regalis*), one of the most successful ferns in bog, is widely distributed in temperate and subtropical regions.

The effect of these marginals, which are similar to those of fen, is to accelerate the reduction of the water surface but as their marshy fringe builds up they help create an area of moist ground in which herbaceous plants such as kingcup (*Caltha palustris*) can grow. Shrubby alders and willows (*Salix*) may eventually be followed by a woodland of birch (*Betula*), oak (*Quercus*) and other trees. In the controlled environment of a garden, all these stages can be maintained although any rapid changes sometimes require a brutal response.

Trees that tolerate wet ground are particularly interesting. In eastern North America the eastern cottonwood (*Populus deltoides*) and silver maple (*Acer saccharinum*) are typical streamside trees, both of which will tolerate prolonged flooding. In the numerous peat bogs of northern North America black spruce (*Picea mariana*) and tamarck (*Larix laricina*) are consistently found together. One of the most impressive of all the swamp trees is the swamp cypress (*Taxodium distichum*) which is, like tamarck, a deciduous conifer. Although in cultivation this conifer does not require wet soil, in the wild it is found in alluvial swamps, which contain fertile soil left after a flood, in the south-eastern states of North America. The curious knee-like protuberances that surround the trunks of old plants are called breathing roots or pneumatophores but there is debate about their function. One of the greatest of all dendrological sensations when it was recognized as a living fossil in the 1940s, the dawn redwood (*Metasequoia glyptostroboides*), shows many parallels with the swamp cypress. In its tiny area of natural distribution, in China's north-west Hubei province, it is found by the edges of streams and rivers. **(For plants in gardens, see pp. 82–83; pp. 84–87).**

Mountainous and Rocky Landscapes

Pleasure in the grandeur of alpine scenery is relatively recent. Partly as a consequence, the horticultural infatuation with alpine plants did not reach its peak until the late 19th and early 20th centuries. The appeal of these naturally trimmed and poised plants remains enormous so that they continue to inspire expeditions of athletic botanists and provide devotees with the material for a challenging kind of gardening.

On the highest mountain peaks, as in the polar regions, there are no plants but below this alpinist's heaven of rock, snow and ice there are various zones of vegetation caused by changes in altitude. These altitudinal zones bear some resemblance to the latitudinal zones between the tropics and the North Pole but the parallels can easily be pushed too far. In the classic mountain zonation a more or less continuous forest cover, known as montane forest, is succeeded at a higher elevation by a more open zone with trees, often stunted and deformed, growing among grasses and herbaceous plants. The upper limit of this sub-alpine zone is the tree line which, unlike the forest edge of the tundra, is clearly marked. Above the tree line is the alpine zone proper, sometimes known as alpine tundra, which looks surprisingly garden-like, despite the generous spacing between plants.

The general pattern of zonation, and in particular the altitude of the tree line, shows considerable variations from one part of the world to another. Temperature is the key factor: the absolute minimum temperature is not crucial (this occurs anyway when trees are dormant) but the length of the growing season is. In Europe the tree line is usually at about 6,550ft (2,000m) but moisture, snowfall and aspect all affect it. In some of the drier areas of North America, the tree line can be at more than 10,000ft (3,048m). In the tropics, where the average daily temperature is about the same throughout the year, other factors come into play, especially the sharp differences between day and night temperatures, more marked with increasing altitude.

Many compact plants are found in sub-alpine meadow or on rocky outcrops below the true alpine zone but it is necessary to go higher for the purist's alpines. The harshness of the conditions is in some ways comparable to the Arctic tundra but there is no underlying layer of permafrost. There may be boggy dips, but here much of the terrain is rough and steep so that water drains quickly. Rainfall is often low but during the growing season melting snow maintains a good supply of moisture. Buffeting winds often rise to a shrieking nightmare and there is negligible soil in which to gain a hold and from which to get

nourishment. During the short growing season plants are exposed to intense light. Within this broad and daunting pattern of conditions there is often a complex pattern of microclimates and soils. Temperature, duration and intensity of sunshine, wind speed, loss of moisture through evaporation and drainage, thickness of snow cover and its persistence are all to some extent affected by the steepness of the slope, the direction it faces and the character of the rock.

The plants that succeed in this inhospitable environment are remarkably consistent in their refinement, even though their flowers sometimes seem a size too large. Some are prostrate shrubs such as dwarf willows (*Salix*). There are also dwarf bulbs, including crocuses, although many other bulbous plants belong to alpine meadows at a lower altitude. A large number are herbaceous perennials, crouching against wind as low mats, neat cushions or packed leaf rosettes. They include mealy leaved alpine primulas, saxifrages with lime-encrusted rosettes and blue gentians. Most of these plants rely on root systems that extend deep into rocky crevices for anchorage, moisture and nourishment. They are all equipped to some extent to withstand desiccation and primed to make quick growth, flower and set seed when conditions are favourable. The heat from the growth of some of the first to flower can even melt the last of the snow that covers them.

Their position in vertical crevices or the stony fragments around them ensure that they never have a soggy collar. Some of these plants, remarkably, manage to keep their balance in the unstable environment of screes, the streams and rivers made of shattered rock fragments that are constantly being replenished by frost action on parent rock. The stone chips of the topmost layer are for ever slipping lower but beneath them there is usually a more stable base, through which water moves freely. The plants that live in these demanding conditions show various specializations. Some have fleshy roots that are deeply bedded in the relatively stable soil beneath the moving surface. Many have leaves that snap off easily without damaging the stem. The underground parts trail up the slope, which is an indication of the gravitational pull on the surface of the scree.

It is the exceptions in nature that are always intriguing. In the equatorial mountains of Central Africa and the Andes giant alpines, including lobelias and members of the sunflower family (Compositae), provide a curious contrast to the more familiar small-scale alpines. In these mountains, the average temperature varies little throughout the year but the swing between day and night temperatures can be dramatic.

Above The Pyrenean *Saxifraga longifolia*, found on the French and Spanish sides but with a restricted distribution, is commonly seen with splendid sprays spilling from a rocky crevice. The symmetrical rosettes, composed of lime-encrusted narrow leaves, build up over several years before the spectacular flowering and then die.

Opposite top The lushness of plants in sub-alpine meadows contrasts with the compact and ground-hugging growth of the true alpines. Typical plants of the meadows in European Alps include species of cranesbill (*Geranium*), *Pulsatilla* (their flowers of silky hairiness followed by heads of feathery seeds), *Ranunculus* and globe flower (*Trollius*).

Opposite centre The colourful bracts of various species of Indian paintbrush (*Castilleja*) make these among the showiest perennials below and above the tree line in the Rocky Mountains of western North America. Most species are parasitic on the roots of other plants and difficult to establish in gardens.

Above left Stunted specimens of *Abies lasiocarpa*, sometimes known as the alpine fir, are found in the upper limits of forest in the Rocky Mountains.

Left The stony hillsides of Crete, like much of the Mediterranean, are rich in plants. The great cliffs of the island, such as the Samaria Gorge shown here, have provided a refuge for a high proportion of endemic plants. The pink-flowered oleander (*Nerium oleander*), seen in the foreground, is particularly common in dry river beds, where there is underground water.

Day temperatures rise quickly to as much as 104°F (40°C) but fall below freezing at night. These giants get by with various methods of insulation such as woolly leaves or using old leaves as overcoats.

Far from all the plants that are grown in rock gardens or raised beds come from the high alpine zone. Although not as refined as the true alpine, there are many compact plants from lower altitudes found in rocky or stony ground. Some of them are pioneers seizing a new opportunity, some are refugees that have found in a harsh environment a kind of peace not to be had in a more competitive one. Among the pioneers are those that make their homes in the stony beds of dry rivers and in moraines, the almost soilless piles of rocky debris left by retreating glaciers. At Glacier Bay in Alaska, where retreat in the last 200 years has been calculated at over 40 miles (64km), species of *Dryas* and *Epilobium* have become established in a succession that leads to dominance by spruce (*Picea*) and hemlock (*Tsuga*). In the Mediterranean region, where the natural vegetation has been modified by centuries of felling, burning and heavy grazing, steep rock faces and gorges, like the Samaria Gorge in Crete, have served as refuges for plants that are not to be found elsewhere. Plants from the gorges of Crete include several bellflowers, such as *Campanula saxatilis,* yellow-flowered flax (*Linum arboreum*) and the Cretan dittany (*Origanum dictamnus*). The Burren in Ireland's County Clare is another example of a rocky refuge, in this case near the sea. Slabs of porous limestone form a broken pavement that has been cracked by enormous pressure during the ice ages and riddled with cavities as a result of erosion. Its clefts and niches shelter a puzzling mix of small plants, such as the spring gentian (*Gentiana verna*), which is most often seen in alpine habitats, and more than 20 species of terrestrial orchid. Although the rock is calcareous (contains calcium carbonate), the soil is sufficiently acid in some hollows to allow heaths (*Erica*), heather or ling (*Calluna vulgaris*) and other acid-loving plants to thrive.

In many rocky and stony habitats where there is a marked dry season, especially in the Mediterranean region, bulbs eclipse most other flowers in spring and sometimes in autumn. This is true in lowlands and sub-alpine zones as well as in true alpine regions. One of the richest areas of the world for bulbs is the Anatolian plateau of Turkey. From it have come some of the most popular dwarf bulbs for gardens, such as crocuses, fritillary (*Fritillaria*), snowdrop (*Galanthus*), iris and scilla, most of which are found in free-draining stony ground that is moist in the growing season, sometimes from snow melt, but later dry. Fortunately, dwarf bulbs, low shrubs and compact perennials from a wide range of rocky habitats work very well together in the garden. **(For plants in gardens, see pp. 92–95).**

Above left **Although rock- and boulder-strewn areas are often very exposed, their shaded chinks and crevices may provide a moist environment in which ferns, such as this species of *Dryopteris*, can become established.**

Centre left **Species of houseleek (*Sempervivum*), a high proportion of which are alpine plants, have succulent leaves arranged in neat rosettes. Further adaptations to conserve moisture are waxy or hairy surfaces to the leaves and, in extreme conditions, an ability to curl up and reduce transpiration.**

Centre right **The purple saxifrage (*Saxifraga oppositifolia*), one of the most widely distributed alpine and tundra plants of the Northern Hemisphere, is shown here on Canada's Somerset Island within the Arctic Circle. The flowers overwinter after being formed in the previous growing season and are ready to open within a few days of the snow cover clearing.**

Above right **In late spring and early summer the Burren, an area of limestone pavement near the sea in County Clare, Ireland, brims with small flowers such as thrift (*Armeria maritima*). The rocky crevices shelter a much wider range of plants than can be found in the surrounding area, some of them lime-lovers, others lime-hating and a few survivors of a flora that existed before the ice ages.**

Right **Some of the world's most majestic rocky landscapes are found in the Colorado Plateau in south-west USA. The vegetation shows considerable altitudinal zonation on cliffs that rise to 2,000–3,000ft (610–914m) and are carved in the desert and semi-desert landscape of Zion National Park, Utah, by the Virgin River.**

DESERT

"Making the desert bloom" is a slogan used to justify irrigation schemes in arid regions. At heavy financial and often environmental cost irrigated deserts have produced remarkable crops from non-desert plants. Still more remarkable are the true desert plants that survive against the odds.

Harsh desert landscapes on a heroic scale are a major feature of the interior of continents, regions where mountain ranges create areas of rain shadow and coastal regions next to cold currents. Low, irregular rainfall, often less than 10in (25cm) a year, and a high evaporation rate limit plant growth. High day temperatures, often well above 100°F (37°C) in the Sahara, can fall to near freezing at night. Desiccating winds and their load of abrasive debris are a constant feature. Deserts, however, show considerable variations of land forms and soils: these include shifting sand dunes, rock surfaces and areas of boulders and stones. The soils are often saline (see "Coastal Areas", pp. 46–47).

A desert is a primed landscape: just after rainfall, plants burgeon, flower, and set seed within weeks. Ephemerals are most tolerant of environmental extremes as seeds with success depending on finely tuned mechanisms to trigger germination when conditions are right.

The desert's brief exuberance after rain is a rare event but, except in the harshest environments, a community of dogged plants survives. To tap available water the roots are well developed for the size of the plants. Cactus root systems are extensive, near the surface and new root hairs develop within hours of the ground being moistened. Many shrubs, such as the creosote bush (*Larrea tridendata*) of the Mohave Desert in south-western USA, have deep far-reaching roots while the New World mesquites (*Prosopis*) have dense shallow roots and deep tap roots. Wide spacing between plants indicates the intense competition for water; creosote bushes are usually 15–30ft (4.5–9m) apart.

Adaptations to minimize water loss include small leaves, usually thick-skinned, and often with a waxy bloom or felting to reduce transpiration. Some plants may shed their leaves in extreme drought. Some shrubs that lose their leaves, such as the mesa palo verde (*Cercidium*

Above Death Valley in eastern California and southern Nevada drops to 282ft (86m) below sea level and its most austere sand dunes and salt flats are plantless.

Bottom left and right Succulent species of *Euphorbia* in arid regions of Africa, such as the Namib Desert (left), seem to mimic the adaptations to extreme drought of cacti in Arizona (right) and other desert areas of the New World.

Below Conspicuous plants of the Sonoran Desert, extending north from western Mexico into south-west USA, include cacti and ocotillo (*Fouquieria splendens*), with flame-red flowers after light winter rains.

microphyllum) from the Sonoran Desert in Mexico and south-west USA, photosynthesize through their bark. Plants are most vulnerable to water loss through their leaf pores. In desert plants, the pores are often reduced in number and recessed or protected by hairs. Closing pores as day temperatures rise reduces water loss but calls for metabolic adjustments. Succulents, which take in carbon dioxide when the pores are open at night, fix the carbon as an organic acid until photosynthesis can start again during the day. Cacti, conspicuously successful succulents of New World deserts, have no leaves and photosynthesize through green stems. Like the succulent euphorbias of Africa, they have relatively few pores and often ridged stems with the pores sheltered in the valleys. This allows for expansion and contraction according to the supply of water.

The miracle of deserts and gardens inspired directly by them is not that they respond to irrigation but that they can support plant communities without it and that these bloom in their own time. **(For plants in gardens, see pp. 90–91).**

Above left and right In arid regions, even small amounts of water allow increases in plant densities. Prickly pear (*Opuntia*) grows thickly along the bed of a dry creek in the Grand Canyon, USA (left), while in the Namib Desert of south-west Africa a succulent *Aloe* is the dominant plant where moisture gathers at the base of this rocky outcrop or inselberg (right).

Below Sparse vegetation, including *Yucca*, grows in the wind-shaped waves of gypsum sand and alkali flats in White Sands National Monument, New Mexico, USA.

Bottom Many drought-tolerant plants survive in this National Monument in the Mojave Desert.

Above left As described by John Gerard, author of the celebrated *Herball* (1597), the yellow horned poppy (*Glaucium flavum*) is a plant of "sandes and bankes of the sea". In fact, it is widely distributed on the coasts of Europe and adjacent regions, even as far as the Canary Islands. Gerard added the name sea poppy but horned has stuck, the seedheads being so conspicuous. The ruffled leaves are glaucous.

Above right Extensive root systems, foliage adapted to minimize water loss, an ability to survive burial by shifting sand, and tolerance of salt are features of many plants that colonize coastal sands, including this species of *Senecio* from the Falkland Islands.

Below left Grasses that tolerate repeated burial by shifting sand are among the first colonizers of sand dunes. As the stabilized sand dunes move inland, a much wider range of plants can become established.

Centre right On rugged and rocky promontories in the Mediterranean, where there is little tidal movement and the splash zone is limited, a hillside mixture of scrub and Aleppo pines (*Pinus halepensis*) often extends almost to the water's edge, as is the case here in Puglia, in south-eastern Italy.

COASTAL AREAS

The meeting place of land and sea is a taxing environment for higher plants. Many just cannot cope with the high levels of salinity. Despite an abundance of water, osmotic pressure prevents its absorption. The soil structure also poses problems: it is often nearly pure sand, draining almost instantaneously and burying plants as dunes move. Pure rock, the firmest defence of land against sea, allows little purchase for higher plants. Breezes that shape whole plant communities can turn to violent gales, desiccating, maiming and searing with their salt content.

Some of the most successful plants of coastal regions are those that do not stand up well in competition with terrestrial plants or even those from fresh-water swamp. Mangroves are among them and this group of about 100 species of evergreen trees and shrubs from various families provides an interesting example of converging evolutionary processes. Mangrove forest and scrub covers more than 50 per cent of tropical shoreline, reaching its fullest development on intertidal mud-flats, where often only the crowns of plants stand above water at high tide. Low tide exposes a clutter of air roots (pneumatophores) and stilt roots. Like other plants that extract water in saline conditions, they tolerate high salt concentrations in their sap, which allows osmosis to occur. They can also excrete excess salt on the surface of their leaves.

The vegetation of salt marshes in temperate regions includes grasses and sedges. In Britain the aggressive cord grass (*Spartina anglica*) is an example of a new species that has evolved from a sterile hybrid. Among other specialized plants is the leafless, fleshy stemmed glasswort (*Salicornia europeae*). This belongs to the beet family (Chenopodiaceae) whose members show remarkable salt tolerance and are widely distributed in saline conditions near coasts and in deserts.

Mangroves provide an example of seed that is transported by sea currents, in their case often germinating on the plant. The remarkably

Above Silver sea holly (*Eryngium maritimum*) is often found on European beaches in much less stable sand and shingle than here. The waxy surface of the leaves helps reduce the loss of moisture while fleshy roots, as much as 6ft (1.8m) long, tap and store any moisture and give the plants a secure anchor. The roots of eryngo, as the plant is also known, are thick enough to have been cooked as a delicacy and candied.

Below right The original home of the coconut may have been in Polynesia or South America but the buoyancy of its fruit, allowing it to be carried on vast oceanic voyages, and its tolerance of salt makes it the characteristic tree of sandy tropical shorelines.

uniform shoreline vegetation of tropical islands is partly because viable fruits and seeds, such as the coconut (*Cocos nucifera*), are transported by sea from one island to another, partly as a result of seed carried by shore birds. The uniformity of the shoreline vegetation is often in sharp contrast to the diversity of the interiors, which are not penetrated by oceanic birds and frequently hold plants unique to individual islands.

As interesting ecologically as the tropical atoll is the more commonplace beach backed by sand dunes. Classic studies of it have identified successive stages that finally result in a plant community in a state of equilibrium. The species mentioned here are European but the stages are roughly the same in many parts of the world. The succession begins with salt-tolerant plants such as sea rocket (*Cakile maritima*) and sand couch grass (*Agropyrone junceiforme*) that germinate at the limit of the highest tide. The vegetation checks wind speed with the result that more sand accumulates. Less frequent inundations from the sea and leaching by rain allow less salt-tolerant species to become established as the dune grows and moves inland. The most successful are those like marram grass (*Amophila arenaria*) and blue lyme grass (*Leymus arenarius*) that grow up through sand if buried. Stabilizing of the dune, further leaching and the accumulation of organic matter allow yet more plants to become established, including shrubs such as sea buckthorn (*Hippophae rhamnoides*) or, on acid dunes, heather (*Calluna vulgaris*), heaths (*Erica* species) and gorse (*Ulex europaeus*). A final but uncommon stage is stable woodland.

Building near the sea is not new. Well before the catastrophic eruption of Vesuvius in AD 79, the Bay of Naples had become the playground of rich Roman society, elegantly established in lavish villas. However, mass tourism and the development that goes with it pose a greatly increased threat to the often fragile plant communities of even remote shorelines which until now have escaped development for farming, forestry and industry.

(For plants in gardens, see pp. 96–97).

PLANTS IN GARDENS

The Garden's Character

A good start to discovering the character of a garden is to look at the climate of the area in which it lies. One of the first factors to consider is the usual temperature range that is likely to be experienced. The upper limits are generally not as important as the lowest temperature, the brutal factor that often decides whether a plant can be grown in a particular place. The broad pattern is sufficiently consistent in the United States, where cold air from the north has such a dominant influence in winter, for the wide use of hardiness zones (1 to 11) based on consistent annual average minimum temperatures, plants being given hardiness ratings that correspond to these zones. For example, Zone 7 represents a temperature range of 0 to 10°F (-18 to -12°C). However, the system is not easily applicable to the west coast of North America, where the influence of the Pacific Coast and topography create their own complex pattern of climate. Hardiness zone ratings comparable to those used in North America can be applied to other land masses such as Europe. The striking feature of coastal Europe is the extent to which the climate is modified by the Gulf Stream, as is seen in the wide range of subtropical plants that can grow in north-west Scotland.

With irrigation, flourishing gardens can even be created in deserts. But increasing demands on water resources everywhere is a good reason to choose plants that do well on the natural water supplies. In most areas the main source of water is rainfall but there can also be moisture from thawing snow, dew and high levels of humidity. Other factors that affect the availability of moisture include the nature of the soil, the slope of the land and the existence of streams and ponds, which may have boggy margins where some plants thrive. Among the most remarkable adaptations are those that get plants through seasonal and long-term drought (see p. 18; pp. 30-31; and pp. 44-45).

Two other climatic factors forming the character of a garden are the amount of light it gets and its exposure to wind. The amount of sunlight varies with latitude, the seasonal differences being more marked in the higher latitudes, but the slope and orientation of the garden are also significant. The amount of wind a garden catches is largely determined by topography with many anomalies ensuring that it is not just gardens on hillsides or near coastlines that are exposed.

There is little that can be done to change the broad pattern of climate affecting a garden but soils can be modified to some extent so that a broader range of plants can be grown. Exploratory digging in various parts of a newly acquired garden gives a good idea of the character of the soil, whether it is light and free-draining or heavy and sticky when wet and baked hard in summer when dry. Plants growing nearby may indicate whether the soil is likely to be acid or alkaline but it is useful to have confirmation by carrying out a test using a simple kit. This involves mixing a soil sample into a chemical solution to produce

Left Many plants, including bulbs such as daffodils (*Narcissus*) and perennials such as *Brunnera macrophylla*, that flower before the tree canopy develops flourish in the cool conditions under deciduous trees.

Far right (top) The shuttlecock fern (*Matteuccia struthiopteris*) and the wake robin (*Trillium grandiflorum*) share a preference for moist neutral to acid soil and light shade. The radiant purity of the wake robin is retained in the double form (*T. grandiflorum* 'Flore Pleno').

Far right (bottom) All roses require well-lit conditions and most only flower freely where they can grow with full sun. Clematis, which in this sunny garden are trained over arches with roses, are adaptable climbers but grow best where their roots are shaded and cool.

Right The hybrid tulips (*Tulipa*) do best in sunny sheltered positions where the soil is fertile and well-drained. Forget-me-nots, cultivars of the woodland *Myosotis sylvatica*, tolerate full sun and light shade.

Below Signet marigolds, derived from the Mexican *Tagetes tenuifolia*, and the purple-flowered South American *Verbena rigida*, a fast-maturing tuberous perennial that is often grown as an annual, are ardent sun-lovers that thrive in fertile well-drained soils.

a colour change which gives an approximate pH reading (see p.20 and p.78). As a general rule, it can be assumed that the structure and nutrient levels of all soils can be improved by the addition of organic matter, such as garden compost and leafmould, which is worked in to the soil or added as a mulch. Waterlogged soils in which many plants will simply die of asphyxiation can be brought to life by improving the drainage but the laying of tiles to achieve this is an expensive and labour-intensive operation. Even after improvement, soils betray their underlying character and the humble gardener bows to it.

Numerous local variations are found within any broad pattern of climate and soil types. Altitude, slope, outcrops of underlying rock, proximity of hills and bodies of water are all factors that modify the growing conditions. In our small-scale gardens, the human environment can also have a major influence. In towns and cities, temperatures, especially in winter, are likely to be a few degrees higher than in the surrounding countryside. The built-up city is also a heavily shadowed world where gentle breezes can quickly turn into turbulent gusts.

Familiarity with your garden will reveal other variations. There are obvious contrasts of sun and shade, the shade being cast by buildings, walls or established trees. The ground may be permanently wet in places while elsewhere even a gentle slope may be sharply drained. Some corners are cool, others are suntraps. Strong winds catch some areas while others remain serenely calm. The recognition of these interlocking microclimates and variations in drainage and soil is the beginning of rewarding gardening in which plants are placed where they will grow best. The section from pp. 52–75 looks at the broad approaches to planting that apply in most of the temperate world while more specialized conditions are covered on pp.76–101.

Below In a classic arrangement a pair of herbaceous borders backed by shrubs flanks a narrow path. Apparently casual repetition in the planting creates a subtle rhythm.

Bottom Compact sun-loving annuals and biennials, such as daisies (*Bellis perennis*) or, as here, *Dianthus* hybrids, are useful low plants for the frontal positions in borders.

SUNNY FLOWER BORDERS AND BEDS

Flower borders of a kind existed long before the 19th century. On the whole, however, they were clearly defined areas in which floral treasures, including choice tulips and carnations (*Dianthus*), were sparingly planted, with a considerable amount of bare soil showing between them. Fashionable and intelligent interest in the large number of herbaceous plants introduced in the 19th and early 20th centuries, the availability of cheap labour and the influence of persuasive and eminent gardening writers such as Gertrude Jekyll, saw the border transformed. From being a collection of individual plants it became a co-ordinated assembly, the beauty of the whole exceeding that of the individual plants of which it was composed.

The herbaceous border of the kind described by Gertrude Jekyll, its most influential exponent, is not well suited to small gardens and requires considerable maintenance. Nonetheless, it continues to exercise a tremendous hold on the imagination of gardeners. Fortunately, there is still much that can be learned from imaginatively planned and well-managed borders and applied to gardening on a smaller scale. It is, however, the new developments in gardening with perennials that are much closer to the spirit of this book.

HERBACEOUS BORDERS

The classic herbaceous border consists of a rectangular plot, rarely less than 20ft (6m) long and 6–12ft (1.8–3.7m) deep, in an open sunny position, backed along its length by a hedge or wall and flanked on its other side by a grassy walk. In the grandest arrangements a pair of borders flanks a broad grassed walk. Sometimes a paved path runs along the edge of a border. Where this is not the case mowing is made easier if a narrow run of paving or bricks is set just below the level of the grass. Plants that flop forward are not then damaged. If the border is deep enough, a narrow gap along the base of the wall or hedge provides useful access and simplifies trimming.

The border's dramatic impact is partly achieved by staged variations in the height of component plants. While avoiding a rigid ranking, the aim is to encourage the eye to work easily backwards and forwards, with the shortest plants at the front and the tallest at the back. Borders composed of dwarf plants (disproportionately numerous in nursery

lists) give an idea of the dulling effect of uniform height. Gertrude Jekyll recommended planting in drifts, with plants of a kind grouped in irregular bands that interweave as they run at an angle across the border. As well as resulting in complex juxtapositions of form and colour, this method of planting helps to introduce a pleasing irregularity in heights but it is not effective in a narrow border. In many interesting borders the occasional straying of a tall airy plant such as *Salvia uliginosa* towards the front makes a slightly eccentric but welcome variation. If there is a backing wall, its planting should make a vertical extension of the border. At Sissinghurst, the garden created by Vita Sackville-West and her husband Sir Harold Nicolson, and now one of the best-known National Trust properties in England, the purple border provides a superb example, with clematis and other climbers providing a remarkable interplay of rich and light tones.

Contrasts of scale, shape and form add to the dynamic aesthetics of the border but nothing counts for quite as much as colour. Among the successes of plant breeders is a remarkable extension in the colour range available in perennials. The choice makes it possible to build up monochrome schemes, lifted by touches of colour; quiet harmonies, silver-greys and pastels, for example; vibrant contrasts, orange, say, intensified by blue; flaunted clashes of reds; and apparently random mixtures, given sense, perhaps, by the repetition of key colours.

The herbaceous border is in its prime in mid- to late summer and there is a long period between autumn and spring when there is very little vegetation and a lot of bare soil showing. In small to medium-sized gardens this is a strong case for a border to be mixed, in which a framework of branches and evergreen leaves gives body and interest even in the winter months. To Edwardian owners of large gardens the border's short season hardly mattered. They might well be away when it was out of season or the spotlight might be turned on other horticultural splendours so that the blankness of the border could be forgotten.

Top left Beds crowded with sun-loving plants that flower in early summer – among them alliums, bearded irises and peonies – risk becoming dull late in the season.

Top The highly bred border phloxes derived from *Phlox paniculata*, a plant from eastern North America usually found in wooded areas near streams and rivers, reach their peak in late summer.

Above The genus *Campanula* includes many species that excel in temperate gardens. *C. latiloba*, from northern Turkey, in the wild found at the edge of woodland, is one of many bellflowers that is suitable for borders.

53

However, it is worth making the effort to extend the border's season. Spring bulbs can be added, tulips being more suitable than daffodils, for their foliage dies down more tidily. The customary practice is to lift tulips annually but, if left in the ground, a surprising number persist from year to year, although they may need to be topped up. Bulbs are often considered a nuisance in the border but, provided their location is well noted, there is no need for them to be disturbed when the ground is being cultivated. Biennial wallflowers planted in autumn provide clumps of green through the winter and deliciously scented warm-coloured distractions in spring. They have to be positioned where their replacements – dahlias are possibilities – will fit in. Other early flowering plants that can help to set the border season going are more often associated with rock gardens but their compact growth makes them suitable for frontal positions. Sea thrift (*Armeria maritima*) or even aubrietas can be used, but aubrietas need to be trimmed after flowering.

Early summer is exaggeratedly lamented in Britain as the June gap. There is no *embarras de richesses* but there are plants of superb quality, especially geraniums, bearded irises, peonies and oriental poppies, as well as old favourites, such as lupins and aquilegias. One pays for the magnificence of the oriental poppies, which are very untidy as they die back and they need to be carefully positioned so that the gap left by the collapsing foliage is obscured as the season advances.

The great wealth of material to choose from for the high season can be a source of frustration. A lifetime is too short for many major reworkings of a border. It is not surprising that some borders long-established in historic gardens have retained their initial colour scheme and a core of good plants, although often enriched by exciting new introductions. The professionally designed border, laid out all of a piece, frequently requires modification, even radical alterations. The amateur can allow a border to evolve more gradually, perhaps in the early stages using annuals and tender plants to try out colour schemes and to experiment with heights and shapes. These same plants – including dahlias, penstemons and salvias – are of great value, too, for extending the border season into late summer and even into autumn. But for really effective autumn displays few plants can match the chrysanthemums.

Cutting back dead growth and tidying the border in autumn and applying a mulch in spring are basic to the maintenance of a border. There must also be a regular programme of renovation. Some perennials, including peonies, are long lived and better left undisturbed. Others, among them delphiniums, are short lived and the performance of many perennials declines after two or three years if they are not lifted and divided. This is best done selectively on an annual basis

during the dormant season, between autumn and spring. Diseased plants should be burned and the old woody centres that no longer produce vigorous growth can be discarded.

Staking is the border chore that gives cause for most complaints. In well-manured soil, close planting and the proximity of a backing wall or hedge tend to encourage lanky growth. The solid background also helps to create turbulent conditions. To prevent the tallest plants, particularly delphiniums, from being knocked about and toppling, some staking is necessary. In a large border this can be laborious work and must be well timed so that plants are not damaged before or while supports are being put in. It comes at a busy time, between mid- and late spring. Bamboo canes that stand above plants when these have reached their ultimate height are unsightly. To be inconspicuous, canes should be kept within the upper limit of the foliage. Soft string looped around stems and two or more canes to a plant should allow a certain amount of free movement. Large areas of a border and smaller groups of plants can be stiffened with brushwood that has had the tops bent over to form an interlocking mesh. Sloping panels of wide-mesh plastic netting can also be used to give support. They need to be about 1ft (30cm) high where they start, set back from the front of the border, and about 3ft (90cm) high at the back. If only a few plants need support, purpose-made frames are an alternative to canes or brushwood.

Island beds, championed by the British nurseryman Alan Bloom, free the border from its backing wall or hedge and reduce the need for staking. Without a wall or hedge there is better air circulation, plants are stronger and more erect, and the tallest, grouped towards the centre, do not lean out and shade lower plants at the edges. Island beds work well in large gardens but are less satisfactory within the rectilinear framework of small to medium-sized gardens.

Above Tall delphinium hybrids demand staking but lupins can usually be left to their own devices.

Below Astilbes, Siberian irises and the royal fern (*Osmunda regalis*) thrive in moist or even boggy ground in sun or partial shade. The feathery plumes of astilbes come in shades of pink, red, mauve or white.

Left Perennials such as aquilegias, tall campanulas and thalictrums are the dominant components of this freely planted sunny hillside garden backed by shrubs and trees.

Below left A deep pink rock rose (*Cistus*), the ornamental onion (*Allium cristophii*) and euphorbias suggest the Mediterranean but this collection of plants is eclectic, the brightest component being hybrid penstemons.

Below In a dry garden (see also pp. 88–91), where texture counts for as much as colour, the purple-flowered *Verbena bonariensis*, which is usually short-lived, and the prickly biennial *Eryngium giganteum* self-seed among perennials. These include the feather grass (*Stipa tenuissima*) and the lemon-yellow *Anthemis tinctoria* 'E. C. Buxton'.

A FRESH APPROACH TO PERENNIALS

A reaction to the sophistication of herbaceous borders and the labour involved in maintaining them has coincided with a growing interest in plant ecology. A freer approach to gardening with perennials, strongly influenced by the ideas of the German nurseryman Karl Foerster, exploits the large number of species and the less highly bred perennials, of which there are sufficient to provide planting material for almost any garden situation. In this style of gardening, which is not constrained by a need to create massed effects, the first principle of planting is to select perennials that suit the growing conditions. It does not rely on a conventional layout of borders and lawns, although these are not necessarily excluded. More commonly it is created in an area defined by trees and shrubs and crossed by paths, well-placed groups of plants being combined in a range of sizes to provide a subtle rhythm.

A different tuning is needed to enjoy this kind of gardening to the full. Flower size is smaller, and flower colour much less vivid and varied than in the border. Texture and form become more important, with greater weight being given to ferns and grasses, plants often poorly represented in traditional borders. The whole plant matters, the poise of its stem and foliage just as much as its flowers, and also its full seasonal progression from first shoots to winter russet foliage and dry seeds and fruits. And the plants need to be seen as only one part of an environment sympathetic to wildlife of all kinds.

For the gardener one of the main attractions of this approach is that it involves relatively low maintenance. There is initial work clearing ground of perennial weeds and lightly working the soil, partly to find out about its character so that a workable planting scheme can be devised. Weeding in the initial stages is necessary but the aim should be to allow plants to develop a reasonably close ground-cover – although not monoculture groundcovers exclusively for weed control. Initial close planting to limit weed competition can be thinned as groups spread. Expansion and self-seeding are taken for granted but the gardener may sometimes have to intervene, controlling plants that threaten to overwhelm less vigorous neighbours. The selection of plants means that watering and protection from cold are only necessary in exceptional circumstances and many of the pest and disease problems resulting from lush growth are eliminated by not feeding. As the following pages show, gardening with a light rein can be applied to many situations, so long as the right plants are chosen.

Above In this meadow-like garden, low perennials, such as violas, are combined with taller plants, including aquilegias, bearded irises and poppies (*Meconopsis* and *Papaver*). Old walls have been colonized by dwarf campanulas, sedums and other rock plants.

Sunny Mixed Borders

The commonsense solution of combining shrubs, perennials, bulbs and a few annuals to form integrated plantings is far from new. All of these components could sometimes be found in Edwardian herbaceous borders and certainly jostled together in the cottage garden. Mixed borders, as these plantings are usually described (the term does not imply that the plantings occupy a geometrically regular space) make sense in small and medium-sized gardens, where they provide the best chance of creating a well-furnished look for all 12 months of the year. They make sense, too, because their own layered structure reflects that of plant communities in the wild. The aesthetic and horticultural interest of a mixed border is much greater than that of a shrubbery, an area

devoted to a close planting of shrubs, usually with an underplanting of vigorous groundcover. Tired remnants of 19th century plantings have been partly responsible for the bad press shrubberies get. There is a place for them at the outer reaches of large gardens but as self-evidently dull solutions they make a garden seem a horticultural problem, not the delight it might be with the leavening power of bulbs and perennials.

SHRUBS FOR FOLIAGE

The spine of a mixed border is usually composed of interlocking shrubs. Evergreen broad-leaved shrubs, including hollies (*Ilex*), some of which are better grown as shrubs than as trees, laurels (*Prunus*), mahonias and *Osmanthus* are rated for the way they provide bulk and weight throughout the year. The varied forms and foliage colour of the dwarf and slow-growing conifers seem to offer a lot but often disappoint. When used in numbers these plants, which have crowded twigs and leaves, can make the border seem congested; the deadening effect of their appalling stillness often leaves one craving bare earth.

Foliage is given much more weight in the mixed than the herbaceous border. As well as giving body to the border, the foliage of evergreens provides a background that shows off a succession of incidents. In intensity these may fall short of high moments in the herbaceous borders but any loss of drama is compensated for by the integration of components that keeps interest alive all year. It is the variation of scale, shape, texture and colour that makes the mixed border such a rich tapestry. The seasonal changes, marked even enough in some evergreens, take a dramatic turn with deciduous shrubs such as the smoke bushes (*Cotinus*) and *Euonymus alatus*.

Below left The jagged leaves and the pale green flowers of *Helleborus argutifolius*, which is a shrubby evergreen perennial, complement a planting of bulbs, from early dwarf irises to late tulips, over a long spring period.

Below right The sumptuous flowers of the perennial *Paeonia lactiflora* 'Sarah Bernhardt' are bedded here with shrubs such as *Rosa glauca* and *Pittosporum tenuifolium*. The cool *Iris pallida* 'Variegata' skirts the front of the border.

Bottom A wave of brightly coloured perennials, including fiery *Crocosmia* 'Lucifer', yellow-flowered *Achillea filipendulina* 'Gold Plate', day lilies (*Hemerocallis*), golden rod (*Solidago*) and rudbeckias, seems poised to overwhelm the shrubs and trees. These include *Buddleja globosa*, *Hypericum* 'Hidcote' and *Robinia pseudoacacia* 'Frisia'.

FLOWERING SHRUBS

Although very satisfying borders can be planted that rely almost exclusively on foliage effects, flowers usually play an important role. Shrubs that flower over a long season – examples include *Abelia* × *grandiflora*, hardy fuchsias, the mophead hydrangeas, several hypericums and shrubby mallows such as *Lavatera* 'Barnsley' – are understandably popular but a border packed with them can become monotonous. Shrubs that offer a welcome pause after their first flush before flowering again include the Mexican orange (*Choisya ternata*) and *Syringa microphylla* 'Superba', a lightly built deciduous lilac.

Shrubs that flower either side of the main season and contribute to the border's interest year round have a special value. A surprising number of the best-scented plants are shrubs that flower in winter and early spring, competing for the attentions of the relatively few pollinating insects that are about. Among the pick are several viburnums, the deciduous *Viburnum* × *bodnantense* bearing fragrant flowers on naked wood over a long period between autumn and spring. Several daphnes are also winter flowering, among them the deciduous mezereon (*Daphne mezereum*) and the evergreen *D. odora*.

All of these are reasonably ornamental, at least while in flower. By comparison the shrubby winter-flowering honeysuckles, of which *Lonicera* × *purpusii* is the best, are nondescript. Dullness when out of flower is a problem with many fragrant shrubs of spring and summer, among them the richly scented viburnums, such as *Viburnum carlesii*, the lilacs (cultivars of *Syringa vulgaris*) and the mock oranges (*Philadelphus*). At least with mock oranges the scent is so far reaching that they do not need a prominent position and the choice of cultivars includes several that are compact. One way of giving dull shrubs a new lease of life is to use them as supports for climbers of moderate vigour, the small-flowered clematis that flower in late summer and autumn being well suited to this purpose (see pp. 179–80). The ornamental shortcomings of important fragrant shrubs make one reappraise several that stand up well throughout the year. The winter-flowering and evergreen *Mahonia japonica*, more richly scented than the hybrid mahonias, is a conspicuously jagged plant throughout the year. And *Choisya ternata*, which continues to flower intermittently after its main spring flush, is furnished year round with glossy aromatic leaves.

Top There is a place for *Buddleja alternifolia* in mixed borders. Here, it dominates a mixture containing *Rosa* 'Fritz Nobis', a white peony (*Paeonia lactiflora*) and *Campanula persicifolia*.

Above *Euphorbia griffithii* 'Dixter' has dramatic orange bracts but on light soils this spurge can spread too freely.

Just as valuable as the shrubs of winter and early spring are those that add a sequel to the main summer season. Many of these flower on the current season's wood and need cutting back in spring. Several in the blue range are very effective at freshening the border in late summer and autumn. Russian sage (*Perovskia atriplicifolia*), a sub-shrub that can be cut back to near ground level in spring, has small violet-blue flowers carried on downy white stems above aromatic grey-green leaves. A blue of great intensity is that of *Caryopteris × clandonensis*, a shrub that also has aromatic foliage. *Ceratostigma willmottianum* has flowers of clear blue and the foliage colours well in autumn.

ROSES

The large-flowered and cluster-flowered bush roses (Hybrid Teas and Floribundas) are remarkable for their long season and the quantity of flower they produce but their gawky stiffness and their cultivation requirements make them far less satisfactory for mixed borders than the old and modern shrub roses. Some of the modern shrubs such as *Rosa* 'Golden Wings' and many of the English Roses bred and introduced by David Austin, repeat well but others, and nearly all the old shrub roses, have a single glorious flush lasting a few weeks.

Many of these roses look perfectly at home in mixed borders but there comes a point when there are enough of them to demand their own territory. If you have admitted defeat on this front, the best solution is to combine them with an underplanting and edging of sympathetic perennials and low shrubs. Lady's mantle (*Alchemilla mollis*), aquilegias, old-fashioned pinks (*Dianthus*), diascias, low geraniums, compact lavenders, lambs' ears (*Stachys byzantina*), *Viola cornuta* and the biennial foxglove (*Digitalis purpurea*) are among plants that will help to sustain a border largely devoted to shrub roses.

BERRIES AND STEMS

Although not a substitute for flowers, berries and stems enrich mixed borders with their colours and textures. Rose hips and many berries are often well coloured by late summer but it is those that persist into autumn and even winter that warrant special plantings. Disappointments are sometimes the result of unfavourable weather or early losses to birds, which seem oddly inconsistent in the interest they show in berry crops. However, the most common causes of failure are to do with pollination. Several berrying trees and shrubs, among them hollies, have male and female flowers on separate plants. Female plants of these kinds must have a male in the vicinity if they are to bear crops. Some other shrubs, among them viburnums, only crop freely when there are two or more specimens in close proximity to ensure cross-pollination. Cotoneasters, somewhat lacking in other respects, are in the first rank of berrying shrubs, with a colour range that extends to black, yellow and coral. Among the most surprising berry colours are the blue of *Viburnum davidii* and the violet of *Callicarpa bodinieri* var. *giraldii*.

Above left Roses do not have to be grown in isolation in a rose garden. Grow them in mixed borders with carpets of low-growing perennials for added interest.

Above *Rosa* 'Iceberg' and other roses are important in this garden but so, too, are numerous perennials and shrubs that anchor the planting.

Main picture opposite A pampas grass, *Cortaderia selloana* 'Sunningdale Silver', and a coppiced yellow-leaved Indian bean tree (*Catalpa bignonioides* 'Aurea') are bracketed with *Dahlia* 'Bishop of Llandaff' and *Sedum spectabile* 'Brilliant' for a strong autumn display.

Below Its flowers do not count for much but the vigorous *Rosa glauca* is a strong candidate for mixed borders. The foliage is blue-green in summer and the hips vivid red in autumn.

The rich colour or greyish bloom on the young stems of several deciduous shrubs and trees, including several dogwoods (*Cornus*) and willows (*Salix*), can be an important winter feature. Plants grown for this need to be cut back (coppiced or pollarded) regularly to ensure a supply of young stems, which are more colourful than old wood.

ANNUALS AND BIENNIALS

While a border is still young and shrubs and perennials have yet to reach their mature size, annuals and biennials are the ideal fillers. The more expensive alternative is to plant closely, thinning as the shrubs and perennials begin to fill out, a necessary operation but calling for resolution that the faint hearted may find it difficult to muster. Some annuals and biennials choose to stay on, self-seeding with differing degrees of success. The poached egg flower (*Limnanthes douglasii*), honesty (*Lunaria annua*) and forget-me-not (*Myosotis*) will come up year after year, as will several short-lived perennials, among them *Campanula persicifolia*, *Salvia sclarea* var. *turkestanica* and the tall *Verbena bonariensis*. Some annuals wheedle their way into one's affections and are difficult to dispense with even though they have to be sown annually. Leaving areas free for annual planting means more work but it is easy to be convinced that clumps of cosmos or the annual mallow *Lavatera trimestris* 'Mont Blanc' will give the border a timely lift.

BULBS

Bulbs that are positioned among other plants tend to get forked up during cultivation. This is a disadvantage, especially when perennials are being lifted and divided, but set against the effect bulbs make in a mixed border it is trivial. Many of the smaller bulbs – among them crocuses, chionodoxas, grape hyacinths (*Muscari*), puschkinias and scillas – can be planted under the canopy of deciduous shrubs. A position under shrubs also suits daffodils (*Narcissus*), the growth of perennials helping to mask the untidiness of their dying leaves. In a more open position spring foliage will grow over the less conspicuous leaves of tulips. By the time the ornamental onions (*Allium*), most with splendid spherical heads, come into flower their foliage is already looking untidy and they need to be planted behind perennials, such as geraniums, that make early growth. The key bulbs later in the season are lilies; there are few bulbs that can give borders such a shot in the arm. They are well suited to planting in bays among shrubs, so that the base of the plant is lightly shaded and the top exposed to full sun.

Far left Bulbs add much to borders but they undoubtedly complicate cultivation. The untidy foliage of alliums, often dying while the plants are still in flower, can be masked by lamb's ears (*Stachys byzantina*) or similar foreground plants.

Left Planting tulips to grow through forget-me-nots (*Myosotis*) is a gardening cliché but it bears repetition. The yellow lily-flowered tulip here is *Tulipa* 'West Point'.

Below The yellow-green foliage of the trees and shrubs enhances the warm colours of late summer flowers. Day lilies (*Hemerocallis*), red hot pokers (*Kniphofia*) and the yellow-flowered *Coreopsis verticillata* all stand up to some degree of frost but where frosts are normal in winter the tubers of dahlias need to be lifted annually.

PERENNIALS

In a mixed border there is room for great variation in the proportion of perennials to shrubs. At one extreme the border can be largely dominated by perennials with a light stiffening of shrubs. At the other, perennials may be used as little more than fillers and edging. In a balanced border on an open site where there are inlets between the shrubby plants it is possible to have a wide seasonal range and various heights, representing preferences for full sun and part shade. Staking for the tallest may be necessary. Frontal open positions can be filled with low-growing plants such as *Campanula carpatica* and *Geranium renardii* mixed with low shrubs such as the rock roses (*Helianthemum*). Taller-growing perennials, such as the catmint *Nepeta* 'Six Hills Giant', can be used to hide the dying leaves of bulbs. For the middle ground some of the most suitable will tolerate part shade. Particularly attractive are those perennials that work their way up through other plants such as *Viola cornuta*. To some extent the scale of the border will dictate the height of the tallest but even very large perennials such as *Crambe cordifolia*, cardoon (*Cynara cardunculus*) and plume poppies (*Macleaya*) do not look out of place overtopping the backbone of shrubs.

ORNAMENTALS COMPETING WITH GRASS

A flowery meadow scattered with splendid trees was a medieval ideal of a paradise garden. The appeal of flowers in grass is easily appreciated but its first great advocate as a style of gardening was the influential 19th-century garden writer William Robinson, who was reacting against the formal bedding that dominated gardens of his day. In our own time the loss of wildflower meadows in agricultural land has encouraged many to create meadows of their own.

The open grasslands that provide the model for flowered lawns and wildflower meadows are far from being truly natural (see p. 32). Human intervention has controlled the growth of trees and shrubs and, in the most flower-rich meadows, annual removal of hay without the application of fertilizers has kept the soil poor so that grasses, usually strongly dominant, do not overwhelm other plants. This delicate balance depends on the grasses being relatively uncompetitive species, not bullies like agricultural rye grass (*Lolium* species).

Encouraging flowers to grow in grass holds out the prospect of relaxed gardening. There is, however, a lot of labour involved in the early stages of creating a wildflower meadow and it may take several years for a stable community of desirable plants to become established that can be maintained by a few cuts a year. In the short term, prospects are brighter for non-purists who are happy to include exotic species in grass that can be cut less often than a conventional lawn.

THE GRASS AND FLOWER COMPONENTS

Commercially available mixtures for sowing wildflower meadows are usually three parts grass, in which several species are represented, and one part wildflowers. Most of the flower seed is of perennials. As well as being appropriate to the acid or alkaline chemistry of the soil and its moisture content, the mixture should contain seed of plants that grow locally. The ideal is to have seed gathered locally, so that one is not bringing in different genetic material. Conservation-minded gardeners are sometimes surprisingly comfortable with the degree to which mixtures are manipulated. Yarrow (*Achillea millefolium*) and oxeye daisy (*Leucanthemum vulgare*) may be common locally but mixtures containing them are sometimes rejected because these are quick developers and do not give other plants a chance to get started.

Many gardeners will be happy to include non-native perennials in a wildflower meadow, or even allow them to dominate. Plants that are suitable for meadows on chalk or lime include *Aster amellus*, the bellflower *Campanula persicifolia*, several pinks (*Dianthus*), the blue flax *Linum perenne* and the silky Pasque flower (*Pulsatilla vulgaris*). Among the most lovely wildflowers for growing on moist soils are the meadow cranesbill (*Geranium pratense*), Jacob's ladder (*Polemonium caeruleum*) and several primulas.

Annuals are opportunists that flourish in disturbed ground, not true grassland plants. But corn cockle (*Agrostemma githago*), cornflowers (*Centaurea cyanus*) and the field poppies (*Papaver rhoeas*) are showy plants and are often included in seed mixtures as a nurse crop. Eventually they are crowded out by others unless the ground is disturbed again.

Top Daffodils are the easiest bulbs to grow in grass and multiply steadily if the mowing regime does not begin until the leaves die down in summer. *Narcissus* 'February Gold' and other Cyclamineus hybrids are better suited in scale than some of the heavily built daffodil hybrids that are often favoured for naturalizing.

Above Lupins on roadsides and railway embankments show their ability to form self-sustaining colonies.

Bulbs are among the easiest and most satisfying plants to establish in grass and if gardeners are prepared to draw on the plants that are not native to their area, the range available is considerable. Many bulbs that are suitable for naturalizing in woodland thrive in sunny open positions. Dwarf bulbs include spring- and autumn-flowering crocuses and winter aconites (*Eranthis*). The most widely planted of the taller bulbs are daffodils such as the Lent lily (*Narcissus pseudonarcissus*) and the Cyclamineus hybrids, but the dwarf *N. cyclamineus* itself and *N. bulbocodium* are of incomparable beauty when planted in large drifts. The snake's head fritillary (*Fritillaria meleagris*), with nodding chequered flowers, and the camassias are suitable for moist soils.

CREATING AND MAINTAINING FLOWERED LAWNS AND MEADOWS

If the prime aim is to create a pleasing ornamental effect rather than to conserve wildflowers, changing the mowing regime of an existing lawn is a simple and reasonably satisfactory option. Unlike a wild-flower meadow, this can be effective even on a small scale. Some wildflowers may establish themselves, daisies (*Bellis perennis*), bird's-foot trefoil (*Lotus corniculatus*) and germander speedwell (*Veronica chamaedrys*) competing with fine lawn grasses. These grasses should be used if sowing a lawn, perhaps with some wildflower seed added. If buying turf, ensure that it is of good quality and contains no rye grass. Bulbs supplemented by plants such as primroses (*Primula vulgaris*) are the obvious plants to enrich this kind of lawn.

Above Damp meadow suits a European species of fritillary, *Fritillaria meleagris*, which holds on as a wild plant or naturalized introduction in parts of Britain. The snake's head fritillary, as it is known, is more commonly a chequered purple but there are many gradations between this and the white form (f. *alba*) on which the tessellation is no more than a greenish shadow.

Below In the wild, Quamash (*Camassia quamash*) is found in very varied habitats, not merely marshy ground, but readily naturalizing in damp grass.

The best chance of establishing wildflowers in grass is on poor soil, especially on chalk or limestone. The removal of topsoil is a drastic measure that is sometimes advocated. Repeated mowing and removal of cut grass is a slower and less radical way of reducing fertility. Sowing cleared ground with an appropriate mixture of grass and wildflower seed is the most economic and effective method of establishing plants. Sowing in small patches of ground that have been cleared in existing areas of grass is usually less effective. Other options include planting out growing mixtures of grass and wildflowers, either as wildflower turfs or, more economically, in the form of small plugs spaced evenly on prepared ground. Large-scale planting into existing turf is generally ruled out on grounds of expense but on a small scale can be a successful way of establishing perennials. To be effective, however, competition from surrounding grasses must be reduced, which usually means applying a weedkiller before planting. Mowing at an early stage helps to control weeds while desirable plants

become established. Thereafter the mowing regime must be geared to the cycle of the plants growing among the grass. The first cut of the year can be made in early summer if crocuses and other dwarf and early-flowering bulbs have been used. Where there are daffodils, the first cut must be delayed until mid-summer. If there are autumn-flowering bulbs, cutting must stop in late summer or early autumn. The cut grass needs to be raked off but if it is left to dry first there is a chance of valuable seeds being left behind. Closely mown paths through flowery lawns and meadows are practical and provide scope for imaginative contrasts of short and long grass.

Above With a backdrop of trees it is possible to create the impression that the garden is emerging from the edge of woodland.

Below The Japanese maples (*Acer japonicum* and *A. palmatum*) do well in sheltered sites on moist soils and can eventually develop into large shrubs or small trees. The foliage is beautiful from its delicate unfolding in spring to its smouldering and incandescent climax in the autumn.

TREES

Trees are the ultimate plant sculptures, wonderfully varied in the structure of their woody frames and in the canopies that these support. Compared with other plants they are slow to reach maturity but once mature they seem, at least when set against a human's life span, permanent features of the garden. Their presence in woods and forests or even in assembled clumps in parkland can be on an awesome scale. Some trees are planted in the knowledge that it will be for future generations to appreciate their mature beauty, but there are a surprising number of trees for medium-sized gardens that will even give pleasure to impatient gardeners. Others are planted principally because they make rapid growth, providing shelter at the boundaries of gardens.

WOODLAND GARDENS

Lucky are the gardeners who start with established woodland. The shaded and sheltered environment under trees provides conditions in which a wide range of shrubs, perennials and bulbs will thrive. The broadest range of plants can be grown if the shade is dappled and where there are glades resulting from occasional breaks in the canopy.

A woodland effect of sorts can be created on a surprisingly small scale, perhaps using an existing tree or clump as the nucleus. The remnants of an old orchard could be the starting point, although the ordered planting of an orchard goes against the free spirit of woodland, where the art is to seem artless. This is a point to bear in mind when choosing trees to supplement the nucleus or when starting from scratch. A large variety of trees grouped in contrasting shapes, colours and textures is too self-conscious for woodland.

SPECIMEN TREES AND FORMAL PLANTING

The ornamental qualities of individual trees are particularly important when there is room for only one or two trees and where specimens are to be isolated, for example as focal points in lawns. The shape and stance of a tree can be its principal recommendation. Most trees growing naturally have a strong central leader supporting a balanced

arrangement of branches, as in *Liquidambar*, or develop a more rounded branched head, as in ornamental cherries (*Prunus*) and crab apples (*Malus*). Gardeners show an interest in shapes that are less common in nature, often preferring weeping trees, those with tiered horizontal branches or contorted stems and others with growth that is narrowly upright (fastigiate) or densely columnar.

Flowers are a principal feature of many trees, among them the thorns (*Crataegus*), the magnolias and the crab apples. In their flowering season some of these trees can make a sensational impact and it is asking a lot to expect their ornamental qualities to be sustained throughout the whole year. Fortunately, among the small trees there are a good number that are beautiful in flower and produce impressive crops of fruits. The crab apples and the thorns are outstanding, while some of the ornamental cherries follow their high point in spring with richly coloured foliage in autumn. The flowers of *Sorbus* are less impressive but the genus includes trees suitable for small gardens that have good autumn colour and plentiful crops of attractive fruits.

Colourful foliage year-round, or in the case of deciduous trees from spring to autumn, has both merits and drawbacks. Distinctive bark, on the other hand, is invariably a feature worth noting. The rich patterning of *Parrotia persica*, the cinnamon-red of *Arbutus* × *andrachnoides*, the burnished red-brown of *Prunus serrula* and the ghostly whiteness of *Betula utilis* var. *jacquemontii* are enough to make these plants stand out in any garden.

The shade that trees create can be a vice or a virtue. Too near the house and it takes light from rooms – and the roots of trees may cause damage to foundations and to drains. Too dense and over too large an area and the garden becomes dank and sunless. There is no denying that the range of trees for small gardens is limited. The most suitable, like the Mount Etna broom (*Genista aetnensis*), have an airy canopy that lets plenty of light through. Thinning the canopy of denser trees can help to let more light in but this is work for a qualified arboriculturist. An easier operation is the removal of lower branches, allowing light to reach under the canopy at an angle. Trees of fastigiate growth are widely recommended but they often make awkward and graceless substitutes for close relatives that are well balanced. In a small garden it may be better to create height and manageable shade with climbers growing on a well-proportioned pergola or arch (see pp. 68–69).

Except in orchards, the formal planting of trees is now largely confined to ordered rows forming avenues. To achieve an even and regular appearance the plants should be of the same clone or grafted on to the same reliable stock.

Above Topiary and even gentle shaping of trees, in this case the silver-leaved *Pyrus salicifolia* 'Pendula', arouses strong feelings. There is, however, a place for it in firmly ordered areas of the garden.

Below Some botanists consider that the magnolias belong to one of the most primitive families of flowering plants. It is universally acknowledged that they are in the first rank of ornamental trees.

Bottom Gardeners who plant *Prunus* 'Shirotae' and other flowering cherries must be reconciled to the brief duration of their blossom.

CLIMBERS

Climbers are the athletic opportunists of the vegetable world, relying on more plodding growers to provide support as they rush skyward. Their questing nimbleness which makes them so successful in the wild is also their great asset in the garden. They provide a link between garden floor and canopy and where no canopy exists make their own. With their supple grace they create an impression of profusion and yet are not space-consuming. Climbers are malleable, readily responding to the hand of the gardener, who can train them round architectural features, up screens to block out unsightly views, and over pergolas and arches to create shade. And they do not necessarily have to climb. Wisterias trained as standards, roses trailing down banks, ivies sprawling along a woodland floor and clematis spilling out of a tall jar are reminders of the versatility of this group of plants.

CLIMBERS ON LIVING SUPPORTS

The most natural way of growing climbers, training them through other plants, is curiously neglected by many gardeners, despite its many advantages. The tapestry interweaving of climber with shrubs or trees, climber with climber, even climber with herbaceous perennials, is one of the most effective ways of creating an integrated planting. At its simplest it mimics the airy nonchalance of plants growing in the wild. The effect is particularly telling when the climber adds another season of beauty to its support. In the classic combination rambler roses climb into old fruit trees that are no longer yielding useful crops but produce a good display of blossom and a few colourful fruit in autumn. A vigorous rambler such as *Rosa* 'Bobbie James' needs little encouragement to race high into the canopy, from where in midsummer it spills showers of fragrant flowers, like a magically improved second crop of blossom. It has to be said that the rose's embrace can eventually be too much for an old fruit tree and that pruning of the rose (ramblers flower most freely if stems are cut out after they have flowered) is problematic.

The success of these marriages depends on matching the vigour of climber and support. Climbers also need help to start. Where trees have made a close network of roots near the surface, the climber may need to be planted outside the area of the canopy and then trained in. Large forest trees are needed for giant climbers such as *Hydrangea anomala* subsp. *petiolaris*, *Vitis coignetiae* and wisterias. For shrubs and trees with light frames clematis are often the climbers of first choice. They are particularly useful for shrubs that flower in spring or early summer, some of which, like the cultivars of the common lilac (*Syringa vulgaris*), are ponderously dull when not in flower. A slender climber of great appeal in late summer is the flame creeper (*Tropaeolum speciosum*). It is, however, in danger of becoming something of a cliché as a wandering decoration on dark hedges, yew showing off the vivid scarlet of its flowers to perfection.

CLIMBERS ON WALLS

The most common way of training climbers in the garden, in two planes on walls, is highly effective at integrating house and garden and producing dramatic effects in small enclosures where there is barely

Top left In the wild, clematis climb from shade to light, clinging to supports with hitches of their leaf stalks. In the garden, moderately vigorous Viticella hybrids, such as 'Etoile Violette' and 'Abundance', can be planted to scramble over and through vigorous shrubs.

Top The ornamental gourds (*Cucurbita pepo*) are hardskinned and inedible versions of squashes, pumpkins and marrows. Their romping growth and quaintly shaped and coloured fruits make them amusing annual climbers.

Above The rambling *Rosa* 'Albertine' often cursed by mildew but glorious in midsummer is backed by the sweetly scented *Lonicera periclymenum* 'Graham Thomas', a yellow-flowered form of the European woodbine.

room for narrow borders. By combining climbers and wall-trained shrubs there is plenty of scope for well-timed coincidences of flowering and long successions of bloom. In fully paved yards climbers and shrubs can be planted in containers but when grown in this way they need more attention than those in the open ground and regular watering is essential. Walls that are in good condition are not likely to be damaged by self-clinging climbers such as ivy (*Hedera*) and Virginia creeper (*Parthenocissus*). Climbers that pull themselves up by other means need wires or trellis to get a purchase.

Whatever the support, it should stand out from the wall by about 4in (10cm); climbers growing tightly against a wall tend to be more prone to disease than those that have air moving more freely about their leaves and stems.

Preference for sun or shade, less critical when climbers are growing in three dimensions, becomes an issue when the orientation is dictated by a wall. One that gets full sun (in the Northern Hemisphere a south-facing wall) seems on the face of it a choice position. It does provide conditions in which growth ripens well, encouraging frost resistance and generous flowering. When grown on a shady wall, wisterias and other sun-lovers are likely to produce lush foliage but poor crops of flowers. However, the growing conditions at the wall's base often pose problems. Most climbers like well-drained but moist rather than dry soil and the base of a wall, particularly a sunny wall, is often the driest area of a garden, partly because a wall creates its own rain shadow, and it is sometimes rubbly. Measures that help get round these problems include the addition of generous quantities of well-rotted compost or similar organic material that boosts the humus content, planting about 18in (45cm) from the wall with the roots trained away from it, and additional planting – but not so that there is strong competition for moisture and nutrients – to shade the roots of climbers. (See also p.75 for shade-tolerant climbers.)

Top right Solanum crispum 'Glasnevin', usually grown as a wall shrub, is here trained on a metal arch, with a hybrid of the small-flowered *Clematis viticella* making a bright accent at the base.

Above The ivies, including large-leaved kinds such as *Hedera canariensis* 'Gloire de Marengo', are as useful covering ground as they are on walls.

CLIMBERS ON FREESTANDING SUPPORTS

Architectural features in a garden are prime sites for climbers. Pergolas and arches that are not clothed with climbers barely make sense; an ornamental bridge festooned with blossom is a delicious and romantic surprise. It has already been suggested that a simple structure such as an arch supporting climbers can be a more manageable way of introducing height in a small garden than the planting of a tree (see p.67). The same principle can equally be applied when a larger garden is being established; a pergola can be smothered by ramping vines long before trees are making an impression. Screens that are made of trellis and planted with climbers are an alternative to hedges. Sprinters for quick cover include annuals (and perennials that are grown as annuals) such as morning glory (*Ipomoea*), the canary creeper (*Tropaeolum peregrinum*) and the cup and saucer plant (*Cobaea scandens*). Matching the sturdiness of the support and the vigour of the climber is, of course, very important. Tall focal points can be created in borders with pyramids of trellis and metal frames around and through which plants are trained. Less pretentious and just as pleasing are tripods and wigwams of bamboo canes or brushwood loaded with sweet peas (*Lathyrus odoratus*).

Top The contrast between formal and informal components, full sun and shade, and areas of dense and spare planting can create dramatic tensions in a garden. A yew hedge (*Taxus baccata*), one of the best hedging plants in shade, marks the divide between two contrasting areas, one under trees planted informally with shrubs such as *Viburnum* x *burkwoodii* and another consisting of an expanse of grass.

Above The brilliant, even shrieking, colours of some azaleas and rhododendrons, such as *Rhododendron augustinii*, can strike a harsh note in a woodland setting. The company of other shade-tolerant shrubs that thrive in acid conditions helps establish a balance. *Corylopsis*, a small Asiatic genus of deciduous shrubs with dangling clusters of pale yellow flowers, is ideal.

Above right Since the late 19th century, a large number of rhododendron species have been introduced from Asia and their hybrids are legion. In scale, flower colour, leaf size and shape they show great diversity but all need acid growing conditions and most benefit from light overhead protection.

SHRUBS IN WOODLAND

Woodland gardening as a style is surprisingly modern. It represents an important shift in taste in the latter half of the 19th century but it was also a response to the dramatic increase in plant introductions from temperate regions of the world, especially the Himalayas, western China and Japan. In woodland gardening at its best there is an effortless combination of exotic and native plants creating an impression of perfected nature.

Many of the shrubs best suited to the woodland garden are to some extent shade tolerant but few thrive in dense shade. In the wild they are often plants of glades and woodland margins, where they get filtered sunlight and often direct sunlight during part of the day. A large number thrive only on soils that are neutral to acid, well-drained but moist and rich in organic matter. Non-native shrubs are usually vigorous enough to compete with many existing plants but aggressive spreaders should be cleared before shrubs are planted.

The tree canopy of a woodland garden is the protector of the plants layered beneath it. The microclimate (see p. 16) it creates reduces the risk of frost damage, cuts water loss and gives shelter from wind. The ideal canopy is that of deep-rooting trees that cast dappled shade, such as oak (*Quercus*). Woodland gardens in exposed areas need the additional defence of well-maintained shelter belts (see p. 96) composed of tough plants such as Leyland cypress (x *Cupressocyparis leylandii*).

RHODODENDRONS

The great woodland gardens of the 19th and early 20th centuries were repositories for the hundreds of rhododendron species introduced from the Himalayas and western China and were also nurseries for the breeding of hybrids. The rhododendron in its many forms remains the

woodland shrub par excellence. This is especially so on acid soils in north-west North America, New Zealand and areas of western Europe where the climate is mild and moist. Enthusiasts extol the varied ornamental qualities of the genus. In size plants range from midgets to large trees and show considerable variation in plant growth. There is also an impressive choice of flower size and shape, colour and a judicious selection can give a very long flowering season. The foliage itself can also be a feature, some of the evergreens being interesting for the colour, texture and size of the leaves, while many deciduous azaleas colour well in the autumn. Detractors, however, point out the conflict between the character of the rhododendron hybrids and their use in naturalistic planting. The colours of some have a synthetic stridency, the dense massing of the flowers is like that of bedding plants writ large, and out of flower many are lugubrious. By a discriminating choice of species and hybrids, and a willingness to use them with other shrubs, however, the pitfalls of woodland gardening with rhododendrons and azaleas can be avoided. Their fibrous root system allows them to be moved with relative ease so there should be no hesitation rectifying mistakes in initial planting.

Below Shrub planting in gardens is more often inspired by woodland edge than by woodland depths, where only very shade-tolerant species thrive under a full deciduous or even denser evergreen canopy. Here, autumn sunshine lights the bright foliage of deciduous shrubs such as maples (*Acer*).

Bottom The tiered branches of *Viburnum plicatum* 'Mariesii', laden with a greenish show of sterile florets, stand out in a glade-like setting or backed by larger shrubs and trees.

BEYOND RHODODENDRONS

Other plants for dappled shade on moist neutral to acid soils include the calico bush (*Kalmia latifolia*) and the Japanese *Enkianthus campanulatus*. Quite outside the ericaceous camp are the hydrangeas. By far the most widely grown are the mophead and lacecap forms of *Hydrangea macrophylla*. On acid soils, where they do best, there are strong blues, on alkaline soils they are pink. The mopheads can look very townish and it is easy to feel that they strike a false note in a woodland setting. More suitable choices can be found among the lacecaps and other species, including the oak-leaved hydrangea (*H. quercifolia*).

Some shrubs, including species of *Corylopsis* and *Fothergilla*, that are valued for their spring flowers are also impressive for their autumn colour. A continental climate is needed to bring a woodland garden to its full autumn climax but even where the contrasts between summer and winter are less marked it is worth planting for a blaze of colour at leaf fall. Maples (*Acer*) are the supreme genus for autumn colour. The Asiatic species *A. japonicum* and *A. palmatum* tolerate lime but need moist soils rich in organic matter. A sheltered position in woodland protects their delicate foliage from cold winds and rapid thaw following frost. The pleasing outlines of these trees and shrubs and the rich colours of their autumn leaves are seen to best effect against broad-leaved and coniferous evergreens such as holly (*Ilex*) and yew (*Taxus*).

Those who garden on a grand scale can include shrubs and small trees that thrive in the sheltering embrace of woodland but do not need shade. These include dogwoods such as *Cornus kousa*, winter-flowering witch hazels (*Hamamelis*) and spring-flowering magnolias.

THE WOODLAND FLOOR

Shade-tolerant bulbs and perennials make the tapestried beauty of the woodland floor. The mix is usually international, including daffodils (*Narcissus*) and primroses (*Primula vulgaris*) from Europe, trilliums and trout lilies (*Erythronium*) from North America, hostas from Japan and blue poppies (*Meconopsis*) from the Himalayas and China. Few of these plants will grow in deep shade, and even ferns, more tolerant of shade than most flowering plants, do best in reasonably bright conditions. Many of the bulbs make their growth, flower and start to die down before deciduous trees overhead are in full leaf. Most of the perennials do best beneath the edges of the tree canopy, where they get some angled light for at least part of the day as well as filtered light from overhead. In comparison, the dark shade under conifers or the secondary canopy of evergreen rhododendrons is a hostile environment. Most of the bulbs, as well as the perennials, flourish in soils that are moist and rich in organic matter, and some require neutral to acid conditions. Few will grow in dry shade under beech trees (*Fagus sylvatica*) and even trees that cast light shade but are surface rooting, such as birches (*Betula*), leave little moisture for bulbs and perennials.

Below left In the wild many lilies are plants of forest glades and this kind of setting suits even such spectacular hybrids as *Lilium* 'Casa Blanca'.

Below The hellebores (*Helleborus*) are a major group of winter- and spring-flowering perennials which are particularly suitable for woodland conditions. Here, purple-flowered *Hepatica nobilis* 'Rubra Plena' has been planted with a long-flowering Lenten rose (*Helleborus orientalis*). The prettily silvered leaves of the autumn-flowering *Cyclamen hederifolium* last until early summer.

Once established, many native and non-native plants are capable of looking after themselves with a very low level of maintenance. Some are altogether too successful. In a large piece of woodland there is a place for coarse and vigorous plants such as comfrey (*Symphytum*), yellow archangel (*Lamium galeobdolon*) and the greater periwinkle (*Vinca major*) but they are bullies that will overwhelm choicer plants and a decision to plant them should not be taken lightly.

For the choicest of the woodland plants, including the blue poppies (*Meconopsis*) and trilliums, the garden needs stronger management. Although the charm of wildness is to some extent sacrificed, the ground needs to be cleared, dug over and improved with the addition of well-rotted organic matter. A mulch, ideally of leaf mould, helps to keep down weeds and conserve moisture. This level of management is less a problem where a limited area under the canopy of a small cluster of trees is gardened to create a woodland effect. For the area covered, the proportion of bulbs and perennials used will be higher than in woodland proper but the aim must still be to convey in the casual grouping of clumps and the placing of individual specimens an impression that plants have found their own way into the garden.

Above Bulbs that flower early and are dormant by mid-summer are an important feature of natural woodland in the temperate Northern Hemisphere. Among the easiest plants to naturalize under deciduous trees are the yellow-flowered winter aconite (*Eranthis hyemalis*) and snowdrops (*Galanthus* species).

Below When allowed to spread freely in semi-wild conditions, either under trees or in more open conditions, the English bluebell (*Hyacinthoides non-scripta*) produces a unique massed spring display of blue flowers. In the more ordered parts of the garden it can quickly become a nuisance.

BULBS

The woodland garden bright with bulbs before the leaves of deciduous trees unfurl is the epitome of spring. A relatively narrow range of plants is enough and should not contain large-flowered hybrids. The vigorous hybrid daffodils may seem to offer more than small flowered hybrids and species such as *Narcissus pseudonarcissus* but in a woodland garden they look showy and overdressed. For a large area, expense will probably dictate the choice of the common snowdrop (*Galanthus nivalis*), say, rather than named selections, which are best reserved for a small-scale special feature.

Bulbs should be planted, not too densely, in small irregular groups with a few outliers. Winter aconite (*Eranthis hyemalis*) and snowdrops (*Galanthus*) settle down more quickly if planted "in the green", that is immediately after flowering, rather than as dry bulbs. In time, some bulbs, including wood anemone (*Anemone nemorosa*) and winter aconite will form very large colonies if grown in conditions that suit them. *Crocus tommasinianus*, best in a glade-like opening, also spreads freely but small rodents may take a heavy toll. *Cyclamen hederifolium* will even self-seed in quite dry shade. The blue tides of English bluebells (*Hyacinthoides non-scripta*), it must be admitted, are at the expense of other plants.

Many lilies and their close relatives are well suited to woodland conditions. The turk's-cap lily (*Lilium martagon*) naturalizes easily but the bulb sensation in woodland conditions is the giant lily (*Cardiocrinum giganteum*), which has a massive stem up to 12ft (3.7ft) high and steeply angled, richly scented, white trumpets.

PERENNIALS

Cool refinement rather than starry glamour marks the best of the woodland perennials. Their character is typified by plants such as the Lenten roses (*Helleborus orientalis*) and Solomon's seal (*Polygonatum × hybridum*) of spring, early summer geraniums such as the sombre mourning widow (*Geranium phaeum*), the elegantly poised autumn-flowering *Kirengeshoma palmata* and subtle foliage plants such as epimediums. Even the most eye-catching plants have an aristocratic reserve. With their improbable azure, the Himalayan blue poppies such as *Meconopsis grandis* seem as envoys from a remote and magical region. They tend to be monocarpic, dying once they have flowered, but in lime-free conditions where the atmosphere and soil are moist it is worth taking considerable trouble to maintain colonies.

73

BORDERS IN SHADE

Trees and shrubs in the garden create shady conditions that relate closely to those of forest and woodland. In small gardens additional shade is cast by buildings, walls or fences. In Mediterranean heat architectural shade may have a special value as a place of retreat but in cooler climates we want to sit on sunny lawns or patios, surveying an idyll of foliage and flowers that is often relegated to shady areas.

Some of the problems attributed to shade are to do with other aspects of the growing conditions. The soil at the base of walls is commonly the poorest in the garden, choked with limy builder's rubble and dry, the walls themselves causing areas of rain shadow. In addition, walls cause turbulence, which can wreck long-stemmed and fragile plants. Removing rubble and replacing it with organic-rich soil is worth it where practicable. The minimum aim should be to work in plenty of organic material every year. The perennial problem of rain shadow can only be overcome by regular watering, even in spring and autumn, combined with the use of a mulch. The answer to turbulence is to use sturdy plants closely planted for mutual support.

The problems that are specific to shade are largely the consequence of inappropriate planting. Plants with a low tolerance of shade become drawn and their weak growth is prone to disease. Some plants that are reasonably tolerant of shade although essentially sun loving produce foliage at the expense of flowers when grown in shade. There is, however, compensation in that flowers in shade usually last longer than those in full sun. Tall and upright plants tend to lean out when planted close to walls. Staking is time-consuming, difficult to conceal and plants, when fettered, lose much of their grace. A better solution is to rely more heavily on plants of rounded growth set 2–3ft (60–90cm) from walls and backed by climbers or wall-trained shrubs.

Most of the shrubs, perennials and bulbs suitable for woodland can be grown in the shade of walls and buildings, provided the soil is rich in organic matter and kept reasonably moist. To these can be added a very large number of plants that grow well with little or no direct sunshine provided they get plenty of light and there is no over-

head shade. A deeply shaded courtyard surrounded by high walls will always present problems but there are plants even for these conditions and light levels can be raised by painting walls white.

USEFUL QUALITIES IN SHADE

Plants that flower with unstinting generosity despite the conditions have a special value. In some important categories of ornamentals there are relatively few plants that flower freely in shade. Roses, for example, disappoint, although among old roses Albas such as *Rosa × alba* 'Alba Maxima' perform reasonably well and a few climbers, famously the white 'Madame Alfred Carrière', flower blithely even on a wall that gets little direct sun. The selection is thin among annuals, biennials and bedding plants but among those suitable several provide a broad colour range, notably busy lizzies (*Impatiens*), polyanthus (*Primula* Polyanthus Group) and the numerous pansy and viola hybrids (*Viola*). The colour range of tobacco plants (*Nicotiana*) is limited but their height, especially of *N. sylvestris*, is an advantage.

In other categories of plants, including climbers and shrubs, the choice is wider. Most honeysuckles (*Lonicera*) are best in shade and many clematis flower just as freely as in sun without the flowers being bleached of colour. Major groups of shrubs that flower prolifically include camellias, fuchsias, hydrangeas and mock oranges (*Philadelphus*). The camellias need shade where the flowers are not caught by early sun (rapid thawing of frost on flowers causes browning of the petals). Some shrubs, notably skimmias and pyracanthas, are more colourful in berry than they are in flower.

Bulbs and perennials provide flowers for most of the year, starting with snowdrops (*Galanthus*) and lungworts (*Pulmonaria*) and continuing into autumn and beyond with monkshood (*Aconitum*) and Japanese anemones (*Anemone × hybrida*). Flowers that are white or pale give the shady border a special lift. Plants that add touches of cool bright radiance include *Narcissus* 'Jenny', *Camellia japonica* 'Alba Plena', *Philadelphus* 'Sybille', *Hydrangea macrophylla* 'Madame Emile Mouillère' and *Anemone × hybrida* 'Honorine Jobert'.

Foliage with light-enhancing qualities also has a special value. Matt dark leaves, especially heavy purples, weigh down a shady border but leaves with polished surfaces reflect light. Evergreen shrubs with glossy leaves include the Mexican orange (*Choisya ternata*), *Fatsia japonica* and camellias. Several hostas, such as *H. plantaginea*, have leaves with sheeny surfaces but for lustrousness nothing can quite match bears breeches (*Acanthus mollis* Latifolius Group). Variegation

is a more light-enhancing effect with which to freshen shady borders, but overuse can create a hectic look. The contrast of white and near whites with green is very crisp in *Hosta undulata* varieties, *albomarginata* and *univittata*, as well as in many hybrids. A striking white-variegated shrub is *Cornus alba* 'Elegantissima', silvery in summer and with red stems in winter. In theory plants with yellow leaves or yellow variegation should seem like patches of sunshine in shady borders. In practice, yellow foliage, which often burns in full sun, can look a jaundiced green in full shade. Relatively die-fast yellows include cultivars of *Euonymus fortunei*, several ivies and the hollies (*Ilex*).

Below A position in the shade of a wall often provides the shelter from cold winds and late frosts that camellias need. But they also require lime-free soil and plenty of moisture. *Camellia japonica* 'Gloire de Nantes' starts flowering in winter.

Left Many species of columbine, including the granny's bonnet (*Aquilegia vulgaris*), are woodland plants that adapt well to the walled and confined conditions of town gardens, provided the ground is reasonably moist. Plants are short-lived but they self-seed freely.

Special Conditions and Solutions

The rainless hearts of deserts and regions of permanent ice and snow are almost the only parts of the world where there is no natural vegetation. It is a point to bear in mind when contemplating a garden that seems to present impossible growing conditions. For every "problem" garden there are suitable plants that have highly specific requirements or, looked at in another way, remarkable tolerances. Matching these plants with particular growing conditions is the subject of the following section (pp. 78–101). Far from being concerned with joyless gap-filling, we are touching here on some of the most passionately pursued branches of horticulture, where the combination of special growing conditions and the plants that thrive in them produces features or gardens with a highly distinctive character.

For novice gardeners the dislike some plants show for soils containing lime seems a perverse complication. It is, however, a fact to which gardeners quickly become reconciled, partly because there are many good plants that happily straddle the acid-alkaline divide, partly because gardens on acid or alkaline soils appeal so directly. A large number of shrubs of the understorey that flourish in moist acid soils have already been touched on under woodland (see pp. 70–71).

Moisture-loving plants are not simply a solution to planting boggy areas. From a very early stage in the history of garden making, still and moving water has been used to create special features. Pools, channels or lotus lakes existed in the gardens of Ancient Egypt, in those of Persia at the time of Cyrus the Great and in the earliest gardens of China, a country with the longest continuous tradition of garden making. The water garden has taken on a life of its own but so too has the bog garden, a feature developed to accommodate the lush water-loving plants from the Himalayas, China and South America that in the 19th century were added to the plants known from Europe and North America.

Many drought-resistant plants have a long history in cultivation simply by virtue of being native to the classical world. Rosemary (*Rosmarinus officinalis*) is characteristic of Mediterranean plants in

Above Planted in paving, *Tulipa sprengeri* and border geraniums produce flowers and leaves that dissolve the sharp edges between paths and borders in a lightly shaded garden, where a true peony (*Paeonia suffruticosa*) is in bloom.

Below right Violet purple *Salvia nemorosa* stands out in a dry garden of drought-tolerant plants, which include *Euphorbia characias*, with large heads of green bracts, and ornamental onions (*Allium*).

Below Deciduous rhododendrons, *Meconopsis* and *Primula* thrive in the cool, damp, lime-free soils of a woodland edge.

being well adapted to long hot summers followed by moderate rainfall in a mild winter. Plants from the Mediterranean region and areas with a similar climate have acquired new status as components of dry gardens that have to get through hot summers without being watered. Although pursuing the subject takes us outside the temperate regions, it is incomplete to speak of drought-tolerant plants without referring to the most successful among them, the succulents and other desert plants that miraculously manage to survive in areas of low or negligible rainfall. Like the plants for tropical and subtropical gardens, they do not feature heavily in the "Plant Directory", but their tenacity, their sculptural forms and the often improbable splendour of their flowers have earned them a keen following and a branch of gardening, known as desert gardening or xeriscaping, uses them extensively in arid areas where nothing else would thrive without heavy watering.

Alpines and rock garden plants are another group of ornamentals that have inspired a special branch of gardening. Many can be grown without the creation of a specialized area, for example on well-drained banks, at the front of borders, in dry stone walls and in cracks among paving. They almost all require sharp drainage but many of them also need a good supply of moisture during the growing season. Gardeners in the 19th century felt that they had to represent miniaturized alpine scenery in their grandiouse rock gardens. However, a raised bed filled with a gritty compost is a much simpler special feature than these. Many of the plants show adaptations that are very similar to those found among some plants of coastal areas, especially against the desiccating effects of strong winds. But coastal plants are equipped to deal with yet another problem, the presence of salt.

The section on tropical and subtropical gardens completes the parallels between wild and cultivated plants. Those of us who garden in the temperate world will recognize some of them. Some are annuals, such as the African and French marigolds (*Tagetes*) that have to be started off under glass in cool climates. In a back-to-front way other plants, such as the Swiss cheese plant (*Monstera deliciosa*), seem to have strayed outdoors from the conservatory or sitting-room. But these are figures overwhelmed in a vast crowd and the colourful richness of it is a reminder of the extent and variety of the plant world.

Top *Iris sibirica*, a perennial found in the wild from central and eastern Europe to Russia, and the Chinese *Primula bulleyana* form a naturalized swathe at the base of a slope in moist soil that is rich in organic matter.

Above Damp ground by the side of a stream, on which float the leaves of a water lily (*Nymphaea*), provides the growing conditions that suit a wide variety of lush foliage plants, including perennial hostas and ferns.

Above The mock oranges (*Philadelphus*), heavily scented shrubs of mid-summer, do well even on poor thin chalky soils. *Crambe cordifolia*, a perennial that makes a large cloud of small white flowers, will also grow in similar conditions.

Above right Highdown, near Worthing, Sussex, is an inspiration to British gardeners on chalk, having been developed from the early 20th century in the unpromising setting of a chalk pit. A remarkable range of plants was grown there by its creators Sir Frederick Stern and Lady Stern.

Below Red valerian (*Centranthus ruber*), to some gardeners a bothersome weed, especially when its roots become established in walls, is a splendid perennial on dry chalky slopes.

THE ACID-ALKALINE DIVIDE

The terms calcifuge and calcicole express one of the great divides in the plant world. Lime-hating plants (calcifuges), which take their stand on acid soils, and plants that flourish in lime-rich conditions (calcicoles) seem like the adherents of a major religion ranged either side of a fundamental dogma. By far the most rigid are the calcifuges, yellowing with disapproval when a trace of lime pushes the pH over 7, the point of neutrality. Most of the lime lovers and their loose adherents, however, tolerate soils that are neutral to slightly or even markedly acidic. In practice, therefore, it is gardeners on alkaline soils that have to be most particular in choosing plants and this section is focused on their needs. Other sections of this book cover woodland gardens on acidic soils (see "Shrubs in Woodland", pp. 70–71) and acid-loving plants (see "Specialized Gardens on Acid Soils", pp. 80–81).

Some gardeners are so besotted with rhododendrons and other calcifuges that even on strongly alkaline soils they contrive conditions to suit them, resorting to dependence on chemicals. Far better, though, to embrace lime-tolerant plants with enthusiasm and to delight in their very varied ornamental qualities. Most of the plants that give gardens on chalk and lime their distinctive character belong to families that are enthusiastic lime lovers or are so easy going that it makes no odds. Wild flowers in grassland on chalk, a model for meadow gardening (see p. 65), give an idea of their beauty. Others come from families that show a mixture of responses to lime, some genera and species implacable in their hatred of it, others often tolerant to a remarkable degree.

LIME ENTHUSIASTS AND EASY-GOING PLANTS

The genus *Dianthus*, which includes pinks, carnations and sweet Williams, is among the pick of the lime-loving families. Many have an old world charm but their ornamental value in borders and raised beds, as well as in many other open positions where the soil is free draining, does not depend on mere sentimental association. The peonies (*Paeonia*), shrubby and herbaceous, have also long been in cultivation, their sumptuous beauty being appreciated in China and Japan long before the Asiatic species and hybrids were added to those grown for centuries in Europe. The winter- and spring-flowering hellebores (*Helleborus*), currently riding on a crest, have a subdued beauty, most exciting in the Lenten roses (*H. orientalis*), with white, green, pink and plum flowers, in some cases heavily speckled. Clematis do not need lime to make healthy vigorous growth, as was once often asserted, but the fact remains that the genus as a whole is a great success where there is lime in the soil. In the temperate garden there are no climbers to match them for seasonal and colour range.

These few genera are the tip of an iceberg. There are also trees, on the large scale beeches (*Fagus*), on a smaller scale most species and hybrids of *Prunus* (the ornamental cherries from Japan being something of a surprise since many plants from this region are lime hating). The dove or handkerchief tree (*Davidia involucrata*), breathtaking when it hangs out its large white bracts, is representative of the

numerous plants from western China that grow readily on alkaline soils. In gardens Asiatic shrubs such as buddlejas grow well with species and hybrids of *Cistus* and other shrubs of the Mediterranean, where limestone formations are common. The choice among perennials also includes plants from many parts of the world. Most of the perennials belonging to the following genera flourish where there is lime in the soil: *Acanthus, Agapanthus, Campanula, Euphorbia, Kniphofia, Gypsophila* and *Scabiosa*. To these can be added numerous annuals and biennials such as wallflowers (*Erysimum*) and stocks (*Matthiola*). And there is almost the whole gamut of bulbous plants, with the notable exception of lilies (see below).

LIME-TOLERANT PLANTS AMONG THE LIME-HATERS

No group of plants is more notorious for its intolerance of lime than the vast ericaceous family, with its mobs of rhododendrons. It has even given its name to lime-free composts. Nonetheless, the winter-flowering ericas, including *Erica carnea* and its numerous cultivars, tolerate lime. The family also contains the evergreen strawberry trees (*Arbutus*), of which *A. andrachne, A. unedo* and the hybrid between them, *A. × andrachnoides*, can be grown on alkaline soils.

Undoubtedly the majority of lilies do best in neutral to acid soils. Many, including one of the most spectacular, the golden-rayed lily (*Lilium auratum*) object to the slightest trace of lime. There are, however, glorious lime-tolerant exceptions. In the first rank are two Chinese species, the regal lily (*L. regale*) and the orange-flowered *L. henryi*. The martagon or Turk's-cap lily (*L. martagon*), which is the most widely distributed of the European species, and the splendid *L. monadelphum* from Turkey and the Caucasus, also tolerate lime but these, like the Chinese species, are not suitable for dry chalky soils. The Madonna lily (*L. candidum*) is undeniably capricious but is certainly found in a wild or semi-wild state in the eastern Mediterranean growing in hot dry niches among limestone rocks. Lime tolerance has been passed on to the Nankeen lily (*L. × testaceum*), the first of all the lily hybrids and a cross between *L. candidum* and *L. chalcedonicum*.

The magnolias, among the most beautiful of all flowering trees and shrubs, are best known as plants for acid to neutral soils but a surprising number tolerate lime. Few will thrive on the free-draining conditions of chalk, although *Magnolia grandiflora* can succeed even here if nursed through its first years. Others that do well on moist soils containing lime include *M. kobus, M. × loebneri* and *M. stellata*. Plants that stand out in other genera on account of their lime tolerance include *Acer griseum* among the maples, *Eucryphia cordifolia* and the hardier *E. × nymansensis* in the eucryphias, *Gentiana septemfida* among the autumn-flowering alpine gentians and *Hydrangea aspera* and the vigorous climbing *H. anomala* subsp. *petiolaris* among the hydrangeas.

The roses are also mixed in their reactions to lime. The least satisfactory are the large-flowered modern bush roses (hybrid teas), but even many of these do reasonably well on a heavy soil that contains lime. The most satisfactory are the climbers and ramblers, the cluster-flowered modern bush roses (floribundas) and vigorous old and modern shrub roses, the Albas, for example, and hybrids such as 'Nevada'.

Above Although camellias are said to be slightly more tolerant of lime than rhododendrons, healthy growth can only be expected on moist lime-free soil. A high broken canopy, as here, helps protect the flowers from frost and wind.

Below The early-flowering hybrid *Clematis* 'Proteus' makes a starling appearance among the variegated leaves of *Actinidia kolomikta*, often with more white to give a distinctive tricolour effect. Both plants tolerate alkaline soils but clematis do not require lime, as is sometimes asserted.

SPECIALIZED GARDENS ON ACID SOILS

Two distinctive and contrasting garden features are associated with plants that prefer or require acid soils. Heather gardens exploit the capacity of plants of moorland and heath to form a dense interlocking cover that excludes weeds. As a result, they are usually intended as low-maintenance features over extensive areas. The plants used are heather or ling (*Calluna vulgaris*) and heaths (*Daboecia* and *Erica*), all small-leaved and small-flowered members of the ericaceous family. Species from the great stronghold of ericas in the wild, South Africa, are excluded from the typical heather garden of temperate regions by their relative tenderness. Several ericas, notably the winter heath (*E. carnea*) and the Darley Dale heath (*E. × darleyensis*), will grow on chalky soils. Nevertheless, extensive gardening with heaths and heathers is largely confined to acid soils.

On a much smaller scale raised beds with moist acid soil that are positioned in light or partial shade provide growing conditions suitable for a number of alpines and small woodland plants that will not tolerate lime. The height of the bed allows the refinement of these plant treasures to be appreciated. Raised beds with acid soil are sometimes referred to as peat beds; peat blocks were commonly used to construct the walls and peat was added to the soil as a lime-free conditioner. Because of the ecological damage done to wetlands by the large-scale extraction of peat, peat substitutes should be used in the construction and as the growing medium. Some gardeners fight against the conditions of their gardens and construct raised beds with an acid growing medium in gardens on chalk, isolating the bed with a liner. This is a perversity that deserves to fail.

HEATHER GARDENS

As an allusion to wild heathland and moorland, heather gardens cannot fail to disappoint. The scale and openness to the elements of wild landscapes covered with heathers are heightened by the poverty of the vegetation and the broad effects of the seasonal changes. The model does not translate well to suburban gardens, where the view ends with a house wall or a boundary marks an incongruous juxtaposition of heather garden and lawn or heather garden and colourful border.

The strongest reason for planting heathers extensively is that they provide relatively low-maintenance cover that gives foliage and flower colour over a long season, even the dead flowers having a quiet serene beauty for weeks. The work involved in planting and maintaining a heather garden is not, however, negligible. The ground for planting must first be cleared of any weeds. The young plants, set deeply, about 18in (45cm) apart, closer in the case of the less vigorous kinds, will

Top The taller heaths – the Portuguese heath (*Erica lusitanica*) and the tree heaths (*E. arborea* and *E. a.* var. *alpina*) – together with shrubs and trees can help to make the heather garden a more interesting association of plants than the conventional mixture of low heaths and dwarf conifers.

Centre Many dwarf cultivars of heath (*Erica*) and heather (*Calluna vulgaris*) give long-lasting effects in cool temperate gardens. However, real variety in the genus is found in the Cape heaths.

Bottom On reasonably moist soils, amelanchiers make good two-season shrubs to back heaths. In spring they are a mass of small flowers and colour well in autumn.

take several years to knit together to form a weed-suppressing ground cover and during this time some weed control will be necessary. Fire, the means of rejuvenating heather on grouse moorland, is not an option open to the gardener. Mechanical trimming in spring or after flowering for winter- and spring-flowering heaths, will help to keep the plants vigorous and bushy but after 8 to 10 years the cover will become sparse and replanting will be necessary.

One of the few places where a heather garden can hardly be bettered is as a transition to a wild open landscape. An effect that is too managed would jar but planting heaths or heathers in groups of 6 or more can give a year-round textured succession of flower and foliage colour. There are strong advocates for the use of dwarf and slow-growing conifers as incidents in the heather garden but the match is usually ill-starred, reducing the garden to a state of static joylessness. A better option, if the garden is large enough, is to plant a small cluster of trees such as birch (*Betula*) or rowan (*Sorbus aucuparia*) that are tolerant of acid soils. The more wind-blasted they look the better.

RAISED BEDS ON ACID SOILS

An ideal position for a raised bed is on a sheltered sloping site that faces away from the sun and is lightly shaded but not overhung by trees. However, raised beds can also be constructed in well-lit positions partly shaded by buildings. The most common substitutes for peat blocks are railway sleepers that have been treated with a non-toxic wood preservative. Wood is on the whole preferable to brick as the building material. Lime in the mortar of a brick wall will eventually leach into the soil unless the bed is lined or the inside of the wall is treated with a sealant. A wall height of approximately 10–20in (25–50cm) is adequate. The acid-loving plants suitable for peat gardens can be grown in a mixture of neutral to acid soil (2 parts) with an acid peat substitute (2 parts) as conditioner and lime-free grit (1 part). This needs to be well mixed with the addition of a slow-release fertilizer before being put into the bed. Beds should be watered and then left to settle for a few days before being planted. Once planted, a mulch, say of bark chippings, will help to conserve moisture and keep the bed free of weeds.

To some extent these small-scale features inevitably become repositories for less common and in some cases undeniably difficult plants. However, a raised bed can be of interest over a long season, particularly if the range of plants it contains goes beyond acid-loving shrubs such as *Cassiope*, *Gaultheria* and dwarf rhododendrons and classic perennials such as the autumn-flowering *Gentiana sino-ornata*. Those plants that thrive in the cool moist conditions of a peat bed include a selection of bulbs, among them erythroniums, and woodland perennials like trilliums, the harebell poppy (*Meconopsis quintuplinervia*) and bloodroot (*Sanguinaria canadensis*).

Below left Bloodroot (*Sanguinaria canadensis*) is widely distributed in north-east North America, usually growing in moist deciduous forest. In cultivation it is best known for its double form, 'Plena', a plant of startling whiteness for a peat bed.

Below Most of the trilliums show a marked preference for neutral to acid soil and in gardens as well as in the wild thrive in partial, even quite dense shade. The glistening radiance of the wake robin (*Trillium grandiflorum*), with its parts arranged in threes, makes it a choice plant to grow with erythroniums.

Moisture-Retentive and Heavy Soils

In principle, a soil that has moisture-retaining qualities is a great asset. It will see plants through periods when the natural water supply falters. Even in open sunny borders it will allow many plants to be grown that are strongly associated with boggy places and the waterside. Astilbes, the ornamental rhubarb (*Rheum palmatum*), globe flowers (*Trollius*) and the arum lily (*Zantedeschia aethiopica*) are just a few of the plants that grow happily in moist soils quite divorced from the specialized conditions in which they are often seen.

In a moist and well-drained soil there is a balanced supply of water and air, for the majority of plants the one just as important as the other. In soils that have a high clay content, however, there is no happy equilibrium. In their fine-textured stickiness, their particles so small that they do not leave the myriad pockets of air that give buoyant life to soils, they hold on to water with a sullen tenacity. Clay soils are nearly the despair of gardeners. In a sodden state plants growing in them drown. When they dry out, they bake and crack. They are slow to warm up in spring so that plants make a late start. They fully justify their description as "heavy", being backbreaking to work. They are temperamental about when they can be handled. They are gluey to work on when wet and quickly compact so that what little structure they have is seriously damaged. The best time to dig clay soils is in autumn or early winter, where there are frosts the alternation of freezing and thawing helping to break down large slabs. In spring the gardener has to wait patiently until the clay can be worked. And yet clay soils are redeemed by their fertility and their capacity for improvement and in moderation their water-retaining qualities are invaluable.

Improving Clay Soils

A seriously waterlogged garden on clay soil can only be remedied by the installation of a drainage system in which sloping pipes, laid in a herringbone pattern about 2ft (60cm) below the surface, carry water to a soakaway or ditch. For the amateur gardener with a less serious problem the most important method of improving the soil's structure is to incorporate copious quantities of well-rotted organic matter, preferably worked into the soil and also laid as a mulch while the soil is moist but after it has started to warm up. Although the soil will not be transformed overnight, applications over several years will greatly increase the openness of the soil, creating a better balance between moisture retention and aeration. Other measures that help improve the structure include the addition of generous quantities of horticultural grit or coarse sand and liming. Liming helps the clay particles form into crumbs but inevitably alters the acid-alkaline balance of the soil and is generally advisable only where the conditions are highly acidic.

While overall improvement of clay soils is desirable, it is often better to concentrate resources of time and energy by improving limited areas of the garden. Raised beds that can be worked without being walked on, either loosely mounded or with low walls of board or brick, have a much more general application than the vegetable garden and are particularly appropriate on clay. Even after years of cultivation and the application of generous quantities of organic matter, clay soils will remain heavy but once they are aerated a broad range of plants can take advantage of their fertility.

Planting on Heavy Soils

Given the labour involved in working heavy soils, it makes sense when planting to aim for broad effects that in the long term will require only low-level maintenance. A large part of the garden can be devoted to mixed plantings relying heavily on sturdy shrubs and plants that have a good ground-covering capacity. Well-chosen trees, shrubs and perennials are usually slow to get started but eventually outstrip the same

Top The fat buds of these drumstick primulas (*Primula denticulata*) push through heavy soils in late winter or early spring. The seed-raised plants of this Himalayan species show a colour range from washy mauve to deep purple and white.

Above Golden groundsel (*Ligularia dentata*), cannas and dahlias make a hot colour scheme for the second half of summer on heavy moist soils, on which they do well.

Right Joe Pye weed (*Eupatorium purpureum*) is impressive in scale and has a long autumn season. This clump, at least 8ft (2.5m) high, dwarfs a knotwood (*Persicaria*) and coneflower (*Rudbeckia*).

Opposite A mauve tradescantia and Bowles' golden sedge (*Carex elata* 'Aurea') are key plants in a cluster thriving in moisture-retentive soil.

plants growing on free-draining soils. Some of the best hedging plants, including hornbeam (*Carpinus betulus*), hawthorn (*Crataegus*), holly (*Ilex*) and yew (*Taxus*) do well on heavy soils. Major genera of ornamental trees in temperate gardens, such as maples (*Acer*), crab apples (*Malus*), oaks (*Quercus*) and *Sorbus* species thrive on, or are adaptable to, these conditions. There are many popular shrubs, from the solid spotted laurel (*Aucuba japonica*) to the more showy flowering quinces (*Chaenomeles*) and forsythias, that can be relied on but also shrubs or small trees of real class, including the witch hazels (*Hamamelis*), magnolias and roses. It is sometimes stated that roses require a clay soil. This is not true but they flourish on well-drained clay. Smaller plants with good ground-covering capacity – *Alchemilla mollis*, bergenias and ivies (*Hedera*) – greatly reduce heavy work on a clay soil. They can be used extensively or in combination with more distinguished but hearty perennials such as monkshood (*Aconitum*), day lilies (*Hemerocallis*), heleniums, primulas and coneflowers (*Rudbeckia*). Almost all of these plants, woody and herbaceous, will benefit if soil mixed with grit or coarse sand is worked around the roots in the planting hole.

Plants that cannot be expected to do well on heavy soils unless special provision is made for them include those of marginal hardiness and broad categories that thrive in free-draining soils. These include most rock garden plants, almost all plants with silver foliage, many Mediterranean plants (*Euphorbia characias* is an exception) and numerous annuals. It must be expected that bulbs, too, are ill-suited to heavy soils but there are in fact a number that are highly successful. These include snowdrops (*Galanthus*) and daffodils (*Narcissus*), and a sprinkling of other bulbs, including camassias, bluebells (*Hyacinthoides*) and the summer snowflake (*Leucojum aestivum*). Few lilies can be added to these but the Caucasian *Lilium monadelphum* is a distinctive exception. Any measures that improve the drainage of heavy soils will greatly increase the range of bulbs that can be grown. Even on an improved clay soil it is worth planting individual bulbs, especially lilies and fritillarias, on a bed of grit or coarse sand.

WATER AND WATERSIDE GARDENS

Mirror reflections, cascades of splintered light, the splash of fountains or the gentle murmur of a quiet current all add a dimension to the garden that has an age-old fascination. While it is uncommon for a garden to contain natural bodies of water, whether still or moving, the ready availability of flexible and rigid liners and simple pumps to circulate water have made it easy to install ponds, streams and fountains. Even a tiny paved garden has space for a tub or pot.

These water features provide scope for a range of different plantings but, even with the fringe of plants that thrive in shallow water, the water garden itself is much less important as an area for planting than the moist ground that sometimes lies close to streams, ponds and lakes. The combination of fertile soil and an unfailing supply of moisture produces rapid growth in trees and shrubs and prodigious size and lushness in perennials.

The wonderful exuberance of plants that can plug in to a dependable supply of moisture means that water and waterside gardens demand regular maintenance and vigilance. Weeds thrive in the same conditions and can romp away in spring before they are crowded out by dense growth. During and after the growing season the gardener almost certainly has to step in and re-establish a balance of forces that has tilted in favour of the most aggressively vigorous plants. And initial caution about what to introduce is well justified, for the beguiling can turn into monsters.

DEEP WATER AND SUBMERGED PLANTS

Water lilies (*Nymphaea*) are by far the best known and most varied of aquatics for planting in the deepest water, with species and hybrids that thrive in tropical and temperate conditions. The most vigorous are suitable for lakes but many thrive in ponds less than 2ft (60cm) deep. All, however, are best suited to still water. Their many-petalled starry flowers are of ravishing beauty but it is the shade cast by their foliage and that of other plants with floating leaves that is of critical importance to the ecological balance of a pool. A combination of light, warmth and nutrients encourages the growth of aquatic algae, which can make the water of a pond as turbid as pea soup or fill it with blankets of green filaments. These unsightly although perfectly natural growths are only temporarily and ineffectually checked by chemical control. A much more certain long-term solution is to plant so that about a third of the water surface is covered by leaves. The inclusion of submerged plants such as hornwort (*Ceratophyllum demersum*) or curled pondweed (*Potamogeton crispus*) also helps, for these compete for the salts that encourage the growth of algae. They also play an important role as oxygenators and they provide cover and

Top left Water irises such as the plain-leaved and variegated yellow flag iris (*Iris pseudacorus*) give double value with their reflections when planted in the shallow margins of ponds.

Above Water lilies (*Nymphaea*) vary greatly in their vigour, some tolerating a depth of almost 10ft (3m) but several of the pygmy water lilies will grow in less than 1ft (30cm) of water.

Top In the south-eastern states of America the swamp cypress (*Taxodium distichum*) lives up to its name, stands of it draped with Spanish moss (*Tillandsia usneoides*) being found in alluvial valleys. This deciduous conifer, however, makes an adaptable waterside tree.

Above A small stream and pool allow scope for the imaginative use of waterside and floating plants.

breeding sites for fish. Keeping nutrients to a minimum will help to control algal growth. If possible, ponds should be topped up with rainwater rather than more nutrient-rich tap water and fertilizers should not be used with the planting medium. Small pools are more likely to suffer from the problem of algal growth than larger bodies of water because the rapid fluctuations in temperature make it difficult to establish a steady balance while the water level requires a more frequent topping up.

In natural bodies of water and in clay-puddled pools water lilies and other aquatics can be planted directly in the soil on the bottom. In pools made from flexible or rigid liners it is best to plant in micro-mesh or lined baskets that are topped with a layer of gravel so that the soil particles do not dirty the water.

THE WATER MARGINS

Plants that tolerate their feet being plunged in water are a godsend to the gardener who wants to create a natural-looking pond. The challenge in establishing such a pond is to make it sit in its setting so that it seems to have been there always. Marginals help the eye slip over the give-away seam where land and water meet, particularly when they are backed by planting that is all of a piece with the waterside setting. With their reflections they can provide a continuous line that extends from the heart of a pool to a distant backing of shrubs and trees. An

85

over-exuberant planting of marginals would spoil the outline of a formal body of water but even here they have a role and when planted in ordered groups they can discreetly underline the geometry of a pool.

The succession observable in natural bodies of water, where reeds and other swamp lovers that colonize shallow water trap debris and silt until they eventually extend the shoreline, serves as a warning to gardeners planting the shallow margins of their ponds. Many marginals are extremely vigorous, often, like the common reed (*Phragmites australis*), forming large stands that exclude all other plants and only limited in their extent by lack of moisture on the land side and on the other side by deep water. These aggressive colonizers have a place in landscape planting but are not suitable for a garden pond. They inevitably include plants that are well suited to ponds that are intended to attract wildlife, giving particularly valuable cover to birds and insects. There is, however, an irony in the degree of management required if they are planted in a small-scale pond. Even much less vigorous marginals usually need to be controlled and their roots are best contained by planting them in baskets, which can be positioned on ledges that are an intrinsic part of the design of many ponds. Where ledges do not exist, stacked bricks can be used as an underwater plinth.

Many marginals are plants with striking foliage, among the most distinctive being several with linear or strap-shaped leaves with vertical variegation. The leaves of *Iris laevigata* 'Variegata' are stiffly upright while the blades of some grasses arch gracefully over the water. But marginals also include plants from many corners of the world with flowers of great distinction. Among them are the kingcup or marsh marigold (*Caltha palustris*), which is a radiant spring flower widely distributed in northern temperate regions, the arum lily (*Zantedeschia aethiopica*) from southern Africa, with swirling white funnels above dark green foliage, and the sumptuous cultivars of the Japanese iris (*I. ensata*), which for centuries have had a special status in their homeland.

WATERSIDE AND BOG PLANTINGS

An area of naturally moist soil is the ideal place to create a waterside or bog garden as background to a pond or stream, even in a depression where there is no open water nearby. To maintain the moisture level water may have to be diverted from a stream or channelled from the overflow of a dam. Because of its impermeable lining, an artificial water feature, unless specially constructed with an overflow, does not provide moisture to replenish the reserves of a bog garden. To compound the artificiality, a flexible liner, sparingly pierced and laid in an excavated hole and then filled with soil rich in organic matter can provide an area moist enough to plant up in the manner of a bog garden.

Although the divide is not clear-cut, a workable distinction can be made between marginals that thrive in shallow water and those that

require wet conditions but do not tolerate indefinite flooding of their roots. This second category of plants, catered for by the dependably moist conditions of a bog garden, includes some of the most sensational giants among herbaceous plants. There is nothing in the temperate garden that can quite match the splendour and scale of *Gunnera manicata*. Its handsome, rough, rhubarb-like leaves thrust out on prickly stalks and its floral cones lurk within the massive clump. Other impressive perennials include species of *Ligularia*, *Rheum* and *Rodgersia*, plants with superb foliage and flowers that are by no means insignificant, those of *Ligularia* 'The Rocket' sparking into life as if to launch the tall dark stems. Combined with such plants as the paddle-leaved skunk cabbages (*Lysichiton*), clumps of the royal fern (*Osmunda regalis*) and tall grassy plants, they create a rich pattern of shapes and textures, which can be infinitely varied with the addition of light fronds, broad leaves such as those of the large hostas and erect or lax straps and blades. The bog garden can, of course, be given a much more strongly floral character and for this purpose few plants surpass the candelabra primulas and astilbes, the finest of the astilbes providing a combination of long-lasting flowers and superb foliage.

Above left Like the yellow skunk cabbage (*Lysichiton americanum*) of North America, the species from Kamchatka, *L. camtschatcensis*, thrives in bog but it is a more refined plant and its flowers are sweet smelling.

Above The candelabra primulas, which have their flowers arranged distinctively in whorls up the stems, seed themselves freely in moist-retentive soil.

Left *Miscanthus sinensis* 'Gracillimus' is an elegant waterside plant but the species and its cultivars adapt to a wide range of conditions.

Top right Moisture and nutrient-rich soil fuel the growth of gunneras and skunk cabbages (*Lysichiton*).

Bottom right Even a narrow channel can be planted with moisture lovers such as these water irises.

WATERSIDE TREES AND SHRUBS

Most moisture-loving trees grow rapidly and when mature take up enormous quantities of water in summer, drying out small areas of bog and ponds to which their roots have access. They create shade and shed leaves that accumulate at the bottom of ponds. Although shade is needed to discourage the growth of algae, that cast by a high canopy is indiscriminate. There is little scope for the successful planting of tall moisture-loving trees except on the margins of large ponds and lakes in a landscape setting. In such a context the large alders (*Alnus*), poplars (*Populus*), willows (*Salix*), and two deciduous conifers, the American swamp cypress (*Taxodium distichum*) and the Chinese dawn redwood (*Metasequoia glyptostroboides*), come into their own.

Even small trees like the snowy mespilus (*Amelanchier*) are best kept back from the edges of medium-sized garden ponds, for which the most suitable woody framework is provided by moisture-loving shrubs. Among the most elegant of the evergreens are bamboos, but non-running kinds must be chosen or the waterside will become a thicket. The smaller willows are among the most useful of the deciduous shrubs. Some, like *Salix hastata* 'Wehrhahnii', are slow growing. Others, such as *S. alba* subsp. *vitellina* 'Britzensis', can be kept to a moderate size by regular cutting back, which ensures a succession of young stems that become brilliant orange-red in winter. Regular stooling of dogwoods such as *Cornus alba* 'Sibirica' also maintains a supply of straight stems.

DRY AND DESERT GARDENS

Many gardens are predictably dry. They lie, for example, in areas of seasonal or consistently low rainfall and low humidity. An additional or separate problem may be that the soil is fast draining sand, gravel, chalk or limestone. Even when the overall picture of a garden does not suggest problems of drought there will inevitably be areas within it that are drier than others. Buildings, walls and trees, just to mention the most conspicuous features, all create their own microclimates, often exaggerated by differences of level and steepness of slope.

Low or seasonal rainfall and fast-draining soils are familiar norms but more and more gardeners are having to cope with relatively dry conditions. Patterns of climate seem to be changing in many regions of the world, in part at least as a consequence of human activity. Irregularities in rainfall have coincided with accelerating demand for water. Rationing and substantial increases in the cost of supply have shocked gardeners into recognizing the extent to which the plants they grow rely on watering and irrigation. By taking measures to conserve moisture and by choosing drought-tolerant plants, many of the problems posed by dry gardens can be solved in a way that is aesthetically pleasing. Even in true desert conditions the garden can bloom without the lavish use of scarce water reserves.

CONSERVING MOISTURE

Quite simple measures can help to reduce water loss in vulnerable gardens. Shelter belts and hedges (see also p. 96) reduce the amount of water lost through evaporation. Building up the level of organic matter content in the soil makes it more efficient at retaining moisture. Various materials can be used, the most practical being garden waste composted on site. A mulch covering the soil helps to hold in moisture and discourages the growth of weeds, which compete with plants for available moisture and nutrients. Mulches also help to maintain an even temperature and protect the soil from violent deluges. One of the most useful general-purpose organic mulches is pulverized bark, which should be laid about 4–6in (10–15cm) deep. Gravel and pebbles are effective as mulches in dry gardens, especially around succulents and other plants that resent moisture accumulating around the collar. Newly planted trees and shrubs are especially vulnerable. Black plastic sheeting or strips of old carpet are effective mulches around newly planted trees and shrubs but as with all mulches should only be laid on ground that has been well watered.

In using scarce water resources gardeners have to rank priorities according to their own judgment. The lawn, a great guzzler if it is to attain velvety perfection and unsightly as a parched dust bowl, is the first feature to consider axing. It can be replaced with paving, decking or a less thirsty kind of planting consisting of drought-tolerant plants, perhaps growing in beds of gravel or pebbles. Vegetables and fruit require a regular supply of moisture if they are to produce worthwhile crops. Young plants of all kinds need more regular watering than those that are established. Planting in a slight depression ensures that the maximum amount of water gets to the roots and the minimum is lost through run-off. Although not without their disadvantages, low-level drip or trickle systems of irrigation that are used in conjunction with timing devices are generally considered the most efficient way of

Left The blue oat grass (*Helictotrichon sempervirens*) grows with the oriental poppy, *Papaver orientale* 'Cedric Morris', and a large spurge, *Euphorbia characias* subsp. *wulfenii*, in a dry bed planted in gravel.

Below The silvery biennial *Eryngium giganteum* makes a prickly bouquet planted with a late-flowering member of the onion family (*Allium*), while other earlier flowering ornamental alliums are already forming seedheads.

Bottom The Mediterranean scrub, which survives a long dry summer, is rich in aromatic plants such as lavenders (*Lavandula*) and other plants that make valuable culinary herbs. The yellow-flowered Jerusalem sage (*Phlomis fruticosa*) is native to the eastern Mediterranean.

directing scarce water to the plants that need it most. As a general principal, watering little and often is potentially harmful and it is certainly less effective than less frequent soaking that is long and slow.

PLANTS FOR DRY GARDENS

Desert gardens are a special case that deserve their own discussion (see pp. 90–91). For less extreme conditions the astonishing range of plants that are drought tolerant to varying degrees must be selected according to their hardiness. It has already been acknowledged that the range of plants for dry shade is relatively limited (see p. 75) but the case is quite different where the site is open. Those who garden in the Mediterranean region and roughly comparable climates such as parts of coastal California come off extremely well. Many plants of great ornamental value are native to these regions and they translate easily from one geographical area to another. A surprising number of these adapt reasonably well to cool climates. Their greatest problems result from low temperatures combined with winter wet, compounded sometimes by insufficient sun and warmth in summer to ripen the tissues of woody plants and bulbs.

The pick of the trees, climbers and large shrubs suitable for wall training – including acacias or wattles, bougainvilleas, coral trees (*Erythrina*) and the showiest of the eucalypts – need a mild climate to succeed. There are, however, reasonably hardy plants among the evergreens, including the strawberry tree (*Arbutus unedo*), Californian lilac (*Ceanothus*), other eucalypts, the almost leafless Mount Etna broom (*Genista aetnensis*), the holm oak (*Quercus ilex*) and numerous conifers. Among deciduous trees are the Judas tree (*Cercis siliquastrum*) and the oleaster (*Elaeagnus angustifolia*).

The grey and silver theme introduced by the oleaster can be extended with many shrubs and perennials with felted or hairy foliage. Artemisias, *Convolvulus cneorum*, lavenders (*Lavandula*), salvias and santolinas, in some cases powerfully aromatic, are pleasing aesthetically and equipped to survive dry conditions. These grey- and silver-leaved plants look at home mixed with airy and tufted grasses, such as species of *Pennisetum* and *Stipa*, globe thistles (*Echinops*),

Above Annuals, including pretty selections of the field poppy (*Papaver rhoeas*) and love-in-a-mist (*Nigella damascena*), add an airy touch to beds planted with drought-tolerant perennials, bulbs and shrubs, among which the candles of mulleins (*Verbascum*) are conspicuous. The planting and design is by Beth Chatto, one of the foremost British exponents of imaginative planting to suit the growing conditions.

Below The crown imperial (*Fritillaria imperialis*) looks at home with drought-tolerant plants, as here, and is reasonably tolerant of dry conditions. However, it grows most vigorously in moderately heavy soil.

Above The Canary Island date palm (*Phoenix canariensis*) is much planted as an ornamental where frosts are rare or non-existent but its dates, although edible, do not have the succulence of the fruits of the date palm (*P. dactylifera*). Once established, the Canary Island date palm tolerates considerable drought.

Above right Yuccas and a flowering *Agave* are major plants in a French Mediterranean garden consisting almost entirely of rock. Agaves take many years to reach flowering maturity but not the 100 years implied in the name "century plant" sometimes applied to *A. americana*.

Opposite top *Aeonium arboreum* is a succulent subshrub with leaf rosettes that have a flower-like symmetry. In frost-prone areas it is best grown as a container plant so that it can be given protection in winter.

Opposite centre and bottom Small succulents, barrel and columnar cacti and specimens of the Joshua tree (*Yucca brevifolia*) form part of an impressive collection of North American desert plants at the Huntington Botanic Garden, in Pasadena, California. Although primarily botanical, it is an inspiration to those who garden in conditions of extreme drought.

and even more thistly sea hollies (*Eryngium*) as well as towering spires of mulleins (*Verbascum*). Ideas can be borrowed from the desert garden with the inclusion of impressive succulents such as the agaves.

Summer can be a colourful season with a generous use of annuals and long-flowering plants. There are few that can match pelargoniums, often treated as annuals but shrubby in character. Even in areas with a cool climate, they can be overwintered easily under glass. It is hardly surprising that they have become such popular container plants because they are remarkably tolerant of neglect. But summer in the dry garden never quite matches the blithe freshness of spring, echoed faintly in autumn, when bulbs detonate in a series of colourful explosions. Those of Mediterranean origin are supplemented by a rich selection from western North America, South Africa and even Central Asia, where spring is a brief interlude between a cruelly cold winter and a parched summer.

DESERT GARDENS

The Koranic vision of the paradise garden, with running water and cool shade, presents an idealized contrast to the dusty rigours of a harsh desert landscape. The Islamic tradition of garden making which elaborates this theme has had a profound influence in arid regions. It presupposes, however, a plentiful supply of water with which to create fountains and pools and to irrigate ground for ornamental flowers and fruit. Another landscape approach is represented by the work of the great American architect Frank Lloyd Wright, whose own house and studio at Taliesen West was designed to harmonize with the austere beauty of the desert. Xeriscaping, to use the fashionable term, has taken off and garden-making or landscaping in arid regions increasingly rejects the oasis effect in favour of open rocky surfaces with carefully grouped specimens of true desert plants.

As in the ungardened desert a stone's throw away, plants in desert gardens have to keep a decent distance from one another if they are to find enough water to survive (see p. 44). Plants are spread out horizontally, not arranged in integrated layers as they are in temperate regions. Trees are rare. The few that tolerate low and irregular rainfall and might be used in gardens include several Australian desert gums (*Eucalyptus* species) and the spiny deciduous mesquite (*Prosopis* species) of North and South America. The honey mesquite (*P. glandulosa*) has weeping branches and bright green leaves but most of this genus must be treated with caution for they can be aggressive weeds.

The supremely successful plants of desert conditions are, however, the succulents. A bald statement of the principal way they survive long periods of drought by storing water in the fleshy tissues of leaves, stems and the base of stems is an inadequate preparation for their range of scale and sculptural form. To achieve their stark beauty they must have sharp drainage. They quickly succumb in the misery of a cold wet climate but a few are surprisingly hardy and most will tolerate a few degrees of frost, as they do in the cold nights of the desert, provided their growing conditions are dry.

Of all plant families the cacti from the Americas have most wholeheartedly embraced succulence as a way of life, jettisoning leaves and carrying out photosynthesis through the skin of their swollen stems. Their range includes the tree-like saguaro cactus (*Carnegiea gigantea*), up to 60ft (18m) high with columnar stems that are often branched, its gaunt presence lending authenticity to countless old western films. The cylindrical shapes of other cacti, single or in family-like huddles, are equally familiar. The vertical ribbing and clusters of spines that ensure that part of the barrel cactus (*Ferocactus cylindraceus*) is always in shade make a characteristic pattern in the desert garden. A shaggy coat of hairs, another self-shading device, gives several cacti a highly distinctive appearance. This feature has earned *Cephalocereus senilis*, a columnar Mexican species up to 40ft (12m) high, the common name old man cactus. Among the most widespread of all cacti in cultivation are the prickly pears and chollas (*Opuntia* species). Their almost 2-dimensional oval extensions root with great ease when they fall, accounting for their dismaying proliferation in many desert landscapes. Their cultivation is prohibited in Australia, where their outrageous success in covering miles of desert was only checked by the introduction of a biological control. Where they can be grown, they make interesting contrasts of scale and form and *O. macrocentra* is unusual for the violet-grey colouring of its pads. Their remarkable durability in harsh conditions is undoubtedly the principal reason for growing the very varied members of the cactus family but their flowers, sadly short-lived, are of such sheeny magnificence that it is worth much patient waiting to see them in their sumptuous fullness.

Other tree-like giants that seem to mirror cactus forms include several spurges, the grandest, *Euphorbia candelabrum*, found wild from Somalia to South Africa, growing to 50ft (15m) or more. Just as important in the desert garden, where contrasts of scale, form, and texture count for so much, are the numerous succulents with fleshy leaves. The rosettes in the Mexican *Agave americana* are on a monumental scale and strikingly handsome in the plain-leaved and variegated forms. One of the most important groups of African succulents are the aloes, the poker-like spikes of flowers being a distinctive feature of many, including the tree-like *Aloe ferox*. Many succulents have leaf rosettes of almost flower-like quality. Those of one of the hardiest aloes, *A. aristata*, are speckled with soft white spines; *Aeonium* 'Zwartkop' has burnished purple leaves arranged like the petals of a sinister bloom. Spiky leaves, such as those of the Joshua tree (*Yucca brevifolia*), introduce a very different graphic quality as do the strange tufts of the Australian grass trees (*Xanthorrhoea* species). Like many plants that survive in arid conditions, these are for the patient gardener, the clump of narrow grassy leaves painstakingly rising on a trunk made up of old leaf bases gummed together with a resin and erratically producing spears of creamy flowers, in the wild most commonly after bush fires.

PLACES FOR ROCK PLANTS

Despite the windswept harshness of the environment above the tree line, which is often blanketed in snow for months of the year, the alpine zone is astonishingly rich in plants of refined beauty. The plants of high rocky crevices and the screes beneath them, composed of rock shattered by a constant cycle of freezing and thawing, first entered gardens on a large scale in the 19th century. The ridiculed rock piles of the Victorian era have been swept away but the man-made rock garden, which attempts to convey a natural geological formation, continues to be used as a setting for these small plants. The emphasis has shifted to providing the free-draining growing conditions that most of them need and a range of settings – small pockets, crevices, vertical cracks, overhangs and slopes of rocky debris – that allow alpines to be grown in a natural way. These plants have been augmented by numerous small shrubs and perennials from lower altitudes, usually from harsh rocky environments, that also need to be grown in open free-draining conditions. All of these compact or trailing perennials and small shrubs, and sometimes, too, the dwarf bulbs that look so effective planted with them, are commonly bundled together in the term "rock plants".

Left Open, well-drained positions often require little special preparation before being planted with easy-going alpines and rock garden plants.

Right *Geranium dalmaticum* clambers over the dark and densely clustered rosettes of a houseleek (*Sempervivum*).

Far left A low dry stone wall can be planted at various levels with houseleeks (*Sempervivum*), pinks (*Dianthus*), sisyrinchiums and thymes (*Thymus*).

Below Low-growing campanulas and geraniums tumble over rocks on a terraced slope.

Bottom Pasque flowers (*Pulsatilla vulgaris*) and the rock rose *Helianthemum* 'Wisley Primrose' stand out on a rocky slope.

For a serious and generous fraternity of gardeners, the true alpines are the elite among the rock plants. Not all of these plants adapt well to outdoor conditions in lowland gardens. The snow that covers them for months of the year in mountainous country is a surprisingly protective mantle, keeping them dry and providing a relatively stable temperature, without sudden highs that might start plants into premature growth. When the snows melt and the short growing season begins, there is plenty of moisture but it is constantly on the move and well oxygenated, draining quickly through a soil that is low in nutrients and organic matter. In lowland areas where the atmosphere is sluggish, the winters wet rather than snowy, with temperatures fluctuating from well below freezing to spring-like highs, they are like uprooted sherpas, pining for the exhilarating clear air of the Himalayas. The alpine house in which they are sometimes grown is in effect an unheated but well ventilated greenhouse where the conditions are never allowed to become soggy. The plants are usually potted individually, with the pots sometimes sunk in a bed of sand.

The rock garden still has its adherents but the recognition that rock plants, including the less temperamental alpines, do not have to be associated with the imitation of a geological form is a substantial advance. Raised beds are much more flexible components of gardens, especially those that are small, and allow a very wide range of plants to be grown in conditions that can be tailored to their needs. Many robust rock plants and some of the true alpines are highly adaptable and can be fitted into many positions where there is good drainage.

ROCK GARDENS AND SCREE BEDS

The conventional rock garden is usually designed as a stratified outcrop and is commonly combined with a pool or flowing water. The advice generally given is to use local rather than imported rock and large rather than small pieces. Choice, however, is often limited, partly the consequence of measures to conserve natural rock landscapes that have already been heavily exploited. The most favoured readily available materials are various stratified sandstones, which absorb moisture and are relatively cool in summer. Weathered limestones are sometimes available secondhand. The scale of a rock garden may well be determined by the high cost of the rock and its transportation. It is as well from the outset to consider if there are better ways to provide the growing conditions that rock plants need. A skimpy modern rock garden can be as absurd in its way as the rock follies of the 19th century.

An open and sheltered position, preferably sloping to catch the sun, that has unimpeded drainage can be made into a rock garden feature. In constructing a rock garden the aim should be to establish a free-draining base of coarse rubble and to set the rock pieces tipped back so that they are at least half covered by soil, with the strata forming more or less continuous lines. A suitable soil consists of equal parts of garden loam, grit and peat substitute. A rock garden can be partly planted during construction but the final planting should be left until the soil has settled. A topping of stone chippings is an attractive finish and is a weed-suppressing mulch that keeps the soil cool and moist.

A scree bed made of very free-draining material can be formed as an integral part of a rock garden but is also an alternative, requiring less rock and more easily adapted to a small space. The essential requirement is a foundation of rubble or graded rock providing perfect drainage, over which is laid soil having the same constituents as for a rock garden but with the quantity of grit doubled or trebled, then topped with a layer of stone chippings or coarse gravel. Provided there is a good supply of freely moving water beneath the apparently dry surface layer of stones, this provides ideal conditions for carpeting and cushion plants such as *Dianthus alpinus* and several other pinks.

RAISED BEDS AND DRY STONE WALLS

Raised beds are alternatives to rock gardens that attempt to mimic natural formations. The raised level of the beds has the advantage of making gardening possible even from a wheelchair. A wide range of materials can be used, including mortared brick, unmortared stone, sawn logs and railway sleepers. A more or less flat surface, suitable for bulbs as well as low perennials and shrubs, and dry, that is unmortared, stone walls is a winning combination. The crevices in the walls, sunny and shaded, according to the bed's orientation, provide planting sites and a cool root run for trailing plants such as many of the campanulas and niches well suited to plants that resent moisture around the crown. The individual stones, usually 4–8in (10-20cm) thick, need to be set so that they slope back gently to ensure stability and good drainage. The maximum height should be 30in (75cm); higher walls may need to be

Above left Logs leaning into a bank form an unusual retaining wall, the weathered grey of the wood showing off the plants trailing from above. There are drawbacks to making a retaining wall in this way: water escapes freely and the logs will eventually rot.

Above *Tulipa saxatilis* and the grape hyacinth (*Muscari armeniacum*) grow freely in a garden that has levels defined by large lumps of chalk.

Opposite top A highly finished drystone wall has openings at the base so that excess water behind the wall can drain off easily. Although the stones are closely set, there is still space for a few rock garden plants and there is further scope for planting along the top.

Opposite centre Low-growing geraniums and rock roses (*Helianthemum*) are the sort of rock garden plants that are suitable for frontal positions in borders.

Opposite bottom Rock garden plants, including the vigorously spreading *Campanula portenschlagiana*, play a strong role in this garden which has retaining free-standing walls.

reinforced. The same soil mixture can be used as for rock gardens, modified if necessary to suit the special requirements of selected plants, and topped with stone chippings.

On a sloping site retaining walls for terracing can be constructed in much the same way as the walls of raised beds and planted with equally pleasing mixtures of trailing and rosette-forming plants. It is important to get professional advice before constructing retaining walls on a steep site, where the strength of the wall must match the potential pressures of water and soil.

Small collections of rock plants can be gathered together in containers, in effect miniature raised beds. Stone sinks and troughs are very appealing visually but they are difficult to obtain and expensive. Furthermore, they tend to be shallow, so that plants do not have a cool root run. To some extent this can be overcome by positioning rocks on the surface and the use of a dressing of stone chippings or gravel. Tufa is often used with them. This form of water-deposited lime is soft and porous. Small plants can be established directly in drilled holes that are topped up with soil once the plant has been inserted. The surprising thing is that plants that usually dislike lime as well as those that are lime lovers will extend their roots into the tufa and grow happily.

Troughs made of hypertufa, a mixture of concrete and peat or peat substitute, and glazed sinks with a hypertufa coating simulate stone containers reasonably well once they have weathered. Terracotta containers stand in their own right and are much less trouble. Whatever the material of the container, good drainage is essential. Because of their weight when filled, position containers while still empty, setting them in an open position raised on bricks or similar supports to ensure that water can get away. Drainage holes should be covered with broken crocks or wire gauze and the bottom 2–3in (5–8cm) filled with gravel, stone chippings or other fast-draining material before the compost is added. A suitable mixture consists of equal parts of a soil-based compost such as John Innes No. 2, peat substitute and coarse grit.

FREE-RANGE ROCK PLANTS

The toughest of the rock plants are suitable for planting in cracks or larger gaps between paving in paths and other areas of hard surface, sometimes merging with other low plants in frontal positions in borders. The combination of very free-draining conditions and cool moist areas under paving slabs provides a good balance. It is important that the planting cover should not be overdone, partly because many plants will not stand the wear and tear but partly because firm clean areas are needed for access and often, too, for placing tables and chairs. It is sometimes recommended that gaps should be left in paving to make planting easier but even at the edges of a path or paved area they can present an ankle-cracking hazard.

Tough low plants such as the aromatic thymes are the most suitable plants for general use in paving but in out of the way corners it is worth introducing contrasting shapes, including the uprights of spring bulbs, summer-flowering sisyrinchiums and, particularly good in shade, large-leaved bergenias. The planting can extend from paving on the flat to steps. The free-draining conditions suit many plants to perfection and running along in cracks between treads and risers they have the effect of bedding the steps in the planting.

Above The hybrid pelargoniums, often thought of as a Mediterranean speciality, are mainly derived from South African species. They do extraordinarily well in sunny coastal areas and flower for many months.

Below The Isles of Scilly, off the south-west tip of Britain, are windswept but the careful planting of shelter belts around the gardens of Tresco Abbey has created an environment in which plants from many parts of the temperate and subtropical world thrive.

GARDENS NEAR THE SEA

At its bright and sunny best the seaside seems a perfect place for relaxed gardening. Coastal conditions do, however, present real challenges for the gardener. The great tyrant in seaside gardens is wind, not just a pleasant on-shore breeze but roaring gales, which come laden with salt picked up over miles of open water and, from the shoreline, an abrasive mixture of small pebbles and sand. Wind breaks brittle stems and branches, drags moisture out of the ground and from leaves, and damages young shoots and tender foliage. Salt drift scorches plants, sometimes far inland, and when washed into the ground creates difficult growing conditions. The soil is likely to present additional problems. There is also a good chance of it being sandy, holding water only briefly and leached of nutrients. Even more difficult is pure rock with a negligible layer of soil except for shallow accumulations in small pockets.

Happily there are plants well-suited to these conditions, which to some extent can be ameliorated. There are, too, advantages in gardening near the sea. The proximity of a vast body of water has a moderating influence on temperature, seaside gardens often escaping the worst effects of frost. Warm currents have a benign effect, as can be seen in some of the remarkable coastal gardens of western Scotland that benefit from the Gulf Stream.

CREATING SHELTER

Buildings and people as well as plants benefit if the seaside garden can be sheltered from prevailing winds. Walls and fences are not the ideal way of creating a calmer microclimate, for on the leeward side of these solid defences there are wild and damaging downdrafts and eddies. Shelter belts and hedges are much more effective baffles, filtering wind and sapping it of its force. The plants used for these living screens must themselves be tolerant of the growing conditions. The range is surprisingly extensive, including numerous conifers and tough and sinewy broad-leaved trees and shrubs. Until a living barrier becomes established a temporary windshield, such as brushwood or openwork fencing, will almost certainly be necessary. Trees and shrubs used as shelter belts or hedging are space-consuming. Even planted in a single row they occupy far more room than walls or fences and for a garden right on the coast several ranks are needed. They are also heavy consumers of moisture and nutrients.

IMPROVING THE SOIL AND MULCHING

Sandy soils warm up quickly in spring and provide conditions in which many annuals germinate freely but they are less successful at sustaining mature and long-lived plants. It is idle to think that sandy soils can be totally transformed. Nonetheless, it is worth taking trouble to improve them, giving plants more leeway during dry weather and broadening the range of ornamentals that can be grown. Organic matter such as garden compost added to the soil

or used as a mulch is invaluable. Stone mulches of gravel or pebbles are not a source of nutrients but they are highly effective at keeping the ground cool and conserving moisture by reducing evaporation. Where a garden is being created on almost bare rocky ground the addition of bought-in topsoil may help to get key plants established but sparse planting is still possible without resorting to such measures.

THE STRENGTHS OF SEASIDE GARDENS

Those that are new to seaside gardening often feel that they are getting a raw deal when they recognize the large number of ornamentals that cannot be grown in their robust conditions. And it is true that only heartbreak can follow if gardeners near the sea persist with plants that are of brittle character, that have lush and delicate foliage, or that are highly bred and carry large flowers on tall upright stems. Once reconciled to their lot, however, seaside gardeners discover that there is ample material with which to create planted havens of great character.

Where space is adequate, there is a choice of distinctive trees, predominantly evergreen with leathery leaves, such as the holm oak (*Quercus ilex*) and strawberry trees (*Arbutus*). There is hardly a more distinctive tree of the Mediterranean than the wide-crowned umbrella pine (*Pinus pinea*). The Canary Island palm (*Phoenix canariensis*) and other highly ornamental members of this group are also a feature of Mediterranean and similarly favoured gardens.

The tough shrubs and perennials that relish the full glare of seaside light provide a pleasing mixture of compact rounded shapes and jagged outlines. Much of their ornamental value derives specifically from characteristics that allow them to survive the onslaught of salty desiccating winds. Some, like the sea thrift (*Armeria maritima*), form low clumps of narrow leaves. Others, like the seakale (*Crambe maritima*), have handsome foliage protected by a waxy coating. Many, such as *Phormium tenax*, have leathery or glossy leaves. Even more are grey with a covering of fine hairs (*Santolina chamaecyparissus*). And some, such as the aloes, are spectacular succulents.

In the most successful seaside gardens such distinctive plants combined with sun roses (*Cistus*), brooms (*Cytisus* and *Genista*) and other free-flowering shrubs form close associations that defy the wind. When these are given a skirt of Californian poppies (*Eschscholzia californica*) and other bright annuals or even tender shrubs such as pelargoniums the garden is filled with dazzling colour that seems just right for a prominent position near the sea.

Above Evergreen shrubs and small trees in a French Mediterranean garden give an impression of the maquis (see pp. 30–31). Some have been clipped, their simple shapes giving the appearance that they have been browsed by goats.

Below An impressive example of planting in coastal conditions is provided by the famous Scottish garden in Inverewe, where the first attempts at making a garden on a bare rocky site at the edge of the sea loch began in the 1860s. The warming influence of the Gulf Stream allows a very wide range of plants to be grown.

TROPICAL AND SUBTROPICAL GARDENS

Mention of tropical gardens summons up an image of a seasonless hot and steamy environment in which dense foliage and a profusion of brightly coloured and bizarrely shaped flowers provide an endless display. Not surprisingly, this stereotype is misleading. The broad equatorial belt bounded by the tropics of Cancer and Capricorn, covering about 40 per cent of the earth's surface, includes areas that are enormously varied in their natural vegetation, reflecting considerable differences in climate, geography, geology and altitude. In many areas there are more or less dramatic alternations of wet and dry seasons and in some regions the rainfall is so low that semi-desert or desert conditions prevail. Gardens in the subtropical zone, extending to about the 35th parallel north and south and taking in places with an equable climate such as Madeira, have their tropical character diluted by a high proportion of temperate plants.

THE CHARACTER OF TROPICAL AND SUBTROPICAL GARDENS

Tropical and subtropical gardening does not represent a style but reflects a choice of plants for particular conditions. Nevertheless, the way plants are used does draw on old traditions of palace and temple landscaping, especially in parts of South-east Asia; sometimes shows the strong influence of traditional European gardens, a legacy of colonial rule; and is increasingly dominated by modern trends in town planning and design, as can be seen in the gardens of many large international hotels. There is a long history of plants being introduced into one tropical area from another, points at the intersections of sea routes, such as Tenerife in the Canaries, acting as botanical entrepôts. Selection of plants on the basis of their economic and ornamental value has almost invariably been at the expense of native species.

Shade trees are an important feature of almost all tropical gardens, creating places of refreshing retreat, supports for epiphytes and climbers and providing, too, an environment that suits shade-tolerant plants that grow at ground level. Among the most impressive of the shade trees are species of fig (*Ficus*), some making vast buttressed

Above In the tropics, as in the temperate world, plants of different origins but similar requirements are brought together in an imaginative way to make successful gardens.

Below left In the intensity of their foliage colour some cultivars of *Cordyline fruticosa* are the equal of many tropical flowers. The flowers of *Anthurium* clearly show that they belong to the arum family.

Below The cycads – including species of genera such as *Cycas*, *Dioon* and *Encephalartos* – have proved successful survivors of a distant geological past. Some are of economic importance, the stems being used to make sago, and the seeds, although toxic, being treated to make a flour.

structures dangling curtains of aerial root. The prominence of flowering trees is perhaps even more striking. Those from regions with a high and evenly distributed rainfall are evergreen and in many cases flower spasmodically throughout the year. One of the most handsome of these is the African tulip tree (*Spathodea campanulata*), a native of tropical West Africa. Leaf loss often makes trees that are geared to an alternation of dry and wet seasons particularly conspicuous. The jacarandas of tropical America – the best known, *Jacaranda mimosifolia*, being much used as a street tree – drop their leaves during the dry period and produce their clouds of violet-blue flowers shortly before the new leaves emerge. The same pattern can be seen in the flamboyant or flame tree (*Delonix regia*) from Madagascar, valued for its light shade and the brilliance of its flowers massed in a broad umbrella-like dome.

There are shrubs and climbers like some of the trees that follow a clear seasonal cycle. Frangipani (*Plumeria alba*), a plant native to the West Indies, loses its leaves at the beginning of the dry season, the richly fragrant flowers being borne on a stark and almost leafless shrub. The success of bougainvilleas in Mediterranean climates is an indication of their tolerance of dry periods. It is a common practice in the tropics to withhold water from these climbers as a way of bringing them into flower. There are, of course, many other shrubs and climbers where there seems to be no conventional seasonal rhythm. Common shrubs such as the Chinese hibiscus (*Hibiscus rosa-sinensis*), from tropical Asia, and flame of the woods (*Ixora coccinea*), from India and Sri Lanka, are in flower for much of the year. The vigour of the numerous climbers expresses the surging energy of the tropical garden. There is hardly a pause in the flowering of some, like the blue trumpet vine (*Thunbergia grandiflora*) from northern India.

The palms that are such a distinctive feature of tropical and subtropical gardens come from widely separated geographical regions and demonstrate a considerable range in growing requirements and tolerances. A large number thrive in open positions in full sun. Of these one of the most remarkable is the coconut palm (*Cocos nucifera*). As might be guessed from the tropical holiday brochures, it is tolerant of salt-laden winds. Others include the drought-tolerant Canary Island date palm (*Phoenix canariensis*), one of the most widely planted palms in subtropical regions. In contrast to these the royal palm (*Roystonea regia*), a magnificent Cuban species much planted as an avenue tree, thrives in moist soil. So, too, does the fish-tail palm (*Caryota mitis*), an unusual species from South-east Asia that in the wild is part of the forest understorey and does best in partial shade. The contrasts in requirements extend to several palm-like trees. The traveller's tree of

Top right Shade has a special importance in tropical and subtropical gardens as do plants such as ferns that grow in it.

Centre right Crotons (*Codiaeum*) have insignificant flowers but they are among the most widely planted tropical perennials on account of their startling foliage.

Bottom right The flowers that have given angel's trumpets (*Brugmansia*) their fanciful common name are often highly fragrant. The species from which the hybrids are derived are mainly from tropical South America as is the climber golden shower (*Pyrostegia venusta*).

Above The most important bromeliad economically is the pineapple (*Ananas comosus*) and the bromeliad with the widest natural distribution is Spanish moss (*Tillandsia usneoides*). In this large and varied family, with a distribution almost entirely confined to the New World, many of the mainly epiphytic species and their hybrids are distinctive ornamentals, often for their foliage as well as their flowers. The water tank formed in the leaf bases of many that live in the dry tropics is an ingenious but sinister feature. Malaria-carrying mosquitos can use these small bodies of water to breed.

Below The terrestrial orchid *Phaius tankervilleae*, an early species to be cultivated under glass in the West, is widely distributed in lowland and lower montane forest from Sri Lanka to China. It is difficult to think of orchids as weeds but this species is now widely spread in Florida and other areas outside its natural distribution.

Below right The tropical water lilies (*Nymphaea*) fall into two main categories according to the time of day the flowers are open. Some bloom from sundown to mid-morning, others from mid-morning to early evening. Most have fragrant flowers.

Madagascar (*Ravenala madagascariensis*), with its symmetrical fan of banana-like leaves (it is a banana relative), is a plant for full sun in areas of high rainfall. The cycads or fern palms – neither ferns nor palms but an ancient group lying somewhere between conifers and true flowering plants – are in the wild mainly plants of open dry woodland or semi-desert.

The epiphytic dimension of humid tropical gardens is on a scale far beyond anything imaginable in the temperate garden, the piled and cascading foliage and flowers creating an impression of fullness and luxuriance. The most numerous of the flowering epiphytes are orchids (see below) but other important groups include waxy flowered anthuriums, rosette-forming bromeliads (species of *Aechmea* and *Guzmania*, for example) and epiphytic climbers such as the Swiss cheese plant (*Monstera deliciosa*). Competing with them for space are numerous ferns, including large species such as the staghorn fern (*Platycerium grande*), the fronds of which form massive bracts.

Foliage often counts for as much as flowers in the low shrubs and perennials that make up the floor of the tropical garden. Plants for shade in the humid tropics include caladiums and dieffenbachias, both widely grown as houseplants, species of *Spathiphyllum*, which tolerate deep shade, and various gingers, among them species of *Alpinia*. Foliage plants for more open positions include the vividly coloured cordylines and crotons (*Codiaeum*), almost a match in their colouring for the extraordinary heliconias, plants producing zigzag arrangements of brightly coloured boat-like bracts that cradle the flowers. Luxuriant growth is inevitably a problem in water gardens. Isolation is sometimes the best course, appropriately so in the case of the sacred lotus (*Nelumbo nucifera*), which is worthy of veneration for its beauty alone.

ORCHIDS

Even in the context of the tropical garden with its bewildering variety of plant form and flower colour, orchids stand out as an exceptionally diverse family. It is one of the largest among flowering plants with a total of about 20,000 species. Far from all of these species are tropical or subtropical. Orchids are found in almost every geographical region except for Antarctica and a few isolated islands and in all but the most extreme environments. About half are terrestrial, growing in soil, from

which the roots extract nutrients. The other half, all tropical or subtropical, are epiphytes, not parasitic but perching on other plants or rocks. Although there are many terrestrial orchids in tropical and subtropical regions, it is the epiphytes and lithophytes (to use the correct term for those that grow on rocks), with their curiously coarse and tangled aerial roots, that are the most conspicuous. The green root tips absorb moisture and nutrients while the active tissues within are protected by a greyish layer of dead cells.

There are many intriguing characteristics of orchids. A large number of those growing in the tropics and subtropics are surprisingly well equipped for extreme conditions. The leaves are very varied but in many cases are strap shaped and leathery. The pseudobulbs possessed by most tropical terrestrial and epiphytic species are swollen stems that store water and nutrients. The tissues in these as well as in other parts of the plants apart from the leaves are actively involved in photosynthesis. The seeds of orchids are minute but usually produced in prodigious quantities. Successful germination depends on a mycorrhizal association of orchid and fungus, a symbiotic relationship that appears to continue throughout the life of an orchid. Inevitably, however, it is the flowers of orchids that grab attention.

The variety of their form and colour is so extraordinary that it is difficult to take in the essential structure that most share. This consists of a whorl of 3 sepals and an inner whorl of 3 petals that surrounds the sexual organs, united to form a single structure, the column. The confusing and fascinating feature of these flowers is that while the 2 lateral petals are often similar to the sepals, the dorsal petal has a character all its own. The lip or labellum, as this petal is known, is usually much larger than the other segments and of highly distinctive shape and sometimes colour and texture. The apparently fantastic and whimsical character of the flowers is, of course, deceptive. Their business is to ensure pollination. The spectacular variety that has made tropical orchids so attractive to collectors and growers is an indication of the highly specific relationship between an individual species and its pollinator. "Various contrivances", as Charles Darwin called them, ensure a precise match between flower and pollinating agent, be it insect, hummingbird, bat or even frog.

Darwin demonstrated that the flowers were structured to ensure cross-pollination. Even in the wild, hybrids sometimes occur; orchids have more naturally occurring hybrids than any other plant family. Since the first artificially produced orchid hybrid was flowered in 1856 numerous deliberate crosses have been made, resulting in tens of thousands of different hybrids. The ease with which many orchids hybridize even extends to crosses between different genera. Plants have been bred combining as many as 20 species and 5 genera. The promiscuity of these plants is the basis of a major orchid growing and breeding industry with its centre in the USA but with other countries, including Germany, Malaysia, Singapore and Thailand, playing an active part.

Far from all the tropical and subtropical species and their hybrids can be grown in the same conditions. They have different temperature, light and humidity requirements, as might be expected when the species are found in so many different habitats, from equatorial lowland to mountainous misty jungle north of the tropic of Cancer and south of the tropic of Capricorn. Their sheer numbers mean, however, that in most tropical and subtropical regions where the climate is reasonably humid a large selection can be grown outdoors. Unfortunately, most of these plants cannot be grown outdoors in temperate regions and so are not a strong feature of the "Plant Directory". They can, however, be grown in cool, medium and warm greenhouses.

Above left Trees in the tropical garden can be ornamental on their own account, provide essential shade and support galleries of epiphytic plants, including orchids. The largest orchid genus is *Dendrobium*, numerous hybrids such as that grown here adding to a species total of 900 to 1,400, most of them epiphytic.

Above and below The Singapore Botanic Gardens, on the present site since 1859, played a key role in the development of the Malayan rubber industry. In the 20th century the gardens became less concerned with economic botany but initiatives in orchid breeding in the 1920s led to several south-east Asian countries playing an active role in the modern orchid business. A major orchid garden, displaying orchids among other tropical plants, offers a wealth of ideas for ambitious gardeners.

PLANT DIRECTORY

Using the Directory

The "Plant Directory" is divided into ten categories: Trees; Shrubs; Conifers; Climbers; Roses; Perennials; Bulbs, Corms and Tubers; Annuals and Biennials; Bamboos, Grasses and Grass-like Plants; and Ferns.

In every category, there is an introduction to each genus describing its main qualities. Each introduction is accompanied by concise information on Cultivation; Propagation; Potential Problems; and a Warning for any plant that can have harmful effects. This is followed by plant entries organized alphabetically according to their internationally accepted botanical name.

A plant entry might be a species, a hybrid or group of hybrids, a variant or a cultivar although these also appear within other entries. Some genera such as tulips are further sub-divided into species and hybrids. As well as a brief description, information is given on a plant's natural origins; height and spread; time of interest for flowers, foliage and fruits/berries/hips; and hardiness. Descriptions of other plants may appear within a genus introduction or a plant entry.

Genera that appear in more than one category, such as *Acer* in "Trees" and "Shrubs", are cross-referenced within the Directory. However, botanical and common names and genus synonyms are cross-referenced in the "Plant Index" (pp. 342–351). Plants with an AGM (Award of Garden Merit) also appear here.

Family name
This is the botanical family (group of related genera) to which the genus belongs.

Genus introduction
This is a general description of the genus and gives the number of species, some indication of preferred conditions and natural habitat, and sometimes advice on how the plants can be used in the garden.

Additional plants
A plant that has not been given its own entry is often described within the genus introduction. In the same way, additional plants are sometimes described under the main plant entry when they have similar characteristics as the entry. In both cases, the plant is in bold.

Propagation
Only the main methods of propagation are given with the most likely appearing first followed by any other methods. The season for each method is also given.

Potential problems
This lists the most common pests to which a plant is susceptible followed by the most common diseases. These are given in order of susceptibility. "Usually none" is used to describe genera that are not really susceptible to any problems.

Warning
This states whether any part of a plant is potentially harmful.

Main plant entry
This gives the current botanical name of the plant in bold. Occasionally, there is one entry for a group of hybrids. For example, *H.* **hybrids** is used to denote *Hemerocallis* hybrids in "Perennials".

Foliage; Flowers; Fruits; Berries; Hips
Where appropriate, these headings indicate when a plant has interesting, attractive foliage; the period when it flowers; and when any fruits or berries appear. An evergreen plant is denoted by the term "year-round".

Height and spread
This gives a range of heights and spreads to show the difference in growth rates that gardeners may experience depending on location and conditions. If the height and the spread are the same, then only one measurement is given. There is no spread given for climbing or rambling roses in "Roses" or for "Climbers". Imperial always precede metric measurements.

Variants and cultivars
The descriptions of cultivars (cv.), plants raised in cultivation; subspecies (subsp.), plants below species but higher in rank than varietas (var.) and forma (f.), both naturally occurring variants of a species or subspecies, appear within main plant entries. Heights and spreads are only added if they differ from the main entry.

RUTA •

• RUTACEAE Rue •

• The best-known species in this small genus of 8 aromatic shrubs and sub-shrubs has long been cultivated for its supposed medicinal properties. In the wild it is found in sunny stony places. Fringed rue (**R. chalepensis**), a subshrub, also has blue-green aromatic leaves. *CULTIVATION* Tolerate full sun or
• partial shade and require well-drained soil. Cut back old stems to fresh growth.
• *PROPAGATION* From seed, sown in spring. From semi-ripe cuttings, in mid-summer.
• *POTENTIAL PROBLEM* Phytophthora root rot.
• *WARNING* Contact with the foliage may cause photodermatitis. Swallowing any part will cause severe stomach upset.

***Ruta graveolens* 'Jackman's Blue'**

• **R. graveolens** *S.E. Europe*
Common rue •
• Flowers: mid- to late summer. Foliage: year-round. H 2–3ft (60–90cm), S 24–30in (60–75cm). FH•
The pungently aromatic blue-green leaves make a low bush bearing greenish yellow flowers in summer. The form usually seen in gardens is
• **'Jackman's Blue'**, with very dense and glaucous foliage.

Genus name
This gives the botanical name for a group of related species.

Common name or names
These apply to the whole genus and are not intended to be exhaustive. Where a genus is monotypic (there is only one species in the whole genus), any common name appears with the genus heading rather than with the main entry heading.

Cultivation
This section gives the aspect (level of sun or shade) which the plants described in the selection either require or tolerate. Where a plant definitely requires those conditions. If a plant can be grown in a container (whether indoors or outdoors) this is followed in parentheses by the type of John Innes compost that is most suitable. If one particular plant in a genus requires slightly different growing conditions to the norm, this is also described here. The planting out time is given only for "Bulbs, Corms and Tubers"; the planting times for the other categories are given in each category introduction. Where appropriate, there is also advice on pruning for "Roses" (for each different category of rose); "Shrubs"; and "Climbers".

Caption
The full botanical name is given with each picture.

Country or countries of origin
The geographical distribution of the plant is given in alphabetical order. If no location is given, then the plant is of garden origin. This means that it has been developed in cultivation and does not occur naturally in the wild.

Common name or names
Gives the common name or names for the main plant entry.

Hardiness
Each main plant entry has a hardiness rating, denoted by the following symbols:

FH   Fully hardy (withstands temperatures down to 5°F/-15°C)

FrH   Frost hardy (withstands temperatures down to 23°F/-5°C)

HH   Half hardy (withstands temperatures down to 32°F/0°C)

FT   Frost tender (damage may occur in temperatures below 41°F/5°C). Note: in temperate areas frost-tender plants should be grown under glass or outdoors during the summer only.

trees

Trees are the natural component that gives the landscape scale and their diverse forms, variations on a crown of branches supported by a main stem, create the skyline. In gardens, trees have several important functions: they break the force of winds, provide shade and privacy, and block out unsightly views. They also have highly individual ornamental qualities, a seasonally changing compound of foliage colour, flowers and fruit, belonging to a structure of distinctive character. An established tree determines what can be grown in its vicinity and is large enough to damage buildings when badly placed. However, a well-chosen tree, as beautiful in its movement and in the sound it makes as in its more obvious ornamental qualities, seems to belong by right where it is planted.

The following selection is limited to flowering deciduous and evergreen trees, while conifers are covered on pp. 166–74. Brief advice on pruning is given where necessary with individual entries. It is as well to repeat here that large-scale pruning and felling of trees is potentially highly dangerous and should not be undertaken by an amateur. The best planting time for deciduous trees is in frost-free weather between autumn and early spring while evergreen trees are best planted in spring.

Top Liquidambar styraciflua
Centre Cornus controversa 'Variegata'
Bottom Magnolia × *loebneri* 'Leonard Messel'

ACER

ACERACEAE Maple

The maples are an important genus of ornamental trees and shrubs, with about 150 evergreen and deciduous species found in the temperate Northern Hemisphere. A few are canopy trees of woodland but most are plants of the under-storey. Several have interesting flowers and winged fruits and a number have handsomely patterned bark but the lobed leaves, often colouring brilliantly in autumn, make the maples outstandingly beautiful. See also SHRUBS.

CULTIVATION Tolerate sun or partial shade and require fertile, moist, well-drained soil.

PROPAGATION From seed, sown as soon as ripe; plants raised this way are variable. By grafting, in late winter or budding in summer (cultivars).

POTENTIAL PROBLEMS Aphids, scale insects, caterpillars, mites; leaf scorch, honey fungus and other fungal diseases.

A. griseum *C. China*
Paper-bark maple
Foliage: autumn. Flowers: spring.
H and S 20–30ft (6–9m). FH.
For the quality of its deciduous foliage alone this is an outstanding small tree. The dark green leaves, divided into 3 leaflets and in summer dark green with blue-green undersides, turn scarlet in autumn. The buff-coloured bark, peeling to reveal orange-brown layers beneath, is intriguing at all seasons.

Acer negundo 'Variegatum'

A. negundo *North America*
Ash-leaved maple, box elder
Foliage: spring to autumn. Flowers: spring. H 40–50ft (12–15m),
S 20–30ft (6–9m). FH.
The bright green leaves of this

deciduous maple turn clear golden yellow in autumn. In spring, bright golden yellow flowers are produced in broad flat clusters before the leaves emerge. 'Flamingo' has pink-edged leaves that turn white in summer while 'Variegatum' has pink shoot tips in spring and mid-green leaves marbled with creamy white flecks.

Acer pensylvanicum

A. pensylvanicum *E. North America*
Moosewood, striped maple
Foliage: autumn. Flowers: spring.
H 40ft (12m), S 30ft (9m). FH.
This is an especially striking maple by virtue of its green-and-white-striped bark and mid-green leaves which turn yellow in autumn. The pendent clusters of greenish yellow flowers are also a feature. Other species with conspicuously striped bark and good autumn colour, several going under the common name snake-bark maple, include *A. capillipes*, *A. grosseri var. hersii* and *A. rufinerve* 'Hatsuyuki', the last having leaves with bold white mottling. All grow eventually to 30ft (9m).

A. platanoides *Europe*
Norway maple
Foliage: autumn. Flowers: spring.
H 100ft (30m), S 50ft (15m). FH.
Flat clusters of conspicuous golden yellow flowers emerge before the leaves on this vigorous deciduous maple. 'Crimson King' produces red-purple foliage and yellow flowers tinged red. It reaches 50ft (15m) in height. 'Drummondii' has mid-green leaves with a broad creamy white margin and grows to 40ft (12m). *A. pseudoplatanus* 'Brilliantissimum' is another strikingly variegated tree, with foliage that unfolds pink, then turns yellow before becoming green. The tree slowly grows to a height of 20ft (6m).

A. rubrum *E. North America*
Red maple, scarlet maple, swamp maple
Foliage: autumn. Flowers: spring.
H 70ft (22m), S 30ft (9m). FH.
The dark green leaves, which turn vivid red in autumn, are 5-lobed, the centre lobe being the longest. An acid soil ensures optimum autumn colour. 'October Glory' has shiny leaves that turn dark orange-red or bright crimson in autumn, while the columnar dense 'Scanlon' has deep red autumn foliage.

A. saccharinum *E. North America*
Silver maple
Foliage: autumn. Flowers: spring.
H 80ft (25m), S 50ft (15m). FH.
A light breeze ruffling the pale green leaves shows the silvery underside that gives this fast-growing spreading maple its common name. Autumn colour is of variable quality.

AESCULUS

HIPPOCASTANACEAE

These woodland deciduous trees and shrubs, with all 15 species in the genus from the Northern Hemisphere, have fingered leaves and flowers arranged in upright panicles. Glossy brown seeds (conkers) ripen and burst out of spiny or smooth capsules in autumn. Among the most magnificent species are the common horse chestnut (*A. hippocastanum*), decked with candle-like white flowerheads in late spring, and the yellow buckeye (*A. flava*), displaying yellow flowers and rich autumn colours, but reaching a height of 80ft (25m) or more these are too large for most gardens.

CULTIVATION Tolerate sun or partial shade and require fertile, moist but well-drained soil.

PROPAGATION From seed, sown as soon as ripe in autumn (species and natural varieties).

POTENTIAL PROBLEM Scale insects.

WARNING All parts of the tree are toxic if eaten.

Aesculus hippocastanum

A. × *carnea*
Red horse chestnut
Foliage: autumn. Flowers: early to mid-summer. H 70ft (22m), S 50ft (15m). FH.
Dark green leaves set off red or deep pink flowers. Spiny fruits contain the seeds. **'Briotii'** has dark rose flower candles and glossy leaves that turn gold in autumn.

Aesculus × carnea 'Briotii'

A. *indica* N.W. Himalayas
Indian horse chestnut
Foliage: autumn. Flowers: summer. H and S 50ft (15m). FH.
The leaves open bronze and turn dark green then yellow in autumn. The flowers are white or pinkish. Pear-shaped smooth fruit contains almost black shiny conkers.

A. × *neglecta* S.E. USA
Foliage: autumn. Flowers: mid-summer. H 30ft (9m), S 25ft (7.5m). FH.
Smooth fruit capsules follow yellow or yellow-flushed red flowers. The mid-green leaves are richly coloured in autumn. The sunrise horse chestnut, **'Erythroblastos'**, has bright pink leaves which turn yellow then green and finally golden in autumn.

ALNUS

BETULACEAE Alder

The alders are deciduous trees of the Northern Hemisphere, many of the 35 species tolerating wet growing conditions. The Italian alder (*A. cordata*), a fast-growing conical tree with bright green glossy leaves, is remarkably tolerant of a wide range of soils, thriving even on dry thin soils on chalk. The drooping male catkins and the shorter female catkins, which later become seed-bearing cones, are borne on the same tree.
CULTIVATION Require full sun and moist but well-drained soil.
A. cordata tolerates dry soil; *A. glutinosa* tolerates wet soil.
PROPAGATION From seed, sown as soon as ripe.
POTENTIAL PROBLEM Phytophthora on wet soil.

Alnus glutinosa 'Imperialis'

A. *glutinosa* Europe, N. Africa, W. Asia
Common alder
Flowers: late winter to early spring; H 80ft (25m), S 30ft (9m). FH.
The dark yellow male catkins, 4in (10cm) long, make a distinctive winter display before the dark green leaves. **'Imperialis'**, a light, graceful tree, has deeply cut leaves.

ARBUTUS

ERICACEAE

Evergreen foliage, distinctive bark and clusters of small bell-shaped flowers followed by strawberry-like fruits are outstanding features of several species of this genus. There are about 14 in all, which are found in North and Central America, the Mediterranean and, in the case of the Killarney strawberry tree (*A. unedo*), also in Ireland. The madrone (*A. menziesii*) is conspicuous among Californian evergreens for its smooth reddish brown bark. All need protection from cold winds.

Arbutus unedo

CULTIVATION Require full sun and fertile well-drained soil. *A. menziesii* needs acid soil.
PROPAGATION From seed, sown fresh. From semi-ripe cuttings, taken in late summer.
POTENTIAL PROBLEMS Aphids; leaf-spot.

A. × *andrachnoides* S.E. Europe, S.W. Asia
Foliage: year-round. Flowers: late spring to early summer. H and S 20–25ft (6–7.5m).
The fully hardy Killarney strawberry tree and the frost-hardy Grecian strawberry tree (*A. andrachne*) are the parents of this lime-tolerant hybrid. It has leathery leaves, orange-red peeling bark, clusters of white bell-shaped flowers and orange-red fruits.

BETULA

BETULACEAE Birch

The 60 or so species of birch are deciduous trees and shrubs that are found in a wide range of habitats in the Northern Hemisphere. The genus includes a number of elegant small to medium-sized trees with attractive bark and delicate foliage, which usually turns shades of yellow in autumn. Male and female catkins are borne on the same tree.
CULTIVATION Require full sun and well-drained neutral to acid soil.
PROPAGATION From seed, sown in early spring. By grafting, under protection in early spring.
POTENTIAL PROBLEMS Aphids, caterpillars, weevils, mites; honey fungus, mildew.

Betula pendula

B. *pendula* Europe, N. Asia
Silver birch
Foliage: autumn. H 70–80ft (22–25m), S 20–30ft (6–9m). FH.
The silver birch takes its common name from its white bark but the base of the trunk becomes darkly fissured as the tree ages. It is a lightly elegant tree with pendent branchlets and diamond-shaped leaves that turn yellow in autumn. **'Laciniata'** has deeply divided, mid-green leaves; **'Youngii'** (Young's weeping birch) grows to about 30ft (9m) and weeps to the ground.

Betula utilis var. *jacquemontii*

B. utilis *China, Himalayas*
Himalayan birch
Foliage: autumn. H 50–60ft
(15–18m), S 25–30ft (7.5–9m). FH.
The tree is variable but the bark is
beautiful, whether copper-brown,
pink-grey or white. The long leaves
are dark green, turning butter-
yellow in autumn. The graceful
var. jacquemontii has pure white
bark; **var. jacquemontii 'Jermyns'**
has white bark and large catkins.

CARPINUS

CORYLACEAE Hornbeam

The 35 to 40 species are deciduous
trees and occasionally shrubs of
woodland in the temperate
Northern Hemisphere. The veined
leaves are borne on zigzag twigs.
The flowers, produced in catkins,
male and female on the same plant,
are followed by conspicuous
clusters of fruit, the nuts having
wing-like bracts. The American
hornbeam (**C. caroliniana**), a small
tree to 40ft (12m) high with blue-
green leaves, is sometimes known
as ironwood, an allusion to the
hardness of the wood.
CULTIVATION Tolerate sun or partial
shade and require well-drained soil.
Clip hedges annually in mid-
summer.
PROPAGATION From seed, sown in
autumn.
POTENTIAL PROBLEMS Usually none.

Carpinus betulus

C. betulus *Europe*
Common hornbeam
Foliage: autumn. Flowers: spring.
H 70–80ft (22–25m), S 60–70ft
(18–22m). FH.
The trunk of this conical, later
more rounded, tree is grey and the
dark green toothed leaves turn
yellow in autumn. As a hedge, it
holds on to brown leaves in winter.

CATALPA

BIGNONIACEAE

The 11 species of *Catalpa* are
deciduous and usually spreading
trees from E.Asia and North
America, which in their native
habitat are plants of woodland and
the banks of streams and rivers.
They produce dramatically large
heart-shaped leaves and upright
clusters of bell-shaped flowers,
which are followed by long,
slender, bean-like pods. The seeds
eventually released from the pods
are winged at both ends.
CULTIVATION Prefer full sun and
fertile, moist, free-draining soil and
shelter from strong winds. Can be
regularly cut back to near the base
in early spring to produce extra-
large leaves.
PROPAGATION From seed, sown in
autumn. From softwood cuttings,
taken in spring or summer. From
hardwood cuttings, taken in winter.
By grafting (winter) or budding
(summer).
POTENTIAL PROBLEMS Usually none.

Catalpa bignonioides 'Aurea'

C. bignonioides *S.E. USA*
Indian bean tree, Southern catalpa
Flowers: summer. H and S 40–50ft
(12–15m). FH.
The magnificent heart-shaped
leaves, tinged purple before
turning light green, are late to
develop on the open spreading
tree. The frilled foxglove-like
flowers are white with yellow and
purple markings. These are
followed by long drooping pods
that turn black and remain on the
tree throughout winter. '**Aurea**',
which grows to 30ft (9m), has
yellow leaves which are bronze
when young.

CERCIS

CAESALPINIACEAE

The half dozen species are shrubs
or trees of woodland and more
open rugged terrain in C. and
E.Asia, North America and the
Mediterranean. They have heart-
or kidney-shaped leaves and
pretty pea-like flowers, which are
followed by flat pods. The
E. Mediterranean Judas tree
(**C. siliquastrum**), which grows to
30ft (9m), fizzes with purple-pink
flowers, even on the trunk, before
the leaves open.
CULTIVATION Require full sun and
fertile, moist, free-draining soil.
PROPAGATION From seed, sown in a
coldframe in autumn. From semi-
ripe cuttings, taken in summer. By
budding, in summer (cultivars).
POTENTIAL PROBLEMS Scale insects;
coral spot, canker.

Cercis canadensis 'Forest Pansy'

C. canadensis *North America*
Eastern redbud
Foliage: autumn. Flowers: late
spring. H and S 25–30ft (7.5–9m),
FH.
This large shrub or small tree needs
hot summers to produce bright
pink flowers in profusion. The
heart-shaped leaves are bronze
when young, yellow in autum.
'**Forest Pansy**' has rich purple
leaves which turn red and orange
in autumn.

CORDYLINE

AGAVACEAE

Leathery strap-like leaves held in
tufts or rosettes give several of the
cordylines a palm-like appearance.
The 15 species are widely
distributed in India and the
Southern Hemisphere, most being
found in tropical and subtropical
zones. They are grown mainly as
foliage plants, outdoors and under
glass, but the mass of sweetly
scented flowers can be impressive
in its abundance. The flowers are
followed by round berries.
CULTIVATION Tolerate full sun or
partial shade and require fertile
well-drained soil (JI No. 3).

PROPAGATION From suckers, taken in spring. From stem-section cuttings, taken in early summer. From seed, sown in spring.
POTENTIAL PROBLEMS Usually none outdoors; mealy bug, scale insects, red spider mite under glass.

Cordyline australis

C. australis *New Zealand*
New Zealand cabbage palm or cabbage tree
Foliage: year-round. H 20–30ft (6–9m), S 6–9ft (1.8–2.7m). HH.
This small upright tree usually forms a single trunk with short stout branches that are topped with a large dense mass of sword-like grey-green leaves. After 8–10 years they produce large plumes of fragrant creamy white flowers in early summer. The **Purpurea Group** has purple-flushed leaves.

CORNUS

CORNACEAE Cornel, dogwood

These decorative deciduous small trees and multi-stemmed shrubs, contribute flowers and showy bracts, berry clusters and colourful stems to the garden at different seasons. The 45 or so species are found in a wide range of habitats in the temperate Northern Hemisphere. See also SHRUBS.
CULTIVATION Require full sun and fertile well-drained soil. Prune plants grown for their coloured stems in alternate years in spring.
PROPAGATION From seed, sown in autumn. From hardwood cuttings, taken in winter.
POTENTIAL PROBLEMS Usually none.

C. alternifolia *E. North America*
Green osier, pagoda dogwood
Foliage: autumn. Flowers: late spring to early summer. Fruits: autumn. H and S 20–25ft (6–7.5m). FH.
Tiered branches carry alternate, oval, mid-green leaves that colour red in autumn. The clusters of small white flowers are followed by black berries. '**Argentea**' is an outstanding variegated shrub or small tree, 15ft (4.5m) tall, with white-margined bright green leaves.

C. controversa *China, Himalayas, Japan*
Foliage: autumn. Flowers: early summer. H and S 40–50ft (12–15m). FH.
The tiered tree has dark green leaves, glossy above and glaucous on the underside, which turn purple in autumn. Flat clusters of white flowers are followed by bluish black fruits. '**Variegata**' has leaves edged creamy white. It is half the size of the species.

Cornus controversa 'Variegata'

C. florida *E. North America*
Flowering dogwood
Foliage: autumn. Flowers: late spring to early summer. Fruits: autumn. H and S 20–30ft (6–9m). FH.
The clusters of greenish flowers are inconspicuous but the white bracts surrounding them make this large shrub or small tree highly ornamental. There are red fruits in autumn and the leaves turn red and purple. '**Cherokee Chief**' has deep pink bracts and '**Rainbow**', growing to 10ft (3m), has white bracts and yellow variegated leaves colouring vividly in autumn. The bracts of **f. rubra** are pink.
C. 'Eddie's White Wonder', with white bracts and brilliant autumn foliage, grows to 20ft (6m).

Cornus florida f. rubra

C. mas *Europe, W. Asia*
Cornelian cherry
Foliage: autumn. Flowers: late winter. Fruits: late summer.
H and S 15–20ft (4.5–6m). FH.
Clusters of small yellow flowers stud the branches before the dark green glossy leaves appear. Bright

red fruits form in late summer. White-edged leaves distinguish the slow-growing '**Variegata**', which grows to 8ft (2.5m) tall.

CRATAEGUS

ROSACEAE Hawthorn

Crowded clusters of white to vivid pink flowers are followed by round, mostly red, berries (haws) in winter on the deciduous, sometimes evergreen, trees. The foliage of some species provides rich autumn colour. The 200 or more species, found in woodland and more open habitats, are widely distributed in the temperate zone of the Northern Hemisphere. Because of their ornamental qualities, adaptability, hardiness and moderate size, hawthorns are among the finest trees for specimen planting in gardens. Thorny branches make many species suitable as sturdy hedging plants, among them the common hawthorn, **C. monogyna**.
CULTIVATION Tolerate full sun or partial shade and any garden soil that is not waterlogged. Trim hedges in autumn.
PROPAGATION From seed (which may take 18 months to germinate), sown in early spring. By grafting (cultivars).
POTENTIAL PROBLEMS Usually none.

Crataegus laevigata 'Rosea Flore Pleno'

C. laevigata *Europe to India, N. Africa*
May, Midland hawthorn
Flowers: late spring. Fruits: autumn. H and S 25ft (7.5m). FH.
Clusters of white flowers, sometimes tinted pink and followed by red haws, brighten a rounded thorny tree with glossy mid-green leaves. '**Paul's Scarlet**' has double red flowers and '**Rosea Flore Pleno**' has double pink flowers. All have a cloying scent.

C. × _lavalleei_ 'Carrierei'
Foliage: autumn. Flowers: early
summer. Fruits: late autumn to early
winter. H 15–25ft (4.5–7.5m),
S 20–25ft (6–7.5m). FH.
The tree is lightly thorned and it
often holds its glossy dark green
leaves until early winter. The
orange-red fruits that follow
the clusters of white flowers
are long-lasting.

Crataegus persimilis 'Prunifolia'

C. _persimilis_ 'Prunifolia'
Foliage: autumn. Flowers: early
summer. Fruits: autumn. H 25ft
(7.5m), S 30ft (9m). FH.
The broad-headed thorny tree has
distinctive glossy dark green foliage
that colours well in autumn, and
round bright red haws, which
follow dense clusters of white
flowers and persist into winter.

DAVIDIA

DAVIDIACEAE Dove tree, ghost tree,
handkerchief tree

The single deciduous species is a
woodland tree from China, rare in
the wild and with a scattered
distribution. The adventurous
search for it by E. H. Wilson,
culminating in large-scale
introduction to the west at the
beginning of the 20th century, has
added glamour to an already
remarkable tree.
CULTIVATION Tolerate full sun or
partial shade and require fertile
moist but well-drained soil.
PROPAGATION From seed, sown in
autumn. From semi-ripe cuttings,
taken in early summer.
POTENTIAL PROBLEMS Usually none.

Davidia involucrata

D. _involucrata_ _S.W. China_
Foliage: autumn. Flowers: late
spring. H 50ft (16m), S 30ft (9m).
FH.
When in flower the tree,
improbably, seems decked with
drooping handkerchiefs. The
flowers themselves are small and
clustered in a rounded head, each
of which is surrounded by an
unequal pair of white bracts. The
leaves are heart-shaped and a vivid
green with a coating of dense
hairs on the underside; in autumn
they turn bright golden-yellow
with a red tinge around the margin.
The greenish brown fruits are
ridged and egg-shaped. The leaves
of **var. _vilmoriniana_** are hairless.

EUCALYPTUS

MYRTACEAE Gum, gum tree

The eucalypts, a large genus of
more than 500 species of
evergreen trees and shrubs, most
native to Australia, are notable for
their bark, their foliage and for
their petalless but showy flowers.
These are usually creamy white but
the half-hardy species (**_E. ficifolia_**)
has red flowers. Juvenile and
mature leaves often differ in shape,
size and arrangement on the stems,
changing from opposite to
alternate as they age. Plants are
usually fast-growing and many are
heat- and drought-tolerant. Only a
few are hardy enough to grow in a
cool temperate climate. The
spreading Tasmanian blue gum
(**_E. globulus_**) makes a splendid
large tree where the climate is mild
enough but is also grown as a
bedding plant for its silvery blue-
green juvenile leaves.
CULTIVATION Require full sun and
fertile, well-drained, neutral to acid
soil. Some shelter may be necessary
while plants are young.
PROPAGATION From seed, sown in
spring.
POTENTIAL PROBLEMS Silver leaf,
oedema.

E. _gunnii_ _Tasmania_
Cider gum
Foliage: year-round. Flowers:
summer. H 60–80ft (18–25m),
S 20–40ft (6–12m). FH to FrH.
The rounded blue leaves of the
young plant give way to sickle-
shaped grey-green leaves, although
the plant can be pruned hard each
year to maintain the blue juvenile
foliage. On mature trees, the older
green-white bark is shed in
summer, revealing new grey-green
bark, sometimes with a pink or
orange flush. Clusters of small
cream-white flowers are borne
in summer.

Eucalyptus gunnii

**E. _pauciflora_ subsp.
niphophila** _S.E. Australia,
Tasmania_
Alpine snow gum, snow gum
Foliage: year-round. Flowers:
summer. H 20–40ft (6–12m),
S 20–30ft (6–9m). FH.
The bark, likened to the skin of a
python, is marked in shades of
green, grey and cream. The grey-
green leaves are long and leathery.
The flowers are creamy white.

Eucalyptus pauciflora subsp.
niphophila

EUCRYPHIA

EUCRYPHIACEAE

The 5 or 6 deciduous and
evergreen trees and shrubs of this
genus from Chile and S.E. Australia
bear white cup-shaped flowers
with golden stamens from late
summer until early autumn. The
mid- to dark green leaves are
leathery with a crinkled margin.
CULTIVATION Require full sun and
shelter from cold winds with the
roots kept cool and damp.
PROPAGATION From semi-ripe
cuttings with a heel, taken in
early autumn.
POTENTIAL PROBLEMS Usually none.

E. × *nymansensis* *South America*
Leatherwood
Foliage: year-round. Flowers: late
summer to early autumn. H 36ft
(11m) S 6-8ft (1.8-2.5m). FH to
FrH.
This is a small columnar evergreen
tree, and the hardiest most lime-
tolerant of the eucryphias. It bears
both simple and compound leaves,
reflecting the leaf shapes of its
parents, **E. *cordifolia*** and
E. *glutinosa*. *E. × nymansensis*
'Nymansay' spreads 8-15ft
(2.5-4.5m) and grows and matures
quickly. It has pure white flowers
2¼in (6cm) across which are more
numerous than on the species.

Eucryphia × nymansensis

FAGUS

FAGACEAE Beech

The 10 species of woodland trees,
all from the temperate Northern
Hemisphere, produce foliage that
colours well in autumn. Their size
limits their use in small or medium-
sized gardens. The inconspicuous
flowers are followed by woody
fruits, which contain nuts (mast).
CULTIVATION Tolerate full sun or
partial shade and require well-
drained soil. Trim hedges in late
summer.
PROPAGATION From seed, sown in
autumn. By grafting (cultivars).
POTENTIAL PROBLEM Beech bark
disease.

Fagus sylvatica **'Dawyck'**

Fagus sylvatica **'Purpurea Pendula'**

F. *sylvatica* *C. Europe*
Common beech
Foliage: autumn. H 80-100ft
(25-30m), S 40-60ft (12-18m). FH.
Oval leaves emerge clear green
then turn dark green and golden
and finally copper and brown in
autumn on this gracefully
spreading deciduous tree. The bark
is silver-grey in maturity. As a
specimen tree the species and
upright purple-leaved forms such
as **'Riversii'** are too large for most
gardens but are excellent hedging
plants, holding their brown leaves
in winter. There are several
cultivars of more manageable
proportions. **'Dawyck'** is columnar
with copper leaves in autumn. The
narrow leaves of **var. *heterophylla***
'Aspleniifolia' are deeply cut. The
branches of the weeping beech
(**'Pendula'**), which is up to 60ft
(18m) tall, hang to the ground. An
equivalent with purple foliage,
'Purpurea Pendula' rarely exceeds
15ft (4.5m).

FRAXINUS

OLEACEAE Ash

There are about 65 species of ash,
all but a few deciduous trees and
the majority woodland plants of
the temperate Northern
Hemisphere. The common ash
(**F. *excelsior***), is a fast-growing
vigorous tree eventually reaching
about 100ft (30m) and has far-
reaching surface roots, making it
unsuitable for all but large gardens.
F. *excelsior* **'Pendula'**, known as
the weeping ash, rarely exceeds
50ft (15m) and its hanging
branches form a curtained bower.
CULTIVATION Require full sun and
neutral to alkaline, moist but well-
drained soil.
PROPAGATION From seed, stratified
over winter, sown in autumn or
spring.
POTENTIAL PROBLEMS Usually none.

F. *ornus* *S. Europe, S.W. Asia*
Manna ash
Foliage: autumn. Flowers: late
spring to early summer. H and S
50ft (15m). FH.
This bushy rounded species, the
best known of the "flowering
ashes", produces clustered plumes
of fluffy cream-white flowers,
which are heavily scented. The
pinnate dark green leaves turn
purple-red in autumn.

Fraxinus ornus

GENISTA

PAPILIONACEAE Broom

The Mount Etna broom
(*G. aetnensis*) rises above most of
the 90 or so species in this genus
to form an open and airy small
deciduous tree. It is drought-
tolerant and, despite its green
appearance, nearly leafless. See
also SHRUBS.
CULTIVATION Requires full sun and
well-drained light sandy soil.
Tolerates acid and alkaline soils.
PROPAGATION From seed, sown in
spring. From semi-ripe cuttings
with a heel, taken in early autumn.
POTENTIAL PROBLEM Aphids.

Genista aetnensis

G. *aetnensis* *Italy (Sardinia,
Sicily)*
Mount Etna broom
Flowers: summer. H and S 18-25ft
(5.5-7.5m). FrH.
This is an elegant large shrub or
small tree with many slender,
drooping, bright green branches.
Large quantities of heavily scented
golden yellow pea flowers are
produced in mid-summer. It casts
only light shade.

GLEDITSIA

CAESALPINIACEAE

The 14 or so species of this deciduous spiny tree, distantly related to the garden pea, are grown for their attractive leaves, which are pinnate or bipinnate with up to 32 leaflets. The flowers are greenish white and give rise to long brown pods in autumn.
CULTIVATION Require full sun, fertile well-drained soil and shelter from wind in spring. Tolerant of atmospheric pollution.
PROPAGATION From seed, sown in spring (species). By grafting, in early spring (named cultivars).
POTENTIAL PROBLEMS Usually none.

G. triacanthos *C. and E. North America*
Honey locust
Foliage: autumn. Flowers: mid-summer. H 60–80ft (18–25m), S 30–50ft (9–15m). FH to FrH.
This is a formidably armoured tree with frond-like foliage that turns clear yellow in autumn. Where summers are warm enough the insignificant flowers are followed by twisted seed pods. 'Sunburst', thornless and growing to 40ft (12m), has yellow young foliage, which turns lime green before colouring yellow again in autumn. It does not produce seed pods.

Gleditsia triacanthos 'Sunburst'

ILEX

AQUIFOLIACEAE Holly

In a genus of more than 400 species of mainly evergreen trees and shrubs distributed in forests and woodlands in temperate, subtropical and tropical regions, the best-known hollies are species and hybrids with more or less spiny evergreen leaves and showy berries in autumn. Male and female flowers usually grow on separate trees (the sex is indicated following

plant names in the entries) although some plants are self-fertile. Hollies are tolerant of wind and pollution and so are valuable hedging plants. Shrubby evergreen hollies that are fully hardy include the Japanese holly (*I. crenata*), the berries of which are usually black, and the blue holly (*I. × meserveae*) with blue-green leaves. The American holly (*I. opaca*), also fully hardy, is more tree-like and has matt green leaves.
CULTIVATION Tolerate full sun or partial shade and prefer moist well-drained soil.
PROPAGATION From seed, sown in autumn (seed may not germinate for 2–3 years). From semi-ripe cuttings, taken in late summer or early autumn.

Ilex × altaclerensis 'Camelliifolia'

I. × altaclerensis
Highclere holly
Foliage: year-round. Flowers: spring to early summer. Berries: autumn to winter. H 50–70ft (15–22m), S 25–50ft (7.5–15m). FrH.
These fast-growing hollies, useful for hedging, have glossy sparsely spiny leaves that set off the red berries. Cultivars include: 'Belgica Aurea' (f), with grey-green mottled leaves edged cream; 'Camelliifolia' (f), purple-stemmed and with large berries and deep green almost spineless leaves; and 'Golden King' (f), with yellow leaf margins.

Ilex aquifolium 'Madame Briot'

I. aquifolium *N. Africa, W. Asia, W. and S. Europe*
Common holly, English holly
Foliage: year-round. Flowers: spring to early summer. Berries: autumn to winter. H 50–70ft (15–22m), S 15–25ft (4.5–7.5m). FrH.
As a young tree this forms a loose dark green pyramid of glossy and prickly leaves. Mature foliage is only spine-tipped. The long-lasting berries are red, occasionally orange or yellow. Cultivars include: 'Ferox Argentea' (m), dark green cream-margined leaves covered in spines; 'Golden Milkboy' (m), spiny leaves with irregular yellow centres; 'Handsworth New Silver' (f), purple stems and white-margined spiny leaves; 'Madame Briot' (f), spiny leaves with yellow margins; 'Pyramidalis' (f), lightly spined green leaves, self-fertile and fruiting freely; and 'Silver Queen' (m), purple-stemmed and dense with spiny leaves, their creamy edges tinged pink on emerging.

Ilex aquifolium 'Ferox Argentea'

KOELREUTERIA

SAPINDACEAE

Showy seedpods follow sprays of small flowers on the 3 species of these spreading deciduous trees and shrubs from dry valley woodlands in Asia. The leaves are long and decorative.
CULTIVATION Requires full sun and well-drained soil.
PROPAGATION From seed, sown under glass in autumn. From root cuttings, taken in autumn.
POTENTIAL PROBLEMS Usually none.

K. paniculata *China, Korea*
Golden-rain tree, Pride of India
Foliage: autumn. Flowers: mid- to late summer. Fruits: late autumn. H 30–50ft (9–15m), S 20–30ft (6–9m). FH.
The long elegant pinnate leaves are reddish when they emerge, mid-green in summer and yellow in autumn. The prominent seedpods that follow sprays of small yellow flowers are green flushed red. Hot summers are needed for a good display.

Koelreuteria paniculata

LABURNUM

PAPILIONACEAE Golden rain

The genus comprises 2 similar deciduous species, **L. alpinum** and **L. anagyroides**, both from South and Central Europe, which make small trees producing trailing clusters of yellow pea-like flowers in late spring or early summer. The plant described is a hybrid between them.
CULTIVATION Require full sun and well-drained soil. *Laburnum ×
watereri* 'Vossii' has a brittle root system and must be permanently staked.
PROPAGATION From seed, sown in spring. By grafting, in spring (cultivars).
POTENTIAL PROBLEMS Black fly; honey fungus, powdery mildew, silver leaf.
WARNING All parts of the tree are toxic if eaten.

Laburnum × watereri 'Vossii'

L. × watereri 'Vossii'
Flowers: late spring. H 20–30ft (6–9m), S 18–25ft (5.5–7.5m). FH.
In late spring the tree drips with clusters of deep yellow flowers, to 60cm (24in) long, which are followed by grey-brown pods filled with black seeds (these are the most toxic part of the plant). The grey-green leaves have a glossy upper surface and a paler underside.

LIQUIDAMBAR

HAMAMELIDACEAE

The 4 species, deciduous woodland trees from Asia, North America and Mexico, have maple-like leaves with 3 to 7 lobes. *L. styraciflua* is notable for its complex colouring in autumn.
CULTIVATION Tolerate full sun or partial shade and require moderately fertile, moist but well-drained soil, preferably acid or neutral.
PROPAGATION From greenwood cuttings, taken in summer. From seed, sown under glass in autumn.
POTENTIAL PROBLEMS Usually none.

L. styraciflua E. USA, Mexico
Sweet gum
Foliage: autumn. Flowers: late spring. H 70–80ft (22–25m), S 25–30ft (7.5–9m). FH.
The glossy palmate leaves of this rather conical-shaped tree have 5 to 7 lobes. In autumn, the colour shifts through orange and red to purple.

Liquidambar styraciflua

LIRIODENDRON

MAGNOLIACEAE Tulip tree

The 2 fast-growing deciduous trees in this genus make fine specimen plants where there is space. Green cup-shaped flowers appear on trees that are about 15 years old. The remarkable leaves are almost straight across the top.
CULTIVATION Tolerate full sun or partial shade and require reasonably fertile, moist, well-drained soil.
PROPAGATION From seed, sown in autumn (species). By grafting, in early spring (cultivars).
POTENTIAL PROBLEMS Usually none.

Liriodendron tulipifera

L. tulipifera E. North America
Tulip tree
Foliage: autumn. Flowers: mid-summer. Fruits: autumn. H 80–100ft (25–30m), S 40–50ft (12–15m). FH.
The pale green tulip-shaped flowers have orange markings at the base and enclose long crowded stamens. The leaves are dark green, turning yellow in autumn. In the slower-growing 'Aureomarginatum' the leaves have gold-green edges and the tree grows to about 70ft (22m).

MAGNOLIA

MAGNOLIACEAE

Magnolia campbellii

This genus of 125 deciduous and evergreen species, from Asia and the Americas, includes some of the most splendid flowering trees and shrubs for temperate gardens. The flowers, usually borne prolifically on mature plants, are beautifully formed – sometimes saucer-, bowl- or goblet-shaped, sometimes starry with numerous petals – and in some cases fragrant. See also SHRUBS.
CULTIVATION Tolerate sun or partial shade and require moist, well-drained, fertile soil and protection from winds.
PROPAGATION From greenwood cuttings, taken in early summer (deciduous plants). From semi-ripe cuttings, taken in late summer (evergreens). From seed, sown in spring.
POTENTIAL PROBLEMS Usually none.

M. campbellii India, Nepal, S.W. China
Flowers: late winter to spring. H 50–70ft (15–22m), S 25–33ft (7.5–10m). FH.
Large goblets appear on the bare branches of this deciduous tree after 20 or more years. The usual colour is deep pink but the range extends from white to purplish pink. 'Charles Raffill' has flowers that are deep pink on the outside, white with a pinkish flush inside. It and **subsp. mollicomata**, which usually has purple-pink flowers, flowers after 10 to 15 years.

M. denudata China
Lily tree, yulan
Flowers: spring. H and S 20–30ft
(6–9m). FH.
The cup-shaped white flowers are
lemon-scented and open before the
mid-green leaves on this spreading
deciduous tree, which comes into
flower in 3 to 5 years. Primrose-
yellow flowers appear on
M. 'Elizabeth' before and at the same
time as the coppery leaves unfurl,
once the tree is 2 to 3 years old.

Magnolia grandiflora

M. grandiflora S.E. USA
Bull bay
Foliage: year-round. Flowers: late
summer to autumn. H 20–60ft
(6–18m), S 20–40ft (6–12m). FrH.
This evergreen magnolia is often
wall-trained but makes a handsome
free-standing specimen. The
scented creamy white flowers, up
to 10in (25cm) across, nestle
among large, dark green, glossy
leaves. 'Exmouth', with narrower
paler leaves, and 'Goliath', with
very large flowers up to 1ft (30cm)
across, come into flower at a
relatively young age.

Magnolia × loebneri 'Leonard
Messel'

M. × loebneri 'Leonard Messel'
Flowers: mid-spring. H 20–25ft
(6–7.5m), S 15–20ft (4.5–6m). FH.
Crosses between *M. kobus*, a
Japanese species that is slow to
come into flower, and *M. stellata*
have produced small deciduous
trees or large shrubs of great
quality that flower when young.
'Leonard Messel' has starry pink
flowers that are tinged mauve. *M. ×
loebneri* 'Merrill', which can grow

to 33ft (10m), produces numerous
white goblets that are fragrant and
starry when open.

M. salicifolia Japan
Willow-leaved magnolia
Flowers: mid-spring. H 30–40ft
(9–12m), S 15–25ft (4.5–7.5m).
FH.
The star-shaped flowers are pure
white and faintly fragrant and open
before the long lance-shaped leaves
on this deciduous tree.

MALUS

ROSACEAE Apple, crab apple

The thousands of eating and
cooking apple cultivars are
themselves highly ornamental.
There are about 35 species, all
deciduous and found in woodland
or more open habitats in Europe,
Asia and North America. They and
some of their hybrids include
relatively small trees valuable for
their blossom, their colourful fruits
and, in some cases, autumn foliage.
CULTIVATION Best in full sun but
tolerate partial shade. Require
moist but well-drained soil.
PROPAGATION From seed, sown in
autumn. Trees are propagated
commercially by budding in late
summer or grafting in mid-winter.
POTENTIAL PROBLEMS Canker,
fireblight, honey fungus. (Crab
apples are less prone to disease
than orchard apples.)

M. coronaria var. *dasycalyx*
'Charlottae'
Foliage: autumn. Flowers: late
spring to early summer. Fruits:
autumn. H 20–30ft (6–9m),
S 15–20ft (4.5–6m). FH.
Clustered semi-double fragrant
flowers of palest pink are followed
by yellowish fruit. The leaves turn
scarlet in autumn.

Malus floribunda

M. floribunda Japan
Japanese crab apple
Flowers: mid- to late spring. Fruits:
autumn. H and S 20–30ft (6–9m).
FH.
Clustered crimson buds open to
pale pink blossoms, which are

followed by tiny yellow fruits.
Another Japanese crab apple,
M. toringo subsp. *sargentii*, which
rarely exceeds 12ft (3.7m), bears
white flowers that are followed by
long-lasting deep red fruits.

M. 'John Downie'
Flowers: late spring. Fruits: autumn.
H 20–30ft (6–9m), S 15–20ft
(4.5–6m). FH.
The tree is narrowly upright when
young but broadens with age. The
display of white flowers opening
from pink buds is generous but
even more outstanding is the crop
of orange and red conical fruits.

M. × robusta 'Red Sentinel'
Flowers: late spring. Fruits: autumn
to winter. H and S 20–25ft
(6–7.5m). FH.
A heavy crop of long-lasting, glossy,
deep red fruits follows the white
flowers. The foliage is dark green.
M. × robusta 'Yellow Siberian',
which eventually may grow to 40ft
(12m), bears clusters of yellow
fruits, which are long-lasting.

Malus × schiedeckeri 'Red Jade'

M. × schiedeckeri 'Red Jade'
Flowers: late spring. H 12–18ft
(3.7–5.5m), S 8–15ft (2.5–4.5m).
FH.
Pink buds open to white blossoms
on weeping branches. Red fruits
follow.

M. tschonoskii Japan
Foliage: autumn. Flowers: late
spring. Fruits: autumn. H 30–40ft
(9–12m), S 18–23ft (5.5–7m). FH.
This species, upright at first, later
spreading, is one of the best crabs
for autumn colour, turning shades
of red, orange, yellow and purple.
Yellow-green fruits follow the pink-
flushed white blossoms.

M. × zumi 'Golden Hornet'
Flowers: spring. Fruits: autumn to
winter. H 18–25ft (5.5–7.5m),
S 12–18ft (3.7–5.5m). FH.
Long-lasting bright yellow fruits
hang thickly from the branches of
this small rounded tree in autumn
and winter. The flowers open white
from pink buds.

MORUS

MORACEAE

The genus comprises about 10 species of shrubs and trees from a range of habitats in Africa, Asia and the Americas. Two species have long been cultivated, the white mulberry (**M. alba**), the leaves of which were used to feed silkworms, and the species described, which produces edible loganberry-like fruits and is a characterful tree with a rounded crown when mature.

CULTIVATION Require full sun, well-drained soil and shelter. Any pruning should be carried out in late winter or early autumn; at other times wounds are likely to bleed.

PROPAGATION From hardwood cuttings, taken in early winter and rooted out in the open ground.

POTENTIAL PROBLEMS Bacterial blight, coral spot.

M. nigra *S.W. Asia*
Black mulberry
Foliage: autumn. Flowers: early spring. H and S 25–40ft (7.5–12m). FH.
The purplish red fruits are delicious but the deciduous tree is also a distinctively gnarled ornamental when mature, with large, heart-shaped, dark green leaves that turn yellow in autumn. The flowers are inconspicuous.

Morus nigra

NYSSA

NYSSACEAE Tupelo

Vivid colouring of the foliage in autumn marks out the best of the nyssas, a genus of about 5 deciduous species, plants of woodland and swampy conditions in China and North America. The Chinese species **N. sinensis**, usually a large shrub rather than a tree, colours with exceptional brilliance in autumn.

CULTIVATION Tolerate sun or partial shade and require moist lime-free soil.

PROPAGATION From seed, sown in early spring. By layering, in autumn.

POTENTIAL PROBLEMS Usually none.

Nyssa sylvatica

N. sylvatica *E. North America*
Black gum, sour gum, tupelo
Foliage: autumn. Flowers: spring to early summer. H 50–70ft (15–22m), S 25–30ft (7.5–9m). FH.
This is a handsome, slow-growing, medium to large tree with a broadly conical to columnar habit. The dark glossy green leaves turn a rich red, orange and yellow in autumn. The flowers and fruits are inconspicuous.

PARROTIA

HAMAMELIDACEAE

The single species of this genus is a deciduous forest tree with ornamental bark and foliage that colours well in autumn.

CULTIVATION Tolerate full sun or light shade and alkaline conditions but require a well-drained soil.

PROPAGATION From softwood cuttings, taken in summer. By layering, in autumn. From seed, sown in autumn.

POTENTIAL PROBLEMS Usually none.

P. persica *Caucasus, N. Iran*
Persian ironwood
Foliage: autumn. Flowers: late winter to early spring. H and S 20–30ft (6–9m). FH.
The flaking bark on the older branches of this spreading shrub or tree creates a random patchwork of cream, grey and fawn. The flowers, which appear before the leaves, are mere tufts of crimson stamens. They easily go unnoticed but not so the rich tints of the leaves in autumn. **'Pendula'** is a weeping form.

Parrotia persica

PLATANUS

PLATANACEAE Plane

This genus of about 6 species of deciduous trees includes the American sycamore, **P. occidentalis**, native to E. and S. North America, and the Oriental plane, **P. orientalis**, found from Europe to W. Asia. Generous proportions, bright green leaves, multi-coloured bark and long-lasting fruits are common characteristics.

CULTIVATION Require full sun and well-drained soil.

PROPAGATION From hardwood cuttings, taken in early winter.

POTENTIAL PROBLEM Anthracnose.

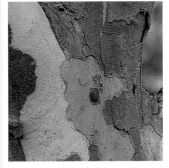
Platanus × hispanica

P. × hispanica
London plane
Foliage: autumn. Fruits: summer to the following spring. H 80–100ft (25–30m), S 50–70ft (15–22m). FH.
This columnar round-topped tree, which has large leaves that have 5 to 7 lobes, is widely planted in towns because it tolerates atmospheric pollution and heavy pruning. The bark of the straight trunk and branches is mottled brown, cream and grey. Strings of 2 to 6 ball-like fruit clusters hang during autumn and winter.

POPULUS

SALICACEAE Poplar

This genus of some 35 species of deciduous trees and shrubs, which are distributed throughout the Northern Hemisphere, includes some of the most rapidly growing trees. The balsam poplars, including **P. balsamifera**, have aromatic young buds. Trees are single sex. The more decorative reddish male catkins are borne on bare branches in spring. Female catkins are followed by small green fruits carried in a white cotton-like mass of threads. All plants have a wide-spreading root system which takes up large quantities of water in the growing season. The leaves of **P. × candicans 'Aurora'** have splashy green, cream and pink variegation.

CULTIVATION Tolerate sun or partial shade and require moist well-drained soil.
PROPAGATION By hardwood cuttings, taken in winter; instant young trees can be created by rooting cuttings up to 6ft (1.8m) in length.
POTENTIAL PROBLEM Silver leaf fungus kills large branches and eventually the whole tree.

P. alba *Asia, Central Europe*
Abele, white poplar
Flowers: spring. H 80ft (25m), S 30ft (9m). FH.
A broad spreading habit, dark grey-green fissured bark and young shoots covered with a thick white felt are appealing but the main attraction is the fluttering foliage, the leaves dark green with a silvery and downy underside. They turn yellow in autumn. **'Raket'** is narrow with erect branches.

Populus alba

P. tremula 'Pendula' *France*
Weeping aspen
Flowers: spring. H 20–30ft (6–9m), S 18–25ft (5.5–7.5m). FH.
This small female tree of pendulous habit produces greyish green catkins before the almost circular leaves emerge. It is one of the best and most robust weeping trees for the garden. The American aspen (*P. tremuloides*), similar to *P. tremula* but with yellow bark and finely toothed leaves, also has a weeping form **'Pendula'**.

PRUNUS

ROSACEAE

The genus comprises about 200 species of deciduous and evergreen trees and shrubs, most of which are native to the temperate Northern Hemisphere, with a few found in South America. It is horticulturally important for the large number of plants – including almonds, apricots, cherries,

peaches and plums – that are grown for their edible fruits. Their ornamental value, sometimes considerable, is eclipsed by that of several species and numerous hybrids that are grown for their prolific displays of flowers and, in some cases, colourful autumn foliage. Many have bark circled with glossy bands, the most outstanding for its coppery lustre being *P. serrula*. See also SHRUBS. The plants are listed under "Species" and "Hybrids".
CULTIVATION Tolerate full sun or partial shade and require moist but well-drained fertile soil. Trim hedges after flowering.
PROPAGATION From seed, sown in autumn. From greenwood cuttings, taken in early summer.
POTENTIAL PROBLEMS Aphids, caterpillars; silver leaf.

SPECIES

P. avium *Europe, N. Africa, Russia, S.W. Asia*
Gean, wild cherry
Foliage: autumn. Flowers: mid-spring. H 60–75ft (18–23.5m), S 30–40ft (9–12m). FH.
The trunk of this spreading tree has red-banded bark and the leaves open bronze, turn dark green, then crimson in autumn. The clusters of white flowers are followed by reddish fruits. **'Plena'**, to 40ft (12m), has double white flowers.

P. cerasifera *S.E. Europe, S.W. Asia*
Cherry plum, myrobalan
Flowers: early spring. H and S 25–33ft (7.5–10 m). FH.
The bare shoots of this deciduous tree bear small white flowers in profusion. These may be followed by yellow or red edible fruits. Purple-leaved forms include **'Nigra'**, with pink flowers, and **'Pissardii'**, with very pale flowers. All make a dense hedge.

P. dulcis *C. and S.W. Asia, N. Africa*
Common almond
Flowers: early spring; H 25–40ft (7.5–12m), S 25–30ft (7.5–9m). FH.
An erect, later spreading, deciduous tree bears early pink blossom, the flowers solitary or paired. The green fruits contain edible nuts.

P. mume *China, Korea*
Japanese apricot
Flowers: late winter to early spring. Foliage: deciduous. H and S 20–30ft (6–9m). FH.
This small deciduous tree has long been cultivated in Japan for its almond-scented pink or white

flowers, which are borne on bare shoots. They are followed by sour edible fruits. The flowers of **'Beni-chidori'** are deep pink and double, those of **'Omoi-no-mama'** white with a pink flush and semi-double. Both of these cultivars are shrubby, growing to about 8ft (2.5m).

Prunus × subhirtella 'Autumnalis Rosea'

P. × subhirtella **'Autumnalis'**
Foliage: autumn. Flowers: late autumn to early spring. H and S 20–30ft (6–9m). FH.
The clusters of semi-double white flowers are tinged pink and appear intermittently over a long period. The leaves turn yellow in autumn. **'Autumnalis Rosea'** has pinkish flowers. *P. pendula* **'Pendula Rosea'** has weeping branches and pink flowers which rarely appear before early spring.

HYBRIDS

Foliage: autumn. Flowers: early spring to early summer. H and S 12–30 ft (3.7–9 m). FH.
This group includes the Japanese ornamental cherries. Cultivars include: **'Accolade'**, deep pink buds opening to semi-double pink flowers; **'Chôshû-hizakura'**, bronzy red young leaves and pink blossoms; **'Kiku-shidare-zakura'**, compact, weeping and with crowded pink double blossoms; **'Kursar'**, dark pink flowers preceding the leaves; **'Shirofugen'**, large, scented, double white flowers and leaves that turn from bronze to green to red; **'Shirotae'**, scented white flowers on arched branches and rich autumn foliage; **'Shôgetsu'**, hanging clusters of pink and white flowers, and orange and red autumn foliage; **'Spire'**, pale pink flower clusters and orange and red autumn leaves; and **'Taihaku'** with clusters of large white single blossoms.

Prunus 'Shirofugen'

PYRUS

ROSACEAE Pear

Clusters of decorative white spring blossoms characterize these deciduous trees and shrubs, found in woodland and on hillsides in Europe, Asia and N. Africa. There are about 30 species as well as many cultivars of the dessert and culinary pears, which are ornamental in their own right.
CULTIVATION Requires full sun and fertile well-drained soil.
PROPAGATION From seed, sown in autumn.
POTENTIAL PROBLEMS Aphids, caterpillars; honey fungus, powdery mildew.

P. salicifolia 'Pendula'
Flowers: spring. H 20–30ft (6–9m), S 12–20ft (3.7–6m). FH.
Dense creamy white blossom clusters on weeping branches with the grey-felted foliage, which is narrow, willow-like and turns grey-green in summer.

Pyrus salicifolia 'Pendula'

QUERCUS

FAGACEAE Oak

The oaks constitute a major genus of about 600 species of deciduous to evergreen trees and shrubs, which are widely distributed in woodland and more open habitats, mainly in the temperate Northern Hemisphere. The grand presence of many oaks, including the fast-growing Turkey oak (*Q. cerris*), can be appreciated only when they are given generous space. Leaf size and shape vary enormously but the foliage is often distinctively ornamental, particularly on several species that colour well in autumn. The insignificant male and female flowers, borne separately on the same tree, are followed by egg-shaped brown nuts (acorns) in basal cups.
CULTIVATION Tolerate sun or partial shade and require deep well-drained soil. The evergreen *Q. ilex* is best grown in full sun. *Q. rubra* and *Q. coccinea* need lime-free soil.
PROPAGATION From seed, sown as soon as ripe under glass or in a seedbed.
POTENTIAL PROBLEMS Aphids; honey fungus, powdery mildew and other fungal diseases.

Quercus coccinea 'Splendens'

Q. coccinea E. North America
Scarlet oak
Foliage: autumn. Flowers: late spring to early summer. Fruits: autumn. H 65–80ft (20–25m), S 40–50ft (12–15m). FH.
This fast-growing, eventually broad deciduous tree has deeply cut glossy leaves that in autumn turn from dark green to bright red. The bark is grey-brown. '**Splendens**' has red-purple foliage in autumn.

Q. ilex S.W. Europe
Holm oak
Foliage: year-round. Flowers: late spring to early summer. Fruits: autumn. H 70–80ft (22–25m), S 60–70ft (18–22m). FrH.
The broad rounded head is dense with glossy dark green leaves that are grey on the underside. Branches on mature specimens of this evergreen are pendulous. Acorns are small and roundish and are borne singly or in clusters.

Q. palustris E. USA
Pin oak
Foliage: autumn. Flowers: late spring to early summer. Fruits: autumn. H 60–80ft (18–25m), S 40–50ft (12–15m). FH.
This fast-growing tree has weeping lower branches and deeply cut glossy mid-green leaves that turn red-brown in autumn.

Quercus robur

Q. robur Europe
Common oak, English oak, pedunculate oak
Flowers: late spring to early summer. Fruits: autumn. H 120ft (36m), S 80ft (25m). FH.
The broad and often irregularly domed head of this deciduous species is heavily branched. The almost stalkless deep green leaves have rounded lobes. Acorns are carried singly or in clusters of 2 or 3. '**Concordia**', with a height and spread of 30ft (9m), has golden young foliage. The sessile oak, *Q. petraea*, has stalkless acorn cups.

Q. rubra E. North America
Red oak
Foliage: autumn. Flowers: late spring to early summer. Fruits: autumn. H 80ft (25m), S 70ft (22m). FH.
On this fast-growing tree, long dark green leaves with pointed lobes turn reddish and yellow-brown in autumn.

Quercus rubra

ROBINIA

PAPILIONACEAE

The fast-growing and generally suckering trees and shrubs in this genus (about 20 species, according to some authorities) are all from North America. Most are plants of wooded or more open dry habitats. The mid-green leaves are divided into many small leaflets along a central rib up to 18in (45cm) long, held on thorny, very brittle branches. The pea-like flowers are carried in long hanging racemes; where the summers are hot enough these are often followed by long, shining, brown seed pods. The shrubby and fully hardy rose acacia (**R. hispida**), usually about 8ft (2.5m) high and bearing deep pink flowers, is sometimes grafted and grown as a small tree.

CULTIVATION Require full sun and moist well-drained soils but tolerate drier conditions.

PROPAGATION From seed, sown in spring (species). By grafting, in early spring (cultivars).

POTENTIAL PROBLEMS Usually none.

Robinia pseudoacacia 'Frisia'

R. pseudoacacia *E. USA*
Black locust, false acacia, locust
Foliage: autumn. Flowers: late spring to early summer. H 70–80ft (22–25m), S 40–50ft (12–15m). FH.
This elegant upright tree has a loose open habit and slightly arching thorny branches, which break very easily. The dark green leaves consist of up to 13 small oval leaflets. They turn butter yellow in autumn. The scented flowers are creamy white. **'Frisia'** is a small tree up to about 50ft (15m) high with bright yellow foliage.

SALIX

SALICACEAE Willow

About 300 deciduous trees and shrubs are widely distributed, mainly in temperate regions but in a wide variety of habitats. Willows have tiny seeds, each with a tangle of long hairs that aid wind dispersal, and need moist conditions to germinate. Most of the ornamental tree willows are plants of moist lowlands and riversides. Several with weeping shoots are shown to best effect planted near water. These include the weeping willow (*S. babylonica*) and the golden weeping willow, *S.* × *sepulcralis* var. *chrysocoma*. Their roots travel far, however, and these trees are not for planting near buildings or within striking distance of drains. The shape and poise of the trees, the elegance of the foliage and the catkins, male (usually the more showy) and female on separate trees, are all attractive features. There are some, too, with young stems that are colourful or that have a distinctive bloom in winter. Pollarding and coppicing are traditional methods of pruning that maintain a supply of young growths. See also SHRUBS.

CULTIVATION Require full sun and moist well-drained soil. To ensure crops of colourful young stems on *S. alba* cut back to a framework of permanent branches annually in early spring.

PROPAGATION From greenwood cuttings, taken in summer. From hardwood cuttings, taken in winter.

POTENTIAL PROBLEMS Aphids, leaf beetles; honey fungus.

S. alba *C. Asia, Europe, N. Africa*
White willow
Catkins: spring. Stems: winter. H 65–80ft (20–25m), S 30–40ft (9–12m). FH.
As a landscape tree this quickly provides a mass of silvery foliage, the reverse of the leaves being blue-green and silky. The metallic lustre of the silver willow (**var. sericea**), which grows to 50ft (15m), is even more pronounced. Young stems of some cultivars are strongly coloured in winter. Those of **subsp. vitellina** 'Britzensis' are orange-red.

Salix alba var. *sericea*

S. babylonica var. **pekinensis** 'Tortuosa'
Catkins: late winter to early spring. H 40–50ft (12–15m), S 20–25 ft (6–7.5m). FH.
The twisted branches and contorted bright green leaves of this upright fast-growing willow make it a tree of character at all seasons. Yellow-green catkins precede the leaves.

SOPHORA

PAPILIONACEAE

In a genus of about 50 species widely distributed in temperate and tropical regions there are deciduous and evergreen shrubs and trees of woodland and dry, more open, habitats. The flowers are pea-like and the division of the pinnate leaves gives the foliage a light ferniness. The frost-hardy New Zealand kowhai (**S. tetraptera**), an evergreen that grows to 30ft (9m), produces dense clusters of golden flowers in late spring.

CULTIVATION Require full sun and fertile well-drained soil. These plants flower best in hot dry conditions.

PROPAGATION From seed, sown in early spring under protection.

POTENTIAL PROBLEMS Usually none.

Sophora japonica

S. japonica *China, Korea*
Japanese pagoda tree
Flowers: late summer to early autumn. H 60–80ft (18–25m), S 40–60ft (12–18m). FH.
This deciduous species, although not native to Japan, long cultivated there, has leaves about 1ft (30cm) long composed of up to 15 leaflets. It is slow to reach flowering age but in maturity produces masses of creamy white pea flowers when grown in regions with hot dry summers. The seed pods 2–4in (5–10cm) long, often stay on the tree all winter.

SORBUS

ROSACEAE

About 100 species of these deciduous trees and shrubs are found in the temperate Northern Hemisphere, many of them in woodland but some in more open, sometimes mountainous, habitats. The genus includes several ornamental trees of moderate size, with elegant foliage that usually colours well in autumn, conspicuous berries that can be long-lasting and flowers that attract attention, despite being soberly unshowy.
CULTIVATION Tolerate full sun or partial shade and require well-drained soil.
PROPAGATION From seed, sown in autumn. From greenwood cuttings, taken in early summer.
POTENTIAL PROBLEMS Aphids; fireblight.

S. aria Europe
Whitebeam
Foliage: spring to autumn. Flowers: late spring. Berries: autumn. H 50–80ft (15–25m), S 30–40ft (9–12m). FH.
In the wild this rounded tree is commonly seen on lime-rich soils and is sensational when silvered with young spring foliage. Although the grey felt persists on the reverse of the simple leaves, the upper surface becomes bright green. The clusters of berries that follow white flowers become crimson before the leaves turn gold and brown. 'Lutescens', rarely more than 30ft (9m) high, is exceptionally silvery in spring and later grey-green. 'Majestica' has large leaves and fruit.

Sorbus aria

S. aucuparia Asia, Europe
Mountain ash, rowan
Foliage: autumn. Flowers: late spring. Berries: late summer to autumn. H 40–50ft (12–15m), S 15–25ft (4.5–7.5m). FH.
On an open elegant tree bright red berries, which follow scented white flowers, stand out against still green pinnate leaves. The foliage colours well in autumn.

'Aspleniifolia' has distinctively cut leaflets. Cultivars growing 25–30ft (7.5–9m) high include 'Fructu Luteo', with yellow berries, and the narrowly upright 'Sheerwater Seedling'.

Sorbus cashmiriana

S. cashmiriana W. Himalayas
Foliage: autumn. Flowers: late spring. Berries: autumn to early winter. H 20–25ft (6–7.5m), S 15–20ft (4.5–6m). FH.
Clusters of white or pink flowers are succeeded by long-lasting white berries on this open tree. The long pinnate leaves are dark green. The Hubei rowan (S. hupehensis) from China, of similar size, has bluish green foliage that turns red in autumn and white berries with a pink tinge.

S. 'Joseph Rock'
Foliage: autumn. Flowers: late spring. Berries: autumn to winter. H 25–30ft (7.5–9m), S 15–20ft (4.5–6m). FH.
Bright green pinnate leaves that turn orange, red and purple in autumn and long-lasting yellow to orange-yellow berries are features. This highly ornamental upright tree is unfortunately prone to fireblight.

S. vilmorinii S.W. China
Foliage: autumn. Flowers: late spring to early summer. Berries: autumn. H and S 12–18ft (3.7–5.5m). FH.
The elegant ferny foliage of this shrub or small tree turns red to purple in autumn. The berries, drooping in clusters from arching branches, change from red to pink and eventually pink tinged white.

STEWARTIA

THEACEAE

The 15 to 20 species include deciduous and evergreen woodland trees and shrubs growing on acid soils in E.Asia and S.E. USA. Several of the deciduous species have colourful autumn foliage as well as summer flowers and attractive bark.

CULTIVATION Require partial shade, well-drained neutral to acid soil and protection from strong winds.
PROPAGATION From seed, sown in autumn. From greenwood cuttings, taken in early summer. From semi-ripe cuttings, taken in mid- to late summer.
POTENTIAL PROBLEMS Usually none.

S. pseudocamellia Japan
Foliage: autumn. Flowers: mid- to late summer. H 50–70ft (15–22m), S 20–25ft (6–7.5m). FH.
Good reasons for growing this open tree as a specimen if space allows include cup-shaped white flowers with prominent stamens, leaves that turn yellow-orange to red-purple in autumn and pink to red-brown flaking bark.

Stewartia sinensis

S. sinensis C. and E. China
Foliage: autumn. Flowers: mid-summer. H 20–30ft (6–9m), S 15–20ft (4.5–6m). FH.
This large shrub or small tree has peeling red-brown bark, fragrant cup-shaped white flowers and foliage that turns rich crimson in autumn.

STYRAX

STYRACACEAE

Among the 100 or so species of this genus of deciduous and evergreen trees and shrubs, widely distributed in temperate and tropical regions of the Northern Hemisphere, several are woodland plants producing graceful displays of pendulous white flowers in spring or summer.
CULTIVATION Tolerate full sun or partial shade and require moist well-drained soil and shelter from cold winds.
PROPAGATION From seed, sown in a coldframe in autumn. From semi-ripe cuttings, taken in mid-summer.
POTENTIAL PROBLEMS Usually none.

Styrax japonicus

S. japonicus *China, Japan, Korea*
Japanese snowbell
Foliage: autumn. Flowers: summer.
H 30ft (9m), S 9ft (2.7m). FH.
This attractive large shrub or small
tree has a loose open habit. The
spear-shaped leaves are dark green
on the upper surface and have a
silver-white underside. They turn
red or yellow in autumn. Short
drooping clusters of large, fragrant,
white, bell-shaped flowers are
carried on the undersides of the
shoots in early summer. Other
notable species that are fully
hardy and deciduous include
S. hemsleyanus, from China,
which grows to 30ft (9m) and the
more shrubby **S. obassia**, from N.
China to Japan, which has fragrant
flowers and peeling bark.

TILIA

TILIACEAE Lime, linden

The limes are deciduous woodland
trees of the temperate Northern
Hemisphere, different authorities
giving a total of between 20 and 45
species. Several, including the
common lime (**T. × europaea**),
have been much planted as stately

Tilia × europaea

avenue trees or pleached, having
pliable stems and being tolerant of
heavy pruning. The magical
fragrance of the small creamy
white to yellow flowers, which are
carried in numerous clusters, has
understandably inspired much
poetry and song.
CULTIVATION Tolerate full sun or
partial shade and require moist
well-drained soil. *T.* × *euchlora* and
T. 'Petiolaris' do not sucker strongly.
PROPAGATION From seed, sown as
soon as ripe in autumn. From semi-
ripe cuttings, taken in summer.
POTENTIAL PROBLEMS Aphids,
except *T.* × *euchlora* and
T. 'Petiolaris', gall mites; honey
fungus.

T. × euchlora
Flowers: mid-summer. H 60–70ft
(18–22m), S 40–50ft (12–15m). FH.
Unlike many limes, this rounded
tree is free of aphids and therefore
does not shed honeydew. The
arching branches bear dark green
rounded leaves, paler on the
underside, and drooping clusters of
yellow-green flowers that are
wonderfully fragrant but narcotic
to bees.

T. 'Petiolaris'
Pendulous silver lime
Flowers: late summer. H 80–100ft
(25–30m), S 50–70ft (16–22m).
FH.
Weeping branches, dark green
leaves with silvery undersides and
strongly scented pale yellow flower
clusters distinguish this handsome
deciduous tree. The flowers are
narcotic to bees.

Tilia platyphyllos 'Rubra'

T. platyphyllos *Europe*
Large-leaved lime
Flowers: early to mid-summer.
H 80–100ft (25–30m), S 50–70ft
(15–22m). FH.
Drooping branchlets give the
columnar tree a weeping character.

The leaves are heart-shaped, on the
underside downy and pale green,
and the yellow-green flowers,
which are narcotic to bees, exhale
a scent of summer contentment.
This species suckers less freely
than the common lime but like it
attracts aphids, which shed
honeydew. The shoots of the red-
twigged lime ('**Rubra**') are
conspicuous in winter.

TRACHYCARPUS

ARECACEAE

The 6 species of evergreen palms
comprising this genus are forest
trees from the Himalayas and East
Asia. The only species that is
commonly grown, the Chusan
palm *T. fortunei*, is the hardiest of
the palms and notable for the size
of its fan-shaped leaves.
CULTIVATION Tolerates full sun or
light shade and requires well-
drained soil and protection from
strong winds.
PROPAGATION By division, removing
basal growths with 2 or more
leaves in late spring. From seed,
sown under glass in spring.
POTENTIAL PROBLEMS Usually none.

Trachycarpus fortunei

T. fortunei *China*
Chusan palm
Foliage: year-round. Flowers: late
spring to early summer. H 30–50ft
(9–15m) S 8–10ft (2.5–3m). FrH.
The mid-green leaves are about 3ft
(1m) across and are pleated and
split at the ends, giving a jagged
tooth-like appearance. They are
held on sharply toothed leaf stalks
up to 3ft (1m) long that arch out
from the top of an upright stem
that is covered with the fibrous
remains of dead leaves. The small
yellow flowers appear in large
dense bunches that can be 24in
(60cm) long. Where summers are
hot enough, they produce small,
black, date-like fruits.

shrubs

In the strict sense, shrubs are woody plants with several main stems developing at or near ground level. Many shrubs such as the evergreen Portugal laurel (*Prunus lusitanica*) can be grown on a single stem while large multi-stemmed plants like the Persian ironwood (*Parrotia persica*) are usually regarded as trees. Plants with a woody base and soft stems are known as sub-shrubs. Shrubs are found under the canopy of forests, as a tough component of vegetation like that of the Mediterranean maquis and garrigue (see pp. 30–31) and beyond the tree line, as in the case of many Himalayan rhododendrons and dwarf shrubs of mountainous and tundra areas. This selection includes compact shrubs for rock gardens, shrubs for cool moist areas under and among trees and others for sunny areas. Flowers, foliage and fruits can all be of ornamental value.

In theory container-grown shrubs can be planted at any time of the year, provided the ground is not frozen. In practice the best time to plant deciduous shrubs is from autumn to early spring and evergreens from early to mid-spring. Many shrubs need little pruning except for the removal of dead, diseased and damaged wood. However, specific advice on pruning is given with individual entries.

Top Pyracantha 'Golden Charmer'
Centre Viburnum tinus 'Gwenllian'
Bottom Camellia japonica 'Gloire de Nantes'

ABELIA

CAPRIFOLIACEAE

About 30 species, from Asia and Central America, are represented in gardens by a small number of semi-evergreen and deciduous shrubs with neat foliage. They bear small foxglove-like flowers in great profusion. Abelias do well in a sunny border. The most colourful species, the half-hardy Mexican *A. floribunda*, which is evergreen, dangles tubular flowers of reddish pink. For success in cool temperate gardens it needs a favoured position at the foot of a warm wall where it can grow to a height of 10ft (3m) or more.

CULTIVATION Require full sun and fertile well-drained soil. Prune out old straggly stems in mid-spring. In frost-prone areas, grow plants against a south- or west-facing wall or fence.

PROPAGATION From cuttings, in summer.

POTENTIAL PROBLEMS Usually none.

Abelia × grandiflora

A. × grandiflora

Flowers: mid-summer to autumn. H 6–9ft (1.8–2.7m), S 4–7ft (1.2–2.2m). FrH.

Slightly fragrant pink and white flowers, densely clustered above the glossy semi-evergreen foliage, are undramatic but the season is long and late. '**Francis Mason**', which has dark green leaves with a yellow margin, is attractive as a foliage plant but the variegated leaves do not go well with the flowers. The semi-evergreen **A. 'Edward Goucher'**, of which *A. × grandiflora* is a parent, is more compact and the glossy bronze of its young leaves is a prelude to the mauve-pink flowers.

ABUTILON

MALVACEAE

The genus, with well over 100 species, is widely distributed in tropical and subtropical regions. Several shrubby species and a number of hybrids are notable for their bell-shaped flowers and maple-like leaves. In cool temperate regions the tender species need greenhouse conditions but in mild areas the hardiest abutilons can be grown outdoors, preferably with the backing of a warm wall. The handsomely shaped leaves of *A. pictum* '**Thompsonii**' can look sickly with its yellow and green mottling. However, because of this, rather than despite it, the shrub is a favourite to include in subtropical bedding schemes.

CULTIVATION Require full sun and well-drained soil (JI No. 2). Prune weather-damaged shoots in early spring and prune crossing shoots after flowering.

PROPAGATION From seed, sown in spring at 59–64°F (15–18°C). From cuttings, taken in spring and summer.

POTENTIAL PROBLEMS Under glass: red spider mites, whiteflies, mealybugs, scale insects.

A. megapotamicum *Brazil*

Trailing abutilon
Flowers: summer to autumn. H and S 4–6ft (1.2–1.8m). FrH.

Vivid heart-shaped buds dangle from flopping slender stems, which are improved by wall training. The crimson calyces open just enough to allow yellow petals and purple stamens to protrude. Among several hybrids that owe some of their character to this species, **A. 'Kentish Belle'** features larger pale apricot petals which have striking reddish veins.

**Abutilon vitifolium
'Veronica Tennant'**

A. vitifolium *Chile*

Flowers: early summer. H 12–15ft (3.7–4.5m), S 6–8ft (1.8–2.5m). FrH.

Almost tree-like when it romps away, this fast-growing deciduous shrub has downy vine-like leaves and clusters of large saucer-shaped flowers of mauve blue. '**Veronica Tennant**' is very pale, edging towards the purity of '**Tennant's White**'. The species is a parent of the hybrid *A. × suntense*, a smaller shrub with a colour range from white to violet blue.

ACER

ACERACEAE Maple

Their poise as shrubs or small trees, the elegant cut of their foliage, and its colour range, with spectacular transformations in autumn, has earned for a small group of deciduous Asiatic maples a special place in Japanese gardens. In the West they have been grown for well over 100 years, most impressively as a shrub storey in woodland glades where the soil is moist and there is shelter from cold winds. Autumn colour is said to be most brilliant on acid soils. Their qualities are also easily appreciated in small gardens, even those in no way inspired by a Japanese aesthetic. These maples, outstanding in a genus of about 150 species, are easily accommodated, being slow-growing and of moderate size. They do not rely on flowers to grab attention but are, at the least, pleasing and sometimes superbly ornamental when in leaf and remain interesting when reduced to an intricate pattern of twigs and stems. See also TREES.

CULTIVATION Tolerate sun or partial shade and require well-drained, moist, fertile soil and shelter from late spring frosts; temperatures below 25°F (–4°C) will kill new foliage. Prune out crossing and unsightly shoots in late autumn to mid-winter.

PROPAGATION From seed, sown as soon as ripe. By grafting, in late winter. By budding, in late summer.

POTENTIAL PROBLEMS Aphids, mites, scale insects, caterpillars; tar spot, verticillium wilt, leaf scorch.

A. japonicum *Japan*

Full-moon maple, Japanese maple
Foliage: mid-spring to autumn.
Flowers: early to mid-spring; H 20–30ft (6–9m), S 10–20ft (3–6m). FH.

In spring, the purplish red flowers, hanging in clusters, are an attractive feature. However, the species and its named cultivars are grown mainly for their rounded outline and the elegance of their leaves. The deeply lobed leaves of '**Aconitifolium**' and the broader fans of '**Vitifolium**' turn from soft green to rich shades of red in autumn.

A. palmatum *China, Japan, Korea*

Japanese maple
Foliage: mid-spring to autumn.
Flowers: spring. Fruits: late summer.
H 15–25ft (4.5–7.5m), S 10–20ft (3–6m). FH.

In the wild the Japanese maple is said to make a tree as much as 40ft (12m) in height but in cultivation

Acer palmatum Dissectum Atropurpureum Group

its numerous forms are better known as slow-growing bushes, eventually forming large shrubs or small trees of rounded outline. The Japanese fascination with this species over many centuries accounts for the extraordinary range of leaf colour and shape, all variations on a 5- to 7-lobed green pattern with bronze to red colouring in autumn. The flowers are insignificant but in some of the cultivars the red-winged fruits are conspicuous in late summer. Many cultivars, not just the deeply lobed **f. atropurpureum**, have dark purplish or bronze foliage in summer, turning red in autumn. **'Bloodgood'**, for example, has rich purple leaves with 5 deeply divided lobes, and is richly coloured in autumn with bright red fruits. Deep division of the leaves in **var. dissectum** gives them a soft ferny texture, the effect of which is heightened by the weeping growth of mounded shrubs about 6ft (1.8m) high. The leaves have as many as 11 lobes, each finely cut and toothed. Some of the cultivars with finely divided foliage have copper-red or purplish foliage in summer, the **Dissectum Atropurpureum Group** making mushroom shapes of bronze-red. **'Inaba-shidare'** is a more open bush, with large, red-stalked, dark leaves that become intense crimson in autumn. The larger-leaved forms include the tree-like **'Osakazuki'**, the 7-lobed leaves, more than 4in (10cm) long, turning in autumn from mid-green to incandescent reds. Also tree-like, **'Sango-kaku'**, sometimes known as the coral bark maple, makes a beautiful transition from light green to soft yellow in autumn but is most remarkable for bright red stems in winter.

A. shirasawanum 'Aureum'
Foliage: mid-spring to autumn. Flowers: spring; H and S 12–20ft (3.7–6m). FH.
The prettily fan-shaped leaves, with 7 to 11 elegant points, are carried in overlapping tiers on a compact

rounded bush that can slowly attain tree-like proportions. The lime-green foliage turns to orange and red in autumn.

Acer shirasawanum 'Aureum'

AMELANCHIER

ROSACEAE Snowy Mespilus

White starry flowers in spring and foliage that colours brilliantly in autumn are the winning ornamental characteristics of a mainly North American genus of deciduous shrubs and small trees. It also has representatives in Asia and Europe. There are altogether about 25 species, some of which have proven difficult to distinguish one from another, and because of this have been much confused in commerce.
CULTIVATION Tolerate sun or partial shade and require well-drained, moist, fertile, acid soil. In winter, remove any branch which spoils the shape of the plant.
PROPAGATION From seed, sown as soon as ripe. From cuttings, taken in summer. Some species develop suckers which can be lifted.
POTENTIAL PROBLEM Fireblight.

Amelanchier lamarckii

A. lamarckii
Foliage: autumn. Flowers: mid-spring. Fruits: mid-summer.
H and S 10–25ft (3–7.5m). FH.
The 5-petalled white flowers are massed among young foliage that is copper red and silky. This large shrub or small tree is spectacular again in autumn, when the leaves colour red and orange. The purple-black berry-like fruits, which ripen

in summer, are edible. Two similar North American species are the suckering shadbush (**A. canadensis**) and the Allegheny service berry (**A. laevis**). The latter is a parent of a fine hybrid, **A. × grandiflora 'Ballerina'**, which carries a profusion of large flowers.

ARALIA

ARALIACEAE

This very mixed genus of about 40 species, distributed in Asia and the Americas, includes several deciduous shrubs or small trees that are notable for their compound leaves. Variegation refines the already elegant foliage of the species described.
CULTIVATION Tolerate sun or partial shade and require moist soil that is rich in organic matter. Prune unwanted stems in autumn and winter.
PROPAGATION From seed, sown as soon as ripe or in spring after stratification. From root cuttings, in winter. By removal of suckers, in autumn or winter. By grafting *A. elata* variegated cultivars in winter.
POTENTIAL PROBLEM Aphids.

A. elata E. Asia
Japanese angelica tree
Foliage: late spring to autumn. Flowers: late summer to early autumn; H and S 20–30ft (6–9m). FH.
The species, usually an upright tree, has spiny sparsely branching stems topped by magnificent leaves which are up to 4ft (1.2m) long, doubly divided and with about 80 leaflets. The frothy clusters of tiny cream flowers appear just as the leaves begin to turn red and yellow.
'Aureovariegata', with leaflets margined yellow to cream, and the paler **'Variegata'** are less vigorous, usually making large shrubs about 10–15ft (3–4.5m) in height and spread. The tendency to sucker needs to be carefully watched, particularly on the variegated cultivars, which are usually grafted on plain-leaved stocks.

Aralia elata 'Aureovariegata'

AUCUBA

CORNACEAE

The fate of the spotted laurel (*A. japonica*) is to be taken for granted, for it has long been used as a shrub of last resort, expected to tolerate heavy pollution and to flourish in dismal corners where other plants would certainly fail. The 3 or 4 species in the genus are evergreen and bear male and female flowers on different plants. For female clones to produce berries there must be a male plant in close proximity.
CULTIVATION Tolerate full sun or partial or full shade and most soil conditions (JI No. 2). Remove unwanted stems during dormancy.
PROPAGATION From seed, sown in autumn. From semi-ripe cuttings, in mid-summer.
POTENTIAL PROBLEMS Usually none.
WARNING Swallowing any part may cause mild stomach upset.

A. japonica *Japan*
Spotted laurel
Foliage: year-round. Flowers: mid-spring. Fruits: autumn to spring (female plants only). H and S 6–10ft (1.8–3m). FH.
Even in dense shade, this is a bushy shrub that is well covered with large glossy leaves. The small purplish flowers are easily overlooked but the long-lasting berries, when they eventually colour, are a lustrous scarlet. There are numerous plain-leaved and variegated cultivars. The female **f. longifolia** and the male 'Lance Leaf' have narrow plain leaves. 'Crotonifolia' (female) is brightly splashed and speckled with yellow. The plain-leaved and compact 'Rozannie', which grows to about 3ft (90cm) in height, is self-pollinating and regularly bears heavy crops of berries. The original spotted laurel, and once widely planted 'Variegata' (female), has toothed leaves that are densely spotted with gold. Reverted growths that appear on the variegated cultivars should be removed promptly.

Aucuba japonica 'Variegata'

BALLOTA

LAMIACEAE

Among the 30 to 35 species are several evergreen subshrubs of Mediterranean origin that thrive in hot stony places. Their woolly grey mounds become more white the drier the conditions.
CULTIVATION Require full sun and poor, dry, well-drained soil (JI No. 2). Cut the plant back in mid-spring.
PROPAGATION From cuttings, in summer.
POTENTIAL PROBLEMS Usually none.

Ballota pseudodictamnus

B. pseudodictamnus *Crete, Greece, W. Turkey*
Foliage: mid-spring to late autumn (year-round in frost-free zones). Flowers: late spring to early summer; H and S 18–24in (45–60cm). FrH to FH.
Erect white-felted stems carry rounded yellow-green leaves silvered with a covering of grey wool. The small purplish pink flowers, carried in whorls, are much less important ornamentally than the foliage. **B. acetabulosa** is a similar plant with greener leaves and the flowers have larger calyces.

BERBERIS

BERBERIDACEAE Barberry

Many of the barberries seem rather gauche plants. But in this large genus comprising about 450 species of deciduous and evergreen shrubs are numerous plants of ornamental value, grown for their flowers, foliage and large crops of berries. The spininess of many plants makes them difficult to work among but this is an asset when they are used for hedging. They are found in a wide range of habitats throughout the Northern Hemisphere and also in Africa and South America.
CULTIVATION Require sun and tolerate any well-drained soil. Prune only to maintain a balanced shape. Prune evergreen shrubs and trim evergreen hedges after flowering; prune and trim deciduous specimens and hedges in late winter.
PROPAGATION From seed, sown in winter; from cuttings, taken in summer.
POTENTIAL PROBLEMS Aphids; powdery mildew.
WARNING Contact with the spines may irritate the skin. Swallowing any part may cause stomach upset.

Berberis × stenophylla

B. darwinii *Argentina, Chile*
Flowers: mid- to late spring. Fruits: autumn. H and S 8–10ft (2.5–3m). FH.
Clusters of small, cup-shaped, orange-yellow flowers hang in profusion among the glossy spiny leaves and are followed by blue berries. This evergreen species makes a highly ornamental informal hedge. It is a parent of **B. × stenophylla**, which is of similar height but makes a wider thicket. It is one of the most graceful barberries, putting out arching stems that in late spring have deep yellow strongly fragrant flowers. The crop of berries that follows is sparse. **B. × stenophylla** 'Corallina Compacta', usually under 1ft (30cm), has flowers that open yellow from coral buds.

Berberis darwinii

B. julianae *China*
Flowers: late spring. Fruits: autumn. H and S 8–10ft (2.5–3m). FH.
A hedge of this spiny-stemmed and spiny-leaved evergreen is almost impenetrable. The leaves are coppery when young and the scented yellow flowers, which have a red tinge, are followed by blue-black berries.

B. × ottawensis

Flowers: late spring. Fruits: autumn.
H and S 6–8ft (1.8–2.5m). FH.
The plain-leaved hybrid is a
pleasing deciduous shrub with
arching stems giving it a rounded
outline. The yellow flowers, which
have a red tinge, are followed by
dangling clusters of red berries.
'Superba' carries purplish red
leaves that turn bright crimson
in autumn.

B. 'Rubrostilla'

Flowers: late spring. Fruits: autumn.
H 4–6ft (1.2–1.8m), S 6–8ft
(1.8–2.5m). FH.
The glaucous leaves of this
gracefully arching deciduous shrub
colour well in autumn. Clustered
pale yellow flowers are followed by
distinctively pear-shaped coral-red
berries that are broadest at their
base, not their tip.

B. thunbergii *Japan*

Flowers: early summer. Fruits:
autumn. H 4–5ft (1.2–1.8m), S 6–8ft
(1.8–2.5m). FH.
The straw-coloured flowers have a
warm tint and the leaves of this
spiny deciduous species colour
bright red and orange in autumn at
the same time as the small ovoid
berries turn scarlet. The plain-
leaved form is useful for hedging
but it is the numerous purple-
leaved variations that are most
commonly grown. The full-scale
f. *atropurpurea* has bronze
purple foliage. Less vigorous is
'Rose Glow', with pale pink or
white streaking of the leaves.
Dwarf purple-leaved forms include
'Atropurpurea Nana', up to 2ft
(60cm) high, and the even more
compact 'Bagatelle'.

Berberis thunbergii 'Rose Glow'

BRACHYGLOTTIS

ASTERACEAE

Daisy flowerheads and leaves that
are usually grey- or white-felted on
the underside are characteristic of
a group of about 30 evergreen
shrubs, native to New Zealand and
Tasmania, that have been moved
from *Senecio* to this genus. They
are found in a wide range of
habitats but most species, like the
hybrid that is described, are
sun-lovers and are remarkably
tolerant of wind and salt spray so
that they are useful shrubs for
seaside gardens.
CULTIVATION Require full sun and
well-drained soil. Prune the older
straggly stems back to new lower
growths in mid-spring.
PROPAGATION From semi-ripe
cuttings in mid-summer.
POTENTIAL PROBLEMS Usually none.

Brachyglottis Dunedin Group
'Sunshine'

B. Dunedin Group 'Sunshine'

Foliage: evergreen. Flowers: mid-
summer to autumn; H 4–5ft
(1.2–1.5m), S 4–6ft (1.2–1.8m). FH.
The sprawling mound gives a very
silvery impression when covered
by young hairy leaves and felted
buds. The mature leaves are grey-
green but their wavy margins are
outlined in silver-grey. The brash
yellow daisies are borne in great
profusion. The less hardy 'Moira
Read' has an irregular yellow and
pale green variegation.

BUDDLEJA

BUDDLEJACEAE

Self-sown seedlings of the common
butterfly bush (*Buddleja davidii*),
apparently thriving in the cracks of
old walls or on rubbly waste
ground, show the resilience of
these plants in dry conditions. This
is a large and very mixed genus of
about 100 species, from Asia, Africa
and the Americas, but all the shrubs
in general cultivation share a
preference for open sunny
positions and well-drained soils,
and are tolerant of lime. The
individual tubular flowers, which
are sweetly scented, are small
but their densely clustered
arrangements are conspicuous.
Buddlejas that flower in late
summer are highly attractive to
butterflies and other insects. They
are fast-growing and very useful in
young gardens.
CULTIVATION Require full sun and
fertile well-drained soil (JI No. 3).
Prune buddlejas that flower in late
summer and autumn in early
spring, cutting back to a low
framework of stems. Prune
B. alternifolia after flowering,
cutting the flowered shoots back to
lower young growths and
removing about a quarter of the
old shoots. Prune *B. globosa* lightly
after it has flowered.
PROPAGATION From semi-ripe
cuttings, in summer; *B. davidii* from
hardwood cuttings in autumn.
POTENTIAL PROBLEMS Capsid bugs,
caterpillars, figwort weevil, mullein
moth, red spider mites.

B. alternifolia *China*

Flowers in early summer. H 12–
15ft (3.7–4.5m), S 10–15ft
(3–4.5m). FH.
The long arching branches,
generously covered along their
length with clusters of small
purplish mauve flowers, are seen to
best effect when specimens are
trained on a main stem to form a
weeping standard. The flowers are
borne on growths made in the
previous season. The species is
unusual in having alternate leaves.

Buddleja alternifolia

B. crispa *Himalayas*

Foliage: mid-spring to autumn.
Flowers: mid to late summer. H and
S 6–10ft (1.8–3m). FrH. to FH.
This deciduous white-felted shrub
is a study in soft tones, its scented
flowers, borne in cylindrical spikes,
being white centred and pale
mauve. Where the shrub's
hardiness is borderline it is best
trained against a warm wall and
pruned annually to a framework of
branches. The flowers are produced
on the wood of the current season.

Buddleja 'Pink Delight'

B. davidii *China, Japan*
Butterfly bush
Flowers: mid-summer to early autumn. H and S 8–12ft (2.5–3.7m). FH.
The scented nectar-rich flowers densely cluster in arching plumes up to 20in (50cm) long and draw butterflies to the garden over a long season. The fast-growing broad bushes have lance-shaped grey-green leaves, felted on the underside. The flower colour in the wild and of most of the self-sown seedlings that spring up on waste ground is pale purple. The many white and richly coloured forms in cultivation include **'Dartmoor'**, with short magenta plumes; **'Empire Blue'**, violet-blue with orange eye; **'Royal Red'**, purplish red; and **'White Profusion'**, white with a yellow eye. **'Nanho Blue'**, with pale mauve flowers, is an example of several of slender build. The pink flowers of **B. 'Pink Delight'**, a hybrid, have orange eyes and are borne on long spikes.

B. fallowiana *W. China*
Flowers: late summer to early autumn. H 6–8ft (2–2.5m), S 10ft (3m). FrH.
This species, less vigorous and more tender than the better known *B. davidii*, produces mauve-blue flowers with an orange eye against felted grey foliage. The young foliage of **B. 'Lochinch'**, probably a hybrid between this species and *B. davidii*, is silvery grey. It bears narrow plumes of violet-blue flowers with orange centres.

B. globosa *Argentina, Chile*
Orange ball tree
Flowers: early summer. H and S 10–15ft (3–4.5m). FrH.
The arrangement of the yellow flowers, which are clustered in tight balls, is unique among the buddlejas. The balls are about 2cm (¾in) across, 8 to 10 balls standing above the partially evergreen foliage in a branched arrangement at the end of the stems. The underside of the leaves is buff and downy.

BUXUS

BUXACEAE Box, Boxwood

Of about 70 species, all evergreen, several are remarkably tolerant of regular clipping and as a consequence have long been grown as hedging plants and as subjects for topiary. Specimens hold their shape well even with only a single annual trim. In southern Europe *B. balearica* is used in much the same way as the most widely grown of the species, the common box (*B. sempervirens*). The starry, yellow-green flowers are inconspicuous nestling among the leathery leaves. Male and female flowers are carried on the same plant.
CULTIVATION Tolerate full sun or partial shade and a wide range of well-drained soils but best in light shade and fertile conditions. Clip hedges and topiary species in mid- to late summer; prune old hedges in late spring.
PROPAGATION From semi-ripe cuttings, in mid-summer.
POTENTIAL PROBLEMS Box sucker, red spider mites.
WARNING Contact with the sap may irritate the skin.

B. sempervirens *Europe, N. Africa, Turkey*
Common box
Foliage: year-round. Flowers: mid-spring. H and S 10–15ft (3–4.5m). FH.
The glossy dark green leaves of this species are its main attraction and on unclipped specimens form dense sprays on untidy bushes or small trees. Clipping results in even denser growth that holds its shape well. The many cultivars of this species, including several that are variegated, show a considerable range of vigour and leaf size. An irregular creamy margin to the leaves of **'Elegantissima'** gives this slow-growing box a silvery look. Bearing plain leaves **'Handsworthiensis'**, which is vigorous and of upright growth, is much favoured for hedges. It can even reach heights of 6ft (1.8m)

Buxus sempervirens 'Elegantissima'

or more. In marked contrast, **'Suffruticosa'**, which is compact and very slow-growing, is mainly used in formal gardens for edging flowerbeds. Dense slow-growing clones of the small-leaved box (*B. microphylla*) such as **'Green Pillow'** can be used in the same way and only require an occasional clip to keep their shape.

CALLICARPA

VERBENACEAE

In a genus of well over 100 species many are tropical and subtropical shrubs and trees. The beauty berry is one of the hardiest and makes a startling autumn discovery in temperate gardens when thinning leaves expose clustered fruits of unusual colouring. Several plants of different clones need to be grown together to ensure good crops.
CULTIVATION Tolerate sun or partial shade and require well-drained fertile soil (JI No.2). Prune in early spring, cutting back to new shoots.
PROPAGATION From seed, sown in autumn or spring. From cuttings, in spring and summer.
POTENTIAL PROBLEMS Usually none.

Callicarpa bodinieri var. *giraldii*

C. bodinieri var. **giraldii**
C. and W. China
Beauty berry
Flowers: mid-summer. Fruits: autumn. H 6–10ft (1.8–3m), S 5–8ft (1.5–2.5m). FH.
In summer this deciduous shrub is bushy with dark green leaves but has no distinctive feature to attract attention until, late in the season, it produces numerous tiny flowers of mauve-pink. From these develop small round fruits and when these colour the shrub is transformed, clusters of shiny violet-purple berries encrusting the stems before leaf-fall and remaining afterwards on the bare stems. **'Profusion'** is a particularly outstanding form, freely producing strongly coloured fruits. Its foliage has a purplish tint in the spring and turns an attractive reddish purple in the autumn.

CALLISTEMON

MYRTACEAE Bottlebrush

The "bottlebrushes" of these Australian evergreens bristle with colourful stamens, the other flower parts being insignificant. In the wild the long-lasting seed capsules that cluster along the stems only open after bush fires. These shrubs or small trees are curious in that the stems continue to grow beyond the faded flowers. There are about 25 species, most of which are plants of open or lightly forested land where the soil is reasonably moist. Where their hardiness is marginal, these are best at the base of a warm wall. *CULTIVATION* Require full sun and well-drained soil (JI No. 2), which is neutral or slightly acid. Prune back any unsightly shoots to lower new growths in early spring. *PROPAGATION* From seed, sown in spring at 61–64°F (16–18°C). From semi-ripe cuttings, in late summer. *POTENTIAL PROBLEMS* Red spider mites, mealybugs, scale insects.

C. citrinus Australia (Victoria, New South Wales)
Crimson bottlebrush
Flowers: late spring to early summer. H and S 4–20ft (1.2–6m). HH.
The specific name of this shrub refers to the lemon scent of the bruised leaves. This species must stand as representative of several very beautiful half hardy callistemons. It is especially impressive in the form '**Splendens**', when the arching branches carry numerous crimson flower spikes. '**White Anzac**' is 3–10ft (1–3m) tall and produces white flowers which can have attractive touches of pink when they are fully open. Alternatives to the more tender species include the fully hardy Tonghi bottlebrush (*C. subulatus*), which reaches a height of 5ft (1.5m) and has red flowers. The frost hardy alpine bottlebrush (*C. alpina*) is about the same size but has pale yellow flowers.

Callistemon citrinus

CALLUNA

ERICACEAE Heather, ling

In the Northern Hemisphere vast stretches of mountainside, moorland and heathland are transformed in late summer and autumn by the dense clusters of purple bell-shaped flowers produced by the single species in this genus. The leaves are generally dark green in colour. The soils on which this low evergreen shrub is found in the wild are acidic and usually of low fertility. As garden plants the hundreds of cultivars are restricted to being grown in areas where the soil is lime-free. *CULTIVATION* Require full sun and well-drained, acidic, organic-rich soil. Trim annually after flowering or in early spring. *PROPAGATION* From semi-ripe cuttings, in mid-summer. By layering, in spring. *POTENTIAL PROBLEMS* Grey mould (*Botrytis*), Phytophthora root rot, rhizoctonia.

Calluna vulgaris 'Firefly'

C. vulgaris Azores, N. and W. Europe to Russia (Siberia), Morocco, Turkey
Flowers: mid-summer to late autumn. H 4–24in (10–60cm), S 4–30in (10–75cm). FH.
Few plants of such intrinsic beauty so defeat the gardener. Heather has a way of looking alien in the domesticated order of a garden with beds, borders and lawn. To look its best, heather needs a setting on the wild side. The many cultivars available include singles and doubles in white, mauve, pink, purple and ruby. Even the dead flowers can look attractive in winter. There are differences in height and spread and also great variations in foliage colour (admittedly, not always matching the flowers), often with seasonal changes that make their strongest effects in winter. In the following selection, flowering in late summer to early autumn unless stated otherwise, the average height and spread are given: '**Allegro**', 20 by 24in (50 by 60cm), mid- to dark

Calluna vulgaris 'County Wicklow'

green foliage and deep red flowers in autumn; '**Anthony Davis**', 18 by 24in (45 by 60cm), grey-green foliage and white flowers; '**County Wicklow**', 10 by 12in (25 by 30cm), dark-green foliage and double pink flowers in mid- to late summer; '**Darkness**', 10 by 14in (25 by 35cm), bright green foliage and crimson flowers; '**Firefly**', 18 by 24in (45 by 60cm), red-brown foliage turning orange-red in winter and purplish pink flowers; '**Foxii Nana**', 6 by 12in (15 by 30cm), foliage making a bright green tight mound with only a few mauve flowers; '**Gold Haze**', 18 by 24in (45 by 60cm), yellow-green to gold foliage with white flowers; '**H.E. Beale**', 18 by 24in (45 by 60cm), mid- to dark green foliage and double bright pink flowers in autumn; '**Inshriach Bronze**', 10 by 14in (25 by 35cm), yellow-gold leaves and lilac-pink flowers; '**Robert Chapman**', 10 by 24in (25 by 60cm), yellow-green foliage in spring, strongly tinted orange and red in winter, and purple flowers; '**Sister Anne**', 4 by 10in (10 by 25cm), grey-green foliage bronzing in winter and mauve-pink flowers; '**White Lawn**', 2 by 16in (5 by 40cm), bright green foliage and white flowers; and '**Tib**', 12 by 16in (30 by 40cm), dark green foliage and purple flowers from mid-summer to mid-autumn.

Calluna vulgaris 'Robert Chapman'

CAMELLIA

THEACEAE

This Asiatic genus of evergreen shrubs and small trees comprises about 250 species, of which relatively few are widely grown, but the cultivated forms are numbered in their thousands. The attention of breeders and selectors over centuries, originally in China and Japan, accounts for the curious contrasts of simple grace and formal artifice that make such striking contrasts in the many cultivars. The colour range is relatively limited, covering white and shades of pink and red, as well as a number of bicolours. Admittedly, there is the yellow-flowered *C. nitidissima*, from South China and Vietnam, but the colour has yet to make a significant mark among the hardier hybrids. In flower form, however, the range includes singles and semi-doubles, with the stamens forming a prominent central boss. Others have anemone- and peony-like centres, in which some of the stamens are petal-like, making very full flowers in the peony forms. There are also doubles, sometimes showing stamens at the centre, surrounded by numerous tiers of petals but in the case of the formal doubles the numerous petals overlap symmetrically right to the centre. Being in essence woodland plants of moist neutral to acid soils, camellias do well under a light deciduous canopy, which protects the flowers from frost and reduces the risk of any bruising caused by rapid thawing in early morning sunshine. Many of the cultivated camellias have travelled so far from their origins that they look out of place in a wild garden and are much more plants for sheltered town gardens. Here they do well when planted in the shade of walls and buildings, even as container-grown specimens, their glossy leaves being ornamental year round. They are also suitable for hedges and screens.

CULTIVATION Require partial shade and moist, well-drained, acid soil that is rich in organic matter (ericaceous potting compost). Can be grown under glass for perfect blooms. Mulch annually in late winter. Prune any straggly shoots from plants in early spring.

PROPAGATION From leaf bud and semi-ripe cuttings, in late summer to late winter. Also by grafting, in late winter.

POTENTIAL PROBLEMS Aphids, scale insects, vine weevils; sooty mould, viruses, leafy gall and leaf spot.

Camellia japonica 'Adolphe Audusson'

C. japonica China, Japan, Korea
Common camellia
Flowers: Late winter to late spring. H 6–25ft (1.8–7.5m), S 6–20ft (1.8–6m). FH.
Shrubs or trees in the wild, sometimes more than 30ft (9m) high, are said to have undistinguished single red flowers but the foliage is glossy and handsome. The many cultivars exhibit the whole gamut of camellia flower form and considerable differences in growth, some being compact, others spreading. Even when flowers are caught by frosts, the season is usually long enough for some flowers to attain perfection. A drawback is that blooms do not fall when they are over, so that, unless picked off, the browned flowers vie for attention with those that are pristine. The following is a small selection: 'Adolphe Audusson', vigorous but compact and free-flowering, with semi-double, large, blood-red flowers; 'Alba Plena', upright but slow-growing, with white formal double flowers of medium size; 'Bob Hope', upright and compact, with very dark red, large, semi-double flowers, sometimes peony-like in form; 'Bob's Tinsie', upright and compact, with small bright red flowers of anemone form; 'Elegans', spreading, with large, anemone-form, deep pink flowers; 'Gloire de Nantes', upright and medium-sized, with large, semi-double and red-pink flowers; 'Hagoromo', upright and medium-sized, with semi-double pale pink flowers; 'Jupiter', vigorous and upright, with medium-

Camellia japonica 'Jupiter'

sized single flowers, the bright red petals cradling yellow stamens; and 'Lavinia Maggi', vigorous and open, with medium-sized, formal, double flowers that are white with pink or crimson streaks and spots.

C. reticulata China
Flowers: early spring. H 10–50ft (3–15m), S 5–15ft (1.5–4.5m). HH. The wild plant, a large shrub with dark green matt leaves that are net veined, bears deep pink flowers with conspicuous stamens. The species, long cultivated in China, was first known in the West as a sumptuous semi-double, an early introduction being 'Captain Rawes', with carmine flowers that can be more than 6in (15cm) across. Some magnificent hybrids, of which *C. reticulata* is a parent, are hardier than the cultivars. *C.* 'Leonard Messel', which makes a rounded shrub to about 12ft (3.7m), is fully hardy and has large clear pink flowers that are semi-double or of peony form.

Camellia 'Leonard Messel'

C. sasanqua Japan
Flowers: mid- to late autumn. H 10–20ft (3–6m), S 10–15ft (3–4.5m). FH. The shrub is hardy but the small sweetly scented flowers are often damaged by frost. The flowers can be single and white in the wild but the cultivars are often semi-double or double and in shades of pink or red. Plants need moisture but Mediterranean or Californian sun does wonders for their performance. 'Crimson King' is a bright red single and 'Narumigata' a pink-tinged single white.

C. × *williamsii*
Flowers: late autumn to mid-spring. H 6–15ft (1.8–4.5m), S 3–10ft (90–300cm). FH.
This name covers a range of hybrids raised from crosses between *C. japonica* and *C. saluenensis*, the latter a leafy shrub from Yunnan in China that has single flowers in white or shades of pink. The hybrids, hardier than *C. saluenensis* and very free-flowering, have the great merit of

Camellia saluenensis

dropping their blooms once they have faded. The foliage is glossy and the flowers, white to deep pink, are single or semi-double, occasionally of anemone or peony fullness. **'Donation'**, upright and compact, with semi-double soft pink flowers that are darkened by carmine veining, is a magnificent and free-flowering camellia but it is too widely planted to seem the treasure it undeniably is. **'Brigadoon'**, dense and upright, also has semi-double flowers of lovely form and deep pink. Among the finest of the singles are the white **'Francis Hanger'** and the pale pink **'J.C. Williams'**.

Camellia × williamsii 'Donation'

CARYOPTERIS

VERBENACEAE

The half dozen plants in this genus include several small aromatic shrubs that are Asiatic in origin. One of these, *C. mongolica*, a plant that in the wild experiences hot dry summers and very cold winters, is a parent of the widely grown hybrid described below.
CULTIVATION Require full sun and light well-drained soil. Prune to a low woody framework annually in early spring.
PROPAGATION From seed, sown in autumn. From cuttings, in late spring to early summer.
POTENTIAL PROBLEM Capsid bugs.

C. × *clandonensis*
Flowers: late summer to early autumn. H 2–3ft (60–90cm), S 30–48in (75–120cm). FH.
The bushy plants have grey-green

leaves, silvered with fine hairs on the underside, and clusters of small tubular flowers in shades of blue. **'Heavenly Blue'** is a compact upright cultivar which has dark blue flowers.

Caryopteris × clandonensis 'Heavenly Blue'

CASSIOPE

ERICACEAE

The dozen dwarf evergreen shrubs of this genus are heather-like plants originating from the arctic and alpine regions of N. Europe, N. Asia and North America. Some have a very wide distribution. The stems seem leafless but are in fact tightly clasped by overlapping green or grey scale-like leaves. The small bell- or urn-shaped flowers dangle prettily on fine stalks, but to achieve their exquisite best these little shrubs need to be grown in cool acid conditions. Several species are prostrate.
C. lycopodioides, for example, makes a wiry mat that rarely reaches more than 3in (8cm) in height but as much as 18in (45cm) across. It is topped by nodding creamy flowers in late spring. More upright plants include
C. 'Edinburgh' and other hybrids that are usually easier to please as garden plants than the species.
CULTIVATION Tolerate sun or partial shade and require moist acid soil that is rich in organic matter.
PROPAGATION From seed, sown in autumn. From cuttings, in summer. Also by layering prostrate species, in autumn or early spring.
POTENTIAL PROBLEMS Usually none.

Cassiope lycopodioides

Cassiope 'Edinburgh'

C. **'Edinburgh'**
Flowers: late spring. H and S 10in (25cm). FH.
The upright clump of dark-green stems is enlivened in spring by white bells with green-red calyces.

CEANOTHUS

RHAMNACEAE California lilac

Ceanothus × veitchianus

The common name is a misleading introduction to a genus of deciduous and evergreen shrubs with dense heads of very small flowers, usually in shades of blue or white. There are about 55 species, all from North America and many from California, where they are an important constituent of the dense scrub known as chapparal. The deciduous kinds are generally hardier than the evergreens. Plants are fast growing and come into flower when young. A number of ceanothus are low growing and make effective ground cover. Others are tree-like, with bushy growth developing above a short trunk to a height of 20ft (6m) or more. Notable among these is the frost-hardy *C. arboreus* and its fine cultivar **'Trewithen Blue'**, which has flowers of a deep tint.
C. × *veitchianus*, an evergreen shrub about 10ft (3m) high, with dark blue flowers in late spring, is a naturally occurring hybrid.
CULTIVATION Require full sun and well-drained fertile soil. Prune straggly stems from evergreens after flowering. Prune deciduous plants in early spring by cutting old shoots back close to the wood.

PROPAGATION From seed, sown in autumn. From cuttings, in mid- to late summer.
POTENTIAL PROBLEM Honey fungus.

C. 'Autumnal Blue'

Flowers: late summer to early autumn. H 8–10ft (2.5–3m), S 6–10ft (1.8–3m). FH.
The hardiness of this evergreen hybrid and its long season in late summer or autumn, sometimes, too, with flowers in spring, are great assets. The flowers are sky blue, the leaves glossy green. The less hardy C. 'A.T. Johnson', a slightly smaller evergreen hybrid, produces rich blue flowers in 2 distinct seasons, in spring and then again in late summer and autumn.

Ceanothus 'Cascade'

C. 'Cascade'

Flowers: late spring to early summer. H 10–15ft (3–4.5m), S 10–12ft (3–3.7m). FrH.
The arching branches, loaded with bright blue flowers, show to good effect when this vigorous evergreen is trained up a wall.

C. × delileanus 'Gloire de Versailles'

Flowers: mid-summer to autumn. H and S 5–6ft (1.5–1.8m). FH.
The deciduous hybrids include some of the hardiest ceanothus. 'Gloire de Versailles' bears large panicles of soft blue flowers but the darker indigo tint of 'Topaze' makes more point. C. × *pallidus* 'Perle Rose' is of similar character but has pink flowers.

Ceanothus × *delileanus* 'Gloire de Versailles'

C. griseus var. horizontalis

Flowers: late spring to early summer. H 2–3ft (60–90cm), S 7–10ft (2.2–3m). FrH.
This is a low-growing variant of the Carmel ceanothus, itself a medium-sized to large evergreen shrub. In 'Yankee Point' bright blue flowers stand out against glossy dark-green leaves. C. 'Blue Mound', an evergreen hybrid of which C. *griseus* is a parent, also flowers in late spring and summer, when the sprawling pile of glossy foliage, up to 5ft (1.5m) high, is obscured by massed heads of dark blue flowers.

C. impressus USA (California)

Santa Barbara ceanothus
Flowers: mid- to late spring. H 5–6ft (1.5–1.8m), S 7–8ft (2.2–2.5m). FrH.
Deep veining of the small leaves is a distinctive feature of this densely branched evergreen species. The small clusters of deep blue flowers are borne in great profusion. This species is a parent of several medium-sized to large hybrids that flower from mid-spring to early summer. C. 'Concha', with a height and spread of up to 10ft (3m), has purplish red buds opening to dark blue flowers. C. 'Puget Blue', of similar size, makes a dense shrub covered for a long season with flowers of a rich and deep blue.

C. thyrsiflorus var. repens

USA (N. California)
Creeping blueblossom
Flowers: late spring. H 3–4ft (90–120cm), S 6–8ft (1.8–2.5m). FH.
One of the hardiest of the evergreen species, C. *thyrsiflorus*, is a large shrub or small tree with dark-green leaves and pale-blue flowers. The creeping blueblossom, a low-growing variant found in coastal areas, makes a wide-spreading mound well covered in spring with clustered heads of light blue flowers.

CERATOSTIGMA

PLUMBAGINACEAE

The blue flowers of a few Asiatic species are great fresheners of the garden in late summer and early autumn. In cool temperate gardens even C. *willmottianum*, the most widely grown shrub in this small genus, is commonly cut to the ground in winter. The autumn-flowering C. *plumbaginoides*, with brilliant blue flowers in autumn on a spreading plant about 16in (40cm) high, is a woody based perennial.
CULTIVATION Require full sun and light, moist, well-drained soil. Prune in early spring.

PROPAGATION From cuttings, in summer.
POTENTIAL PROBLEM Powdery mildew.

Ceratostigma willmottianum

C. willmottianum W. China

Flowers: late summer to early autumn. Foliage: autumn. H 2–3ft (60–90cm), S 3–5ft (90–150cm). FH.
Small clusters of rich blue flowers, tubular and opening out to 5 lobes, are sprinkled generously among diamond-shaped leaves that take on red tints in autumn. The Himalayan C. *griffithii* is a more tender evergreen or semi-evergreen species with dark blue flowers and leaves that turn scarlet in autumn.

CHAENOMELES

ROSACEAE Flowering quince, Japanese quince, japonica

The 3 species of this genus, which are all early-flowering, thorny, deciduous shrubs, are natives of China and Japan and in the wild they are found in high wooded country. The fresh beauty of their saucer-shaped flowers, especially when clustered thickly on bare stems, is their chief interest. Flowering continues after the leaves emerge. The green or yellow-green fruits that follow are not highly ornamental but are aromatic and delicious jellies can be made from them. The species described and the hybrids make dense and tangled bushes when they are grown as specimens in the open garden. They are also suitable for hedging and for fan training against walls in the same way as apples trees.
CULTIVATION Tolerate full sun or partial shade and require well-drained soil. Trim hedges and cut back most of the previous year's growth on wall-trained specimens after flowering.
PROPAGATION From semi-ripe cuttings, in mid-summer. By layering, in autumn. Also from seed, sown in autumn.
POTENTIAL PROBLEMS: Aphids, scale insects; canker.

C. speciosa *China*

Japonica

Flowers: late winter to early spring. Fruits: autumn. H 6–8ft (1.8–2.5m), S 8–12ft (2.5–3.7m). FH.

In mild weather, clusters of single red flowers are sometimes produced on this plant as early as mid-winter and the season can continue until well after the leaves have developed. Eventually this species makes a large spreading shrub that is tallest when it is wall trained. There is a good colour range in the cultivated forms, the best including **'Moerloosei'**, a mixture of pink and white, and **'Nivalis'**, which has pure white flowers. **'Simonii'** has semi-double blood-red flowers on a low shrub, and grows to a height of about 3ft (90cm).

Chaenomeles speciosa 'Simonii'

C. × superba

Flowers: mid-spring to early summer. Fruits: autumn. H 3–6ft (90–180cm), S 5–6ft (1.5–1.8m). FH.

The free-flowering hybrids going under this name are the result of crosses between *C. speciosa* and the shorter-growing Japanese species *C. japonica*. Most plants are low spreading shrubs with cup-shaped flowers that are white, pink, crimson or scarlet. **'Crimson and Gold'** owes its name to the contrast of yellow anthers and dark red petals. Other cultivars include: **'Knap Hill Scarlet'**, in fact orange-red; **'Nicoline'**, with single to semi-double scarlet flowers; and **'Pink Lady'**, a low spreading bush with clear pink flowers.

Chaenomeles × superba 'Nicoline'

CHIMONANTHUS

CALYCANTHACEAE Wintersweet

Only one of the half dozen species in this Chinese genus is widely cultivated but, as its common name suggests, the wintersweet holds its place in temperate gardens because of its winter flowers and beguiling scent. The wood ripens more fully and produces flowers more freely when the shrub is trained against a warm wall.

CULTIVATION Requires full sun and fertile well-drained soil. Prune immediately after flowering.

PROPAGATION From seed, sown when ripe.

POTENTIAL PROBLEMS Usually none.

Chimonanthus praecox

C. praecox *China*

Winter sweet

Flowers: late winter. H 10–12ft (3–3.7m), S 8–10ft (2.5–3m). FH.

Out of its flowering season the shrub is a nonentity and even the flowers themselves are more curious than ornamental, being almost stalkless and with dull, pale yellow, almost translucent outer segments surrounding the small maroon inner segments. The scent, though, is invigorating even in a cold garden and when the flowers are brought into a warm room the spicy fragrance expands generously.

CHOISYA

RUTACEAE

The choisyas are aromatic evergreen shrubs from Mexico and southern USA. Of about 8 species one has a surprisingly strong foothold in cool temperate gardens, making a densely leafy bush pleasing for its year-round dark green glossiness and for its citrus-scented flowers.

CULTIVATION Require full sun and fertile well-drained soil. Prune after first flush of flowers has finished. Cut back frost-damaged stems in spring.

PROPAGATION From semi-ripe cuttings, in summer.

POTENTIAL PROBLEM Usually none.

C. ternata *Mexico*

Mexican orange blossom

Foliage: year-round. Flowers: late spring and late summer to autumn. H 5–8ft (1.5–2.5m), S 6–8ft (1.8–2.5m). FH.

Rounded bushes are covered to the ground with shining leaves, which are divided in threes and pungently aromatic when crushed. Single and clustered white fragrant flowers spangle the bushes in spring, usually with a second flush in autumn, and there are often flowers at other times of the year, even in winter. An unblemished plant is a splendid sight but except where the climate is mild this is only achieved in a sheltered position. There is inexplicable enthusiasm for **Sundance ('Lich')**, a form with sickly greenish yellow leaves. *C.* **'Aztec Pearl'** is smaller, usually less that 6ft (1.8m) high, and carries leaves that are divided into 5 to 10 linear leaflets and almond-scented white flowers that are pink in bud.

Choisya 'Aztec Pearl'

CISTUS

CISTACEAE Rock rose, sun rose

Rock roses are among the most common medium-sized shrubs of the Mediterranean region and the Iberian peninsula, where they bask in hot sun and survive months with negligible rainfall. Their saucer-shaped flowers, crumpled and silky, shatter within a day but a shrub carries many at a time and the season lasts for many weeks. The colour range covers white, often with dark blotches at the bases of the petals, and various shades of pink, extending to bright magenta. These are among the first evergreen shrubs to consider for dry sunny gardens and do well near the sea. In cool temperate regions there is a risk of losses in winter.

CULTIVATION Require full sun and well-drained soil. Prune after flowering.

PROPAGATION From seed, sown when ripe and in spring. From cuttings, in summer.

POTENTIAL PROBLEMS Usually none.

C. × hybridus *S. Europe*
Flowers: late spring to early summer. H 3–4ft (90–120cm), S 5–6ft (1.5–1.8m). FrH.
The dark green leaves of this naturally occurring hybrid are a good foil for the reddish buds and white flowers, which are stained yellow at the centre. It has one of the best records among cistuses for surviving hard winters.

C. ladanifer *S.W. Europe to N. Africa*
Common gum cistus, laudanum
Flowers: late spring to early summer. H 5–6ft (1.5–1.8m), S 4–5ft (1.2–1.5m). FrH.
The large flowers, white often with chocolate blotches around a yellow centre, are borne on a leggy shrub with narrow dull green leaves that are slightly sticky and aromatic. This species is a parent of some of the most important hybrids.
C. × aguilarii, a cross with **C. populifolius** that is found wild in the Iberian peninsula and North Africa, is a smaller plant with a height and spread of 4ft (1.2m). Its leaves have a wavy margin; the white flowers have a yellow centre and, in the case of **C. × aguilarii** '**Maculatus**', have bold crimson blotches. **C. × cyprius**, a hybrid of **C. ladanifer** and **C. laurifolius**, is one of the hardiest of the cistuses, making an upright shrub, with a height and spread of about 5ft (1.5m). Its large white flowers have dark crimson blotches at the bases of the petals and yellow stamens.

Cistus ladanifer

C. laurifolius *S.W. Europe*
Flowers: early to late summer. H and S 5–6ft (1.5–1.8m). FrH.
Yellow-centred white flowers are produced freely on an upright bush with leathery dark-green leaves. The relative hardiness of this species is a character also found in **C. 'Silver Pink'**, a sprawling hybrid of which it is a parent. The cross, which grows to a height of about 30in (75cm), is well named for the cool pink of its numerous crumpled flowers.

C. × purpureus *S. Europe*
Flowers: late spring to mid-summer. H and S 3–4ft (90–120cm). FrH.
C. ladanifer is credited as a parent but this hybrid may owe the deep pink of its flowers to *C. creticus*, a frost-hardy species from the eastern Mediterranean. The flowers of the hybrid, a small shrub with reddish stems, are distinguished by the deep crimson blotches around the yellow centre.

Cistus × purpureus

CONVOLVULUS

<small>CONVOLVULACEAE</small> Bindweed

The large family of bindweeds is best known for its climbers and scramblers. There are also some shrubby species. *C. cneorum* is a Mediterranean plant with hairy grey leaves, a clear indication of its preference for well-drained soils and sun. It is short-lived, often succumbing in cold clammy winter weather, but it is always worth having rooted cuttings of this lightweight charmer in reserve. See also CLIMBERS.
CULTIVATION Requires full sun and well-drained gritty soil (JI No.1). Cut back to new growths in spring.
PROPAGATION From seed, sown in spring at 55–64°F (13–18°C). From cuttings, in late spring and summer.
POTENTIAL PROBLEMS Under glass: red spider mites, aphids.

Convolvulus cneorum

C. cneorum *Mediterranean*
Flowers: late spring to late summer. Foliage: evergreen. H and S 2–3ft (60–90cm). FrH.

The silvery silkiness of the foliage of this compact bushy shrub is the perfect complement to the funnel-shaped white flowers. These are meticulously folded in pink bud, yellow centred when open and produced in succession over a long season.

CORNUS

<small>CORNACEAE</small> Dogwood, cornel

The dogwoods are plants of various habitats in northern temperate regions that show great diversity in their ornamental qualities. Almost all of about 45 species are deciduous shrubs or trees but the creeping dogwood (*C. canadensis*) is a low creeping perennial notable for the pure white bracts surrounding its insignificant flowers. See also TREES.
CULTIVATION C. kousa tolerates full sun or partial shade and requires a fertile well-drained soil that is not alkaline. Those grown for their winter stems require full sun and moist soil but are tolerant of lime. *C. canadensis* requires moist acid soil.
PROPAGATION From cuttings, in summer. From hardwood cuttings, in winter of winter-stemmed dogwoods (grown for winter stem colour). From seed, sown in autumn.
POTENTIAL PROBLEM Anthracnose.

Cornus alba '**Elegantissima**'

C. alba *N. China to Korea, Siberia*
Red-barked dogwood
Flowers: late spring to early summer. H and S 8–10ft (2.5–3m). FH.
The real interest of this deciduous suckering shrub does not lie in its modest white flowers or the bluish white berries that follow but in the foliage and stems. Annual or biennial coppicing ensures a supply of young wood, which is a lustrous scarlet in winter. Outstanding for its brightness is '**Sibirica**', usually under 8ft (2.5m) tall. Of several forms with yellow to white variegated foliage the first choice must be the vigorous

'**Elegantissima**', with a creamy white variegation brightening the grey-green leaves. It, too, makes a thicket of vivid young stems if coppiced. In sober contrast, '**Kesselringii**' has dark-purple stems and leaves that turn purplish red in autumn. *C. stolonifera* '**Flaviramea**', a form of the red osier dogwood of eastern North America that has greenish yellow young wood, also needs cutting back regularly to maintain a supply of well-coloured stems.

Cornus kousa var. *chinensis*

C. kousa Japan, Korea
Foliage: autumn. Flowers: early summer. Fruits: late summer. H 10–20ft (3–6m), S 9–15ft (2.7–4.5m). FH.
The flowers are insignificant but the large white bracts surrounding them makes this a dazzling large shrub or small tree in early summer. The pointed bracts stand upright along the spreading branches, the general effect being of unevenly tilted broad tiers. As the bracts age they often take on a pink tint. There are strawberry-like fruits and the foliage colours well in autumn. In '**Satomi**' the bracts are a strong pink and the autumn foliage reddish purple.
Var. *chinensis* is a more tree-like shrub and its structure is less obviously tiered.

CORONILLA

PAPILIONACEAE

The shrubby species in this genus of about 20 species are mainly sun-loving plants from southern Europe. The plant described is an easy-going self-seeder where the climate is mild enough, but at the limit of its range it needs a sheltered position at the base of a warm wall.
CULTIVATION Require full sun and well-drained soil. Prune the plant after the main flowering season in spring.
PROPAGATION From seed, sown as soon as ripe or in spring at 50–55°F (10–13°C) after stratification. From cuttings, in summer.
POTENTIAL PROBLEMS Usually none.

Coronilla valentina subsp. *glauca*

C. valentina subsp. *glauca*
Flowers: late winter to early spring, also in late summer. H 24–30in (60–75cm), S 24–30in (60–75cm). FrH to FH.
Although flimsy and likely to succumb to hard frosts, this is an easy plant where the weather is mild enough, cheerfully producing a profusion of pea flowers in spring and a trickle at almost all times of the year. Their yellow goes well with the hint of blue in the foliage; even better is the lemon-yellow of '**Citrina**'.

CORYLOPSIS

HAMAMELIDACEAE

The genus is Asiatic and the species, about 10 in all, are deciduous woodland shrubs or small trees that flower in spring. They are not attention seeking but a leafless plant hung with catkin-like racemes of small fragrant flowers is a very lovely sight.
CULTIVATION Require partial shade and well-drained, moist, fertile, acid soil.
PROPAGATION From cuttings, in summer. By layering, in autumn. From seed, sown in autumn.
POTENTIAL PROBLEMS Usually none.

Corylopsis sinensis

C. pauciflora Japan, Taiwan
Flowers: early to mid-spring. H 5–6ft (1.5–1.8m), S 6–8ft (1.8–2.5m). FH.
Numerous short racemes of primrose yellow flowers hang stiffly from a densely branching shrub with twiggy stems. The leaves, hornbeam-like but small, are copper or pink when first open but

then become bright green.
C. sinensis is a taller shrub, growing to 10ft (3m), with scented pale yellow flowers on racemes up to 3in (8cm) long.

CORYLUS

CORYLACEAE Hazel

The hazels and filberts belong to a small genus comprising about 15 species of deciduous shrubs and trees that are mainly woodland plants of the temperate Northern Hemisphere. The Turkish hazel (*C. colurna*) is a handsome pyramidal tree that thrives where there is a marked contrast between hot summers and cold winters. The shrubs that are grown for their nuts include several that are of ornamental value.
CULTIVATION Tolerate full sun or partial shade and a range of well-drained fertile soils. Coppice forms with coloured foliage in spring to encourage new growth with large leaves. Remove suckers from grafted plants.
PROPAGATION By layering, in autumn. From seed, sown as soon as ripe. By grafting, in winter.
POTENTIAL PROBLEMS Aphids, caterpillars, mites, sawflies; powdery mildew, silverleaf.

Corylus maxima '**Purpurea**'

C. avellana Europe, Turkey
Hazel, cob-nut
Flowers: late winter to early spring. H 15–20ft (4.5–6m), S 15–20ft (1.5–6m). FH.
This nut-bearing shrub or small tree is appealing when the male catkins hang from the bare branches and again in autumn when the leaves turn soft yellow. '**Aurea**', rarely more than 6ft (1.8m) in height, has yellow-green leaves, that are greener in late summer. '**Contorta**' grows with tormented slowness to 10ft (3m). The leaves are unattractively puckered but the writhing twigs and branches are graphic in winter. A vigorous purple-leaved form of the filbert, *C. maxima* '**Purpurea**', grows to 20ft (6m), and is a shrub of brooding darkness, even down to its tinted catkins.

133

COTINUS

ANACARDIACEAE Smoke brush

Curious wispy plumes surrounding the tiny flowers and fruits and the rich colours of the foliage in autumn are the main features of the 2 species included in this genus, both of which are deciduous shrubs occurring in poor stony ground and open positions.

C. obovatus, originating from southern USA, often develops into a small tree. It is less ornamental in flower than the European species but outclasses it in the brilliance of its autumn foliage colour.

CULTIVATION Tolerate full sun or partial shade and require well-drained soil. Autumn foliage colour is less intense on rich soils. Prune only lightly; coppicing in spring produces the maximum foliage effect but few or no inflorescences at all develop.

PROPAGATION From seed, sown in autumn. By layering, in spring. From cuttings, in summer.

POTENTIAL PROBLEMS Verticillium wilt, powdery mildew.

C. coggygria S. Europe to C. China
Smoke bush, Venetian sumach
Foliage: autumn. Flowers: mid-summer. H and S 10–15ft (3–4.5m) FH.

The shrub is often almost enveloped by the smoky plumes of the inflorescences, which sometimes have a pink tint before they turn grey in late summer. The oval green leaves colour well in autumn. 'Notcutt's Variety' features dark-red leaves with purplish pink plumes. The light green leaves of **f. *purpureus*** are orangey red in autumn. The plant also produces purplish pink inflorescences. 'Royal Purple' carries red-purple leaves that turn scarlet in autumn. Even more spectacular in autumn are the vigorous tree-like hybrids *C.* 'Flame', with purple-pink plumes, and *C.* 'Grace', with leaves that are purple throughout spring and summer, and scarlet in autumn.

Cotinus coggygria f. *purpureus*

COTONEASTER

ROSACEAE

Many of the cotoneasters bear masses of flowers, usually pink in bud and white on opening, but they are small and they make nothing like the effect of the fruits that follow, which enrich the garden for weeks and sometimes months in autumn and winter. There are more than 200 species, most of them from the temperate regions of Europe and Asia. In the wild some are shrubs of open rocky places but many are plants of woodland fringes. They are found on a wide range of soils, but in cultivation their tolerance extends to stiff clays, sandy soils and chalk. There are deciduous, semi-evergreen and evergreen species and in scale they range from compact low mounds and prostrate carpets to tree-like large shrubs.

CULTIVATION Require full sun (dwarf evergreens and deciduous species) or tolerate sun or partial shade and need shelter from cold winds (medium and large evergreens). All require well-drained soil.

PROPAGATION From seed, sown as soon as ripe in autumn. From cuttings, in summer.

POTENTIAL PROBLEMS Webber moth caterpillars, woolly aphids, scale insects, aphids; honey fungus, fireblight.

WARNING Swallowing the seeds may cause mild stomach upset.

C. conspicuus S.E. Tibet
Flowers: early summer. Fruits: late summer to mid-winter. H 5–6ft (1.5–1.8m), S 5–8ft (1.5–2.5m). FH. The plant usually grown is 'Decorus', which makes a dense mound closely covered with glossy evergreen leaves. The white flowers that crowd the stems are followed by rounded and lustrous orange-red fruits that are usually ignored by birds and therefore last well into winter.

C. dammeri China (Hubei)
Flowers: early summer. Fruits: all autumn. H 5–8in (13–20cm), S 5–7ft (1.5–2.2m). FH.
The creeping stems, which root as they spread, make an evergreen carpet that is bright with scarlet berries in autumn. Other evergreen cotoneasters that make useful low groundcover plants include *C. salicifolius* 'Gnom', which may make a mound up to 2ft (60cm) high but quickly spreads as much as 6ft (1.8m). The bright red berries show up well against glossy dark green leaves.

Cotoneaster frigidus

C. frigidus Himalayas
Flowers: early summer. Fruits: late summer to late winter. H 15–25ft (4.5–7.5m), S 12–25ft (3.7– 7.5m). FH.
A small tree can be made of this deciduous species by training up a main stem. Great crops of pea-sized crimson fruits are borne in heavy clusters. The semi-evergreen 'Cornubia', loaded with bright red fruits among its dark leaves, is one of the most spectacular of all large berrying shrubs. *C. frigidus* is a parent of several semi-evergreen hybrids, including those listed under *C.* × *watereri*. One of these, 'John Waterer', has a height and spread of about 15ft (4.5m) and its arching branches seem weighed down by its red fruits. Two large evergreens that are sometimes grouped with these hybrids are *C. salicifolius* 'Exburyensis' and *C. s.* 'Rothschildianus'. Both have a height and spread of about 15ft (4.5m) and produce heavy crops of long-lasting yellow fruits.

Cotoneaster × *watereri* 'John Waterer'

C. horizontalis W. China
Foliage: autumn. Flowers: late spring. Fruits: late summer to late winter. H 2–4ft (60–120cm), S 5–6ft (1.5–1.8m). FH.
The herringbone pattern of the stems is highly distinctive, especially when set with small bright red fruits. This is a deciduous shrub, with tiny, glossy, dark green leaves that turn red when the fruits are already ripe. *C. atropurpureus* 'Variegatus' has white margins to the leaves, giving it a silvered look.

C. lacteus *China (Yunnan)*
Flowers: early to mid-summer.
Fruits: mid-autumn to late winter.
H 10–15ft (3–4.5m), S 8–12ft
(2.5–3.7m). FH.
The milky white flowers are borne
in great profusion but the shrub's
chief season is autumn and winter,
when the broad clusters of egg-
shaped fruits stand out bright red
against the dark-green leaves,
which are felted on the underside.
This species is suitable for hedging.

CYTISUS

PAPILIONACEAE Broom

The brooms, including those that
belong to other genera (see also
Genista and *Junceum*) are mainly
sun-loving shrubs with pea-like
flowers, often fragrant and usually
yellow, produced with great
prodigality. The flowers are
followed by green, often hairy, seed
pods. The genus, which contains
about 50 species, has its centre
of gravity in Europe but is also
represented in north Africa and
western Asia. Most of the species
are found on free-draining, even
poor soils, the common broom
(*C. scoparius*), for example, being
a common shrub of sandy
healthland. The fact that they are
fast-growing shrubs makes them
very useful in newly established
gardens.
CULTIVATION Require full sun and
well-drained soil (JI No. 2).
PROPAGATION From seed, sown in
autumn or spring. From cuttings,
in summer.
POTENTIAL PROBLEMS Usually none.
WARNING Swallowing any part, but
especially the seeds, may cause
stomach upset.

Cytisus battandieri

C. battandieri *Morocco*
Pineapple broom
Flowers: mid- to late summer.
H 12–15ft (3.7–4.5m), S 10–15ft
(3–4.5m). FrH.
The common name refers to the
fruity scent of the yellow flowers,
which are clustered in cone-like
spikes. This is a large lax shrub with
laburnum-like leaves that are

divided into 3, the fine hairs giving
them a silky grey finish. Where it is
of marginal hardiness this is a
shrub worth wall training.

Cytisus × kewensis

C. × beanii
Flowers: late spring. H 18–24in
(45–60cm), S 3ft (90cm). FH.
The sprawling *C. ardoinoi* from
the Maritime Alps, itself a pleasing
miniature for a raised bed or rock
garden, is a parent of this hybrid,
which is at its best when its stems,
well set with dark-yellow flowers,
arch over from the top of a
retaining wall. *C. × kewensis* is a
larger shrub, up to 2ft (60cm) high
but spreading as much as 6ft
(1.8m), that also owes its semi-
prostrate habit to *C. ardoinoi*. It
needs a raised position to show off
its cascades of creamy flowers.

C. hybrids
Flowers: late spring to early
summer. H and S 3–5ft
(90–150cm). FH.
The complex hybrids by which
brooms are best known in gardens
usually owe much to the common
broom of Western Europe,
C. scoparius, an upright
deciduous shrub 5–6ft (1.5–1.8m)
high, commonly seen in summer
brightening wasteland and
heathland with a profuse display
of large rich yellow flowers. The
flowers of many of the hybrids
are bicoloured or two-toned. The
following is a small selection:
'**Hollandia**', has cream and dark
pink flowers; '**Lena**', yellow and
reddish brown; '**Windlesham
Ruby**', dark crimson; and '**Zeelandia**'
creamy white and mauve-pink.

C. × praecox
Flowers: mid to late spring. H 4–6ft
(1.2–1.8m), S 5–6ft (1.5–1.8m). FH.
The free-flowering *C. multiflorus*
from the Iberian peninsula and
north Africa is a parent with
C. purgans of several compact
deciduous hybrids, the first,
'**Warminster**', bearing masses of
creamy yellow flowers. The arching
stems of '**Allgold**' are loaded with
flowers of bright clear yellow.

DABOECIA

ERICACEAE

The 2 evergreen species are low
shrubs of coastal and mountain
heathland in western Europe, the
half-hardy *D. azorica* being
confined to the Azores. In
appearance they are close to the
ericas and, like many of them,
require a neutral to acid soil. The
flowers are not retained as they are
by other heaths but fall when they
are spent. The flowering season is,
however, exceptionally long.
CULTIVATION Require full sun and
well-drained acid soil. Shear off the
previous year's flowers in early to
mid-spring.
PROPAGATION From semi-ripe
cuttings, in mid-summer.
POTENTIAL PROBLEM Phytopthora
root rot.

D. cantabrica *W. Europe*
Cantabrian heath, St. Dabeoc's
heath
Flowers: early summer to mid-
autumn. H 10–24in (25–60cm),
S 2–3ft (60–90cm). FH.
The urn-shaped flowers are carried
on one-sided spikes above glossy
dark-green foliage. The flower
colour is usually purplish pink but
ranges from white to magenta. The
eccentric '**Bicolor**' can have white,
pink, red or striped flowers on the
same plant, even on the same stem.
D. × scotica is a frost-hardy hybrid
between the 2 species.

Daboecia cantabrica

DAPHNE

THYMELAEACEAE

The scented flowers are the great
delight of this genus, which
comprises about 50 Asiatic and
European species. Many are
woodland plants, the European
spurge laurel (*D. laureola*)
tolerating heavy shade and making
a mound of glossy evergreen leaves
up to 5ft (1.5m) high. Others are of
more open habitats and in
cultivation need positions in full
sun. Even the easiest in cultivation
tend to be unpredictable and some
of the dwarf species provide the

sort of challenge that sets the pulse of alpine specialists racing. Triumph for them is a flower-studded hummock less than 6in (15cm) high of **D. petraea** 'Grandiflora', an evergreen from the European Alps.
CULTIVATION Tolerate sun or partial shade and require moist, well-drained soil that is neutral to slightly acid or slightly alkaline and rich in organic matter.
PROPAGATION From seed, sown as soon as ripe. From cuttings, in summer. By grafting, in winter. By layering, in spring.
POTENTIAL PROBLEMS Aphids; leaf spot, grey mould, viruses.

Daphne cneorum 'Eximia'

WARNING Contact with the sap may irritate the skin. All parts are toxic if eaten.

D. cneorum *Mountains of C. and S. Europe*
Garland flower
Flowers: late spring. H 6–8in (15–20cm), S 2–5ft (60–150cm). FH.
The scent of low plants often goes unnoticed but not the piquancy of this evergreen. Sprawling 'Eximia' bears crimson buds opening to deep pink flowers. Semi-evergreen hybrids between this species and the deciduous *D. caucasica* are among the easiest daphnes to grow. *D.* × *burkwoodii* 'Somerset' has purple-pink fragrant flowers.

Daphne mezereum

D. mezereum *Caucasus, Europe, Siberia, Turkey*
Mezereon
Flowers: late winter to early spring. H 4–5ft (1.2–1.5m), S 2–4ft (60–120cm). FH.
The small scented flowers of this deciduous species are stemless and cluster densely along the upper portions of the bare stems, making a mauve- to purple-pink or white sleeve. The flowers are followed by fleshy red berries. The white-flowered **f. alba**, also well scented, has yellow fruits.

D. odora *China, Japan*
Flowers: mid-winter to early spring. H and S 5–6ft (1.5–1.8m). FrH.
Tight posies of starry flowers at the tips of twiggy stems exhale an incomparable fragrance. They are surrounded by ruffs of glossy leaves and the combination of purplish red reverse and crystalline white interior to the flowers gives the clusters a bicoloured effect. This is a sprawling evergreen shrub for a sheltered position. '**Aureomarginata**', with irregular yellow margins to the leaves, has the reputation of being slightly hardier than the plain-leaved plant.

DEUTZIA

HYDRANGEACEAE

The deutzias, mainly plants of woodland and scrub in the Himalayas and further east in Asia, are free-flowering shrubs that are easily grown in a wide range of conditions. Of about 60 species, most are deciduous and of medium height. A large number are hardy enough for gardens in cool temperate regions, although those that flower in spring are sometimes damaged by frost. Among the largest is *D. scabra*, which grows up to 10ft (3m), and has white or pink-tinted fragrant flowers in dense upright clusters. Like many deutzias, it has peeling bark.
CULTIVATION Require full sun and well-drained soil. Cut one-fifth of the oldest branches back to ground level and the flowered shoots down to new strong growths annually after flowering.
PROPAGATION From seed, sown in autumn. From cuttings, in summer. From hardwood cuttings, in autumn.
POTENTIAL PROBLEMS Usually none.

D. × **elegantissima**
Flowers: late spring to early summer. H and S 4–5ft (1.2–1.5m). FH.
The medium-sized Chinese species **D. purpurascens**, with fragrant

purple-tinted flowers, is a parent of this and several other hybrids. The cross is an upright shrub with arching stems carrying loose heads of starry flowers that are pink or, in '**Rosealind**', white with carmine tips. Another hybrid of similar size with *D. purpurascens* in its make-up is *D.* × *rosea*, which produces graceful sprays of pink or white bell-shaped flowers in early summer; '**Carminea**' has deep pink flowers that open from purplish buds.

D. longifolia *W. China*
Flowers: early to mid-summer; H 4–6ft (1.2–1.8m), S 6–10ft (1.8-3m). FH.
The comparatively large flowers arching out in graceful clusters put this in the top flight of deutzias. The stars open white but the reverse is purple; '**Veitchii**' has mauve-pink flowers outlined in white. *D. longifolia* and the small Chinese species *D. discolor* are the parents of several shrubs, listed under *D.* × *hybrida*, that flower freely in early summer. '**Magicien**' has mauve-pink flowers that are edged with white, displaying a purple reverse, and '**Mont Rose**' has purplish buds that open to pink flowers with wavy petals. The hybrids are generally 4–5ft (1.2–1.5m) in height and spread.

Deutzia × *hybrida* 'Mont Rose'

ELAEAGNUS

ELAEAGNACEAE

The bell-shaped flowers, in several cases deliciously scented, are inconspicuous and it is largely for their foliage that these shrubs are grown. Silvery or bronzy scaliness is a feature of the young foliage, often persisting on the underside of leaves, and sometimes showing also on stems and flowers. There are about 45 species altogether, the majority of Asiatic origin, some deciduous and some evergreen. They are found in a variety of habitats, but all are tolerant of dry conditions and the evergreens do well near the sea.
CULTIVATION Require full sun

(deciduous) or tolerate full sun or partial shade (evergreens). All need well-drained soil. Cut out reverted shoots on variegated cultivars.

PROPAGATION From seed, sown in autumn. From cuttings, in summer. By grafting, in late winter. From rooted suckers of deciduous species, in autumn.

POTENTIAL PROBLEM Usually none.

Elaeagnus angustifolia

E. angustifolia *S. Europe to C. Asia, Himalayas, China*
Oleaster
Foliage: spring to autumn. Flowers: early summer. Fruits: late summer. H and S 12–20ft (3.7–6m). FH.
The tiny pale yellow flowers would go unnoticed among the silvery willow-like leaves were it not for their penetrating fruity scent. This is a spreading deciduous shrub or small tree, to some extent spiny, that tolerates shaping. The amber-coloured fruits are edible.
E. 'Quicksilver' is a more compact silvery shrub in the same mould.

E. × ebbingei
Foliage: year-round. Flowers: early to mid-autumn. Fruits: spring. H 10–12ft (3–3.7m), S 10–12ft (3–3.7m). FH.
Fast-growing, although not shapely, this evergreen hybrid is useful for creating shelter in coastal gardens. The leaves are large and silver on the underside and the tiny flowers, which declare themselves by their rich spicy fragrance, also have a silvery quality. The leaves of **'Gilt Edge'** have a splendid golden margin to the dark centre.

E. pungens *Japan*
Foliage: year-round. Flowers: early to mid-autumn. Fruits: late winter. H 8–12ft (2.5–3.7m), S 10–15ft (3–4.5m). FH.
Glossy dark green leaves, which are grey-white on the underside and have wavy margins, hide the small scented flowers of this shrub, which are sometimes followed by red berries. This usually spiny plant is much used for hedging and shelter in gardens, and is most commonly seen in its variegated

forms. The leaves of **'Maculata'** have a rich yellow centre and are outlined in dark green.

ENKIANTHUS

ERICACEAE

Subtle beauty in flower and brilliance of leaf colour in autumn distinguish the deciduous shrubs or small trees in this Asiatic genus of about 10 species. These are predominantly woodland plants and like most of the members of the heath family, the ericaceous plants, they need a lime-free soil.
CULTIVATION Tolerate full sun or partial shade and require moist, well-drained, neutral to acid soil that is rich in organic matter.
PROPAGATION From seed, sown in late winter or early spring at 64–70°F (18–21°C). From semi-ripe cuttings, taken in mid-summer. By layering, in autumn.
POTENTIAL PROBLEMS Usually none.

E. campanulatus *Japan*
Foliage: autumn. Flowers: late spring to early summer. H 8–12ft (2.5–3.7m). S 5–10ft (1.5–3m). FH.
The reserve of this shrub in flower is as appealing as the brilliance of its foliage in autumn. Red veining usually adds a warm tinge to the creamy yellow of small bells, which hang closely and profusely in pretty clusters. There is, in fact, considerable variation in flower colour, the range including white and pale yellow-green. Another Japanese species, **E. perulatus**, about 6ft (2m) in height and spread, has white urn-shaped flowers and foliage that outdoes in intensity most autumn scarlets.

Enkianthus campanulatus

ERICA

ERICACEAE Heath

A handful of mainly European species provides the large number of low-growing heaths that are widely grown, especially on lime-free soils, in cool temperate regions. The genus is, however, a very large one and a high proportion of the 700 or more

Erica vagans 'Saint Keverne'

evergreen species are from South Africa. It is only because of their relative tenderness that beautiful plants such as **E. bauera**, **E. cerinthoides**, **E. perspicua** and many others do not relieve the sometimes monotonous effect of the most familiar heaths, which, like ling (**Calluna vulgaris**), are rarely as beautiful in cultivation as they are in the wild. Although most heathers need a neutral to acid soil, some including the Cornish heath (**E. vagans**) and its cultivars, such as **'Saint Keverne'**, tolerate mildly alkaline conditions. They come into their own when they can be planted in broad groups away from the lushest areas of the garden.
CULTIVATION Require full sun and, although there are some exceptions that tolerate lime, well-drained acid soil (ericaceous compost and sharp sand). Shear off spent flowers after flowering.
PROPAGATION From semi-ripe cuttings, in mid- to late summer.
POTENTIAL PROBLEM Fungal diseases.

E. arborea *N. Africa, mountains of central E. Africa, Mediterranean, S.W. Europe*
Tree heath
Flowers: late spring. H 12–20ft (3.7–6m), S 6–10ft (1.8–3m). FH.
The bell-shaped flowers that cover tall upright plants with grey-white snow have a honeyed scent. As specimens age, they become lanky but cutting back into old wood will rejuvenate them. The more compact **var. alpina** grows to about 6ft (1.8m). The Portuguese heath (**E. lusitanica**) is a frost-hardy species that grows to about 10ft (3m). From late autumn to early spring the feathery stems are crowded with white tubular flowers that open from pink buds.

E. carnea *C. Alps, E. Europe, N.W. Balkans, N.W. Italy*
Winter heath, alpine heath
Flowers: late winter to early spring. H 8–12in (20–30cm), S 15–24in (38–60cm). FH.
The species, a dwarf evergreen alpine shrub, is represented in

gardens by numerous cultivars, some of which are prostrate while many others are more or less upright. In the wild the flowers are usually purplish pink and the foliage mid- to dark green but there is considerable variation in the cultivars. The following is a small selection from those that are well-established but new additions are always being made: **'Ann Sparkes'**, golden foliage with bronze tips in spring, and pink flowers that darken to purple; **'Myretoun Ruby'**, deep green foliage, with pink flowers deepening to crimson; **'Springwood White'**, bright green foliage on a vigorous spreading shrub, with a great profusion of white flowers; and **'Vivellii'**, bronzed foliage in winter and pink flowers that darken to carmine.

Erica carnea 'Myretoun Ruby'

E. cinerea *Europe*
Bell heather
Flowers: early summer to early autumn. H 1-2ft (30-60cm), S 15-30in (38-75cm). FH.
Th bell heather, typical of the genus in being intolerant of lime, has deep green leaves that curl back at the margins. In the wild, flowers are usually purplish red, fading to russet. Cultivars include: **'C.D. Eason'**, with vibrant magenta-pink flowers; **'Pink Ice'**, compact, growing to about 6in (15cm), with clear pink flowers and bronze winter foliage; and **'Velvet Night'**, with deep purple bells. The cross-leaved heath (**E. tetralix**), another fully hardy species from western Europe that flowers from early summer to early autumn, is found wild in boggy lime-free ground. It grows up to about 1ft (30cm) and the hairy leaves seem grey-green. The flowers are usually soft pink but the white of **'Alba Mollis'** goes well with the grey foliage.

E. × darleyensis
Darley Dale heath
Flowers: late winter to early spring. H 18-24in (45-60cm), S 24-30in (60-75cm). FH.
Like *E. carnea*, one of its parents, this hybrid is reasonably lime-tolerant and makes calf-high ground cover with a long flowering season. **'Darley Dale'**, the original plant, has pale pink flowers. **'Arthur Johnson'** has long dense sprays of bright purplish pink flowers. **'Silberschmelze'** has white flowers and dark-green foliage tinted red in winter.

ESCALLONIA

ESCALLONIACEAE

Glossy evergreen foliage and a long flowering season are attractive characteristics of many escallonias, which are invaluable shrubs or small trees for hedging and shelter belts in coastal areas where the climate is reasonably mild. The 50 or so species in this South American genus are mainly plants of scrubland and are found on a wide range of soils, most of them tolerating lime. In gardens the hybrids are in general more widely grown than the species. However, one of the finest escallonias for hedging is undoubtedly **E. rubra 'Crimson Spire'**, a vigorous upright shrub with deep crimson flowers. Where they are of borderline hardiness, escallonias are best when grown against a warm wall.
CULTIVATION Require full sun and fertile well-drained soil.
PROPAGATION From cuttings, in summer. From hardwood cuttings, in late autumn.
POTENTIAL PROBLEMS Usually none.

Escallonia 'Iveyi'

E. hybrids
Flowers: early summer to autumn. H 6-10ft (1.8-3m), S 8-10ft (2.5-3m). FrH to FH.
Although in their overall appearance they are reasonably homogenous, these vary somewhat in hardiness, vigour, growth and flowering season. The following small selection samples the range: **'Apple Blossom'**, a frost hardy, bushy, evergreen shrub about 6ft (1.8m) in height and spread, with pink and white flowers in early to mid-summer; **'Edinensis'**, a fully hardy evergreen shrub up to 10ft (3m) in height and spread, with arching stems bearing red buds opening to dark pink flowers in early to mid-summer; **'Iveyi'**, a frost hardy tall evergreen shrub, up to 10ft (3m) in height and spread, with white flowers in late summer and autumn; and **'Langleyensis'**, fully hardy evergreen or semi-evergreen shrub, about 6ft (1.8m) in height but spreading, with pink flowers among small leaves in the first half of summer.

EUONYMUS

CELASTRACEAE Spindle tree

The ornamental qualities of the shrubs and trees in this large genus of around 175 species are very mixed. The flowers count for little but at their best the evergreens are variegated shrubs of bright effect and the deciduous species include several with foliage that colours vividly in autumn, at the same time as the intriguing round-shaped fruits ripen. In the wild the few European species, as well as the Asiatic majority, are found in woodland and scrubland on a wide range of soils, including those containing lime. To get good crops on species that bear colourful fruits it is advisable to grow several specimens of different clones in close proximity. Several evergreen species can also make useful hedging shrubs. The Japanese spindle (**E. japonicus**), for example, with its dense foliage, which is in some forms variegated, is particularly good when cultivated in coastal areas where the climate is mild enough.
CULTIVATION Tolerate full sun or partial shade and require well-drained soil.
PROPAGATION From seed, sown as soon as ripe. From cuttings, taken in summer.
POTENTIAL PROBLEMS Caterpillars, scale insects and vine weevils (evergreens); powdery mildew, leaf spot.
WARNING Swallowing any part may cause stomach upset.

E. alatus *China, Japan*
Winged spindle
Foliage: autumn. Flowers: late spring; fruits: autumn. H 6-7ft (1.8-2.2m), S 8-10ft (2.5-3m). FH.
The corky wings to the branches are almost obscured by the dense growth when the plant is covered in leaves. The reliable brilliance of its pink and crimson foliage in the autumn is exceptional and far more important ornamentally than the purple-red fruits. These fruits burst open to reveal orange-coated

seeds. As its name suggests, **'Compactus'** is of very dense growth and rarely exceeds 3ft (90cm) in height.

Euonymus alatus 'Compactus'

E. europaeus *Europe, W. Asia*
Spindle
Foliage: autumn. Flowers: late spring. Fruits: autumn. H and S 6–10ft (1.8–3m). FH.
What might be despised as a dull deciduous shrub or small tree in spring and summer, useful in the past for its hard wood, is transformed in autumn when rich leaf colours coincide with the ripening of purplish pink fruits, which split to show orange-coated seeds. **'Red Cascade'** is sensational, heavy crops among scarlet leaves weighing down the branches.
E. hamiltonianus **subsp.** ***sieboldianus***, a Japanese plant sometimes more than 20ft (6m) high, is in the same mould but the exterior of the fruits is strong pink.

Euonymus fortunei 'Silver Queen'

E. fortunei *Japan*
Foliage: year-round. H as shrub 2–4ft (60–120cm), H as climber 8–15ft (2.5– 4.5m), S 4–6ft (1.2–1.8m). FH.
Given support, what is usually seen as a prostrate or mound-forming evergreen shrub becomes a self-clinging climber. There are juvenile and adult stages and it is the juvenile foliage of the non-flowering stage that is of prime value ornamentally. It is a very variable plant and has numerous variegated forms, usually seen as bushy shrubs. These include **Emerald Gaiety**, with an irregular white outline surrounding the dark green centre of the leaves; **Emerald 'n' Gold**, the margins to the dark-green leaves bright gold, paler in winter; and **Silver Queen**, with a striking contrast between a dark green and an irregular white outline to the leaves. In most cases the yellow or white variegation becomes pinkish in winter.

EXOCHORDA

ROSACEAE Pearl bush

Their profusion of pure white flowers makes these deciduous shrubs a dazzling, although short-lived, spectacle in late spring or early summer. The 4 species, all Asiatic, are plants of woodland margins that flower most freely in full sun. More common in cultivation is the hybrid described below but a lovely alternative to it is ***E. giraldii*** **var.** ***wilsonii***, a bush as much as 10ft (3m) high and wide, covered in late spring with flowers up to 2in (5cm) across.
CULTIVATION Require full sun and well-drained, moist, fertile soil. Cut back flowered shoots to lower, new, strong growth after flowering. Each year remove about a fifth of the oldest shoots to the base.
PROPAGATION From seed, sown in autumn. From cuttings, in summer.
POTENTIAL PROBLEMS Usually none.

E. × ***macrantha*** **'The Bride'**
Flowers: late spring to early summer. H and S 3–6ft (90–180cm). FH.
Arching branches become white garlands that coincide with late spring bulbs. This is a lower growing plant than the species but its growth is so lax that it may need some support.

Exochorda × macrantha 'The Bride'

FATSIA

ARALIACEAE

Of the 2 or 3 species in this genus, native to E. Asia, one is widely grown, most commonly as an evergreen houseplant. It is a woodland plant and tolerant of shade; more surprisingly, it also stands up well to coastal conditions and the pollution of urban gardens. Where the climate is mild enough the deeply lobed glossy leaves are a great asset in the open garden. The tree-ivy (× ***Fatshedera lizei***), a hybrid between it and ivy (*Hedera*), with 5- to 7-lobed leaves, is another glossy foliage plant that is less hardy but handsome when container grown.
CULTIVATION Tolerate full sun or partial shade and require well-drained, moist, fertile soil (JI No.3). Variegated cultivars all require partial shade.
PROPAGATION From seed, sown in autumn or spring at 59–70°F (15–21°C). From cuttings in early or mid-summer. By air layering in spring or late summer.
POTENTIAL PROBLEMS Under glass: mealy bugs, scale insects.

Fatsia japonica 'Variegata'

F. japonica *Japan, S. Korea*
Foliage: year-round. Flowers: mid-autumn; H and S 5–12ft (1.5–3.7m). FH.
The shining dark green leaves, up to 16in (40cm) across and wavy at the edges, are thrust out on long stems from a spreading shrub. In autumn stiff sprays composed of numerous globular clusters of tiny creamy flowers stand above the bold foliage. These are followed by small black berries. **'Variegata'** is less hardy but is a very striking variegated plant, with the tips of the lobes splashed creamy white.

FORSYTHIA

OLEACEAE

If they were seen less often, forsythias would be splendid shrubs. Perhaps the secret of enjoying their uncompromising radiance is to observe them in a neighbour's garden, so avoiding the problem of masking the dullness of forsythias for much of the year. There are about 7 species in the genus, usually deciduous and, with the exception of a single European example, they are Asiatic. The species are plants of open woodland but like the hybrids, which are more commonly seen, are adaptable to a wide range of conditions. All have yellow flowers. The species have their merits. *F. giraldiana*, which eventually reaches about 12ft (3.7m), often starts to bear its solitary flowers on arching stems in late winter. Its fault is lankiness but the relative sparseness of its flowers can be thought a point in its favour. Golden bell (*F. suspensa*) is usually a lax shrub but can grow to 10ft (3m) when trained on a wall, which is the best way to show off its pendulous flowers.

CULTIVATION Tolerate full sun or partial shade and require well-drained moist soil. Each year, after flowering, remove about a fifth of the oldest shoots on established plants and cut back the remaining flowered shoots to strong lower shoots or buds.

PROPAGATION From cuttings, taken in summer.

POTENTIAL PROBLEMS Forsythia gall, honey fungus.

F. × *intermedia*

Flowers: early to mid-spring. H and S 5–7ft (1.5–2.2m). FH. Numerous hybrids have been raised, most of them medium to large shrubs, the stems crowded with starry flowers in spring. **'Lynwood'** bristles with large rich yellow flowers. Those of **'Spectabilis'** are only marginally smaller. These are large shrubs but even **'Minigold'** grows to 6ft (1.8m). **'Spring Glory'** is of similar size but its paler yellow flowers are less assertive.

Forsythia × *intermedia* 'Spectabilis'

FOTHERGILLA

HAMAMELIDACEAE

The fothergillas have two high seasons but in between they are inconspicuous shrubs. The 2 species, deciduous woodland shrubs of acidic soils in south-east USA, bear bottlebrush spikes of creamy white flowers in spring and the autumnal smouldering of the foliage is outstanding. The witch alder (*F. gardenii*) is similar to the

plant described but in height and spread rarely exceeds 3ft (90cm).

CULTIVATION Tolerate full sun or partial shade and require moist well-drained acid soil that is rich in organic matter.

PROPAGATION From seed, sown in autumn or winter. From cuttings, taken in summer. By air layering, in summer.

POTENTIAL PROBLEMS Usually none.

F. major USA (Allegheny Mountains, Virginia to South Carolina)

Foliage: autumn. Flowers: late spring to early summer. H 6–8ft (1.8–2.5m) S. 4–6ft (1.2–1.8m). FH. The stems are bare or just breaking into leaf when the fragrant flower spikes of this shrub start to open. The flowers are without petals, the bottlebrush consisting of a mass of stamens. Before falling, the leaves turn a stunning bright orange-yellow and red.

Fothergilla major

FREMONTODENDRON

STERCULIACEAE Flannel bush

Although the shrubs themselves are somewhat coarse in appearance, they bear magnificent yellow flowers over a long season. These are petal-less, but have a large and waxy calyx. The few species in the genus, which are evergreen or semi-evergreen, are plants that grow on dry and scrubby terrain in northern Mexico and southern USA. Where they are of borderline hardiness, fremontodendrons will fare best planted at the bottom of a warm wall.

CULTIVATION Require full sun and well-drained neutral to alkaline soil.

PROPAGATION From seed, sown in spring at 55–65°F (13–18°C). From cuttings, in summer.

POTENTIAL PROBLEM Phytophthora root rot.

WARNING Contact with the foliage (even brushing against the shoots) may irritate the skin. Inhalation of leaf and stem hairs may cause severe asthmatic attacks.

Fremontodendron 'California Glory'

F. 'California Glory'

Flowers: late spring to mid-autumn. H 12–20ft (3.7–6m), S 8–12ft (2.5–3.7m). FrH.

This free-flowering hybrid and its parents, *F. californicum* and *F. mexicanum*, all show a strong family resemblance. 'California Glory', marginally the hardiest, makes rapid growth vertically and then becomes more spreading but at an early age starts producing large flowers more than 2in (5cm) across. The leaves of all of these plants are backed with a rusty felting and the stems, too, are hairy; the warning given above should be noted.

FUCHSIA

ONAGRACEAE

Relatively few of the evergreen and deciduous species, about 100 in all, are widely grown. However, the hybrids, numbered in thousands, are enormously popular and are often grown as half-hardy perennials that are overwintered under glass. Some make erect and bushy plants, others have lax and trailing stems. The flowers of the hybrids, borne very freely over a long season, dangle with a balletic charm inherited from their parents. The typical flower consists of a waxy tube that opens out into 4 sepals, which curl back from or partly cover a bell (the corolla) of 4 overlapping petals. It is, however, the protruding stamens and style that give the flowers their special poise and without them the dancing blooms would seem like amputees. The colour range is largely restricted to mauve, purple, pink, red and white but in many cases there is a pleasing colour contrast between the body and overskirt, composed of tube and sepals, and the bell-like skirt itself. Semi-double hybrids have 5 to 7 petals, the doubles sometimes many more than 8, making a very full, even cluttered corolla. Some species, including the deciduous trailing fuchsia from New Zealand (*F. procumbens*) have erect flowers. Where the weather is mild enough, this is a appealing frost-hardy rock garden plant, but it is more interesting when it is bearing plum-like red fruits than when it is in flower. In the following selection, an entry for the best-known species is followed by the hybrids, which are grouped broadly according to their hardiness.

CULTIVATION Tolerate full sun or partial shade and require soil that is fertile and moist but well-drained. Under glass plants require loam-based compost (JI No. 3).

PROPAGATION From seed, sown in spring at 75°F (24°C). From softwood cuttings, in spring. From semi-ripe cuttings, in late summer.

POTENTIAL PROBLEMS: Whiteflies, capsid bugs, aphids; rust.

Fuchsia magellanica

SPECIES

F. magellanica *Argentina, Chile*
Flowers: summer. H and S 5–10ft (1.5–3m). FrH.
The hardiest species and the parent of many hybrids is a shrub of rare refinement. The arching stems carry neat pointed leaves and drip with small crimson flowers, their long sepals almost hiding the short purple corolla. Its numerous forms, some variegated and usually less hardy, are all graceful shrubs. The narrow leaves and slender scarlet and violet flowers give **var. *gracilis*** an added delicacy. '**Versicolor**' is one of the loveliest of variegated shrubs. The foliage, pink-tinted when young, becomes grey-green, making a soft foil for the crimson flowers.
F. 'Riccartonii' is like a particularly vigorous version of the species, the flowers with broader sepals of a darker red. Where the climate is mild enough, it makes a good, although rather broad, informal flowering hedge.

HYBRIDS

Frost hardy
Flowers: summer. H 6–60in (15–150cm), S 12–36in (30–90cm). FrH.
Some of the hybrids are

Fuchsia 'Tom Thumb'

surprisingly tough and, where frost does not penetrate the ground deeply, are often grown in the open garden. They vary considerably in size but are usually erect and bushy and their flowers are much larger than those of *F. magellanica*. The following selection is no more than a sample: '**Alice Hoffman**', up to 2ft (60cm) in height and spread, has bronze and purple-tinted foliage and single flowers with a deep pink tube and sepals above a pink-veined white corolla; '**Genii**', an upright bush reaching 3ft (90cm), has yellow-green foliage, red shoots and small single flowers that are red with a violet corolla; '**Mrs Popple**', a vigorous bush up to 4ft (1.2m) high, has large single flowers that have a scarlet tube and sepals and violet petals, from which protrude conspicuous crimson stamens and style; '**Phyllis**', a fast-growing bush reaching 3ft (90cm), has semi-double flowers, the tube and sepals reddish pink, with the corolla a deeper shade; and '**Tom Thumb**', a compact bush up to 1ft (30cm) high, with small single flowers that have scarlet sepals and a mauve corolla.

Fuchsia 'Jack Shahan'

Half hardy
Flowers: summer. H 6–30in (15–75cm), S 12–24in (30–60cm). HH.
The half-hardy hybrids, the most varied of the fuchsias, are widely used for summer bedding and container gardening, those with trailing stems being particularly popular for tall pots and hanging baskets. The following all make upright bushes: '**Annabel**', up to

2ft (60cm) in height and spread, has double white flowers, the tube and sepals flushed pink, the corolla veined pink, and the stamens pink; '**Dollar Princess**', up to 18in (45cm) high, has double flowers the tube and sepals red, the corolla deep purple; '**Flash**', 2–3ft (60–90cm) in height, has large numbers of small uniformly red single flowers; and '**Royal Velvet**', up to 30in (75cm) high, has double flowers, with the tube and sepals crimson, and the corolla deep purple. The following have lax or trailing stems, unless stated otherwise growing up to 18in (45cm) high with a spread of 2ft (60cm). They are suited to growing in tall pots or hanging baskets. '**Bicentennial**' has double flowers, with the tubes near white, the sepals pale orange, and the corolla orange and magenta; '**Golden Marinka**', 1ft (30cm) high and as much as 18in (45cm) across, has variegated green and yellow foliage and single red flowers, the corolla slightly darker than the sepals; '**Jack Shahan**', with large single pink flowers, with the corolla darker than the tubes and sepals; '**La Campanella**', with many small semi-double flowers, with the tube pink, the sepals white with pink flush and the corolla purple; and '**Red Spider**', up to 1ft (30cm) high and almost twice this in spread, bears long, narrow, single flowers, with the tube and sepals crimson, and the corolla reddish pink.

Fuchsia 'Thalia'

Frost tender
Flowers: summer. H 24–30in (60–75cm), S 18–36in (45–90cm). FT.
These include a group derived from *F. triphylla*, a species native to Haiti and Santo Domingo. This parent bears long-tubed orange-scarlet flowers with small sepals at the tips of arching stems and the leaves, arranged in threes, are purple on the underside. '**Gartenmeister Bonstedt**' and '**Thalia**' are two similar hybrids with velvety bronze-red leaves and long-tubed flowers of a uniform orange-red.

GARRYA

GARRYACEAE

The dozen or so evergreen shrubs in this small genus from western USA, Central America and the West Indies are mainly of interest to gardeners on account of their long and slender catkins. Male and female catkins are borne on separate plants, the male catkins being the more ornamental. The species are found in a range of habitats. The plant described flowers best in full sun and where it is of borderline hardiness should be planted at the base of a warm wall.
CULTIVATION Tolerate full sun or partial shade and require well-drained soil.
PROPAGATION From seed, sown in autumn or spring. From semi-ripe cuttings, in mid-summer.
POTENTIAL PROBLEMS Fungal leaf spot.

G. elliptica W. USA
Silk-tassel bush
Flowers: mid-winter to early spring. H 8–13ft (2.5–4m), S 6–12ft (1.8–3.7m). FrH.
For much of the year this is a plodding evergreen with rather dull, grey-green, leathery leaves. The winter transformation of the male plants is dramatic, the whole shrub being draped with pliant grey-green catkins swaying gently.
In the male clone 'James Roof' the seagreen catkins can be as much as 8in (20cm) long. The plainer catkins that are borne by female plants are followed by clusters of purplish fruits.

Garrya elliptica 'James Roof'

GAULTHERIA

ERICACEAE

The lustrous berries are the chief interest of these ericaceous shrubs but their evergreen foliage is an asset in the lime-free conditions on

which they insist. There are about 170 species, which are found in woodland and more open rocky habitats in the Americas, Asia, including the Himalayas, and Australasia. They spread readily by suckers and some such as the salal or shallon (G. shallon) from western North America can become a nuisance once established.
G. cuneata and G. miqueliana are less troublesome low but spreading plants about 1ft (30cm) high, with white or pink-tinted fruits, and are suitable for a raised bed. The plant described is, however, by far the showiest.
CULTIVATION Require partial shade and moist, peaty, acid or neutral soil.
PROPAGATION From seed, sown in autumn. From semi-ripe cuttings, in mid-summer. By sucker removal, in spring.
POTENTIAL PROBLEMS Usually none.
WARNING Swallowing any part except for the fruit may cause stomach upset.

Gaultheria mucronata 'Indian Lake'

G. mucronata Argentina, Chile
Flowers: late spring to early summer. Fruits: mid-autumn to late winter. H and S 2–4ft (60–120cm). FH.
A thicket of wiry stems is densely covered with glossy spiny leaves but plants become leggy with age. The white urn-shaped flowers, often tinged pink, are less conspicuous nestling among the foliage than the marble-like fruits that follow and remain on the plants through autumn and winter. In colour the fruits range from white and pink through to purplish red. Male and female flowers are usually borne on separate plants, a male plant, such as the compact and free-flowering 'Thymifolia', being needed to ensure that female plants carry good crops. Cultivars with red to purple fruits include 'Indian Lake' and 'Mulberry Wine'. The fruits of 'Parelmoer' are light pink, while those of 'Sneeuwwitje' are white flecked with pink. 'Bell's Seedling' is hermaphroditic and its fruits are dark red.

GENISTA

PAPILIONACEAE Broom

Genista lydia

The brooms in this genus, like those in the closely related genus Cytisus, are valued for their profusion of pea flowers. Almost all are deciduous, but their green stems give the impression that they are in leaf year round. Most of the species, about 90 in all, are from Europe and W. Asia and almost all are plants of open habitats that are dry rather than moist. In some areas, as in parts of Australia, they are so successful in dry conditions that they have become weeds. Their adaptability is, however, a big asset in gardens with hot dry banks and stony free-draining ground. See also TREES.
CULTIVATION Require full sun and light well-drained soil.
PROPAGATION From seed, sown in autumn or spring
POTENTIAL PROBLEM Aphids.

G. lydia E. Balkans
Flowers: early summer. H 2–3ft (60–90cm, S 3–4ft (90–120cm). FH.
The grey-green hummock of slender arching stems becomes a mound of bright yellow flowers, particularly effective when cascading over a retaining wall.

G. pilosa var. minor W. and C. Europe
Flowers: late spring to early summer. H 18in (45cm), S 2–3ft (60–90cm). FH.
The overlapping stems of this prostrate shrub make a tangled

Genista pilosa 'Vancouver Gold'

mat, in '**Procumbens**' not more than 8in (20cm) high and thickly sprinkled with yellow flowers. The taller '**Vancouver Gold**' also flowers generously.

G. sagittalis

Flowers: early summer. H 6–8in (15–20cm), S 3–4ft (90–120cm). FH. The real leaves are small and scattered but the colour and broad wings of the stems gives this shrub a very leafy appearance. The yellow flowers are clustered in dense heads. A diminutive version from the Pyrenees, **subsp. *delphinensis***, makes a sunny little mound rarely more than 6in (15cm) high.

G. tinctoria *Europe, Turkey*

Dyer's greenweed
Flowers: early summer to early autumn. H 18–36in (45–90cm), S 3–4ft (90–120cm). FH. Slender short spires of bright yellow flowers stand out against dark green leaves and stems over a long season. The double-flowered '**Flore Pleno**' is especially noticeable. The free-flowering '**Royal Gold**' is richly coloured.

HAMAMELIS

HAMAMELIDACEAE Witch hazel

The winter encrustation on bare branches of fragrant spidery flowers in shades of yellow and dull red is the principal ornament of most of the half dozen species. However, the autumn colouring of the foliage is also an asset of some of these deciduous shrubs and small trees from Asia and North America. The moisture-loving Ozark witch hazel (**H. vernalis**) from central USA has an outstanding form, '**Sandra**', with leaves that are purplish when they first open and which turn vivid shades of orange, scarlet and red before falling. All the witch hazels are woodland plants of neutral to acid soils.
CULTIVATION Tolerate full sun or partial shade and require well-drained, moist, neutral to acid soil.
PROPAGATION From seed, sown as soon as ripe. By grafting, in late winter. By budding, in late summer.
POTENTIAL PROBLEMS Honey fungus, coral spot.

H. × intermedia

Foliage: autumn. Flowers: early to mid-winter; H 10–12ft (3–3.7m), S 10–12ft (3–3.7m). FH. Crosses between the Japanese witch hazel (**H. japonica**) and the Chinese witch hazel (**H. mollis**), strongly stamped with the family characteristics, have produced a varied range of hybrids. All have

Hamamelis × intermedia 'Pallida'

flowers consisting of 4 narrow crimpled petals that are to some extent scented. '**Arnold Promise**', upright when young but spreading with age, has large yellow flowers in thick clusters from mid- to late winter. '**Diane**' has dark-red flowers at the same time, '**Jelena**' copper-red flowers a little earlier; both have colourful autumn foliage. The ultimate in these shrubs is, however, the cool yellow of '**Pallida**', in mid- to late winter, one of the supreme shrubs of the woodland garden. Hybrids are commonly grafted onto stocks of the Virginian witch hazel (**H. virginiana**). Suckers should be removed.

HEBE

SCROPHULARIACEAE

About 100 species of evergreen shrubs or, rarely, trees are the woody versions of the veronicas. A very high proportion are natives of New Zealand, where they are found among other shrubs in a range of habitats, many in coastal regions, some in gravelly river valleys and others in high country and mountainsides. The foliage is usually dense but the size of the leaves varies considerably, those with small leaves being the hardiest. The white-flowered **H. rakaiensis**, which makes a spreading dome about 3ft (90cm) high, has leaves under 1in (2.5cm) long and is frost hardy to fully hardy. The "whipcord hebes" have closely overlapping scale-like leaves so that superficially they resemble some of the dwarf conifers. The flowers are tubular, opening out to 4 lobes, and are usually tightly packed in spike-like arrangements. Where the weather is mild enough, and especially in coastal and exposed gardens, these are very useful shrubs but where they are growing at the margins of

their hardiness losses are common.
CULTIVATION Tolerate full sun or partial shade and require moist, well-drained, neutral or slightly alkaline soil (JI No.2).
PROPAGATION From seed, sown as soon as ripe. From semi-ripe cuttings, in late summer.
POTENTIAL PROBLEMS Aphids; phytophthora root rot, leaf spot, downy mildew.

Hebe rakaiensis

H. cupressoides *New Zealand (South Island)*

Foliage: year-round. Flowers: early to mid-summer; H 3–4ft (90–120cm), S 3–4ft (90–120cm). FrH. The closely packed tiny leaves give this whipcord hebe the appearance of a cypress. Mature plants are studded with short spikes of pale blue flowers. '**Boughton Dome**', a dwarf and very dense form that makes a pleasing green mound about 1ft (30cm) high, seldom flowers. The fully hardy **H. ochracea** '**James Stirling**' is another whipcord type, with tiered sprays of ochre-yellow foliage tinted orange in winter. It makes a low mound about 16in (40cm) high with white flowers in late spring and summer.

H. 'Midsummer Beauty'

Foliage: year-round. Flowers: mid-summer to late autumn. H 4–6ft (1.2–1.8m), S 4–5ft (1.2–1.5m). FrH. A large number of hybrids, many with the rather tender **H. speciosa** as a parent, bear impressive tapering or bottlebrush spikes of flowers over a long period in summer, the colour range including blue, violet, pink, purplish red and pure white. 'Midsummer Beauty' has lance-shaped leaves, purplish red on the underside, and its mauve spikes, fading to white, can be as much as 6in (15cm) long. Other hybrids in the same mould are '**Alicia Amherst**', with dark-green leaves and violet-blue flowers; '**Great Orme**', flowers pink turning to white; and '**La Séduisante**', usually no more than 3ft (90cm) in height, with purple-tinted foliage and wine-red flowers.

Hebe pinguifolia 'Pagei'

H. 'Pewter Dome'

Flowers: late spring to early summer. H 12–18in (30–45cm), S 18–24in (45–60cm). FrH. Several dwarf hebes that make low mounds of grey-green foliage are appealing plants for rock gardens, raised beds and edging. 'Pewter Dome' has short spikes of white flowers. *H.* 'Red Edge', a similar plant in size and hardiness but with blue-grey leaves veined and margined with red, is particularly conspicuous in winter. It has mauve-blue flowers that fade to white. Hardier than these is *H. pinguifolia* 'Pagei', a blue-green sprawling plant about 1ft (30cm) high but making a mat up to 3ft (90cm) wide. It has short spikes of white flowers in late spring or early summer. Slightly more compact and equally hardy is *H.* 'Youngii' but its foliage is dark green and it bears its violet flowers in early to mid-summer.

HELIANTHEMUM

CISTACEAE Rock rose, sun rose

The genus comprises about 100 species, which are found in many parts of the world, including parts of Asia, Europe, North Africa as well as North and South America. They are best known in gardens by their hybrids that are derived from crosses of European species such as *H. nummularium*. This low spreading plant with bright yellow flowers is an ardent sun lover and thrives on poor dry soils.
CULTIVATION Require full sun and well-drained neutral or alkaline soil. Cut back to the woody clump in early spring.
PROPAGATION From seed, sown as soon as ripe or in spring. From softwood cuttings, in late spring or early summer.
POTENTIAL PROBLEMS Usually none.

H. hybrids

Flowers: early to mid-summer. H 6–12in (15–30cm), S 10–20in (25–50cm). FH.
Sprawling shrubs with variable foliage but often grey-green carry masses of single or double papery flowers in a wide range of colours. The individual flowers are short lived but there are a few dwarf shrubs that reliably give a long display in sunny well-drained positions, particularly in raised beds and rock gardens. The colour range includes many shades of pink, red and orange, as well as yellow and white. Three singles with grey or silver-grey foliage are representatives from a range in which almost all are worth growing: 'Rhodanthe Carneum', soft pink flowers with a yellowish centre; 'The Bride', milky white flowers with a yellow centre; and 'Wisley Primrose', pale yellow flowers with a deeper coloured centre.

Helianthemum 'The Bride'

HIBISCUS

MALVACEAE

This very varied genus of about 200 species, including annuals and perennials as well as trees and shrubs, is best known for one of the most popular tropical and subtropical shrubs, the Chinese hibiscus (*H. rosa-sinensis*). The numerous cultivars of this evergreen species produce single or double flowers in a colour range including crimson, yellow and white over a very long season. The species described is the most reliable in cool temperate gardens.
CULTIVATION Require full sun and moist, well-drained, neutral or slightly alkaline soil that is rich in organic matter (JI No. 2).
PROPAGATION From seed, sown in spring at 55–64°F (13–18°C). From cuttings, in late spring and mid-summer. By layering, in spring or summer.
POTENTIAL PROBLEMS Aphids, scale insects, mealybugs, whiteflies; powdery mildew.

H. syriacus *China to India*

Flowers: late summer to mid-autumn. H 6–10ft (1.8–3m), S 4–6ft (1.2–1.8m). FH.
The penalty of being so late into leaf and late into flower is that the blooms are sometimes damaged by frost, despite the shrub's relative hardiness. The mallow-like flowers are borne on an upright shrub, the single cultivars being of much more pleasing shape than the doubles. 'Oiseau Bleu' has violet-blue flowers with purplish veining; 'Red Heart' has white flowers with magenta blotches and veining, and 'Woodbridge' has rich pink flowers, a darker pink centre and veining.

Hibiscus syriacus 'Oiseau Bleu'

HYDRANGEA

HYDRANGEACEAE

In the garden, the main ornamental value of the hydrangeas lies in their flattened or dome-shaped flowerheads. These generally consist of fertile flowers, which are small but numerous, surrounded by sterile flowers or ray-florets, usually much less numerous but of greater size. Flower colour, especially of *H. macrophylla*, is affected by the alkalinity or acidity of the soil. The most intense blues are produced on neutral to acid soils; on alkaline soils an otherwise blue hydrangea becomes purplish or pink. Almost all the 80 or so species in the genus are climbers or shrubs of moist woodlands in east Asia or North and South America. All the shrubs described are deciduous and the leaves of some are richly coloured in autumn. See also CLIMBERS.
CULTIVATION Tolerate sun or partial shade and require moist, well-drained soil that is rich in organic matter (JI No. 2). Cut a third of the oldest stems of *H. macrophylla*, *H.* 'Preziosa' and *H. serrata* down to the base in early spring. Cut out weak crossing stems and prune the previous year's flowered shoots down to the next pair of healthy buds.
PROPAGATION From seed, sown in spring. From softwood cuttings, taken in early summer. From hardwood cuttings, taken in winter (deciduous shrubs). From semi-ripe cuttings, taken in mid-summer (evergreens).
POTENTIAL PROBLEMS Aphids, red spider mites, vine weevil, capsid bugs, scale insects; grey mould

(*Botrytis*), powdery mildew, honey fungus, leaf spot, hydrangea virus. *WARNING* Contact with the foliage may aggravate skin allergies. Swallowing any part may cause stomach upset.

H. aspera *E. Asia*
Foliage: early summer to autumn. Flowers: mid- to late summer. H and S 8–10ft (2.5–3m). FH.
Several shrubs, sometimes tree-like and previously regarded as separate species, are grouped under this name. All have flattened flowerheads consisting of mauve to purplish blue fertile flowers surrounded by a broken ring of sterile flowers that are white, usually with a pink or mauve tint. The roughly hairy leaves and flowerheads of '**Macrophylla**' are very large. Coming into flower slightly earlier is **subsp. sargentiana**, with large leaves that are bristly on the underside. The most refined of these hydrangeas are those of the **Villosa Group**, in which the foliage has a soft velvety texture.

Hydrangea macrophylla 'Madame Emile Mouillère'

H. macrophylla *Japan*
Common hydrangea
Flowers: mid- to late summer. H 4–6ft (1.2–1.8m), S 4–8ft (1.2–2.5m). FH.
By far the best known of the hydrangeas are the numerous mophead cultivars of this species, with large rounded flowerheads composed almost entirely of single or double sterile florets. They can be criticized for their graceless excess but they give value for a very long period and are even beautiful when they have faded. They are, not surprisingly, popular in town gardens and as container plants. '**Générale Vicomtesse de Vibraye**' flowers early and carries good pale blue or pink flowers in large flowerheads. '**Madame Emile Mouillère**' is a handsome white that flowers well into autumn. The flowers become pink-tinged with age. More at ease in a woodland garden are the lacecap cultivars,

with flat heads of fertile flowers ringed by sterile florets. On acid soils '**Mariesii Perfecta**' is rich blue with a constellation of paler florets. The fertile flowers of '**Lanarth White**' are often mauve or pink tinted but the florets are white. *H.* '**Preziosa**', a particularly fine mophead, grows to about 5ft (1.5m). The young leaves are purplish and colour well in autumn; the flowers are strong pink, darkening to purplish red. *H. serrata* '**Bluebird**' is like a compact lacecap, up to 4ft (1.2m) high, with rich blue flowers.

Hydrangea paniculata

H. paniculata *Russia (Sakhalin), China, Japan*
Flowers: late summer to early autumn. H 10–20ft (3–6m), S 8–10ft (2.5–3m). FH.
Large conical flowerheads are made up of small creamy white sterile flowers and large ray florets, white at first but pink as they age. '**Grandiflora**' has flowerheads up to 1ft (30cm) tall.

H. quercifolia *S.E. USA*
Oak-leaved hydrangea
Foliage: autumn. Flowers: mid- to late summer. H 5–6ft (1.5–1.8m), S 4–8ft (1.2–2.5m). FH.
The boldly lobed "oak" leaves turn shades of purple and bronze just as the white ray-florets in the cone-like flowerheads take on pink tints.

Hydrangea quercifolia

HYPERICUM

CLUSIACEAE St. John's wort

In a genus of over 400 species the numerous shrubs, evergreen and deciduous, are widely distributed and found in a variety of habitats, including woodland and open rocky places. Most of those in cultivation produce their bright yellow flowers, which have prominent stamens, in the second half of the summer. In some cases the flowers are followed by ornamental fruits. The rose of Sharon (*H. calycinum*), a low semi-evergreen shrub growing to about 2ft (60cm), spreads energetically by runners to the point of becoming a weed but is a useful shrub for covering ground in dry shady places. Its cup-shaped yellow flowers, filled with long stamens, are borne most freely in sun.
CULTIVATION Tolerate sun or partial shade and require moist well-drained soil (large species) or require full sun and very well-drained soil (dwarf species). The small alpine species need protection from winter wet (JI No. 1). Prune deciduous species and *H. calycinum* down to the woody base in early spring.
PROPAGATION From seed, sown in autumn. From cuttings, in summer.
POTENTIAL PROBLEMS Rust (*H. calycinum* and *H.* × *inodorum*).

H. 'Hidcote'
Flowers: mid-summer to early autumn. H and S 3–5ft (90–150cm). FH.
This semi-evergreen and aromatic shrub bears saucer-shaped yellow flowers over a long season but its great popularity has rather blunted its effect. The deciduous and fully hardy *H. forrestii*, which originates from south-west China, is a pleasing alternative which has a long season of clustered yellow flowers and good foliage colour in autumn.

H. × inodorum
Flowers: mid-summer to mid autumn. H 3–4ft (90–120cm), 4–6ft (1.2–1.8m). FH.
The small, starry, yellow flowers are produced freely on a semi-evergreen shrub with dark-green aromatic leaves. They are followed by clusters of conical fruits. '**Elstead**' has copper-tinted autumn foliage and coral-red fruits but is prone to rust. The compact Chinese species, *H. kouytchense*, which grows to a height of about 3ft (90cm), also has bright red fruits following a long season of yellow flowers.

Hypericum olympicum

H. olympicum *N. Greece, N.W. Turkey*
Flowers: late summer. H 9–12in (23–30cm), S 1ft (30cm). FH.
Bright yellow flowers are scattered over a loose blue-green hummock. This is an appealing dwarf deciduous shrub for full sun but even more beautiful as a rock garden miniature is the
f. uniflorum 'Citrinum', which has lemon-yellow flowers.

H. 'Rowallane'
Flowers: late summer to early autumn. H 4–6ft (1.2–1.8m), S 3–5ft (90–150cm). FrH.
Where the climate is mild enough this semi-evergreen hybrid is the pick of the hypericums. The dark green leaves make a good background to bowl-shaped golden flowers, sometimes nearly 3in (8cm) across, borne on arching branches.

KALMIA

ERICACEAE

The kalmias are firmly in the same lime-intolerant camp as the rhododendrons. One species is found in Cuba, the other half dozen in North America, always on acid soils and usually in woodland or swamp. They can do well in a shrub border or a woodland garden. The large species described below is the pick of these shrubs but the sheep laurel (**K. angustifolia**) makes pleasing low thickets growing to 2–3ft (60–90cm) high that are brightened by crowded clusters of reddish pink flowers in early summer. It is also fully hardy.
CULTIVATION Tolerate full sun or partial shade and require acid soil that is rich in organic matter. Mulch in late winter with leafmould.
PROPAGATION From seed, sown in spring at 45–54°F (6–12°C). From cuttings, in late spring and mid-summer. By layering, in late summer.
POTENTIAL PROBLEMS Usually none but tends to resent continued containerization.
WARNING Swallowing any part may cause severe discomfort.

K. latifolia *E. USA*
Calico bush, Mountain laurel
Flowers: late spring to mid-summer. H 6–10ft (1.8–3m), S 8–10ft (2.5–3m). FH.
Bushes are densely clothed with dark green leathery leaves but these can be nearly obscured when the large flower clusters are open. The bowl-shaped flowers are pink – although there is great variation in the precise shade – and they are prettily detailed, with conspicuous stamens and a ring of darker colour. There are numerous slight variations on this very beautiful theme. 'Ostbo Red' has bright red buds opening to pale pink flowers.

Kalmia latifolia

KOLKWITZIA

CAPRIFOLIACEAE Beauty bush

The single species, from rocky mountainous slopes in western China, is a graceful deciduous shrub that is grown for its wonderful profusion of bell-shaped flowers.
CULTIVATION Require full sun and fertile well-drained soil. Cut about a fifth of the oldest stems down to ground level after flowering. Prune flowered shoots down to strong healthy growths.
PROPAGATION From cuttings, taken in late spring or early summer. By removal of suckers, in spring.
POTENTIAL PROBLEMS Usually none.

K. amabilis *China (Hubei)*
Flowers: late spring to early summer. H 6–12ft (1.8–3.7m), S 6–12ft (1.8–3.7m). FH.
Masses of pink flowers, yellow in

Kolkwitzia amabilis

the throat, cover a densely twiggy arching bush. 'Pink Cloud' is a particularly good selection with flowers of deep colouring.

LAURUS

LAURACEAE Laurel

The crown of laurels, the accolade of classical heroes and subsequent paragons, was fashioned from the foliage of the bay laurel (*L. nobilis*). This and one other species, *L. azorica*, from the Canary Islands and the Azores, are aromatic evergreens that are capable of developing into small trees. The culinary value of the bay laurel justifies its place in the garden.
CULTIVATION Tolerate full sun or partial shade and require soil that is fertile, moist but well-drained. Laurels also need shelter from wind.
PROPAGATION From seed, sown in autumn. From semi-ripe cuttings, in summer.
POTENTIAL PROBLEMS Bay sucker; powdery mildew.

Laurus nobilis

L. nobilis *Mediterranean*
Bay laurel, sweet bay
Flowers: spring. H 10–30ft (3–9m), S 8–16ft (2.5–5m). FrH.
The glossy leaves are this shrub's feature. Untrained, the shrub is of irregular growth but it is very tolerant of trimming and, shaped as a standard, cone or pyramid, makes a splendid container plant, easily moved under cover where it is vulnerable to winter cold outdoors. The flowers are small and greenish yellow, with male and female on separate plants. Female plants bear purple-black berries.

LAVANDULA

LAMIACEAE Lavender

The lavenders are strongly associated with southern Europe and the Mediterranean region but the distribution of about 25 species extends from the Canary Islands in the west to India in the east. Almost everywhere, however, these evergreen shrubs or subshrubs are plants of dry and sunny habitats.

They have long been grown for their spikes of small two-lipped flowers, which are strongly scented and much loved by bees. The grey-green of their aromatic foliage is also appealing and has made them popular as dwarf hedging. The most interesting of the lavenders for foliage, such as the white woolly *L. lanata* from southern Spain, abhor cold wet weather.
CULTIVATION Require full sun and well-drained soil. Shear off spent flower spikes immediately after flowering. Prune straggly plants in late spring down to buds which have just broken.
PROPAGATION From seed, sown in spring. From semi-ripe cuttings, in mid-summer.
POTENTIAL PROBLEMS Froghoppers; honeyfungus, grey mould (*botrytis*).

L. angustifolia *W. Mediterranean*
Flowers: mid- to late summer. H 2–3ft (60–90cm), S 2–4ft (60–120cm). FH.
Many of the plants that have been grown under this name are now recognized as hybrids (see *L. × intermedia*). The aromatic grey-green shrub is represented in gardens by several clones, typically with violet-blue spikes but some have pink or white flowers. '**Hidcote**' and '**Twickel Purple**', broader in leaf, are compact, growing to about 2ft (60cm), with dark purple flowers. '**Munstead**' is a useful dwarf about 18in (45cm) high, but less intense in colouring.

Lavandula angustifolia 'Hidcote'

L. × intermedia
Flowers: mid- to late summer. H and S 1–2ft (30–60cm). FH.
This plant, a cross between *L. angustifolia* and *L. latifolia*, often has spoon-shaped leaves, like the latter species. The **Dutch Group** with silver-grey leaves and grey-blue flowers belongs here.

L. stoechas *Mediterranean*
French lavender
Flowers: late spring to mid-summer. H and S 20–30in (50–75cm). FrH to FH.
Bushy strongly aromatic plants

Lavandula stoechas 'James Compton'

with grey-green leaves are topped by short spikes of dark purple flowers with showy bracts as finials. The flower stalks of **subsp. pedunculata** are longer and the ear-like bracts can be more than 2in (5cm) long, although slightly shorter in '**James Compton**'.

LAVATERA

MALVACEAE Mallow

In this mixed genus of about 25 species there are several shrubby species that are plants of open and dry habitats. The plants that are most commonly grown are fast-growing and vigorous subshrubs that produce a long succession of funnel-shaped flowers among downy lobed leaves. They are often short-lived but are good on light soils and do well in coastal gardens.
CULTIVATION Require full sun and well-drained light soil. Cut the previous year's growth down to woody base stems in early spring.
PROPAGATION From seed, sown in mid- to late spring. From softwood cuttings, in spring.
POTENTIAL PROBLEMS Rust, stem rot, fungal diseases.

L. 'Barnsley'
Flowers: mid- to late summer. H and S 5–6ft (1.5–1.8m). FH.
Throughout summer, airy branches carry innumerable funnel-shaped flowers that are pale pink animated by a darker centre. Others in the same mould include '**Burgundy Wine**', with deep pink flowers darkened by rich veining.

Lavatera 'Barnsley'

LEUCOTHOE

ERICACEAE

Several shrubs in this widely distributed genus of about 50 species are grown for their foliage as much as for their flowers. Most are plants of woodland and swampy ground and all show the heath family's dislike of lime.
CULTIVATION Require partial or deep shade and moist acid soil that is rich in organic matter.
PROPAGATION From seed, sown in spring. From semi-ripe cuttings, in mid-summer. By division of suckering species, in spring.
POTENTIAL PROBLEMS Usually none.

Leucothoe walteri

L. walteri *S.E. USA*
Switch ivy
Foliage: autumn and winter. Flowers: late spring; H 4–6ft (1.2–1.8m), S 4–5ft (1.2–1.5m). FH.
Few evergreens colour so dramatically in autumn and winter but in spring it is the many clusters of white urn-shaped flowers dangling all along the arching stems that are the main ornament. The leathery leaves, which are lance-shaped and narrow to a pointed tip, colour most strongly when grown in exposed positions, taking on purplish to betroot-red tints. *L. Scarletta*, usually not more than 2ft (60cm) high, is similar to the species but has young reddish purple leaves which turn dark green and later bronzy purple.

LEYCESTERIA

CAPRIFOLIACEAE

The half dozen species in the genus are deciduous shrubs of rugged and wooded country in India and China. The arrangement of the flowers in tassel-like racemes is unusual, as are the hollow stems.
CULTIVATION Tolerates full sun or partial shade and requires well-drained soil. Cut back flowered shoots to strong lower buds in spring.
PROPAGATION From seed, sown in autumn. From cuttings, in summer.
POTENTIAL PROBLEMS Usually none.

Leycesteria formosa

L. formosa *Himalayas, W. China*
Himalayan honeysuckle
Flowers: mid-summer to early
autumn. Fruits: winter. H and S
5–8ft (1.5–2.5m). FrH–FH.
In winter the upright stems, at first
covered with a glaucous bloom,
later polished and dark green, form
a highly ornamental thicket. In
summer they are obscured by the
elegant foliage. Dangling among
the pointed leaves are racemes
about 4in (10cm) long of funnel-
shaped white flowers set among
long-lasting wine-red bracts. The
round berries that follow are
purplish black.

LIGUSTRUM

OLEACEAE Privet

The adaptability of the privets to a
wide range of conditions is their
major asset but from about
50 species of evergreen, semi-
evergreen and deciduous shrubs
there are few that are notable
ornamentals. The nearest to a plant
of distinction is the Asiatic
L. lucidum, an evergreen large
shrub or tree, which may reach
30ft (9m) in height. It has glossy,
dark evergreen leaves and in late
summer or early autumn there are
frothy sprays of creamy flowers,
followed by blue-black fruits. Even
more striking is yellow variegated
'**Excelsum Superbum**'. The shrub
described below is humdrum but
undeniably useful as a hedging plant.
CULTIVATION Tolerate full sun or
partial shade and require well-
drained soil.
PROPAGATION From seed, sown in
autumn or spring. From semi-ripe
cuttings, in mid-summer. From
hardwood cuttings, in winter.
POTENTIAL PROBLEMS Thrips,
aphids, scale insects, leaf miners;
leaf spots, honey fungus, wilt.
WARNING Swallowing any part can
cause severe discomfort.

L. ovalifolium *Japan*
Flowers: mid-summer. H 10–15ft
(3–4.5m), S 10–15ft (3–4.5m). FH.
This species is most commonly
seen as an evergreen or semi-

evergreen hedging plant but if left
untrimmed makes a large open
shrub. Its creamy flowers, which
have a disagreeably sour smell, are
followed by round black fruits.
'**Aureum**', known as the golden
privet, is bright, with leaves edged
with a broad yellow margin.

Ligustrum ovalifolium 'Aureum'

LITHODORA

BORAGINACEAE

The star of the genus, a low
evergreen subshrub with flowers
of ravishing blue, is a lime-hater
but about half a dozen other
species with less arresting blue or
white flowers tolerate alkaline
conditions. They are plants of the
Mediterranean region, including
parts of north Africa and east to
Greece and Turkey, and are found
in a variety of habitats, including
the margins of woodland and sandy
coasts.
CULTIVATION Require full sun and
well-drained neutral or alkaline soil
(equal parts loam, leafmould and
sharp sand). *L. diffusa* 'Heavenly
Blue' requires acid soil that is rich
in organic matter. Cut back
flowered shoots down to strong
lower growths. Plant in spring.
PROPAGATION From semi-ripe
cuttings, taken in mid-summer.
POTENTIAL PROBLEMS Under glass:
aphids, red spider mites.

L. diffusa *S. Europe*
Flowers: late spring to early
summer. H 6–12in (15–30cm),
S 18–24in (45–60cm). FH.
The sprawling mat of intricately
branched stems, so ordinary when

Lithodora diffusa

merely covered with narrow hairy
leaves, is transformed by the blue
of numerous flowers, in '**Heavenly
Blue**' of a piercing azure intensity.
This subshrub is at its loveliest
spilling over a raised edge or
trailing from a rock garden ledge.

LONICERA

CAPRIFOLIACEAE Honeysuckle

The twining plants in this genus of
over 150 species are certainly more
showy than most of the evergreen
and deciduous shrubs. The dense,
glossy, dark green leaves of
L. nitida, a fully hardy evergreen
that can grow to more than 6ft
(1.8m), qualifies it and the yellow-
leaved form '**Baggesen's Gold**' as a
hedging plant. Another hardy
evergreen, **L. pileata**, makes good
ground cover up to 2ft (60cm) high
in almost any conditions. More
decorative are some of the
deciduous species, like the pink-
flowered **L. tatarica**, which have
red berries to follow the late spring
or early summer floral display.
Where there is space, however, the
shrubby honeysuckles to include
are those that flower in winter and
make their point with scent. See
also CLIMBERS.
CULTIVATION Tolerate full sun or
partial shade and require moist
well-drained soil that is rich in
organic matter (JI No. 3). After
flowering cut flowered shoots
down to strong lower growths.
Remove about a fifth of old stems
down to ground level.
PROPAGATION From seed, sown
when ripe. From semi-ripe
cuttings, in mid-summer
(evergreen). From semi-ripe
cuttings, in summer or hardwood
cuttings, in autumn (deciduous).
POTENTIAL PROBLEM Aphids.
WARNING Swallowing the berries
can cause mild stomach upset.

Lonicera × purpusii

L. × purpusii
Flowers: mid-winter to early spring.
H 5–6ft (1.5–1.8m), S 6–8ft
(1.8–2.5m). FH.
The parents are two very similar
Chinese species, **L. fragrantissima**

and *L. standishii*, but their hybrid is freer flowering, especially in the form **'Winter Beauty'**. The creamy flowers, which are carried on the bare stems, can easily go unnoticed so that the fragrance is a delicious mystery. The parent species produce red berries, the hybrid only rarely.

MAGNOLIA

MAGNOLIACEAE

The magnolias are in the first rank of flowering trees and shrubs. A high proportion of the evergreen and deciduous species, about 125 in total, as well as numerous hybrids bear flowers of exceptional quality. The colour range is limited, but in many cases individual blooms are of superb form and texture and on mature plants they are borne in profusion. The species are mainly plants of woodland and scrub, with a distribution ranging from the Himalayas to south-east Asia and from North to South America. The foliage, although generally pleasing, does not match the distinction of the flowers. In many cases the clusters of fruits are a curious, even moderately colourful feature in autumn. See also TREES.
CULTIVATION Tolerate sun or partial shade and require moist, well-drained, acid soil that is rich in organic matter.
PROPAGATION From semi-ripe cuttings, in late summer.
POTENTIAL PROBLEM Honey fungus.

M. liliiflora China
Flowers: mid-spring to mid-summer. H 8–10ft (2.5–3m), S 6–12ft (1.8–3.7m). FH.
This rather open deciduous shrub has slender tulip-like flowers that are mauve-pink on the outside, white inside. More commonly seen is the more compact **'Nigra'**, which has upright purplish red flowers, white with purple staining on the inside. The species is a parent of many fully hardy deciduous hybrids that flower freely in mid- to late spring. *M.* **'Susan'**, one of these, is of upright growth, bearing long buds, usually arching to form a crescent and then opening to fragrant flowers with long reddish purple segments that twist slightly to show the paler inside.

M. sieboldii China, Korea, Japan
Flowers: late spring to late summer. H 15–25ft (4.5–7.5m), S 20–40ft (6–12m). FH.
The white bowl-shaped flowers, up to 4in (10cm) across and refined in fragrance as well as in form, are borne among dark green foliage.

They look out or down, showing their conspicuous wine-red anthers. The shrub is deciduous and its leaves are downy and grey-green on the underside.

Magnolia × soulangeana

M. × soulangeana
Flowers: mid- to late spring. H 12–15ft (3.7–4.5m), S 15–20ft (4.5–6m). FH.
Despite their profusion, the large goblet-shaped flowers have a dignified eloquence matched by the flowers of few other spring shrubs and trees. Although this deciduous hybrid can make a spreading tree, it is most often seen as a large rounded shrub. The sculpted blooms, which can be as much as 6in (15cm) across, are seen at their best before the young leaves develop. Several fine forms, some of which produce a few flowers in autumn as well as the main flush in spring, vary in colour from the familiar white with a purple stain at the base. The fragrant flowers of the tree-like **'Alba Superba'** are almost pure white. **'Lennei'** has purplish pink goblets, **'Rustica Rubra'** goblets of a deeper reddish purple, but in both cases the flowers are milky white on the inside.

***Magnolia stellata* 'Royal Star'**

M. stellata Japan
Star magnolia
Flowers: early to mid-spring. H 8–10ft (2.5–3m), S 8–12ft (2.5–3.7m). FH.
Twigs of grey-green flower buds have a sombre beauty of their own but the shrub's great moment is when the narrow snowy segments

spill out to make fragrant slightly limp stars up to 4in (10cm) across. **'Royal Star'**, which is pink in bud, and **'Waterlily'** both have slightly larger flowers, with about 30 segments.

MAHONIA

BERBERIDACEAE

The handsome evergreen foliage and yellow flowers in winter or early spring, followed in many cases by blue-black berries, are important features of shrubs that adapt well to a wide range of conditions. There are about 70 species, which are found in woodland and more open rugged country in Asia, from the Himalayas to China, as well as in North and Central America.
CULTIVATION Require partial or full shade and moist well-drained soil that is rich in organic matter.
PROPAGATION From seed, sown as soon as ripe or in autumn. From semi-ripe or leaf-bud cuttings, in mid- to late summer.
POTENTIAL PROBLEMS Mildew, rust.

M. aquifolium W. North America
Oregon grape
Flowers: early spring. Fruit: late spring. H 2–3ft (60–90cm), S 3–5ft (90–150cm). FH.
Although never in the first rank of shrubs, this mahonia performs astonishingly well, forming dense suckering thickets even in the least favoured corners of the garden. The pinnate leaves are shiny green, often turning red-purple in winter. The yellow flowers are densely clustered and are followed by grape-like, blue-black berries.

M. japonica China
Foliage: year-round. Flowers: early winter to early spring. H 5–9ft (1.5–2.7m), S 8–12ft (2.5–3.7m). FH.
The evergreen foliage has a severe and graphic boldness, the large leaves, arranged at the end of branches in whorls, consisting of paired spiny leaflets. The leaflets are leathery and dark green but in full sun sometimes turn red. In winter, clustered flower sprays spill from the centre of the leaf rosettes. They are crowded with lemon-yellow bells that provide one of the best scents in the winter garden, carrying well when the weather is mild. Inexplicably, the laxness of the flower sprays is sometimes considered a failing but it is in fact a concession to gracefulness that is lacking in most of the hybrids. After the flowers, there are blue-black berries, which often contain no seeds.

149

M. × media

Foliage: year-round. Flowers: late autumn to late winter. H 12–15ft (3.7–4.5m), S 10–12ft (3–3.7m). FH. The hybrids that go under this name are the result of crosses between *M. japonica* and another winter-flowering Chinese species, the frost-hardy *M. lomariifolia*. This is an often leggy upright shrub to 10ft (3m), with erect clustered sprays of yellow flowers. The hybrids lean towards one or other parent. 'Charity' has numerous sprays of yellow flowers that at first are upright, later spreading; on the long upright sprays of 'Lionel Fortescue' the bright yellow flowers open early. The flowers of these 2 hybrids are faintly scented; those of 'Winter Sun', which has erect sprays, are more fragrant.

Mahonia × media 'Charity'

MYRTUS

MYRTACEAE Myrtle

Only 2 evergreen shrubs remain in *Myrtus*, their close relatives having been shunted off to other genera. Both are Mediterranean and thrive in hot dry conditions. The common myrtle (*Myrtus communis*), long in cultivation, has a happy horticultural connection with the classical world where it was emblematic of love.
CULTIVATION Require full sun and moist well-drained soil.
PROPAGATION From seed, sown in autumn. From semi-ripe cuttings, taken in mid-summer.
POTENTIAL PROBLEMS Usually none.

M. communis *Mediterranean*

Common myrtle
Flowers: mid- to late summer. Fruits: autumn. H and S 8–10ft (2.5–3m).
These bushy plants are dense with small glossy leaves that are spicily aromatic when bruised. Specimens are usually left untrimmed but myrtle can be clipped into simple topiary shapes, very much like box (*Buxus sempervirens*). The fragrant white flowers, which are carried in profusion, have 5 petals and a central puff of stamens. Where the

climate is warm enough, there are dark purple berries to follow. The compact **subsp. *tarentina***, with a height and spread of up to 5ft (1.5m), has narrow leaves, flowers that are tinted pink and grey-white berries. Where these shrubs are grown at the margins of their hardiness, they are best planted at the foot of a warm wall.

Myrtus communis

NANDINA

BERBERIDACEAE Heavenly bamboo

The single species in this genus, bamboo-like but really an evergreen *Berberis* relative, is a streamside and woodland shrub of mountainous country in China, India and Japan.
CULTIVATION Require full sun and moist well-drained soil.
PROPAGATION From seed, sown as soon as ripe. From semi-ripe cuttings, taken in mid-summer.
POTENTIAL PROBLEM Viruses.

Nandina domestica

N. domestica *China, India, Japan*

Heavenly bamboo
Foliage: early spring to late autumn. Flowers: mid-summer. Fruits: autumn and winter. H 4–6ft (1.2–1.8m), S 3–5ft (90–150cm). FrH.
The unbranched stems carry large leaves consisting of many narrow segments. They are purplish red when young and colour well again in autumn. Where the climate is warm enough, the clusters of starry white flowers with long yellow anthers are followed by red berries. 'Firepower' is compact and colours richly.

OSMANTHUS

OLEACEAE

Although relying simply on their polished leaves and small but fragrant flowers, several shrubs in this genus have an irresistible appeal. There are about 15 species, all of them evergreen woodland shrubs or trees, generally flowering most freely when they are growing in plenty of sun. Some are natives of southern USA and the Pacific Islands but the best known are Asiatic. The plants described all respond well to clipping and are suitable for hedging and simple topiary.
CULTIVATION Tolerate sun or partial shade and require well-drained fertile soil.
PROPAGATION From seed, sown as soon as ripe. From semi-ripe cuttings, in mid-summer. By layering, in autumn or spring.
POTENTIAL PROBLEMS Usually none.

Osmanthus delavayi

O. delavayi *W. China (Sichuan, Yunnan)*

Flowers: mid- to late spring. H 6–15ft (1.8–4.5m), S 6–12ft (1.8–3.7m). FH.
The slow-growing dark green bush has neat glossy leaves, which set off to perfection the clusters of tubular white flowers. Their scent is sweet and refined. There are sometimes blue-black fruits to follow. A fully hardy hybrid of which this is a parent, *O. × burkwoodii*, is more compact, slightly coarser and less well scented but it is being measured against a paragon.

O. heterophyllus *Japan, Taiwan*

Flowers: late summer to early autumn. H 8–15ft (2.5–4.5m), S 8–12ft (2.5–3.7m). FrH to FH. Its dark green glossy leaves are toothed and prickly so that the shrub seems to be faking a holly. Tiny white flowers, rather lost among the leaves, are sweetly scented. They are sometimes followed by blue-black berries. There are several variegated forms; 'Variegatus' has a pale yellow edging to the leaves.

PACHYSANDRA

BUXACEAE

This small genus of 4 species of evergreen or semi-evergreen woodland plants includes a subshrub that is useful for carpeting bare ground under trees.
CULTIVATION Require partial or full shade and tolerate any soil.
PROPAGATION By division, in spring. From softwood cuttings, in early summer.
POTENTIAL PROBLEMS Slugs and snails.

P. terminalis *N. China, Japan*
Flowers: mid- to late spring. H 8–12in (20–30cm), S 18–24in (45–60cm). FH.
The glossy dark-green leaves clustered at the tips of short stems are the plant's principal asset. The upper half of the leaves is often toothed. The overlapping rosettes make very dense cover and the plants spread freely at the roots, especially in moist soils rich in organic matter. Male and female flowers, which are borne on separate plants, are small, greenish white or white and without petals.

Pachysandra terminalis

PAEONIA

PAEONIACEAE Peony

The common name 'tree peony' is misleading for the woody plants in this genus, which are shrubby and usually of short stature. In the sumptuous beauty of their flowers many of these deciduous shrubs rank with the finest of the more numerous herbaceous peonies and the foliage of some is of a very high order. With such qualities, they can be forgiven for the gauntness of their bare stems out of season. There are about 30 peony species in all, the tree peonies coming from lightly wooded country or more open terrain in west China and bordering areas of Tibet. The current interest in the tree peonies may make them seem a novelty but they have long been cultivated in China and Japan. See also PERENNIALS.

CULTIVATION Tolerate full sun or partial shade and require deep, moist, well-drained soil rich in organic matter.
PROPAGATION From seed, sown in autumn or winter. From semi-ripe cuttings, in mid-summer. By grafting in winter.
POTENTIAL PROBLEMS Swift moth larvae, eelworms; viruses, honey fungus, peony wilt.
WARNING Swallowing any part may cause mild stomach upset.

Paeonia delavayi

P. delavayi *China*
Foliage: late spring to autumn. Flowers: late spring. H 5–6ft (1.5–1.8m), S 4–5ft (1.2–1.5m). FH.
The nodding flowers are short-lived and rather lost in the foliage, but combine splendidly sober maroon-red petals and yellow stamens. The large leaves are composed of jagged leaflets with a hint of blue on the underside. The Tibetan **var. ludlowii**, with a height and spread of about 8ft (2.5m), is also impressive in its foliage and its single flowers, as much as 5in (13cm) across, are rich yellow.
P. × lemoinei 'Souvenir de Maxime Cornu', one of the best and most fragrant of several good hybrids raised between *P. delavayi* and *P. suffruticosa*, has very double ruffled flowers with orange-yellow petals edged red.

Paeonia delavayi var. *ludlowii*

P. suffruticosa *China*
Moutan peony
Flowers: late spring to early summer. H 6–7ft (1.8–2.2m), S 5–7ft (1.5–2.2m). FH.
This species is represented in

Paeonia suffruticosa subsp. *rockii*

gardens by a range of single to double cultivars, many of which are fragrant. They compensate by their magnificence for the shortness of their flowering season. The leaves, deeply cut and with pointed lobes, set the flowers off well. The following are selected from a court of near equals: **'Hana-daijin'**, a violet-purple double; **'Mrs William Kelway'**, a white double; **subsp. rockii** a semi-double white with maroon touches; and **'Yae-zakura'**, a soft pink double.

PHILADELPHUS

HYDRANGEACEAE Mock orange

The best of the mock oranges produce masses of heavily scented pure white or tinted flowers in early to mid-summer. At their peak they are highly seductive so that their dullness out of flower is inevitably disappointing. This shortcoming is not such a disadvantage in a large garden or when the more compact mock oranges are grown and a compensation is the way these shrubs tolerate a wide range of conditions. There are about 40 species, mainly deciduous, and they are found in Europe, Asia and North and Central America, usually in scrub or lightly wooded country. The species have largely been displaced in cultivation by numerous hybrids but the yellow-leaved form of a fully hardy European species, **P. coronarius 'Aureus'**, is widely grown as a foliage plant. The yellow burns in full sun and the shrub is better seen as a lime-green accent, as much as 10ft (3m) high, in partial shade.
CULTIVATION Tolerate full sun or partial shade and require well-drained soil (JI No. 3). Cut out about a fifth of the oldest growths down to ground level after flowering. Cut back the flowered shoots to new strong shoots lower down the stems.
PROPAGATION From cuttings, taken in summer. From hardwood cuttings, in autumn or winter.
POTENTIAL PROBLEMS Aphids; powdery mildew.

P. hybrids

Flowers: early to mid-summer.
H and S 4–10ft (1.2–3m). FH.
Some gardeners will insist on pure white in the flowers but good fragrance and suitable size are more to the point. The following small selection includes compact and large hybrids: '**Beauclerk**', single very fragrant white flowers with a mauve stain on an arching shrub up to 8ft (2.5m) tall; '**Belle Etoile**', single strongly scented creamy flowers with a purplish centre on a bushy plant up to 8ft (2.5m) high; '**Dame Blanche**' semi-double, scented, pure white flowers on an arching shrub up to 6ft (1.8m) high; '**Manteau d'Hermine**', double, very fragrant, milk-white flowers on a spreading bush only 30in (75cm) high; '**Sybille**', strongly scented pure white single flowers with purple centres on a broad shrub about 4ft (1.2m) high; and '**Virginal**', double pure white flowers with rich scent on a shrub that at 10ft (3m) can be gawky.

Philadelphus '**Dame Blanche**'

PHOTINIA

ROSACEAE

The photinias, an Asiatic genus found in the Himalayas and further east, are shrubs and trees of woodland and scrub. There are about 60 species, mainly evergreen, some of which have bright coloured young leaves in spring. In gardens or alkaline soils they are substitutes for the colourful forms of *Pieris*, which are intolerant of lime.
CULTIVATION Tolerate full sun or partial shade and require fertile, moist, well-drained soil.
PROPAGATION From seed, sown in autumn. From semi-ripe cuttings, in mid-summer.
POTENTIAL PROBLEMS Fireblight, leaf spot, powdery mildew.

P. davidiana *China, Vietnam*

Foliage; late summer to autumn.
Flowers: mid-summer. Fruits: autumn. H 12–20ft (3.7–6m), S 10–18ft (3–5.5m). FH.
The main ornament of this large evergreen shrub or small tree is the crop of red matt berries, hanging in loose bunches. The hawthorn-like flowers have an unpleasant smell. Odd leaves turn scarlet as they age. '**Palette**' is slow-growing and its leaves are streaked and blotched with cream and pink.

Photinia × *fraseri* '**Red Robin**'

P. × fraseri

Foliage: late spring to early summer. Flowers: mid to late spring. H 12–15ft (3.7–4.5m), S 10–15ft (3–4.5m). FrH–FH.
The small white flowers are of little importance but the intense copper red of the young leaves makes this evergreen shrub or small tree an arresting plant in spring. The young foliage of '**Red Robin**' is exceptionally vivid.

PIERIS

ERICACEAE

The connection with the heath family shows not only in botanical characteristics but also in a dislike of lime. There are 7 species, all evergreen, the pick of them being Asiatic woodland plants. The sprays of small pitcher-shaped flowers are borne in great profusion but even in winter, long before they open, the buds look attractive against the glossy leaves. More dramatic on some *Pieris* is young foliage of vivid and lustrous red.
CULTIVATION Tolerate full sun or partial shade and require moist, acid, well-drained soil rich in organic matter.
PROPAGATION From seed, sown in spring or autumn. From cuttings, in summer.
POTENTIAL PROBLEMS Leaf spot, phytophthorta root rot.
WARNING Swallowing the leaves may cause severe stomach upset.

P. formosa *China, Himalayas*

Foliage late spring to early summer. Flowers: mid to late spring. H 6–15ft (1.8–5m), S 10–12ft (3–3.7m). FrH to FH.
Where the climate is mild enough this makes a large dark green bush loaded with drooping sprays of waxy flowers. The young foliage is usually tinted copper but in **var. forrestii** '**Wakehurst**' is spectacular scarlet. *P. japonica*, a more compact species than *P. formosa* and good in foliage and flower, is probably a parent with it of several hybrids, including *P.* '**Forest Flame**'. This bears masses of fragrant flowers and the young leaves in spring are bright red before changing through pink and cream to green.

Pieris formosa var. *forrestii* '**Wakehurst**'

PITTOSPORUM

PITTOSPORACEAE

Good foliage and scented flowers distinguish several of the evergreen shrubs and small trees in this large genus of about 200 species. A high proportion of those in cultivation are Australasian but plants are also found in regions as far apart as Japan and South Africa.
CULTIVATION Require full sun and well-drained, moist, fertile soil (JI No. 3).
PROPAGATION From seed, sown as soon as ripe or in spring. From semi-ripe cuttings, in mid-summer. By layering or air-layering, in spring.
POTENTIAL PROBLEMS Under glass: red spider mites. Leaf spot and powdery mildew.

Pittosporum tenuifolium '**Irene Patterson**'

P. tenuifolium *New Zealand*

Kohuhu
Foliage: year-round. Flowers: late spring to early summer. H 12–30ft (3.7–9m), S 6–15ft 91.8–4.5m). FrH.
Light green leaves with wavy

margins make a pretty contrast to the very dark stems and as a consequence the shrub, sometimes a small tree, is savaged by flower arrangers. The small fragrant flowers are maroon. Where the climate is mild enough, it is an attractive shelter or hedging plant. There are forms with purple and variegated leaves; those of '**Irene Patterson**' are almost white but speckled with grey and green.

P. tobira *China, Japan, Korea*
Japanese mock orange
Foliage: year-round. Flowers: late spring to early summer. H 6–33ft (1.8–10m), S 5–10ft (1.5–3m). HH.
In warm air a luxurious scent spreads far from the clusters of small cream flowers, which are surrounded by dark green leaves. The capsules split to show orange seeds. This slow-growing species can be used for hedging but at the margins of its hardiness needs the protection of a warm wall. The leaves of '**Variegatum**' have an irregular creamy white margin.

POTENTILLA

ROSACEAE Cinquefoil

Small **5**-petalled flowers, like miniature single roses, liberally decorate the shrubby potentillas over a long season. They, like the perennials, annuals and biennials in this large genus of about 500 species, are found in a range of habitats throughout the Northern Hemisphere. The most important species for gardeners, *P. fruticosa*, has an astonishing distribution in the wild so that its adaptability in the garden is not surprising. See also PERENNIALS.
CULTIVATION Require full sun and well-drained soil. Cut off the tips of the flowered shoots after they have flowered.
PROPAGATION From seed, sown in autumn or spring. From cuttings, in early summer.
POTENTIAL PROBLEMS Usually none.

P. fruticosa *Europe, N. Asia, North America*
Flowers: late spring to mid-autumn. H 3–4ft (90–150cm), S 4–5ft (1.2–1.5m). FH.
This deciduous species is represented in gardens by numerous cultivars with a good range of flower colour that includes white and shades of yellow, pink, red and orange. Bushes are usually compact, with dark green to grey-green leaves, but there is variation in scale, as can be seen in the following selection: '**Abbotswood**', up to 4ft (1.2m)

high), has dark grey-green leaves and white flowers; '**Manchu**', a spreading plant but only about 1ft (30cm) high, has white flowers over grey green foliage; '**Primrose Beauty**', about 3ft (90cm) high, has soft yellow flowers over grey-green foliage; '**Red Ace**', up to 30in (75cm) high, has vermilion flowers, the petals having a yellow reverse; and '**Vilmoriniana**', a tall plant up to 4ft (1.2m) high, has creamy flowers and silvery foliage.

Potentilla fruticosa '**Abbotswood**'

PRUNUS

ROSACEAE Ornamental cherry

The cherries and their close relatives refuse to be typecast. There are over 200 species, many of which are tree-like, as are a large number of the numerous fruiting and ornamental hybrids. However, the Fuji cherry (*P. incisa*) is one of several lovely deciduous shrubs that are laden with blossom on bare stems in winter or spring. '**Kojo-no-mai**' is a gnarled form, ancient in appearance even in youth, which has pale pink flowers and slowly reaches 6ft (1.8m). The main interest of the evergreen shrubs described here is their foliage but their flowers and fruit are far from insignificant. See also TREES.
CULTIVATION Require full sun (deciduous) or tolerate full sun or partial shade (evergreen). All require moist well-drained soil.
PROPAGATION From seed, sown in autumn. From cuttings, in summer. By budding cultivars, in summer or grafting in early spring.
POTENTIAL PROBLEMS Bullfinches, aphids, caterpillars; silver leaf, honey fungus, blossom wilt.
WARNING Swallowing the leaves and fruits of some plants may cause severe discomfort.

P. laurocerasus *E. Europe, S.W. Asia*
Laurel, cherry laurel
Foliage: year-round. Flowers: mid- to late spring. H 15–25ft (4.5–7.5m), S 20–30ft (6-9m). FH.
The cherry laurel is so widely

Prunus laurocerasus

planted and naturalized that it is hard to appreciate the splendid glossiness of its dark green leaves and to give it full credit as an evergreen shelter and hedging plant. The sprays of white flowers, the scent regrettably tainted, are followed by small "cherries", which turn from red to black. It is worth seeking out a distinctive clone, such as the compact '**Otto Luyken**', which grows to about 3ft (90cm).

P. lusitanica *S.W. Europe*
Portugal laurel
Foliage: year-round. Flowers: early summer. H and S 15–40ft (4.5–12m). FH.
As a dense shrub or small tree this is a very satisfying evergreen, its dark glossy foliage given class by the red leaf stalks. Slender sprays of scented white fowers are followed by red fruits that blacken as they start to ripen.

PYRACANTHA

ROSACEAE Firethorn

The firethorns come into their own in autumn and winter for it is then that these more or less spiny evergreen shrubs are laden with prodigious quantities of colourful berries. There is a corresponding mass of hawthorn-like white flowers in early summer but relying for effect on quantity rather than refinement. There are 7 species, some such as the fully hardy and red-berried *P. coccinea*, from southern Europe and south-west Asia. Others are from the Himalayas and further east, one of the finest, *P. rogersiana*, coming from China. This frost-hardy species has fragrant flowers and orange-red or, in the case of '**Flava**', yellow berries. The species have been overtaken in popularity by the hybrids, some of which show resistance to fireblight and scab, to which some of these shrubs are particularly prone. All can be wall-trained or grown as hedges.
CULTIVATION Tolerate full sun or partial shade and require fertile well-drained soil.

PROPAGATION From seed, sown in autumn. From semi-ripe cuttings, in mid-summer.

POTENTIAL PROBLEMS Aphids, caterpillars, scale insects, leaf miners; fireblight, scab, coral spot.

WARNING Swallowing the seeds may cause mild stomach upset.

P. hybrids

Flowers: early summer. Fruits: late summer to early spring. H 8–15ft (2.5–4.5m), S 10–15ft (3–4.5m). FrH to FH.

Despite various species being involved in the crosses, the family resemblance among these hybrids is strong. The following 4 are fully hardy and among the best: 'Golden Charmer', up to 10ft (3m), has orange-red berries; 'Orange Glow', up to 10ft (3m), has long-lasting orange or orange-red berries; 'Soleil d'Or', up to 10ft (3m), has rich yellow berries; and 'Teton', up to 15ft (4.5m), has yellow-orange berries and good resistance to fireblight.

Pyracantha 'Golden Charmer'

RHAMNUS

RHAMNACEAE

Although the genus contains well over 100 species, relatively few of these evergreen and deciduous shrubs or trees find a place in gardens. *R. alaternus* is a widely distributed adaptable species that is usually found with sun-living shrubs in dry stony terrain.

CULTIVATION Requires full sun and well-drained soil. Prune out reverted shoots on *R. alaternus* 'Argenteovariegata' as they appear.

PROPAGATION From seed, sown as soon as ripe. From semi-ripe cuttings of evergreen species, in summer. From greenwood cuttings of deciduous species, in autumn.

POTENTIAL PROBLEMS Usually none.

R. alaternus 'Argenteovariegata'

Foliage: year-round. Flowers: late spring to early summer. H 10–15ft (3–4.5m), S 8–12ft (2.5–3.7m). FrH to FH.

The species is a fast-growing evergreen with glossy green

foliage. Small yellow-green flowers are followed by red berries, which ripen to black. It is, however, variegation that transforms a pedestrian shrub into a plant of some distinction. The grey-green leaves of 'Argenteovariegata' are irregularly outlined in creamy white.

Rhamnus alaternus 'Argenteovariegata'

RHODODENDRON

ERICACEAE

Those who disparage rhododendrons and azaleas point to the colour crudities and funereal dullness of the foliage, which are sometimes the lasting impressions of massed plantings. However, even the critics must acknowledge the extraordinary importance of this genus. Well over 500 species are found in various parts of the world, although not in the African continent, a high proportion of the most valuable horticulturally coming from the Himalayas and further east in Asia.

The species range in scale from tiny shrublets to small or medium-sized trees and they are found in a very wide range of habitats where the soil is neutral to acidic. Hybridizing, once almost exclusively a pastime of dignified rivalry between aristocrats but increasingly plebeian, has resulted in countless crosses. Some of these are large and only suitable for woodland gardens, but many are small enough and sufficiently shade tolerant to find a place in tiny urban gardens or rock gardens. A particularly useful compact group is derived from *R. yakushimanum*. A very large number of species, as well as the hybrids, carry flowers of remarkable beauty. Many are bell- or funnel-shaped, but there is considerable variation from tubular to an open saucer shape. The leaves of many rhododendrons also have ornamental value. In some species they are of impressive size and in many the underside has a felt-like hairiness, the nap being referred

to as the indumentum. Most rhododendrons are evergreen but among the azaleas, a group that is popular for abundant displays of small flowers on small to medium-sized shrubs, some are deciduous. In the following selection, which provides only a small glimpse of the genus, rhododendrons and azaleas are listed separately and in both cases the species that are described precede the hybrids. In some cases a hybrid name is applied to a group and to a particular clone.

CULTIVATION Require dappled shade (in a sheltered woodland area for larger species) and well-drained, moist, acid soil (ericaceous compost). Deadhead immediately after flowering.

PROPAGATION From seed, sown as soon as ripe or in spring on ericaceous compost. From semi-ripe cuttings, in mid-summer. By layering, in autumn. By grafting, in late winter or late summer.

POTENTIAL PROBLEMS Vine weevil, lacebugs, scale insects, caterpillars, aphids, leafhoppers, rhododendron and azalea whiteflies; bud blast, honey fungus, leafy gall, powdery mildew, petal blight, rust, silver leaf, phytophthora root rot.

WARNING Swallowing the nectar of some rhododendron flowers may cause severe stomach upset.

Rhododendron yakushimanun

RHODODENDRON SPECIES

R. augustinii China

Flowers: mid to late spring. H 6–10ft (1.8–3m), S 6–8ft (1.8–2.5m). FH.

At its best this is a startling evergreen shub when it bears clusters of violet-blue flowers among its dark leaves. The throat is spotted olive green. Forms which have mauve flowers are definitely inferior.

R. falconeri E. Himalayas

Foliage: year-round. Flowers: mid to late spring. H 25–40ft (7.5–12m), S 10–20ft (3–6m). FH.

Whether growing as a large shrub or as a small tree this is magnificent for its foliage as well as for its flowers. Thick-textured bells, creamy or yellow, usually with purple marks on the inside, stand in bold trusses above large paddle-shaped leaves. These are deeply veined and felted brown on the underside.

R. moupinense *W. China*
Flowers: late winter to early spring. H and S 3–4ft (90–120cm). FH.
As a parent of many fine hybrids this is an important species but it is also a fine dwarf evergreen shrub in its own right provided it can be sheltered from early frosts. The rounded shiny leaves, paler and scaly on the reverse, are a quiet background for pale to dark pink funnel-shaped flowers, spotted with purple, that are usually borne in clusters of 2 or 3.

R. orbiculare *W. China*
Flowers: mid- to late spring. Foliage: year-round. H 8–10ft (2.5–3m), S 8–10ft (2.5–3m). FH.
The domed outline of this evergreen shrub and its heart-shaped pale green leaves, blue-green on the underside, are very pleasing. The bell-shaped flowers, borne in clusters of 7 to 10, are deep pink with a bluish tinge.

R. sinogrande *Burma, China, Tibet*
Foliage: year-round. Flowers: mid- to late spring. H 25–40ft (7.5–12m), S 25–35ft (7.5–11m). FH.
Just for the scale of its leaves, sometimes more than 30in (75cm) long and as much as 1ft (30cm) across, this is an impressive evergreen tree or large shrub. The upper surface is lustrous deep green, the underside downy with a silver or buff indumentum. The flowers are cream or yellow bells, usually stained purple inside, and they are borne in clusters of 20 to 30.

R. williamsianum *W. China*
Flowers: mid- to late spring. H and S 3–5ft (90–1.5cm). FH.
The spreading evergreen dome has bronze-tinted young growth, the mature leaves, often kidney shaped, becoming dark green and blue-green on the underside. The bell-shaped flowers borne singly or in small clusters, are red in bud, paling to soft pink on opening.

R. yakushimanum *Japan (Yakushima Island)*
Foliage: late spring to mid-summer. Flowers: late spring to early summer. H and S 6–7ft (1.8–2.2m). FH.

This parent of many very fine dwarf hybrids makes a compact evergreen dome, the leaves with a thick brown indumentum on the underside and, when young, with a fawn indumentum on the upper surface. Trusses of up to 10 deep pink buds open to paler pink, later white, funnel-shaped flowers.

RHODODENDRON HYBRIDS

R. 'Anna Baldsiefen'
Foliage: winter. Flowers: early spring. H and S 30–36in (75–90cm). FH.
The leaves of this dwarf evergreen turn bronze in winter. It has bright pink flowers with wavy darker margins, borne in dense clusters.

Rhododendron 'Anna Baldsiefen'

R. Bow Bells Group
Foliage: late spring to early summer. Flowers: late spring. H and S 6–7ft (1.8–2.2m). FH.
The long-stalked, bell-shaped flowers, which are borne in loose clusters, are deep pink in bud and a paler pink on opening. The foliage is copper tinted when young.

R. Cilpinense Group
Flowers: early spring. H and S 3–4ft (90–120cm). FH.
This evergreen rounded bush, which is one of the loveliest of the compact hybrids, carries numerous loose trusses of bell-shaped white flowers that are lightly tinged with pink. A light overhead canopy will help reduce the risk of frost damage to the flowers.

R. 'Curlew'
Flowers: mid-spring. H and S 20–24in (50–60cm). FH.
The pale yellow flowers with greenish brown markings on the inside cluster together in twos and threes on a dwarf spreading evergreen shrub. This is a small-leaved hybrid suitable for a cool raised bed.

R. 'Dopey'
Flowers: late spring. H and S 5–6ft (1.5–1.8m). FH.
The deep red bells carried in

rounded trusses fade slightly as they age but they are long lasting. This free-flowering and compact evergreen hybrid owes much to *R. yakushimanum*.

Rhododendron 'Dopey'

R. 'Fastuosum Flore Pleno'
Flowers: late spring to early summer. H and S 10–12ft (3–3.7m). FH.
This "iron-clad" rhododendron is of exceptional hardiness. It bears semi-double flowers that are mauve-blue.

R. 'Hydon Dawn'
Flowers: mid-spring to early summer. H and S 5–6ft (1.5–1.8m). FH.
Like one of its parents, *R. yakushimanum*, this compact evergreen shrub produces leaves that are covered with a pale indumentum on the upper surface when they are young. Frilly pale pink flowers, which fade almost to white, are carried in numerous dense trusses over the low mound of foliage.

Rhododendron 'Loderi King George'

R. 'Loderi King George'
Flowers: late spring to early summer. H and S 10–12ft (3–3.7m). FH.
The large evergreen rhododendrons of the Loderi group include several large shrubs or small trees that bear very large trusses of fragrant trumpet-shaped flowers. The pink buds of **'King George'** open to white flowers with a hint of green suffusing the throat.

R. 'Mrs G.W. Leak'

Flowers: mid-spring. H 10–12ft (3–3.7m), S 10–12ft (3–3.7m). FH.
The funnel-shaped flowers, borne in loose trusses on a large dark evergreen shrub, are pink with conspicuous deep brown and crimson interior markings.

Rhododendron 'Mrs G.W. Leak'

R. 'Pink Pearl'

Flowers: mid- to late spring. H and S 10–12ft (3–3.7m). FH.
Although tending to become lanky, especially if grown in shade, this tall large-leaved evergreen bears funnel-shaped pink flowers in splendid conical trusses. Brown markings give an attractive accent to the centre of the flowers.

R. 'Sappho'

Flowers: early summer. H 10–12ft (3–3.7m), S 8–10ft (2.5–3m). FH.
Although long in cultivation, this stands up well to the competition offered by other large hybrids. The funnel-shaped flowers, which are tightly clustered in dome-shaped trusses, are white with conspicuous purple and black markings in the throats.

AZALEA SPECIES

R. luteum *E. Europe to Caucasus*

Flowers: late spring to early summer; foliage: autumn. H 8–12ft (2.5–3.7m), S 7–10ft (2.2–3m). FH.
Funnel-shaped yellow flowers, sticky in bud and borne in trusses of up to 12, are strongly scented. The deciduous foliage often colours richly in autumn.

R. schlippenbachii *China (N. Manchuria), Korea*

Foliage: autumn. Flowers: mid- to late spring. H 8–13ft (2.5–4m), S 8–10ft (2.5–3m). FH.
This deciduous species is the perfect answer to those who find fault with the brash colours of many azaleas. The flowers, nearly saucer-shaped and borne up to 6 in a cluster, are pink or white, spotted with red. The leaves are purple, tinted when young, and colour well in autumn.

AZALEA HYBRIDS

R. 'Gibraltar'

Flowers: mid-spring. H and S 4–5ft (1.2–1.5m). FH.
This deciduous azalea is one of the numerous Knap Hill-Exbury crosses. The flowers, deep coloured in bud, are frilly and orange-red with a yellow flash. Another from the same background is **'Klondyke'**, with vibrant orange-yellow flowers of large size. The young foliage has copper tints.

R. 'Hino-mayo'

Flowers: mid-spring to early summer. H and S 24–30in (60–75cm). FH.
The evergreen Kurume azaleas, of which this is a fine example, originated in Japan. They flower prolifically and in colours that sometimes hurt the eye. **'Hinode-giri'** is bright crimson. 'Hino-mayo' is clear pink.

Rhododendron 'Narcissiflorum'

R. 'Narcissiflorum'

Flowers: late spring to early summer. H and S 5–8ft (1.5–2.5m). FH.
This deciduous shrub is a lovely representative of the **Ghent hybrids**, a group producing clusters of fragrant flowers. Those of 'Narcissiflorum' are pale yellow with darker shading on the outside and at the centre.

Rhododendron 'Spek's Orange'

R. 'Spek's Orange'

Flowers: late spring to early summer. H and S 6–8ft (1.8–2.5m). FH.
This bushy deciduous shrub bears dense clusters of bright orange-red flowers. It is scentless, like other **Mollis hybrids** but is untypical in flowering so late; most bloom just after mid-spring.

RHUS

ANACARDIACEAE Sumach

Most of the sumachs in cultivation are deciduous and are grown for the brilliant colouring of their foliage in autumn. However, this is a large genus comprising about 200 species of shrubs, trees and climbers, some of which are evergreen. Species are found in many parts of the temperate and tropical world. The poison ivy of North America (**R. radicans**) belongs to this genus.
CULTIVATION Require full sun and moist well-drained soil. In early spring coppice prune *R. typhina*.
PROPAGATION From seed sown in autumn. From semi-ripe cuttings in mid-summer. From root cuttings taken in winter. From removal of suckers when dormant.
POTENTIAL PROBLEMS Verticillium wilt, coral spot.
WARNING Contact with the foliage of some species of *Rhus* may cause allergic skin reactions.

R. glabra *North America*

Scarlet sumach, smooth sumach
Foliage: early to mid-autumn. Flowers: summer. Fruits: autumn. H and S 6–12ft (1.8–3.7m). FH.
The smooth leaflets turn dashing shades of red and yellow in autumn, when the scarlet and hairy fruit clusters are also conspicuous.

R. typhina *E. North America*

Stag's horn sumach, Velvet sumach
Foliage: autumn. Fruits: autumn to winter. H 10–15 ft (3–4.5m), S 12–20ft (3.7–6m). FH.
Its suckering nature is tiresome but this is a striking shrub or small tree. The large pinnate leaves, with lance-shaped paired leaflets, are impressive throughout summer and magnificent when they turn brilliant yellow, orange and purplish red in autumn. Male and female flowers are borne on separate plants. On female plants the dense clusters of dark crimson hairy fruits stand out as the leaves fall and remain as dark brown accents throughout winter. The sparsely branched irregular shape of the shrub also shows in winter but it is only young stems that have a velvet coating of red-brown hairs.
'Dissecta' is a female form with much divided leaves that are especially vivid in autumn. Another fully hardy ferny-leaved shrub

colouring sensationally in autumn is *R. × pulvinata* '**Red Autumn Lace**', a female plant with smooth stems.

Rhus typhina

RIBES

Grossulariaceae Flowering currant

As well as the culinary currants and gooseberries, this genus of about 150 mainly deciduous, occasionally evergreen, species contains a number of ornamental flowering shrubs. A few species come from South America but most are plants of temperate regions of the Northern Hemisphere, many of them growing in woodland or scrub. Their main use is in mixed borders but *R. sanguineum* can make an informal hedge.
Cultivation Require full sun and well-drained soil. After flowering cut about a fifth of the oldest stems down to ground level and reduce the flowered shoots down to lower, strong, new growths.
Propagation From hardwood cuttings, in winter (deciduous). From semi-ripe cuttings, in mid-summer (evergreens).
Potential problems Aphids; coral spot, honey fungus, leaf spot, powdery mildew.

R. sanguineum *W. North America*
Flowering currant
Flowers: mid-spring. H 6–7ft (1.8–2.2m), S 5–6ft (1.5–1.8m). FH.
This deciduous shrub has very upright growth and in spring is covered with numerous sprays of bright red flowers, their colour often being forced to fight it out with the bright yellows of forsythias and daffodils. At first the flower sprays droop, later they stand more erect. '**Pulborough Scarlet**' is a vigorous deep red cultivar with white-centred flowers and '**Tydeman's White**' is a good clean white. The strong coarse smell of the flowers is a shortcoming but this is not the case with the clove-scented
R. odoratum, a fully hardy species from central North America that grows to a height and spread of about 6ft (1.8m). In mid- to late spring it carries small sprays of bright yellow flowers.

R. speciosum *USA (California)*
Fuchsia-flowered currant
Flowers: mid- to late spring. H 6–8ft (1.8–2.5m), S 4–6ft (1.2–1.8m). FrH to FH.
Slender bright red flowers dangling in clusters of 3 or 4 give this plant a fuchsia-like grace. It is semi-evergreen and upright, the lobed leaves dark green and glossy and the stems thickly covered with reddish bristles. It is worth a place on a warm wall.

Ribes speciosum

ROSMARINUS

Lamiaceae Rosemary

Common rosemary is one of the happiest transfers from the physic to the ornamental garden. In a genus of 2 species it is the one that is known and loved for its evergreen aromatic foliage and usually pale blue flowers. In its Mediterranean homeland it is usually found with other sun-loving shrubs in stony dry ground. Many of these plants effortlessly make the transition to sunny well-drained gardens, rosemary growing among them or making a scented informal hedge.
Cultivation Require full sun and well-drained soil. Cut back any straggly stems to strong, lower, new growths in spring.
Propagation From seed sown in spring. From semi-ripe cuttings in summer.
Potential problems Honey fungus.

R. officinalis
Rosemary
Foliage: year-round. Flowers: mid-spring to early summer (often again in autumn and mild winters). H 5–6ft (1.5–1.8m), S 5ft (1.5m). FH.
Stems densely clothed with grey-green needle-like leaves, grey-white on the underside, are more or less upright but the shrub is of irregular shape and often sprawls. When the usual colour form produces its small flowers the effect is of a grey-

blue shrub. '**Severn Sea**', a spreading plant, is one of several rosemaries with flowers of brighter blue. '**Miss Jessopp's Upright**' is very erect, at least when young, a contrast to the **Prostratus Group**, regrettably the first to succumb in cold weather, with trailing stems.

Rosmarinus officinalis

RUBUS

Rosaceae

The best-known plants in this large genus of about 250 species are the blackberries and raspberries grown for their edible fruits. There are, however, several species that are ornamental on account of their flowers, fruits or stems. They are often plants of woodland but species are found in a very wide range of habitats almost worldwide.
Cultivation Tolerate sun or partial shade (species grown for winter stem colour require full sun) and require well-drained fertile soil. Cut stems of *R. cockburnianus* in early spring down to near ground level. Prune *R.* 'Benenden' after flowering, cutting about a fifth of old stems down to ground level and reducing the flowered shoots down to strong new growths.
Propagation From greenwood cuttings in summer (deciduous). From semi-ripe cuttings in summer (evergreens).
Potential problems Grey mould (*Botrytis*)

R. '**Benenden**'
Flowers: late spring to early summer. H 7–10ft (2.2–3m), S 8–10ft (2.5–3m). FH.
The large, saucer-shaped, white flowers, with a boss of yellow stamens, are of an unaffected and radiant splendour. Crowding spoils the superb effect of this large deciduous shrub with flowers so beautifully spaced along its arching thornless stems.

157

R. cockburnianus *China*
Flowers: early summer. H 7–9ft
(2.2–2.7m), S 6–8ft (1.8–2.5m).
FH.
The purplish flowers do not count
for much but in winter this arching
deciduous species has a ghostly
charm, the purplish ground colour
of its prickly stems being overlaid
by a white bloom.

Rubus cockburnianus

RUTA

RUTACEAE Rue

The best-known species in this
small genus of 8 aromatic shrubs
and subshrubs is said to have
medicinal properties. In the wild it
is found in sunny stony places.
CULTIVATION Tolerate full sun or
partial shade and require well-
drained soil. Cut back old stems to
fresh growth.
PROPAGATION From seed, sown in
spring. From semi-ripe cuttings, in
mid-summer.
POTENTIAL PROBLEMS Phytophthora
root rot.
WARNING Contact with the foliage
may cause photodermatitis.
Swallowing any part will cause
severe stomach upset.

Ruta graveolens 'Jackman's Blue'

R. graveolens *S.E. Europe*
Common rue
Flowers: mid- to late summer.
Foliage: evergreen. H 2–3ft (60–
90cm), S 24–30in (60–75cm). FH.
The pungently aromatic blue-green
leaves make a low bush bearing
greenish yellow flowers in summer.
The form usually seen in gardens is
'Jackman's Blue', with very dense
and glaucous foliage.

SALIX

SALICACEAE Willow

Many of the tree willows are fast-
growing and far too large for
modern gardens but this important
genus, with about 300 species,
contains a number of compact,
even dwarf shrubs. The genus is
represented in many parts of the
world but the deciduous shrubs
grown for their ornamental value
are essentially from temperate
regions of the Northern
Hemisphere. In the wild, however,
they are found in a surprising range
of habitats. The willows produce
male and female catkins, the male
catkins usually being the more
ornamental. See also TREES.
CULTIVATION Require full sun and
moist well-drained soil. Alpine and
dwarf species require very well-
drained gritty soil. Cut stems of
Salix grown for winter stems down
to about 6in (15cm) above ground
level in early spring annually or
according to the desired
dimensions of the shrub.
PROPAGATION From hardwood
cuttings, in winter. From cuttings,
in early summer.
POTENTIAL PROBLEMS Aphids,
sawflies, caterpillars, leaf beetles;
rust, anthracnose, honey fungus.

S. 'Boydii'
Foliage: late spring to autumn.
Flowers: early spring. H 1–2ft (30–
60cm), S 8–12in (20–30cm). FH.
Only a few dull catkins are
produced but the gnarled slow
growth and small grey-green leaves
that are deeply veined make this a
useful little shrub to combine with
alpines. It is a female clone.

S. caprea *Europe, W. Asia*
Goat willow
Flowers: early spring. H 25–30ft
(7.5–9m), S 20–25ft (6–7.5m). FH.
The goat willow is usually a large
shrub or small tree, the female with
silver catkins ("pussy willow"), the
male with large yellow catkins. The
weeping male form '**Kilmarnock**'
is grafted to make a miniature tree
about 6ft (1.8m) high.

Salix hastata 'Wehrhahnii'

S. hastata '**Wehrhahnii**'
Flowers: early spring. H and S 3–4ft
(90–120cm). FH.
The species is represented in
gardens by a slow-growing shrub,
which is decked in spring with
upright silver catkins that later turn
yellow. This is a male clone.

S. irrorata *S.W. USA*
Flowers: early spring. H 8–10ft
(2.5–3m), S 8–12ft (2.5–3.7m). FH.
The catkins appear before the
glossy green leaves, the male
having red anthers that turn
yellow. The shrub, though, is most
interesting in winter, when the
purplish stems are covered with
a white bloom.

S. lanata *N. Europe*
Woolly willow
Foliage: late spring to autumn.
Flowers: late spring; H 2–4ft (60–
120cm), S 2–5ft (60–150cm). FH.
In a rock garden the slow growth
rate is an advantage. This willow
gets its common name from its
felted grey-white leaves. The male
catkins are yellow, the longer
female catkins grey yellow.

SALVIA

LAMIACEAE Sage

It is difficult to draw a sharp line
between the shrubs and subshrubs
in this very large genus of about
900 species, which also includes
annuals, biennials and perennials.
Several of the Mediterranean
species, aromatic plants of sunny
dry habitats, do well in open
positions where there is free
drainage. See also PERENNIALS.
CULTIVATION Require full sun and
moist, light, well-drained soil that is
rich in organic matter (JI No. 2 or 3).
Protect frost-hardy species from
too much winter rain. Cut straggly
shoots back to lower new growth in
spring.
PROPAGATION From seed, annuals at
61–64°F (16–18°C) in mid-spring;
biennials in summer; perennials in
spring.
POTENTIAL PROBLEMS Slugs, snails.

S. officinalis *N. Africa,*
Mediterranean
Common sage
Flowers: early to mid-summer.
H 24–30in (60–75cm), S 2–3ft
(60–90cm). FH.
Its value as a culinary herb ensures
a place for this in the garden but its
grey-green aromatic leaves are also
ornamental. The colour variations
in the foliage can be used for
contrast. The variegated '**Icterina**'
has yellow and green leaves. In
purple sage (**Purpurascens Group**)

the purple colour is particularly pronounced in young foliage. The leaves of the frost hardy and less vigorous 'Tricolor' are grey-green with an irregular cream margin and are tinged with purplish pink. *S. lavandulifolia*, frost to fully hardy and up to 20in (50cm) tall, has narrow lavender-scented leaves and bears generous sprays of violet-blue flowers.

Salvia officinalis Purpurascens Group

SAMBUCUS

CAPRIFOLIACEAE Elder

The common elder (*S. nigra*) is such a weed that most gardeners would reject outright any advice to plant it. Some of its forms are, however, really handsome. 'Guincho Purple' is exceptional when the dark purple leaves, which turn red in autumn, provide a background for heads of dark pink buds and pale pink flowers. The American elder (*S. canadensis*) also has striking forms, the yellow-leaved 'Aurea' having red berries. These fully hardy plants, like many other shrubs and trees in this genus of about 25 species, are coarse but tolerate a wide range of conditions. *CULTIVATION* Tolerate full sun or partial shade and require moist, well-drained soil that is rich in organic matter. Coloured leaved kinds require dappled shade and should be cut down to within 1ft (30cm) of ground level in early spring. *PROPAGATION* From seed, sown in autumn. From cuttings, in summer. From hardwood cuttings, in winter. *POTENTIAL PROBLEMS* Blackfly; verticillium wilt. *WARNING* Contact with the foliage may irritate the skin. Swallowing any part may cause severe stomach upset.

S. racemosa Europe, Russia (W. Siberia) Red-berried elder Flowers: mid-spring. Fruits: mid to late summer. H 8–10ft (2.5–3m), S 8–10ft (2.5–3m). FH. In the plain green plant the pinnate

Sambucus racemosa 'Sutherland Gold'

leaves, divided into 5 to 7 leaflets, are a relatively subdued feature, the creamy flowers and especially the scarlet berries being more conspicuous. The picture changes when the leaflets are deeply cut and are bright yellow, as they are in 'Sutherland Gold'. 'Tenuifolia' makes a ferny green mound only about 3ft (90cm) high.

SANTOLINA

ASTERACEAE

The santolinas are aromatic evergreen shrubs of dry stony habitats in the Mediterranean. There are about 18 species in all, many of which have tightly packed grey leaves. These species tolerate heat and drought to a remarkable degree and even the green-leaved santolinas, such as the frost hardy *S. rosmarinifolia*, do well in dry conditions. The foliage is topped in summer by button-like flowerheads. *CULTIVATION* Require full sun and well-drained soil. Shear off spent flower stems in early spring. Older plants can be renovated by hard pruning. *PROPAGATION* From seed, sown in autumn or spring. From cuttings, in summer. *POTENTIAL PROBLEMS:* Usually none.

Santolina chamaecyparissus

S. chamaecyparissus C. and W. Mediterranean Cotton lavender Foliage: year-round. Flowers: mid to late summer. H 18–24in (45–60cm), S 18–24in (45–60cm). FH. The stems of this plant are grey-

white and felted, the leaves silvery and finely dissected. Plants lose their tight shape when they produce their yellow button flowerheads.

S. pinnata subsp. *neapolitana* Foliage: evergreen. Flowers: mid-summer. H 24–30in (60–75cm), S 2–3ft (60–90cm). FrH to FH. The foliage is very feathery and silvery white in exceptionally dry conditions and the flowerheads are bright lemon yellow.

SARCOCOCCA

BUXACEAE Christmas box, sweet box

These small bushy evergreens seem modest in every way but in winter their refined character shows in the sweet scent wafting from little tassel-like flowers. The berries of most species are purple or black. The dozen or so species, which are distributed from the Himalayas eastwards, are mainly plants of moist woodland. In gardens they will tolerate a wide range of conditions, doing well under trees, and make no distinctions between acid and alkaline soils. *CULTIVATION* Require partial or deep shade and moist well-drained soil. *PROPAGATION* From seed, sown in autumn or spring. From semi-ripe cuttings, taken in midsummer. By sucker removal, in late winter. *POTENTIAL PROBLEMS* Usually none.

Sarcococca hookeriana var. digyna

S. hookeriana var. *digyna* W. China Flowers: late winter. H and S 3–4ft (90–120cm). FH. The erect bush is filled with narrow glossy leaves, which almost hide the small creamy flowers. There are sometimes a few dark berries to follow. In 'Purple Stem' the young stems and even the leaf-stalks have a purplish colour. *S. confusa*, also fully hardy, is a slightly taller plant and carries heavy crops of purplish black berries into summer.

SKIMMIA

RUTACEAE

It is fortunate for gardeners that birds dislike the brilliant red berries produced by female plants of the best-known species. It is a member of a small evergreen genus, in the wild plants of woodland in the Himalayas and east Asia. Its shade tolerance, neat growth and long-lasting berries have made *S. japonica* a favourite of town gardeners.
CULTIVATION Require partial or full shade and moist well-drained soil that is rich in organic matter.
PROPAGATION From seed, sown in autumn. From semi-ripe cuttings, in mid-summer.
POTENTIAL PROBLEMS Scale insects.
WARNING Swallowing the fruits may cause mild stomach upset.

Skimmia japonica

S. japonica China, Japan, S.E. Asia
Flowers: mid- to late spring. Fruits: late summer to autumn. H 20–48in (50–120cm), S 20in (50cm). FH.
The species is variable but is usually a compact dome-shaped bush dense with oval leathery leaves, sometimes tinted on the reverse. The male plant **'Rubella'**, which grows to about 4ft (1.2m), has red stalks and a thin red rim to its dark green leaves. The tint is picked up in the numerous clusters of red-brown buds that stand through winter before opening in spring to sweetly scented white flowers. **'Nymans'**, a free-fruiting dwarf female clone, grows to about 3ft (90cm). **'Veitchii'**, also female, is more vigorous. These clones need a male plant nearby to produce berries. The fragrant hermaphrodite flowers of **subsp. *reevesiana* 'Robert Fortune'**, a low mound up to 3ft (90cm) high, produce colourful berries without the presence of a male plant.

SPARTIUM

PAPILIONACEAE Spanish broom

The single species brightens dry hillsides, open woodland and waste ground throughout the Mediterranean region. In the garden it is useful for covering dry sunny banks and as a fast-growing filler in new plantings.
CULTIVATION Requires full sun and well-drained soil. Coppice poor specimens in early spring to give them a new lease of life.
PROPAGATION From seed, sown in autumn or spring.
POTENTIAL PROBLEMS Usually none.

Spartium junceum

S. junceum N. Africa, S. Europe, Syria, Turkey, Ukraine (Crimea)
Flowers: early summer to early autumn. H 8–10ft (2.5–3m), S 7–10ft (2.2–3m). FrH to FH.
This shrub is deciduous but the green of its upright stems lasts throughout the year. The pea flowers, rich yellow and fragrant, are borne very freely. The seed pods that follow are brownish black in colour.

SPIRAEA

ROSACEAE

The best of the spiraeas are graceful deciduous or semi-evergreen shrubs with good foliage but it is for their flowers that most are grown. There are about 80 species found throughout temperate regions of the Northern Hemisphere and as far south as Mexico. Many are plants of moist woodland or woodland margins but several species are found in more open habitats. As garden plants they can be roughly divided into two main groups according to their season of flowering. Those that flower in spring do so on growths that are made in the previous year. Those that flower in summer do so on the current season's shoots.
CULTIVATION Require full sun and moist, fertile, well-drained soil. Cut down the flowered stems of plants that flowered on the previous year's stems to strong lower growths or buds. Cut down the stems of plants that flowered on the current season's shoots to within a few inches of ground level after flowering.

PROPAGATION From cuttings, in summer. By dividing suckering species, in late autumn.
POTENTIAL PROBLEMS Usually none.

S. 'Arguta'
Foam of May, bridal wreath
Flowers: mid- to late spring. H and S 6–8ft (1.8–2.5m) FH.
Wiry arching stems are crowded with small white flowers, a reliable display being maintained provided the twiggy growths are cut back annually after flowering.

Spiraea 'Arguta'

S. japonica China, Japan
Flowers: mid- to late summer. H 4–6ft (1.2–1.8m), S 4–5ft (1.2–1.5m). FH.
There are numerous cultivars of this variable summer-flowering species, usually with small pink flowers borne in flattish heads.
'Anthony Waterer', which grows to about 5ft (1.5m), has dark pink flowers and there are random shoots with cream or bronze-red leaves. **'Shirobana'**, only about 2ft (60cm) high, produces white and pink flowers in the same head. The popularity of **'Goldflame'** is a puzzle; the mound of bronzed orange foliage, about 30in (75cm) high, assertive in spring, fights with the pink of the flowers.

Spiraea japonica 'Goldflame'

S. × vanhouttei
Flowers: early summer. H 6–7ft (1.8–2.2m), S 4–5ft (1.2–1.5m). FH.
This earns a place in late spring or early summer with its snowy mass of tiny white flowers borne in dense clusters on every twig.
Thereafter it is a dull plant.

STACHYURUS

STACHYURACEAE

The best-known species are grown for their flowers in late winter or early spring. The individual flowers are small but the short catkin-like racemes are pretty hanging stiffly from bare stems and are conspicuous from late autumn, when the flowers are still in bud. The half dozen species of deciduous and semi-evergreen shrubs and small trees in the genus are mainly woodland plants that originate from the Himalayas and from east Asia.
CULTIVATION Tolerate full sun or partial shade and require well-drained moist soil that is rich in organic matter. Cut about a fifth of the oldest stems down to ground level annually.
PROPAGATION From seed, sown in autumn. From semi-ripe heel cuttings, taken in mid-summer.
POTENTIAL PROBLEMS Usually none.

Stachyurus praecox

S. praecox *Japan*
Flowers: late winter to early spring. H 6–12ft (1.8–3.7m), S 6–10ft (1.8–3m). FH.
Small pale yellow bells are closely set in short racemes about 4in (10cm) long and contrast well with purplish brown bare twigs. Another fully hardy species, **S. chinensis**, has slightly longer racemes and the flowers open a little later. **'Magpie'** is a variegated form which has oval finely tapered leaves that are grey-green with a broad creamy margin that often shows pink tints.

STEPHANANDRA

ROSACEAE

The flowers are pleasing enough but it is for their general character as graceful shrubs that these plants are grown. The 4 species, all from east Asia, are plants of woodland margins or shrubby thickets with moist conditions.
CULTIVATION Tolerate full sun or partial shade and require well-drained, moist, fertile soil. Cut the

stems down to strong lower growths or buds after flowering.
PROPAGATION From cuttings, in summer. By rooted sucker separation, in autumn. From hardwood cuttings, in late autumn.
POTENTIAL PROBLEMS Usually none.

Stephanandra tanakae

S. tanakae *Japan*
Foliage: autumn. Flowers: early to mid-summer. H 5–8ft (1.5–2.5m), S 6–8ft (1.8–2.5m). FH.
This suckering shrub forms a thicket of arching stems that are bright greenish or orange-brown in colour. The broad leaves, sharply toothed and tapering to a point, turn rich shades of yellow and orange in autumn. Airy clusters of yellow-green flowers are a diversion in summer. **S. incisa** **'Crispa'**, also fully hardy, makes a low dense thicket of arching stems to a height of about 2ft (60cm) with a good showing of greenish white flowers and splendid foliage colours in autumn.

SYMPHORICARPOS

CAPRIFOLIACEAE Snowberry

The best-known species and hybrids are valued for their white berries, which are shunned by birds and therefore longlasting. However, the berry colour varies among the 15 or so species, all deciduous and found in a range of woodland and more open habitats, mainly in North and Central America. The coral berry or Indian currant (**S. orbiculatus**), best known in its fully hardy variegated forms, has purplish red fruits. Their tolerance of shade and adaptability to a wide range of soils makes the snowberries useful, but to produce heavy crops of berries they need sun and good growing conditions.
CULTIVATION Tolerate full sun or partial shade and require well-drained soil. Cut straggly stems down to ground level in early spring.
PROPAGATION: From cuttings, in summer. From hardwood cuttings, in autumn. By division of suckering specimens, in autumn.
POTENTIAL PROBLEMS Usually none.

WARNING Contact with the fruits may irritate the skin. Swallowing the fruits may cause mild stomach upset.

S. × doorenbosii
Flowers: mid- to late summer. Fruits: early autumn to mid-winter. H 6–7ft (1.8–2.2m), S 6–20ft (1.8–6m). FH.
Several of the best snowberries go under this name. **'Mother of Pearl'** is a bushy dense shrub with heavy crops of white berries that are flushed pink. **'White Hedge'**, usually no more than 5ft (1.5m) high, is compact and erect with marble-like white berries. In the background of these hybrids is another fully hardy hybrid, **S. × chenaultii**, often grown in its own right, especially in the dwarf form **'Hancock'**. This makes good ground cover at about 3ft (90cm) high but produces rather thin crops of pink berries.

Symphoricarpos × doorenbosii 'White Hedge'

SYRINGA

OLEACEAE Lilac

When the period bridging spring and summer is spoken of as "lilac time" what people have in mind is the common lilac (*S. vulgaris*) and its numerous cultivars, with their fragrant flowers densely clustered in cone-shaped panicles. But it is, too, the season of several other graceful and somewhat neglected lilacs. Some of these are large but there are also several compact shrubs that are suitable for small gardens. There are about 20 species of lilac, all of them deciduous shrubs and trees, most of them found in woodland and scrub. Many are Asiatic in origin; some come from eastern Europe.
CULTIVATION Require full sun and well-drained neutral to alkaline soil that is rich in organic matter.
PROPAGATION From greenwood cuttings, in early summer.
By layering, in early summer. By grafting or budding, in mid-summer.
POTENTIAL PROBLEMS Leaf miners, thrips; lilac blight, honey fungus.

S. komarovii subsp. reflexa
C. China

Flowers: late spring to early summer. H 10–14ft (3–4.3m), S 6–10ft (1.8–3m). FH.
Where there is space this justifies inclusion with its long drooping panicles, the flowers purplish pink in bud, paler on opening. It is a parent of a fine fully hardy hybrid of similar size, **S. × josiflexa** 'Bellicent', with large panicles of fragrant clear pink flowers and the "Canadian Hybrids" (**S. × prestoniae**), large, though less elegant shrubs that have been bred for hardiness. One of the best of these is 'Elinor', with erect panicles of mauve-pink flowers opening from darker buds.

Syringa pubescens subsp. *microphylla* 'Superba'

S. pubescens subsp. microphylla W. China

Flowers: early summer, often in autumn. H 6–10ft (1.8–3m), S 5–8ft (1.5–2.5). FH.
The form most widely grown is 'Superba', a twiggy bush with small rounded leaves which at its main flush bears numerous panicles of small fragrant flowers that are rich pink in bud, paler on opening. It continues to flower intermittently until autumn, especially if encouraged with watering and feeding. Another fully hardy small twiggy lilac is **S. meyeri var. spontanea** 'Palibin'. It grows slowly to a height of 4–5ft (1.2–1.5m) and the bushes are well covered in early summer with panicles of mauve-tinted pink flowers that are sweetly scented.

Syringa vulgaris 'Primrose'

S. vulgaris E. Europe

Flowers: late spring to early summer. H and S 22ft (7m). FH.
In gardens numerous cultivars have taken the place of the species, a vigorous large suckering shrub or small tree bearing small mauve flowers. They are clustered in cone-shaped panicles when the leaves, more or less heart-shaped, are well developed. The flowers of the cultivars have retained the refined scent of the parent but are larger and the panicles are more densely packed. There are singles and doubles and the colour range includes white and cream as well as various shades of mauve and purple, some leaning to blue, others to pink and red. Well-established cultivars include: 'Andenken an Ludwig Späth', with slender panicles of single wine-red flowers on a spreading shrub; 'Firmament', with panicles of single mauve-blue flowers; 'Katherine Havemeyer', with double flowers mauve-pink in bud making dense purplish blue panicles; 'Madame Lemoine', with creamy buds opening to make dense white panicles; 'Mrs Edward Harding', with long panicles of red-purple double flowers; and 'Primrose' with single pale yellow flowers.

TAMARIX

Tamaricaceae Tamarisk

Several of the tamarisks are astonishing survivors of extreme conditions. In the deserts of north Africa and the Middle East, for instance, the shade tree, *T. aphylla*, survives great heat and drought and tolerates high levels of salinity. There are just over 50 species of these deciduous trees and shrubs, and several are good for gardens, especially in coastal areas. Despite the light feathery foliage, they make useful windbreaks. If grown freely, they can become angular trees and it is better to maintain them as shrubs by pruning.
Cultivation Require full sun and well-drained soil. Require protection from drying winds in inland gardens.
Propagation From semi-ripe cuttings, in summer. From hardwood cuttings, in winter.
Potential problems Usually none.

T. ramosissima S.E. Europe to Asia

Flowers: late summer to early autumn. H and S 12–15ft (3.7–4.5m). FH.
Arching red-brown stems carry pale grey-green foliage and plumes of soft pink flowers, more richly

Tamarix ramosissima

coloured in 'Pink Cascade', are carried on growths made in the current year. *T. tetranda*, also fully hardy, has greener foliage, and carries sprays of pink flowers on growths made the preceding year.

TEUCRIUM

Lamiaceae

Only a few species are widely grown and these are mainly shrubs or sub-shrubs from southern Europe and the Mediterranean area. The genus, however, has about 300 species, distributed worldwide.
Cultivation Requires full sun and well-drained soil.
Propagation From softwood cuttings, in early summer with bottom heat. From semi-ripe cuttings, in mid-summer with bottom heat.
Potential problems Usually none.

Teucrium fruticans

T. fruticans W. Mediterranean
Shrubby germander

Flowers: summer. H 24–39in (60–100cm), S 12ft (4m). FrH.
The stems and undersides of the leaves are covered with a white, silvery felt. The long-lipped flowers of this aromatic evergreen are pale blue and borne over a long season. In cold gardens it is best grown at the foot of a warm wall.

THYMUS

Lamiaceae Thyme

The common thyme (*T. vulgaris*) was long ago brought into gardens so that its aromatic foliage could be gathered fresh for medicinal and

culinary purposes. Other thymes also please with the piquant scent of their crushed leaves, particularly when planted in paving. Some have attractive golden or variegated foliage and most flower freely. Thymes are sun-lovers, most cultivated species coming from southern Europe and the Mediterranean region. The genus is large with 300 to 400 species of evergreen shrubs and subshrubs distributed in Europe and Asia.
CULTIVATION Require full sun and well-drained neutral to alkaline soil.
PROPAGATION From seed, sown in spring. From semi-ripe cuttings, in mid to late summer.
POTENTIAL PROBLEMS Usually none.

T. × citriodorus
Lemon thyme
Flowers: summer. H 8–12in (20–30cm), S 10–18in (25–45cm). FH.
The leaves are broad and valued for their lemon scent and the flowers are mauve-pink. There are several golden-leaved and variegated forms, most retaining the citric scent. The leaves of '**Silver Queen**' have cream variegation.

T. serpyllum *Europe*
Flowers: summer. H 2–3in (5–8cm), S 12–18in (30–45cm). FH.
Purple flower spikes cover mats of hairy leaves. There are numerous named forms. '**Pink Chintz**' bears masses of pink flowers.

Thymus serpyllum

T. vulgaris *W. Mediterranean*
Flowers: late spring to early summer. H 6–12in (15–30cm), S 16in (40cm). FH.
Bushes are variable in size but, at least when young, the wiry stems are densely covered with dark green leaves. The flowers are pink or white. '**Silver Posie**' has leaves with a cool white variegation.

VIBURNUM

CAPRIFOLIACEAE

The viburnums are mainly shrubs and trees of woodland and thickets in the temperate regions of the Northern Hemisphere but the genus extends into south-east Asia and South America. Among the 150 or so species there are several fine deciduous and evergreen shrubs for temperate gardens, several outstanding for their winter flowers.
CULTIVATION Tolerate full sun or partial shade and require fertile moist but well-drained soil. Shelter evergreen plants from wind in cold areas.
PROPAGATION From seed, in autumn. From greenwood cuttings, in summer (deciduous); semi-ripe cuttings, in summer (evergreens).
POTENTIAL PROBLEMS: Aphids, viburnum beetles; honey fungus.

V. × bodnantense
Flowers: late autumn to spring. H 8–12ft (2.5-3.7m), S 5–8ft (1.5-2.5m). FH.
Two winter-flowering deciduous species, the Chinese *V. farreri* and the Himalayan *V. grandiflorum*, are the parents of this rather stiff upright shrub, which eventually makes more arching growth. Dense clusters of pink-tinged white flowers that hang from bare stems open over several months. '**Charles Lamont**' and '**Dawn**' are rich pink.

Viburnum carlesii '**Charis**'

V. carlesii *Japan, Korea*
Flowers: mid- to late spring. H and S 5–6ft (1.5-1.8m). FH.
The rounded bush is in leaf when pink buds open to fragrant white flowers. The fruits that follow are deep black. '**Aurora**' has pink flowers opening from red buds. The flowers of the compact form '**Diana**' are similar but fade to near white and its young foliage is purple tinted. This deciduous species is a parent of several fine fully hardy hybrids with fragrant flowers in mid- to late spring. '**Charis**' has a profusion of white flowers. Those going under the name *V. × burkwoodii* are semi-evergreen, with clusters of pink buds opening to white flowers. '**Anne Russell**' is a compact shrub about 6ft (1.8m) high and '**Park Farm Hybrid**' as much as 8ft (2.5m) in height and spread. By unfair comparison *V. × carlcephalum* is a less refined deciduous shrub but its foliage is tinted in autumn and it is handsome when the large heads of pink buds open to white flowers. It is an upright plant to about 8ft (2.5m). *V. × juddii* is bushy and more compact, with a height and spread of about 5ft (1.5m), and has pink-tinged white flowers.

Viburnum davidii

V. davidii *W. China*
Flowers: late spring. H and S 3–5ft (90–150cm). FH.
The glossy oval leaves, three nerves boldly cutting into their surface, create low tiers of dark green foliage. The flat heads of small white flowers are followed by long-lasting egg-shaped berries of turquoise blue. Several specimens must be planted close together to ensure worthwhile crops of these lustrously metallic berries.

V. opulus *Europe, N. Africa, C. Asia*
Guelder rose
Flowers: late spring to early summer. H 10–15ft (3-4.5m), S 8–12ft (2.5-3.7m). FH.
This is a large deciduous shrub of many parts. Its maple-like deciduous foliage colours well during the autumn months. Its heads of white flowers are ringed by sterile florets and the bunches of red fruits gleam enticingly. '**Compactum**', with a height and spread of 5ft (1.5m), flowers and fruits freely. '**Xanthocarpum**' bears yellow fruits. The snowball tree ('**Roseum**') carries rounded heads of white flowers, often tinted pink, that are sterile.

Viburnum opulus

V. plicatum

Japanese snowball bush
Flowers: late spring. H 8–12ft
(2.5–3.7m), S 10–15ft (3–4.5m). FH.
This deciduous shrub is variable in
its growth, most forms being
spreading but some having a
markedly tiered arrangement of
horizontal branches that easily
spoiled by crowding. In its various
forms there are differences also in
the flowerheads, some consisting
entirely of crowded white infertile
florets, others with small creamy
white fertile flowers surrounded
by a ring of infertile florets.
'**Grandiflorum**' has large heads of
sterile flowers that are tinged pink.
The branches of '**Mariesii**' are in
tiered layers and the flowerheads
consist mainly of infertile florets.
'**Nanum Semperflorens**' is a
compact plant which slowly
reaches a height of 5ft (1.5m) or
so and produces small white
flowers from late spring to early
autumn.

V. tinus *Mediterranean*

Laurustinus
Flowers: late winter to spring.
H and S 8–12ft (2.5–3.7m). FH.
Municipal planting has made the
lauristinus seem dull but a dense
evergreen bush of dark foliage
flowering generously from autumn
through to spring is not to be
despised. The flat heads of pink
buds open to small white flowers,
which are followed by blue-black
fruits. '**Eve Price**' and '**Gwenllian**'
are both compact and have flowers
that are strongly pink tinted in bud.
'Gwenllian' fruits freely.

WEIGELA

CAPRIFOLIACEAE

The weigelas most commonly seen
in gardens are hybrids that are
valued as reliable and easy shrubs.
The dozen species in the genus are
plants of woodland margins or
more open scrub in temperate east
Asia. The flowers, borne on growth
made in the previous year, are
bell- or funnel-shaped. The
predominant colours are pinks and
reds. **W. middendorffiana** carries
soft yellow flowers, with orange
spots accenting the throat. This is a
lovely and reasonably hardy shrub
growing to about 5ft (1.5m) but its
precocious early shoots are
sometimes damaged by frost.
CULTIVATION Tolerate full sun or
partial shade and require fertile
well-drained soil.
PROPAGATION From hardwood
cuttings, in autumn to winter.
POTENTIAL PROBLEMS Leaf and
bud eelworm.

***Weigela florida* 'Foliis Purpureis'**

W. florida *N. China, Korea*

Flowers: late spring to early
summer. H and S 6–8ft (1.8–2.5m).
FH.
This is a vigorous bush with
arching stems well covered with
light green leaves and in its season
numerous clusters of reddish pink
flowers with a pale interior. '**Foliis
Purpureis**', a compact plant about
3ft (90cm) high, combines purplish
foliage and soft pink flowers. The
attractive leaves of '**Variegata**', with
a creamy yellow margin, contrast
with the pink flowers.

W. hybrids

Flowers: late spring to early summer.
H and S 6–8ft (1.8–2.5m). FH.
The family resemblance of these is
very strong even though some may
show characteristics hinting at one
or other parent. '**Abel Carrière**' is a
spreading bush with purplish red
buds opening to deep pink flowers
with a gold spot in the throat.
'**Bristol Ruby**' is vigorous with
erect dark red flowers. '**Candida**' is
compact with green buds opening
to white flowers and '**Newport
Red**' is erect with dark red flowers
and contrasting off-white anthers.

YUCCA

AGAVACEAE

Impressive spikes of bell-shaped
flowers contrast with rosettes of
evergreen sword-like leaves. The
yuccas, some stemless, others tree-
like, are plants of dry or desert
habitats in North and Central
America and the West Indies. There
are about 40 species in this genus,
some which are of great value in
desert gardens and several add a
jagged exoticism when translated
to sunny positions in temperate
gardens. The heights given in the
head information are for foliage
rosettes.
CULTIVATION Require full sun and
well-drained soil.
PROPAGATION From seed, sown in
spring with bottom heat. From
rooted suckers, in spring.
POTENTIAL PROBLEMS Aphids;
leaf spot.

Y. filamentosa *USA (New Jersey to Florida)*

Adam's needles
Flowers: mid- to late summer.
H 5–6ft (1.5–1.8m), S 3–4ft
(90–120cm). FH.
The stiff grey-green leaves forming
a stemless rosette are edged with
thread-like curling hairs. The
compact flowering spike of creamy
bells reaches 5ft (1.5m). The leaves
of '**Bright Edge**' have yellow
margins. Our Lord's candle
(**Y. whipplei**) is magnificent but
less hardy. A spiked narrow grey-
blue rosette has massive clusters of
lemon-scented ivory bells, over 10ft
(3m) high. Plants take many years
to flower and, having flowered, die.

Y. flaccida *USA (N. Carolina to Alabama)*

Flowers: mid- to late summer.
H and S 4–5ft (1.2–1.5m). FH.
The rosettes on this almost stemless
shrub have narrow grey-green limp
leaves that arch at the tips and have
threads along their margins. The
graceful flower spikes, up to 5ft
(1.5m) high, have many creamy
bells, greenish in bud. '**Golden
Sword**' has yellow variegated leaves,
'**Ivory**' is impressive in flower.

Y. gloriosa *USA (N. Carolina to Florida)*

Spanish dagger
Flowers: late summer to autumn.
H 6–8ft (1.8–2.5m), S 4–6ft (1.2–
1.8m). FrH.
The woody trunk bears rosettes of
blue-green to dark-green leaves. The
spike of bell-shaped flowers,
creamy white with a pink tinge,
can be more than 6ft (1.8m) high.
'**Variegata**' has leaves with a
yellow edge. The fully hardy
Y. recurvifolia has dark grey-green
foliage, the outer leaves of each
rosette recurving. The flower
spikes of creamy white bells are up
to 6ft (1.8m) high.

Yucca gloriosa

conifers

Cone-bearing trees, which are mainly evergreen, include the giants of the plant world. Two Californian species that set records are the coastal redwoods (*Sequoia sempervirens*), for height, and the giant redwoods (*Sequoiadendron giganteum*), for bulk. Compact and slow-growing species are found in harsh environments, such as tundra and rocky mountains. Many conifers propagated from sports are also dwarf, some never living down their freakish origins. In between the giants and the pygmies are many conifers of intermediate size, some of which make very large stands in the wild. An addition is the maidenhair tree (*Ginkgo biloba*), a living fossil but not a true conifer.

Conifers, more primitive than flowering plants, have separate male and female flowers. Pollen from the male flowers, borne on a spike (strobilus), is carried by wind to female strobili that are usually round- or barrel-shaped. When the naked ovules of the female strobilus are fertilized the scales usually become woody, forming the familiar cones. Even the "berries" of conifers such as junipers (*Juniperus*) are simply fleshy cones. Many species are best raised from seed but cultivars are raised commercially from cuttings or grafted. The best time to plant is in early to mid-spring. Little pruning is generally required.

Top Cedrus deodara
Centre Juniperus horizontalis 'Blue Chip'
Bottom Larix decidua

ABIES

PINACEAE Silver fir

There are more than 50 species of fir widely distributed throughout the Northern Hemisphere. Many grow to a prodigious size; the giant fir (**A. grandis**) of western North America can exceed 300ft (90m). Most species have compact or dwarf forms. Some of these are of considerable garden value, although they lack the majestic conical shape and tiered horizontal branches that make these trees so impressive in the wild.
CULTIVATION Tolerate full sun or partial shade and require moist soil that is neutral to acid.
PROPAGATION From seed, sown outdoors in late winter. From grafting, under glass in early autumn or late winter to early spring (cultivars).
POTENTIAL PROBLEM Adelgids.

A. balsamea f. hudsonia
C. and E. Canada, E. USA
Foliage: year-round. H and S 2–3ft (60–90cm). FH.
The balsam fir (**A. balsamea**) grows to 80ft (25m), but this curiosity makes a compact spherical mound. It does not produce cones.

Abies balsamea f. hudsonia

A. concolor *S.W. USA to N. Mexico*
White fir
Foliage: year-round. H 50–100ft (15–30m), S 15–25ft (4.5–7.5m). FH.
An alternative to the handsome but tall upright species, which has blue- or grey-green foliage, '**Compacta**' grows to 6ft (1.8m) and can have a spread of 10ft (3m). It seldom produces cones and its short leaves are steely blue.
A. lasiocarpa '**Arizonica Compacta**', a slow-growing form of the corkbark fir from south-west USA, is another blue-grey conifer of moderate size, reaching 15ft (4.5m).

A. koreana *S. Korea*
Korean fir
Foliage: year-round. H 20–30ft (6–9m), S 10–20ft (3–6m). FH.
This very hardy and slow-growing fir is exceptional in producing its

Abies koreana

violet-blue cones when only 5 to 10 years old and as small as 3ft (90cm) high. It makes a broad pyramid, the spiky foliage dark green on the upper surface and bright silver underneath. Even slower in growth is '**Silberlocke**'. This has a silvery sheen caused by the leaves as they twist on themselves and show their silvery undersides. Young pale green cones ripen to a dark yellow.

ARAUCARIA

ARAUCARIACEAE

Most of the 18 species of this genus from the Southern Hemisphere need a warm temperate climate. The curiously symmetrical Norfolk Island pine (**A. heterophylla**) is sometimes grown as a shade-tolerant house plant. The hardiest is the monkey puzzle (**A. araucana**), which is best grown as a specimen, uncluttered by close planting.
CULTIVATION Require an open position and moist but well-drained soil. Water young plants well.
PROPAGATION From seed, sown in a propagator or greenhouse with a temperature of 68°F (20°C).
POTENTIAL PROBLEMS Usually none.

Araucaria araucana

A. araucana *Argentina, Chile*
Chilean pine, monkey puzzle
Foliage: year-round. H 50–80ft (15–25m), S 20–30ft (6–9m). FH.
On the highly distinctive mature specimens, the long branches, which are densely clothed with darkly glossy spine-tipped leaves, sweep downwards, sometimes almost to ground level. The spiky cones take 3 years to mature.

CALOCEDRUS

CUPRESSACEAE Incense cedar

The hardiest of the 3 species of evergreen conifers in this genus, the North American *C. decurrens* makes a handsome specimen tree for parks and large gardens. Other species are Asiatic.
CULTIVATION Requires an open sheltered position and a well-drained, preferably acid, soil.
PROPAGATION From seed, sown outdoors in late winter or early spring. From hardwood cuttings, in early autumn (essential for variegated forms).
POTENTIAL PROBLEM Scale insects.

Calocedrus decurrens

C. decurrens *W. North America*
Foliage: year-round. H 40–130ft (12–39m), S 2–10ft (60–300cm). FH.
The dark green column is tightly packed with sprays of aromatic scale-like leaves which are carried on short horizontal branches. The cylindrical cones, rust-coloured when mature, are about 1in (2.5cm) in length.

CEDRUS

PINACEAE Cedar

Mature cedars are among the most magnificent trees of parkland. The 4 species, all evergreens from the Himalayas and the Mediterranean region, are conical when young but, with age, they become broad and irregular in outline. The needle-like leaves grow in dense clusters and the barrel-shaped cones ripen slowly from purplish green to brown.

CULTIVATION Require full sun and well-drained soil.

PROPAGATION From seed, sown outdoors in spring. From grafting, in a propagator in late winter to early spring. From cuttings, in late summer (cultivars).

POTENTIAL PROBLEMS Root rot, stem rot, honey fungus.

Cedrus deodara

C. deodara *W. Himalayas*
Deodar cedar
Foliage: year-round. H 60–120ft (18–36m), S 15–30ft (4.5–9m). FH. The drooping tips of the branches give this fast-growing blue-grey conifer a languid air. '**Aurea**', which slowly attains a height of 15ft (4.5m), has yellow-green foliage.

Cedrus libani **subsp.** *atlantica*

C. libani **subsp.** **atlantica** *Asia minor, Syria*
Atlas cedar
Foliage: year-round. H 80–130ft (25–39m), S 15–30ft (4.5–9m). FH. The ascending branches and upright leader are distinctive but, eventually, specimens can develop

the flat-topped outline associated with the cedar of Lebanon. The foliage is green or grey-green but in the blue cedars (**Glauca Group**) it is a silvery blue. '**Glauca Pendula**' has weeping branches and glaucous leaves and rarely exceeds 15ft (4.5m) tall; the branches may need to be staked. The cedar of Lebanon (**C. libani** subsp. **libani**) has tiered arching branches, which can spread to 100ft (30m) or more, with dense flat layers of grey-green foliage. The cones are grey-green with a hint of pink. **C. libani** subsp. **libani** '**Sargentii**' is slow-growing, to 5ft (1.5m), but the weeping branches with blue-green leaves can ultimately have a spread of more than 20ft (6m).

CHAMAECYPARIS

CUPRESSACEAE False cypress

Although there are only 7 species of these natives of eastern North America, Japan and Taiwan, the false cypresses are represented in gardens by numerous cultivars, offering a vast choice in shape, size, growth rate and foliage colour, often at its best during the coldest winters. A standard feature is the broad frond-like foliage which has a flattened appearance. Young plants are usually conical in outline but spread with age.

CULTIVATION Tolerate full sun or partial shade and a wide range of soils, but best on neutral to acid soils. Trim hedges between late spring and early autumn.

PROPAGATION From seed, sown outdoors in late winter. From semi-ripe cuttings, taken in late summer to early autumn. By grafting, under cover in early spring (cultivars).

POTENTIAL PROBLEMS Aphids; phytophthora, honey fungus, root rot.

C. lawsoniana *North America*
Lawson cypress
Foliage: year-round. H 50–130ft (15–39m), S 6–15ft (1.8–4.5m). FH. This elegant and narrow columnar tree, with its characteristic drooping leading shoot, will quickly outgrow all but the largest of gardens. The dense dark green leaves are arranged in pairs along shoots which are a rich reddish brown when young, ageing to a dull grey-brown. The cones are small and round. '**Green Hedger**', vigorous and upright, with light green leaves, makes a good hedge when clipped. Columnar forms that usually grow to 15–25ft (4.5–7.5m) high include '**Alumnii**', with upright branches and large sprays of blue-grey foliage; the

narrow 30ft (9m) tall '**Ellwoodii**', with dense sprays of grey-green leaves which are bluer in winter; and the slow-growing '**Fletcheri**', dense and erect with grey-green foliage. Dwarf cultivars include '**Minima Aurea**', compact and very hardy, making an oval mound some 3ft (90cm) high of two-tone foliage, golden on the upper surface and yellow underneath; and '**Minima Glauca**', which forms a 6ft (1.8m) ball of sea-green sprays.

Chamaecyparis obtusa '*Crippsii*'

C. obtusa *Japan*
Hinoki cypress
Foliage: year-round. H 50–70ft (15–22m), S 15–20ft (4.5–6m). FH. This cone-shaped tree has horizontal spreading branches with shiny, aromatic, dark green leaves, the undersides marked white and the leaf tips blunt. The small rounded cones ripen from green to brown. '**Crippsii**', slow-growing to 50ft (15m), has bright golden new growth which fades to yellow-green. It reaches a height of around 30ft (9m). Semi-dwarf cultivars include '**Nana Gracilis**', which grows to 8ft (2.5m) with glossy dark green foliage, and '**Tetragona Aurea**', which reaches twice this height, with bright gold foliage at its best in full sun. '**Kosteri**', one of several dwarf cultivars, makes a tight cone of bright green, eventually reaching 4ft (1.2m).

Chamaecyparis obtusa '*Kosteri*'

C. pisifera *Japan*
Sawara cypress
Foliage: year-round. H 50–70ft
(15–22m), S 12–15ft (3.7–4.5m).
FH.

The species is conical, with sharply pointed, scale-like, aromatic leaves which are bright green with a white line on the underside. Its cultivars include one of the most popular of all conifers, **'Boulevard'**, outstanding for its soft steely blue foliage, tinged purple in winter. It grows to 30ft (9m). **'Filifera Aurea'**, which is slow to exceed 10ft (3m) but commonly spreads to 15ft (4.5m), has slender, elongated, yellow foliage on drooping stems.

Chamaecyparis pisifera
'Filifera Aurea'

CRYPTOMERIA

TAXODIACEAE Japanese cedar

The single species is an elegant fast-growing evergreen that is generally represented in gardens by its compact cultivars.
CULTIVATION Tolerate full sun or partial shade and a wide range of soils, but perform best on those that are moist and slightly acid.
PROPAGATION From semi-ripe cuttings with a heel, taken in early autumn and placed in a coldframe over winter.
POTENTIAL PROBLEM Honey fungus.

C. japonica *Japan*
Foliage: year-round. H 50–80ft
(15–25m), S 15–20ft (4.5–6m). FH.
The attractive, soft, orange-red bark shreds into fine strips as the tree ages. The thin, needle-like, evergreen leaves are mid-green, deepening to dark green, and densely packed in spirals along the extended, slender, lateral branches.
'Elegans', which eventually forms a small tree 20–30ft (6–9m) high, retains its soft and feathery juvenile foliage, although this changes colour through the year, from silver in spring and green in summer, to blue-red in autumn and bronze-red in winter. **'Elegans Compacta'**, slower growing to 12ft (3.7m), has even softer more feathery foliage, which turns dark purple in winter.

'Vilmoriniana', with a height and spread of only 3ft (90cm), has dense light green foliage that turns reddish brown in winter.

Cryptomeria japonica **'Vilmoriniana'**

× CUPRESSOCYPARIS

CUPRESSACEAE

Leyland cypresses are fast-growing with dense, resilient, scale-like foliage, which makes them suitable for shelter belts, even coastal areas. However, their rapid growth counts against them as hedging plants since they require frequent cutting.
CULTIVATION Tolerate full sun or partial shade and a wide range of soils, although prefer moist neutral to acid soils. Trim hedges several times annually between late spring and early autumn.
PROPAGATION From semi-ripe cuttings, taken in spring or autumn.
POTENTIAL PROBLEMS Canker, honey fungus.

× *Cupressocyparis leylandii*

× C. leylandii
Leyland cypress
Foliage: year-round. H 100–120ft
(30–36m), S 15–20ft (4.5–6m). FH.
As a specimen tree, this cypress forms a dense column of dark green or grey-green foliage which is held in flat dense sprays. The small cones are round and dark brown. The bronze-yellow **'Castlewellan'** is less vigorous, forming a straighter column with a flatter crown.

CUPRESSUS

CUPRESSACEAE Cypress

The true cypresses, of which there are 20 or so species, are plants of dry landscapes. They have scale-like aromatic leaves, and the round cones, which are green when new and woody from the second year, often remain on the tree for years. Included among them are the Monterey cypress (*C. macrocarpa*), which is columnar when young but gauntly cedar-like as an old specimen; the gracefully weeping but only half-hardy Kashmir cypress (*C. torulosa* **'Cashmeriana'**) and the Arizona cypress (*C. arizonica*).
CULTIVATION Require full sun, well-drained soil and protection from cold winds.
PROPAGATION From semi-ripe cuttings with a heel, taken in early to mid-autumn and placed in a coldframe or with bottom heat.
POTENTIAL PROBLEMS Phytophthora, canker, honey fungus.

Cupressus sempervirens

C. sempervirens *Mediterranean, West Asia*
Italian cypress, Mediterranean cypress
Foliage: year-round. H 30–60ft
(9–18m), S 3–15ft (90–450cm). FH.
This narrow upright tree, so evocative of the Tuscan landscape, has upward-pointing branches and erect sprays of dark green leaves. The leaves are short, stubby and closely packed together, completely covering the twigs. Young plants may be damaged by freezing winter winds. The pencil pine (**'Stricta'**) is a narrower tree with flaking grey-brown bark.

GINKGO

GINKGOACEAE Maidenhair tree

To use Charles Darwin's term, the single species in this genus is a "living fossil", an astonishing survivor of a primitive plant group. It is thought to be unknown in the wild but was widely grown in imperial and temple gardens of China. Its tolerance of pollution makes it a useful city tree.

CULTIVATION Tolerate sun or partial shade and require well-drained soil.
PROPAGATION From seed, sown in spring. From semi-ripe cuttings, taken in summer.
POTENTIAL PROBLEMS Usually none.

Ginkgo biloba

G. biloba *S. China*
Foliage: spring to autumn. H 80–100ft (25–30m), S 15–25ft (4.5–7.5m). FH.
This upright deciduous conifer spreads with age. The bright green leaves, which form a notched fan up to 3in (8cm) across, turn clear yellow in autumn. If fertilized, the female trees produce fruits with edible kernels in late summer and autumn; the outer coating has a rank smell. **'Pendula'** is smaller than the species and has spreading or weeping branches.

JUNIPERUS

CUPRESSACEAE Juniper

This important genus of evergreen conifers includes 50 to 60 species that are native to dry forests and hillsides of the Northern Hemisphere, and hundreds of ornamental varieties. Nearly all the plants are hardy and show remarkable tolerance of heat and considerable resistance to drought. There are forms for almost every situation, and the full conifer palette of greens, blues, yellows and greys is covered. Sharp, needle-like, young leaves mature into fleshy stem-hugging scales. Juvenile and mature foliage are present at the same time on some junipers. As the plants mature, the reddish bark peels and flakes.
CULTIVATION Tolerate full sun or light shade (the gold forms are best in full sun) and a wide range of soils.
PROPAGATION From semi-ripe cuttings with a heel, taken in early autumn. From seed, sown in containers and placed in a coldframe in late winter (species).
POTENTIAL PROBLEMS Aphids; fungal root, phytophthora.
WARNING Contact with the young needles may irritate the skin.

J. chinensis *China, Japan*
Chinese juniper
Foliage: year-round. H 60–80ft (18–25m), S 15–20ft (4.5–6m). FH.
In old Chinese gardens, this is a tall, conical or columnar tree of imperial solemnity, but in the wild it is very variable. The aromatic foliage is grey-green, composed of needle-like juvenile leaves and scale-like adult leaves. Male and female strobili are borne on separate plants. The fruits on female plants are berry-like and blue-black when ripe. The dull brown bark peels away in strips as the tree ages. Some of the smaller cultivars are very popular: **'Aurea'** is about half the size of the species, making a tall slender tree with green juvenile foliage and golden adult foliage. A male form, it is slow to establish but grows quickly thereafter. The golden foliage has a tendency to scorch when the plant is grown in full sun. The shrub **'Blue Alps'** has a vigorous and spreading habit, to 10ft (3m) or more, although compared to other junipers this is quite modest. It reaches a height of 12ft (3.7m). The shoots arch over at the tips when young and the foliage is silver-blue to steel-blue. **'Obelisk'** is a tall narrow shrub growing to 8ft (2.5m) with bluish green dense foliage. **'Pyramidalis'** (pyramidal juniper) slowly makes a dense blue-green column, about 6½ft (2m) high.

J. communis *N. Hemisphere*
Common juniper
Foliage: year-round. H 2–25ft (60–750cm), S 3–20ft (90–600cm). FH.
The common juniper ranges from a small spreading shrub to a large upright tree. The needle-like, glossy and aromatic leaves are mid-green or yellow-green with silver undersides. The rounded fleshy fruits, which are sometimes used as a flavouring in, for example gin, are

Juniperus communis 'Hibernica'

black with a glaucous bloom. The very slow-growing **'Compressa'** will reach a height of 3ft (90cm) after a number of years, and is covered in sharp, grey-green or green needles. **'Hibernica'** (Irish juniper) is similar but more vigorous, eventually making a silver-blue column about 10ft (3m) high. **'Hornibrookii'** is a low creeping plant that moulds itself to the contours it covers, spreading to 6½ft (2m) or more. Its blue-green needles are silvery on the underside.

Juniperus conferta

J. conferta *Japan, Russia (Sakhalin)*
Shore juniper
Foliage: year-round. H 10–12in (25–30cm), S 3–4ft (90–120cm). FH.
The creeping stems with raised tips are densely clothed with needle-like leaves to make grey-green to bright green mats. The berry-like fruits are purplish black with a light bloom.

Juniperus horizontalis 'Blue Chip'

J. horizontalis *North America*
Creeping juniper
Foliage: year-round. H 12–20in (30–50cm), S 6–10 ft (1.8–3m). FH.
The creeping juniper eventually forms a large mat of blue-green or blue-grey aromatic needles. The berries are pale blue but are rarely produced in cultivation. Dwarf cultivars, none reaching much more than 1ft (30cm) high, include: **'Blue Chip'**, with bright blue foliage throughout the year; **'Emerald Spreader'**, which is a very flat shrub with bright green foliage; and the vigorous **'Hughes'**, with upward pointing branches and grey-green leaves.

Juniperus × *pfitzeriana*

J. × *pfitzeriana*

Foliage: year-round. H 6–10ft (1.8–3m), S 8–15ft (2.5–4.5m). FH.
The long branches of this juniper rise at an angle of about 45 degrees from a short trunk and have drooping tips. The green scale-like leaves are carried in tiered sprays, among which there is a scattering of more glaucous juvenile leaves. The spherical fruits are purple at first, becoming paler later. **'Aurea'** is a golden version that becomes yellow-green in winter. **'Old Gold'**, which is a sport of it, is more compact and remains bronzed yellow throughout the year. **'Mint Julep'**, another of the numerous junipers covered by this hybrid name, resembles *J.* × *pfitzeriana* but has bright green foliage.

Juniperus sabina 'Tamariscifolia'

J. *sabina* C. Europe to N. China

Savin
Foliage: year-round. H and S 6–15ft (1.8–4.5m). FH.
The savin shows considerable variation over its wide natural distribution but is usually a spreading shrub and only rarely tree-like. Its flaking red-brown bark is, therefore, generally obscured. The foliage, which consists mainly of adult scale-like leaves, is grey-green and produces a rank smell when bruised. Low spreading cultivars include the very hardy **'Blaue Donau'**, which has light grey-blue foliage and spreads to around 6ft (1.8m); and the form it is best known by, **'Tamariscifolia'**, which grows to 4ft (1.2m) across and carries bright green needle-like leaves arranged in tiers.

J. *scopulorum* North America (Arizona, British Columbia, Texas), N. Mexico

Rocky Mountain juniper
Foliage: year-round. H 30–50ft (9–15m), S 12–15ft (3.7–4.5m). FH.
The species is a cypress-like conical tree, sometimes with several main stems. Although the foliage can vary in colour, it is often blue-green, while the bark, which peels in shreds, is red-brown. The garden cultivar **'Skyrocket'** is a narrow column of feathery blue-grey foliage, which slowly reaches 20ft (6m) in height but not much more than 1ft (30cm) in diameter.

Juniperus squamata 'Blue Star'

J. *squamata* Asia

Flaky juniper
Foliage: year-round. H 3–30ft (90–900cm), S 3–25ft (90–750cm) FH.
This prostrate or bushy juniper has rusty brown bark that flakes off the trunk as the plant ages. All forms have short triangular-shaped leaves, which are silvery blue to green with a white or pale green line on the upper surface, and drooping tips to each shoot. Spreading branches carry the blue-grey foliage of **'Blue Carpet'**, which grows to 8–12in (20–30cm) by 5–6½ft (1.5–2m). The densely bushy **'Blue Star'** makes a mound of silvery blue foliage, 12–16in (30–40cm) by 18–36in (45–90cm). **'Meyeri'** has ascending angular branches with densely packed glaucous blue foliage. Although usually seen as a shrub with a height and spread of about 5ft (1.5m), it can reach over 20ft (6m) by 20ft (6m).

Juniperus virginiana 'Grey Owl'

J. *virginiana* E. USA

Pencil cedar
Foliage: year-round. H 50–100ft (15–30m), S 15–25ft (4.5–7.5m). FH.
The pencil cedar is a slow-growing columnar or conical tree that resembles the Chinese juniper. The foliage is grey-green, with patches of glaucous juvenile leaves occurring among the scale-like adult leaves. The brown bark comes away in shreds. The brown-blue fruits are like berries, with a white bloom. **'Grey Owl'** is a wide-spreading open shrub, eventually growing to more than 8ft (2.5m) high and as much as 12ft (3.7m) across, with tiered sprays of grey-green foliage. Its fruits are a glaucous purple.

LARIX

PINACEAE Larch

The larches make up a small genus of 10 to 14 species, all deciduous and all belonging to temperate regions of the Northern Hemisphere. Most are fast-growing and tolerant of a wide range of conditions. Several, including the European larch (*L. decidua*), are widely used in commercial forestry. Although their size may count against them as garden trees, the green of the young foliage and their brilliant autumnal colours, especially the yellow, make them highly ornamental. Pretty strobili, sometimes pink or red, are followed by small neat cones that persist long after they have shed their seeds.

Larix kaempferi 'Pendula'

CULTIVATION Require full sun and well-drained soil.
PROPAGATION From seed, sown from late winter to mid-spring. By grafting (cultivars).
POTENTIAL PROBLEMS Woolly aphids; stem canker (especially *L. decidua* cultivars).

L. kaempferi *Japan*
Japanese larch
Foliage: autumn. H 80–100ft (25–30m), S 15–25ft (4.5–7.5m). FH.
Purplish red twigs make this vigorous columnar larch highly distinctive in winter. The needle-like leaves are grey-green or bluish; the light pink, sometimes light lime-green, strobili are followed by small oval cones with scales that turn outward and downward at the tips. **'Pendula'** is a tall elegant cultivar with long weeping branches that can look particularly striking in autumn.

METASEQUOIA

TAXODIACEAE Dawn redwood

The genus was first described in 1941, based on the fossil specimens of 3 species. Remarkably, a fourth living species was found in 1945 in N.E. Sichuan in western China. Seed gathered from this deciduous conifer and distributed in Europe and North America germinated freely and the tree has grown vigorously in a wide range of conditions, shooting to stardom after millennia of obscurity.
CULTIVATION Requires full sun and fertile, preferably acid, moist soil.
PROPAGATION From seed, sown in autumn. From cuttings, taken in mid- to late autumn, with bottom heat.
POTENTIAL PROBLEMS Usually none.

Metasequoia glyptostroboides

M. glyptostroboides *China*
Foliage: autumn. H 60–120ft (18–36m), S 12–20ft (3.7–6m). FH.
During the summer, this fast-growing conical tree has bright green feathery leaves, which turn rusty pink and gold before falling. Male and female strobili are borne on the same tree, the females developing into small cones which hang on long stalks. The flaking bark is red-brown.

PICEA

PINACEAE Spruce

Between 30 and 40 species of spruce are distributed in the temperate Northern Hemisphere, many in rugged mountainous country. The typical arrangement of the main branches in tiered whorls on an erect trunk gives the trees their conical or columnar shape; the pendulous branchlets of some give them their weeping character. The needle-like leaves are borne on stubby projections. Male and female strobili are carried on the same tree and the cones, which are ovoid or cylindrical and pendent, usually fall late in the second year. Several handsome species, including the Serbian spruce (**P. omorika**) and the oriental spruce (**P. orientalis**), both capable of growing to 100ft (30m), are too large for most gardens. The compact cultivars do not usually produce cones.
CULTIVATION Require a sunny sheltered site and a deep moist but well-drained soil, preferably neutral to acid.
PROPAGATION From seed, sown under glass in late winter. Grow on seedlings for two to three years before planting out.
POTENTIAL PROBLEMS Aphids, red spider mite (particularly on dwarf spruces); *P. omorika* is susceptible to honey fungus.

P. abies *S. Scandinavia to C. and S. Europe*
Common spruce, Norway spruce
Foliage: year-round. H 70–130ft, (22–39m), S 15–25ft (4.5–7.5m). FH.
Much used in parts of Europe as a Christmas tree, this fast-growing pyramidal conifer has needles that are shiny dark green above and a lighter green underneath. Dark red strobili are followed by conspicuous cigar-shaped glossy cones, 4–8in (10–20cm) long, ripening from green flecked with purple to light brown. **'Little Gem'** is a slow-growing dwarf cultivar with spreading branches that form a neat mound. Older trees have a

Picea abies 'Nidiformis'

slight depression on top. The new spring needles are light green; the older ones are dark. **'Nidiformis'**, a low bush, eventually reaching up to 5ft (1.5m) tall but even more than twice this across, has a nest-like depression in the centre.

Picea breweriana

P. breweriana *USA (N. California, S. Oregon)*
Brewer's weeping spruce
Foliage: year-round. H 30–50ft (9–15m), S 10–15ft (3–4.5m). FH.
Although the main branches dip slightly before turning up at the ends, the tree gets its weeping character from hanging shoots that create a blue-green curtain of foliage. The morinda spruce (**P. smithiana**) of the western Himalayas is another fully hardy species of weeping habit, although its foliage is dark green. Green cones, 4in (10cm) long and pointed at both ends, mature to purple.

Picea glauca var. **albertiana 'Conica'**

P. glauca *Canada, N.E. USA*
White spruce
Foliage: year-round. H 80–120ft (25–36m), S 10–20ft (3–6m). FH.
This large cone-shaped tree, with down-turned branches lifting at the tips, has glaucous green leaves that produce a fetid smell when bruised. The oval cones, growing to 2in (5cm) in length, are green at first, later light brown. Although slow to reach its ultimate size, it will be too large for most gardens. The compact **var. albertiana 'Conica'** very slowly makes a bright green bushy shrub to 6ft (1.8m) high and ultimately can exceed 10ft (3m).

Picea pungens 'Koster'

P. pungens *N. USA*
Colorado spruce
Foliage: year-round. H 50–100ft
(15–30m), S 12–18ft (3.7–5.5m). FH.
This hardy species, a handsome,
medium to large, conical tree with
blue-green foliage, has been
neglected in favour of the blue
spruce (**f. glauca**), with its
markedly glaucous leaves and
numerous compact forms with
blue foliage. '**Globosa**' makes a
bright blue flattened mound, 30in
(75cm) high and wide, while, in
contrast, the light blue '**Hoopsii**' is
a narrow conical tree reaching 15ft
(4.5m) tall with a spread of 5ft
(1.5m). '**Koster**' is a similar shape
but smaller and slow-growing. It
has curved silver-blue needles.

PINUS

PINACEAE Pine

Over 100 species of pine are
distributed in the Northern
Hemisphere, and several are found
further south in mountainous
country. These evergreen conifers
range in size from tall trees to low
shrubs. They include some of the
oldest living trees – specimens of
the bristle cone pine (**P. aristata**),
of south-western USA are said to be
more than 4000 years old – and
very fast-growing trees that are
widely planted for forestry. The
needle-like leaves are bundled in
clusters of 2 to 5. Male and female
strobili are borne on the same tree,
the females developing into woody
cones which are usually conical,
although they can be spherical or
banana-shaped. In most species the
nut-like seeds are winged.
CULTIVATION Require full sun and
well-drained soil. Species with
needles in fives, such as *P. parviflora*,
do best on acid soils.
PROPAGATION From seed, sown
under glass in late winter or in the
open in late spring. Plant out when
at least 2 years old. By grafting
(cultivars).
POTENTIAL PROBLEMS Adelgids,
sawflies, pine shoot moth
caterpillars; honey fungus,
phytophthora, rust.

P. mugo *C. Europe*
Dwarf mountain pine
Foliage: year-round. H 10–15ft
(3–4.5m), S 15–25ft (4.5–7.5m). FH.
This spreading shrubby conifer,
which grows along the ground and
then bends upwards, has rigid,
curved, dark green leaves in pairs
and oval brown cones. '**Gnom**'
makes a dense, dark green, rounded
mound about 6ft (1.8m) high.
Dwarf cultivars include the slow-
growing densely branched '**Mops**',
eventually about 3ft (90cm) high,
and the creeping but bushy **var.
pumilio**, up to 6ft (1.8m) high but
with a spread of 10ft (3m).

Pinus mugo var. *pumilio*

P. parviflora *Japan*
Japanese white pine
Foliage: year-round. H 30–70ft
(9–22m), S 20–25ft (6–7.5m). FH.
This slow-growing pine is conical
when young but develops a flat top
when mature. A popular bonsai
tree, it has abundant, soft, bluish
needles in fives with a blue-white
stripe on the underside, purple-
brown smooth bark and blue-green
oval cones 2–4in (5–10cm) long.
'**Adcock's Dwarf**' is slow-growing,
to about 8ft (2.5m), and has closely
packed grey-green leaves.

P. sylvestris *British Isles*
Scots pine
Foliage: year-round. H 50–100ft
(15–30m), S 25–30ft (7.5–9m). FH.
Easily recognized by its attractive
reddish brown young bark, this
usually upright conifer, which
develops a tall clean trunk, is
sometimes seen as a low spreading
tree. Only then is this natural forest
tree suitable for the average garden.
The twisted paired leaves are grey-
or blue-green; the green cones,
which ripen to pale grey- or red-
brown, are 3in (8cm) long. '**Aurea**'
has blue-green leaves which turn
golden yellow in winter. The
miniature '**Beuvronensis**' makes a

compact blue-green dome 3ft
(90cm) high. '**Watereri**' is a slow-
growing blue-grey bush or small
tree which reaches 12ft (3.7m).

Pinus sylvestris 'Beuvronensis'

P. wallichiana *Himalayas, from
Afghanistan to N.E. India*
Bhutan pine, blue pine
Foliage: year-round. H 70–120ft
(22–36m), S 20–40ft (6–12m). FH.
Conical young specimens develop
into tall trees with blue-green
foliage, the needles arranged in
fives. The cones are banana-shaped.

Pinus wallichiana

PSEUDOLARIX

PINACEAE Golden larch

Like the larches (*Larix*), from
which it is distinguished by small
botanical differences, the single
species is deciduous and colours
magnificently in autumn. This is an
excellent specimen tree but is
slow-growing, especially in areas
where the growing tips are caught
by late frosts.
CULTIVATION Requires a warm
sheltered site in full sun and deep,
well-drained, slightly acid soil.
PROPAGATION From seed, sown
under protection in spring.
POTENTIAL PROBLEMS Usually none.

P. amabilis *S. and E. China*
Foliage: autumn. H 50–70ft
(15–22m), S 20–40ft (6–12m). FH.
On mature specimens, the conical
shape often gives way to a flatter
profile and an open crown. The
long larch-like leaves are light
green in summer but turn clear
yellow, orange and then reddish
brown in autumn before falling.

The erect cones, which are up to 3in (8cm) long, go through similar colour changes, from pale green to light orange.

Pseudolarix amabilis

TAXODIUM

TAXODIACEAE Swamp cypress

The 2 species of deciduous conifers in this genus form columnar or conical trees with frond-like foliage that turns rusty orange in autumn. In the wild, they are found in the shallows of lakes and on marshy waterlogged ground. On wet sites the trunks, flared at the base, are usually surrounded by numerous knee-like stumps, which are aerial roots (pneumatophores).
CULTIVATION Tolerate sun or partial shade and require moist, preferably acid, soil, thriving even in waterlogged conditions.
PROPAGATION From seed, sown in spring; plant outside in autumn the following year. From hardwood cuttings, taken in autumn.
POTENTIAL PROBLEMS Usually none.

T. distichum North America
Swamp cypress
Foliage: autumn. H 70–130ft (22–39m), S 20–30ft (6–9m). FH.
This strikingly beautiful, slow-growing and large, deciduous cypress is the tree most typical of the southern wetlands of the United States. It has fibrous, reddish

Taxodium distichum

brown, peeling bark and a broadly conical habit. The branches are bright orange-brown with grey-green young shoots, producing small narrow leaves which are a vivid yellow-green, turning russet-brown in autumn. **Var. *imbricatum* 'Nutans'** makes a narrow column of short branches.

TAXUS

TAXACEAE Yew

The common yew (*T. baccata*), widely grown in temperate regions as a superlative plant for hedging and topiary, is one of half a dozen or so evergreen species, distributed in the Northern Hemisphere and extending to Central America and the Philippines. Plants are male or female, the females carrying red or orange fruits, each with a single seed. The seed, like most parts of the plant, is poisonous.
CULTIVATION Tolerate a wide range of conditions, provided the soil is well-drained. Trim hedges in summer or early autumn. Yews tend to respond well to heavy renovative pruning.
PROPAGATION From cuttings with a heel, taken in early to mid-autumn.
POTENTIAL PROBLEMS Usually none.
WARNING All parts of yew, except the flesh of the fruits, are highly toxic. They should never be planted where animals graze.

Taxus baccata

T. baccata Asia minor, Europe
Common yew, English yew
Foliage: year-round. H 30–70ft (9–22m), S 25–30ft (7.5–9m). FH.
Whether grown as a bushy, often multi-stemmed specimen, or clipped as a fine-textured hedge, the common yew is a tree of dark steadfastness, tolerant of a wide range of conditions. There is an unexpectedly jaunty side to this evergreen; the fleshy red covering of the seeds are gaily translucent when seen against the light. The numerous forms include several with yellow foliage. One of the best for hedging is **'Elegantissima'**, which matures from rich gold to light green. It is female, as is

'Standishii', which slowly makes a narrow golden column to a height of 5ft (1.5m). **'Fastigiata'**, the Irish yew, another female clone, makes a dark green column, 30ft (9m) tall.

Taxus baccata 'Standishii'

T. × *media*
Foliage: year-round. H and S 10–25ft (3–7.5m). FH.
This vigorous very wide-spreading but variable shrub produces stiff, needle-like, flattened leaves held on olive-green stems. Female plants bear bright red fruits. **'Hicksii'**, which makes a broad dark green column, like a more open *T. baccata* 'Fastigiata', is suitable for hedging.

THUJA

CUPRESSACEAE Arbor-vitae

Pleasing dense foliage, extending to the ground, and a neat conical or columnar form are the chief attractions of these hardy evergreen trees and shrubs. The juvenile foliage is soft and feathery; the mature leaves are scale-like and held in flat sprays. Both leaves and cones are aromatic. A small genus of 6 species, thujas are native to temperate regions of the Northern Hemisphere. They can be long-lived and make useful screen or hedging plants, and attractive freestanding specimens. Several of the species have numerous cultivars, some of which are slow-growing or dwarf.
CULTIVATION Prefer a sheltered position in full sun and deep, moist, well-drained, acid soil. Young plants may be damaged by cold winds. Trim hedges in late spring or early autumn.
PROPAGATION From semi-ripe cuttings, taken in spring or autumn.
POTENTIAL PROBLEMS Usually none. *T. plicata* is susceptible to honey fungus.
WARNING Contact with the sap may aggravate skin allergies.

Thuja occidentalis 'Rheingold'

T. occidentalis *E. North America*
American arbor-vitae
Foliage: year-round. H 30–70ft
(9–22m), S 9–15ft (2.7–4.5m). FH.
The leaves of this slow-growing
columnar conifer are glossy light
green above and matt below,
turning bronze in winter. When
crushed, they give off a pleasing
scent of apples. The peeling bark
is reddish brown; the small cones
are yellow-green, ripening to
brown. It is a tidy tree when young.
'Holmstrup', an upright small tree,
grows to 12ft (3.7m) and has rich
green foliage throughout the year.
'Rheingold', with golden-yellow
foliage, bronze in winter, makes a
cone shape 3–6ft (90–180cm) high.

T. orientalis *N. and W. China*
Chinese arbor-vitae
Foliage: year-round. H 30–50ft
(9–15m), S 10–15ft (3–4.5m). FH.
This slow-growing large shrub or
small tree has an irregularly
rounded crown. Erect branches
carry scentless pale acid-green
leaves in flattened vertical sprays.
The bark is fibrous and the egg-
shaped cones a glaucous grey,
ripening to brown. At only 2ft

Thuja orientalis

(60cm), **'Aurea Nana'** makes a
dwarf globe-shaped bush with
yellow-green foliage that turns
bronze in winter. The foliage of the
small columnar **'Elegantissima'**,
which grows to 15ft (4.5m), is
golden yellow, developing bronze
tinges and turning green in winter.

T. plicata *North America*
Western red cedar
Foliage: year-round. H 70–120ft
(22–36m), S 20–30ft (6–9m). FH.
This is a vigorous long-lived tree
with a neat conical shape. The bark
is light to reddish brown and peels
and flakes as the tree ages. The
bright green leaves have a white
cross on the underside. Flat and
made up of numerous small scale-
like sections, they release a strong
pineapple-like aroma when
crushed. It is an excellent plant
for growing as a freestanding
specimen but is also easily
controlled to make a dense hedge
or screen. **'Atrovirens'**, very
upright and suitable for hedging,
has exceptionally dark and glossy
leaves. **'Rogersii'** slowly forms a
compact cone 3–4ft (90–120cm)
high with gold and bronze foliage
that darkens in winter. **'Stoneham
Gold'**, with a height and spread of
6ft (1.8m), is green with coppery
shoots. **'Zebrina'** makes a conical
tree up to 50ft (15m) high, with
yellow banding to the leaves that is
particularly marked on specimens
grown in full sun.

Thuja plicata 'Zebrina'

TSUGA

PINACEAE Hemlock

Elegant sweeping branches and a
broadly conical outline are typical
of the 10 or 11 species of these
evergreen conifers which originate
from North America and north and
eastern Asia. The needles are blunt
and short, often white underneath
against the dark or blue-green

upper surface. The small cones are
pendulous and remain on the tree
for as long as 3 years.
CULTIVATION Tolerate partial shade
and require moist but well-drained
soil, preferably neutral to acid,
and shelter from cold winds. Trim
hedges during summer. Can be
pruned.
PROPAGATION From seed, sown in
spring. From ripe cuttings, in
autumn (cultivars).
POTENTIAL PROBLEMS Honey
fungus; sensitive to environmental
pollution.

Tsuga canadensis 'Pendula'

T. canadensis *E. North America*
Canada hemlock, eastern hemlock
Foliage: year-round. H 50–80ft
(15–25m), S 20–30ft (6–9m). FH.
The grey shoots of this broadly
conical conifer produce dark green
leaves which are often inverted to
reveal silver lines beneath. The oval
cones are light brown and up to
1in (2.5cm) long. **'Jeddeloh'**, up
to 5ft (1.5m) high and as much as
6ft (1.8m) across, makes a light
green bush with branches arching
out from a low centre. The slow-
growing spreading **'Pendula'** builds
into a mound up to 6ft (1.8m) high
of drooping branches.

T. heterophylla *W. North
America (Alaska to California)*
Western hemlock
Foliage: year-round. H 70–100ft
(22–30m), S 20–30ft (6–9m). FH.
As well as being an extremely
valuable and fast-growing timber
tree with light straight-grained
wood and tannin-rich bark that is
used in the leather industry, the
western hemlock is one of the
most graceful of all conifers. This
narrowly conical tree, displaying
cracked purple-brown bark, has
slender branches, the lower ones
drooping. The flattened needle-like
leaves are dark green with silvery
bands underneath and the small
shoots are lightly pendulous.
The oval pale green cones ripen
to dark brown. Tolerant of shade,
this makes a handsome specimen
tree and is also an excellent
hedging plant.

climbers

True climbers have given up relying on their own stems for support and instead take a helping hand from other plants or rocky outcrops. Some twine; some cling with aerial roots or sucker pads; some grasp with tendrils. All have one ambition: to get at least part of themselves into a fairly well-lit position. The most dramatic ascents are made by tropical lianas but even temperate climbers, such as *Vitis coignetiae*, can be prodigiously vigorous. In gardens climbers play several important roles (see also pp. 68-69). They can obscure the unsightly and, on fences or walls, make visual links to the world beyond the garden. Grown on supports, from which they cast light shade, they provide the quickest way of asserting that a garden is 3-dimensional.

This selection includes a few annual and perennial climbers as well as plants with woody stems. Climbing and rambling roses appear with the other roses and the so-called wall shrubs are in the shrub category. Climbers are best planted in frost-free weather from autumn to mid-spring. Some initial tying in and training is usually advisable. Pruning is mainly concerned with ensuring regular and heavy flower crops but an element of control may be important. No spread dimensions are given in the entries as this depends on the training method.

Top Clematis viticella **'Purpurea Plena Elegans'**
Centre Jasminum polyanthum
Bottom Campsis × tagliabuana **'Madame Galen'**

ACONITUM

RANUNCULACEAE Aconite, monkshood

This genus of 100 species consists of hardy herbaceous perennials, including some twining climbers, occurring throughout the Northern Hemisphere, often in grassland or scrub. They have slender spires of usually blue or purple, helmet-shaped or hooded blooms, and glossy dark green leaves with deeply divided lobes. See also PERENNIALS.
CULTIVATION Prefers partial shade but tolerates full sun and requires fertile, moist but well-drained soil.
PROPAGATION From seed, sown in spring. By division, in autumn.
POTENTIAL PROBLEMS Aphids, slugs; fungal stem rot, verticillium wilt.
WARNING Contact with the foliage may irritate the skin. All parts of the plant are toxic if eaten.

A. hemsleyanum *C. and W. China*
Flowers: mid-summer to early autumn. H 6–10ft (1.8–3m). FH.
This twining climber's scrambling habit makes it ideal for growing through shrubs. It bears racemes of soft lilac-purple flower spikes.

Aconitum hemsleyanum

ACTINIDIA

ACTINIDIACEAE

This genus contains 40 species of mostly deciduous hardy twining climbers, native to light forests in eastern Asia. They are highly valued for their striking, often variegated, ornamental foliage. Male and female flowers, generally less interesting than the foliage, are usually carried on separate plants, although hermaphrodite plants do occur. The vigorous Chinese gooseberry, also known as kiwi fruit (*A. deliciosa*), mainly grown as a fruiting climber, has impressively large heart-shaped leaves that are carried on hairy shoots. Tara vine (*A. arguta*) is another vigorous species that is capable of clambering high into tall trees; its leaves are light green and heart-

shaped, with toothed margins, and turn a rich golden colour in autumn. It bears edible but insipid green-yellow fruits. Some species, including Chinese gooseberry (*A. deliciosa*) and *A. kolomikta*, induce delirious rapture in cats, who chew the stems.
CULTIVATION Require full sun, shelter from strong winds and moist but well-drained soil. Thin out overcrowded growth in spring.
PROPAGATION From semi-ripe cuttings, in late summer. From seed, sown in autumn or spring.
POTENTIAL PROBLEMS Usually none.

Actinidia kolomikta

A. kolomikta *E. Asia*
Foliage: early summer. Flowers: early summer. H 10–15ft (3–4.5m). FH.
This deciduous twining climber is grown for the striking variegation of its dark green leaves: the tips or sometimes even the whole leaf may be white with a pink tinge. The coloration is most marked early in the season, and in leaves that are in full sun. Female plants bear fragrant but insignificant white flowers which may be followed by edible, yellow-green fruits in autumn.

AKEBIA

LARDIZABALACEAE Chocolate vine

The genus comprises about 5 deciduous and semi-evergreen twining climbers from forest margins in east Asia. They are valued both for their elegant foliage, with compound leaves composed of 3 or 5 leaflets, and for their ornamental, spicily fragrant flowers. These are borne in pendent racemes, with small male flowers at the tip, and larger, cup-shaped female flowers near the base. If different clones are grown together, attractive grey-violet, sausage-shaped seed pods may form in early autumn.
A. trifoliata is similar to *A. quinata*, except it is fully deciduous and its leaves have 3 radiating leaflets.
CULTIVATION Tolerate light shade or full sun, preferably in a sheltered

site, and require fertile, moist but well-drained soil. To fruit well, need warm springs and hot summers.
PROPAGATION From semi-hardwood cuttings, taken in summer. By layering, in winter. From seed, as soon as ripe.
POTENTIAL PROBLEMS Usually none.

Akebia quinata

A. quinata *China, Japan, Korea*
Foliage: year-round in mild winters. Flowers: mid-spring. Fruits: early autumn. H 20–30ft (6–9m). FH.
The leaves of this semi-evergreen twining climber are usually made up of 5 rounded, untoothed, dark green leaflets; when young, they are suffused with bronze-purple. The stems are dark purple-red. Vanilla-scented, cup-shaped female flowers have large, dark maroon sepals. If fertilized, they produce long, grey-violet, sausage-like pods, which split open when ripe to reveal white pulp and black seeds.

AMPELOPSIS

VITACEAE

Like the vines in the closely related genus *Vitis*, the 20 or so species of *Ampelopsis* have twining stem tendrils. They are deciduous woodland plants of Asia and North America, mainly grown for their foliage, although the fruits that follow the insignificant flowers are also of ornamental value.
A. aconitifolia is a slender species with pea-sized, dull orange fruits.
CULTIVATION Tolerate full sun or partial shade (they fruit best in full sun) and require moist but well-drained soil.
PROPAGATION From softwood cuttings, in summer. From seed, sown in autumn or spring.
POTENTIAL PROBLEMS Usually none.

A. glandulosa var. brevipedunculata *N. E. Asia*
Foliage: autumn. Flowers: late spring. Fruits: autumn. H 15–25ft (4.5–7.5m). FH.
The hop-like leaves, with 3 or 5 lobes, are dark green and hairy on the undersides. If grown against a

warm wall, this climber will bear attractive, near-spherical, bright blue fruit in autumn. 'Elegans' is a less vigorous form of the species, with irregular, agitated variegation in white, pink and green.

Ampelopsis glandulosa var. brevipedunculata 'Elegans'

BERBERIDOPSIS

FLACOURTIACEAE

Although well established in cultivation, this single species, an evergreen twining climber from moist forests in Chile, is now thought to be extinct in the wild.
CULTIVATION Requires partial shade and neutral to acid, moist but well drained soil.
PROPAGATION From semi-ripe stem cuttings, in late summer. By layering, in autumn.
POTENTIAL PROBLEMS Usually none.

Berberidopsis corallina

B. corallina *Chile*
Coral plant
Foliage: year-round. Flowers: late summer to early autumn.
H 12–18ft (3.7–5.5m). FrH.
The dark green, oblong leaves have spiny margins and are leathery in texture. They form a striking contrast to the drooping clusters of near-spherical, deep red flowers, dangling on red stalks.

BOUGAINVILLEA

NYCTAGINACEAE

Among the 14 species in the genus, all native of forest and scrub in South America, are several scrambling, sometimes thorny climbers. They may be evergreen or partly deciduous. Bougainvilleas seem to be covered for months by vivid, showy flowers. However, it is the bracts surrounding the flowers that are so colourful and long-lasting; the true flowers are insignificant. *B.* 'Scarlett O'Hara' is a vigorous climber, carrying bright crimson to scarlet bracts. The hybrids of *B. glabra*, *B. peruviana* and *B. spectabilis* should be grown under glass in frost-prone areas.
CULTIVATION Require full sun and fertile, well-drained soil (JI No. 3). In early spring, remove all thin weak growths and shorten the main stems to about two-thirds.
PROPAGATION From semi-ripe cuttings, from mid- to late summer.
POTENTIAL PROBLEMS Red spider mites, mealy bugs, scale insects.

Bougainvillea 'Scarlet O'Hara'

B. × buttiana
Flowers: mid-summer to autumn.
H 25–40ft (7.5–12m). FT to HH.
This strong, vigorous, evergreen climber, a hybrid of *B. glabra* and *B. peruviana*, has purple, red, or rich yellow floral bracts. Oval, dull green leaves conceal small sharp spines on the stems. 'Mrs Butt' has crimson-magenta bracts. Numerous newer hybrids of *B. × buttiana* are now available.

CAMPSIS

BIGNONIACEAE Trumpet creeper, trumpet vine

Both of the 2 species in this genus are deciduous climbers, found in woodland in China and North America, usually climbing by aerial roots. They produce trusses of trumpet-shaped flowers in shades of orange and scarlet, and the leaves are pinnate, composed of about 7 leaflets. The Chinese trumpet creeper or vine (*C. grandiflora*) has larger flowers, which are orange and red-veined in the throat, with paler lobes. Its aerial roots are less secure than those of the common trumpet creeper (*C. radicans*), from S.E. USA. Where summers are cool, they tend to flower poorly unless the wood is ripened by exposure to full sun.
CULTIVATION Require full sun, although they will tolerate partial shade in warm climates, and fertile but well-drained soil.
PROPAGATION From semi-ripe cuttings, in late summer or early autumn. By layering or from rooted suckers, in spring.
POTENTIAL PROBLEMS Red spider mites, mealy bugs, scale insects; powdery mildew.

Campsis × tagliabuana 'Madame Galen'

C. × tagliabuana 'Madame Galen'
Foliage: autumn. Flowers: late summer to early autumn.
H 20–40ft (6-12m) FrH.
This hybrid freely produces trusses of up to 12 salmon-red, trumpet-shaped flowers. In autumn, the light to mid-green leaves turn yellow and the young, light grey-green stems age to creamy brown.

CELASTRUS

CELASTRACEAE Bittersweet, staff vine

There are about 30 species of shrubs and twining climbers in the genus, most of which are deciduous and native to thickets and woodland in tropical or subtropical regions. These climbers are particularly attractive when trained into sturdy trees. The flowers are inconspicuous, and in some species male and female flowers are borne on separate plants. Several hardy species are grown for their brightly coloured autumn fruits. American bittersweet (*C. scandens*) bears pea-sized fruits containing scarlet seeds, but both a male and female plant are required. It is fully hardy, but only fruits well in a continental climate.
CULTIVATION Tolerate full sun or partial shade and most soils. Remove up to one-third of the old branches in spring, but leave plants growing in trees unpruned.
PROPAGATION By layering, in spring. By seed, sown as soon as ripe.
POTENTIAL PROBLEMS Usually none.

C. orbiculatus *E. Asia*

Oriental bittersweet, staff vine
Foliage: autumn. Flowers: early
summer. Fruits: autumn. H 25–40ft
(7.5–12m). FH.
The almost rounded, scalloped to
toothed mid-green leaves of this
large, vigorous climber have
pointed tips and turn yellow in
autumn. When the inconspicuous
green flowers are fertilized, they
are followed in autumn by bead-
like, yellow fruits. These split open
when ripe to reveal scarlet-coated
seeds. Male and female flowers are
usually borne on separate plants,
but a single plant of the
Hermaphrodite Group will bear
crops of fruits.

Celastrus orbiculatus

CLEMATIS

RANUNCULACEAE

In this large genus of about 250
deciduous and evergreen species,
a high proportion are subshrubby
climbers. Most are plants of forest
and woodland, widely distributed
in both hemispheres, mainly in
temperate regions. The climbing
species attach themselves to
supports by means of twining leaf
stalks. The flowers are often very
showy, particularly those of the
numerous hybrids, and they vary
greatly in shape, size, colour and
flowering season. The petal-like
segments, which are in fact sepals,
are often of contrasting colour to
the conspicuous central stamens.
Some clematis also carry stamens
that are petal-like, giving a double
effect. Feathery seeds are an
attractive feature of many species
at the end of the season.
　In addition to the climbing species
and hybrids, there are a few
clematis that are lax or semi-
climbing perennials or subshrubs:
they all need supports when
grown in borders. These include
C. × *durandii*, with large, single,
indigo-blue flowers, and
C. × *jouiniana*, with small flowers
that are creamy white and grey-
blue. The climbing clematis
described here are all deciduous,
unless otherwise stated.

Clematis × durandii

CULTIVATION Tolerate full sun or
partial shade, with the roots and
base in shade, and require moist
but well-drained soil (JI No. 3).
Tie in securely initially. Pruning
depends on flowering time,
according to these categories:
(i) Early-flowering species that
flower winter to early spring:
prune immediately after flowering,
removing dead or damaged growth;
most require only light trimming
to restrict size.
(ii) Large-flowered hybrids that
flower late spring to early summer,
in some cases flowering again
later: prune in early spring, before
growth starts, removing dead or
damaged growth and cutting back
stems at the topmost strong buds.
(iii) Large- and small-flowered
species and hybrids, including
herbaceous clematis, that flower
mid-summer to autumn: prune in
late winter, before growth starts,
cutting back the previous season's
stems to a height of about 6in
(15cm), making the cut above a pair
of strong buds.
PROPAGATION From softwood
cuttings, in early spring. From
semi-ripe cuttings, in mid-summer.
By layering, in late winter or
early spring.
POTENTIAL PROBLEMS Aphids,
earwigs, slugs; powdery mildew,
clematis wilt.

SPECIES

C. alpina *Europe*
Alpine clematis
Flowers: spring. H 6–8ft (1.8–
2.5m). FH. Pruning group (i).
The early nodding flowers of this
early-flowering species, usually
mauve-blue, are carried singly on
brownish green stems. The pale
to mid-green leaves are broadly
oval and end in a pointed tip.
Silky seedheads are produced in
the autumn and last well into the
winter. **'Frances Rivis'** is larger
and more vigorous, and is grown
for its deep blue, white-centred
flowers. Also larger, **subsp.
sibirica 'White Moth'** bears
creamy white double flowers.

C. armandii *China*
Foliage: year-round. Flowers: early
spring. H 20–30ft (6–9m). FrH.
Pruning group (i).
The evergreen, glossy, dark green
leaves, each with 3 leathery
leaflets with 3 veins, are copper-
tinted when young. The shiny
green stems are slightly tinged
with red when young, but turn
dull green with age. The densely
clustered fragrant flowers, each
with 5 or 6 sepals, are white or
occasionally, as in **'Apple
Blossom'**, pink and white.

C. cirrhosa *Europe*
Foliage: year-round. Flowers: early
to late winter. H 8–12ft (2.5–3.7m).
FrH. Pruning group (i).
This evergreen clematis has dainty,
fern-like, light to mid-green foliage.
The small, creamy white flowers,
spotted with pink inside, are bell-
shaped and nodding, and borne
singly or in pairs. **'Freckles'** has
sepals with maroon-pink markings.

Clematis florida 'Sieboldii'

C. florida 'Flore Pleno'
Flowers: late spring to early
summer. H 8–10ft (2.5–3m). FrH.
Pruning group (ii).
Flowering in late spring to early
summer, this clematis carries an
abundance of large, double,
greenish cream flowers, up to 5in
(12cm) across. A less vigorous but
striking plant, *C. florida* **'Sieboldii'**,
has deep purple-red, petal-like
stamens at the centre of its large,
creamy white flowers.

C. macropetala *China (Gansu),
Mongolia, Russia (Siberia)*
Flowers: late spring to early
summer. H 8–10ft (2.5–3m). FrH.
Pruning group (ii).
The slender stems carry fern-like
foliage and nodding blue flowers.
The 4 sepals surround numerous
petal-like stamens, which are
usually creamy white, creating a
double effect. The flowers of
'Maidwell Hall' are deep blue on
the outside, with lighter blue,
petal-like stamens. **'Markham's
Pink'** bears rich mauve-pink
flowers.

C. montana *C. and W. China, Himalayas*
Flowers: early summer. H 30–40ft (9–12m). FH. Pruning group (i). Deservedly popular for its vigour, tolerance of a wide range of conditions and its prodigious display of white flowers, this species is best planted where it can grow unchecked. 'Elizabeth' bears large, pale pink, vanilla-scented flowers, which make an attractive contrast to the bronze-green foliage. The flowers of **var. rubens** are mauve-pink, becoming paler with age, and the foliage is purple-flushed.

Clematis montana var. *rubens*

C. tangutica *W. China*
Flowers: late summer to early autumn. H 15–20ft (4.5–6m). FH. Pruning group (iii). Balloon-shaped buds open to nodding, solitary, bell-shaped yellow flowers, with pointed sepals and a prominent central boss of stamens. The flowers are borne above the light green, fern-like foliage, and are followed by silvery white, silky seedheads.

C. tibetana subsp. *vernayi*
Nepal, Tibet
Flowers: autumn. H 20–25ft (6–7.5m). FH. Pruning group (iii). The finely divided leaves are bluish green, with a waxy texture to the upper sides. The nodding bell-shaped flowers range in colour from orange-yellow to greenish yellow with purple flecks. When the flowers open, the thick spongy sepals curl outwards to reveal purple stamens. It is the colour and texture of the sepals that give 'Orange Peel' its name. The hybrid *C.* 'Bill MacKenzie' is similar, with yellow flowers.

C. viticella *Central S. Europe*
Flowers: autumn. H 8–12ft (2.5–3.7m). FH. Pruning group (iii). The numerous small nodding flowers, usually violet-blue or purple, make this a delightful late-season climber. It is a parent of many very fine small-flowered hybrids. They are listed here under *C.* hybrids (small-flowered), under their cultivar names. 'Purpurea Plena Elegans' carries double violet-purple flowers, 3in (8cm) across.

HYBRIDS

C. hybrids (large-flowered)
Flowers: late spring to early autumn. H 6–12ft (1.8–3.7m). FH. Pruning group (ii) or (iii), depending on flowering time (see Cultivation).
The large-flowered hybrids are available in shades of white, cream, pink, red, purple and blue, often with contrasting stamens. The colour, size and form of the flowers are greatly influenced by temperature and other weather conditions during bud development. Some cultivars have a few, quite separate, pointed sepals, while others with a larger number of rounded sepals make an almost circular bloom. The following is a small selection of the large-flowered cultivars available: 'Comtesse de Bouchaud', mauve-pink flowers with cream anthers in summer; 'Countess of Lovelace', deep mauve-blue flowers in early summer (double) to early autumn (single); 'Duchess of Edinburgh', short-growing, to 10ft (3m), with double, creamy white flowers tinged with green, in early to late summer; 'Edith', large white flowers with prominent red-brown anthers, in late spring to early autumn; 'Elsa Späth', deep violet-blue flowers with large sepals and red-purple anthers, in early summer to early autumn (early flowers are large, later flowers are smaller and better formed); 'Général Sikorski', mid-blue flowers with overlapping sepals, purple-tinged at the base, and a central boss of golden yellow anthers, in early summer to early autumn; 'Henryi', with creamy white sepals and a central boss of light brown anthers, in early to late summer; 'Huldine', white flowers with mauve undersides and creamy white stamens, in early to

Clematis 'Lasurstern'

mid-autumn; 'Jackmanii Superba', deep purple flowers with large, rounded sepals, in mid-summer to early autumn; 'Lady Caroline Nevill', mauve-blue flowers with a darker central stripe on the 8 sepals, in summer to autumn; 'Lasurstern', large flat flowers, purple-blue to mauve-blue, the sepals with ruffled edges, appear in 2 flushes: early spring to early summer, and late summer to early autumn; 'Marie Boisselot', very large, pure white flowers with broad, overlapping sepals and light brown anthers, in early and late summer; 'Miss Bateman', pale cream flowers with deep brown anthers, in mid-spring to early summer; 'Niobe', deep velvet-red flowers with 6 sepals with ruffled edges, and a central boss of cream stamens, throughout summer; 'Perle d'Azur', light blue flowers, faintly tinted mauve-pink, with creamy green centres, in mid-summer to autumn; 'Proteus', mauve-pink with cream stamens, in mid-summer (double) and autumn (single); 'Rouge Cardinal', deep crimson-red flowers with a tuft of cream stamens, in early summer to early autumn; 'The President', saucer-shaped flowers in deep blue-purple with a paler stripe, and red-purple anthers, in late spring to early autumn; 'Vyvyan Pennell', double, subtly shaded flowers, purple-carmine with mauve-blue inner sepals, and a central boss of yellow stamens, in late spring to mid-summer.

Clematis 'Abundance'

C. hybrids (small-flowered)
Flowers: mid-summer to early autumn. H 8–12ft (2.5–3.7m). FH. Pruning group (iii). Many small-flowered clematis (cultivars or hybrids of *C. viticella*) revive the garden in late summer and autumn with masses of nodding flowers. Their many merits include a long and reliable flowering period relatively late in the season, ease of pruning and resistance to wilt. Some of the best cultivars include: 'Abundance',

Clematis 'Alba Luxurians'

deep red to pink flowers with
darker veins and 4 sepals; '**Alba
Luxurians**', white flowers with
dark stamens and 4 twisted, green-
tipped sepals; '**Étoile Violette**',
deep violet-purple flowers with 5
to 6 sepals and contrasting, creamy
white stamens; '**Kermesina**', deep
crimson-red flowers; '**Pagoda**',
dainty, nodding, bell-shaped
flowers of pale mauve-pink; '**Royal
Velours**', deep royal-purple,
velvety flowers with black anthers.

Clematis 'Étoile Violette'

COBAEA

COBAEACEAE

About 20 species of these evergreen
climbers are found in forests and
thickets in tropical America. Only
one, *C. scandens*, is widely grown.
In the wild, this can reach 50ft
(15m) or more, but it produces
long-stalked, bell-shaped flowers
in its first year and is commonly
treated as a shorter-growing
annual.
CULTIVATION Require full sun and
moist but well-drained soil
(JI No. 2).
PROPAGATION From seed, sown
under glass at 64°F (18°C) in
spring.
POTENTIAL PROBLEMS Usually none.

C. scandens *Mexico*
Cathedral bell, cup and saucer vine
Foliage: year-round. Flowers: early
summer to mid-autumn. H 12–20ft
(3.7–6m). FT.
The leaves, composed of 4 to 6
rich green leaflets, terminate in
branched tendrils, which hook on
to supports and then tighten their

grip. The honey-scented, bell-
shaped flowers are yellow-green at
first, then purple, and grow from
the upper leaf axils; they are
backed by a 5-lobed, saucer-like
calyx. In the case of **f. alba**, white
flowers age to creamy white.

Cobaea scandens

CODONOPSIS

CAMPANULACEAE

This genus comprises 30 or so
species of perennials, some of
which are twining or scandent
climbers, and annuals. All are
Asiatic and mainly plants of scrub
in mountainous areas. The climbers
look best when their slender stems
are allowed to work their way
through or over a supporting
shrub. The flowers are intricately
marked on the inside.
CULTIVATION Tolerate full sun or
partial shade and require a sheltered
site, particularly *C. convolvulacea*,
and fertile, moist but well-drained
soil rich in organic matter.
PROPAGATION From seed, sown in
autumn or spring. From basal
cuttings, between mid- and late
spring.
POTENTIAL PROBLEMS Slugs, snails.

Codonopsis convolvulacea

C. convolvulacea *Himalayas,
W. China*
Flowers: mid-summer. H 3–6ft
(90–180cm). FH.
This slender-stemmed species bears
star-shaped, pale blue to violet
flowers, up to 2in (5cm) across. The
shorter-growing *C. clematidea* has
pale blue flowers with darker
veining, and gold, black and dark
blue markings inside.

CUCURBITA

CUCURBITACEAE

The 25 species in this genus are
trailing or climbing annuals and
perennials of the Americas, mainly
native to tropical and subtropical
regions. They include marrow,
pumpkin and squash, all of which
are grown primarily for their
edible fruits, but also for their
ornamental qualities, such as their
attractive large, lobed leaves.
Other species are grown simply as
ornamental gourds, since their
flesh is bitter and inedible. Some
of the plants in this genus make
useful short-term ground cover,
but they can also be encouraged to
climb. The ornamental gourds,
with their smaller, lighter fruit,
are more appropriate for climbing
than heavy pumpkins and
marrows.
CULTIVATION Requires full sun and
fertile, moist soil heavily enriched
with organic matter.
PROPAGATION From seed, sown
under glass in mid-spring or where
plants are to grow in late spring.
POTENTIAL PROBLEMS Slugs, snails;
cucumber mosaic virus, grey
mould (*Botrytis*), powdery mildew.

Cucurbita pepo

C. pepo *Mexico and S.W. USA*
Ornamental gourd
Flowers: summer to autumn.
Fruits: late summer to autumn.
H 8–16ft (2.5–5m). FT.
Cultivars of this species include
ornamental gourds and the
vegetable marrow. Their floppy
yellow flowers are followed by
smooth or warty fruits, which vary
greatly in size, shape and colour.
They may be dramatically striped
or bicoloured yellow and green.

ECCREMOCARPUS

BIGNONIACEAE

Of this genus of 5 climbers from
forest margins and scrub in
western South America, only a
single species is widely grown.
The Chilean glory flower (*E. scaber*)
is a short-lived evergreen perennial,
but is often grown as an annual. It

climbs by tendrils at the leaf tips, producing tubular flowers.
CULTIVATION Requires full sun and fertile, well-drained soil.
PROPAGATION From seed, sown under glasss at 61–66°F (16–19°C) in spring.
POTENTIAL PROBLEMS Red spider mites, whitefly (under glass).

Eccremocarpus scaber

E. scaber Chile
Chilean glory flower
Flowers: early summer to mid-autumn. Fruits: autumn. H 10–15ft (3–4.5m). FrH.
This is easily raised from seed in warmth, and flowers profusely in its first year. The narrow mouths of the orange-red tubular flowers are surrounded by 5 lobes. The fruit pods are bladder-like.

FALLOPIA

POLYGONACEAE

The 7 species in this genus are scrambling and climbing perennials native to moist habitats in temperate regions of the Northern Hemisphere. The climbing species are ideal for training through trees and on pergolas; the fast-growing species, such as Russian vine (*F. baldschuanica*), are particularly useful in larger gardens for quickly concealing eyesores.
CULTIVATION Tolerates full sun or partial shade and requires moist but well-drained soil.
PROPAGATION From semi-ripe cuttings, in summer. From hardwood cuttings, in autumn. From seed, sown as soon as ripe.
POTENTIAL PROBLEMS Leaf miners.

F. baldschuanica C. China, Tajikistan to W. China
Mile-a-minute plant, Russian vine
Flowers: mid-summer to early autumn. H 40–50ft (12–15m). FH.
Highly vigorous and attractive, this climber is ideal for quickly concealing unsightly structures. However, it must be used with caution, particularly in a small garden, where its rampant growth may well be cause for regret.
The frothy sprays of tiny pink-tinted funnel-shaped flowers are followed by small pinkish white fruits. The foliage is dark green and heart-shaped.

Fallopia baldschuanica

HEDERA

ARALIACEAE Ivy

Ivies are highly adaptable plants, growing either as climbers, when they attach themselves to surfaces by aerial roots, or trailing along the ground, making thick cover and rooting as they go. There are about 10 species, all evergreen and found chiefly in woodland from North Africa and Europe to Japan. There are 2 distinct phases of growth. In the juvenile stage, the ivy creeps or climbs by its aerial roots. The leaves are usually 3- or 5-lobed, and all grow in the same direction. In the adult phase, the leaves are usually unlobed and arranged spirally on woody stems that do not have aerial roots. The stems bear rounded clusters of small, pale green flowers in autumn, followed by usually black fruits.
CULTIVATION Tolerate full sun, partial or dense shade (some variegation may scorch in full sun, and gold variegation generally becomes green in shade) and a wide range of soils (JI No. 2).
PROPAGATION From softwood cuttings, from mid- to late summer. By layering, in late summer.
POTENTIAL PROBLEMS Red spider mites, scale insects, aphids.
WARNING Contact with the sap may irritate the skin. Swallowing any part may cause great discomfort.

H. canariensis Algeria, Tunisia.
Canary Island ivy, North African ivy
Foliage: year-round. Flowers: winter to early spring. H 15–20ft (4.5–6m). FrH.
The purplish stalks of this ivy carry roughly triangular bright green leaves that are heart-shaped at the base. Their glossy, bright green colour usually turns bronze in winter. '**Gloire de Marengo**', which is a popular houseplant, carries silver-green leaves with irregular creamy white margins.

H. colchica Caucasus, N. Iran
Bullock's heart ivy, Persian ivy
Foliage: year-round. Flowers: winter to early spring. H 20–30ft (6–9m). FH.
Dark green, leathery leaves, almost heart-shaped and lemon-scented when crushed, are as much as 10in (25cm) long. It is highly vigorous, but '**Dentata**', with thinner leaves, slightly toothed at the margins, grows even more rapidly. '**Dentata Variegata**', about 15ft (4.5m) high, has grey-green leaves with irregular yellow, later creamy white margins. '**Sulphur Heart**', of similar height, has light green or yellow splashes in the centre of each leaf.

Hedera colchica 'Dentata Variegata'

H. helix Europe
Common ivy, English ivy
Foliage: year-round. Flowers: winter to early spring. H 30–40ft (9–12m). FH.
The common ivy, with glossy, dark green 3- or 5-lobed leaves, is vigorous and tough, both as a climber and trailing plant. It has produced many fine, highly variable cultivars. '**Congesta**' and '**Erecta**' are shrubby, non-climbing forms, with upright stems and leaves arranged in 2 ranks. The cultivars are usually less vigorous than the species, but many grow as high as 15–25ft (4.5–7.5m). In the selection below, approximate heights are given for shorter-growing cultivars only: '**Adam**', neat, 3-lobed leaves, grey-green with irregular creamy white margins and tinged pink in winter; '**Buttercup**', 5-lobed leaves, yellow-green in sun but pale green in

Hedera helix 'Duckfoot'

shade, 6ft (1.8m); '**Cavendishii**', gently lobed, grey-marbled leaves with a broad, irregular creamy white margin; '**Duckfoot**', small green, shallow-lobed leaves with wedge-shaped bases, 30in (75cm); '**Glacier**', small, 3- to 5-lobed, grey-green leaves with silver-grey patches and irregular creamy white margins, 8ft (2.5m); '**Green Ripple**', glossy, elegantly jagged leaves, with forward-pointing lobes and prominent pale veins, 6ft (1.8m); '**Ivalace**', glossy dark green leaves with paler veins, the 5 shallow lobes with frilly margins, 3ft (90cm); '**Kolibri**', neat, very bright, white-splashed leaves with 5 lobes, the centre lobe long and pointed, 4ft (1.2m); '**Königers Auslese**', slender 5-lobed leaves, the centre lobe very elongated, 6ft (1.8m); '**Oro di Bogliasco**', pink stems and glossy dark green leaves with 3 lobes and a conspicuous yellow splash in the centre; '**Pedata**' (bird's foot ivy), dark green leaves with paler veins and 5 lobes, the centre one long, the basal lobes pointing backwards.

Hedera helix '**Glacier**'

H. hibernica *W. Europe*
Irish ivy
Foliage: year-round. Flowers: winter to early spring. H 20–30ft (6–9m). FH.
Although once classified as a form of common ivy (*H. helix*), this plant has larger leaves with broader, less well-pronounced lobes. '**Anna Marie**', which rarely exceeds 4ft (1.2m), has dainty, 5-lobed, grey-green leaves with creamy white margins. '**Deltoidea**', the shield or sweetheart ivy, reaches 15ft (4.5m) and has heart-shaped, glossy, dark green leaves, up to 4in (10cm) long, with overlapping basal lobes.

HUMULUS

CANNABACEAE Hop

The 2 species in this genus are perennial twining climbers of uncertain origin, but widely distributed in woodland, scrub and hedgerows in the temperate Northern Hemisphere. *H. lupulus* is widely grown as a crop: the overlapping bracts that cover the female flowers provide the hops used in brewing. The species is grown mainly for its foliage, but the bracts are also attractive.
CULTIVATION Tolerate full sun or partial shade and prefer moist but well-drained soil.
PROPAGATION From semi-ripe cuttings, from early to mid-summer.
POTENTIAL PROBLEMS Hop mildew.

Humulus lupulus '**Aureus**'

H. lupulus *N. America, W. Asia*
Hop
Flowers: spring to summer. Fruits: autumn. H 15–25ft (4.5–7.5m). FH.
The deeply lobed, light green leaves, 4–6in (10–15cm) long, are bristly with toothed margins. They are carried on square, thin, bristly twining stems. '**Aureus**', the yellow-leaved form, is a useful plant to brighten up dull corners.

HYDRANGEA

HYDRANGEACEAE

Of the 80 or so species usually considered to belong to this genus, most are deciduous or evergreen shrubs and small trees that are widely distributed in the temperate Northern Hemisphere and Central and South America. However, a few are vigorous climbers that cling to supports by means of aerial roots. They produce flat-topped flower clusters, which are composed mainly of small, fertile flowers. In the most showy species, larger sterile flowers orbit the cluster, as in the shrubby lacecap hydrangeas. The frost-hardy evergreen *H. serratifolia* can grow more than 50ft (15m) into trees, and produces fluffy white flower clusters of usually fertile flowers only. See also SHRUBS.
CULTIVATION Tolerate full sun or partial shade and require fertile, moist but well-drained soil.
PROPAGATION From cuttings, in late summer. By layering, in spring.
POTENTIAL PROBLEMS Aphids, red spider mites; grey mould (*Botrytis*),

hydrangea virus, powdery mildew, leaf spot, honey fungus.
WARNING Contact with the foliage may cause an allergic skin reaction. Swallowing any part may cause stomach upset.

H. anomala subsp. *petiolaris*
Japan, Korea, Russia (Sakhalin), Taiwan
Climbing hydrangea
Foliage: autumn. Flowers: summer. H 30–50ft (9–15m). FH.
In the wild, this deciduous climber is capable of growing 80ft (25m) into the canopy of tall trees, but it is slow to get started and to attach itself to its support. The flower clusters consist of tiny, creamy green fertile flowers surrounded sparingly with sterile flowers, 1in (2.5cm) or more across. When the dark green leaves yellow and fall in autumn, the lattice of red-brown stems is revealed. This species can also be grown without supports to make a wide-spreading shrub.

Hydrangea anomala subsp. *petiolaris*

IPOMOEA

CONVOLVULACEAE Morning glory

This large genus of about 500 species, almost all plants of warm temperate to tropical regions from a wide range of habitats, contains numerous annual and perennial, trailing or twining climbers. The relatively small number that are cultivated have elegant, tubular or funnel-shaped flowers and, in some cases, very intense colouring. Among the most striking of these are the blue dawn flower (*I. indica*), a vigorous, frost-tender perennial with purplish blue flowers, and the red morning glory (*I. coccinea*), a frost-tender annual with yellow-throated scarlet flowers.
CULTIVATION Require full sun and light, moist but well-drained soil (JI No. 2).
PROPAGATION From seed, sown under glass at 64°F (18°C) in mid-spring.
POTENTIAL PROBLEMS Aphids, whitefly (under glass), slugs; viruses, powdery mildew.

I. purpurea *Mexico*

Common morning glory
Flowers: summer to autumn.
H 10–15ft (3–4.5m). FT.
The bristly stems of this vigorous
annual climber carry heart-shaped,
sometimes 3-lobed leaves and
single or clustered flowers, which
unfurl from elegant pointed buds.
Their colour range includes white,
purple-blue and pink, and they are
sometimes striped.

Ipomoea purpurea

I. tricolor *Tropical Central and South America*

Morning glory
Flowers: summer to autumn.
H 8–12ft (2.5–3.7m). FT.
This short-lived perennial is best
grown as an annual. The leaves are
heart-shaped, and the delicate,
funnel-shaped flowers, usually blue
or purple and produced in
succession, fade within a day.
I. '**Heavenly Blue**' has azure flowers
with contrasting white throats.

JASMINUM

OLEACEAE Jasmine, jessamine

A high proportion of the 200 to
300 evergreen and deciduous
shrubs and climbers in this genus
are tropical, found in a variety of
habitats. The climbers have
twining stems, and their tubular
flowers, opening to 5 petal-like
lobes, are borne singly or in
clusters. The best-known species
have white flowers, but some
of the climbers, including
J. beesianum, are pink-flowered,
and many of the shrubby species
bear yellow flowers. An essential
oil extracted from the fine-scented
flowers of several species has been
much used in perfumery. The
flowers of most species are
followed by black, berry-like fruits.
CULTIVATION Prefer full sun (but
tolerate light shade in warm
climates) and moist but well-
drained soil.
PROPAGATION From cuttings, taken
from summer to early autumn. By
layering, in autumn.
POTENTIAL PROBLEMS Aphids; grey
mould (*Botrytis*).

J. officinale *Afghanistan, Caucasus, Himalayas, N. Iran, W. China*

Common jasmine
Flowers: early summer to early
autumn. H 30–40ft (9–12m). FrH.
The beguiling scent of this
deciduous to semi-evergreen
climber, combined with its
extended display of white, star-
shaped flowers set against dark
green foliage, has for centuries
delighted gardeners, poets and
travellers throughout its wide area
of natural distribution. In **f. affine**,
the pointed buds are tinged pink.
Variegated, less vigorous cultivars
include '**Argenteovariegatum**',
with white-edged, grey-green
leaves, and '**Aureum**', in which the
leaves are irregularly splashed with
yellow markings.

Jasminum officinale

J. polyanthum *W. and S.W. China*

Foliage: year-round. Flowers: late
spring to early autumn. H 8–16ft
(2.5–5m). HH.
This evergreen climber, with its
pink- or red-tinted buds in large
clusters opening to strongly
fragrant, usually white flowers,
strongly resembles *J. officinale*
f. *affine*. However, it is significantly
less hardy, and in many temperate
gardens is only suitable for a
conservatory or greenhouse.

Jasminum polyanthum

LAPAGERIA

PHILESIACEAE Chilean bellflower

This single species, the national
flower of Chile (known there as
"copihue"), clambers through
trees and shrubs in moist forests.

CULTIVATION Require partial shade
in a warm site and fertile, well-
drained, neutral to slightly acid soil
or lime-free (ericaceous) potting
compost.
PROPAGATION From seed, in spring.
By layering, in spring or autumn.
POTENTIAL PROBLEMS Aphids, mealy
bugs, scale insects (under glass).

Lapageria rosea

L. rosea *Chile*

Foliage: year-round. Flowers:
summer to late autumn. H 12–16ft
(3.7–5m). FrH.
The wiry, twining stems of this
climber carry leathery, pointed,
dark green leaves, and a succession
of waxy, narrow bell-shaped
flowers, up to 3in (8cm) long,
which hang singly or in groups of
2 or 3. The colour range includes
pink, light crimson and pink-tinged
white. '**Flesh Pink**' is delicately
coloured, and '**Nash Court**' has
soft pink flowers lightly marbled
with a darker shade.

LATHYRUS

PAPILIONACEAE

This genus of approximately 150
species comprises annuals and
herbaceous or evergreen
perennials. They are found in a
wide range of habitats in the
temperate Northern Hemisphere,
north and east Africa and
temperate South America. Their
flowers are pea-like, often scented,
and available in a range of colours.
These climbers have leaves
composed of 2 leaflets and a
branched tendril. Lord Anson's
blue pea (*L. nervosus*), with
fragrant, purplish blue flowers, is a
climbing herbaceous species
which originates from the Straits
of Magellan.
CULTIVATION Require full sun and
well-drained soil (JI No. 2).
L. odoratus requires plenty of
organic matter.
PROPAGATION From seed, sown
under cover in autumn or early
spring.
POTENTIAL PROBLEMS Slugs.
WARNING Swallowing the seeds
may cause stomach upset.

183

L. latifolius *S. Europe*
Everlasting pea, perennial pea
Flowers: summer to early autumn.
H 5–10ft (1.5–3m). FH.
The winged stems of this
herbaceous perennial climber carry
blue-green leaves and clusters of
purplish pink flowers. 'White
Pearl' bears lustrous, pure white
flowers. The Persian everlasting
pea (**L. rotundifolius**) is also fully
hardy, but is more slender and
carries pink flowers.

Lathyrus odoratus

L. odoratus *Italy (including Sicily)*
Sweet pea
Flowers: summer to early autumn.
H 6–10ft (1.8–3m). HH.
The pea-like flowers of this annual
climber, which can be prone to
powdery mildew, have a delicate
beauty and sweet fragrance. There
are numerous cultivars. "Old-
fashioned" sweet peas, the earliest
cultivars, have highly scented
flowers in red, pink, blue and
white. Modern sweet peas
(Spencer cultivars) have larger
flowers, with graceful, wavy-edged
petals, and have a wider colour
range: they are available in single
colours and mixtures. There are
numerous dwarf forms of sweet
peas: cultivars of the bushy **Bijou
Group** grow to approximately
18in (45cm); those of the **Jet Set
Group** and the **Knee-hi Group**
reach about 4ft (1.2m).

LONICERA

CAPRIFOLIACEAE Honeysuckle

Honeysuckles are widely
distributed in the Northern
Hemisphere, occurring in a range
of habitats from woodland to
rocky terrain. Of the 180 or so
species, which include some
shrubs, the most ornamental are
the evergreen and deciduous
twining climbers. Their flowers
are tubular or bell-shaped, either
2-lipped or with 5 equal lobes at
the mouth, and borne in pairs or
in small whorls. The pale to mid-
green leaves in opposite pairs vary
in shape from broadly oval to
almost circular, and in some

species and hybrids the topmost
pair of leaves unites to form a
collar beneath the flowers. Honeysuckles are noted mainly for their
heady fragrance, but some of the
climbers are valuable simply for
the profusion of their flowers. The
most magnificent of all the species
is the half-hardy, giant Burmese
honeysuckle (**L. hildebrandiana**),
capable of growing to 60ft (18m),
with its sweetly scented, creamy
white flowers. Out of their natural
habitats, some species have
become serious weeds, as is the
case with Japanese honeysuckle
(**L. japonica**) in parts of USA. See
also SHRUBS.
CULTIVATION Tolerate full sun or
partial shade and a wide range of
soil types (JI No. 3). Thin out old
wood after flowering.
PROPAGATION From semi-ripe
cuttings, in summer or hardwood
cuttings, in mid-autumn.
POTENTIAL PROBLEMS Aphids;
mildew.
WARNING Swallowing the berries
may cause stomach upset.

L. × americana
Flowers: summer to early autumn.
Berries: autumn. H 20–30ft
(6–9m). FH.
This vigorous, deciduous twining
climber, which flowers prolifically
from summer to early autumn, is
strongly fragrant. The tubular
flowers are 2-lipped and yellow,
tinged with purple. The flowers
are followed in the autumn by
red berries.

**Lonicera × brownii 'Dropmore
Scarlet'**

L. × brownii
Scarlet trumpet honeysuckle
Flowers: mid- to late summer.
H 10–15ft (3–4.5m). FH.
This deciduous or semi-evergreen
twining climber has orange-scarlet,
tubular, slightly 2-lipped flowers,
unfortunately without scent. The
blue- to mid-green leaves are almost
circular and carried in pairs on thin,
twiggy stems. One of the parents
of this hybrid, the coral or trumpet
honeysuckle (**L. sempervirens**), of
the eastern and southern USA, is

splendidly vivid, with tubular,
orange-scarlet, unscented flowers
opening to 5 equal lobes at the
mouth. It is frost hardy to fully
hardy. Cultivars of the hybrid
L. × brownii include the long-
flowering and richly coloured
'Dropmore Scarlet'.

L. caprifolium *Europe, W. Asia*
Italian honeysuckle
Flowers: summer. Berries: autumn.
H 15–20ft (4.5–6m). FH.
One of the most seductively
scented of all honeysuckles, this
deciduous species produces
creamy white to yellow flowers,
flushed with pink. The flowers are
cupped by the blue-green,
uppermost leaves, which are
united in pairs. Orange-red berries
appear in autumn.

L. japonica *E. Asia*
Japanese honeysuckle
Flowers: spring to late summer.
Berries: autumn. H 25–30ft
(7.5–9m). FH.
The foliage is evergreen, the leaves
sometimes lobed, and fragrant,
tubular white flowers, with soft
purple staining, are produced
over a long season. They are
followed in autumn by blue-black
berries.

**Lonicera periclymenum 'Graham
Thomas'**

L. periclymenum *Europe,
Caucasus, North Africa, Turkey*
Common honeysuckle, woodbine
Flowers: mid- to late summer.
Berries: autumn. H 20–25ft
(6–7.5m). FH.
This plant of woodland and
hedgerows is prized for the sweet
fragrance of its flowers; in the
evening, the scent is particularly
strong. The tubular white and
yellow flowers are flushed pink
and red, giving way to bright red
berries in autumn. 'Belgica' (early
Dutch honeysuckle) has reddish
purple flowers, which fade to
white and yellow, in late spring,
sometimes again in late summer.
'Graham Thomas', flowers
throughout summer and is white
in bud, becoming yellow when

open. **'Serotina'** (late Dutch honey-suckle) is similar to 'Belgica' but blooms from mid-summer to mid-autumn.

L. × tellmanniana

Flowers: late spring to mid-summer. H 12–18ft (3.7–5.5m). FH. The striking appearance of the flowers of this deciduous hybrid more than compensates for its lack of scent. Carried in whorls cupped by the topmost pair of leaves, the flowers are large, 2-lipped and glowing amber-coloured, flushed scarlet in bud. The foliage is dark green, with blue-white undersides.

PARTHENOCISSUS

VITACEAE Virginia creeper

This is a small genus of vines, comprising about 10 species of deciduous climbers equipped with tendrils, which in most cases are tipped with adhesive suckers. They are mainly tree-climbing plants of forest and woodland in the Himalayas, east Asia and North America; however, those with sucker-like pads are ideal for climbing walls. Virginia creeper is grown mainly for its lobed or entirely divided, layered leaves, which provide a luxuriant display in summer and are usually brightly coloured in autumn. The flowers are insignificant and are followed by grape-like berries.
CULTIVATION Tolerate full sun or partial shade and require a fertile, well-drained soil.
PROPAGATION From softwood or greenwood cuttings, in summer. From hardwood cuttings, in winter. From seed, sown under glass in autumn.
POTENTIAL PROBLEMS Usually none.
WARNING Swallowing the berries may cause mild stomach upset.

P. henryana China

Chinese Virginia creeper
Foliage: autumn. H 20–30ft (6–9m). FrH to FH.
Attaching itself by disc-like suckers, this handsome species quickly climbs walls and trees. The adult leaves consist of 3 to 5 coarsely toothed leaflets, which achieve their finest coloration in shade. The upper sides are velvety green, sometimes lightly bronzed, with silvery grey veins; the undersides, like the leaf stalks, are reddish. In autumn, the leaves turn vivid red.

P. quinquefolia E. North America

Virginia creeper
Foliage: autumn. Flowers: late spring to early summer. H 40–60ft (12–18m).
Whether growing into lofty trees or on walls, this vigorous, self-clinging vine becomes a vision of glowing crimson in autumn. The leaves are composed of 3 or 5 coarsely serrated leaflets.

P. tricuspidata China, Japan, Korea

Boston ivy
Foliage: autumn. Flowers: spring to summer. H 40–60ft (12–18m). FH.
This is a secure, self-clinging vine of great vigour, although growth may be slow to start. The lustrous leaves are very variable in size and shape: in young plants, they are often indistinctly lobed, while in mature plants they are usually 3-lobed and up to 8in (20cm) across. In autumn, the leaves turn reddish purple to scarlet; the young purple shoots retain their striking colour after the leaves have dropped. Cultivars include **'Beverley Brook'**, with purple-tinted summer foliage that turns bright red in autumn, and **'Veitchii'**, with dark reddish purple foliage in autumn. Both grow to about 23ft (7m) high.

Parthenocissus tricuspidata

PASSIFLORA

PASSIFLORACEAE Passion flower

Tropical South America is the home of many of the 400 or so species in this genus, which are predominantly evergreen climbers that attach themselves to supports with twining tendrils. The common name is a reference to Christ's suffering: the parts of the highly distinctive flowers are interpreted as representing his own attributes and the instruments of his Passion. Each flower has a tubular base and 10 segments, which usually spread out flat. A stalk in the centre of each flower holds a distinctive organ bearing the ovary and stamens, and is surrounded by a ring of filaments, known as the corona (interpreted as the crown of thorns). The flowers, in many species pendent, are followed by egg-shaped or spherical fruits, some of which are highly valued for their flavoursome pulp. The best-known of these is the frost-tender passion fruit (**P. edulis**), which has white flowers and yellow to purple fruit.
CULTIVATION Tolerate full sun or partial shade and require fertile, moist but well-drained soil in a sheltered site. Remove frost-damaged growth in mid-spring. Trim out one-third of the main growths each year, and cut back side shoots to 6in (15cm).
PROPAGATION From semi-ripe cuttings, from mid- to late summer. From seed, sown under glass at 55–64°F (13–18°C) in spring.
POTENTIAL PROBLEMS Viral infections.

Passiflora caerulea

P. caerulea C. and W. South America

Blue passion flower
Flowers: mid- to late summer. Fruits: H 20–30ft (6–9m). FrH.
If cut down in winter, this fast-growing species will shoot up again in the spring to make a fresh tangle of new growth. The divided, finger-like leaves are dark green, and the large, lightly scented flowers contain purplish blue filaments, which stand out against the white segments. Egg-shaped orange-yellow fruits, edible but not flavoursome, sometimes follow. **'Constance Elliot'** is less vigorous, with white flowers.

RHODOCHITON

SCROPHULARIACEAE

This very small genus consists of only 3 species of perennial climbers from woodland in Mexico. They are grown for their attractive pendent flowers, each consisting of a 5-lobed, hat-like calyx, protecting the long-tubed corolla, which opens out into 5 petal-like lobes.
CULTIVATION Requires full sun and fertile, moist but well-drained soil (JI No. 2).
PROPAGATION From seed, sown under glass at 59–64°F (15–18°C) or as soon as ripe, in spring.
POTENTIAL PROBLEMS Red spider mites, whitefly (under glass).

R. atrosanguineus *Mexico*
Flowers: summer to autumn.
H 8–10ft (2.5–3m). FT.
In mild conditions, this slender-stemmed perennial is extremely fast-growing. Also quick to reach flowering maturity, it can be grown as an annual. It has heart-shaped, rich green leaves, small showers of purple-red flowers, and climbs by means of twining leaf and flower stalks.

Rhodochiton atrosanguineus

SCHISANDRA

SCHISANDRACEAE

There are about 25 species of woody, deciduous and evergreen climbers in this genus; all are native to east Asia, except for one plant from North America. They are twining stem climbers of woodland and open scrub. The small, drooping blooms appear in clusters at the leaf joints, male and female flowers usually on separate plants. Provided the female flowers are fertilized, which generally means having male and female plants in close proximity to each other, they are followed by zig-zagging, trailing strings of luscious red fruits. The broad green leaves give good autumn colour. They may take up to 5 years to make substantial growth and to flower well. **S. grandiflora** is a rare species from the Himalayas, with conspicuously veined, leathery leaves and pale pink hanging blooms in late spring to early summer.
CULTIVATION Tolerate full sun or light shade and require fertile, preferably neutral to acid, moist but well-drained soil.
PROPAGATION From greenwood or semi-ripe cuttings, from early to mid-summer. From seed, sown in spring.
POTENTIAL PROBLEMS Usually none.

S. chinensis *E. Asia*
Flowers: late spring. Fruits: summer to autumn. H 20–30ft (6–9m). FrH.
With adequate support, this deciduous climber is a tall-growing species, although it can be trained sideways or allowed to sprawl at the top of a framework. Small, fragrant, white- or pink-flushed flowers in drooping clusters appear in late spring. Where males and females are planted together, the flowers are followed by long-lasting strings of fleshy red fruits.

S. rubriflora *Burma, India, W. China*
Flowers: late spring to early summer. Fruits: summer to autumn. H 15–25ft (4.5–6m). FrH.
Deep red, slightly fragrant flowers, up to 1in (2.5cm) across, open widely when mature. Long skeins of redcurrant-like fruits sometimes follow in summer to autumn. The deciduous foliage is bold, dark green and glossy, with oval to lance-shaped blades, up to 2in (5cm) across.

Schisandra rubriflora

SCHIZOPHRAGMA

HYDRANGEACEAE

The 2 species in this genus are woody stemmed deciduous climbers native to damp, shady woodland in Japan, China and Korea. The elegant flowerheads, which resemble those of a hydrangea, are made up of many tiny fertile flowers, and a few large sterile bracts (actually modified sepals). These climbers, with broadly oval leaves, are self-clinging, supporting themselves with aerial roots. They are slow to become established, but once they begin flowering in earnest they are ideal for climbing on walls or through trees.
CULTIVATION Tolerate full sun or partial shade (although flower best in sun) in a sheltered site to protect from winds and prefer moist but well-drained, neutral to slightly acid soil, rich in organic matter.
PROPAGATION From greenwood cuttings, from early to mid-summer or from semi-hardwood cuttings, in late summer. By layering, in autumn. From seed, sown in spring.
POTENTIAL PROBLEMS Usually none.

S. hydrangeoides
Flowers: summer to early autumn. H 30–40ft (9–12m). FH.
The flat, "lacecap" flowerheads have a scattering of sterile flowers around the rim. Surrounding these is a single, conspicuous, oval- to heart-shaped creamy white bract. The bracts remain on the plant for some time after flowering, prolonging interest. '**Roseum**' has pale pink bracts.

Schizophragma integrifolium

S. integrifolium
Flowers: summer to late autumn. H 30–40ft (9–12m). FH.
The large, flat "lacecap" flower-heads measure up to 12in (30cm) across. They are white and composed of fertile flowers and a few marginal bracts. They are long-lasting and still attractive in autumn and early winter when they turn the colour of parchment. The leaves are large, broad and oval, with finely serrated margins.

SOLANUM

SOLANACEAE

This very large and highly varied genus, with about 1400 species widely distributed throughout the world in a range of habitats, includes important vegetables, such as potatoes (**S. tuberosum**), and several ornamental plants. Among these are several woody-stemmed climbers and shrubs that can be wall trained.
CULTIVATION Require full sun and moist but well-drained soil. Thin out or remove overcrowded or damaged growth in mid-spring.
PROPAGATION From stem cuttings, in late summer.
POTENTIAL PROBLEMS Grey mould (*Botrytis*).
WARNING Swallowing the fruits may cause severe stomach upset.

S. crispum *Chile, Peru*
Chilean potato tree
Flowers: summer. H 12–18ft (3.7–5.5m). FrH.
This evergreen or semi-evergreen, bushy scrambling climber has oval-shaped leaves, with dark green

upper sides and paler green undersides, borne on green woody stems. The star-shaped flowers are purple-blue and have prominent yellow centres. **'Glasnevin'** is hardier than the species, with dark purple-blue flowers that last into autumn.

S. jasminoides *Brazil*
Potato vine
Flowers: summer to early autumn. H 10–15ft (3–4.5m). HH to FrH.
The glossy, pale green leaves of this slender, evergreen or semi-evergreen twining climber are oval- to lance-shaped, occasionally lobed. The star-shaped, slate-blue flowers have prominent golden anthers, and are produced in large, delicate clusters. **'Album'**, with white flowers and yellow anthers, is more widely grown.

Solanum jasminoides 'Album'

THUNBERGIA

ACANTHACEAE

The genus comprises about 100 species of twining climbers, shrubs, evergreen perennials and annuals, a high proportion native to tropical Africa and Asia. Those of ornamental value are grown for their tubular flowers with 5 petal lobes at the mouth. One of the most splendid climbers of tropical gardens is the frost-tender, evergreen Bengal clock or blue trumpet vine (*T. grandiflora*). This produces clusters of pale purple-blue flowers over a long season.
CULTIVATION Require full sun and moist but well-drained soil (JI No. 2).
PROPAGATION From seed, sown under glass at 61–64°F (16–18°C) in early spring.
POTENTIAL PROBLEMS Red spider mite (under glass).

T. alata *Tropical Africa*
Black-eyed Susan
Foliage: year-round. Flowers: summer to autumn. H 5–10ft (1.5–3m). HH
This twining perennial climber, widely naturalized in the tropics and subtropics, is quick to flower

when grown from seed, and makes a cheerful half-hardy annual in temperate gardens. The leaves are triangular and heart-shaped at the base, and the flowers are usually orange-yellow with purplish brown eyes.

Thunbergia alata

TRACHELOSPERMUM

APOCYNACEAE

Found in woodland in China, Japan and Korea, this genus consists of 30 evergreen twining or self-clinging climbers. The small, leathery, lance-shaped leaves make dense cover on established plants, clothing the woody stems to the ground. The small, white, 5-petalled flowers, produced in clusters, are highly fragrant. Their habits become bushier with age, provided they do not suffer from severe winter damage. Plants may remain virtually dormant for the first 2 or 3 years after planting, and are generally slow to establish.
CULTIVATION Tolerate full sun or light shade and require fertile, moist but well-drained soil, rich in organic matter. The site must be sheltered from wind and cold – a warm, sunny wall is ideal.
PROPAGATION From seed, sown in spring. By layering, in summer. From semi-hardwood cuttings, in late summer or autumn.
POTENTIAL PROBLEMS Aphids (on young growth).

T. asiaticum
Foliage: year-round. Flowers: mid- to late summer. H 15–20ft (4.5–6m). FrH.
This is a highly fragrant climber, with masses of small white, cartwheel-shaped flowers, creamy white ageing to yellow. The dark, glossy, oval-shaped leaves are relatively small, up to 2in (5cm) long, providing attractive, dense cover. The stems reach about 12ft (3.7m) at maturity.

T. jasminoides
Confederate jasmine, star jasmine
Foliage: year-round. Flowers: mid-summer. H 20–30ft (6–9m). FrH.

This beautiful, scented, evergreen climber is the most widely available species in the genus. With proper training and extra protection from cold and wind, especially in the early years, the confederate jasmine will make a superb year-round feature: wrap it with insulation from late autumn to mid-spring, and mulch to protect the root system. The small white flowers, up to 1in (2.5cm) wide, look at first sight like those of common jasmine (*Jasminum officinale*), hence the common name, but on closer inspection, you can see that the 5 petals are swirled like a cartwheel. They are carried in clusters at the ends of the shoots. The handsome glossy green, oval to lance-shaped leaves are large, measuring up to 4¼in (11cm) in length. **'Variegatum'** is less vigorous. It has glossy grey-green leaves, variegated creamy white, and developing attractive pinkish red tints in winter.

Trachelospermum jasminoides

TROPAEOLUM

TROPAEOLACEAE

The 80 to 90 species of annual and herbaceous perennials in this genus are mostly trailing or climbing. They are plants of Central and South America, many of them from the Andes. The Canary creeper (*T. peregrinum*), which acquired its common name while being acclimatized in the Canary Islands, is an annual with feathered yellow flowers from Ecuador and Peru. All species have short, broadly trumpet-shaped flowers, some with petals of differing sizes, and a prominent spur at the base of each individual bloom. They usually flower from mid-summer to mid-autumn. One of the most familiar annuals, the nasturtium (*T. majus*), is typical of the genus in climbing by means of a coiling action of the leaf stalks. However, many of its cultivars, such as **'Empress of India'**, with semi-double scarlet flowers, are compact plants suitable for bedding and container gardening.

CULTIVATION Tolerate full sun or partial shade and most soils (JI No. 2).
PROPAGATION From seed (annuals), sown where plants are to flower in mid-spring or under glass at 55–61°F (13–16°C) and planted out when the risk of spring frosts is over. By division of the rootstock, in early spring (*T. speciosum*).
POTENTIAL PROBLEMS Aphids.

T. speciosum Chile
Flame creeper, flame nasturtium
Flowers: summer to autumn. Fruits: autumn. H 10–15ft (3–4.5m). FH.
With its spurred bright scarlet flowers, this is striking against the backdrop of a yew hedge in cool, moist gardens. The slender twining stems grow from a creeping rhizome and carry pretty 6-lobed leaves. The bright blue fruits that sometimes follow the flowers are set against deep red calyces.

Tropaeolum speciosum

VITIS

VITACEAE Vine

Most of the 60 to 70 species are deciduous tendril climbers from temperate regions of the Northern Hemisphere. Many of them grow vigorously into trees, particularly at the margins of woodland. Some have superbly ornamental foliage, the leaves colouring brilliantly in autumn. The flowers of the majority of species are small, green and insignificant, but the fruits (grapes) of some species can be ornamental, edible, or made into wine. The grape vine (*V. vinifera*) is of great economic and cultural importance, but its origins are not known for certain.
CULTIVATION Tolerate full sun or partial shade and prefer a fertile, well-drained soil. Thin out old growths and shorten young growths in late summer.
PROPAGATION From hardwood cuttings, from late autumn to winter. From vine eyes, in mid-winter.
POTENTIAL PROBLEMS Brown scale insects, vine weevils; honey fungus.

Vitis coignetiae

V. coignetiae Japan, Korea
Foliage: autumn. Flowers: late spring. Fruits: autumn. H 50–70ft (15–22m). FH.
The vigour and splendour of this vine puts it in a class of its own. The dark green, heart-shaped leaves, up to 12in (30cm) long and wide, have 3 to 5 lobes, deeply sunken veins and felted rust red undersides. The foliage is attractive in autumn, turning orange, purplish brown and scarlet. The bluish black fruits are inedible.

V. vinifera Probably Asia Minor and the Caucasus
Grape vine
Flowers: late spring to early summer. H 20–30ft (6–9m). FH.
The characteristic leaf of the grape vine is leathery, with 3 to 5 lobes and toothed margins in a broadly rounded outline. A few cultivars have been selected for their ornamental qualities: '**Ciotat**' (parsley vine) has finely cut leaves; '**Purpurea**' has young leaves that are white and downy, becoming claret red and, in autumn, turning deepest purple; *V.* '**Brant**', which is similar to *V. vinifera*, with leaves that turn bronze and purple in autumn, although the veins remain green.

WISTERIA

PAPILIONACEAE

Well known for their beautiful cascades of white, pink, blue or mauve pea-like flowers, this genus consists of 10 hardy deciduous climbers, all of which support themselves with twining stems. The usual flowering season is late spring through to mid-summer, although small flushes of flowers are often produced until early autumn. The two most commonly grown species are Japanese wisteria (*W. floribunda*) and Chinese wisteria (*W. sinensis*), both of which are ideal for covering walls, fences and trellis and growing into large trees, twining anti-clockwise around the support. The flowers of the fully hardy

silky wisteria (*W. venusta*), which comes from Japan, are the largest of all the wisterias, reaching up to 1½in (4cm) in diameter. The slightly fragrant flowers, which appear in early summer, are produced on short, drooping racemes with all the flowers opening at the same time. The young foliage has a silvery sheen.
CULTIVATION Require full sun to flower well and a deep, moist but well-drained soil. Prune side shoots to 2 or 3 buds in late winter, and prune gently in mid-summer to keep size in check.
PROPAGATION From heel or nodal cuttings, in late summer. By layering, in late spring.
POTENTIAL PROBLEMS Aphids, brown scale, red spider mite; fungal leaf spot, honey fungus.
WARNING Swallowing any part may cause stomach upset.

W. floribunda Japan
Japanese wisteria
Flowers: early summer. H 20–30ft (6–9m). FH.
The light to mid-green leaves, composed of up to 19 leaflets, open at the same time as the fragrant violet-blue flowers. These are produced in drooping racemes, 12in (30cm) long, which open successively from the base downwards. Named cultivars of this vigorous species include: '**Alba**', with white flowers, flushed with lilac at the keel and borne in racemes up to 2ft (60cm) long; the spectacular '**Multijuga**', with mauve and blue-purple flowers, borne in large racemes, up to 4ft (1.2m) long.

W. sinensis China
Chinese wisteria
Flowers early summer. H 40–60ft (12–18m). FH.
This classic wisteria produces dense racemes of fragrant mauve flowers, up to 1ft (30cm) long, on small, spur-like growths. They open almost simultaneously, before the dark to mid-green leaves start to develop. Other forms include the white-flowered '**Alba**'.

Wisteria sinensis

roses

The rose holds a unique place among garden plants. Relatively few of the 150 species are widely grown but the hybrid roses are so numerous that the genus *Rosa* represents in itself an important branch of gardening and a major horticultural industry. To take a harsh view, the rose has attracted excessive attention from breeders and gardeners.

The following small selection covers all the major categories of roses. These include the Species Roses and Modern Shrub Roses, which in some cases are similar to the species in character. Among old-fashioned roses are some, like those portrayed in 17th-century Dutch paintings, that flower only once, and others, mainly 19th century, that repeat during summer. There are a few Modern Bush Roses, Large-flowered (Hybrid Teas) and Cluster-flowered (Floribundas), that are much used in bedding schemes, and toy-like Patio and Miniature roses. There are also Climbers and Ramblers, for which no spread is given, as it depends on the training method.

Bare-root roses are generally best planted in autumn. Container-grown roses can be planted at most times of the year. Commercially propagated roses are normally budded on to the rootstock of a wild rose and may produce suckers, which should be removed promptly. Pruning advice is given with each category.

Top Rosa glauca
Centre Rosa 'New Dawn'
Bottom Rosa 'Albertine'

ROSA

ROSACEAE ROSE

The finest roses are plants of truly superlative quality and ranked behind them are thousands that are only slightly inferior. And yet the awful fact must be faced: there is a high cost to pay for the dominant role roses so often play in gardens. The most popular are unspeakably dreary in winter and a very high proportion require the regular use of chemicals to control pests and diseases.

The 150 or so species in the genus are widely distributed in the Northern Hemisphere. Most are thorny shrubs or climbers and they are found in a variety of habitats. In themselves the species are relatively unimportant as garden plants, representing only a tiny proportion of the roses in cultivation. A few, however, have played an enormously important role in the breeding of the old roses and the extraordinary output of the modern rose industry.

The following selection is so small that it risks trivializing a much-loved group of plants but it attempts to reflect their variety and valued qualities such as scent. The roses are grouped into 6 categories, according to a standard horticultural classification: Species and Closely Related Hybrids; Old Shrub Roses; Modern Shrub Roses; Modern Bush Roses; Modern Miniature and Patio Roses; and Climbers and Ramblers.

Information on cultivation, propagation and potential problems follows but advice on pruning is given at the end of the introduction to each section. In addition to following the recommended pruning regimes, gardeners should remove all dead, diseased and damaged growths and, as a general principle, prune to outward-facing buds to maintain an open-centred bush through which air can move freely.

CULTIVATION Most roses require full sun (a few tolerate absence of direct sunlight but need an open well-lit position) and well-drained soil with a plentiful supply of moisture. Many hybrid roses, especially the modern bush roses, perform well only in fertile soil that is rich in organic matter. Rose "replant sickness" occurs when roses are planted in soil where roses have been growing.

PROPAGATION Most hybrid roses are raised commercially by grafting. Species, Modern Shrub Roses and Ramblers from semi-ripe cuttings after flowering or hardwood cuttings in winter; true species from seed, sown in autumn.
POTENTIAL PROBLEMS Aphids, caterpillars, leafhoppers, red spider mites, sawfly larvae, scale insects; black spot, canker, honey fungus, powdery and downy mildews, rose "replant sickness", rust, viruses.

SPECIES AND CLOSELY RELATED HYBRIDS

The small number grown usually have only one flush of flowers in a season but they deserve to be judged by their overall character. The best are well-shaped arching shrubs with attractive foliage, usually single flowers and often highly ornamental hips. They include some of the most disease-resistant roses available.
PRUNING Little required except for the removal at ground level, after flowering, of up to one quarter of the oldest stems.

Rosa 'Geranium'

R. 'Geranium'
Flowers: mid-summer. Hips: autumn. H 6–8ft (1.8–2.5m), S 5–6ft (1.5–1.8m). FH.
The Chinese species *R. moyesii* makes a large open bush as much as 10ft (3m) high that is spangled in summer with pink or red single flowers and laden in autumn with flagon-shaped scarlet hips. *R.* 'Geranium' is a slightly smaller shrub in its parent's mould. Creamy stamens brighten the blood-red single flowers, which are followed by heavy crops of the highly distinctive and long-lasting hips.

R. glauca *Mountains of C. and S. Europe*
Flowers: mid-summer. Hips: autumn. H 5–7ft (1.5–2.2m), S 4–6ft (1.2–1.8m). FH.
The pink starry flowers, borne in clusters, are of fleeting interest but there are splendid clusters of red hips to follow. However, what makes this a rose of great distinction is the cool purple-blue of the foliage.

Rosa glauca

R. xanthina 'Canary Bird'
Flowers: mid- to late spring. H 8–10ft (2.5–3m), S 6–12ft (1.8–3.7m). FH.
The species, a graceful arching shrub from China and Japan, is usually represented in gardens by 'Canary Bird'. Its high season comes early, with single clear yellow flowers nestling thickly among ferny grey-green leaves. The fragrance is light and flowering is sparse after early summer. *R.* 'Cantabrigiensis', flowering in spring and early summer, bears a resemblance but the prickly bush is more compact and the sweetly scented flowers are creamy yellow.

Rosa xanthina 'Canary Bird'

OLD SHRUB ROSES

The hybrid roses that existed before the development of the modern Large-flowered Bush Roses (Hybrid Teas) are very mixed in character but they are consistent in their colour range, which excludes yellow and orange. Each of the main groups – Alba, Bourbon, Centifolia, China, Damask, Gallica, Hybrid Perpetual, Moss and Portland – is now often represented in gardens by a relatively small cluster of survivors, but these include some of the most memorably beautiful of all roses. Many do not repeat.
PRUNING With the exception of Hybrid Perpetuals, cut back stems by about a third and on established plants cut out at ground level up to a quarter of the oldest stems, pruning once-flowering roses as

soon as flowering has finished, repeat-flowering roses in late winter or early spring. Prune Hybrid Perpetuals more drastically, cutting back main stems to about 10in (25cm) above ground level and removing completely up to a third of the oldest stems in late winter or early spring.

R. 'Cécile Brünner'
Flowers: repeat, summer/autumn. H 30–36in (75–90cm), S 18–24in (45–60cm). FH.
Although introduced in the 1880s this is usually listed with the more modern Polyanthas which are low-growing with clusters of small flowers. The pale pink buds of the twiggy 'Cécile Brünner' are exceptional for their miniature elegance. The open flowers are lightly scented. There is a climbing form that can grow to 20ft (6m) but it flowers only once. 'Perle d'Or' has lightly fragrant flowers in shades of apricot and cream.

Rosa 'Céleste'

R. 'Céleste'
Flowers: early summer. H 5–6ft (1.5–1.8m), S 4–5ft (1.2–1.5m). FH.
From their name, it might be thought that the Albas are united in having white flowers. Some of these tough hybrids do, including one of the oldest, the so-called Jacobite rose or White Rose of York (*R.* × *alba* 'Alba Maxima'), a sweet-scented double up to 7ft (2.2m). 'Céleste', however, is an Alba rose with fragrant, double, light pink flowers set against blue-grey leaves.

R. 'Charles de Mills'
Flowers: early summer. H and S 4–5ft (1.2–1.5m). FH.
The Gallicas, one of the oldest groups of roses, include several examples that have a distinctive personality. 'Charles de Mills', like many Gallicas almost thornless, produces flowers that seem to have been sliced through to show their crimson and purple tones. 'Cardinal de Richelieu' grows to 3ft (90cm) and has very double flowers of deep purplish red.

Rosa 'Complicata'

'Complicata', up to 7ft (2.2m) tall, is a more vigorous alternative carrying hot pink single blooms with showy yellow stamens.

Rosa 'Fantin-Latour'

R. 'Fantin-Latour'
Flowers: early summer. H 4–6ft (1.2–1.8m), S 4–5ft (1.2–1.5m). FH.
The Centifolia roses – also known as the "cabbage" or "Provence" roses – so lovingly rendered by Dutch and Flemish painters of the 17th century, originated in Holland during the late 16th century. They are distinguished by their large, usually pink, sweetly scented double blooms, which often droop with their own luscious weight. 'Fantin-Latour', named after the famous 19th-century French painter, makes a strong spreading bush which benefits from support. It bears fully double, flat, pink flowers, which have a delicate sweet scent. 'De Meaux' produces an abundance of small clear pink flowers on arching stems. This is a more compact shrub only 3ft (90cm) high. Nearly twice this in size is 'Tour de Malakoff', which carries sumptuous flowers blending magenta, purple and mauve-grey.

R. 'Madame Hardy'
Flowers: early summer. Hips: autumn. H 5–7ft (1.5–2.2m), S 4–5ft (1.2–1.5m). FH.
The Damasks are a very old group of roses and their fragrant flowers have long been used in the commercial production of attar of roses. 'Madame Hardy' is a white of incomparable beauty with a distinctive lemon scent. The feathery buds, blushing faintly, open to pure white double flowers, the petals perfectly folded around a central green "button eye". 'Celsiana', bears pale pink yellow-eyed blooms with crinkled petals. It has a heavy perfume. 'Ispahan' is a vigorous Damask bearing large, fragrant, blush-pink blooms over a long period. The abundant foliage is grey-green.

Rosa 'Madame Isaac Pereire'

R. 'Madame Isaac Pereire'
Flowers: repeat, summer/autumn. H 7–15ft (2.2–4.5m), S 4–6ft (1.2–1.8m). FH.
Some detect a hint of raspberries in the flowers of this and other Bourbons. 'Madame Isaac Pereire', which can be grown as a climber as well as a shrub, like several Bourbons, has deep purple-pink double flowers. The flowers of 'Boule de Neige', creamy white, and 'Louise Odier', pink with mauve tints, are almost camellia-like. 'Reine Victoria' is lax and needs support to carry its scented, beautifully cupped, rose-pink double flowers.

Rosa 'Louise Odier'

R. 'Madame Knorr'
Flowers: repeat, summer/autumn. H 4–5ft (1.2–1.5m), S 3–4ft (90–120cm). FH.
The Portlands were popular roses in the 19th century, valued because they repeated well and had good scent. 'Madame Knorr' has mauve-pink double flowers, flushed a deeper pink at the centre, and remarkable disease-resistance for an old rose.

Rosa 'Nuits de Young'

R. 'Nuits de Young'
Old black rose
Flowers: early summer. H 4–5ft (1.2–1.5m), S 30–36in (75–90cm). FH.

Moss roses are typified by the soft down or "moss" of glands on the flower buds and upper stems which give off a resinous scent and add to their fragrance. 'Nuits de Young' – said to be the darkest of all the old roses – makes an erect but compact bush. The dark brownish green moss encloses the double scented flowers which are deep purple-maroon with a central boss of yellow stamens. '**Gloire des Mousseuses**', another Moss rose, is similar in habit, with scented flowers in pale sugar-pink, flushed darker at the centre. An occasional bloom in autumn is an added bonus.

Rosa 'Reine des Violettes'

R. 'Reine des Violettes'
Flowers: repeat, summer/autumn. H 5–6ft (1.5–1.8m), S 3–4ft (90–120cm). FH.
The Hybrid Perpetuals were immediate forerunners of the modern Large-flowered (Hybrid Tea) roses, their colour range representing a stage before the introduction of yellow. The well-scented double flowers of '**Reine des Violettes**' show, however, the richness of the old palette. The blooms, set against grey-green foliage, are velvet purple, ageing to lilac. '**Paul Neyron**', although unfortunately carrying little scent, makes a more vigorous shrub, with enormous ruffled flowers in deep pink, flushed lilac. '**Mrs John Laing**'

carries fully double silvery pink flowers with a very good scent. It makes a compact shrub about 3ft (90cm) tall.

MODERN SHRUB ROSES

These roses, which have been developed since the end of the 19th century, are very varied but differ from the Modern Bush Roses in having a more graceful character. Many add to the qualites of the Species or the Old Shrub Roses a repeat-flowering habit. Some are generously described as "groundcover" roses.
PRUNING Carry out pruning of repeat-flowerers in late winter or early spring. Those that flower only once should be pruned in late summer. Cut back main shoots by up to a third and shorten laterals to about 4in (10cm); cut out at ground level 1 or 2 of the oldest stems of mature plants.

Rosa Bonica

R. Bonica
Flowers: continuous, summer/autumn. H 34–36in (85–90cm), S 3½–5ft (108–150cm). FH.
With dense, glossy-green, disease-resistant foliage and large sprays of scented, double, pink flowers borne over a long season, **Bonica** is too good to be pigeon-holed merely as a groundcover rose. Other roses marketed under this name include the slightly smaller **Rosy Cushion**, with single to semi-double bright pink flowers with a white eye, and several in the County Series among them **Kent**, only 18in (45cm) high but spreading to 3ft (90cm) and well-covered in summer with semi-double white flowers.

R. 'Buff Beauty'
Flowers: mid-summer, with flushes onwards into autumn. H and S 4–5ft (1.2–1.5m). FH.
The Hybrid Musks, most of which were bred in the 20th century before World War II, make substantial but graceful shrubs with remarkable disease-resistance and copious dark green leaves.

Rosa 'Buff Beauty'

They flower prodigiously in their first flush and often impressively later in the year. '**Buff Beauty**' carries large double flowers that are beige with a subtle tinge of apricot. '**Cornelia**' has summer flowers that are pale sugar-pink and autumn blooms that are deeper pink with a copper tint. The light pink flowers of '**Felicia**' are flushed apricot. All three are fragrant.

R. 'Fru Dagmar Hastrup'
Flowers: mid- to late summer. Hips: autumn. H and S 3–5ft (90–150cm). FH.
The Rugosa roses are only one stage removed from the rugged wild *R. rugosa*, an exceedingly tough suckering species often found on sand dunes in China, Siberia, Japan and Korea. Rugosas have inherited the constitution of their wild parent, making disease-resistant thorny shrubs that endure drought better than most roses. They come into leaf early, produce scented flowers with fine-textured petals throughout summer and the singles and semi-doubles bear impressive crops of tomato-shaped hips in autumn. '**Fru Dagmar Hastrup**', one of the most compact, bears single pink flowers. The ripening hips coincide with the late blooms. '**Roseraie de l'Haÿ**' carries double purple-red flowers and '**Blanche Double de Coubert**' is a double of purest white. Both grow to a height of 6ft (1.8m) or more and are suitable for planting as informal hedges.

Rosa 'Fru Dagmar Hastrup'

R. 'Frühlingsmorgen'

Flowers: late spring. Hips: autumn. H 5-6ft (1.5-1.8m), S 4-5ft (1.2-1.5m). FH.

The roses bred from the wild Scotch rose or Burnet rose (**R. pimpinellifolia**) inherit that plant's tough constitution and so can adapt to a wide range of conditions. 'Frühlingsmorgen', with sweetly scented peach-pink flowers that have pale yellow centres, is one of the first roses to flower each year, and has a graceful arching habit. There is usually a small second crop of flowers. **Frühlingsgold** bears a magnificent display of soft lemon-yellow blooms that fade to creamy white but there is no follow-on after the first display.

R. 'Golden Wings'

Flowers: continuous, summer/autumn. H and S 4-6ft (1.2-1.8m). FH.

Single saucer-shaped flowers, up to 5in (13cm) across, are carried on an elegantly arching shrub, a cluster of red stamens contrasting with the yellow petals. The sweetly scented blooms are borne in profusion throughout the summer. **Sally Holmes** is another impressive modern shrub with single scented flowers. The ivory-white petals have a delicate pink flush to the margins.

Rosa **Constance Spry**

R. Heritage

Flowers: continuous, summer/autumn. H and S 3-4ft (90-120cm). FH.

In the English Roses, a new group that came to notice in the 1970s, some of the qualities of the old roses, in particular flower shape and fragrance, have been combined with the ability to flower repeatedly throughout summer and the wide colour range of modern bush roses. English roses that repeat-flower well include **Heritage**, with cup-shaped fragrant flowers in soft pink, and **Graham Thomas**, a bushy plant with pure yellow fragrant flowers. **Constance Spry**

disappoints by flowering only once but the soft pink fragrant blooms, up to 6in (15cm) across, have a luminous beauty. This rose can be grown as a shrub or trained as a climber.

R. 'Nevada'

Flowers: early summer with occasional autumn blooms. H and S 7-9ft (2.2-2.7m). FH.

Arching red-brown stems carry masses of large, semi-double, creamy white blooms that are slightly scented. The sparse autumn flowers are often much pinker in colour. '**Marguerite Hilling**' is its equal but produces an abundant display of deep pink scented flowers.

Rosa 'Marguerite Hilling'

R. 'Nymphenburg'

Flowers: continuous, summer/autumn. H 8-9ft (2.5-2.7m), S 5-6ft (1.5-1.8m). FH.

The size and vigour of many modern shrub roses allows them to be trained as climbers as well as grown more conventionally. '**Nymphenburg**', a vigorous Hybrid Musk which lends itself to either treatment, has scented, semi-double, peach-pink flowers. **Dortmund**, an equally versatile rose, has single, cherry-red, white-eyed flowers.

Rosa **Jacqueline du Pré**

R. Pearl Drift

Flowers: continuous, summer/autumn. H and S 3-4ft (90-120cm). FH.

Semi-double pale pink flowers are borne above dark green glossy foliage on a spreading shrub.

Jacqueline du Pré, a taller shrub growing to 6ft (1.8m), has semi-double flowers with a musk-like scent. The flowers are ivory-white with a hint of pink.

R. 'White Pet'

Flowers: continuous summer/autumn. H 18-32in (45-80cm), S 18-24in (45-60cm). FH.

Small white pompon flowers open from tight pink buds to provide a succession of dainty clusters on a compact little bush. This variety can be grown as a small standard. The blooms of this Polyantha are very faintly scented. '**The Fairy**', sometimes described as a groundcover rose, is another pretty Polyantha with sprays of pale pink pompons. It is usually less than 30in (75cm) in height and spread and comes into flower late but continues well into autumn.The clear pink, semi-double, lightly scented flowers of '**Mevrouw Nathalie Nypels**' are carried in abundant clusters.

Rosa 'The Fairy'

MODERN BUSH ROSES

In bloom, the Modern Bush Roses are wonderfully prolific or neurotically hectic, depending on your point of view; out of bloom they are undeniably stiff and gawky. Within this broad category are 2 important groups. The Large-flowered Bush Roses (Hybrid Teas) produce high-centred, usually double, flowers that are borne either singly or in small clusters in several flushes between early summer and autumn. The Cluster-flowered Bush Roses (Floribundas) bloom more continuously and have smaller flowers carried in larger clusters.

PRUNING In late winter or early spring, cut back stems of Large-flowered roses to 6-10in (15-25cm) above ground level. Cluster-flowered roses should have their stems cut back to 10-18in (25-45cm). Established bushes of both types should have 1 or 2 of the oldest stems cut out at ground level.

R. Alexander

Flowers: continuous, summer/autumn. H 6–7ft (1.8–2.2m), S 24–32in (60–80cm). FH.
This very vigorous, erect, long-stemmed rose is ideal for cutting. It is also considered a great improvement on its parent **Super Star**, a Large-flowered bush rose which has a less regular habit and a less consistent flower colour. The dark green foliage of **Alexander** shows good disease-resistance and the lightly scented double flowers are of unfading vermilion.

Rosa Amber Queen

R. Amber Queen

Flowers: continuous, summer/autumn. H 20–24in (50–60cm), S 18–24in (45–60cm). FH.
The dark bronze-green foliage of this Cluster-flowered bush rose, tinted red when young, makes an attractive foil for the fully double, fragrant, amber-yellow flowers. This is a compact spreading rose that is more suitable for bedding than '**Glenfiddich**', which is slightly taller but with flowers of a similar colour. Both roses are in flower over a long season.

Rosa 'Arthur Bell'

R. 'Arthur Bell'

Flowers: continuous, summer/autumn. H up to 2–3ft (60–90cm), S 24–30in (60–75cm). FH.
With shiny bright green leaves and double, fragrant, creamy yellow flowers, this spreading Cluster-flowered rose is useful for bedding. **Mountbatten** is taller with a slender upright habit and is less prone to fading. It has slightly larger flowers of a deeper yellow.

R. Chicago Peace

Flowers: continuous, summer/autumn. H 4–6ft (1.2–1.8m), S 2–3ft (60–90cm). FH.
This sport of the famous **Peace** rose has inherited the robust character and glossy dark green foliage of its Large-flowered parent but in the blooms it shows a stronger pink than in the original gentle mixture of soft pink and creamy white.

R. Double Delight

Flowers: continuous, summer/autumn. H 2–3ft (60–90cm), S 18–24 (45–60cm). FH.
With a more compact habit than most Large-flowered cultivars, this is an unusually good bedding rose for a plant of this group. The highly fragrant double flowers are pale pink, with the edges painted deep carmine-red. Unfortunately, it is susceptible to mildew. **Blessings**, similar in size, is another good Large-flowered bedding type. It has scented, double, salmon-pink flowers, although mildew can also be a problem.

R. Elina

Flowers: continuous, summer/autumn. H 3–3½ft (90–108cm), S 24–30in (60–75cm). FH.
The ivory-white flowers have the classic shape of a Large-flowered bush rose and they are shown off well by the foliage. **Pascali**, with sparse foliage, also has white flowers. Both are doubles and are only lightly fragrant.

R. Escapade

Flowers: continuous, summer/autumn. H 30–36in (75–90cm), S 24–30in (60–75cm). FH.
This Cluster-flowered rose has unusual and sweetly scented semi-double flowers, which are white-centred and pink with violet tints. **Eye Paint** has little scent but is a bolder colour choice, its white eye making a startling contrast with the brilliant scarlet petals of the single flowers. It is taller at 3½ft (1.1m).

Rosa Escapade

R. Fragrant Delight

Flowers: continuous, summer/autumn. H 2–3ft (60–90cm), S 24–30in (60–75cm) FH.
The double salmon-pink blooms have a good scent but uneven growth counts against this Cluster-flowered rose. Pink doubles of neater habit include '**Dearest**' and '**English Miss**'.

R. 'Gruss an Aachen'

Flowers: in flushes, summer/autumn. H and S 24–30in (60–75cm). FH.
Many of the Polyantha roses were interbred with the Large-flowered roses to produce the freer more perpetually flowering Cluster-flowered roses. As such, the oldest varieties are truly "parents" to the modern Cluster-flowered roses which have largely supplanted them. Polyanthas are often smaller-flowered and without scent. This gives exceptions such as the fragrant '**Gruss an Aachen**', with creamy white to pale pink sprays of double blooms, a special attraction. **Yesterday**, a spreading, very free-flowering, rather shrubby modern Polyantha type is similarly scented. The single to semi-double flowers are lilac-pink to rose-violet. It has a height and spread of 3–5ft (90–150cm).

Rosa Iceberg ('Korbin')

R. Iceberg ('Korbin')

Flowers: continuous, summer/autumn. H 3–4ft (90–120cm), S 30–36in (75–90cm). FH.
Despite its susceptibility to black spot, **Iceberg** is a popular Cluster-flowered bush rose because of its graceful carriage and the long succession, even into winter, of lightly scented double flowers. '**Margaret Merril**' is a more compact white with better scent.

R. Mister Lincoln

Flowers: continuous, summer/autumn. H 3–5ft (90–150cm), S 24–30in (60–75cm). FH.
The velvet texture of the shapely buds gives an added depth to their deep crimson. This is an upright

Large-flowered bush rose with leathery dark green foliage. **Royal William** is more compact and carries fragrant flowers with similar colouring.

Rosa Royal William

R. 'National Trust'
Flowers: continuous, summer/ autumn. H and S 24–30in (60–75cm). FH.
The high-centred buds open to bright red double flowers with elegantly pointed petals, displaying the classic form of the Large-flowered bush roses. The scent, however, is disappointing. The double flowers of **Silver Jubilee**, which are pink with shades of peach and cream, are also of elegant form and only lightly scented.

Rosa 'National Trust'

R. Oranges and Lemons
Flowers: continuous, summer/ autumn. H and S 24–30in (60–75cm). FH.
The scarlet striping of orange-yellow double flowers gives this novelty value, even among the highly variable Cluster-flowered roses. Another orange-flowered bicolour, **Tango** is a deeper reddish colour, fading to yellow at the petal margins, with each petal yellow on the reverse.

R. 'The Queen Elizabeth'
Flowers: continuous, summer/ autumn. H 6–7ft (1.8–2.2m), S 3–4ft (90–120cm). FH.
This, one of the most vigorous of the Cluster-flowered bush roses, carries double well-shaped clear pink flowers on long stems.

Chinatown, less vigorous but capable of growing to a height of 6ft (1.8m) if lightly pruned, produces double sweetly scented flowers that are yellow with a hint of pink.

MODERN MINIATURE AND PATIO ROSES

Miniature roses and the Patio roses, which are intermediate between Miniatures and the Cluster-flowered bush roses, need an intimate setting in the open garden or in a container. *PRUNING* Trim Miniatures lightly and reduce stems of Patio roses by about a third in late winter or early spring.

R. Baby Masquerade
Flowers: continuous, summer/ autumn. H and S 12–18in (30–45cm). FH.
This Miniature has flowers like those of the well-known Cluster-flowered rose '**Masquerade**' – slightly scented, yellow-pink, flushed deeper red – but they are only 1in (2.5cm) across. It makes a dense twiggy bush, unlike the more erect '**Little Buckaroo**', which has semi-double orange-red flowers. **Orange Sunblaze** has fully double bright orange-red blooms.

R. Gentle Touch
Flowers: continuous, summer/ autumn. H 15–20in (38–50cm), S 16–20in (40–50cm). FH.
This is a slightly scented dwarf Cluster-flowered rose, which bears perfectly cup-shaped, semi-double, pale apricot-pink flowers, which are large for this group – as much as 2in (5cm) across. **Sweet Magic** makes a smaller bush at 14in (35cm), carrying double flowers in a deeper apricot-orange and yellow.

Rosa Gentle Touch

R. Sweet Dream
Flowers: continuous, summer/ autumn. H 14–20in (35–50cm), S 12–16in (30–40cm). FH.
This neat, upright, bushy plant carries dense clusters of well-

proportioned double flowers. The cupped blooms are lightly scented and a melting blend of apricot and peach shades. Other roses in this increasingly popular group are **Anna Ford**, which has semi-double orange-red flowers and a compact habit, and **Little Bo-peep**, which has a more spreading habit and semi-double pale pink flowers.

CLIMBERS AND RAMBLERS

Most Ramblers are roses of exceptional vigour, producing long flexible stems that can be directed to streak into the branches of a tree or trained on a sturdy support such as a pergola. They do not repeat but they produce masses of small flowers, which are usually well scented. Climbers lack the carefree energy of the Ramblers but in most cases the stiff growths carry flowers either in a couple of flushes or more continuously between early summer and autumn. The spread depends on the method of training used so measurements have not been given here.
PRUNING Cut out up to a third of flowered shoots from established Ramblers as soon as flowering has finished; shorten side-shoots of Climbers to 3 or 4 buds between autumn and spring and reduce main shoots, if necessary, in order to keep the plant within the space available.

R. 'Albertine'
Flowers: early to mid-summer. H 15–20ft (4.5–6m). FH.
For a Rambler '**Albertine**' has large flowers and their shade of copper-pink is distinctive. In mid-summer this vigorous rose provides a deliciously scented mass of blooms, looking most at ease when its stiff arching stems are allowed to sprawl over a fence. Another vigorous Rambler, the semi-evergreen '**Albéric Barbier**' bears rather drooping creamy white flowers, which are lightly scented of apples. Both roses produce shiny foliage.

Rosa 'Albertine'

195

Rosa banksiae 'Lutea'

R. *banksiae* 'Lutea'

Yellow Banksian rose
Flowers: mid-spring. H 20–30ft
(6–9m). FrH.
The Banksian roses, which
are vigorous finely branching
Ramblers of Chinese origin, need
a warm wall and shelter if they are
to be grown in frost-prone areas.
The yellow Banksian, said to be
the hardiest, bears numerous
clusters of small fully double
flowers exceptionally early in
the rose year. The flowers have
little scent. '**Paul's Himalayan
Musk**', another vigorous Rambler
displaying clusters of small double
flowers, in this case pale pink and
scented, is hardier and more
conventional in its summer
flowering.

R. 'Bobbie James'

Flowers: early to mid-summer.
H 20–30ft (6–9m). FH.
Large clusters of semi-double
creamy white flowers shed a far-
reaching scent. '**Wedding Day**',
bearing single, creamy white,
scented flowers opening from
apricot buds, is another vigorous
Rambler suitable for training up a
sturdy tree.

Rosa Golden Showers

R. Golden Showers

Flowers: continuous, summer/
autumn. H 8–10ft (2.5–3m). FH.
This rose is a stiff, upright, almost
thornless climber, which can also
be grown as a shrub. The well-
shaped buds open to scented,
loose double, yellow blooms.
Breath of Life, another of the
short Climbers sometimes known

as "pillar roses", produces double
peach-pink flowers, which have a
light scent.

R. 'Madame Alfred Carrière'

Flowers: in flushes, mid-summer
to autumn. H 15–20ft (4.5–6m). FH.
Old Noisette Climbers such as this
are very vigorous, producing
numerous new soft stems in a
season and a succession of
flowers, not carried continuously
but in prolonged flushes. '**Madame
Alfred Carrière**' is a particularly
lovely delicately scented rose
with very disease-resistant pale
green foliage. It carries double
ivory-white flowers flushed palest
pink. It is best grown on a large
wall or heavy pergola support.
Another old Noisette rose with a
good scent is '**Gloire de Dijon**',
which has double flowers in an
unusual shade of buff-yellow with
a soft pink tinge. In the case of
'**Alister Stella Gray**' the apricot
buds open to buff or creamy white
musk-scented flowers with a
yellowish centre.

R. 'Meg'

Flowers: continuous, summer/
autumn. H 12–13ft (3.7–4m). FH.
The large fragrant flowers, which
are semi-double and nearly flat
when fully open, are an unusual
blend of apricot and pink and have
conspicuous reddish amber
stamens. Another stiff-stemmed
Climber with semi-double flowers,
Parkdirektor Riggers, makes a
more flamboyant statement with
large clusters of semi-double
scarlet blooms that have wavy
petals.

R. 'New Dawn'

Flowers: continuous, summer/
autumn. H 10–20ft (3–6m). FH.
Even on walls that get little direct
sun, this vigorous Climber can
produce numerous small sprays of
silvery pink, lightly scented,
double flowers. The dark green
glossy foliage shows good disease-
resistance. '**New Dawn**' is the
parent of a number of healthy
repeat-flowering climbers such as

Rosa 'New Dawn'

'**Parade**', which carries carmine-
pink double flowers. The dark
glossy leaves have a reddish tinge.
Unfortunately, this rose has not
inherited its parent's scent.

R. 'Veilchenblau'

Flowers: mid-summer. H 10–12ft
(3–3.7m). FH.
This compact, easily controlled,
thornless Rambler has healthy,
disease-resistant, light green
foliage. The clusters of apple-
scented, double flowers have a
curious beauty, the blooms
opening dusky magenta-purple
before fading to soft grey-mauve.
Because of its long pliable stems,
this rambler, more tolerant of
shade than most, is admirably
suited to training on most
moderately sized supports. A taller
compact Rambler '**Félicité
Perpétue**', reaching a height of 15ft
(4.5m), covers itself with a
snowstorm of small double
flowers carried in clusters,
opening from pink-edged buds to
a final gentle white, blushed with
pink. Although remarkable for its
evergreen to semi-evergreen
foliage, it is unlikely to prove
hardy in the very coldest areas.
'**The Garland**' has sprays of small,
light salmon-pink flowers and a
rich orange fragrance.

Rosa 'Veilchenblau'

R. 'Zéphirine Drouhin'

Thornless rose
Flowers: continuous, summer/
autumn. H 9–15ft (2.7–4.5m). FH.
Despite being prone to mildew,
this old Bourbon remains a
favourite. Its almost thornless
stems are easily trained and in
early summer it makes an
extravagant and vivid display of
loose bright pink flowers that are
well scented. There are flowers
later in the season but never in
such profusion. '**Blairii Number
Two**', another vigorous climbing
Bourbon, has few flowers after its
main flush but the full, shapely,
fragrant blooms are of exceptional
quality, with deep pink centres
shading delicately to pale pink at
the edges.

perennials

In a broad sense the term perennial covers all non-woody flowering plants that live for more than two years; that is, they have a life expectancy longer than annuals or biennials but do not have the durable framework of shrubs and trees. Many of these plants are herbaceous, having a seasonal cycle in which annual growth dies down in autumn before a period of winter dormancy. Others, such as the bergenias, are evergreen and semi-evergreen. Sub-shrubs, which have a woody base and soft stems, fall somewhere between typical herbaceous perennials and shrubs. A number of common plants, including hybrid petunias, are strictly speaking perennials but are almost invariably grown from seed annually. More problematic are plants, such as *Salvia patens,* that are treated as annuals where they are too tender to survive winter outdoors but in warmer climates can be reasonably long-lived. Variations in cultivation may account for apparent inconsistencies in the placing of plants. The first step to take if a plant cannot be found where expected is to consult the index.

The generous space devoted to perennials here reflects their value in gardens, whether they are planted in traditional borders or in a more relaxed manner (see pp. 56–57). Planting times are spring or autumn.

Top Euphorbia griffithii 'Fireglow'
Centre Hemerocallis lilioasphodelus
Bottom Houttuynia cordata 'Chameleon'

ACAENA

ROSACEAE Bidi bidi, New Zealand Burr

Good foliage, topped in summer by attractive spiny burrs, makes several of these vigorous mat-forming plants useful as ground cover. There are about 100 species, all from the Southern Hemisphere and most, including *A. buchananii* and *A. novae-zelandiae*, come from New Zealand, where they are usually found in open terrain, including high country and river flats. It is ironical that the introduction to New Zealand of domesticated animals, especially sheep, should have provided the perfect means of seed distribution.
CULTIVATION Tolerate full sun or partial shade and require fertile well-drained soil.
PROPAGATION From self-layered stems, in autumn or spring. From softwood cuttings, in late spring. From seed, sown in autumn.
POTENTIAL PROBLEMS Usually none.

A. microphylla *New Zealand*
Foliage: year-round. Flowers: summer. H 1–2in (2.5–5cm), S 18–24in (45–60cm). FH.
This evergreen species is generally represented by the cultivar 'Kupferteppich', with ground-hugging compound leaves of bronzy green, spherical flowerheads and an encrustation of bright red burrs in late summer.

A. saccaticupula 'Blue Haze'
Foliage: year-round. Flowers: mid-summer. H 4–6in (10–15cm), S 3–4ft (90–120cm). FH.
The evergreen compound leaves, the paired leaflets with finely toothed edges, are a metallic blue-green tinged with purple. Bronzed stems carry spherical flowerheads that turn to reddish brown burrs.

Acaena saccaticupula 'Blue Haze'

ACANTHUS

ACANTHACEAE Bear's breeches

In the dry, stony landscapes of the Mediterranean basin, which is the home of several among the 30 species, their foliage is conspicuously handsome, forming bold clumps from which rise stiff spikes of tubular flowers encased in prickly bracts. It is said that acanthus leaves inspired the classical decorative motif of Corinthian capitals, but which species provided the model is subject to debate. In their combination of foliage and flowers, the latter produced most freely in full sun, several species are among the most impressive perennials and worthy of growing in isolated groups. However, the planting site must be well chosen from the start, the fleshy roots being almost ineradicable. The cut flower spikes, although awkward to handle when dry, are highly decorative.
CULTIVATION Tolerate full sun or partial shade and require well-drained soil (JI No. 2).
PROPAGATION By division, in spring. From seed, sown in spring. From root cuttings, taken in winter.
POTENTIAL PROBLEM Powdery mildew.

A. mollis *N.W. Africa, S. Europe*
Foliage: spring to autumn. Flowers: late summer. H 4–5ft (1.2–1.5m), S 3–4ft (90–120cm). FH.
A large clump produces several spikes of purplish veined white flowers hooded by long-lasting purple bracts and surrounded by dark green leaves. These are glossy and generously lobed. In the **Latifolius Group** the leaves are easily 8in (20cm) across.

A. spinosus *Mediterranean, S. Europe*
Foliage: spring to autumn. Flowers: late summer. H 4–5ft (1.2–1.5m), S 2–3ft (60–90cm). FH.
The spiny, arching leaves, up to 3ft (90cm) long and deeply cut, form a splendid base for tall stems bristling with tiers of white flowers hooded by purple bracts. The very finely cut leaves of the **Spinosissimus Group** are grey-green with silvered midribs and points.

Acanthus spinosus

ACHILLEA

ASTERACEAE Yarrow

The 85 or so species from temperate parts of the Northern Hemisphere and several hybrids provide a range of tough, sun-loving plants. These are suitable for borders and for small-scale planting in rock gardens and among paving. The flat or domed flowerheads, predominantly but far from exclusively yellow and usually densely packed with small daisy flowers, are long-lasting in the garden and in many cases are highly decorative when dried. The foliage is often ferny (*A. ptarmica* is an exception) and in some cases silvered. Those that have invasive roots need careful positioning but even the common yarrow (*A. millefolium*) has bright forms, such as 'Cerise Queen', that have a place in plantings on rough ground.

Achillea millefolium 'Cerise Queen'

CULTIVATION Require full sun and well-drained soil.
PROPAGATION By division in spring (advisable every third year, particularly for *A.* 'Moonshine'). From seed, sown in spring.
POTENTIAL PROBLEMS Aphids; powdery mildew.
WARNING Contact with the foliage may cause an allergic skin reaction.

A. 'Coronation Gold'
Foliage: year-round. Flowers: summer. H 30–36in (75–90cm), S 18–24in (45–60cm). FH.
Although owing much to *A. filipendulina*, this is a more compact plant with greyer leaves and flatter, less densely packed yellow flowerheads.

A. filipendulina *Caucasus*
Flowers: early summer to early autumn. H 3–4ft (90–120cm), S 18–30in (45–75cm). FH.
Cultivars of this species, with their stiff stems bearing broad flowerheads in shades of yellow over a long period, are classic tall border plants, providing a contrast to perennials with more flowing lines. The densely packed,

mushroom-shaped heads of **'Gold Plate'** can be up to 6in (15cm) across. The golden colour is retained if the flowerheads are dried properly.

Achillea filipendulina **'Gold Plate'**

A. 'Lachsschönheit'

Flowers: summer. H 30-36in (75-90cm), S 20-24in (50-60cm). FH. Hybrids of *A. millefolium* and *A.* 'Taygetea' run freely like common yarrow but the best of them have broad heads of delicately tinted flowers. In 'Lachsschönheit', the coral of the newly opened flowers fades to peachy beige, the two colours often being present at the same time. *A.* **'Hoffnung'**, up to 30in (75cm) high, has flowerheads that change from cream to biscuit. Both are Galaxy Hybrids.

A. × lewisii 'King Edward'

Foliage: spring to mid-autumn. Flowers: early and mid-summer. H 4-6in (10-15cm), S 9-12in (23-30cm). FH. This scaled-down version of the border achilleas is a long-flowering plant for the rock garden. The heads are buff yellow and the ferny leaves grey-green.

A. ptarmica 'Boule de Neige'

Flowers: early to late summer. H 1-3ft (30-90cm), S 12-18in (30-45cm). FH. They are invasive but the blithe brightness of the double forms of sneezewort, with their profusion of white button flowerheads nearly obscuring the indifferent foliage, makes it worth taking trouble to position them well. **The Pearl Group** covers seed-raised doubles.

A. 'Taygetea'

Foliage: spring to early autumn. Flowers: mid- to late summer. H 18-24in (45-60cm), S 12-18in (30-45cm). FH. This has its own cool scheme with pale yellow flowerheads, flat and up to 4in (10cm) across, and ferny evergreen leaves, that in reality are a soft grey-green. *A.* **'Moonshine'**, up to 2ft (60cm), is like a larger version with more silvery foliage.

Achillea **'Moonshine'**

ACONITUM

RANUNCULACEAE Monkshood

Despite the fascination of their curious hooded flowers, a colour range that includes wonderfully rich blues, and lobed leaves well above the average in quality, these plants are less widely grown than they deserve. They are highly toxic in all their parts, a fact that may have contributed to their neglect. There are over 100 species from the Northern Hemisphere, of which the dozen or so that are grown and which are the parents of some fine hybrids, are mainly natives of alpine pastures and thin woodland where there is a good supply of moisture. Many, including the common monkshood or helmet flower (*A. napellus*), are sturdy erect plants, suitable for borders or planting in the light shade of shrubs or trees but the tallest may need staking. The rootstock of many is tuberous. When using as cut flowers the warning below should be heeded.

Aconitum napellus

CULTIVATION Tolerate full sun or shade and require moist soil. To maintain vigour, divide plants every third year.
PROPAGATION By division, during autumn. From seed, sown in spring.
POTENTIAL PROBLEMS Aphids; verticillium wilt, fungal stem rot.
WARNING Long recognized as plants of sinister potency. Contact with the foliage may cause an allergic skin reaction. All parts, but especially the roots, are toxic.

A. × cammarum 'Bicolor'

Foliage: spring to autumn. Flowers: mid- to late summer. H 4-5ft (1.2-1.5m), S 12-18in (30-45cm). FH. One of the most striking of the old hybrids this has bicoloured flowers in blue and white arranged in loose clusters up the stem.

A. carmichaelii China

Flowers: early autumn. H 3-4ft (90-120cm), S 12-18in (30-45cm). FH. The late flowering season is a tremendous bonus in a sturdy plant with rich green leaves that give useful body to a border throughout summer. The hooded flowers, borne in branched spires, are violet-blue; in **'Arendsii'** the colour is of exceptional richness. **Wilsonii Group 'Kelmscott'** has purplish blue flowers.

Aconitum carmichaelii **'Arendsii'**

A. 'Ivorine'

Flowers: late spring to early summer. H 2-3ft (60-90cm), S 12-18in (30-45cm). FH. Short spires, closely set with creamy helmets, provide a cool foretaste of the monkshood season.

A. 'Newry Blue'

Flowers: mid- to late summer. H 4-5ft (1.2-1.5m), S 12-18in (30-45cm). FH. The range of blues in the hybrids is impressive. The many branches of this tall aconite are densely packed with mid-blue helmets. Other hybrids flowering in the second half of summer include the violet-blue *A.* **'Bressingham Spire'**, about 3ft (90cm) high, and the deeper coloured, taller *A.* **'Spark's Variety'**.

Aconitum **'Spark's Variety'**

ACORUS

ARACEAE

The 2 species in this genus are waterside plants that are more valuable for their blade-like leaves than for their curious flowers. They are widely distributed in the Northern Hemisphere. Their rhizomes may need to be lifted and divided after several years if they have become congested.
CULTIVATION Require full sun and moist or wet soil (especially pond margins).
PROPAGATION By division, in spring (establish in a pot before planting out).
POTENTIAL PROBLEMS Usually none.

Acorus calamus 'Variegatus'

A. calamus 'Variegatus'
Foliage: spring to autumn. H 2–3ft (60–90cm), S 18–24in (45–60cm). FH.
The sword-like leaves of *A. calamus*, the sweet flag, emit a slightly spicy scent when crushed. 'Variegatus' is a much more distinguished marginal for planting in shallow water along the edge of ponds or streams, its longitudinal striping making an intriguing play of green and cream verticals.

A. gramineus *E. Asia*
Japanese rush
Foliage: spring to autumn. H 6–12in (15–30cm), S 6–8in (15–20cm). FrH.

Acorus gramineus 'Ogon'

The relatively short fans of semi-evergreen linear leaves, beautifully striped cream and yellow in 'Variegatus' and with a broad yellow stripe in 'Ogon', make all of these rush-like plants invaluable marginals for small ponds.

ACTAEA

RANUNCULACEAE Baneberry

The 8 baneberry species, natives of moist woodland in temperate regions of the Northern Hemisphere, are grown more for their late summer display of enticing but toxic berries and pleasing divided foliage than for their clusters of small white flowers.
CULTIVATION Require partial shade and moist fertile soil.
PROPAGATION By division, in early spring. From seed, sown in autumn.
POTENTIAL PROBLEMS Usually none.
WARNING The berries are very poisonous if eaten.

A. alba *E. North America*
Doll's eyes, white baneberry
Flowers: late spring and early summer; fruits: late summer.
H 2–3ft (60–90cm), S 18–24in (45–60cm). FH.
The light green leaves, usually composed of 5 irregularly toothed leaflets, make a pleasing mound of foliage. The fluffy white flowers are followed by mesmerizing clusters of white berries, each with a black eye and on a stalk that thickens and turns red. The red baneberry, *A. rubra*, is a shorter growing plant, reaching a height of about 18in (45cm), and the berries that follow the white flowers are glistening scarlet.

Actaea alba

ADONIS

RANUNCULACEAE

Most of the perennials among the 20 species from Europe and Asia are alpine plants from open grassy slopes or the edges of mountain woodland. The widely distributed European species *A. vernalis* is suitable for growing in a rock garden or the front of a border.
CULTIVATION Require full sun and well-drained fertile soil. The European species tolerate alkaline conditions, but the Asiatic species do best in moist acid soils containing plenty of organic matter.
PROPAGATION By division, after flowering. From seed, sown in autumn.
POTENTIAL PROBLEM Slugs.

Adonis amurensis 'Fukujukai'

A. vernalis *Europe*
Flowers: mid- to late spring.
H 10–16in (25–40cm), S 12–18in (30–45cm). FH.
The bright green leaves, ferny with narrow linear leaflets, are topped by anemone-like yellow flowers that are up to 3in (8cm) across. The Japanese species, *A. amurensis*, has similarly bowl-shaped flowers in yellow but it requires shadier and moister growing conditions in an acid soil. The semi-double 'Fukujukai' is one of many selected forms cultivated in Japan.

AGAPANTHUS

ALLIACEAE African blue lily

There are about 10 species of *Agapanthus* found in southern Africa. Some of them are deciduous, mainly from mountainous grasslands; others are evergreen, mainly plants of coastal areas where the rainfall is lower. In addition there are numerous hybrids, which, like the species, are remarkably consistent in their flower colour, straying into white but otherwise keeping to shades of blue. The hybrids as well as the species are fleshy-rooted plants that usually produce clumps of strap-shaped leaves and stout stems culminating in umbels of trumpet-shaped or tubular flowers. The stalks and their flowers often radiate out from the end of the stem to form a rounded head but sometimes the flowers are more or less loosely pendulous, as in the deciduous and frost hardy *A. inapertus*. Where the climate is mild enough they make well-anchored border plants, with flowers that are good for cutting and seedheads that are also decorative. Agapanthus are excellent container plants and in areas where it is too cold to grow them outdoors, even where a thick mulch might help to get them through the winter, container-growing is the solution for the more tender evergreen species such as **A. africanus** and **A. praecox subsp. orientalis**. They can be positioned outdoors in summer and given protection in a greenhouse or conservatory during the coldest months. Plants need plenty of moisture throughout summer but should be kept dry in winter.

CULTIVATION Require full sun and moist, fertile, well-drained soil (JI No. 3).

PROPAGATION By division, in spring. From seed, sown when ripe or in spring and kept at a temperature of 55–59°F (13–15°C). Plants flower after 2–3 years.

POTENTIAL PROBLEMS Slugs and snails; viruses.

Agapanthus campanulatus 'Isis'

A. campanulatus *South Africa* (*Natal, Northern Cape*)
Flowers: late summer. H 2–4ft (60–120cm), S 16–20in (40–50cm). FH.
The flowers, which are nearly bell-shaped and variable in the depth of their blue, are carried in rounded umbels above a base of narrow grey-green leaves, which are deciduous. It is a fine plant in its own right and a parent of numerous hybrids. The flowers of **var.** *albidus* are white and '**Isis**' is a dark blue version.

A. hybrids
Flowers: late summer. H 12–48in (30–120cm), S 10–20in (25–50cm). FH.
The umbrella term **Headbourne Hybrids** used to describe blue- and white-flowered seedlings noted for their hardiness and floral qualities raised and distributed by the Hon. Lewis Palmer has been cavalierly applied to mixed seedlings, giving no guarantee of quality. For this reason, unless buying plants in flower, it is better to seek out named hybrids, most of which are deciduous. One of the most

substantial is '**Blue Giant**', with flower stems about 4ft (1.2m) high carrying dense umbels of rich blue flowers. '**Lilliput**' has deep blue flowers; at 12–16in (30–40cm) tall it is small enough to be tucked into narrow borders with other sun-loving plants. '**Bressingham White**', about 3ft (90cm) high, is one of the best white hybrids.

Agapanthus 'Lilliput'

AGASTACHE

LAMIACEAE

Among the aromatic, sun-loving plants in this genus of about 30 species are several that are natives of dry hilly country in North America and Mexico. The half-hardy plant **A. mexicana**, producing spikes of small tubular red-pink flowers, can be grown as an annual.

CULTIVATION Requires full sun and well-drained fertile soil.

PROPAGATION By division, in spring. From semi-ripe cuttings, taken in late summer and protected from frosts. From seed, sown in early spring at 55–64°F (13–18°C).

POTENTIAL PROBLEM Powdery mildew.

Agastache foeniculum

A. foeniculum *North America*
Anise hyssop
Foliage: spring to early autumn.
Flowers: mid-summer to early autumn. H 3–5ft (90–150cm), S 12–18in (30–45cm). FrH.
The bruised leaves, downy on the underside, are pleasantly aromatic and the erect stems are topped by long-lasting dense spikes of tiny violet-blue flowers.

AGAVE

AGAVACEAE

The agaves are among the most useful plants for frost-free gardens in hot, dry areas, their rosettes of fleshy leaves retaining their sculptural and jagged appeal even during long periods of drought. In cooler climates they make magnificent container plants but need protection under glass during winter. There are more than 200 species, most of them found wild in areas of low rainfall, sometimes at high altitudes, from North to South America and in the West Indies. Many species are slow to reach maturity and when they have flowered the main rosette dies but usually leaves offsets.

CULTIVATION Require full sun and fertile free-draining soil, preferably neutral to acid (JI No. 2 with added grit).

PROPAGATION From offsets, in spring or autumn. From seed, sown in early to mid-spring at 70°F (21°C).

POTENTIAL PROBLEMS Scale insects and, particularly under glass, mealy bugs.

WARNING The leaves of many species are sharp tipped.

Agave americana 'Variegata'

A. americana *Mexico*
Foliage: year-round. Flowers: (when mature) late summer. H 5–6ft (1.5–1.8m), S 6–8ft (1.8–2.5m). FT.
The impressive rosettes are composed of pointed grey-green leaves imprinted on the reverse with the spiny margins of the outer leaves. When the plant eventually produces its yellow-green tubular flowers the stem may be more than 20ft (6m) high. The variegated cultivars include '**Mediopicta**', with a broad yellow streak down the centre of the leaves; and '**Variegata**', with a cream edge to blue-green leaves.

AJUGA

LAMIACEAE Bugle

The 40 or so plants are shade-loving natives of temperate Europe and Asia. *A. reptans* has a close spreading habit, which makes it useful as groundcover, especially in the variants with distinctively coloured foliage. The glossy green leaves of the pyramidal bugle (*A. pyramidalis*) are less effective for this purpose but the eye is strongly drawn to spikes of intense blue flowers in late spring.

CULTIVATION Require partial shade and moist soil.

PROPAGATION By division, in early summer. From softwood cuttings, taken in early summer.

POTENTIAL PROBLEM Powdery mildew.

A. reptans *Europe, Iran*
Flowers: late spring to early summer. H 4–10in (10–25cm), S 2–3ft (60–90cm). FH.
The glossy green species is irrepressible, colonizing in all directions but in late spring a carpet of the blue flowers carried in short spikes makes a wonderfully bright effect in shade. The forms with coloured foliage, generally less vigorous, provide groundcover year round. The bronzy purple of 'Atropurpurea' is at its best with the flowers but with the variegated forms such as 'Burgundy Glow', a mixture of deep red, pink and cream, the flowers are a distraction.

Ajuga reptans 'Atropurpurea'

ALCHEMILLA

ROSACEAE Lady's mantle

Alchemilla mollis, the best-known species, is a native of woodland margins, especially on moist soils, but the genus is a large one and representatives of the 250 or so species are found in many different parts of the world. After *A. mollis* the most useful as garden plants are small species that follow its formula in combining attractive foliage with showers of frothy lime-green flowers.

CULTIVATION Tolerate full sun or partial shade and require moist but reasonably well-drained soil that is rich in organic matter.

PROPAGATION By division, in spring or autumn. From seed, sown in spring. From self-sown seedlings. Transplant these when small.

POTENTIAL PROBLEMS Usually none.

Alchemilla erythropoda

A. erythropoda *Carpathians, Caucasus, Turkey*
Foliage: spring to autumn. Flowers: late spring to late summer. H and S 8–12in (20–30cm). FH.
The sprays of greenish yellow flowers fall across green hairy leaves with a blue tint that are rounded in outline but divided into 7–9 lobes. The alpine lady's mantle (*A. alpina*) and *A. conjuncta* are other compact species; both have the underside of the leaves covered with silky silvery hairs.

A. mollis *Caucasus, Turkey*
Lady's mantle
Foliage: spring to autumn. Flowers: early summer. H 16–24in (40–60cm), S 20–30 (50–75cm). FH.
The downy softness of the rounded grey-green leaves traps droplets of water and turns them to quicksilver. The intricately branched sprays of tiny greenish yellow flowers remain attractive for weeks. The mounds of sympathetic greenery and the casual looseness of the flower sprays in a related colour are a combination that makes this species one of the best plants to use as a skirt for shrubs and other perennials that are bare at the

Alchemilla mollis

base. The main fault of this very beautiful plant is that it can self-seed too freely but the prompt removal of spent flowers avoids this and in any case unwanted seedlings are easy to remove.

ALOE

ALOEACEAE

This large genus of African succulents, with about 300 species, includes a number of rosette-forming plants of jagged character that are suitable for desert gardens. In frost-prone areas they make interesting container plants that can be moved outdoors during the summer months.

CULTIVATION Require full sun and free-draining soil (JI No. 2 with added grit). Under glass, require ventilation and full light.

PROPAGATION From offsets, removed in late spring or early summer. From seed, sown in spring.

POTENTIAL PROBLEMS Scale insects and mealy bugs, particularly when grown under glass.

A. aristata *S. Africa (Cape Province)*
Foliage: year-round. Flowers: late spring to early summer. H 4–6in (10–15cm), S 6–8in (15–20cm). FT.
The stemless rosettes are composed of densely packed grey-green leaves with toothed margins and a liberal covering of spine-like white eruptions, especially on the underside. The cylindrical flowers are orange. This species produces numerous offsets.

Aloe variegata

A. variegata *S. Africa (Cape Province)*
Partridge-breasted aloe
Foliage: year-round. Flowers: early to mid-spring. H 8–12in (20–30cm), S 6–10in (15–25cm). FT.
The common name is an allusion to the irregular white banding on the dark green leaves, which are V-shaped in section and arranged in 3 ranks. They have white toothed edges. The scarlet tubular flowers are carried on a thick stem.

ALSTROEMERIA

ALSTROEMERIACEAE Peruvian lily

The 50 or so species in this South American genus are plants with running fleshy roots that are mostly natives of high open country. Relatively few species are grown as garden plants. The best-known are 3 that are frost hardy: the orange-yellow *A. aurea*, *A. ligtu*, with flowers dominated by shades of purple and pink, and the curious *A. psittacina*, in an arresting combination of green and deep red with maroon marks. The hybrids are better known, increasingly so as a result of breeding for the cut-flower trade. The amateur gardener stands to benefit from hybrids bred for their beautifully marked trumpet flowers, their wiry stems and their year-round performance when grown commercially. Some of these new alstroemerias go under the name **Princess hybrids**. In frost-prone areas deep planting, with the tubers covered by 9in (23cm) of soil, and mulching in autumn protects plants in winter.
CULTIVATION Tolerate sun or partial shade and require moist but well-drained soil.
PROPAGATION By division, in early spring. From seed, sown as soon as ripe.
POTENTIAL PROBLEMS Slugs, red spider mites under glass; viruses.
WARNING Contact with the foliage may irritate the skin.

Alstroemeria ligtu hybrids

A. ligtu hybrids

Flowers: summer. H and S 2–3ft (60–90cm). FrH.
Until recently these have been the most widely grown of the hybrids and have proved themselves more hardy than the species. The wide range of colours includes strong oranges and coral reds as well as softer shades of cream, yellow and pink. The markings of the topmost segments are an appealing feature of these flowers, clustered at the tops of wiry stems. These hybrids can be invasive and in exposed positions may need support.

ANACYCLUS

ASTERACEAE

This Mediterranean genus of only 9 species contains an excellent perennial daisy that grows wild in open and stony mountainous country. It makes an easy rock garden plant, flowering prettily above feathery foliage, but is adaptable to any sunny position in the garden where the drainage is sharp.
CULTIVATION Requires full sun, very well-drained, light soil (JI No. 2 with added grit) and protection from winter wet.
PROPAGATION From cuttings, taken in spring to early summer. From seed, sown in autumn.
POTENTIAL PROBLEMS Usually none.

Anacyclus pyrethrum var. depressus

A. pyrethrum var. *depressus*
N. Africa (Atlas Mountains)
Foliage: spring to early winter. Flowers: summer. H 2–4in (5–10cm), S 6–12in (15–30cm). FrH.
The finely cut evergreen foliage is ground-hugging but stems turn up at their tips to present the flower-heads. Seen from above these seem simple white daisies with yellow centres but the outside of the ray florets, which show on the buds seen in profile, are crimson.

ANAPHALIS

ASTERACEAE Pearl everlasting

In this genus of about 100 plants the species cultivated have grey-green, often woolly, leaves and produce "everlasting" flowerheads. They come from a wide range of habitats and, surprisingly for grey-leaved plants, tolerate moisture and shade. The erect *A. margaritacea* and the slightly more silvery *A. margaritacea* var. *yedoensis* are useful in broad planting schemes but can be invasive.
CULTIVATION Tolerate full sun or partial shade and require moist soil.
PROPAGATION By division, in spring. From cuttings, in spring and early summer. From seed, sown in spring.
POTENTIAL PROBLEMS Usually none.

Anaphalis triplinervis

A. triplinervis *Himalayas to S.W. China*
Foliage: spring to autumn. Flowers: mid- to late summer. H and S 18–24in (45–60cm). FH.
The 3 veins running down the grey-green leaves, which are woolly on the underside, give this species its name. The small ball-like flowerheads, which remain conspicuous for a long season, are clustered at the ends of stems, a yellow centre just showing among the stiff bracts. It demands a plentiful supply of moisture.
'Sommerschnee' is laundry white and compact, rarely more than 10in (25cm) high.

ANCHUSA

BORAGINACEAE

Anchusa cespitosa

The herbaceous plants in this genus of about 35 species, in the wild found growing in full sun on dry soils, are rather coarse but the best are saved from being commonplace by the blue of their flowers. Intense blue flowers are also a feature of a few alpine species, including the Cretan *A. cespitosa*, a plant that is adamant about sharp drainage. It can be grown as a crevice plant or in scree-like conditions, or in deep pots as an alpine house plant.
CULTIVATION Require full sun and moist but well-drained soil. Trim after flowering.
PROPAGATION From root cuttings, taken in winter. From seed, sown in spring.
POTENTIAL PROBLEM Mildew.

A. azurea *N. Africa, W. Asia, S. Europe*

Flowers: early summer. H 18–48in (45–120cm), S 18–24in (45–60cm). FH.

This hairy-leaved plant is not long-lived and tall cultivars often need staking but the erect stems carry numerous saucer-shaped flowers that are bright blue. '**Little John**' is short-growing, up to 18in (45cm) tall, and has deep blue flowers; '**Loddon Royalist**', usually twice as high but rarely needing staking, has flowers of deep purplish blue.

ANDROSACE

PRIMULACEAE Rock jasmine

About 100 species are distributed in alpine regions throughout the Northern Hemisphere and of these the high alpine species, tiny cushions delectably flower-studded in season, present an exquisite challenge to specialist gardeners. High alpine species include several from the Pyrenees. *A. pyrenaica*, *A. cylindrica* and *A. vandellii* (from mountains of Spain and also the Alps) have white flowers; *A. ciliata* has yellow-throated pink flowers. Winter wet is a lethal enemy and success with them is rare outside the alpine house. Other, easier, species can be grown in rock gardens and scree beds.
CULTIVATION Require full sun and moist, gritty, very well-drained soil (JI No.2 with added grit under glass). Outdoors, protect from excessive water.
PROPAGATION From rooting rosette cuttings, taken in summer. From seed, sown in autumn.
POTENTIAL PROBLEMS Aphids; fungal diseases.

A. lanuginosa *Himalayas*
Flowers: mid- to late summer. H 2–4in (5–10cm), S 9–12in (23–30cm). FH.
This mat-forming evergreen looks best when the stems of silky grey-green leaves trail from a rocky chink, the tight clusters of 5-lobed pink flowers brightening a miniature swag.

Androsace sarmentosa

A. sarmentosa *Himalayas to W. China (Sichuan)*
Flowers: late spring to early summer. H 2–4 in (5–10cm), S 12–15in (30–38cm). FH.
Rosettes of hairy leaves form dense mats topped by tight clusters of deep pink flowers with lime-green eyes. *A. sempervivoides* also has rosettes of leaves and pink flowers.

ANEMONE

RANUNCULACEAE Windflower

The fibrous-rooted species among the 120 or so are mainly plants of glades and woodland fringes on moist soils, and often the mainstays of gardens in late summer and autumn. The basal leaves, usually 3-lobed, are good throughout the summer and the saucer-shaped flowers, cradling a central knob and its surround of yellow stamens, are zestful just at the moment when many other perennials are beginning to look tired. Even tall cultivars do not need staking. Although tolerating partial shade, all of the following flower most freely in reasonably open positions. These anemones are often slow starters but once established they spread freely and can be invasive. A combination of *A. hupehensis* and *A. × hybrida* cultivars gives a flowering season from mid-summer into autumn.

Anemone hupehensis

See also BULBS, CORMS AND TUBERS.
CULTIVATION Require varying culture. *A. hupehensis* and *A. × hybrida*, which are described, tolerate full sun or partial shade and require moist soil that is rich in organic matter. Require protection from winter wet.
PROPAGATION By division, in spring. From root cuttings, taken in late autumn or winter. From seed, sown when ripe.
POTENTIAL PROBLEMS Eelworms, caterpillars, slugs; leaf spot, powdery mildew.
WARNING Contact with the sap of some anemone species may cause an allergic skin reaction.

Anemone hupehensis 'Hadspen Abundance'

A. hupehensis *W. and Central China*
Flowers: mid- to late summer. H 2–3ft (60–90cm), S 16–20in (40–50cm). FH.
The species itself, with white or pink flowers carried on wiry stems above the dark green, 3-lobed basal leaves, is rarely seen. The free-flowering '**Hadspen Abundance**' has alternating small and large segments, their reddish pink paling at the edges. '**September Charm**' is a uniform pale pink; var. *japonica* '**Bressingham Glow**' and var. *japonica* '**Prinz Heinrich**' are semi-double and dark pink, with longer often twisted segments.

A. × hybrida
Japanese anemone
Flowers: late summer to early autumn. H 4–5ft (1.2–1.5m), S 2–4ft (60–120cm). FH.
The pink-flowered Japanese anemone is commonly seen in old gardens, and is a beautiful sight when the numerous semi-double, soft-toned flowers float above the base of mid-green leaves. An old favourite among pink cultivars is semi-double '**Königin Charlotte**'. '**Kriemhilde**' is a purplish pink semi-double and '**Max Vogel**' a single pink. The freshness of the whites places them in a class of their own; they look their best seen against a dark background such as a yew hedge. The vigorous '**Géante des Blanches**' and '**Whirlwind**' are both semi-double but the single '**Honorine Jobert**' is the undisputed queen.

Anemone × hybrida 'Whirlwind'

ANEMONOPSIS

RANUNCULACEAE

The single species is a woodland plant of shy charm, and opens its gently nodding pale violet flowers in summer. It is only happy in conditions that match the cool, moist shade of its mountain habitat in Japan.

CULTIVATION Requires partial shade and moist, deep, fertile, acid soil that is rich in organic matter. Requires shelter from wind.
PROPAGATION By division, in spring. From seed, sown as soon as ripe.
POTENTIAL PROBLEMS Usually none.

Anemonopsis macrophylla

A. macrophylla *Japan*
Foliage: spring to autumn. Flowers: mid- to late summer. H 24–30in (60–75cm), S 16–20in (40–50cm). FH.
From a mound of fresh green leaves, the leaflets irregularly toothed and lobed, rise dark stems with purplish buds nodding at the tips. The demure stance does not change when the 3 waxy sepals spring open, releasing the pale violet petals, white at the centre around a boss of stamens.

ANTHEMIS

ASTERACEAE

Radiant daisy flowerheads, offset by finely cut foliage, are produced in great quantity and usually over a long period by several among the 100 or so sun-loving species. As wild plants they are found on very well-drained, often poor stony soils in North Africa, Europe and eastwards to the Caucasus and Iran. Their cheerful, straightforward qualities show up well when set against more sophisticated plants in sunny borders or rock gardens but they have the disadvantage of being short-lived. Replace them with newly propagated plants on a regular basis.

CULTIVATION Require full sun and light well-drained soil. The plants described should be cut back immediately after flowering to encourage fresh growth and prolong their lifespan.

PROPAGATION By division, in spring. From cuttings, taken in spring. From seed, sown in spring.
POTENTIAL PROBLEMS Aphids, slugs; powdery mildew.

A. punctata subsp. **cupaniana**
Sicily
Flowers: early summer to autumn. H 8–12in (20–30cm), S 2–3ft (60–90cm). FH.
The tireless flowering and the sprawling aromatic grey-green foliage transform a simple daisy, white with a yellow centre, into a valuable plant for a large rock garden or path edging. The Caucasian *A. marschalliana*, which is lower growing and has yellow daisies over silvery, finely cut foliage, can be planted in gritty soil among paving.

A. sancti-johannis *S.W. Bulgaria*
Flowers: summer. H 24–30in (60–75cm), S 18–24in (45–60cm). FH.
The vibrant orange-yellow of these daisies, the stubby ray-florets circling a dense convex centre of the same colour, can be described as brassy without any pejorative overtones. The grey-green foliage is delicately cut.

Anthemis tinctoria 'E.C. Buxton'

A. tinctoria *Europe and east to Iran*
Golden marguerite, ox-eye chamomile
Foliage: year-round. Flowers: summer. H and S 2–3ft (60–90cm). FH.
Stiff-stemmed daisies, the cultivars providing a range of yellows, are crowded above the ferny green

Anthemis tinctoria 'Kelwayi'

leaves, '**E.C. Buxton**', with pale lemon ray florets around a brighter yellow disc, lends itself to subtle colour schemes. '**Sauce Hollandaise**' and '**Wargrave**' both creamy yellow, are also good for cool colour schemes. '**Grallach Gold**' is bright yellow and makes a splash in a border; so do the bold yellow daisies of '**Kelwayi**'.

AQUILEGIA

RANUNCULACEAE Columbine

Aquilegia vulgaris

The columbines are too readily pigeon-holed as old-fashioned flowers, even when this is meant as a compliment. It is true that the European granny's bonnet (*A. vulgaris*) has been grown for centuries but it does not require a nostalgic gloss to make it a very good plant, as are others among about 70 species found in woodland and more open habitats, in some cases alpine, in the temperate Northern Hemisphere. There are also numerous hybrids, most species crossing with indiscriminate freedom. Almost all combine good foliage, with prettily divided leaflets, in some cases in a beautiful grey-blue tone, and graceful, distinctively spurred flowers in a broad colour range. The taller columbines are ideal in dappled shade and among shrubs, where they can be allowed to self-seed freely. In highly regulated gardens their generous self-seeding might be thought a nuisance but it is compensation for the tendency of aquilegias to be short-lived. The alpine species described, which do better in more open positions, can be planted in rock gardens, raised beds or between paving stones.

CULTIVATION Tolerate full sun or partial shade and require moist but well-drained soil.
PROPAGATION From seed, sown as soon as ripe. By division, in spring.
POTENTIAL PROBLEMS Aphids, leaf miners, caterpillars, sawflies; powdery mildew.
WARNING Contact with the sap may irritate the skin.

A. alpina *Switzerland*
Alpine columbine
Flowers: late spring. H 2–3ft (60–
90cm), S 12–14in (30–35cm). FH.
Blue or blue and white flowers
hover above a mound of soft grey-
green leaves. The flowers, 2 or 3 to
a stem, have short spurs. **A. 'Hensol
Harebell'** is a fine blue hybrid
between *A. alpina* and *A. vulgaris*.
A species from S. France and Italy,
A. bertolonii, is like a dwarf form
of *A. alpina*, each stem carrying a
single purplish blue flower.

Aquilegia **'Hensol Harebell'**

A. canadensis *E. Canada to S.
USA (Florida, Texas and New Mexico)*
Flowers: mid-spring to mid-
summer. H 2–3ft (60–90cm),
S 12–14in (30–35cm). FH.
The long-spurred species are
much less widely grown than the
hybrids derived from them but
their airy lightness makes them
highly distinctive. *A. canadensis*
has lemon-yellow flowers with red
spurs. Other long-spurred species
from N. America, both yellow-
flowered, are **A. chrysantha** and
A. longissima, the latter with
slender spurs up to 6in (15cm)
long.

A. flabellata var. pumila
Flowers: early summer. H and S
4–6in (10–15cm). FH.
This does not require coaxing
from an enthusiast as do some of
the alpine species. The blue-green
foliage with neatly lobed leaflets is
itself very beautiful and the blue
and white flowers are large for the
size of the plant.

A. McKana Group
Flowers: late spring to early
summer. H 2–3ft (60–90cm),
S 18–24in (45–60cm). FH.
The promiscuity of aquilegias is
tiresome if you are trying to
maintain pure populations but has
resulted in some fine hybrids. In
the McKana hybrids the mid-green
leaves are topped by showers of
long-spurred flowers, up to 15 per
stem, in a colour range that
includes white and shades of blue,
yellow and red. Some of the

Aquilegia **Biedermeier Group**

flowers in the group are bicoloured.
A. Biedermeier Group are shorter-
growing hybrids, rarely taller than
18in (45cm), the hosts of upturned
flowers usually having blue sepals
and short-spurred white petals.
Their confectionery prettiness,
however, is far removed from the
light grace of the species.

A. viridiflora *E. Siberia and
W. China*
Flowers: late spring to early
summer. H 8–12in (20–30cm),
S 6–8in (15–20cm). FH.
The colour is in itself a surprise,
the 2 or 3 nodding flowers having
greenish sepals and purplish
brown spurred petals, from which
protrude the clustered stamens. In
addition, this is one of the sweetly
fragrant species.

A. vulgaris *Europe*
Granny's bonnet
Flowers: late spring to early
summer. H 2–3ft (60–90cm),
S 18–24in (45–60cm). FH.
The short-spurred flowers that
float in profusion above the pretty
foliage are in shades of violet, blue,
pink and plum or white. In so
many of its variations this is a very
beautiful plant, the white **'Nivea'**,
with light green foliage, being an
irresistible woodland enchantress.
It seems perverse, therefore, that 2
curiosities, the double **'Nora
Barlow'**, which has flowers
reduced to cluttered tufts of pink
and green, and the **Vervaeneana
Group**, with gold variegated leaves
and mixed flower colours should
be so popular.

Aquilegia vulgaris **Vervaeneana Group**

ARENARIA

CARYOPHYLLACEAE Sandwort

Among the 150 or more species
in this genus are many low-
growing evergreen perennials and
subshrubs found wild in
mountainous or arctic regions of
the Northern Hemisphere, the
common name indicating the
kind of free-draining terrain on
which some are found. The dense
cushion-forming species such as
A. tetraquetra are most easily
pleased in an alpine house but the
prostrate stems of several easy
species readily drape themselves
over rocks or the edge of a raised
bed.
CULTIVATION Require full sun and
moist but well-drained, poor, sandy
soil.
PROPAGATION By division, in spring.
From basal cuttings, taken in early
summer. From seed, sown in
autumn.
POTENTIAL PROBLEMS Usually none.

Arenaria tetraquetra

A. montana *S.W. Europe*
Flowers: early summer. H 2–4in
(5–10cm), S 12–18 (30–45cm). FH.
The glistening, saucer-shaped
white flowers nestle among the
narrow leaves that closely cover a
mat of wiry stems. The pink
sandwort (**A. purpurascens**), from
N. Spain, has starry flowers, deep
pink in bud, paler on opening.

ARMERIA

PLUMBAGINACEAE Sea pink, thrift

The thrifts are perennials and
subshrubs of rocky mountains and
seashore in Europe, North Africa
and the Americas, most forming
tight cushions or hummocks of
evergreen grassy leaves. Of about
80 species a few are widely grown
in rock gardens and as edging for
their round heads of small flowers.
CULTIVATION Require full sun and
well-drained soil.
PROPAGATION By division, in early
spring. From semi-ripe cuttings,
taken in summer. From seed, sown
in spring or autumn.
POTENTIAL PROBLEMS Usually none.

A. juniperifolia *Mountains of C. Spain*

Flowers: late spring. H 2–3in (5–8cm), S 4–6in (10–15cm). FH.
In a rock garden crevice this makes a tight hummock of dark green leaves well covered by almost stemless heads of pink flowers. The reddish pink of **'Bevan's Variety'** makes a very bright miniature.

Armeria maritima

A. maritima *Europe including Britain*

Sea thrift

Flowers: late spring to summer.
H and S 6–12in (15–30cm). FH.
This widely distributed plant is found wild near the coast and also in mountainous terrain in many parts of the Northern Hemisphere. The flowerheads, up to 1in (2.5cm) across and held well above the linear dark green leaves, are often a washy pink in the wild but the colour range includes darker shades of pink and red as well as white. Strongly coloured cultivars include **'Bloodstone'**, with deep red flowerheads on short stems; **'Düsseldorfer Stolz'**, wine-red flowerheads on short stems; and **'Vindictive'**, deep pink.

Armeria **'Düsseldorfer Stolz'**

ARTEMISIA

ASTERACEAE Mugwort, sagebrush, wormwood

Most of the perennial species in this genus of around 300 species, found in the Northern Hemisphere, have insignificant flowers but the aromatic grey, pewter or silver foliage of several is outstanding.

Tarragon (*A. dracunculus*), in the first rank of culinary herbs, has green leaves, as does *A. lactiflora*, its dark green foliage being heavily cut and its creamy flowerheads suitable for drying. In the wild the species are plants of open dry country. It is difficult to overstate their value as a calming influence where sunny well-drained borders have been planted with vivid colour schemes, in their mediating role easing tensions in what is often described with approval as a riot of colour. Their silky or felted texture is appealing to the eye and to the touch, and adds another dimension of contrasts. Although many are described as evergreen, they generally look bedraggled in cold wet winters.

CULTIVATION Require full sun and well-drained fertile soil. Cut back in spring to keep plants compact.
PROPAGATION By division, in spring. From cuttings, in summer. From seed, sown in spring or autumn.
POTENTIAL PROBLEMS Aphids; gall (*A. absinthium* and *A.* 'Powis Castle').

A. absinthium *Temperate Asia, Europe*

Absinth, wormwood
Foliage: spring to mid-winter.
Flowers: late summer. H 2–3ft (60–90cm), S 20–24in (50–60cm). FH.
This woody based perennial has finely divided silver leaves and sprays of small yellow flowerheads. As a foliage plant it achieves real distinction in **'Lambrook Silver'**.

A. ludoviciana *W. North America to Mexico*

Western mugwort, white sage
Foliage: spring to autumn. Flowers: mid-summer to autumn. H 2–4ft (60–120cm), S 2–3ft (60–90cm). FH.
The roots run freely in well-drained soil, producing numerous upright stems clothed in clean grey leaves, which become almost white in a hot, droughty summer. The plumes of tiny flowers do not compete with the foliage. The leaves of **var.** *latiloba* and **'Valerie Finnis'** have jagged margins.

Artemisia ludoviciana

A. **'Powis Castle'**

Foliage: spring to late autumn.
Flowers: late summer. H 24–30in (60–75cm), S 2–3ft (60–90cm). FrH.
This woody based perennial may owe some of its character to the shrubby *A. arborescens*, itself a good foliage plant with finely divided silver leaves. The mound of soft, fine, silver-green foliage that **'Powis Castle'** makes has the quality of a pelt, a light breeze bringing to life its texture and subtle colouring.

Artemisia **'Powis Castle'**

A. schmidtiana *Japan*

Foliage: year-round. Flowers: summer. H 8–12in (20–30cm), S 12–18in (30–45cm). FH.
The silky texture of the finely cut leaves is an invitation to touch. The very compact **'Nana'** makes silky cushions of soft thread.

A. stelleriana *N.E. Asia, E. North America*

Dusty miller
Foliage: spring to mid-winter.
Flowers: late summer and early autumn. H 18–24in (45–60cm), S 2–3ft (60–90cm). FH.
The intricately cut outline of the grey-green, almost silver leaves and their felted texture make this a remarkable foliage plant.
'Boughton Silver', which sprawls on prostrate stems, is a superb edging and container plant. The yellow flowerheads are insignificant.

ARUNCUS

ROSACEAE Goat's Beard

The 2 or 3 species tolerate a wide range of conditions but grow wild in high moist woodlands of the Northern Hemisphere. In sun, they need fertile moist soil to achieve the full splendour of their foliage and plumy flowers. The low-growing *A. aethusifolius*, with astilbe-like cream flowers over finely cut leaves, is an appealing plant for a woodland edge.
CULTIVATION Tolerate full sun or partial shade and require fertile moist soil.

PROPAGATION By division, in early spring or autumn. From seed, sown in spring or autumn.
POTENTIAL PROBLEM Sawfly larvae.

A. dioicus *Europe to E. Siberia, E. North America*
Foliage: spring to autumn. Flowers: early to mid-summer. H 4–6ft (1.2–1.8m), S 3–4ft (90–120cm). FH.
In full flower this is a really commanding plant, the broad clump of light green compound leaves perfectly balancing the long plumes of tiny flowers. Male and female flowers are carried on separate plants, the male flowers being a cleaner white but the creamy female flowers are followed by attractive seedheads. It is often consigned to the wild garden (female plants may self-seed to excess) but is undeniably a splendid plant for borders and waterside. **'Kneiffi'**, about 3ft (90cm) tall, has cream plumes over foliage cut away to a ferny lace.

Aruncus dioicus

ASPHODELINE

ASPHODELACEAE Jacob's rod

In dry stony landscapes from the Mediterranean eastwards through Turkey to the Caucasus, king's spear (*A. lutea*) and the related 19 species make conspicuous clumps, with spikes of starry flowers followed by long-lasting seedpods. Asphodel (**Asphodelus albus**), from a closely related genus, survives in similarly parched and stony conditions, in early summer producing spikes of white flowers warmed by pink central veins.

Asphodelus albus

Both this and the species described are bold plants for dry, sunny borders or wild plantings in open positions where the soil is free draining. They may need to be mulched where winters are severe.
CULTIVATION Require full sun and well-drained light soil.
PROPAGATION By division, in late summer or early autumn. From seed, sown in spring.
POTENTIAL PROBLEMS Slugs, snails and aphids.

Asphodeline lutea

A. lutea *C. and E. Mediterranean and W. Turkey.*
King's spear, yellow asphodel
Flowers: late spring. H 3–5ft (90–150cm), S 10–12in (25–30cm). FH.
The fleshy roots produce tall stems furnished with whorls of blue-green, grassy leaves, culminating in a spike of fragrant starry yellow flowers. These are followed by rounded green seedpods that slowly dry to brown.

ASTER

ASTERACEAE

Representatives of this large genus – it contains about 250 species – are found in such a wide range of habitats throughout the Northern Hemisphere and so many of the plants grown are hybrids that the only useful generalization to make is that there are asters for most situations in the garden. Their relationship is evident in the daisy-like flowerheads, which are solitary or clustered, but in scale and colour there is an impressive range, valuable for revivifying borders in late summer and autumn.
CULTIVATION Require varying conditions but the plants described need a moist but well-drained soil.
PROPAGATION By division, in spring. From cuttings, taken in spring and early summer. From seed, sown in spring or autumn.
POTENTIAL PROBLEMS Aphids, eelworms, earwigs, slugs, snails; leaf spot, fusarium wilt, grey mould. *A. novi-belgii* cultivars are very prone to mildew.

A. alpinus *European Alps*
Flowers: early to mid-summer. H 7–10in (17–25cm), S 18–24in (45–60cm). FH.
The leaves are often spoon-shaped and the flowerheads a pale mauve. The deep-coloured selections, such as the rich purple **'Dunkle Schöne'**, are the most attractive.

A. amellus *C. and E. Europe*
Flowers: late summer to autumn. H 1–2ft (30–60cm), S 14–18in (35–45cm). FH.
The species, which has grey-green leaves that are rough to the touch and mauve-blue flowerheads with yellow centres, has been displaced in gardens by cultivars mainly in shades of blue. **'King George'** has large, mauve-blue flowerheads but a more refined plant is the purplish blue **'Veilchenkönigin'**.

Aster amellus 'King George'

A. ericoides *C. and E. North America*
Flowers: late summer to late autumn. H 2–3ft (60–90cm), S 12–18 (30–45cm). FH.
The slender twiggy bush carries a late profusion of tiny white flowerheads. The cultivars include pale blues, the creamy **'Brimstone'**, with strong yellow centres, and pinks such as **'Pink Cloud'**.

Aster ericoides 'Pink Cloud'

A. × frikartii 'Mönch'
Flowers: late summer and early autumn. H 24–30in (60–75cm), S 18–24in (45–60cm). FH.
This early hybrid deserves the praise that has been heaped on it. It is a long-flowering and refined plant with yellow-centred

flowerheads in a lovely shade of purplish blue. Furthermore, it does not require support and is resistant to disease.

Aster × frikartii 'Mönch'

A. *novae-angliae* E. North America

New England aster
Flowers: late summer to mid-autumn. H 4-5ft (1.2-1.5m), S 18-24in (45-60cm). FH.
The stiff-stemmed plants have dull foliage and some of the cultivars that represent the species in gardens are indifferent plants. Reddish pink **'Andenken an Alma Pötschke'** is, however, superbly vibrant. Other good cultivars are the softer **'Harrington's Pink'** and the white **'Herbstschnee'**.

Aster novae-angliae 'Herbstschnee'

A. *novi-belgii* North America

Michaelmas daisy, New York aster
Flowers: late summer to mid-autumn. H tall 2-4ft (60-120cm), short 18-18in (30-45cm), S 18-36in (45-90cm). FH.
This species, which has tough rhizomatous roots, is represented in gardens by several hundred cultivars in a wide range of heights and with flowerheads in white or shades of blue, pink, mauve and purple. Despite being nondescript out of flower and prone to disfiguring diseases, these plants have remained popular for their late display of daisy flowerheads. The following selection gives only a glimpse of the range available from a specialist nursery. Two short-growing examples, about 1ft (30cm) in height, are **'Heinz Richard'**, a large semi-double with

Aster novi-belgii 'Heinz Richard'

bright pink rays surrounding the yellow centre, and **'Kristina'**, a double white. Taller examples, about 3ft (90cm) high, include the pale blue double **'Marie Ballard'** and **'Winston S. Churchill'**, a deep red double.

Aster novi-belgii 'Marie Ballard'

A. *pilosus* var. *demotus* North America

Flowers: mid- to late autumn. H 30-36in (75-90cm), S 18-24in (45-60cm). FH.
This is one of the last perennials of autumn, with constellations of small white daisies caught in its wiry stems. *A. pringlei* **'Monte Cassino'** is like a more slender version, up to 2ft (60cm) high.

ASTILBE

SAXIFRAGACEAE

The best of the astilbes combine to perfection densely ground-covering but highly ornamental foliage and graceful, long-lasting airy plumes of tiny flowers, the vestiges of which remain a decorative etching in winter. The

Astilbe hybrids

species, from S.E. Asia and North America, about 12 in number, are all plants of moist ground, often growing in shade near water. The numerous hybrids are versatile plants, growing equally well in sun and shade, relishing moisture, but tolerant of drier conditions in borders. The short-growing hybrids deserve frontal positions, the large need generous spacing. Their parentage is complex and those described are listed according to their cultivar name. Plants should be divided every 3 to 4 years.
CULTIVATION Tolerate full sun or partial shade and require a moist fertile soil, thriving even in boggy conditions.
PROPAGATION By division, in late winter.
POTENTIAL PROBLEMS Leaf spot, powdery mildew.

A. × *arendsii* 'Brautschleier'

Flowers: mid-summer. H and S 2-3ft (60-90cm). FH.
Open sprays, white changing to cream, froth over bright green leaves. The appealing lightness of form and colour of many astilbes is sacrificed in some of the hybrids with dense, strong-coloured plumes. *A.* × *arendsii* **'Fanal'** has dark green foliage and rich red flowers. It grows to 2ft (60cm).

Astilbe × *arendsii* 'Fanal'

A. 'Bronce Elegans'

Foliage: spring to autumn. Flowers: late summer. H and S 10-12in (25-30cm). FH.
This short-growing astilbe is for a frontal position, its dark foliage, tinted bronze, making a beautiful base for sprays of salmon pink and cream flowers. *A.* **'Sprite'** slightly shorter and later flowering, has more ferny dark green leaves and airy pink sprays.

A. *chinensis* var. *pumila* China

Flowers: late summer. H 12-18in (30-45cm), S 1-2ft (30-60cm). FH.
Although dwarf, this plant makes good groundcover and is more welcome for its reddish green foliage than the mauve-pink of its branched flower spikes.

A. × crispa 'Perkeo'

Foliage: spring to late summer.
Flowers: summer. H and S 8–12in
(20–30cm). FH.
Bronzed finely cut leaves turn dark
green as the tight pyramids of
bright pink flowers develop.

A. 'Deutschland'

Flowers: late spring. H 20–24in
(50–60cm), S 1–2ft (30–60cm). FH.
Loose sprays of white flowers toss
about over decorative divided
bright green leaves.

Astilbe 'Professor van der Wielen'

A. 'Professor van der Wielen'

Flowers: mid-summer. H and S
18–36in (45–90cm). FH.
The pick of the large whites has
arching sprays of creamy flowers
over a large mound of mid-green
leaves. Its match in pink but late
flowering is A. 'Straussenfeder'.

ASTILBOIDES

SAXIFRAGACEAE

The single species is a native of
E. Asia, in the wild growing in
shaded areas near lakes and streams
but with its roots above the water
level. In a cool waterside position,
particularly in a woodland setting,
it is a foliage plant of rare quality.
CULTIVATION Requires partial shade
and fertile moist soil.
PROPAGATION By division, in early
spring. From seed, sown in
autumn.
POTENTIAL PROBLEMS Slugs in
autumn and spring.

A. tabularis N.E. China, N. Korea

Foliage: spring to autumn. Flowers:
early and mid-summer. H 3–5ft
(90–150cm), S 3–4ft (90–120cm).
FH.
The broad satisfying clump of
foliage consists of light green
leaves of soft texture, rounded but
with a wandering edge making
slight lobes, and supported at the
centre by the leaf stalks. If the soil
is reliably moist and fertile, leaves
can be up to 3ft (90cm) across. The
drooping sprays of small cream
flowers are carried on strong stems
well above the foliage base.

Astilboides tabularis

ASTRANTIA

APIACEAE Masterwort

The masterworts, a genus of about
10 species, are found wild in
woodland and alpine meadows
from Europe to W. Asia. They
produce sprays of intriguing
flowerheads, with posies of tiny
flowers surrounded by ruff-like
bracts, usually pale green, giving a
cool finish to the clusters of little
pincushions. These sprays rise
above a good clump of attractively
divided leaves. Provided the soil is
reasonably moist, the plants
described can be grown in a wide
range of conditions and in borders
as well as in woodland or wilder
parts of the garden.
CULTIVATION Tolerate full sun or
partial shade and require a fertile
moist but well-drained soil. A. major
tolerates drier soils.
PROPAGATION By division, in spring.
From seed, sown as soon as ripe.
POTENTIAL PROBLEMS Aphids, slugs;
powdery mildew.

**Astrantia major subsp. involucrata
'Shaggy'**

A. major Austria

Flowers: early and mid-summer.
H 2ft (60cm), S 18in (45cm). FH.
The greenish white flowerheads
with tints of pink and stronger
green make a wonderfully subtle
plant for a shady corner that far
exceeds its common brief to
please in a cottage garden. The
rich coloured cultivars – 'Hadspen
Blood' is dark red and 'Rubra' is
wine red – are undoubtedly useful
in strong colour schemes but look
mournful, especially in shade. An

amusing extravagance is displayed
by subsp. involucrata 'Shaggy' in
the length of its bracts, the tips of
which are strong green. The yellow
and cream markings on the foliage
of 'Sunningdale Variegated' make
it a distinctive foliage plant but the
leaves are at odds with the flowers.

A. maxima Europe

Flowers: early and mid-summer.
H 18–24in (45–60cm), S 12–15in
(30–38cm). FH.
The broad fringed bracts clasp a
dense cluster of tiny flowers, the
whole flowerhead pink but tinged
green at first.

AUBRIETA

BRASSICACEAE

The 12 or so species in this genus
of European and Asian origin are
rarely grown but the hybrids
derived from them share their taste
for rocky ground, especially on
lime. They produce vivid splashes
of colour in the garden in spring,
never better than when cascading
over low walls or from crevices.
Trimming plants after flowering
keeps them compact.
CULTIVATION Require full sun and
fertile well-drained soil that is
neutral or alkaline.
PROPAGATION From cuttings, taken
in summer. From seed, sown in
autumn or spring.
POTENTIAL PROBLEMS Aphids,
eelworms, flea beetles; white
blister.

A. hybrids

Flowers: spring. H 2–3in (5–8cm),
S 15–28in (38–70cm). FH.
The evergreen mounds or carpets
of small hairy leaves are often
almost totally obscured by the
cross-shaped flowers in shades of
blue, purple, pink and red and also
in white. Singles include 'Doctor
Mules', a strong purple;
'Greencourt Purple', rich purple;
and 'Red Carpet', deep red.
'Bressingham Pink' is a double
pink. Among those with variegated
leaves is 'Silberrand', which has
blue flowers.

Aubrieta 'Doctor Mules'

AURINIA

BRASSICACEAE

Changes in nomenclature have brought in to this small genus of 7 species the familiar gold dust, better known as *Alyssum saxatile*. The 2 genera are closely allied and both include sun-loving plants of mountainous and rocky habitats in C. and S. Europe. Gold dust itself is best suited to a position in a rock garden or raised bed where in lazing about it softens hard lines and beams with a sunny radiance. The same could also be said of the yellow-flowered and fragrant *Alyssum montanum* 'Berggold'. Trimming plants after flowering keeps them compact.

CULTIVATION Require full sun and very well-drained soil.

PROPAGATION From cuttings, taken in early summer. From seed, sown in autumn.

POTENTIAL PROBLEM Aphids.

Aurinia saxatilis

A. saxatilis C. and S.E. Europe
Gold dust
Flowers: late spring to early summer. H 8–12in (20–30cm), S 12–18in (30–45cm). FH.
Stems densely clustered with 4-petalled bright yellow flowers sprawl from clumps of hairy grey-green leaves. 'Citrina' is lemon-yellow and 'Dudley Nevill' has distinctive apricot-orange flowers.

BAPTISIA

PAPILIONACEAE False or wild indigo

Most of the 20 or so species of this North American genus have white or yellow pea flowers but the best known has flowers in a wonderful shade of blue. *Baptisia australis* makes a large border plant and its position should be well chosen from the outset as it is deep-rooting and resents disturbance.

CULTIVATION Requires full sun and moist but well-drained and preferably acid soil.

PROPAGATION By division, in early spring. From seed, sown as soon as ripe.

POTENTIAL PROBLEMS Usually none.

Baptisia australis

B. australis E. USA
Foliage: summer to late autumn. Flowers: early summer. Fruits: autumn. H 2–4ft (60–120cm), S 18–24in (45–60cm). FH.
The blue-tinted foliage and the slender spires of deep blue, lupin-like flowers have an unusually soft quality. Dark seedpods remain when frost has blackened and cut down the leaves.

BERGENIA

SAXIFRAGACEAE Elephant's ears

It is difficult with this genus of about 8 Asiatic species to strike a balance between the enthusiasm of its over-generous advocates and the scepticism of those who find the formula of hard flower colour and coarse leafage repeated to excess. The great virtue of several species and most hybrids is that they make dense groundcover in a wide range of conditions, even including shady dry areas, reflecting the diversity of their origins in woodland and moorland. The boldness of the large leathery leaves is indisputable and their glossiness enhances the rich mahogany and purple tones that often develop in winter, especially on plants grown in open positions. The flowers, clustered at the tip of heavy stems, are in themselves beautifully bell-shaped; even those of piercing magenta are not impossible to place and are perhaps best left to scream in isolation. The bergenias described are all suitable as groundcover but some of the smaller species and

Bergenia cordifolia

hybrids are also worth growing. *B. stracheyi*, for example, usually less than 8in (20cm) high, has tight clusters of fragrant pink flowers in early spring.

CULTIVATION Tolerate full sun or partial shade and a wide range of soil conditions but best in well-drained soil rich in organic matter.

PROPAGATION By division, in autumn or early spring. By rooting leafy rhizomes, in autumn.

POTENTIAL PROBLEMS Slugs, snails, caterpillars, vine weevils; leaf spot, dry brown rot.

B. 'Abendglut'
Foliage: year-round. Flowers: mid- to late spring. H 8–12in (20–30cm), S 18–24in (45–60cm). FH.
The clumps of rounded small leaves colour strongly in winter, the reverse becoming a rich purplish red. The semi-double flowers are a vivid reddish pink. Other hybrids with small to medium-sized leaves include 'Baby Doll' with large soft pink bells, and 'Rosie Klose', remarkable for the salmon tint of its flowers. The leaves of these 2 bergenias do not colour strongly in autumn.

Bergenia 'Bressingham White'

B. 'Bressingham White'
Foliage: year-round. Flowers: mid- to late spring. H 12–18in (30–45cm), S 18–24in (45–60cm). FH.
The leaves do not take on purplish tones in winter but out of their deep green rise arching sprays of pure white flowers. The flowers of another white of similar dimensions but earlier flowering, *B.* 'Silberlicht', take on pink tinges as they age.

B. ciliata N. India, Nepal, W. Pakistan
Foliage: spring to mid-autumn. Flowers: early spring. H 12–14in (30–35cm), S 18–20in (45–50cm). FH.
The large rounded leaves are hairy, quite different in their soft texture from the run of bergenias. Frost may damage the light pink flowers and this species is sometimes deciduous.

Bergenia cordifolia 'Purpurea'

B. cordifolia *Siberia*
Foliage: year-round. Flowers: late
winter to early spring. H 18–24in
(45–60cm), S 24–30in (60–75cm).
FH.
The species itself is an impressive
evergreen, with large, almost heart-
shaped, deep green leaves that take
on purple tints in winter. The dark
pink flowers are carried on reddish
stems. In 'Purpurea' the purplish
red of the foliage is intensified in
winter, the flower stem is vivid red
and the flowers bright magenta.

Bergenia 'Morgenröte'

B. 'Morgenröte'
Foliage: year-round. Flowers: mid-
to late spring and early summer.
H 12–18in (30–45cm), S 18–24in
(45–60cm). FH.
Red flower stems emerge from the
rosettes of large deep green leaves
carrying reddish pink flowers on
this good ground-covering hybrid.

B. purpurascens *N. Burma,*
W. China, E. Himalayas
Foliage: year-round. Flowers: mid-
to late spring. H and S 12–18in
(30–45cm). FH.

Bergenia 'Wintermärchen'

In winter the dark green narrow
leaves turn purplish red and an
even brighter red on the reverse.
The flowers, which dangle stiffly
from a red-brown stem, are
purplish pink. *B.* 'Wintermärchen'
is a narrow-leaved hybrid, slightly
more compact, with early flowers
in reddish pink. The leaves are
slightly twisted, showing both the
richly coloured reverse and purple-
tinged glossy surface in winter.

BLETILLA

ORCHIDACEAE

This small genus of about 10
Asiatic terrestrial orchids includes
one well-known woodland species
that can form large colonies in
lightly shaded borders provided
the climate is mild enough. The
pseudobulbs, which are tuber-like,
resent deep planting.
CULTIVATION Tolerates full sun or
partial shade. Requires shelter and
well-drained moist soil rich in
organic matter. In frost-prone
areas, lift and store over winter.
Mulch with bark or leafmould if
left outdoors.
PROPAGATION By division, in spring.
POTENTIAL PROBLEMS Aphids. Under
glass red spider mites, whiteflies
and mealy bugs.

Bletilla striata

B. striata *China, Japan*
Flowers: spring to early summer.
H and S 1–2ft (30–60cm). HH.
In well-established colonies of
these vivacious plants sinuous
stems carry sprays of bell-shaped,
light magenta orchid flowers over
sheaves of pleated, sword-like
leaves.

BRUNNERA

BORAGINACEAE

Forget-me-not flowers are a vivid
attraction of the commonly grown
species in this genus of 3 plants
from woodland in E. Europe and
N.W. Asia. The large, heart-shaped
leaves, slightly coarse companions
for the dainty flowers, make good
groundcover and in the variegated
forms are beautifully marked.

CULTIVATION Tolerate full sun but
grow most successfully in partial
to full shade and require a moist
but well-drained soil that is rich in
organic matter.
PROPAGATION By division, in early
spring. From root cuttings, taken in
late autumn. From seed, sown in
spring.
POTENTIAL PROBLEMS Usually none.

Brunnera macrophylla

B. macrophylla *Caucasus*
Foliage: early summer to early
autumn. Flowers: mid- to late
spring. H 12–18in (30–45cm),
S 2ft (60cm). FH.
The plain-leaved form will thrive in
sun or shade, provided the soil is
reasonably moist, producing
abundant sprays of tiny blue
flowers as the foliage develops.
The variegated forms tend to burn
in full sun. 'Dawson's White', with
nearly white margins, is the most
vulnerable. 'Hadspen Cream' has
an irregular margin of palest
yellow and 'Langtrees' has
metallic-grey spotting.

CALTHA

RANUNCULACEAE Kingcup, marsh
marigold

The buttercup relatives that make
up this genus of about 10 species
are all moisture-loving plants and
those described are most beautiful
when their rich foliage has fed on
fertile boggy ground and their
golden flowers, caught in direct
sunlight, are also lit by reflections
from water. They are possible in
borders but need an unfailing
supply of moisture.
CULTIVATION Require full sun and
water's edge planting but will
tolerate fertile, very moist soil.
PROPAGATION By division, in early
spring or immediately after
flowering. From seed, sown as
soon as ripe.
POTENTIAL PROBLEM Powdery
mildew.

C. palustris *Europe, N. America*
Foliage: spring to late summer.
Flowers: early spring. H 6–15in (15–
38cm), S 18–24in (45–60cm). FH.

Caltha palustris

The cup-shaped flowers of richest yellow shine above kidney-shaped deep green leaves. A heartier version of the species, **var. palustris**, supports waxy golden cups on long stems extending over water. The knob of greenish gold in the double **var. radicans** 'Flore Pleno' unfolds in an ordered but ravishing sunburst.

CAMPANULA

CAMPANULACEAE Bellflower

The genus, which contains about 300 species from temperate parts of the Northern Hemisphere, is astonishingly rich in material for the garden. Some species are compact alpines while others are tall woodland and meadow plants. The nodding or upward-facing flowers, predominantly in shades of blue, can be starry, cup-shaped or tubular but almost all have a shapely elegance and in many instances are borne on plants of rare poise. The taller perennial bellflowers are important components of summer borders, shaded as well as sunny. There are, too, many exquisite compact or low spreading plants ideal for raised beds and rock gardens or for edging paths. Some of the alpine species are, admittedly, difficult plants but a large percentage of the genus is easy to grow and a few representatives are beautiful but invasive weeds. Canterbury bells (*C. medium*), from Southern Europe, is a true biennial, producing single, double or cup-and-saucer flowers in blue, pink or white. The short-lived frost-hardy chimney bellflower (*C. pyramidalis*), which is native to Italy and the Balkans and has fragrant clusters of cup-shaped flowers, is usually grown as one.
CULTIVATION The perennial species described flower most freely in full sun but tolerate partial shade. They require a well-drained soil, particularly the compact rock garden campanulas, and a good supply of moisture. Tall species may need staking.

PROPAGATION By division, in spring or autumn. From cuttings, taken in spring or summer. From seed, sown in spring or, for rock garden campanulas, in autumn.
POTENTIAL PROBLEMS Slugs and snails; rust.

C. alliariifolia Caucasus, Turkey
Ivory bells
Flowers: mid-summer to early autumn. H 15–24in (38–60cm), S 18in (45cm). FH.
Toppling spires of nodding creamy tubular flowers rise on wiry stems from a mound of heart-shaped, grey-green leaves.

C. 'Birch Hybrid'
Flowers: summer. H 4–6in (10–15cm), S 18–24in (45–60cm). FH.
This vigorous evergreen hybrid has arching prostrate stems and ivy-shaped bright green leaves at times almost submerged by the bell-shaped deep violet flowers. Its parents are the very vigorous *C. portenschlagiana* and the even more invasive *C. poscharskyana*. It is difficult not to be taken in by plants that are so beautiful.

Campanula 'Birch Hybrid'

C. 'Burghaltii'
Flowers: mid-summer. H 2ft (60cm), 1ft (30cm). FH.
Dark purplish blue buds contrast with large pale blue open bells that dangle from slender stems.

C. carpatica C. Europe (Carpathian mountains)
Flowers: summer. H 8–12in (20–30cm), S 1–2ft (30–60cm). FH.
The myriad upturned saucer-shaped flowers breaking open from fluted buds are attractive in all the permutations of this variable species, one of the easiest and most appealing for the rock garden. The named selections cover a colour range that includes white, such as 'Weisse Clips', as well as shades of blue, such as 'Blaue Clips', and violet. Pale blue **var. turbinata**, usually less than 6in (15cm) high, is more compact. Even more compact is *C. raineri* with similarly upturned blue

flowers but this, like several alpine species that are covered by snow in winter in their natural environment, is a much more difficult plant, demanding very sharp drainage.

C. garganica S. Europe
Adriatic bellflower
Flowers: summer. H 2–4in (5–10cm), S 12–18in (30–45cm). FH.
This looks its best with the stems, clothed with toothed, heart-shaped, bright green leaves, radiating from a rock crevice. The pale blue starry flowers are borne in great profusion.

Campanula garganica

C. glomerata 'Superba'
Flowers: summer. H 18–24in (45–60cm), S 2–4ft (60–120cm). FH.
The rather tubular flowers clustered at the ends of erect leafy stems are a deep violet-purple, their quality making up for the invasiveness of the species.

C. lactiflora Caucasus, Turkey
Milky bellflower
Flowers: early summer to early autumn. H 4–5ft (1.2–1.5m), S 18–24in (45–60cm). FH.
Although it may need staking, the milky bellflower is still one of the finest tall perennials and superb mixed with shrub roses. The stout leaf stems are crowned with great heads of powder blue bellflowers. There is also a beautiful white and the pink 'Loddon Anna'. 'Prichard's Variety', about 30in (75cm) high, has violet-blue flowers and 'Pouffe', under 12in (30cm), is a mound of light blue.

Campanula lactiflora 'Loddon Anna'

C. latifolia *Europe eastward to Iran and Kashmir*
Flowers: summer. H 4–5ft (1.2–1.5m),S 18–24in (45–60cm). FH.
The leafy stems that emerge straight and stiff from a clump of rich green leaves bear spikes of large blue or white tubular flowers, the topmost being the smallest. In borders remove the spent flowers but in the wild garden this species can be allowed to self-seed.

Campanula persicifolia 'Alba'

C. persicifolia *N. Africa,W. and N. Asia, S. Europe, C. and S. Russia*
Peach-leaved bellflower
Flowers: early to mid-summer. H 1–3ft (30–90cm), S 12–15in (30–38cm). FH.
The wiry stems that rise from rosettes of narrow evergreen leaves carry open bells that are outward facing or nodding.The white '**Alba**' is, if anything, more beautiful than the usual blue or violet-blue and both self-seed freely without being a nuisance. It is a winning plant in all its forms, including doubles such as '**Fleur de Neige**' and the large pale blue '**Telham Beauty**'.
C. latiloba is similar in character to *C.persicifolia* except that the shallowly cup-shaped flowers are stalkless.

Campanula takesimana

C. takesimana *Korea*
Flowers: summer. H 18–24in (45–60cm), S 18–36in (45–90cm). FH.
Above toothed and heart-shaped leaves rise numerous stems hung with narrow white bells that are flushed purplish pink, darker on

the inside and with maroon spots. The position for this great beauty needs to be well chosen for it is invasive, as is the shorter-growing *C. punctata*, with flowers of similar colour.

CANNA

CANNACEAE Indian shot plant

The hybrid cannas, large in leaf and flamboyant in flower, are among the most popular bedding plants in tropical and subtropical countries. Various species have played a role in the breeding of the hybrids but almost all of the 50 or so that are distributed in Asia and North and South America are plants of damp forest glades and margins. In temperate gardens that are not frost-free a tropical effect can be achieved with cannas, either in lavish bedding schemes or by combining a smaller number with other bold plants, but they must be planted annually and the rhizomes need to be lifted as soon as the foliage has been cut down by frost. In these conditions cannas flower less freely than in warmer climates but their foliage, as in the dark-leaved *C. indica* '**Purpurea**', can be superb.They also make an impact in containers.
CULTIVATION Require full sun, moist fertile soil and a sheltered position. In cold areas, mulch deeply in autumn. In frost-prone areas, lift plants in early autumn, remove the stems and leaves and store in slightly moist leafmould or peat over winter in a frost-free place.
PROPAGATION By division of rhizomes, in early spring. From seed, sown in spring at 70°F (21°C) after soaking in warm water for about a day.
POTENTIAL PROBLEMS Slugs, snails, caterpillars; under glass, red spider mites.

C. hybrids
Foliage: summer to autumn.
Flowers: mid-summer to early autumn. H 5–6ft (1.5–1.8m), S 2–3ft (60–90cm). HH.
Most have paddle-like leaves, prominently veined and often bronzed or tinted purple. Stout stems carry spikes, usually somewhat cluttered, of asymmetrical flowers, which are predominantly in shades of red and yellow, sometimes in bold combinations.The following is a mere sample of the great range available from specialist nurseries: '**King Midas**', plain green leaves and bright yellow flowers lightly marked with orange; '**Roi Humbert**', purple foliage and

Canna 'Roi Humbert'

flowers of vivid red; and '**Wyoming**', purple leaves with darker veining and flowers in shades of apricot and orange.

CATANANCHE

ASTERACEAE Cupid's dart

One species of this small Mediterranean genus containing 5 perennials and annuals has long been cultivated in sunny well-drained gardens. The daisy flowerheads, with their "everlasting" bracts, are good for cutting and will also dry well.
CULTIVATION Require full sun and well-drained soil.
PROPAGATION By division, in spring. From root cuttings, taken in winter. From seed, sown in spring.
POTENTIAL PROBLEM Powdery mildew.

C. caerulea *S.W. Europe, Italy*
Flowers: mid-summer to autumn. H 18–30in (45–75cm), S 12–18in (30–45cm). FH.
From a clump of grassy grey-green leaves rise branching wiry stems that terminate in silvered buds.The papery bracts open to reveal dark-centred blue daisies, their strap-shaped ray florets neatly fringed at their square ends. '**Alba**' has white flowerheads with a creamy centre, '**Bicolor**' white with a purple centre and in '**Major**' the blues are exceptionally rich.

Catananche caerulea

CENTAUREA

ASTERACEAE

The genus includes the knapweed or hardhead (*C. nigra*) of chalk grassland in Europe but the annual cornflower (*C. cyanus*) is probably the best known example of this large genus, with 400 to 500 species distributed in a wide range of habitats in many parts of the world. Many of the species show a preference for well-drained alkaline soils and almost all are found in open positions. The flowerheads consist of a central disc, often thistly in appearance, ringed by tubular or trumpet-shaped florets that in the showiest species are usually much dissected. Papery bracts around the flowerheads can be a conspicuous feature, as in the yellow-flowered *C. macrocephala*.

Centaurea macrocephala

See also ANNUALS AND BIENNIALS.
CULTIVATION Require full sun and a reasonably fertile well-drained soil. *C. macrocephala* and *C. montana* are the least tolerant of drought.
PROPAGATION By division, in spring or autumn. From seed, sown in spring (*C. montana* in late summer).
POTENTIAL PROBLEM Powdery mildew.

Centaurea hypoleuca 'John Coutts'

C. hypoleuca *Caucasus, Iran, Turkey*
Flowers: summer. H and S 18–24in (45–60cm). FH.
The deeply cut leaves form a grey-green clump through which thrust a succession of pink flowerheads

over a long season. It is usually represented in cultivation by '**John Coutts**', with deep mauve-pink flowers. A similar but flopping species is *C. dealbata*. It makes a lax clump up to 3ft (90cm).

C. macrocephala *Caucasus, Turkey*
Flowers: early to mid-summer. H 3–5ft (90–150cm), S 20–24in (50–60cm). FH.
The plant is undeniably coarse in foliage and thick stemmed but its brawny solidity is justified by the flowerheads. For a short period it is bright in the garden when the large globes of brown papery bracts are topped by bright yellow tufts. The flowerheads dry well.

C. montana *Europe to Poland and N.W. Balkans*
Flowers: late spring to mid-summer. H 18–24in (45–60cm), S 12–18in (30–45cm). FH.
The stems have a tendency to flop but this species, which has been in cultivation for centuries, presents its reddish violet flowerheads in the gap between spring and high summer. There are several cultivars in a range of shades of pink and violet and '**Alba**' is a lovely white.

Centaurea montana

CENTRANTHUS

VALERIANACEAE Valerian

Red valerian, the only species in a genus of about 10 that is in general cultivation, is found far from its Mediterranean home as a handsome weed colonizing old walls and railway sidings, never happier than when growing on chalky rubble in full sun. Its enthusiastic self-seeding is a drawback in the garden but this easy plant is a welcome filler on rough banks and even in sunny borders that parch in summer and it is a good plant for the seaside.
CULTIVATION Require full sun and poor alkaline soil that is well-drained.
PROPAGATION By division, in early spring. From seed, sown in spring.
POTENTIAL PROBLEMS Usually none.

C. ruber *S. Europe, N. Africa to Turkey*
Red valerian
Flowers: late spring to late summer. H and S 2–3ft (60–90cm). FH.
Erect stems carry dense heads of small starry flowers over a clump of fleshy leaves for a long season. The flowers are usually in shades of red or pink; '**Albus**' has flowers of clean white.

Centranthus ruber

CEPHALARIA

DIPSACACEAE

Few of the 65 or so species, mainly plants of moist meadows and high pastures from Europe to Asia, are in cultivation but one, the giant scabious, is remarkable for its height and the soft primrose-yellow of its flowerheads.
CULTIVATION Tolerate sun or partial shade and require moist soil.
PROPAGATION By division, in early spring. From seed, sown in spring.
POTENTIAL PROBLEMS Usually none.

C. gigantea *Caucasus, N. Turkey*
Giant scabious, yellow scabious
Flowers: early summer. H 6–8ft (1.8–2.5m), S 2–4ft (60–120cm). FH.
The divided leaves form a substantial dark green clump, above which hover the pale yellow scabious flowerheads. The butterfly liveliness of these as they move in a breeze is compensation for the gawky branching of the plant.
C. alpina, about half the height of the giant scabious, is a more compact alternative with flowerheads of similar colour.

Cephalaria gigantea

CHELONE

SCROPHULARIACEAE Turtlehead

The 6 or so species in this North American genus have their origins in mountainous terrain or moist woodland. They include several late-flowering plants, one of which, the intriguingly named turtlehead (*C. obliqua*), provides a long display of tubular pink flowers, in contrast with the predominant yellow of the season. The common and generic name is not so fanciful, given the flower shape.
CULTIVATION Tolerates sun or partial shade. Requires moist, deep, fertile soil but tolerates heavy clay and can be grown in boggy conditions.
PROPAGATION By division, in spring. From tip cuttings, taken in late spring to early summer. From seed, sown in spring.
POTENTIAL PROBLEMS Slugs, snails.

Chelone obliqua

C. obliqua *C. and S.E. USA*
Turtlehead
Flowers: late summer to early autumn. H 18–36in (45–90cm), S 12–18in (30–45cm). FH.
Erect stems forming a dense thicket have prominently veined dark green leaves their whole length and terminate in spikes of pink "turtleheads". These 2-lipped tubular flowers, each about 1in (2.5cm) long, have a yellow beard on the inside.

CHIASTOPHYLLUM

CRASSULACEAE

In cultivation, as in the wild, the single species in this genus is a plant for a cool and shady rocky niche or crevice.
CULTIVATION Requires partial shade and moist well-drained soil.
PROPAGATION From sideshoot cuttings, taken in early summer. From seed, sown in autumn.
POTENTIAL PROBLEMS Slugs, snails.

C. oppositifolium *Caucasus*
Foliage: year-round. Flowers: late spring to early summer. H and S 6–8in (15–20cm). FH.
Creeping rosettes are composed of

Chiastophyllum oppositifolium

fleshy rounded leaves that are coarsely toothed. Branching reddish stems carry drooping sprays of small yellow flowers.

CHRYSANTHEMUM

ASTERACEAE

The following groups of chrysanthemums, in this genus of about 20 species, are the result of complex hybridization, the process starting in China and Japan long before the main introductions to Europe began at the end of the 18th century. As with other florists' flowers that have been popular on the show bench, there are numerous categories, partly reflecting the astonishing range of form in the flowerheads. The direction the ray-florets curve is something to note in the large doubles, some being incurved, others reflexed. Other curiosities are flowerheads with spoon- or quill-shaped ray-florets (in the latter case they are tubular) and even some that are spider-form, looking like bizarre toupees combining thin and long dangling ray-florets with curled shorter ones at the top. After discounting the more tender plants that are not suitable for the garden, there is still a wealth of material here for beds and borders. *C. carinatum* is a striking annual with bold banding on the purple-eyed flowerheads.
CULTIVATION Require full sun and well-drained fertile soil, preferably containing lime (JI No. 2).
PROPAGATION By division, in spring. From basal cuttings, taken in spring. From seed of perennial mixtures, sown in late winter or early spring at 55–61°F (13–16°C).
POTENTIAL PROBLEMS Aphids, earwigs, eelworms; *Botrytis* (grey mould), viruses.

HYBRIDS

Korean
Flowers: late summer to mid-autumn. H 1–3ft (30–90cm), S 1–2ft (30–60cm). FH.
This type of spray chrysanthemum,

produces many flowers – single, semi-double or double. The range includes: '**Brown Eyes**', small double pompon, 2-tone orange-brown; '**Ruby Mound**', double, deep ruby; and '**Wedding Day**', single, white with a green centre.

Chrysanthemum 'Ruby Mound'

Pompon
Flowers: late summer to early autumn. H 1–2ft (30–60cm), S 18–24in (45–60cm). FH.
Dwarf bushes produce dense sprays of small, fully double flowers with recurved ray-florets. Popular examples of these are: '**Anastasia**', pale pink; '**Peterkin**', orange; '**Mei-Kyo**', warm pink; and '**Purleigh White**', white.

Rubellum
Flowers: late summer to mid-autumn. H 30–36in (75–90cm), S 20–24in (50–60cm). FH.
The free-flowering bushy chrysanthemums that take their name from *C. rubellum* are among the most valuable of the hybrids for garden use. The flowerheads, usually single, have yellow centres and ray-florets in a wide colour range: '**Clara Curtis**', single, mauve-pink; '**Duchess of Edinburgh**', single, copper-red; '**Emperor of China**', double with quilled petals, silver-pink; and '**Mary Stoker**', single, yellow to apricot with a green tint to centre.

Chrysanthemum 'Wendy'

Spray
Flowers: late summer to mid-autumn. H 3–4ft (90–120cm), S 2–3ft (60–90cm). FH.
Whether lined out for cutting or

incorporated in general planting schemes, the great value of these hybrids is in the amount of flowers produced, generally 5 to 6 blooms to a stem in a wide colour range, excluding blue, with each bush having about 5 stems. Examples include '**Enbee Wedding**', single, pink; '**Salmon Margaret**', reflexed double, apricot-pink; and '**Wendy**', reflexed double, bronzed orange, darker in the centre.

Chrysanthemum 'Salmon Margaret'

CIMICIFUGA

RANUNCULACEAE Bugbane

The common and the generic name refer to the use of *C. foetida*, a graceful species but rarely cultivated as an ornamental, as an insect repellent. Other tall species among the 18, all from temperate areas, grow in cool moist conditions in the wild. They produce wands of bottlebrush flowers that jostle elegantly over a base of ferny leaves.
CULTIVATION Require partial shade and moist fertile soil that is rich in organic matter.
PROPAGATION By division, in spring. From seed, sown as soon as ripe.
POTENTIAL PROBLEMS Usually none.

C. racemosa *E. North America*
Black snakeroot
Flowers: mid- to late summer. H 4–6ft (1.2–1.8m), S 2–3ft (60–90cm). FH.
Of those species in general cultivation this flowers first, the base of deeply cut leaves topped by branching stems terminating in slender white bottlebrushes.

Cimicifuga racemosa

C. simplex *China, Russia*
Foliage: mid-spring to mid-autumn. Flowers: early to mid-autumn. H 3–4ft (90–120cm), S 20–24in (50–60cm). FH.
The sinuous narrow spires of white flowers swaying gently or waving wildly add dramatic movement to the autumn garden. Purple-tinted buds open white on **var.** *matsumurae* '**Elstead**'. Most striking of all are the forms with dark foliage, exemplified by **var.** *simplex* **Atropurpurea Group**, whose creamy bottlebrushes rise above a dark purple base.

CIRSIUM

ASTERACEAE

There are many more weeds than attractive ornamentals in this thistle genus of about 200 species, which are found in a wide range of habitats in the Northern Hemisphere. The one described is not spectacular but the unusual colouring of the flowerheads, carried on branching stems above dark green leaves, adds an unexpected tone to sunny, reasonably moist borders.
CULTIVATION Requires full sun and moist well-drained soil.
PROPAGATION By division, in autumn or spring. From seed, sown in spring.
POTENTIAL PROBLEM Mildew.

Cirsium rivulare '**Atropurpureum**'

C. rivulare '**Atropurpureum**'
Flowers: early to mid-summer. H 3–4ft (90–120cm), S 18–24in (45–60cm). FH.
The spreading clump produces slightly spiny dark green leaves, and branching stems with glowing ruby-crimson soft thistles.

CONVALLARIA

CONVALLARIACEAE Lily-of-the-valley

The deliciously scented single species, by some authorities considered 3, is found throughout the Northern Hemisphere, usually in damp woodland. It can be quirkish in the garden, in some situations extending its

groundcovering role by thong-like rhizomes to invade areas that should be off limits, elsewhere just holding its ground. It is a good candidate for shady wild gardens where the soil is moist.
CULTIVATION Tolerate full sun, but best in shade, even full shade, and a wide range of soils, provided there is a good supply of moisture.
PROPAGATION From seed, sown as soon as ripe. By division, in autumn.
POTENTIAL PROBLEMS Botrytis (grey mould).
WARNING Swallowing the seeds of *C. majalis* may cause stomach upset.

Convallaria majalis

C. majalis *Europe, Asia and N. America*
Flowers: late spring. H 8–12in (20–30cm), S 12–16in (30–40cm). FH.
Stems dangling the fragrant white waxy bells are nursed between paired oval leaves. The best of the named selections are '**Albostriata**', the leaves of which have beautiful longitudinal creamy stripes, and '**Fortin's Giant**', vigorous with large flowers.

COREOPSIS

ASTERACEAE Tickseed

This North and Central American genus of about 100 species is represented in gardens by several annuals and a few perennials, some of which, like *C. grandiflora*, are short-lived and usually grown as annuals. Yellow is the predominant colour but in the annual *C. tinctoria* the flowerheads are darkened by varying proportions of mahogany and deep crimson. These bright daisies, mainly of open grassland, are easy plants that thrive in sunny gardens, especially on light soils.
CULTIVATION Tolerate full sun or partial shade and require well-drained soil.
PROPAGATION By division, in early spring. From seed, sowing perennials in a nursery bed in mid-spring, and annuals where they are to flower.
POTENTIAL PROBLEMS Slugs, snails.

Coreopsis verticillata 'Grandiflora'

C. verticillata *S.E. USA*
Flowers: summer. H 18–30in (45–75cm), S 12–18in (30–45cm). FH.
Relays of starry daisy flowerheads make a dense yellow cover over dark green, needle-like foliage. 'Grandiflora' is very richly coloured but the lemon-yellow of 'Moonbeam' is more versatile.

CORYDALIS

PAPAVERACEAE

The name of this genus, which includes about 300 species, is from the Greek for a lark, a fanciful allusion to the tubular spurred flowers, larks having spurred feet. Species in cultivation are mainly plants of cool woodland or rocky mountainous terrain in temperate areas of the Northern Hemisphere. They are grown principally for their highly distinctive flowers, although in most cases their divided foliage is of very great beauty. No weed is more beguiling than the yellow-flowered evergreen *C. lutea*, which is widely distributed in Europe.
C. ochroleuca, also European but from further south and east, is another species that self-seeds freely. It resembles *C. lutea* but the flowers are creamy with a yellow throat. Some species are tuberous or fleshy rooted, including the temperamental Himalayan
C. cashmeriana, with flowers of ravishing blue, but all are grouped together here.
CULTIVATION The species have varying requirements but many tolerate full sun or partial shade and require well-drained but moisture-retentive soil. Of those described *C. solida* is suitable for a free-draining position in a sunny rock garden. *C. flexuosa* thrives best in soil that is rich in organic matter. *C. cheilanthifolia* needs fertile well-drained soil.
C. cashmeriana needs lime-free soil.
PROPAGATION By division, in autumn and from offsets of tuberous species in spring. From seed, sown as soon as ripe.
POTENTIAL PROBLEMS Slugs, snails.

C. cheilanthifolia *China*
Foliage: year-round. Flowers: early spring to summer. H and S 8–12in (20–30cm). FH.
The lightly bronzed leaves make a ferny clump, above which the spikes of yellow spurred flowers look sparse but they are borne over a long season.

Corydalis flexuosa 'Père David'

C. flexuosa *China (W. Sichuan)*
Foliage: spring to summer. Flowers: late spring to summer. H 9–12in (23–30cm), S 8–10in (20–25cm). FH.
The impact this species has made since its introduction from W. China in 1989 owes almost everything to real virtues. It is easy to grow in the open garden or in containers, provided the medium is moist and rich in organic matter. The soft divided foliage is a calm blue-green, sometimes marked reddish brown or tinged purple. The flowers, like dashing shoals of little blue fish, are produced over many weeks in spring and sometimes again later. The named selections, such as 'Père David', show slight variations in tone or intensity of blue or in the tint of their foliage. All are beautiful and deserve to remain popular.

Corydalis solida f. *transsylvanica* 'George Baker'

C. solida *Asia, N. Europe*
Flowers: mid- to late spring. H 10–12in (25–30cm), S 6–8in (15–20cm). FH.
This ferny-leaved tuberous species produces upright spikes of tilted flowers that have down-turned spurs. The colour varies

considerably, from near white to mauve and reddish purple. The pink terracotta shade of
f. transsylvanica 'George Baker', usually grown in the alpine house, is a rare colour in flowers.

CRAMBE

BRASSICACEAE

Most of the species, about 20 in number, are plants of dry, open country in Europe, Asia and Africa, sometimes coastal, as in the case of sea kale (*C. maritima*). When the young leaf shoots are blanched, this is a spring vegetable delicacy, but this characterful plant offers large blue-green leaves of waxy texture and wavy margin.
C. cordifolia is space consuming but miraculously weightless in flower.

Crambe maritima

CULTIVATION Require full sun and deep, fertile, well-drained soil.
PROPAGATION By division, in early spring. From root cuttings, taken in winter. From seed, sown in spring or autumn.
POTENTIAL PROBLEMS Club root, soil-borne black rot.

C. cordifolia *Caucasus*
Foliage: spring to mid-summer. Flowers: late spring to mid-summer. H 6–8ft (1.8–2.5m), S 4–5ft (1.2–1.5m). FH.
The puckered and lobed large leaves are hairy and coarse but a criss-cross of branched stems is the almost invisible support for a cloud of small white flowers.

CYNARA

ASTERACEAE

No perennial can match the cardoon for the jagged splendour of its silvery leaves. In the same mould but smaller and less silvered is the globe artichoke. This is not so surprising; in a genus of about 10 species, what was once considered a separate species (*C. scolymus*) is, the pundits assert, the same Mediterranean thistle in another guise (*C. cardunculus* Scolymus Group).

CULTIVATION Requires full sun, fertile well-drained soil and shelter from strong winds. For best foliage effects, remove the flowers as they emerge.
PROPAGATION By division, in spring. From root cuttings, taken in winter. From seed, sown in spring.
POTENTIAL PROBLEMS Slugs, aphids; *Botrytis* (grey mould).

Cynara cardunculus

C. cardunculus *Morocco, S.W. Mediterranean,*
Cardoon
Foliage: spring to mid-autumn. Flowers: early summer to early autumn. H 5–6ft (1.5–1.8m), S 4–5ft (1.2–1.5m). FH.
Blanching of the young leaf stems and leaves produces a connoisseur's vegetable but this treatment is incompatible with the development of the great fountain of silvery foliage. Massive stems carry thistle flowerheads, up to 3in (8cm) across, the heavy prickly base topped by a tuft of violet-purple.

CYNOGLOSSUM

BORAGINACEAE Hound's tongue

Few of the 50 to 60 species, which occur in temperate zones and tropical uplands, are in general cultivation and of these several, including the Chinese forget-me-not (*C. amabile*), are annuals or biennials. These as well as the perennial described are plants of open ground or dappled shade. In the garden, plants may need twiggy supports.
CULTIVATION Tolerate sun or partial shade and require moist well-drained soil of moderate fertility.
PROPAGATION From seed, sown in autumn or spring. By division, in autumn or spring.
POTENTIAL PROBLEM Mildew.

C. nervosum *Himalayas*
Flowers: mid-spring to mid-summer. H and S 18–24in (45–60cm). FH.
Over several weeks the intense azure of the forget-me-not-like flowers transforms a nondescript clump of narrow hairy leaves.

Cynoglossum nervosum

DARMERA

SAXIFRAGACEAE Umbrella plant

The rounded clusters of flowers rise naked on flower stems to 6ft (1.8m) tall before the impressive mound of umbrella leaves develops. In the mountainous woodlands of the western USA where it grows wild, the single species in this genus is a waterside plant. In the garden it thrives in a bog garden but tolerates drier conditions in shade.
CULTIVATION Tolerates sun or partial shade and requires moist or, if growing in full sun, very wet soil.
PROPAGATION By division, in spring. From seed, sown in spring or autumn.
POTENTIAL PROBLEMS Usually none.

Darmera peltata

D. peltata *USA (S.W. Oregon to N.W. California)*
Foliage: early summer to late autumn. Flowers: late spring. H 3–6ft (90–180cm), S 2–4ft (60–120cm). FH.
The thick rhizomes throw up stout stems terminating in dense heads of 5-petalled pink or white flowers. The dark green leaves that follow are up to 2ft (60cm) across, with a scalloped margin and prominent radiating veins. In the autumn the leaves often take on red tints.

DELPHINIUM

RANUNCULACEAE

The tall narrow spires of the hybrid delphiniums represent a phenomenal achievement of plant breeding. The main species used is *D. elatum*. Each spire is densely packed with single, semi-double or double spurred flowers in white, cream, grey and even red, as well as every shade of blue. For the last 100 years hybrid delphiniums have been a mainstay of the traditional herbaceous border. Their popularity has been at the expense of the species themselves, of which there are about 250, including annuals and biennials, well distributed throughout the world. Among the most commonly grown species is *D. grandiflorum*, itself important in the breeding of the hybrids, but cultivars such as **'Blue Butterfly'**, a branching open

Delphinium hybrids

plant about 2ft (60cm) high with small sprays of bright blue flowers, are short-lived and often grown as annuals. *D. tatsienense*, another, but slightly smaller, airy plant with deep blue flowers, violet-purple at the tips, is also short-lived. Like many other species, these are not fussy about soil provided it is free-draining but the magnificent perfection of the hybrids requires generous feeding. A liquid feed every 2 weeks during the growing season and thinning of shoots helps boost flower size. Furthermore, plants need staking, attention to control pests and disease (slugs view young growths as the ultimate delicacy) and frequent propagation.
CULTIVATION Require full sun, fertile, well-drained soil and shelter from strong winds. Require staking when plants are over 1ft (30cm) tall.
PROPAGATION Belladonna and Elatum Group hybrids from sturdy basal cuttings, taken in early spring. From seed, sown in early spring at 55°F (13°C).
POTENTIAL PROBLEMS Slugs, snails, leaf miners, delphinium moth caterpillars; leaf blotch, powdery mildew, crown rot, cucumber mosaic virus.
WARNING Contact with the foliage may irritate the skin. Swallowing any part may cause stomach upset.

219

HYBRIDS

Belladonna Group

Flowers: summer. H 3–4ft (90–120cm), S 18–24in (45–60cm). FH. Since their development in the late 19th century these have been popular as cut flowers and in the garden their loose spikes, branching out above fingered leaves, follow in succession over a long period in the second half of summer, provided the old spikes are removed. Examples include: **'Casa Blanca'**, white; **'Cliveden Beauty'**, sky blue; **'Wendy'**, intense violet blue; and **'Völkerfrieden'**, deep blue.

Delphinium Belladonna Group 'Völkerfrieden'

Elatum Group

Flowers: early to mid-summer. H 5–7ft (1.5–2.2m), S 2–3ft (60–90cm). FH. This range of short-, medium- and tall-growing hybrids produces attractive clumps of soft green divided leaves, from which rise stiff spikes crowded with evenly spaced florets, as the flowers are generally known, some with a dark eye called a "bee", others with a light centre. The largest florets are

Delphinium 'Faust'

at the bottom of the spike and can be 3in (8cm) across. Cutting back the main spikes when they are spent encourages the development of laterals that give a lesser late display. Many of these delphiniums are short-lived, as are the **Pacific Hybrids**, which are similar in character but grown as annuals or biennials. Among the most compact are **'Mighty Atom'**, semi-double, violet-blue with brown-streaked "bees"; **'Rosemary Brock'**, semi-double, soft pink with brown eyes; **'Sandpiper'**, semi-double, white with dark-brown eyes; and **'Sungleam'**, semi-double, cream with yellow eye. Examples of medium height include **'Blue Nile'**, semi-double, medium blue with a white eye; and **'Loch Leven'**, semi-double, light blue with white eye. Among the tallest are **'Bruce'**, semi-double, violet-purple with dark brown eye; **'Fanfare'**, semi-double, soft mauve-blue with white eye; and **'Faust'**, semi-double, rich blue with purple overlay and dark eye.

Delphinium 'Sungleam'

DIANTHUS

CARYOPHYLLACEAE Carnation, pink

Few genera are held in such deep affection by gardeners. About 300 species are widely distributed in the Northern Hemisphere and southern Africa, many of them tough dwarf plants found in mountainous country. The perennial species, including compact plants suitable for rock gardens, raised beds and edging, are, however, quite overwhelmed by the thousands of hybrid pinks and carnations. These flower in great profusion and are long-lasting when cut. Some have a rich clove scent. What has also fascinated gardeners during their long history in cultivation is the form of the flower – single or double, fringed or smooth in outline – and the range of markings, for which a special vocabulary is employed. Picotee carnations, for example, usually white, have petals outlined in a darker colour; laced pinks, such as 'Gran's Favourite', have the

margin and centre in one colour contrasting with the body colour of the flower; while in fancies irregular flakes and streaks contrast with the ground colour. The sentimental attachment to these plants is explained in part by the important role they have played in humble gardens, in part by their status as florists' flowers, one of the group of plants devotedly cultivated for perfection of bloom and competitive showing, particularly in the 18th and 19th centuries. As with all the florists' flowers, the hybrids are complex and their categories sometimes confusing. The entry on hybrids covers the main categories usually grown outdoors but omits the half-hardy perpetual-flowering carnations, grown commercially under glass on a large scale for cut flowers, and the Malmaison carnations, also half-hardy and grown under glass for their large flowers and penetrating fragrance. Propagate all plants frequently as many deteriorate after 2 or 3 years. The short-lived Chinese or Indian pink (*D. chinensis*) is grown as an annual or biennial, sweet William (*D. barbatus*), with clusters of white to red flowers, often prettily marked, as a biennial.

Dianthus 'Gran's Favourite'

CULTIVATION Require full sun and well-drained soil, with few exceptions preferring neutral to alkaline soils. (*D. pavonius* is among those that are best on acid soil.) Alpine species need very sharp drainage.
PROPAGATION From cuttings of non-flowering shoots, in summer. From seed, sown from autumn to early spring (alpine species).
POTENTIAL PROBLEMS Aphids, slugs; rust.

SPECIES

D. alpinus *Europe (S.E. Alps)*

Alpine pink
Flowers: all summer. H 3–4in (8–10cm), S 4in (10cm). FH. The single flowers overlap like interlocking shields to hide tight

dark green cushions of foliage.
The fringed petals are variable in
colouring, the range extending
from pale pink to crimson. There is
often a white eye and some degree
of spotting. **'Joan's Blood'** is bright
magenta with a dark red centre.

D. deltoides *Asia, Europe*
Maiden pink
Flowers: all summer. H 6–9in (15–
23cm), S 12–15in (30–38cm). FH.
The single flowers are small but
borne profusely over a long season
on plants with narrow foliage that
often has a purplish tinge. The
colour range includes pink, bright
crimson in **'Leuchtfunk'**, among
others, and white in **'Albus'**.

D. gratianopolitanus *N.W. and C. Europe*
Cheddar pink
Flowers: mid-summer. H 4–10in (10–
25cm), S 10–16in (25–40cm). FH.
Above a carpet of narrow grey-
green leaves single pink flowers
with fringed petals exhale a
carrying fragrance.

D. pavonius *Europe (S.W. Alps)*
Flowers: summer. H 3–5in
(8–13cm), S 6–8in (15–20cm). FH.
Although the single flowers, which
have fringed and overlapping
petals, are variable in their shade of
pink, they are consistent in the
biscuit colour of the underside.
The tufts of foliage are grey-green.

D. superbus *Mountains of Asia and Europe*
Flowers: mid-summer to autumn.
H and S 8–12in (20–30cm). FH.
The untidy sprawl of lax stems
counts against it but the sprays of
mauve-pink flowers, green-eyed
and ragged, are bewitchingly
fragrant. The hybrid **'Loveliness'** is
a more substantial version.

Dianthus 'Pike's Pink'

HYBRIDS

Alpine pinks
Flowers: summer. H 3–4in
(8–10cm), S 6–8in (15–20cm). FH.
Compact cushions or tufted mats
of narrow grey-green leaves are

covered by short-stemmed flowers,
usually fragrant and large in
proportion. The singles include
the greenish white **'Dewdrop'**, the
dark-eyed **'Inshriach Dazzler'**,
which is a vivid reddish pink, and
'La Bourboule', a clear pink. The
double **'Pike's Pink'** has darker
markings in the muddled centre,
giving a focus to the prettily fringed
pale pink flowers.

Border carnations
Flowers: mid-summer. H 18–24in
(45–60cm), S 12–16in (30–40cm).
FH.
The earliest examples were the
delight of 16th- and 17th-century
gardeners. They are lax plants with
grey-green leaves and need staking
to hold up sprays of fragrant double
flowers. Modern kinds have
unfringed petals giving a rounded
outline about 2in (5cm) across.
The small-flowered, deep crimson
'Fenbow Nutmeg Clove' and a few
others are said to date from the 17th
century. More modern examples
include: **'Bookham Fancy'**, yellow,
flecked and outlined in purplish
red; **'Irene Della-Torré'**, white with
pink outline and streaking; and
'Sandra Neal', rich yellow with
irregular dark pink streaks.

Dianthus 'Doris'

Modern pinks
Flowers: early summer to autumn.
H 10–18in (25–45cm), S 10–16in
(25–40cm). FH.
The usually compact plants
produced by hybridizing old-
fashioned pinks and perpetual-
flowering carnations give a long-
flowering display of rather crisp-
textured flowers. Some, but far
from all, are well scented.
Examples of laced doubles include
'Becky Robinson', with red-pink
markings on soft pink, and the
more muddled **'Gran's Favourite'**,
white with fine edging and central
markings in purplish pink. **'Doris'**,
a double bicolour well-known as a
cut flower, has pale pink flowers
that are soft coral at the centre,
and the very full **'Houndspool
Ruby'** is a sharp pink with darker
tints. All of these are clove-scented.

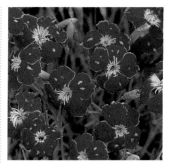
Dianthus 'Sops-in-wine'

Old-fashioned pinks
Flowers: early summer. H 10–18in
(25–45cm), S 10–14in (25–35cm).
FH.
Their season is short and some
make untidy grey-green clumps of
narrow leaves, but these pinks
hold pride of place in gardeners'
affections. The spiced scent of
D. plumarius, said to be one of
the parents, is a hallmark of the
best. Some have been in cultivation
for a very long time but others,
although in the old style, are
relatively modern. Singles include
'Brympton Red', of marbled
crimson, the white but green-eyed
'Musgrave's Pink' and **'Sops-in-
wine'**, with a white patch on each
purplish crimson petal. Many are
laced, among them the semi-
double **'Dad's Favourite'**, white
with crimson edging and a dark
red centre. The creamy white **'Mrs
Sinkins'** is renowned for its scent
but the double flowers are untidy,
petals spilling out of split calyces.

Dianthus 'Mrs Sinkins'

DIASCIA

SCROPHULARIACEAE

About 50 species, annuals as well
as perennials, are native of
southern Africa, where most grow
in open positions with a good
supply of moisture. Although they
are not fully hardy, the perennial
species and a growing number of
hybrids are enjoying a vogue. The
elegant spikes of pink flowers,
varying in shade according to
species and cultivar, are borne in
quantity over a long season. The
individual flowers, which resemble

nemesias, are tubular with 5 lobes, the common name referring to the 2 spurs extending behind the top paired lobes. An attractive feature of diascias is the ease with which they combine with other plants, either at the front of a border or in a container. The flowering season is agreeably long. To keep up the display, old stems should be sheared off as soon as the flowers are spent. Diascias are easily propagated, which partly explains their popularity among nurserymen. In frost-prone areas it is a sensible precaution to over-winter rooted cuttings under glass.
CULTIVATION Require full sun and fertile, moist, well-drained soil.
PROPAGATION By division, in spring. From cuttings, taken in summer. From seed, sown at 61°F (16°C) in spring.
POTENTIAL PROBLEMS Slugs, snails.

Diascia 'Salmon Supreme'

D. barberae 'Ruby Field'
Flowers: summer to early autumn. H 10-12in (25-30cm), S 18-24in (45-60cm). FrH.
Sprays of rich pink flowers sway lightly over a low mat of mid-green leaves. *D. barberae* '**Blackthorn Apricot**', a more recent hybrid of the same height, produces loose spires of apricot pink flowers. The paler apricot *D.* '**Salmon Supreme**' is only 6in (15cm) high.

Diascia barberae 'Ruby Field'

D. rigescens South Africa
Flowers: summer. H 12-18in (30-45cm), S 16-20in (40-50cm). FrH.
Although a trailing plant, the branching angular stems are stiff and more or less upright. They are clothed in toothed heart-shaped leaves and dense spikes of dusty purple-pink flowers.

D. vigilis South Africa (Drakensberg Mountains)
Flowers: all summer to autumn. H 12-18in (30-45cm), S 18-24in (45-60cm). FrH.
This erect, small-leaved species has loose spikes of clear pink flowers. The flowers of *D. fetcaniensis*, a similar plant but slightly smaller and sticky to the touch, are bright pink.

DICENTRA

PAPAVERACEAE

The fanciful common names used to describe several species suggest quaintness rather than beauty. Dutchman's breeches is, admittedly, remarkably descriptive of the unconventional flowers of the E. North American *D. cucullaria*, with upturned white pantaloons that are yellow at the waist, but most of the species and hybrids in cultivation are refined plants, far from grotesque in their flowers and with exceptionally beautiful foliage. Most of the 20 or so species are natives of moist woodland in North America and in Asia from the western Himalayas to eastern Siberia. Apart from *D. spectabilis*, one of the supreme herbaceous perennials for dappled shade, those described have rhizomatous roots by which ferny colonies expand.
CULTIVATION Require partial shade and well-drained but moist soil that is rich in organic matter. *D. spectabilis* tolerates full sun, provided the soil does not dry out.
PROPAGATION By division, in early spring. By root cuttings of *D. spectabilis*, taken in winter. From seed, sown in spring.
POTENTIAL PROBLEMS Slugs, snails.
WARNING Contact with the foliage may cause an allergic skin reaction. Swallowing any part may cause stomach upset.

D. 'Adrian Bloom'
Foliage: spring to autumn. Flowers: late spring and early autumn. H 12-14in (30-35cm), S 18-24in (45-60cm). FH.
After its main flowering this hybrid continues to produce odd stems dangling bright red lockets over grey-green foliage. There is little to choose in quality between the short-growing hybrids but 2 others outstanding for their blue-grey foliage are *D.* '**Langtrees**', with pinkish white flowers, and *D.* '**Stuart Boothman**', deep pink.

Dicentra formosa

D. formosa W. North America
Wild bleeding heart
Foliage: spring to autumn. Flowers: late spring to early summer. H 12-18in (30-45cm), S 2-3ft (60-90cm). FH.
Pink-tinted stems rise from dense low clumps of ferny leaves to dangle pretty clusters of mauve-pink lockets. The wide-spreading hummocks of finely textured foliage contrast well with large-leaved perennials of shady places. The coolness of white lockets in **var.** *alba* is matched by the pale green of the foliage.

Dicentra spectabilis

D. spectabilis Korea, N. China, Siberia
Bleeding heart, Dutchman's breeches, lady's locket, lyre flower
Foliage: spring to autumn. Flowers: late spring to early summer. H 2-4ft (60-120cm), S 18-24in (45-60cm). FH.
The peerless elegance of this species distinguishes it in the spring-summer interregnum but at any season it would be a plant of the first rank. A sheltered position should be reserved for it as it is brittle, down to its roots. When they arch out from the grey-green divided leaves the gently sinuous stems are lightly weighed down by dangling deep pink hearts, from which protrude flashes of white petals. '**Alba**', with pure white lockets, is if anything more beautiful than the species and appears to be a more vigorous plant. For those who can steel themselves to plunder, it is good as a cut flower.

DICTAMNUS

RUTACEAE

Children of all ages are momentarily delighted by the know-all's trick of lighting the volatile oil the plant gives off on a hot day in late summer. Miraculously, the plant is undamaged. The single species, which has a wide distribution in Europe and Asia, is found mainly in open positions on dry, stony ground.

CULTIVATION Require full sun and well-drained, preferably alkaline, soil.

PROPAGATION From seed, sown as soon as ripe. By division, in spring or autumn.

POTENTIAL PROBLEMS Usually none.
WARNING Contact with the foliage may cause photodermititis. Swallowing any part may cause stomach upset.

D. albus *C. and S. Europe to N. China, Korea*
Burning bush, dittany
Flowers: early summer. H 18–36in (45–90cm), S 18–24 (45–60cm). FH.
When bruised, the divided dark green leaves have a strong lemon scent. They are topped by tall spires of white flowers that are followed by appealing star-shaped seed-pods. The flowers of **var. purpureus** are purplish pink with darker veins.

Dictamnus albus

DODECATHEON

PRIMULACEAE American cowslip, shooting star

The dart-like flowers, halted in their plunging descent, are characteristic of the 14 species, all of which are found in North America. Most are woodland plants, growing where there is plenty of moisture in spring, although often much drier later in the year; their leaves die down immediately after flowering. The flower colour of the plants in cultivation ranges from pale pink to carmine, with, in addition, some beautiful albinos. The species described is the most widely grown

but the Californian **D. hendersonii**, with reddish pink petals, and **D. pulchellum**, from W. North America, especially the bright magenta **subsp. pulchellum 'Red Wings'**, are no less appealing and convey the same impression of arrested drama.

CULTIVATION Tolerate full sun but best in partial shade and require well-drained but moist soil rich in organic matter.

PROPAGATION From seed, sown as soon as ripe (germination follows a period of chilling). By division, in spring.

POTENTIAL PROBLEMS Slugs, snails.

Dodecatheon meadia f. *album*

D. meadia *N.W. USA*
Shooting star
Flowers: mid- to late spring.
H 15–24in (38–60cm), S 10–12in (25–30cm). FH.
The erect stems that rise from a rosette of mid-green leaves are charged at their tip with up to 15 toy missiles, the mauve-pink petals swept back from a white base, from which protrude reddish yellow anthers. The creamy **f. album** has yellow anthers.

DORONICUM

ASTERACEAE Leopard's bane

Of about 35 species, several are grown for their spring show of bright yellow daisies. These include **D. austriacum** and **D. orientale**, plants of woodland margins in mountainous country in southern Europe and further east. They may be the parents of the plant described, which is at its best in the wilder parts of the garden.

CULTIVATION Require partial shade and moist soil that is rich in organic matter.

PROPAGATION By division, in autumn. From seed, sown in spring.

POTENTIAL PROBLEMS Leaf spot, root rot, powdery mildew.

D. 'Miss Mason'
Flowers: late spring. H and S 18–24in (45–60cm), S 2ft (60cm). FH.
Yellow flowerheads, about 3in (8cm) across, are carried well

Doronicum 'Miss Mason'

above heart-shaped, bright green leaves. **D. × excelsum 'Harpur Crewe'** has flowerheads about 4in (10cm) across and stems up to 2ft (60cm) high.

DRABA

BRASSICACEAE Whitlow grass

The plants that excite interest in this genus of about 300 species are compact perennials from mountainous screes and rocky outcrops in temperate regions. Their closely packed rosettes of leaves form tight hummocks or mats that in spring or early summer are covered by small cross-shaped flowers. Some of the greatest alpine treasures, such as **D. mollisima**, in flower a tiny cushion of bright yellow, are for the committed specialist.

CULTIVATION Require full sun and very well-drained soil. The cushion types require protection from winter wet and are usually grown in an alpine house (equal parts of loam, leafmould and grit).

PROPAGATION From rosette cuttings, taken in late spring. From seed, sown in autumn after pre-chilling.

POTENTIAL PROBLEMS Aphids and red spider mites under glass.

D. aizoides *Europe*
Yellow whitlow grass
Flowers: late spring. H 4in (10cm), S 6–10in (15–25cm). FH.
The alpine cognoscenti may sneer but this easy-going rock garden plant makes a cheerful show of lemon-yellow flowers clustered over rosettes of bristly leaves.

Draba aizoides

ECHINACEA

ASTERACEAE Coneflower

The central cone, which gives these plants their common name, is a conspicuous, sometimes glistening, feature of the daisy flowerheads. There are about 9 species, all found in North America, most in prairie-like conditions. The species in general cultivation is usually a plant of reasonably moist fertile soils. The flowering season can be prolonged by removing flowerheads as soon as they fade.

CULTIVATION Require full sun and well-drained fertile soil rich in organic matter.
PROPAGATION By division, in autumn or spring. From root cuttings, taken in winter. From seed, sown in spring.
POTENTIAL PROBLEMS Usually none.

Echinacea purpurea

E. purpurea *North America (Ontario S. to Georgia)*
Flowers: mid-summer to early autumn. H 3–4ft (90–120cm), S 18–24in (45–60cm). FH.
As compensation for the coarseness of the plant, with its bristly dark green leaves and stout stems, the large flowerheads consist of a splendidly textured orange-brown cone, around which radiate the purplish red ray-florets. The flowerheads of '**Magnus**' can be well over 6in (15cm) across. In '**White Lustre**' the greenish white ray-florets hang down from a brassy cone.

ECHINOPS

ASTERACEAE Globe thistle

Bees and butterflies throng to feast from the spherical flowerheads, which in the most ornamental are steely blue. There are more than 100 species, widely distributed in the Northern Hemisphere and parts of Africa. Many are found wild among grass on dry stony ground but those cultivated do best in reasonably fertile borders. Flowers can be dried but lose their colour unless cut promptly.

CULTIVATION Require full sun and well-drained soil, tolerating even poor soils.
PROPAGATION By division, in autumn, winter or spring. From root cuttings, taken in winter. From seed, sown in mid-spring.
POTENTIAL PROBLEM Aphids.

Echinops ritro 'Veitch's Blue'

E. ritro *S. Central and S.E. Europe to C. Asia*
Flowers: late summer. H 2–4ft (60–120cm), S 18–24in (45–60cm). FH.
Tall stems rise above prickly green and silver leaves carrying metallic-blue maces that soften in colour as the flowers open. '**Veitch's Blue**' is darker in colour and grows to 3ft (90cm). A plant of similar character is **E. bannaticus** '**Taplow Blue**', with flowers of a brighter hue.

EPIMEDIUM

BERBERIDACEAE Barrenwort, bishop's mitre

Above a thicket of thin wiry stems a low canopy of overlapping, heart-shaped leaflets, often bronze-tinted in spring and richly coloured again in autumn, make a distinctive and superior kind of groundcover. There are over 30 species of these rhizomatous perennials widely distributed in the Northern Hemisphere, most of them growing in shady moist conditions but some, including **E. alpinum**, a deciduous fully hardy species from southern Europe, tolerant of drier soils in the open. The light sprays of small flowers, in many cases extravagantly spurred, are an appealing feature in late spring or

Epimedium alpinum

early summer, but for these to be seen well it is generally necessary to trim back the tattered foliage that has over-wintered. The flower colour is usually white, yellow, pink or crimson but the evergreen fully hardy **E. × warleyense** is unusual with its combination of dull orange and yellow.

CULTIVATION Tolerate full sun but best in partial shade and require well-drained but moist soil that is rich in organic matter. See also under entries.
PROPAGATION By division, in autumn. From rhizome cuttings, taken in winter and kept under glass. From seed, which may take 18 months to germinate, sown as soon as ripe.
POTENTIAL PROBLEMS Vine weevils; mosaic virus.

Epimedium 'Rose Queen'

E. grandiflorum *China, Korea, Japan*
Foliage: spring to autumn. Flowers: mid- to late spring. H 8–12in (20–30cm), S 12–16in (30–40cm). FH.
In spring, when mauve-pink spurred flowers hover above them, the small immature leaflets are coppery brown but later change to light green. The foliage of '**Rose Queen**' is more purplish when young and the deep pink flowers have white-tipped spurs. '**White Queen**' shows a hint of mauve in the flowers. *E. grandiflorum* is one parent of **E. × rubrum**, with deep pink flowers. In spring, green veins run through copper-red leaves, which turn green in summer but colour richly in autumn.

E. perralderianum *Algeria*
Foliage: year-round. Flowers: mid- to late spring. H 10–14in (25–35cm), S 18–24in (45–60cm). FH.
The slowly spreading evergreen clump has large leaves, composed usually of 3 toothed leaflets, which are bronze when young and then turn glossy green. The flowers are bright yellow. The species is one parent of of the slightly taller **E. × perralchicum**, with yellow flowers and foliage with warm tints in spring, maturing to deep green.

Epimedium perralderianum

E. × *versicolor* 'Sulphureum'

Foliage: spring and autumn.
Flowers: mid- to late spring.
H 12-14in (30-35cm), S 1-2ft
(30-60cm). FH.
The leaves, generally composed of
numerous toothed leaflets, are
exceptional for their coppery
tones in spring, and colour well in
autumn too. They hide the spurred
yellow flowers unless cut away.

Epimedium × *versicolor*
'Sulphureum'

E. × *youngianum*

Foliage: spring. Flowers: mid- to
late spring. H 8-12in (20-30cm),
S 12-18in (30-45cm). FH.
Although less effective as groundcover than many barrenworts, this
fully deciduous species has dainty
small leaves. The foliage of 'Niveum'
is flushed soft brown in spring,
when the sprays of white flowers
are carried on reddish stems.

EREMURUS

ASPHODELACEAE Desert candle,
foxtail lily

The flowering of the tallest species
is one of the great events of the
year in a dry garden but a cold
winter period is necessary for
them to produce their sensational
candles. *E. robustus*, a species
from the Tien Shan and Pamir
Mountains, can grow to 10ft (3m),
the foxtail flowerhead itself,
densely packed with pink starry
flowers, being up to 4ft (1.2m)
long. In the wild the 50 or so
species are found in near-desert
conditions in Asia. They die down
after their extravagant display.

Inevitably the large species leave
awkward gaps after flowering, a
problem compounding the
difficulties posed by the space
required for the starfish-shaped
crowns of fleshy roots, which need
to be set about 6in (15cm) deep.
The smaller species and a group of
hybrids are more suitable as
dramatic verticals in dry borders.
CULTIVATION Require full sun and
fertile well-drained soil. However,
young growths may be damaged
by thawing frost if touched by
early morning sun.
PROPAGATION By careful division,
after flowering. From seed, sown as
soon as ripe (seedlings may take 5
years to reach flowering maturity).
POTENTIAL PROBLEMS Slugs, snails.

Eremurus × isabellinus **Ruiter
Hybrids**

E. hybrids

Flowers: early summer. H 3-6ft
(90-180cm), S 18-24in (45-60cm).
FH.
A number of hybrid cultivars and
their mixed seedlings are sometimes
listed under *E. × isabellinus*. They
have strap-shaped leaves and stiff
stems, the dense flowerhead
bristling with stamens. Among the
tallest are the **Ruiter Hybrids** in a
colour range that includes bright
pink and rusty shades. The **Shelford
Hybrids** are slightly shorter,
growing to about 4ft (1.2m);
colours include orange and yellow.

ERIGERON

ASTERACEAE Fleabane

The 200 or so species are found in
many parts of the world. In
gardens the numerous hybrids
between North American species,
plants of prairies and mountainous
areas, predominate. The wide
colour range in the daisy
flowerheads makes these useful
plants for sunny borders, especially
as they often flower a second time
if cut back after their first display.
The tall hybrids need staking and
all plants deteriorate unless
divided about every 3 years.
CULTIVATION Require full sun and
fertile well-drained soil.

PROPAGATION By division, in spring.
From cuttings, taken in spring.
From seed, sown in spring.
POTENTIAL PROBLEMS Slugs;
powdery mildew.

E. hybrids

Flowers: early to mid-summer.
H 10-24in (25-60cm), S 12-18in
(30-45cm). FH.
Leafy stems are topped by single
or semi-double flowers – usually
yellow-centred. The following are
semi-double: '**Dimity**', 10in (25cm),
mauve-pink with an orange centre;
'**Dunkelste Aller**', 2ft (60cm), deep
violet; and '**Foersters Liebling**',
20in (50cm), reddish pink.

Erigeron 'Dimity'

E. *karvinskianus* Mexico to
Panama

Mexican daisy
Flowers: all summer. H 6-12in (15-
30cm), S 2-3ft (60-90cm). FH.
The Mexican daisy has the
manners of a weed, spreading
vigorously and self-seeding
indiscreetly. It is, nonetheless, an
exceptionally pretty plant, and the
random airy mixture of open
white flowerheads with the pink
and purple of buds and faded
daisies is most appealing in plants
that have taken chance lodgings in
walls and paving.

ERODIUM

GERANIACEAE Heron's bill, stork's
bill

The 5-petalled flowers, small but
often delicately veined and artfully
blotched, show the genus's kinship
with *Geranium*. Many of the 60 or
so species, widely distributed, are
compact plants of rocky limestone
country that make neat mounds of
foliage in rock gardens. The larger
species are suitable for the front of
a border.
CULTIVATION Require full sun and
very well-drained, neutral or
alkaline soil.
PROPAGATION By division, in spring.
From basal cuttings, taken in late
spring. From seed, sown as soon as
ripe.
POTENTIAL PROBLEMS Usually none.

Erodium manescaui

E. manescaui *Spain (Pyrenees)*
Flowers: early summer to early
autumn. H 12–20in (30–50cm),
S 1–2ft 30–60cm). FH.
The best-known large species is
colourful over a long period, the
cluster of bright magenta flowers,
with darker blotches on the upper
2 petals, carried over a clump of
hairy, carrot-like foliage. It self-
seeds freely without being
excessively troublesome. A much
more compact Pyrenean species,
E. glandulosum, has silvery tufted
foliage and mauve-pink flowers
blotched purple.

Erodium reichardii

E. × variabile
Flowers: all summer. H 6–8in (15–
29cm), S 12–16in (30–40cm). FH.
The parents of this hybrid,
E. corsicum and **E. reichardii**, are
themselves attractive plants, the
former, found in the wild on the
rocky coastline of Corsica and
Sardinia, having downy grey-green
leaves and white to pink flowers
with conspicuous magenta
veining. In the hybrid the cushion
of scalloped leaves is topped by
deep red flowers. There are several
cultivars of *E. × variabile*, including
a double, **'Flore Pleno'**, and the
dark-veined, pink **'Roseum'**.

ERYNGIUM

APIACEAE Eryngo, sea holly

Flower arrangers will scavenge for
those that when dry retain in their
branched stems and the jagged
ruffs of the cone-like flowerheads
the metallic lustre of the living
plant. There are 230 species, some
of which have deep tap roots and
thrive in dry rocky conditions in
Asia, Europe and North Africa and,
in the case of the sea holly
(**E. maritimum**), on pebbly
shorelines. The silver-green
biennial Miss Willmott's ghost
(**E. giganteum**), the common name
a barbed compliment, as perhaps
the Edwardian gardener deserved,
is of this persuasion. In contrast
most of the species from Mexico,
Central and South America, such as
E. agavifolium from Argentina,
which has an impressive rosette of
toothed leaves, are fibrous-rooted
plants of moister, more fertile soils.
CULTIVATION Require full sun and
well-drained soil; the species
described tolerate dry conditions.
PROPAGATION From seed, sown
when ripe. By division, in spring.
From root cuttings, in winter.
POTENTIAL PROBLEMS Slugs, snails;
powdery mildew, root rot.

E. alpinum *Europe (Alps, Jura,
mountains of W. and C. Balkans)*
Flowers: mid-summer to early
autumn. H 24–30in (60–75cm),
S 18–24in (45–60cm). FH.
The upper part of the branched
stems as well as the flowerheads
and their softly lacy ruffs seem to
be dyed a steely violet-blue. Silvery
'Slieve Donard' is one of several
good selections. *E. × oliverianum*,
of which *A. alpinum* may be a
parent, is large-flowered and silvery
blue, with stiffly spiny bracts.

Eryngium alpinum **'Slieve Donard'**

E. bourgatii *Spain (Pyrenees)*
Foliage: spring to autumn. Flowers:
mid- to late summer. H 1–2ft (30–
60cm), S 12–18 (30–45cm). FH.
Curled and prickly jagged leaves,
veined and spangled with silver,
are the base for branched blue
stems and their silver-spined blue
or grey-green flowerheads.

E. × tripartitum
Flowers: mid-summer to early
autumn. H 2–3ft (60–90cm),
S 20–30in (50–75cm). FH.
Numerous small blue cones with
sparse but darker and spiny bracts
are supported by a wiry
framework, itself metallic blue.
E. amethystinum is similar with
very blue flowerheads later in the
season.

EUPATORIUM

ASTERACEAE

This very mixed genus of about 40
species, some of them annuals and
evergreen shrubs, is widely
distributed in temperate,
subtropical and tropical regions. It
contains a few perennials that are
suitable for large-scale planting in
moist soils. The double form of the
European hemp agrimony
(**E. cannabinum** **'Flore Pleno'**),
like the species described, is an
impressive waterside plant.
CULTIVATION Tolerate full sun or
partial shade and require moist soil.
PROPAGATION By division, in spring.
From seed, sown in spring.
POTENTIAL PROBLEMS Aphids, slugs
and snails.

Eupatorium purpureum

E. purpureum *E. USA*
Joe Pye weed
Flowers: mid-summer to early
autumn. H 6–8ft (1.8–2.5m),
S 3–4ft (90–120cm). FH.
Purplish red stems rise through
coarse leaves bearing soft domes
of pink-purple flowers. In **subsp.
maculatum 'Atropurpureum'** the
stems are slightly shorter and the
flowers have a brighter pink tone.

EUPHORBIA

EUPHORBIACEAE Milkweed, spurge

The curious structure of the
flowers is a feature shared by
about 2000 species in this very
large genus but in other respects
the character of the plants can be
very different, for they include
flimsy annuals, evergreen and
deciduous perennials and shrubs,
as well as tree-like succulents,
some bearing a strong
resemblance to columnar cacti.
Representatives of the genus are
found in a very wide range of
habitats in temperate, subtropical
and tropical regions. The most
useful perennials as garden plants,

at least in temperate regions, are those with good clumps of foliage and long-lasting clusters or heads of flowers, the conspicuous feature being the bracts surrounding the small cup that cradles the tiny male and female flowers. Some of these are plants of dry rocky terrain but others are plants of moister woodland conditions.

CULTIVATION Tolerate full sun or partial shade and a wide range of well-drained soils. Many thrive in dry conditions but of those described the following prefer moist soils in light shade: *E. amygdaloides, E. griffithii, E. polychroma* and *E. schillingii.*

PROPAGATION By division, in early spring. From cuttings, taken in spring (dip cut surfaces in lukewarm water to stop sap bleeding). From seed, sown in spring.

POTENTIAL PROBLEMS Aphids; rust, *Botrytis* (grey mould).

WARNING Contact with the sap may cause skin problems. Swallowing any part may cause severe stomach upset.

E. amygdaloides *Caucasus, Europe, Turkey*
Wood spurge
Flowers: mid-spring to early summer. H 1–2ft (30–60cm), S 1ft (30cm). FH.
The evergreen wood spurge is itself an indifferent plant but '**Purpurea**' combines maroon and purplish red in its stems and young foliage and sharp yellow in the flowerheads. On poor soils in shade **var. robbiae** makes outstanding evergreen ground cover, the dark rosettes topped by yellow-green flowers over a long season.

E. characias *Portugal, W. Mediterranean*
Foliage: year-round. Flowers: early spring to early summer. H 3–5ft (90–150cm), S 3–4ft (90–120cm). FrH.
In reality this is shrubby but in character is not far removed from perennial species thriving in dry

Euphorbia characias **subsp.** *wulfenii*

conditions. The narrow blue-green leaves densely clothing stiff stems are attractive throughout the year and especially beautiful when beaded with drops of water. The flowering stems carry huge heads dense with green bracts, nearly black nectar glands creating a dark eye. In **subsp.** *wulfenii* the nectar glands are greenish yellow.

Euphorbia griffithii

E. griffithii *Bhutan, S.W. China (Yunnan), Tibet*
Foliage: autumn. Flowers: early summer. H 2–3ft (60–90cm), S 20–24in (50–60cm). FH.
Spreading by questing rhizomes, this native of light moist woodland, most frequently represented by cultivars such as '**Fireglow**', can make large patches vivid with the brick-red or coral of its bracts. The narrow leaves are usually green with red tinged midribs, but in '**Dixter**' they are darker, with copper tints.

Euphorbia myrsinites

E. myrsinites *C. Asia, S. and E. Europe to Turkey*
Foliage: year-round. Flowers: spring. H 4–6in (10–15cm), S 12–15in (30–38cm). FH.
At the edge of a rocky outcrop the prostrate stems of this evergreen seem to writhe with the spiral arrangement of the blue-green fleshy leaves. The long-lasting flowerheads are greenish yellow.

E. polychroma *C. and S. Europe, Turkey*
Flowers: mid-spring to mid-summer. H 18in (45cm), S 18–24in (45–60cm). FH.

The clump makes a tidy dome of bright greenish yellow in dry as well as moist soils. All the selections are worth growing, including the extra large '**Major**'.

Euphorbia polychroma

E. schillingii *E. Nepal*
Foliage: spring to autumn. Flowers: mid-summer to mid-autumn. H 30–36in (75–90cm), S 1–2ft (30–60cm). FH.
The very long season in which the bracts remain an attractive greenish yellow make this clump-forming plant, only described as a new species in 1987, a valuable addition to those that thrive in moist soils. **E. sikkimensis** is slightly taller and also does best in moist soils. It is remarkable for the display of pink leaves and red stems in early spring.

FILIPENDULA

ROSACEAE

Except for dropwort (**F. vulgaris**), best known for the creamy double '**Multiplex**', the 10 or so species in this genus are moisture-loving plants from temperate regions in the Northern Hemisphere. They are well suited to waterside planting in the wilder reaches of the garden, where their plumy flowerheads do not seem over-sophisticated. They can be incorporated, too, in borders with a reliable supply of moisture but the giant among them, the queen of the prairies (**F. rubra**), up to 8ft (2.5m) high, requires a very generous border, where its spreading clumps may get out of hand.

CULTIVATION Most tolerate full sun or partial shade and require a moist soil, thriving even in boggy conditions. *F. vulgaris* needs sun and well-drained soil and is best in alkaline conditions.

PROPAGATION By division, in autumn or spring. From root cuttings, taken in early spring. From seed, sown in autumn or in spring at 50–55°F (10–13°C).

POTENTIAL PROBLEMS Leaf spot, mildew.

F. palmata *China, Japan, Mongolia, Siberia*
Foliage: spring to autumn. Flowers: mid-summer. H 4–6ft (1.2–1.8m), S 3–4ft (90–120cm). FH.
The lobed dark green leaves are hairy and white underneath. They form a good clump through which rise stiff stems with flat heads of pink, fluffy flowers. 'Elegantissima' has deep pink flowers followed by bronzy red seedheads.

Filipendula purpurea

F. purpurea *Japan*
Flowers: late summer. H 3–4ft (90–120cm), S 18–24in (45–60cm). FH.
This is a much more manageable plant than *F. rubra* but still makes an impressive mound of fingered leaves. The branched purplish red stems carry reddish pink flowers that fade as they age.

Filipendula ulmaria

F. ulmaria *Europe, W. Asia*
Meadowsweet, queen of the meadows
Foliage: spring. Flowers: summer. H 2–3ft (60–90cm), S 1–2ft (30–60cm). FH.
The specific name is a reference to the elm-like leaves while the common name is a reminder that the creamy flowers are fragrant. The gold-variegated 'Aurea' is the plant to grow. It tolerates bog conditions, demanding an unfailing supply of moisture, and some shade will prevent the leaves from scorching as they change from yellow, through cream to light green. The flowerheads are inferior and should be removed to prevent plain green-leaved seedlings becoming established.

FOENICULUM

APIACEAE Fennel

The aniseed-scented herb, the single species in this genus of European origin, likes rather moister conditions than its close relative the giant fennel (***Ferula communis***). The latter is another impressive perennial, a plant that grows on dry rough ground in the Mediterranean and further east, and which can reach a height of 10ft (3m).
CULTIVATION Require full sun and moist well-drained soil.
PROPAGATION By division, in spring. From seed, sown in spring.
POTENTIAL PROBLEMS Aphids, slugs; mildew.

Foeniculum vulgare

F. vulgare *S. Europe*
Flowers: mid- to late summer. H 6ft (1.8m), S 18in (45cm). FH.
The feathery foliage of fennel is most beautiful in the tinted 'Purpureum', emerging as tight coppery plumes and maturing to grey-green, tinged with bronze. The leaves are topped by branched stems carrying heads of small yellow flowers. Remove well before the seeds drop or you will be cursed with unwanted seedlings with deep tap roots.

GAILLARDIA

ASTERACEAE Blanket flower

The perennial blanket flowers in cultivation, hybrids of the North American prairie species, are showy plants with daisy flowerheads that have a domed disc surrounded by ray-florets in yellow, orange or red, sometimes banded in combination. Hard cutting back in autumn helps extend their lives. Among the 30 species from North and South America are several annuals and biennials, the annual fully hardy **G. pulchella** being widely grown for single and double flowerheads in red, yellow or combinations of these colours.
CULTIVATION Require full sun and well-drained soil.

PROPAGATION From seed, sown in spring at 55–64°F (13–18°C). By division, in spring. From root cuttings, taken in winter.
POTENTIAL PROBLEMS Slugs and snails; downy mildew.

Gaillardia 'Kobold'

G. hybrids
Flowers: early summer to early autumn. H 10–34in (25–85cm), S 18in (45 cm). FH.
An average height is given for each of the following cultivars, which all make bushy plants that produce colourful flowerheads, usually 3–4in (8–10cm) across, over a long season: 'Burgunder', 2ft (60cm), wine red; 'Dazzler', 30in (75cm), maroon disc and orange-red ray florets with yellow tips; 'Kobold', 1ft (30cm), dark red disc surrounded by a band of bright red ray florets with yellow tips; and 'Wirral Flame', 30in (75cm), deep reddish brown with yellow tips.

GALEGA

PAPILIONACEAE Goat's rue

The genus comprises about 6 species, most from southern Europe to west Asia. A tendency to sprawl, particularly when grown in rich soils, has counted against these plants, once popular in cottage gardens and herbaceous borders. If they are given body with twiggy supports they make leafy clumps topped with numerous spikes of small pea-like flowers. They are pleasingly unpretentious plants suitable for wild gardens and mixed or herbaceous borders.
CULTIVATION Tolerate sun or partial shade and require moist soil.
PROPAGATION By division, in late autumn and spring. From seed, sown in spring (soak before sowing).
POTENTIAL PROBLEMS Pea and bean weevils.

G. officinalis *C. and S. Europe, Turkey to Pakistan*
Flowers: late spring to early summer. H 3–5ft (90–150cm), S 3–4ft (90–120cm). FH.

This bushy plant has pinnate leaves, with as many as 17 narrow leaflets, making a soft green base for flowers of pale mauve-pink or, in 'Alba', white. Most of the hybrids of which it is a parent are mauve with a pink or blue bias and a few, such as *G.* × *bartlandii* 'Alba', are white. *G.* 'His Majesty', a bicolour, has white and mauve-pink flowers. *G. orientalis* is a similar species with violet-blue flowers but it is rhizomatous and can be invasive.

Galega officinalis

GAURA

ONAGRACEAE

One prairie perennial from a genus of about 20 North American species is a lively component in dry sunny borders late in the season, its long succession of small flowers dancing lightly on a graceful plant.
CULTIVATION Tolerates full sun or partial shade and dry to moist soils but best in full sun and moist well-drained conditions.
PROPAGATION From seed, sown in spring. By division, in spring. From cuttings, taken in spring and summer.
POTENTIAL PROBLEMS Usually none.

G. lindbeimeri USA (Louisiana, Texas)
Flowers: late spring to early autumn. H 4–5ft (1.2–1.5m), S 30–36in (75–90cm). FH.
The slender stems with willow-like leaves, often dark-spotted, sway freely with their light charge of starry 4-petalled flowers, which are pink in bud but open white.

Gaura lindheimeri

GENTIANA

GENTIANACEAE Gentian

The gentians are best known for the alpine species with trumpet-like flowers in a colour range extending from pale sky blue to intense lapis lazuli. However, the genus, with about 400 species widely distributed in temperate zones, holds some surprises. Some of the larger species are woodland or meadow plants. The bitterwort (*G. lutea*), up to 5ft (1.5m) tall, with clustered whorls of star-shaped yellow flowers, is an example that escapes the stereotype in colour as well as in scale. These larger plants, including the willow gentian (*G. asclepiadea*), are easy to grow and even many of the alpine species are less daunting as charges than their status might suggest. The most easy-going is *G. septemfida*; the most insistent on lime-free conditions are the Asiatic autumn-flowering species such as *G. sino-ornata*; and the most vexing is the European trumpet gentian (*G. acaulis*), which is not difficult to grow but remains impenetrably fastidious about the conditions that will coax it into producing its deep blue, green-throated trumpets.
CULTIVATION Tolerate full sun or partial shade (shade necessary where summers are hot and dry) and require well-drained but moist soil rich in organic matter (JI No. 1 with added grit and leafmould). *G. sino-ornata* and its hybrids require lime-free soil or compost.
PROPAGATION By division, in spring. From cuttings, taken in spring. From seed, sown as soon as ripe.
POTENTIAL PROBLEMS Slugs and snails, aphids and red spider mites under glass; gentian rust fungus, stem-rotting soil fungi.

Gentiana asclepiadea

G. asclepiadea Mountains of C. and S. Europe, Turkey
Willow gentian
Flowers: late summer to early autumn. H 2–3ft (60–90cm), S 18–24in (45–60cm). FH.
The deep blue gentian flowers are paired on arching stems in the axils of willow-like leaves. The white var. *alba* is equally fine as an autumn-flowering perennial for light shade.

Gentiana × *macaulayi* 'Kingfisher'

G. × *macaulayi*
Flowers: late summer to mid-autumn. H 3–6in (8–15cm), S 4–8in (10–20cm). FH.
G. sino-ornata and *G. farreri* are among the species that have been used in hybridizing autumn-flowering alpine gentians. This hybrid, although of deeper blue, takes after *G. farreri*, a species with narrow pale blue trumpets, white in the throat. *G.* × *macaulayi* 'Kingfisher' may be a selected seedling of this hybrid and is like a compact version of *G. sino-ornata*.

G. septemfida Caucasus, Iran to C. Asia, Turkey
Flowers: late summer. H 6–8in (15–20cm), S 10–14in (25–35cm). FH.
This is a great treasure among the alpines, being easy to grow and producing tufts of leafy stems with terminal clusters of blue or purplish blue bells.

G. sino-ornata W. China, Tibet
Flowers: autumn. H 3–6in (8–15cm), S 12–14in (30–35cm). FH.
Subsequent introductions of Asiatic species have not damaged the standing of one of the most splendid autumn-flowering alpines. The funnel-shaped flowers of vibrant azure with greenish yellow vertical bands are borne singly on prostrate stems that radiate from overwintering rosettes.

Gentiana sino-ornata

Gentiana verna

G. verna *Mountains in Europe from Ireland to Russia*
Spring gentian, star gentian
Flowers: spring or early summer.
H 2–3in (5–8cm), S 4–6in
(10–15cm). FH.
Sky-blue stars, usually white in the throat, are scattered over small rosettes of dark green leaves. This small but startling beauty is regrettably short-lived.

GERANIUM

GERANIACEAE Cranesbill

Few perennials are less in need of an apologist than the cranesbills. The combination of dense and attractive foliage, in many cases prettily cut and lobed, and the generous production of small saucer- or star-shaped flowers has made several species and hybrids enormously popular as groundcover plants. Their good qualities and their tolerance of a wide range of conditions suit them well for wild and woodland gardens and, more importantly, as a furnishing to gardens that must be managed with a minimum of labour. Many are rhizomatous and are quick to build up colonies. Others, however, are clump-forming, with fibrous roots, and a few, including the spring-flowering but summer-dormant **G. tuberosum**, are tuberous. The genus, which comprises about 300 species, is inevitably much more interesting than might be guessed from its stereotyped use. The alpines and some larger species from dry, sunny habitats are good among paving and in gravel as well as in the rock garden. A few of the larger species are impressive in their scale and deportment, none more so than the frost-tender **G. maderense**, a Madeiran native, with triumphant stands up to 5ft (1.5m) high of pink-magenta flowers above a podium of beautifully textured dark green leaves. This magnificent plant is, however, short-lived and usually dies after one season of flowering. Almost all are pleasing not only in

their general effect but also when examined in detail, pencilled markings and contrasting eyes in the flowers being an exquisite refinement. Many geraniums will flower a second time if they are cut back as the first crop of flowers fades. An unfortunate source of confusion is the continued but incorrect use of the generic name as a common name for the species and hybrids of *Pelargonium*.
CULTIVATION Most tolerate full sun or partial shade and require well-drained fertile soil that is reasonably moist. In general the small species and hybrids prefer full sun and sharp drainage (JI No. 2 with added grit).
PROPAGATION By division, in spring. By cuttings, rooted with bottom heat, in spring. From seed, sown in spring.
POTENTIAL PROBLEMS Vine weevil larvae, sawfly larvae, slugs and snails; downy mildew, powdery mildew, viruses.

Geranium maderense

G. cinereum *Pyrenees*
Flowers: late spring to early summer. H 6in (15cm), S 1ft (30cm). FH.
The cup-shaped white or pink flowers, large for the size of this dwarf species, are held on short stalks above a rosette of grey-green basal leaves. In '**Ballerina**' they are pink, veined with darker purplish pink. A slightly larger plant, **var. subcaulescens**, which is from the Balkans and N.E. Turkey, produces black-eyed, bright magenta flowers over a very long season.

Geranium cinereum 'Ballerina'

Geranium endressii

G. endressii *France (Pyrenees)*
Flowers: early summer to early autumn. H 18in (45cm), S 2ft (60cm). FH.
Rounded mounds of light green leaves, which are 5-lobed and toothed, are covered with pink flowers for months. This rhizomatous species is a parent of **G. × oxonianum**, which has several named selections. '**Claridge Druce**', height and spread about 3ft (90cm), is the most vigorous and suitable for large-scale planting as groundcover. The lobed leaves are grey-green and the flowers are dark pink and veined.

G. himalayense *Himalayas*
Foliage: autumn. Flowers: early summer to early autumn.
H 12–18in (30–45cm), S 2ft (60cm). FH.
From running rhizomes this species quickly builds into large colonies, even in full shade. Over a base of deeply lobed leaves there is a main display of white-eyed, violet-blue flowers in the first half of summer, followed by a steady trickle until autumn.

Geranium 'Johnson's Blue'

G. 'Johnson's Blue'
Flowers: summer. H 12–18in (30–45cm), S 24–30in (60–75cm). FH.
Saucers of blue flowers that are lightly tinted purple follow in long succession over a dense cover of elegantly divided leaves, colonies spreading by rhizomes. One parent is probably the airy clump-forming meadow cranesbill (**G. pratense**), up to 3ft (90cm) tall, suitable for naturalizing in wilder parts of the

garden. The flowers are usually violet-blue but in **G. pratense 'Mrs Kendall Clark'** are opalescent. Doubles such as **G. pratense 'Plenum Violaceum'** are better in ordered parts of the garden, the singles self-seeding to excess.

Geranium macrorrhizum

G. macrorrhizum *S. Europe*

Foliage autumn. Flowers: early summer. H 12–20in (30–50cm), S 20–30in (50–75cm). FH.
The species from which geranium oil is extracted has sticky aromatic, light green leaves that are rounded but have a scalloped edge. It is rhizomatous and semi-evergreen but the foliage often colours well in autumn. Several fine cultivars offer alternatives to the plant with magenta flowers: 'Album' is pale pink with red calyces, and 'Ingwersen's Variety' is of a stronger but still soft pink. The species is a parent of **G. × cantabrigiense**, also aromatic but a more compact plant up to 1ft (30cm) high, which spreads by runners. **G. × cantabrigiense 'Biokovo'** is a clone forming a mound of deeply divided, smooth leaves with pink-tinged white flowers.

G. × magnificum

Foliage: year-round. Flowers: early to mid-summer. H 18–24in (45–60 cm) S 16–18in (40–45cm). FH.
The glossy violet-blue flowers are darkly veined and abundant. In autumn the hairy rounded leaves, which are deeply cut, usually colour well on this clump-forming geranium.

Geranium × magnificum

G. psilostemon *S.W. Caucasus, N.E. Turkey*

Armenian cranesbill
Foliage: spring and autumn. Flowers: early to late summer. H 2–4ft (60–120cm), S 2–3ft (60–90cm). FH.
The riveting dark-eyed magenta of the flowers provides scope for dramatic colour schemes in summer. The deeply cut leaves make a large clump, signalling autumn with random red tints. **G. 'Ann Folkard'**, of which this species is a parent, is a vigorous hybrid remarkable for its long flowering period but the yellow-green of the foliage is not comfortable with the purple-magenta of the flowers.

Geranium psilostemon

G. renardii *Caucasus*

Foliage: spring to autumn. Flowers: early summer. H and S 1ft (30cm). FH.
The flowers, white with purple veining, are sometimes only sparingly produced but the mound of sage-green, velvety leaves, which are corrugated, deeply veined and have a scalloped edge, make this an exceptionally good foliage plant.

Geranium × riversleaianum

G. × riversleaianum

Flowers: summer. H 9–12in (23–30cm), S 3ft (90cm). FH.
The trailing stems make good groundcover with their grey-green leaves and the flowers in shades of soft to dark pink are borne over a long season. The flowers of 'Russell Prichard' are deep magenta.

G. sanguineum *Europe, N. Turkey*

Bloody cranesbill
Foliage: autumn. Flowers: early summer. H 8–12in (20–30cm), S 12–18in (30–45cm). FH.
The hummock of dark green, finely cut leaves is bright with magenta-pink flowers, white-eyed and with dark veins, right through summer and into autumn. There are numerous cultivars. 'Glenluce' has large soft pink flowers. 'Shepherd's Warning', rarely more than 6in (15cm) across, is deep pink. A similarly compact plant is **var. striatum**, the pale pink flowers with darker veins nestling among bright green foliage.

G. sylvaticum *Europe, N. Turkey*

Wood cranesbill
Flowers: late spring to early summer. H 30–36in (75–90cm), S 18–24in (45–60cm). FH.
The clump-forming wood cranesbill, with violet-blue, white-eyed flowers over soft divided foliage, is transformed into something ethereal in the white-flowered 'Album'. 'Mayflower' combines light purple and violet-blue in a prodigal display of large flowers. The colour range extends to purplish pink in **subsp. sylvaticum var. wanneri**, the flowers of which are veined red. Another slightly smaller species for planting under a leafy canopy is **G. phaeum**; the cultivar 'Mourning Widow' is a pleasingly sombre plant with deep maroon flowers; 'Album' is fresh and light-enhancing for dark corners.

G. wallichianum

N. E. Afghanistan to Kashmir
Flowers: late summer to early autumn. H 10–12in (25–30cm), S 3–4ft (90–120cm). FH.
With its trailing stems working their way through other plants, this produces delightful surprises. In the wild the flowers are purplish in late summer and early autumn. 'Buxton's Variety', which has white-eyed clear blue flowers and dark stamens, is favoured in gardens.

Geranium wallichianum

GERBERA

ASTERACEAE

One of the 40 or so species, a frost-tender daisy from grasslands in southern Africa, is a familiar cut flower as a result of large-scale commercial cultivation under glass. With their astonishing colour range gerberas complement stylish interiors to perfection. In frost-free areas and well-drained positions in full sun they are no mean plants for the garden.

CULTIVATION Requires full sun and well-drained soil (JI No. 2).

PROPAGATION From seed, sown in autumn or spring at 55–64°F (13–18°C). By division, in early spring. From basal cuttings, taken in summer.

POTENTIAL PROBLEMS Aphids, leaf miners, white flies, tarsonemid mites; leaf spot, root rot.

Gerbera jamesonii

G. jamesonii *South Africa (Northern Transvaal, Eastern Transvaal, KwaZulu/Natal), Swaziland*
Barberton daisy, Transvaal daisy
Flowers: late spring to late summer. H 12–18in (30–45cm), S 18–24in (45–60cm). FT.
From a deep-rooted rosette of hairy leaves rise a succession of long-rayed, yellow-centred daisies, one flowerhead per stem. In the wild plant the flowerheads are orange-red but seed-raised selections include singles and doubles, some with heads as much as 4in (10cm) across, in a wide range of pastel and deep colours. The giants, however, have become too worldly and have lost the grace of the species.

GEUM

ROSACEAE Avens

Water avens (**G. rivale**), widely distributed in the Northern Hemisphere, is a plant of cool moist soils but many of the species in this genus, about 50 in number, are found in drier, sometimes rocky and mountainous habitats throughout the temperate and arctic regions of the world. The Chilean species **G. chiloense** is a parent of several hybrid doubles, the main representatives of the genus in cultivation. Specialist nurseries, however, offer a few rock garden plants, one of which is described here, and good selections of water avens itself, such as '**Leonard's Variety**', in which the pendent flowers are a rare shade of copper pink, which is intensified by the maroon of the calyces.

CULTIVATION Tolerate full sun or partial shade and require well-drained soil that is rich in organic matter. **G. rivale** requires moister conditions than most species.

PROPAGATION By division, in autumn or spring. From seed, sown in autumn or spring.

POTENTIAL PROBLEM Sawfly larvae.

G. 'Borisii'
Flowers: early to mid-summer. H 12–20in (30–50cm), S 12–18in (30–45cm). FH.
Orange-red flowers with conspicuous bosses of yellow stamens show well against the rich green clumps of hairy leaves.

Geum 'Borisii'

G. 'Lady Stratheden'
Flowers: all summer. H and S 18–24in (45–60cm). FH.
The rounded terminal leaflet of the hairy foliage is a feature of this and other hybrids. The semi-double, clear yellow flowers are saucer shaped and the notched petals are slightly wavy. **G. 'Mrs J. Bradshaw'**, a semi-double scarlet, shows the same good breeding.

Geum 'Lady Stratheden'

Geum montanum

G. montanum *Mountains of C. and S. Europe*
Flowers: spring to early summer. H 6in (15cm), S 1ft (30cm). FH.
This alpine species makes a dense tuft of hairy leaves from which emerge erect stems carrying rich yellow, saucer-shaped flowers.

GUNNERA

HALORADIGACEAE

The genus, comprising more than 40 species of perennials from Australasia, southern Africa and South America, takes in extremes of scale. There are New Zealand species that make ground-hugging cushions and even the better-known **G. magellanica**, with mats of scalloped leaves, barely reaches 6in (15cm) when in flower. In contrast the vast leaves of their large relatives, especially those of **G. manicata**, are among the prodigies of annual foliage growth. Most species are plants of moist soils and the giants need a rich deep medium and an unfailing water supply to produce their phenomenal leafage. The dead leaves can be used to protect the crowns in winter.

CULTIVATION Tolerate sun or partial shade and require permanently moist deep soil that is rich in organic matter. Large-leaved species need shelter from strong winds.

PROPAGATION From seed, sown as soon as ripe and kept frost-free during winter. From basal leaf bud cuttings, taken in spring. By division, in spring.

POTENTIAL PROBLEMS Slugs and snails.

G. manicata *Columbia to Brazil*
Foliage: spring to autumn. Flowers: early summer. H 6–8ft (1.8–2.5m), S 8–12ft (2.5–3.7m). FH.
In a large garden or landscape this is the ultimate perennial for waterside or bog. Massive prickly stalks support overlapping dark green leaves, bristly and coarse in texture but magnificent not only for their size – they can be 6ft (1.8m) across – but also for their

lobed and toothed outline and prominent veining. Curious cone-shaped, brownish green flower spikes, about 2ft (60cm) high, lurk within the clump. *G. tinctoria*, from Chile, still impressive but a slightly smaller plant, has a distinctive knobbly fruit spike composed of small green fruits flushed with red. The deep green leaves are heart-shaped to rounded and sharply toothed.

Gunnera manicata

GYPSOPHILA

A preference for alkaline conditions is a marked characteristic of most representatives of a genus comprising more than 100 species of annuals and perennials. Many are compact plants, unlike the best-known species, *G. paniculata*, a florists' cliche in the way its frothy sprays have been used to accompany bolder flowers. In the wild almost all species are found in dry stony or sandy places from the E. Mediterranean to the Caucasus, Asia, and N.W. China and in general they are most successful in gardens on light soils. The annual *G. elegans* is another species much grown for cutting.
CULTIVATION Require full sun and well-drained alkaline soil.
G. 'Rosenschleier' prefers reasonably moist conditions.
PROPAGATION From seed, sown in spring. From root cuttings, taken in late winter (species). By grafting in late winter (named cultivars).
POTENTIAL PROBLEM Stem rots.

G. paniculata C. Asia and C. and E. Europe
Baby's breath
Flowers: mid to late summer.
H and S 3–4ft, (90–120cm). FH.
Its vogue as a cut flower may have waned but baby's breath is an infallible, although often short-lived, charmer in dry borders, the hazy mound of tangled fine stems and tiny white stars masking not only its own grass-like leaves but also untidy remnants of plants that die down early. Most of the

cultivars, including '**Bristol Fairy**', are double and some, such as '**Flamingo**', have a pink tint.
G. '**Rosenschleier**', a hybrid between *G. paniculata* and *G. repens*, makes a low hazy mound about 18in (45cm) high, the myriad tiny double flowers turning from white to pale pink.

Gypsophila 'Rosenschleier'

G. repens Mountains of C. and E. Europe
Flowers: all summer. H 2–4in (5–10cm), S 10–15in (25–38cm). FH.
The mat of wiry stems and grey-green leaves nearly obscured by sprays of small white or pink flowers looks its best flowing over a ledge or from a crevice. '**Dorothy Teacher**' carries pale and older dark pink flowers at the same time.

HELENIUM

Helen's flower, sneezeweed

Of the 40 or so species, all from North and Central America, few are common garden plants, but the hybrids, mainly derived from *H. autumnale*, often dominate sunny moist borders from mid-summer with profuse displays of daisy flowerheads. They are often disparaged for their lack of subtlety rather than appreciated for the frank mixture of rich mahogany, bronze and copper with brighter yellows and orange.
H. hoopesii, which grows to about 3ft (90cm) and has yellow or orange ray-florets surrounding a brown centre, is useful for its tolerance of drier conditions than the hybrids. All of these plants have distinctive flowerheads; as these mature, the ray-florets reflex to form a skirt beneath the velvety central knob. The taller hybrids need support and all deteriorate after 2 to 3 years unless divided.
CULTIVATION Require full sun and moist well-drained soil.
PROPAGATION From seed, sown in spring (species). From basal cuttings, in spring (cultivars). By division, in autumn or spring.
POTENTIAL PROBLEM Leaf spot.

WARNING Contact with the foliage may cause an allergic skin reaction. Swallowing any part may cause severe stomach upset.

H. hybrids
Flowers: early summer to early autumn. H 30–60in (75–150cm) S 16–24in (40–60cm). FH.
Selecting for season and colour will give a display of warm and bright tones over a period of about 4 months. The mid-green foliage on the branching clumps is undistinguished, a disadvantage that can be overcome by careful foreground planting for the first half of summer. All of the following have velvety central discs in shades of brown unless stated otherwise. Among the earliest to flower and both about 30in (75cm) in height are: '**Crimson Beauty**', red-brown; and '**Goldene Jugend**', rich yellow with a paler disc. In the next wave is '**Moerheim Beauty**', copper changing to orange-brown, about 3ft (90cm) in height. Among those still flowering in autumn are '**Butterpat**', 2ft (60cm) tall, yellow with yellow-brown disc, and '**Coppelia**', 2ft (60cm) tall, orange and red-brown with brown disc. One of the tallest and also late flowering is '**Sonnenwunder**', which grows to 5ft (1.5m) and bears yellow flowerheads with greenish yellow discs.

Helenium 'Moerheim Beauty'

HELIANTHUS

Sunflower

The best-known species is certainly the annual sunflower (*H. annuus*) but other species from North and South America include yellow-flowered perennial daisies from soils that are generally alkaline but range from swampy to dry. They are often dismissed as coarse plants and generally have the disadvantage of running roots and needing staking, which is best done as plants start to make growth in spring. The tall species and hybrids placed well back give a boost to borders in the second half of summer. *H. salicifolius* can even reach 10ft (3m), its stout stems carrying drooping narrow leaves which are more important than the small flowerheads. This species does better on dry soils than most of the hybrids. These deteriorate unless divided every 3 years.

CULTIVATION Require full sun and well-drained soil, preferably neutral to alkaline, that is moisture-retentive.

PROPAGATION By division, in spring or autumn. From basal cuttings, taken in spring. From seed, sown in spring.

POTENTIAL PROBLEMS Slugs; powdery mildew, *Sclerotinia*.

WARNING Contact with the foliage may cause an allergic skin reaction.

Helianthus 'Loddon Gold'

H. 'Loddon Gold'

Flowers: late summer to mid-autumn. H 4–5ft (1.2–1.5m), S 30–36in (75–90cm). FH.
The thin-leaved sunflower (*H. decapetalus*) is a parent of several tall-growing hybrids, sometimes listed under *H. × multiflorus*. All are in shades of yellow, 'Loddon Gold' having double flowerheads of rich colouring.

Helianthus 'Monarch'

H. 'Monarch'

Flowers: early to mid-autumn. H 5–6ft (1.5–1.8m), S 3–4ft (90–120cm). FrH.
The dark-eyed sunflower (*H. atrorubens*), which has rough, hairy leaves, has produced this fine plant with semi-double rich yellow flowerheads. The ray-florets radiate from the deep maroon disc and curl back at the edges.

HELLEBORUS

RANUNCULACEAE Hellebore

The qualities of most of the 15 species transcend the conspiracy of self-conscious good taste that is sometimes apparent in devotees of the genus. The leaves, usually leathery but boldly lobed and divided, are often an attractive feature. Some species are fully herbaceous, losing their leaves in winter. *H. purpurascens*, for example, produces its slate-tinted green flowers in late winter before the new leaves develop. Other hellebores, among them the Lenten roses (*H. orientalis*), retain the old foliage until spring, when, in a tattered state, it is replaced by new growth. Several, including *H. argutifolius*, are shrub-like in character, producing sturdy stems that bear flowers in their second year, which then die back as new stems develop. The flowers are never frivolous but their sober dignity, often in unexpected shades of green and plum, sometimes softened by delicate shading and freckling, is long-lasting at a time of the year when few other perennials are in flower. The thickly textured segments, backed by leafy bracts, often remain long after seed has set. In the wild the species are found in woodland and more open habitats from Europe to Asia, usually on alkaline soils that get a plentiful supply of moisture in winter and spring, although often dry in summer. In the garden they are long-lived plants and are among the most useful and beautiful perennials as an underplanting to shrubs and in shade cast by buildings. In tamed woodland there is little that can match self-seeding drifts of Lenten roses, which are perfect companions for early bulbs.

CULTIVATION Most hellebores tolerate full sun or partial shade and require well-drained, preferably alkaline soil, containing plenty of organic matter. *H. niger* and *H. orientalis* do well on heavy soils. *H. foetidus* is tolerant of deep shade.

PROPAGATION From seed, sown as soon as ripe (dried seed may take 18 months to germinate). Seedlings usually take 3 years to flower. By careful division, as soon as plants have flowered in early spring or in late summer.

POTENTIAL PROBLEMS Snails, aphids; black rot, leaf spot.

WARNING Contact with the sap may irritate the skin. Swallowing any part may cause severe stomach upset.

Helleborus argutifolius

H. argutifolius Corsica, Sardinia

Corsican hellebore
Foliage: year-round. Flowers: late winter, early spring. H 2–3ft (60–90cm), S 3–4ft (90–120cm). FH.
The jagged, heavily veined leaves, divided into 3 and with a strongly toothed margin, make an impressive mound of foliage. Up to 30 cupped pale green, slightly pendent flowers cluster at the end of stems in their second year. This superb study in green will remain in good condition for several months. Plants self-seed freely.
H. × sternii, a hybrid between this species and the frost-hardy *H. lividus* from Majorca, which is remarkable for the silvery veining of its dark evergreen leaves, is also shrub-like but only 18in (45cm) in height. Its beauty is partly the effect of the purplish pink suffusion that tints stalks and creamy green flowers.

Helleborus foetidus Wester Flisk Group

H. foetidus W. and C. Europe

Bear's foot, dungwort, stinking hellebore, stinkwort
Foliage: year-round. Flowers: mid-winter to mid-spring. H and S 18–24in (45–60cm). FH.
The clump of dark green deeply cut foliage is of sombre beauty throughout the year and the clusters of maroon-rimmed pale green bells a delightful discovery in winter. The stems and flower-stalks are tinged red in the **Wester Flisk Group**. It is often confined to the wild garden but is worth a place anywhere.

H. niger *S. and E. Europe*
Christmas rose
Foliage: year-round. Flowers: early
winter to early spring. H and S
12–18in (30–45cm). FH.
Saucer-shaped flowers, white but
often tinged pink and with a boss
of yellow stamens, face out or nod
gently above toothed dark leaflets.
The large flowers of 'Potter's
Wheel' are tinged green at the
centre. Despite its great potential,
the Christmas rose often
disappoints.

Helleborus niger

H. orientalis *C. and W.
Caucasus, N.E. Greece, N. Turkey*
Lenten rose
Foliage: year-round. Flowers: mid-
winter to mid-spring. H and S
18–24in (45–60cm). FH.
The plants that go under this
name, apparently of complex
hybrid origin, are indisputably
perennials of the first rank. The
colour range of the saucer-shaped
nodding flowers is unusual,
extending from white and pale
yellow through pink and purple to
darkest plum. In almost all cases
the colour is nuanced by shades of
green and many plants have
speckled flowers. They are borne
on sturdy stems. The dark-fingered
foliage makes an attractive clump
in summer. After overwintering it
looks tired and is best removed
before flowering, a measure that
helps to control the spread of grey
mould (*Botrytis*). The number of
named clones, some double, is
increasing, many being remarkable
for their spotting or very deep,
even blue-black, colouring.

Helleborus orientalis

HEMEROCALLIS

HEMEROCALLIDACEAE Day lily

There are only about 15 species of
day lily, all of which are native to
China, Korea or Japan, but plant
breeders, especially in the United
States, have taken up the genus
with such enthusiasm that there
are now many thousands of named
hybrids. These plants are
principally valued for their
trumpet-like flowers, which vary
considerably in size and shape as
well as in their colour. Although
individual flowers last only a day,
the numerous buds on a stem
open in succession over several
weeks. By planting early and late-
flowering day lilies to extend the
main season it is possible to have a
display lasting 4 to 6 months. The
foliage is often praised for its
lushness and the fact that dense
clumps make good groundcover.
The new growth in spring is
exceptionally beautiful, fresh green
and tightly arching. However, in
maturity the strap-shaped leaves
are often disappointing, forming a
rather coarse base to a floral
display that in the heavyweight
hybrids has moved a long way
from the grace of the species. A
few day lilies have rhizomes and
can spread aggressively. This is
true of *H. fulva*, valued by the
Chinese for its edible tawny-orange
flowers and cultivated in the West
for several centuries. There are
several selections with long-lasting
double flowers, including the
orange and yellow 'Green
Kwanso'. Most of the species are
plants of moist soils and grow in
open positions such as meadows
or in light shade at the edge of
woodland. Although the hybrids
are remarkably tolerant of a wide
range of conditions, they develop
to their full potential in fertile,
moist soils. Plants deteriorate
unless divided about every 3 years.
CULTIVATION Require full sun and
tolerate a wide range of soils but
best in well-drained soils with a
plentiful supply of moisture.
PROPAGATION By division,
evergreen day lilies in mid- to late
spring, deciduous kinds in spring
or autumn. From seed, sown in
spring or autumn.
POTENTIAL PROBLEMS Hemerocallis
gall midge, slugs and snails (young
foliage); rust.

H. dumortieri *Korea, E. Russia,
Japan*
Flowers: early summer. H 18–24in
(45–60cm), S 16–20in (40–50cm).
FH.
From a clump of stiff narrow

leaves rise arching stems bearing
red-brown buds that open to rich
yellow, starry flowers. This
compact species is fragrant.

Hemerocallis 'Pink Damask'

H. hybrids
Flowers: mid-summer. H 14–36in
(35–90cm), S 18–40in (45–103cm).
FH.
The following is an intentionally
small and conservative selection.
A constant stream of new hybrids
will be found in the lists of
specialist nurseries; if at all
possible see trial plantings before
buying so that foliage and flowers
can be judged as a whole. An
average height is given for each
hybrid while the season of
flowering is mid-summer unless
stated otherwise. The colour range
also includes off-whites and bicolours. Day lilies with cream to
rich yellow flowers include:
'Cream Drop', 18in (45cm),
scented, creamy yellow flowers
over a low clump of foliage;
'Golden Chimes', 28in (70cm),
early to mid-summer, star-shaped,
rich yellow flowers, reddish brown
on the reverse and in bud;
'Hyperion', 3ft (90cm), finely
shaped flowers, clear yellow and
deliciously fragrant, over narrow
leaves; and 'Stella de Oro', 16in
(40cm), remarkable for its
compactness and for producing
bright yellow flowers circular in
outline, from mid- to late summer.
One of the best of the pink day
lilies is an old hybrid, 'Pink
Damask', 2ft (60cm), mid- to late
summer: the starry reddish pink
flowers are yellow in the throat.

Hemerocallis 'Bonanza'

235

Among hybrids in shades of apricot and orange are: '**Bonanza**', 30in (75cm), pale orange with strong maroon marks; '**Cartwheels**', 3ft (90cm), glowing yellow-orange flowers, sometimes more than 6in (15cm) across; and '**Thumbelina**', 18in (45cm), numerous small flowers of golden orange. Red, maroon and purple hybrids include: '**Black Magic**', 3ft (90cm), yellow-throated flowers of deep brown; '**Buzz Bomb**', 28in (70cm), yellow buds open to red-brown flowers that are yellow in the throat; '**Lilac Wine**', 15in (38cm), a compact hybrid having mauve-purple flowers with darker veins and green throat; and '**Stafford**', 28in (70cm), mahogany-red flowers with yellow mid-stripe and throat.

Hemerocallis lilioasphodelus

H. lilioasphodelus *China*

Flowers: early summer. H and S 30–36in (75–90cm). FH.
The first species to find its way to the West provides a standard of elegance that is unflattering to many hybrids. The finely shaped, lemon-yellow flowers are perfectly matched by their sweet scent. The plant is rhizomatous and spreads freely in moist soils.

HEPATICA

RANUNCULACEAE

The 10 or so hepatica species, which are *Anemone* relatives, are woodland plants from temperate regions of the Northern Hemisphere that are usually found on alkaline soils. In the garden they are bright companions for early spring bulbs. The star- to bowl-shaped flowers, which are bluish, pink or white, usually appear before the new leaves are fully formed. They are particularly useful in shady corners of rock gardens as well as under shrubs and trees.
CULTIVATION Require partial shade and moist, well-drained soil that is neutral or alkaline.
PROPAGATION From seed, sown as soon as ripe. By division, in spring.
POTENTIAL PROBLEMS Slugs; snails.

H. nobilis *Europe*

Flowers: early spring. H 3–4in (8–10cm), S 6–12in (15–30cm). FH.
The starry flowers, one per stem, rise above a tuft of 3-lobed leaves as the old foliage tires and the new begins to shoot. The colour is usually purplish blue, but flowers can also be pink, white or soft blue. Doubles, once widely cultivated, are now uncommon.
H. transsilvanica is like a larger version of this plant.

Hepatica nobilis

HEUCHERA

SAXIFRAGACEAE Coral flower

Dense clumps of evergreen or semi-evergreen foliage, the leaves scalloped or elegantly cut and often richly tinted or marbled, would secure a place for several species and hybrids as groundcover plants of quality even without their numerous spires of dainty flowers. Many of the 55 species are from mountainous woodland in North America but most of those in cultivation are adaptable, growing well in the open as well as in dappled shade. Replant or apply a top-dressing of organic material when plants lift out of the soil. The evergreen hybrid genus × *Heucherella*, the result of crosses between *Heuchera* and *Tiarella* species, is similar in character to *Heuchera* but the flowers are borne earlier. A pretty example, × *Heucherella alba* '**Bridget Bloom**', has sprays of pale pink flowers up to 16in (40cm) high over lobed leaves with brown tints along the veins.

× *Heucherella alba* '**Bridget Bloom**'

CULTIVATION Tolerate sun or partial shade and require moist well-drained soil (JI No. 2).
PROPAGATION By division, in autumn. From seed, sown in spring.
POTENTIAL PROBLEMS Vine weevil larvae, leaf eelworms.

H. americana *C. and E. North America*

Foliage: spring to autumn. Flowers: early summer. H 15–18in (38–45cm), S 10–12in (25–30cm). FH.
When young the lobed leaves are glistening fresh but tinted and veined soft brown. They grow to nearly 6in (15cm) in length, forming dark green clumps of satiny texture. Wiry bare stems carry the small brown-green flowers.

H. cylindrica *W. North America*

Foliage: spring to autumn. Flowers: mid-spring to mid-summer. H 12–20in (30–50cm), S 12–18in (30–45cm). FH.
Metallic glints relieve the dark green mound of lobed and scalloped leaves. The flowers are green-brown but among several selections showing variations is '**Greenfinch**', with numerous stiff bare stems up to 3ft (90cm) high, bearing creamy green bells. '**Green Ivory**', probably a hybrid, is similar but about 30in (75cm) high.

Heuchera micrantha var. *diversifolia* '**Palace Purple**'

H. micrantha *W. North America*

Foliage: spring to winter. Flowers: early summer. H and S 18–24in (45–60cm). FH.
Several selections have outclassed the species, which has hairy leaves with grey marbling. Over-familiarity may yet blunt an appreciation of the foliage qualities of **var. *diversifolia* 'Palace Purple'**. Jagged, dark bronze-red leaves, with a metallic lustre and lighter on the underside, overlap to form dense clusters. Dark stems support a creamy haze of tiny flowers, which are followed by pink seedheads. It contrasts well with lighter colours in containers.

Heuchera 'Snow Storm'

H. 'Snow Storm'

Foliage: spring to mid-autumn. Flowers: early summer. H and S 12–14in (30–35cm). FH.
The rounded leaves, hairy and with a scalloped edge, resemble in shape and texture those of coral bells (**H. sanguinea**), the species with the most colourful flowers and the parent of several hybrids, such as *H.* '**Red Spangles**', notable for their sprays of small red flowers. The flowers of *H.* 'Snow Storm' are also red but the leaves are creamy white with green edging. In the garden it can look a vulnerable curiosity but it comes into its own as a container plant.

HOSTA

HOSTACEAE Plantain lily

Hosta lancifolia

Hostas were first introduced to Western gardens from China and Japan in the late 18th century but their current popularity is a recent development. Even when the hosta craze eventually abates, a core of really good perennial foliage plants of various textures will remain. **H. lancifolia** is sheeny but others have waxy or mat, often puckered, leaves. Some have quiet but distinguished flowers, in a few cases sweetly scented. In the wild the 70 species are found in a wide range of habitats, mainly in temperate Asia. In cultivation they are remarkably versatile. The full magnificence of their foliage is usually seen when they are grown in partial shade on moist but well-drained soil rich in organic matter.

In full sun they are less lush but tend to flower more readily while many prove tolerant of quite dry conditions. The dramatic and subtle qualities of their foliage are shown to good effect when they are grown in containers. They are little troubled by diseases but their succulence makes them irresistible to slugs and snails. Because new foliage is usually produced only in spring and early summer any damage to young leaves spoils plants for the whole season. The following small selection, with the species described first followed by the hybrids, is chosen to give a fair representation of the extraordinary range of plain and variegated foliage that is found in the genus.
CULTIVATION Tolerate full sun or partial shade and require well-drained but moist soil rich in organic matter. (JI No. 2 with added leafmould).
PROPAGATION By division, in late summer or spring. From seed, sown in spring.
POTENTIAL PROBLEMS Slugs and snails, vine weevils; viruses.

SPECIES

H. fortunei *Japan*
Flowers: mid-summer. H 2–3ft (60–90cm), S 18–32in (45–80cm). FH.
The variegated and yellow-leaved forms have diverted attention from the plain plant with long-stalked, mat, grey-green leaves and mauve flowers. Although its variegation later fades, **var. albopicta** is superb in spring, the bright yellow leaf edged with pale green, the balance gradually changing until there are 2 shades of green. In **var. aureomarginata** the edge is yellow, the leaf colour dark green.

Hosta fortunei var. *albopicta*

H. plantaginea *China*
Foliage: late spring to autumn. Flowers: late summer to early autumn. H 20–30in (50–75cm), S 2–3ft (60–90cm). FH.
The heart-shaped, light green leaves are glossy and conspicuously veined, the flowers, a late surprise, pure white and

sweetly fragrant. The relaxed clumps of **var. japonica** are composed of narrower and longer wavy leaves.

H. sieboldiana *Japan*
Foliage: late spring to autumn. Flowers: early summer. H 30–36in (75–90cm), S 3–4ft (90–120cm). FH.
The heavily textured and veined blue-green leaves make an impressive quilted mound barely cleared by the dense head of palest mauve flowers. More commanding still is **var. elegans**, the puckered blue-grey leaves, which are thick and waxy, topped by mauve-white flowers. The foliage of both these plants turns tawny gold in autumn.

Hosta sieboldiana var. *elegans*

H. undulata var. albomarginata
Foliage: late spring to autumn. Flowers: early to mid-summer. H and S 20–24in (50–60cm). FH.
The smooth dark green leaves have an irregular creamy white margin that barely reaches the pointed tip. The flowers, which come early, are mauve. **H. crispula** is a similar plant but the undulating edge of the leaves has a broader white margin. *H. undulata* var. *albomarginata* makes good-sized clumps quickly, is one of the most adaptable hostas in the garden and is handsome enough to isolate in a container. A dynamic relative, **var. univittata**, has twisted, rich green leaves, the spiral movement of which is emphasized by bold and irregular creamy white striping in the centre.

Hosta undulata var. *albomarginata*

HYBRIDS

H. 'Frances Williams'

Foliage: late spring to autumn. Flowers: early summer. H and S 2–3ft (60–90cm). FH

Although slow to develop, as a mature clump this is one of the most impressive and subtly variegated of all hostas. Heart-shaped leaves, which are puckered and strongly veined, have a waxy blue centre extending fingers into an irregular beige-yellow margin, which later turns yellow-green. The flowers are white. Among hybrids with much stronger contrasts between bright margins and green or blue-green centres are *H.* 'Shade Fanfare', 18in (45cm) high, with heart-shaped leaves edged cream changing to near white, and *H.* 'Wide Brim', which grows to 18–24in (45–60cm) and has a broad yellow margin to puckered blue-green leaves. Both have mauve flowers. Several hybrids provide the contrast in reverse. The oval to heart-shaped leaves of *H.* 'Gold Standard' start green but the centre changes to greenish yellow or yellow with an irregular green edge. It grows to 26in (65cm) and the flowers are pale mauve.

Hosta 'Gold Standard'

H. 'Ginko Craig'

Foliage: late spring to autumn. Flowers: mid-summer. H 10–12in (25–30cm), S 16–20in (40–50cm). FH.

The white edge to the narrow green leaves is broadest when plants are grown in heavy shade and gives a lively effect to close

Hosta 'Francee'

plantings of tight clumps. The flowers are mauve. The contrast of white margin and dark green is striking in the larger *H.* 'Francee', superb as a container plant and reaching a height of 22in (55cm), with a spread of 3ft (90cm). The elongated heart-shaped leaves are puckered and slightly dished.

Hosta 'Krossa Regal'

H. 'Krossa Regal'

Foliage: late spring to autumn. Flowers: late summer. H 4–5ft (1.2–1.5m), S 30–36in (75–90cm). FH.

The waxy blue-green leaves, pointed and prominently veined, are held on long stems, making a vase-shaped clump that is topped by spires of mauve flowers. Other outstanding hostas with blue-green leaves include *H.* Tardiana Group 'Hadspen Blue', 10in (25cm) high, with a spread of 2ft (60cm). The deeply veined leaves are heart-shaped and the flowers in mid-summer are mauve. The more upright *H.* 'Halcyon', 14–16in (35–40cm) high, with a spread of 28in (70cm), has narrow pointed leaves and mauve-blue flowers on purple stems in late summer.

H. 'Royal Standard'

Foliage: late spring to autumn. Flowers: late summer. H 2–3ft (60–90cm), S 2–4ft (60–120cm). FH. The large, heart-shaped leaves, undulating at the margins and deeply veined, create a bold effect in glossy light green. This hybrid flowers freely and the white bells are sweetly scented. Fragrant flowers, in this case mauve, are also a feature of *H.* 'Honeybells', another plain-leaved hosta that grows to 30in (75cm), with a spread of 4ft (1.2m).

H. 'Sum and Substance'

Foliage: late spring to autumn. Flowers: mid- to late summer. H 30–36in (75–90cm), S 3–4ft (90–120cm). FH.

The glossy, heavily textured leaves, heart-shaped and up to 20in (50cm) long, are yellow or greenish yellow and the flowers,

carried on tall stems, pale mauve. *H.* 'Zounds', which slowly reaches 22in (55cm), with a spread of 3ft (90cm), is another hosta with large yellow leaves and mauve flowers. The foliage is heavily puckered.

HOUTTUYNIA

SAURURACEAE

In the wild, the single species in the genus, from E.Asia, rampages through damp, shady places with rapidly spreading rhizomes.

CULTIVATION Tolerate full sun or partial shade and require moisture-retentive soil (JI No. 2 with added leafmould).

PROPAGATION From seed, sown as soon as ripe. By division, in spring. From softwood cuttings, taken in late spring.

POTENTIAL PROBLEMS Slugs, snails.

H. cordata *China, Japan*

Flowers: spring. H 10–12in (25–30cm), S indefinite. FH. The heart-shaped leaves of this rampant groundcover smell of oranges when bruised and the short, cone-like spikes of tiny greenish-yellow flowers have 4 white petal-like bracts at their base. These features are not reason enough to throw caution to the wind unless you are wild gardening on a grand scale. The variegated 'Chameleon' is less rampageous but so brilliant that it is a difficult plant to place in the garden: its startling mixture of colours – various shades of red, yellow and green – make it a useful foliage plant for containers.

Houttuynia cordata 'Chameleon'

INCARVILLEA

BIGNONIACEAE

The flared trumpet flowers of several perennials among the 14 species from mountainous areas of Asia make a show in rock gardens and the front of borders. The plants described have deep tap-roots and are generally long-lived.

CULTIVATION Tolerate full sun or partial shade and require well-drained soil that is moist and fertile.

Incarvillea mairei

PROPAGATION From seed, sown in spring or autumn. From basal cuttings, taken in spring. By division, in spring.
POTENTIAL PROBLEM Slugs.

I. delavayi *China (Yunnan)*
Flowers: early to mid-summer. H 18–24in (45–60cm), S 12–18in (30–45cm). FH.
Above a rosette of divided leaves sturdy stems carry several yellow-throated, rich pink trumpet flowers up to 3in (8cm) across, the lobes wavy in outline. There is a good white, '**Alba**', and the pale '**Bee's Pink**', a slightly shorter plant, has very large flowers. *I. mairei*, rarely more than 1ft (30cm) tall, but in the same mould, carries up to 5 purple flowers per stem.

INULA

ASTERACEAE

A few representatives of this genus of about 100 species are grown ornamentally. They are valued, despite a tendency to coarseness, for their yellow daisy flowerheads. Although most species are plants of open sites, they come from a wide range of habitats in Africa, Asia and Europe. Several, including *I. ensifolia*, a densely bushy plant, about 2ft (60cm) in height, are plants of dry grassland on chalk. The species in cultivation that is most tolerant of shade, *I. hookeri,* rapidly colonizes moist soils.
CULTIVATION Most species, including *I. magnifica*, require full sun and well-drained but moist soil. *I. hookeri* requires partial shade. Stake tall species.
PROPAGATION By division, in autumn or spring. From seed, sown in spring or autumn.
POTENTIAL PROBLEM Powdery mildew.

I. magnifica *E. Caucasus*
Flowers: late summer. H 5–6ft (1.5–1.8m), S 30–36in (75–90cm). FH.
Rough, dark green leaves, up to 10in (25cm) long, the largest at the base, are stacked on stout stems and topped by rich yellow daisies

up to 6in (15cm) across. This is a blunt-speaking but impressive perennial, if not crowded by other plants, and best near water or in a bog. *I. royleana*, rarely more than 2ft (60cm) high, has similarly large flowerheads but of vibrant orange-yellow, which open from dark buds. The pale yellow flowerheads of *I. hookeri* are half the size.

Inula hookeri

IRIS

IRIDACEAE

Even discounting the wonderful riches to be found among the bulbous irises, this genus holds an astonishing number of delectable plants, some as valuable for their foliage as are others for their flowers. The 300 or so species are widely distributed in the Northern Hemisphere. The rhizomatous irises that are described here, like the bulbous species, have distinctive flowers composed of 6 segments. The 3 large outer ones, known as the falls, are in many instances drooping or reflexed, while the standards, the 3 inner segments, are usually smaller and more erect. In addition to these elements there are petal-like style branches or arms that give protection to the stigmas.

For the gardener the most important group among the rhizomatous irises are those described as bearded. These are plants with thick rhizomes (many of the species are from sunny dry habitats) and sword-like leaves that have flowers with a hairy 'beard' on the falls. The classic in this group is the familiar *I. germanica*, with purple falls, brightened by a yellow beard, and mauve-blue standards. Along with its exquisite and even more fragrant white counterpart, *I.* '**Florentina**', it has long been cultivated and remains desirable, even despite the flood of bearded hybrids in almost every combination of bold and subtle colours imaginable. Numerous irises have been involved in their breeding, with dwarf species such as *I. pumila* helping to extend the

range from miniatures less than 8in (20cm) in height to tall hybrids that can grow to 28in (70cm) or more. For more adventurous gardeners there are also bearded irises that become dormant in summer, such as the sublime *I. hoogiana* of the Regelia group, but these are demanding in their requirements and regretfully have been omitted from this selection.

The beardless irises are a large but mixed bag that includes the Laevigatae water irises. These thrive in moist soils, in some cases even in shallow water, and include the numerous Japanese irises, which are the result of hybridization over several centuries. Beardless irises come from a wide range of habitats. Many of the species grow on moist acid soils, but there are some, including the Algerian iris (*I. unguicularis*) that in the wild are plants of sharply draining alkaline soil.

The crested Evansia irises are a smaller group not represented

Iris 'Florentina'

here. In species such as *I. japonica* there is a crest instead of a beard on the falls. See also BULBS, CORMS AND TUBERS.
CULTIVATION Bearded irises require full sun and well-drained soil, preferably neutral to slightly acid. Beardless irises tolerate full sun or partial shade, many preferring well-drained neutral to slightly acid soil but some having special requirements: *I. sibirica* and the Siberian iris hybrids thrive in sunny positions where the soil is moist; the water irises, such as *I. ensata* and *I. pseudacorus* require moist even wet soils; *I. foetidissima* tolerates dryness and full shade; and *I. unguicularis* requires full sun, sharp drainage and prefers alkaline conditions.
PROPAGATION By division of rhizomes or clumps, shortly after flowering or in early autumn.
POTENTIAL PROBLEMS Slugs and snails; viral diseases, including cucumber mosaic virus, and fungal diseases, particularly rust and rhizome rot.

SPECIES

I. ensata Japan, N. China, E. Russia

Flowers: mid-summer. H 1–3ft (30–90cm), S 12–18in (30–45cm). FH.
This species has purple beardless flowers with short standards and broad drooping falls. The colour range of its numerous progeny, long prized in Japan, includes white, many shades of blue, mauve, pink and purple, some flowers having ruffled falls, and some being double. The most beautiful retain the grace of the species despite the size and velvety luxuriance of their flowers. New cultivars from Japan and the United States join old favourites such as: 'Alba', a breathtaking white; 'Rose Queen', dusky pink; and 'Variegata' with young foliage with vertical white stripes and purple flowers.

Iris foetidissima

I. foetidissima Azores, Canary Islands, N. Africa, S. and W. Europe

Stinking gladwyn, stinking iris
Flowers: early summer. H 18–24in (45–60cm), S 1–2ft (30–60cm). FH.
This beardless iris, burdened with unflattering names (references to the unpleasant smell of the bruised leaves), is a dull cousin of the splendid plants described here until pods split to reveal orange seeds. The dark evergreen foliage provides a good contrast to low groundcover in shade. The flowers are small and purplish brown but in **var. citrina** larger and yellow, with purplish brown markings.

I. innominata USA (S.W. Oregon, N.W. California)

Flowers: late spring early summer. H 6–10in (15–25cm), S 9–12in (23–30cm). FH.
Beardless flowers, 1 or 2 to a stem and up to 3in (8cm) across, are carried above tufts of narrow evergreen leaves. The colour is variable, the predominant range being from cream through yellow to orange, with fine veining in purplish brown. The fullest range is seen in the hybrids, which include shades of mauve and purple. This

Iris innominata

species is one of the Pacific Coast irises from North America, which share a number of similarities. Another of these Pacific Coast species, the taller *I. douglasiana*, has veined flowers in shades of blue-mauve and blue-purple.

Iris laevigata 'Variegata'

I. laevigata C. Russia to N. China, Korea, Japan

Flowers: early to mid-summer. H 18–30in (45–75cm), S 9–18in (23–45cm). FH.
In permanently moist soil or shallow water this beardless iris produces fans of broad, pale green leaves and stems usually carrying 3 flowers of soft mauve-blue, with a thin white central streak on the falls. 'Alba' is a very lovely white. 'Variegata' has soft blue flowers and ivory-white vertical stripes on the leaves.

Iris pallida 'Argentea Variegata'

I. pallida Croatia

Foliage: spring to autumn. Flowers: late spring to early summer. H 3–4ft (90–120cm), S 12–18in (30–45cm). FH.
This tall bearded iris has soft

mauve-blue flowers. In **subsp. pallida** the fans of broad leaves are exceptionally fine but more eye-catching are 'Argentea Variegata', with white stripes and 'Variegata', with strong yellow stripes.

Iris versicolor 'Kermesina'

I. pseudacorus Caucasus, Europe to W. Siberia, Iran, N. Africa, Turkey

Yellow flag
Flowers: mid- to late summer. H 3–5ft (90–150cm), S 12–18in (30–45cm). FH.
This vigorous beardless iris flourishes in marshy ground and in shallow water, the blue-green leaves making a lush fringe to ponds and lakes. Stems carrying yellow flowers are shorter than the leaves. Plants tolerate drier conditions but are shorter growing. The vertical yellow stripes of 'Variegata' stand out in spring but by mid-summer have become green. The blue flag (*I. versicolor*) from eastern North America, a shorter plant for moist soils, has a distinctive red-purple clone, 'Kermesina', with flowers that are veined white.

Iris sibirica 'Perry's Blue'

I. sibirica C. and E. Europe, Russia, N.E. Turkey,

Siberian iris
Flowers: early summer. H 30–48in (75–120cm), S 18–24in (45–60cm). FH.
Small blue to white flowers with darker veining hover above clumps of grassy leaves. In the wild this species of beardless iris is found in swamps and damp meadows but it tolerates drier conditions. It is the

parent of a steadily increasing number of very fine hybrids, which are at their best in reasonably moist soils. Taller hybrids growing to 39in (1m) include: **'Caesar's Brother'**, velvety violet-blue; **'Perry's Blue'**, light blue; and **'Sparkling Rose'**, pinkish purple with a veined yellow base to the falls. Slightly shorter hybrids include: **'Tropic Night'**, violet-blue; and **'White Swirl'**, ruffled white petals and yellow throat.

I. unguicularis *Algeria, Greece, W. and S. Turkey, W. Syria, Tunisia*
Flowers: late winter to early spring. H 1–2ft (30–60cm), S 12–15in (30–38cm). FH.
The delicacy of the fluttering, scented flowers is a surprise when they emerge from untidy clumps of tough, grass-like, evergreen leaves, the succession lasting over several months, provided plants get a good baking during summer. This is a beardless iris, the colour range including white as well as the more usual shades of mauve-blue and purple, with veining and a central yellow band on the falls. **'Mary Barnard'** is a rich violet-purple, **'Walter Butt'** silvery mauve-blue.

HYBRIDS

Flowers: early spring to early summer. H 6–60in (15–150cm), S 6–24in (15–60cm) but see notes on dimensions under entries. FH.
The trembling, fine-textured flowers, usually well scented, held above fans of blade-like, grey-green leaves, come in an astonishing range of colours, often combined with breathtaking flair. Ruffling of the falls and standards is a feature of many of the new hybrids, sometimes to such an extent that the essential character of the flower is obscured. This selection gives an idea of the range but even the most ravishing of these plants are often quickly superseded by new introductions from specialist nurseries. The elaborate classification used for exhibition purposes is of limited application to the ordinary gardener and here 3 groups only are distinguished.

Tall bearded
Their height, 28–60in (70–150cm), is not always an advantage but a fluttering display of well-grouped sturdy specimens is a highlight of early summer: **'Frost and Flame'**, pure white with bright red beard; **'Jane Phillips'**, clear pale blue with ruffled falls and white beard; **'Kent Pride'**, red-brown standards

and red-brown margins to yellow falls; **'Party Dress'**, soft pink and heavily ruffled; **'Stepping Out'**, white with dark purple edges; and **'Titan's Glory'**, an even deep blue-purple.

Iris **'Kent Pride'**

Intermediate bearded
These range from 15–27in (38–68cm) in height: **'Green Spot'**, white with green veins and spot on falls; **'Rare Edition'**, white with a central streak and broad margins of violet on the standards and narrow violet edge on the falls; and **'Red Orchid'**, dark red with gold beard.

Dwarf bearded
The standard dwarf bearded irises are 8–16in (20–40cm) in height, but the new classification allows for miniatures that are under 8in (20cm): **'Eyebright'**, yellow with dark brown marks and streaking on the falls; **'Lilli-white'**, pure white with a wavy edge; **'Melon Honey'**, apricot, the falls darker and the orange beard with white tips; **'Pogo'**, strong yellow with rusty markings; and **'Tinkerbell'**, bright blue with darker markings.

KIRENGESHOMA

HYDRANGEACEAE

The 2 species are found in Japan and Korea and it is tempting to see in the refinement of the woodland plant described an expression of traditional Japanese aesthetic values. Where conditions match those of its native habitat, it is not difficult but it is a plant that would be worth a great deal of trouble.
CULTIVATION Requires partial shade and moist neutral to acid soil that is rich in organic matter.
PROPAGATION By division, in spring. From seed, sown as soon as ripe or in spring.
POTENTIAL PROBLEMS Slugs, snails.

K. palmata *Japan*
Foliage: late spring to autumn. Flowers: late summer to early autumn. H 3–4ft (90–120cm), S 24–30in (60–75cm). FH.

In sheltered woodland the clump of vine-like leaves is a dignified quiet presence throughout summer. Fine dark stems eventually arch from the clump bearing loose clusters of rich creamy shuttlecocks. The whole plant has a crafted finish, especially the flowers, which have thick, waxy petals meticulously overlapping at the base.

Kirengeshoma palmata

KNAUTIA

DIPSACACEAE

There are about 40 species of these scabious relatives, mainly plants of open or scrubby limestone country in Europe and N. Africa, but few find their way into gardens. The one described produces a long succession of pincushion flowers in an unusual colour among garden plants.
CULTIVATION Requires full sun and well-drained, preferably alkaline, soil.
PROPAGATION From seed, sown in spring. From basal cuttings, taken in spring.
POTENTIAL PROBLEM Aphids.

K. macedonica *C. Balkans to Romania*
Flowers: mid- to late summer. H 24–30in (60–75cm), S 1–2ft (30–60cm). FH.
Above the basal clump of leaves rise curved and branching stems terminating in domed buds surrounded by green bracts that have soft bristles. The open flowerheads are a dark reddish purple and very attractive to bees.

Knautia macedonica

KNIPHOFIA

ASPHODELACEAE Red hot poker, torch lily

A base of linear or strap-like leaves, upright stems and a spike-like arrangement of tubular flowers, often strongly coloured in shades of yellow, orange or red, is a formula allowing for a surprising number of variations. There are about 70 species in the genus, all of them coming from southern or tropical Africa, most being plants of soils that are well-drained but moist early in the growing season. In addition to the species, there are numerous garden hybrids, which follow their parents in showing a preference for well-drained ground. Although they need a good supply of moisture early in summer, excessive wet in winter, especially in areas that experience low temperatures, spells disaster. The evergreen *K. uvaria*, which can grow to 5ft (1.5m), is largely responsible for the image of red hot pokers as coarse plants with untidy leaves, even when they make a bold show of flaming torches in late summer and autumn. Several species, including *K. triangularis*, which has flame-coloured flowers on wiry stems, are much more refined and these have played a role in the development of lighter and more compact hybrids. As a general rule, the species and hybrids with narrow, grass-like leaves are deciduous and those with broad, strap-shaped leaves are evergreen.

Kniphofia uvaria

CULTIVATION Require full sun and tolerate a wide range of well-drained soils, preferably moist and rich in organic matter.
PROPAGATION From seed, sown in spring. By division, in late spring.
POTENTIAL PROBLEMS Thrips; violet root rot.

Kniphofia 'Goldelse'

K. hybrids
Flowers: summer to early autumn. H 20–60in (50–150m), S 9–36in (23–90cm). FH.
The tallest, 5ft (1.5m) or more in height include: **'Green Jade'**; evergreen, with a spread of 24–30in (60–75cm), and flower colour graduating from lime-green to cream and then white; **'Ice Queen'**, autumn-flowering, with a spread of 30in (75cm), buds fading from lemon-yellow to ivory on opening; and **'Prince Igor'**, with a spread of 3ft (90cm), which brandishes incandescent orange-red torches in autumn. In the middle range, mainly 3–4ft (90–120cm) in height, are: **'Bees' Sunset'**, with a spread of 2ft (60cm), flowers in a blend of apricot and yellow throughout summer; **'Royal Standard'**, with a spread of 2ft (60cm), scarlet buds open to yellow flowers in the second half of summer; and **'Sunningdale Yellow'**, with a spread of 18in (45cm), yellow flowers from mid- to late summer. Short hybrids, generally 20–30in (50–75cm) in height, which are slim-lined and not dwarfishly compressed,

Kniphofia 'Little Maid'

include: **'Bressingham Comet'**, with a spread of 9in (23cm), orange-red and yellow flowers in early to mid-autumn; **'Goldelse'**, with a spread of 1ft (30cm), yellow spikes in early summer; and **'Little Maid'**, with a spread of 18in (45cm), a hybrid of refinement, with green-yellow buds turning to pale cream when open.

LAMIUM

LAMIACEAE Dead nettle

Many of the 50 or so dead nettles are plants of moist woodland and the species most commonly seen in gardens are valued as groundcover in shade, their pretty hooded flowers coming second to their foliage, which in many cases is silvered with exquisite variegation. As the common name implies, the leaves are nettle-like in appearance but do not sting. The yellow dead nettle (*L. galeobdolon*) is so remorseless in its spread that even with leaves as beautifully frosted as they are in **'Florentinum'**, this plant should be reserved for large-scale wild planting under trees or shrubs.
CULTIVATION Tolerate full sun or shade, being particularly good in shade, and require well-drained but moist soil.
PROPAGATION By division, in autumn or early spring. From stem-tip cuttings in summer. From seed, sown in autumn or spring.
POTENTIAL PROBLEMS Slugs, snails.

Lamium maculatum 'Roseum'

L. maculatum *Europe and North Africa to W. Asia*
Foliage: spring to mid-autumn. Flowers: summer. H 6–8in (15–20cm), S 1–3ft (30–90cm). FH.
Flower colour that varies from white to reddish pink and degrees of variegation have resulted in numerous selections, all of which, however, spread vigorously, especially in moist shade. Those with yellow leaves, such as **'Aureum'**, are slightly sickly in appearance. The clear pink flowers and silvered leaves of **'Roseum'** are

a happy combination. The leaves of **'White Nancy'** have a narrow green margin to the frosted centre and the flowers are icy white.

LEUCANTHEMUM

ASTERACEAE

The 10 species are found in high ground and grassland in Europe and temperate Asia. The Pyrenean *L. maximum* is a parent of numerous single and double white daisies that are good as fillers in borders, although often short-lived, especially the doubles.
CULTIVATION Tolerate full sun or partial shade and require well-drained but moist soil.
PROPAGATION By division, in early spring or late summer. From seed, sown as soon as ripe.
POTENTIAL PROBLEMS Aphids, slugs, chysanthemum eelworm; leaf spot.

Leucanthemum × superbum
'Wirral Supreme'

L. × superbum
Shasta daisy
Flowers: early summer to early autumn. H 18–36in (45–90cm), S 18–30in (45–75cm). FH to FrH.
The white daisies, one per stem, are borne in long succession over a clump of rather fleshy dark green leaves. Singles include **'Beauté Nivelloise'**, which grows to 3ft (90cm) and **'Snowcap'**, usually less than 20in (50cm). Neither of these need support but semi-doubles such as **'Aglaia'** and doubles such as **'Esther Read'**, both about 24–30in (60–75cm) in height, should have their clumps stiffened with twiggy sticks. This is even more important with tall doubles such as **'Wirral Supreme'**, which grows to 3ft (90cm). Seed selections are available as an alternative to these named clones.

LEWISIA

PORTULACACEAE

In flower several representatives of this North American genus of about 20 species are among the showiest plants for growing in rock gardens or the alpine house.

They dislike lime and any hint of sluggish drainage, the reason they are often grown in an alpine house being to protect them from excessive wet in winter. Those, like the peach-pink *L. tweedyi*, with a rosette of evergreen fleshy leaves, prefer light shade, in the wild lodging in rocky cracks and crevices, while the deciduous species, such as *L. brachycalyx*, squat and pale pink or white, are plants of more open stony ground. A niche in a retaining wall provides the best position for planting in the open garden.
CULTIVATION Require full sun (deciduous species) or partial shade (evergreen species) and very well-drained neutral to acid soil that is rich in organic matter (equal parts loam, lime-free sharp sand and leafmould).
PROPAGATION From offsets, separated from evergreen species in early summer. From seed, sown in autumn.
POTENTIAL PROBLEMS Slugs and snails, neck rot; under glass: aphids.

L. cotyledon USA (N.W. California)
Flowers: mid-spring to early summer. H 8–12 (20–30cm), S 6–8in (15–20cm). FH.
The most easily satisfied species is evergreen, with spoon-shaped leaves, often with a wavy edge, making a tight rosette, from which emerge several stems carrying sprays of sumptuous many-petalled flowers. Although pinkish purple is the usual colour, the range includes white, yellow and soft orange, the petals often pencilled with dark stripes. In their size and brilliance the hybrids of *L. cotyledon* are not to all tastes an improvement.

Lewisia cotyledon

LIATRIS

ASTERACEAE Blazing star, gayfeather

Of the 40 species, few are in cultivation. They are mainly plants of prairie or lightly wooded country in eastern and central North America and show a strong family resemblance, one peculiarity

being that the dense spikes open from the top downwards (spikes of flowers usually open from the bottom first). They are carried on stiff stems. The long-lasting effect of the spikes, which are good for cutting as well as for creating vertical accents in sunny borders, is of wispy, vividly coloured bottlebrushes.
CULTIVATION Require full sun and well-drained but moist soil.
PROPAGATION By division, in spring. From seed, sown in autumn.
POTENTIAL PROBLEMS Slugs and snails, mice.

Liatris spicata

L. spicata E. and S. USA
Gayfeather
Flowers: late summer to early autumn. H 2–3ft (60–90cm), S 12–18in (30–45cm). FH.
The stiff stems that emerge from a clump of grassy leaves are clothed in whorls of short linear leaves and in the top two-thirds by tightly packed buds that open to purplish pink flowerheads. The compact **'Kobold'** is usually less than 20in (50cm) tall and there are also white cultivars, such as **'Alba'**. The Kansas feather (*L. pycnostachya*) is similar to *L. spicata* but slightly taller.

LIGULARIA

ASTERACEAE

Relatively few of the 150 species of this moisture-loving genus are cultivated. Most are found in Asia although the genus includes some European representatives. They and a number of hybrids, although on the coarse side, at their best combine pleasing foliage and tall spires of daisy flowers. The plants are suitable for borders where the soil never dries out but are seen to best effect forming waterside colonies in semi-wild gardens.
CULTIVATION Tolerate full sun or partial shade and require deep moist soil and shelter from strong winds.
PROPAGATION By division, in spring or after flowering. From seed, sown in autumn or spring.
POTENTIAL PROBLEMS Slugs, snails.

Ligularia dentata **'Desdemona'**

L. dentata *Japan, China*
Golden groundsel
Foliage: late spring to autumn.
Flowers: mid-summer to early
autumn. H 3–5ft (90–150cm),
S 30–36in (75–90cm). FH.
The strong stems that rise above
dark green, heart-shaped leaves
break into loose heads of orange-
yellow daisy flowers. **'Desdemona'**,
rarely more than 3ft (90cm) in
height, has flowerheads of a
deeper hue. It is outstanding for its
foliage, but a breeze is needed to
show that the dark bronze-green
leaves are vibrant red-brown on
the underside.

L. 'Gregynog Gold'
Foliage: late spring to autumn.
Flowers: late summer to early
autumn. H 5–6ft (1.5–1.8m),
S 30–36in (75–90cm). FH.
A powerful stem carries the loosely
conical spike of orange-yellow
flowers, which are brown at the
centre, well clear of a handsome
clump of heart-shaped leaves. The
stately height of the plant makes
an impact in a border.

Ligularia **'The Rocket'**

L. przewalskii
Foliage: late spring to autumn.
Flowers: mid- to late summer.
H 5–6ft (1.5–1.8m), S 30–36in
(75–90cm). FH.
Slender ebony-dark stems rise fom
a clump of fingered dark green
leaves, which have irregularly
jagged lobes. The small flowerheads
are clear yellow. **L. 'The Rocket'** a
hybrid of similar character, splutters
to take off with a shower of orange-
yellow sparks.

LINARIA

SCROPHULARIACEAE Toadflax

The best-known species is the
annual **L. maroccana** but in this
genus of about 100 plants there
are several short-lived perennials,
mainly plants of dry open habitats
in southern Europe, that are of
ornamental value for their spurred
snapdragon-like flowers, which,
although small, are borne freely
over a long period. The large
species are slender plants that
easily fit between more substantial
perennials and sun-loving shrubs,
and the small species, such as
L. alpina, with yellow-lipped violet
flowers, are suitable for planting in
rock gardens or among paving. See
also ANNUALS AND BIENNIALS.
CULTIVATION Require full sun and
light well-drained soil.
PROPAGATION From seed, sown in
early spring.
POTENTIAL PROBLEMS Aphids;
powdery mildew.

Linaria purpurea

L. purpurea *S. Europe*
Flowers: early summer to early
autumn. H 30–36in (75–90cm),
S 12–18in (30–45cm). FH.
The purple-blue flowers are tiny
but they are closely set on slender
stems that wave nonchalantly
when stirred by a breeze. Variants
include the pale pink **'Canon
Went'** and **'Springside White'**.

L. triornithophora *N. and C.
Portugal, W. Spain*
Flowers: early summer to early
autumn. H 30–36in (75–90cm),
S18–24in (45–60cm). FrH.
It is not too fanciful to see in the
spurred buds, loosely clustered
above blue-green leaves, a
resemblance to a chattering flock
of budgerigars poised for flight.
The flowers are purple or pink
with yellow lips.

LINUM

LINACEAE Flax

The flax grown for linen and
linseed oil (**L. usitatissimum**) is
one of the annuals in this large

genus of about 200 species. The
flowering flax (**L. grandiflorum**)
is an annual of purely ornamental
value, **'Rubrum'** bearing flowers
of brilliant crimson. The genus
includes several rock garden
plants, among them the shrubby
yellow-flowered **L. arboreum**, and
a small number of short-lived
perennials. These are blithely free-
flowering in sunny, free-draining
conditions as are found in the
open grasslands and scrub of the
temperate Northern Hemisphere
where they grow wild.
CULTIVATION Require full sun and
light well-drained soil.
PROPAGATION From seed, sown in
spring or autumn. From stem-tip
cuttings, taken in early summer.
POTENTIAL PROBLEMS Slugs and
snails, aphids.

L. flavum *C. and S. Europe*
Golden flax, yellow flax
Flowers: all summer. H 12–18in
(30–45cm), 8–10in (20–25cm). FH.
This woody-based perennial
produces clear yellow funnel-
shaped flowers, about 1in (2.5cm)
across. **'Compactum'** is a neat
edging plant.

L. narbonense *W. and C.
Mediterranean*
Flowers: early to mid-summer.
H 1–2ft (30–60cm), S 12–18in
(30–45cm). FH to FrH.
This is worth replanting regularly
for the rich blue of the satiny,
funnel-shaped flowers, individually
short-lived but lightly borne in
long succession on a twiggy plant.
'Heavenly Blue' is aptly named.
L. perenne is a similar but smaller
plant that is also short-lived.

Linum narbonense

LIRIOPE

CONVALLARIACEAE Lilyturf

The 5 or 6 species in this Asiatic
genus of woodland plants have
grass-like leaves and some that are
rhizomatous, including **L. spicata**,
colonize very rapidly. The clump-
forming species described flowers
best in an open position, although
the foliage is better in moist shade.

CULTIVATION Tolerate full sun or partial shade and require light, well-drained, acid soil.
PROPAGATION By division, in spring. From seed, sown in spring.
POTENTIAL PROBLEM Slugs.

L. muscari China, Japan, Taiwan
Foliage: mid-winter. Flowers: early to late autumn. H and S 12–18in (30–45cm). FH.
The autumn-flowering period is a compensation for blemishes in the evergreen strap-shaped leaves. Spikes densely packed with tiny violet flowers that never seem to open fully bear a resemblance to those of grape hyacinths. Black berries follow.

Liriope muscari

LOBELIA

CAMPANULACEAE

This large genus contains nearly 400 species, showing considerable differences of character and coming from a wide range of habitats in tropical and temperate regions. They are very well represented in the New World. The species described are plants of moist habitats (some lobelias are desert plants) and their hybrids also need to be in fertile ground where the water supply does not fail. All of the plants described tend to be short-lived and even those that are described as fully hardy do not fare well in wet winters unless given a dry mulch. Tall lobelias may need staking. The numerous compact and trailing cultivars of **L. erinus** are grown as annuals, although the species is a half-hardy perennial. They hold their place because of their long flowering season and a delicacy of form that makes them easy companions for other plants.
CULTIVATION Tolerate full sun or partial shade and require deep, moist soil.
PROPAGATION By division, in spring. From seed, sown as soon as ripe at 55–65°F (13–18°C).
POTENTIAL PROBLEMS Slugs; leaf blotch.
WARNING Contact with the sap may irritate the skin.

L. cardinalis E. Canada (New Brunswick) to USA (Michigan to Florida and Texas)
Cardinal flower
Flowers: late summer to early autumn. H 30–36in (75–90cm), S 12–18 (30–45cm). FH.
Erect, branching stems, which rise from a basal rosette of glossy, often bronzed leaves, carry flaming spikes of 2-lipped tubular flowers.

Lobelia cardinalis

L. hybrids
Flowers: mid-summer to mid-autumn. H 30–36in (75–90cm), S 12–18 (30–45cm). FH.
The hybridizing of several species, especially *L. cardinalis*, the less hardy but similar **L. fulgens** and the blue-flowered *L. siphilitica*, has resulted in a range of upright, moisture-loving plants with flowers of intense colouring. The 3 following have deep purplish red or maroon leaves and stems: '**Bees' Flame**', bright crimson; '**Dark Crusader**', ruby-red; and, one of the oldest of the hybrids, '**Queen Victoria**', vivid scarlet. See also under *L. siphilitica*.

Lobelia 'Bees' Flame'

L. siphilitica E. USA
Blue cardinal flower
Flowers: late summer to mid-autumn. H 2–4ft (60–120cm), S 12–18in (30–45cm). FH
The ridged upright stems that rise from rosettes of softly hairy leaves carry numerous flowers that are tubular, 2-lipped and bright blue.
L. × gerardii 'Vedrariensis', a hybrid between this species and *L. fulgens*, has narrow spikes with flowers of intense violet-purple.

L. tupa Chile
Flowers: late summer to mid-autumn. H 5–6ft (1.5–1.8m), S 3–4ft (90–120cm). FrH.
Grey-green leaves, up to 1ft (30cm) long, form a downy base from which rise purple stems terminating in a spike of tubular flowers that are 2-lipped and curiously curved. The calyces are the same colour as the stems but the flowers are rich red or brick-coloured. According to some authorities, even the smell may have harmful effects.

LUPINUS

PAPILIONACEAE Lupin

Lupins are often recommended for cottage gardens as if they had been prized by cottagers in an ill-defined but golden age of rural bliss. The hybrid lupins, with sturdy and magnificent spikes, often bicoloured and in a wide range of colours, are, however, hybridizing triumphs of this century. There are in all about 200 species, the major parent of the hybrids being the blue-flowered **L. polyphyllus**, from western North America. Other American species, including the shrubby, yellow-flowered **L. arboreus**, itself an underrated plant for dry gardens, and **L. perennis**, have played their part. The hybrids are short-lived and seed selections offer an alternative to the plants raised from cuttings. The annual **L. nanus**, which grows to about 20in (50cm), is available in mixtures such as '**Pixie Delight**' that include pinks, blues, purple and white, sometimes as bicolours.
CULTIVATION Tolerate full sun or partial shade and require well-drained, slightly acid, sandy soil (equal parts loam, leafmould and grit).
PROPAGATION From seed (which may need to be soaked for a day or so before sowing), sown in spring. From basal cuttings, in mid-spring.
POTENTIAL PROBLEMS Slugs, aphids; fungal and bacterial rot, gall, mildew, leafspot and viruses.
WARNING Swallowing the seeds may cause severe stomach upset.

Lupinus arboreus

L. hybrids

Flowers: early to mid-summer.
H 3–4ft (90–120cm), S 30–36in
(75–90cm). FH.
The mounds of soft green foliage
are decorative long before the
flower spikes emerge, the minute
hairs that cover the fanned soft
green leaflets trapping droplets of
moisture. The dense columns of
keeled pea flowers should be cut
back as they fade to encourage a
later display of smaller spikes. As
summer advances, the foliage
becomes untidy so it as well to
have foreground planting that will
mask it. Named selections include:
'Chandelier', yellow flowers; 'The
Chatelaine', pink and white; and
'The Governor', deep blue and
white flowers.

LYCHNIS

CARYOPHYLLACEAE Campion

Several species, easy plants that
have held their place in gardens, are
remarkable for their unsophisticated
but vividly coloured flowers. All
15 or so biennial and perennial
species are from temperate or
arctic regions of the Northern
Hemisphere but they come from a
range of habitats, some preferring
moist soils, while others, especially
dusty miller (*L. coronaria*), flourish
in dry conditions.
CULTIVATION Tolerate full sun or
partial shade and require well-
drained soil. *L. chalcedonica* and
L. viscaria do best in fertile moist
soil.
PROPAGATION By division, in early
spring. From basal cuttings, taken
in early spring. From seed, sown as
soon as ripe or in spring: plants
will flower the following year.
POTENTIAL PROBLEM Slugs.

Lychnis chalcedonica

L. chalcedonica *European Russia*

Jerusalem cross, Maltese cross
Flowers: early to mid-summer.
H 3–4ft (90–120cm), S 12–18in
(30–45cm). FH.
Small scarlet flowers with notched
petals are densely packed in domed
heads up to 5in (13cm) across.

L. coronaria *S.E. Europe*

Dusty miller, rose campion
Foliage: year-round. Flowers: late
summer. H 30–36in (75–90cm),
S 12–18in (30–45cm). FH.
Dusty miller self-seeds prolifically
in compensation for being short-
lived, but it is easy to get rid of
unwanted seedlings. The leaves
forming the basal tuft are silver-
grey and woolly, as are the wide-
branching stems that carry velvety
flowers of vivid red-purple. The
foliage and flowers are a happy
combination and even more subtle
in the white-flowered **Alba Group**
and the **Oculata Group**, in which
white flowers have a deep pink
eye. Flower of Jove (*L. flos-jovis*) is
a shorter plant with less silvery
foliage; the flowers, with notched
petals, are purplish pink.

Lychnis viscaria

L. viscaria *Europe to W. Asia*

German catchfly
Flowers: early to mid-summer.
H and S 12–18in (30–45cm). FH.
Numerous sticky stems emerge
from a grassy clump of basal leaves
carrying clustered sprays of bright
pink flowers. In 'Splendens Plena'
the frilly double flowers are of a
brilliant magenta pink.

LYSICHITON

ARACEAE Skunk cabbage

The 2 species in this genus are
slow-growing waterside plants
producing large arum-like spathes,
each surrounding an erect spadix
tightly packed with minute flowers.
The huge leaves that emerge as the
flowers are maturing remain an

Lysichiton americanus

impressive feature throughout the
summer, making a telling contrast
to the linear or strap-shaped foliage
of reeds and irises. The American
species, *L. americanus*, wins in
terms of scale, for its glossy leaves
can be up to 4ft (1.2m) long. But it
has a rank scent and the bright
yellow of its spathes is aggressive.
CULTIVATION Tolerate full sun or
partial shade and require
permanently damp soil rich in
organic matter, preferably at the
water's edge.
PROPAGATION From seed, sown as
soon as ripe in wet compost. From
offsets, separated in spring or
summer.
POTENTIAL PROBLEMS Usually none.

L. camtschatcensis *N.E. Asia*

White skunk cabbage
Foliage late spring to autumn.
Flowers: early spring. H and S
30–36in (75–90cm). FH.
The pointed white spathe, up to
16in (40cm) high, looks like a white
napkin furled around the green
spadix. In flower the plants exhale
a sweet scent. Although overall a
smaller plant than *L. americanus*,
individual leaves can be more than
3ft (90cm) in length.

LYSIMACHIA

PRIMULACEAE Loosestrife

The common name is confusingly
shared, as is a liking for moist soils,
with the genus *Lythrum*. Relatively
few of about 150 species of
Lysimachia, found in subtropical
regions and temperate parts of the
Northern Hemisphere, are much
used in gardens and even these are
generally relegated to wild areas,
where other vigorous spreaders
can help to keep them in check.
One of the most invasive is
L. punctata, undeniably appealing
when spikes densely packed with
yellow cup-shaped flowers top
clumps of dark green leaves but
not a plant for beds and borders.
CULTIVATION Tolerate full sun or
partial shade and require moist
well-drained soil.
PROPAGATION By division, in
autumn or spring. From seed, sown
in spring.
POTENTIAL PROBLEMS Slugs, snails.

L. clethroides *China, Japan, Korea*

Flowers: mid- to late summer.
H 30–36in (75–90cm), S 18–24in
(45–60cm). FH.
This runs in fertile moist soil but a
large patch is a lovely sight, the
tapering flower spikes, packed
with white stars, flexing sinuously
above the leafy base.

Lysimachia nummularia 'Aurea'

L. nummularia 'Aurea'
Golden creeping Jenny
Foliage: year-round. Flowers:
summer. H 2–4in (5–10cm),
S indefinite. FH.
Where the climate is mild and the
soil moist this is a plant to treat
with caution in the garden, rooting
stems creating large patches dense
with lime-green to yellow heart-
shaped leaves, among which nestle
cup-shaped bright yellow flowers.
It is, however, a useful trailing plant
for container gardening.

LYTHRUM

LYTHRACEAE

Lythrum virgatum 'The Rocket'

The 38 species are found in
temperate parts of the Northern
Hemisphere. The slender spires of
purple loosestrife (*L. salicaria*)
make lightly swaying colourful
drifts over several weeks late in the
season. The similar but slighter
L. virgatum and its cultivars,
including '**The Rocket**', flower
earlier in summer. These loosestrifes
are the only 2 species with any
standing as garden plants in a genus
that shows a strong preference for
moist growing conditions. These
loosestrifes are happy in a bog
garden or a wild waterside planting
but flourish also in borders where
the water supply does not fail.
CULTIVATION Require full sun and
moist soil.
PROPAGATION By division, in spring.
From basal cuttings, taken in
spring or early summer. From seed,
sown in spring.
POTENTIAL PROBLEMS Slugs, snails.

L. salicaria *Temperate Asia, Europe*
Purple loosestrife
Flowers: mid-summer to early
autumn. H 2–5ft (60–150cm),
S 18–24in (45–60cm). FH.
The strongly upright stems that
rise from a clump of downy leaves
are closely set with small starry
flowers, pink or purplish red in
colour. Among several cultivars the
palest is '**Blush**' while '**Robert**' is a
brighter pink and '**Feuerkerze**' an
intense reddish pink.

Lythrum salicaria

MACLEAYA

PAPAVERACEAE Plume poppy

Colonies of plume poppies, with
tall stems, delicately feathered
above lobed leaves, have a
choreographed beauty when they
flex lightly in a breeze. In the wild,
the 2 or 3 species, found in China
and Japan, form large patches at
the edge of woodland and in
grassy places. In the garden, the
running roots are a minor
drawback of these graceful plants
of real stature.
CULTIVATION Require full sun and
moist, well-drained soil.
PROPAGATION By division, in late
autumn or spring. By separation of
rooted rhizomes when dormant.
From seed, sown as soon as ripe.
POTENTIAL PROBLEM Slugs.

Macleaya cordata

M. cordata *China, Japan*
Foliage: summer to autumn.
Flowers: mid- to late summer.
H 7–8ft (2.2–2.5m), S 2–3ft
(60–90cm). FH.
The leaves are grey-green with a

white and downy underside. The
tiny flowers are off-white or, in
'**Flamingo**', pink. The more
invasive *M. microcarpa* is similar
to it but in '**Kelway's Coral Plume**'
the buds are apricot pink before
opening to buff cream.

MECONOPSIS

PAPAVERACEAE

Meconopsis cambrica

The Welsh poppy (*M. cambrica*)
the single European plant among
45 or so species in the genus, is a
cheeky but endearing self-seeder
with bright lemon or orange
flowers. It is totally outclassed,
however, by its close relatives from
the Himalayas and mountainous
country further east, especially the
fabulous blue poppies. These
created a sensation when first
introduced to the West and they
have retained their power to
command a reverential awe,
especially when seen planted in
quantity to fill a woodland glade.
Some of the species, such as the
yellow-flowered Nepalese
M. regia, are monocarpic, dying
after they have flowered. Another
of this persuasion is *M. horridula*,
from Nepal, Tibet and China, which
grows to about 3ft (90cm). It has
spiny foliage but is a much more
appealing plant than its name
might suggest, with blue or reddish
blue flowers. Those described tend
to be short-lived unless grown in
ideal conditions. The harebell
poppy (*M. quintuplinervia*), a
paragon of woodland elegance,
with nodding mauve-blue flowers
usually less than 1ft (30cm) tall,
has spreading roots and is one of
the most reliably perennial of the
genus.
CULTIVATION Require partial shade
and moist well-drained soil that is
neutral or slightly acid and rich in
organic matter.
PROPAGATION From seed, sown as
soon as ripe or in spring. By
division, after flowering. From
offsets, in spring.
POTENTIAL PROBLEMS Slugs and
snails; downy mildew.

M. betonicifolia Burma, S.W. China, Tibet

Himalayan blue poppy, Tibetan blue poppy

Flowers: early summer. H 3–5ft (90–150cm), S 12–18in (30–45cm). FH.

Hairs give a slight rust-like tint to basal and stem leaves. The bright or purplish blue flowers, growing from the top and also from the leaf axils, open in true poppy fashion with their petals crumpled before they reflex elegantly from the central boss of yellow stamens. *M.* × *sheldonii*, a hybrid between this species and *M. grandis*, is generally considered the most reliably perennial of the large-flowered blue poppies and its colour is free of purple tint.

Meconopsis grandis

M. grandis Bhutan, E. Nepal to India (Sikkim), E. Tibet

Himalayan blue poppy

Flowers: early summer. H 3–5ft (90–150cm), 24–32in (60–80cm). FH.

There is a rosette of erect, toothed leaves, tinted rust from a sparse pile of reddish hairs, and a whorl of leaves below the nodding flowers. These are up to 6in (15cm) across and usually have 4 petals. At their best their blue is of heart-stopping brilliance but they often show a purple tint.

MENTHA

LAMIACEAE Mint

The mints, aromatic plants of moist or wet soils, are mainly grown for their use as culinary herbs, although the Corsican mint (*M. requienii*) is worth planting to creep among paving just for the peppermint scent released when the minute leaves are bruised. The 25 species are from Africa, Asia and Europe. Variegation lifts some of the mints into another category but as foliage plants they need to be treated with caution for they are always in search of *Lebensraum*.

CULTIVATION Require full sun and tolerate a wide range of soils that are moist.

PROPAGATION By division, in spring or autumn. By rooting rhizomes, during the growing season. From tip cuttings, taken in spring or summer. From seed, sown in spring.

POTENTIAL PROBLEMS Powdery mildew, rust.

Mentha suaveolens 'Variegata'

M. suaveolens 'Variegata'

Flowers: summer. H 10–18in (25–45cm), S indefinite. FH.

The brilliant mixture of ivory and green on strongly aromatic leaves shows well in shade and makes this a very good container plant. The contrast of yellow and green in the scented leaves of *M.* × *gracilis* 'Variegata' is most remarkable in full sun.

MERTENSIA

BORAGINACEAE

About 50 species of these borage relatives are found in a wide range of habitats in the Northern Hemisphere. Several are true alpines, growing on stony slopes that are fast-draining, others are coastal species, surviving in almost pure sand, and an even greater number, including the species described, are plants of moist woodland. These form bright decorative patches in the shade of deciduous trees.

CULTIVATION Requires partial shade and well-drained but moist soil that is rich in organic matter.

PROPAGATION By division, in spring. From cuttings, taken in early winter. From seed, sown in autumn.

POTENTIAL PROBLEMS Slugs, snails.

Mertensia pulmonarioides

M. pulmonarioides North America

Blue bells, Virginia cowslip

Foliage: spring. Flowers: mid- to late spring. H 18–24in (45–60cm), S 8–12in (20–30cm). FH.

The long-tubed flowers, which flare at the mouth, are carried in arching sprays over grey-green leaves. They can be white but usually the buds are violet-pink, opening to violet-blue. The foliage of this clump-forming plant dies down in mid-summer.

MIMULUS

SCROPHULARIACEAE Monkey flower

Mimulus aurantiacus

A puzzle of horticulture is that in about 1914 the penetrating scent of musk (*M. moschatus*), once widely grown as a pot plant, disappeared in wild and cultivated populations – and has not returned. Many of the 150 or so species in this widely distributed genus are moisture-lovers, and one, the monkey musk or yellow monkey flower (*M. luteus*) from Chile, is naturalized in ditches and other watery places in many parts of the world. It is a parent of numerous hybrids that are usually treated as annuals. *M. cupreus*, another Chilean species that has been used in hybridizing, is a low-growing plant, under 12in (30cm) in height, and in the short-lived **'Whitecroft Scarlet'** produces flowers of an intense vermilion. Those plants that tolerate drier conditions include the 2 species described and even drier soils suit the shrubby, frost hardy *M. aurantiacus*, from western North America, an excellent container plant. See also ANNUALS AND BIENNIALS.

CULTIVATION The plants described tolerate full sun or partial shade and require fertile moisture-retentive soil (JI No.2).

PROPAGATION By division, in spring. From seed, sown in autumn or early spring

POTENTIAL PROBLEMS Slugs and snails; powdery mildew.

M. cardinalis *W. USA to Mexico*
Scarlet monkey flower
Flowers: summer. H 18–36in
(45–90cm), S 9–24in (23–60cm).
FH to FrH.
Erect stems carry snapdragon
flowers over downy foliage. Most
commonly the full lips are red and
the constricted throat yellow but
there are variations in this colour
range as well as pink.

M. lewisii *North America (Alaska
to California)*
Flowers: summer. H 1–2ft (30–
60cm), S 12–18in (30–45cm). FrH.
The leaves of this lax species are
sticky and the pink or sometimes
white flowers have wispy hairs on
the lip.

MONARDA

<small>LAMIACEAE</small> Bergamot

The common name refers to the
scent of the foliage, which is said
to resemble that of the bergamot
orange. Two perennial plants from
this small North American genus of
about 15 species are involved in
the sun-loving hybrids that provide
colour in borders in summer and
early autumn. Although wild
bergamot (***M. fistulosa***) is tolerant
of drier conditions than the
moisture-loving bee balm
(***M. didyma***), sometimes known as
Oswego tea, in practice most of
the hybrids do best in soils rich in
organic matter that do not dry out.
CULTIVATION Tolerate full sun or
partial shade and require well-
drained but moist soil.
PROPAGATION By division, in spring.
From basal cuttings, taken in
spring. From seed, sown in autumn
or spring.
POTENTIAL PROBLEMS Slugs,
powdery mildew.

Monarda 'Cambridge Scarlet'

M. hybrids
Flowers: mid-summer to early
autumn. H 2–3ft (60–90cm),
S 14–20in (35–50cm). FH.
From a base of aromatic pointed
leaves rise square stems carrying
hooded sage-like flowers clustered
in dense whorls. '**Cambridge**

Scarlet', an old cultivar, remains
one of the most intense of the
reds, the colour intensified by deep
purple-red calyces. The softest of
the pinks is '**Beauty of Cobham**',
and the darkest in mauve-purple is
'**Prärienacht**'. The white
'**Schneewittchen**' has smaller
flowerheads than the other
hybrids.

MORINA

<small>MORINACEAE</small>

The thistle-like appearance of the
most widely grown of the 4 or 5
species is misleading but adds to
the fascination of this plant. In the
wild it is found in stony open land
from eastern Europe to Asia.
CULTIVATION Tolerates partial shade
but best in full sun and requires
very well-drained soil of moderate
fertility.
PROPAGATION From seed, sown as
soon as ripe. From root cuttings,
taken in winter.
POTENTIAL PROBLEM Slugs.

Morina longifolia

M. longifolia *Himalayas*
Whorlflower
Flowers: mid-summer. H 30–36in
(75–90cm), S 12–18in (30–45cm).
FH.
The plant has a deep tap root and
forms a rosette of prickly aromatic
leaves. The sturdy reddish purple
stems carry tiered whorls of
tubular flowers, each whorl
cupped in a thorny bract. The
flowers open white, change to pale
pink and, once fertilized, turn red.
Even when the flowers are over,
the tall stems retain a sketchy
graphic quality.

NEPETA

<small>LAMIACEAE</small> Catmint

The best-known catmints are
plants of well-drained soils but this
is a large genus with well over 200
species, some of which require
plenty of moisture. They are found
in temperate parts of the Northern
Hemisphere. The shy star among
those for cool moist conditions is
N. govaniana, more than 3ft

(90cm) in height, bearing light
sprays of pale yellow flowers. The
mauve- or purple-blue catmints
described are naturals for romantic
gardens and soften the effect of
bare-stemmed roses and other
bedding over a long season.
CULTIVATION Tolerate partial shade
but best in full sun and those
described require well-drained soil.
PROPAGATION From seed, sown in
autumn. By division, in spring or
autumn. From softwood cuttings,
taken in early summer.
POTENTIAL PROBLEMS Slugs;
powdery mildew.

Nepeta 'Six Hills Giant'

N. × faassenii
Flowers: early summer to early
autumn. H and S 18–24in
(45–60cm). FH.
As an edging plant or skirt to bare-
stemmed shrubs, including roses,
this is hard to beat. The close stems
of grey-green aromatic leaves are
topped by generous sprays of small
mauve-blue flowers. *N.* '**Six Hills
Giant**', nearly twice the height,
creates an even fuller effect and
makes a long-flowering border
plant. Cutting back after flowering
encourages further flushes.

Nepeta sibirica

N. sibirica *E. Asia, Siberia*
Flowers: mid- to late summer.
H 30–36in (75–90cm). S 18–24
(45–60cm). FH.
The roots spread freely, sending up
erect stems that are clothed with
aromatic leaves and terminate in
spikes of mauve-blue flowers.
'**Souvenir d'André Chaudron**' is
dark flowered and usually under
20in (50cm) in height.

NYMPHAEA

NYMPHAEACEAE Water lily

No other genus provides such a range of floating ornamentals for still water in lakes, ponds and small pools. There are about 50 species distributed in temperate and tropical regions of the world, few of which are cultivated but there are many hybrids providing a long season of elegant flowers. Some are sweetly scented. All have floating leaves that are themselves decorative, give cover to fish and, by casting shade, inhibit the growth of algae. The tender and tropical species, some of which bloom at night, usually hold their flowers well above the surface of the water. Most of the hardy water lilies flower during the day and their blooms float on or are held close to the water. Water lilies can be planted directly into the silt at the bottom of a pond or lake but in small pools it is advisable to use lined or micro-mesh baskets filled with an aquatic compost or loam. A mulch of pea shingle helps to keep the soil or compost in place. Very vigorous water lilies, such as the common white water lily (**N. alba**), can be planted at up to depths of 10ft (3m) but the hardy hybrid water lilies described are suitable for more shallow water. The surface spread of a water lily is about one-and-a-half times its planting depth. However, the area covered by the pads varies considerably according to the growing conditions, a water lily planted in the muddy bottom of a large pool spreading more freely than the same plant container-grown in a small body of water. When first establishing water lilies, it is best to start them in shallow water, the crown of miniatures at a depth of about 3in (8cm). They can be put at their final depth as soon as they are making vigorous growth.
CULTIVATION The hardy water lilies described require full sun and, as an alternative to the mud on the floor of a pond, a loam-based or specially formulated aquatic compost.
PROPAGATION By division, in spring. From offsets, taken in spring. From seed, sown as soon as ripe submerged under 1in (2.5cm) of water and, for hardy water lilies, at a temperature of 50–55°F (10–13°C).
POTENTIAL PROBLEMS Water lily beetle, water lily aphid, brown china-mark moth, false leaf-mining midge; brown spot, crown rot, water lily leaf spot.

Nymphaea 'Marliacea Chromatella'

N. hybrids

Foliage: late spring to autumn. Flowers: early to late summer. S 1–5ft (30–150cm). FH.
One of the most striking for large ponds with a depth of up to 6ft (1.8m) is **'Escarboucle'**. It has deep green leaves, 1ft (30cm) across, and fragrant crimson flowers with white-tipped outer petals and bright yellow stamens. The many water lilies of moderate vigour are suitable for water that is 18–30in (45–75cm) deep. Popular examples include: **'Gonnère'**, with bright green leaves, bronzed at first, and fully double white flowers lit by yellow stamens; **'Froebelii'**, its tulip-like deep red flowers opening out among purplish green leaves; **'Marliacea Chromatella'**, with bronze- and purple-marked olive-green leaves and yellow flowers, the sepals and outer petals sometimes tinted pink; **'Odorata Sulphurea Grandiflora'**, with heavily mottled dark green leaves setting off large bright yellow star-shaped flowers; and **'Sioux'**, with leaves mottled purple and starry flowers that change from yellow to orange and crimson. Toy-like water lilies suitable for water 10–18in (25–45cm) deep include: **'Aurora'**, with cream buds emerging among purple mottled leaves and passing on opening through shades of yellow, orange and blood red; **'Pygmaea Helvola'**, with heavily mottled olive-green leaves and lightly scented yellow flowers; and **'Laydekeri Lilacea'**, leaves blotched brown and fragrant pink flowers that deepen to crimson.

Nymphaea 'Sioux'

OENOTHERA

ONAGRACEAE Evening primrose

The common evening primrose, **O. biennis**, naturalized as a charming and common biennial weed of waste ground in many parts of the world, is not in the same league as some of the perennials in this genus of about 125 species from North and South America. These sun-loving plants, many of which thrive in the dry poor soils that suit *O. biennis*, have silky flowers, sometimes fragrant, that individually are fleeting in their beauty but which follow one another in hurried succession for many weeks in summer.
CULTIVATION Require full sun and well-drained soil, most tolerating even poor growing conditions.
PROPAGATION By division, in early spring. From softwood cuttings, taken in late spring to mid-summer. From seed, sown in early spring.
POTENTIAL PROBLEMS Slugs; leaf spot, mildew, root rot.

O. fruticosa E. North America
Sundrops
Flowers: late spring to late summer. H 1–3ft (30–90cm), S 12–18in (30–45cm). FH.
In gardens the species, with yellow flowers up to 2in (5cm) across, is usually represented by **subsp. glauca**, with reddish young foliage, or by named selections like **'Fyrverkeri'**, with purple-tinted leaves and bright blooms opening from red buds. Another species from the eastern United States, **O. perennis**, which grows to 18in (45cm), has much smaller flowers.

Oenothera macrocarpa

O. macrocarpa S. Central USA
Ozark sundrops
Flowers: late spring to early autumn. H 4–6in (10–15cm), S 18–24in (45–60cm). FH.
The slouching reddish stems, clothed with silky leaves, suit a rock garden ledge or the front of a border. The magnificent lemon-yellow flowers are cup-shaped and sometimes more than 4in (10cm) across.

O. speciosa *S.W. USA to Mexico*
Flowers: early summer to early
autumn. H and S12–18in
(30–45cm). FH.
The cup-shaped flowers of this
low, running plant are usually
white and yellow-centred but in
'**Rosea**' and '**Siskiyou**' they are
pink, with exquisite veining.

OMPHALODES

BORAGINACEAE Navelwort

The 28 or so species in this genus
are widely distributed in N. Africa,
Asia and Europe. Some come from
habitats other than the moist
woodland where the most
commonly grown species is found
wild. Its flowers are larger than
those of a forget-me-not but also
blue and borne with an airy grace.
CULTIVATION Require partial shade
and moist organic-rich soil.
PROPAGATION By division, in early
spring. From seed, sown in spring.
POTENTIAL PROBLEMS Slugs, snails.

Omphalodes cappadocica
'Cherry Ingram'

O. cappadocica *Turkey*
Flowers: early spring. H 8–10in
(20–25cm), S 16–24in (40–60cm).
FH.
Small sprays of bright blue flowers
float above a clump of oval leaves.
Named clones include the deep
blue '**Cherry Ingram**' and '**Starry
Eyes**', with a white stripe in the
centre of each petal.

OPHIOPOGON

CONVALLARIACEAE Lilyturf

The grass-like leaves are the main
feature of these 50 or so perennials
from E. Asia, most of which are
plants of shade. Variegated forms of
O. jaburan and **O. japonicus** are
bright alternatives to the dark tufts
of the plant described.
CULTIVATION Tolerate full sun but
best in partial shade and require
well-drained but moist slightly acid
soil rich in organic matter (JI No. 2
with added leafmould).
PROPAGATION By division, in spring.
From seed, sown as soon as ripe.
POTENTIAL PROBLEM Slugs.

Ophiopogon planiscapus
'Nigrescens'

O. planiscapus '**Nigrescens**'
Foliage: year-round. Flowers: mid-
summer. H and S 6–12in
(15–30cm). FH.
Without the contrast of light-
coloured foliage or flowers, the
clumps of near-black leaves are
simply sullen curiosities but in a
skilfully planted scheme they take
on a sinister charm, especially
when the small mauve flowers are
followed by shiny black berries.

ORIGANUM

LAMIACEAE

Aromatic foliage is a distinctive
feature of this genus from the
Mediterranean, which comprises
about 20 species of perennials and
subshrubs, in the wild usually
found on free-draining alkaline
soils. Dittany (**O. dictamnus**), for
example, a choice plant for alpine
gardeners with white, felted leaves
and tiny flowers set in purplish
bracts, clings to limestone cliffs in
the gorges and mountains of Crete.
Several are grown as herbs, the
most highly prized being sweet
marjoram (**O. majorana**), a frost-
hardy subshrub that is often grown
as an annual or biennial. The
slightly hardier pot marjoram
(**O. onites**), another subshrubby
perennial, is coarser in flavour. The
slowly spreading low mound of
the golden-leaved common
marjoram (**O. vulgare** '**Aureum**')
makes a sunny patch beside a path
or in a rock garden. The leaves
become greener late in the season.
The most ornamental of the
species are grown for their small
tubular or funnel-shaped flowers
set among conspicuous bracts.
These bracts are often beautifully
tinted and are long-lasting.
CULTIVATION Require full sun and
well-drained, preferably alkaline,
soil (compost consisting of equal
parts loam, leafmould and sharp
sand).
PROPAGATION By division, in spring.
From basal cuttings, taken in late
spring. From seed, sown in autumn.
POTENTIAL PROBLEMS Usually none.

O. 'Kent Beauty'
Flowers: summer. H and S 4–8in
(10–20cm). FH.
This is one of the several hybrids
that have been raised from
O. rotundifolium, a native of
Turkey and neighbouring countries
further east. This lax-stemmed
species has blue-green leaves and
its soft pink tubular flowers are set
in hop-like bracts of pale apple-
green. The plant is of the same
scale as 'Kent Beauty', but in the
hybrid the tumbling bracts are
flushed pink.

O. laevigatum *Cyprus, Turkey*
Flowers: late spring to autumn.
H 18–24in (45–60cm), S 12–18in
(30–45cm). FH.
The wiry stems that rise from a
clump of almost scentless grey-
green leaves carry sprays of tiny
purplish pink flowers. The young
foliage of '**Herrenhausen**' has a
purple tint and the densely
clustered purplish pink flowers are
surrounded by darker bracts.

Origanum laevigatum 'Herrenhausen'

OSTEOSPERMUM

ASTERACEAE

The daisy flowers close and sulk in
shade or dull weather but in an
open position and full sun, even
where the skies are a pale
imitation of the radiance of
southern Africa, the home of most
of the 70 or so species, these are
wonderfully bright and free-
flowering plants for beds, borders
and containers, regular
deadheading prolonging the
flowering season. They are
commonly grown as annuals but
often survive short periods of low
temperatures in winter when
grown on a spartan diet on free-
draining ground.
CULTIVATION Require full sun and
well-drained soil (JI No. 2 with
added grit).
PROPAGATION From softwood
cuttings, in late spring or semi-ripe
cuttings, in late summer. From seed,
sown in spring at 64°F (18°C).
POTENTIAL PROBLEMS Aphids;
downy mildew, verticillium wilt.

Osteospermum 'Blue Streak'

O. ecklonis *South Africa (Eastern Cape)*

Flowers: late spring to autumn. H 18–24in (45–60cm), S 2–3ft (60–90cm). FrH.
The daisies of this subshrubby species provide a striking contrast: the disc is dark blue, the ray florets dazzling white but indigo blue on the back. In *O.* 'Blue Streak' the contrast is between white and slate blue. The daisies topping the low mat of *O.* 'Prostratum', 6–10in (15–25cm) high, are purplish blue when closed; when open the white ray-florets surround a blue-grey disc.

Osteospermum 'Buttermilk'

O. hybrids

Flowers: late spring to autumn. H 10–24in (25–60cm), S 1–3ft (30–90cm). HH to FrH.
Numerous hybrids have been raised, the contrast between the upper surface and back of the ray florets and dark disc florets being characteristic of most. The colour range includes purple, as in 'Nairobi Purple', and yellow in 'Buttermilk', in which the reverse

Osteospermum 'Whirligig'

of the ray florets is bronzed. One of the most striking is 'Whirligig', in which a white and blue contrast is emphasized by the way the ray florets are pinched in the middle, the tip being spoon-like.

Osteospermum jucundum

O. jucundum *E. South Africa*

Flowers: late spring to autumn. H 12–18in (30–45cm), S 1–2ft (30–60cm). FH.
Narrow aromatic leaves make sprawling clumps from which the daisies rise in steady succession over several months. The purple disc, which changes to gold as it ages, is surrounded by purplish pink ray florets, usually darker but duller on the underside. A shorter plant, var. compactum, little more than 6in (15cm) high, is said to be more hardy.

PAEONIA

PAEONIACEAE Peony

From the 30 or so species that are widely distributed in temperate regions of the Northern Hemisphere and the many hybrids derived from them (often listed under *P. lactiflora*) it would be very easy to make a long list of exceptionally beautiful and long-lived garden plants that are suitable for sun or partial shade in well-drained soil. Most have pleasing foliage, in some cases drawing attention to itself in spring or autumn with rich tints, and flowers, often well scented, that are remarkable for their refinement. In the wild these plants have single flowers, which are usually cup- or bowl-shaped, with prominent bosses of stamens. The species and the single hybrids derived from them have an entrancingly innocent but short-lived beauty when in bloom. A very long history of selection and hybridizing, beginning centuries ago in China and Japan, has led to the development of numerous double and semi-double peonies as well as a group of anemone forms, which are sometimes called imperial or Japanese peonies. In

these peonies, the stamens have been replaced by crowded ribbon-like petals. These are correctly known as petaloids or staminodes. Miraculously, elaboration has not coarsened these hybrids, which are longer-lasting in their beauty than the single hybrid peonies. See also SHRUBS.
CULTIVATION Tolerate full sun or partial shade and require well-drained soil that contains generous quantities of organic matter.
PROPAGATION From seed, sown in autumn or early winter. By division, in autumn or early spring. From root cuttings, taken in winter.
POTENTIAL PROBLEMS Swift moth, eelworms; peony grey mould blight, honey fungus, viruses.
WARNING Swallowing any part may cause stomach upset.

Paeonia 'Sarah Bernhardt'

P. hybrids

Flowers: early summer. H and S 2–4ft (60–120cm). FH.
The key species in the development of the magnificent large-flowered cultivars is *P. lactiflora*, a native of north and west China and neighbouring regions. Its fragrant, bowl-shaped flowers are white or pale pink. The result of centuries of breeding and selection is a range of exceptionally opulent plants in a colour range extending from white and pale pink to shades of crimson and maroon. The following small selection is intended to give an idea of the seductive choice presented in specialist catalogues. Single hybrids include: 'White Wings', with ruffled creamy white petals around the boss of yellow stamens. Among 19th-century double hybrids that still hold their own are: 'Félix Crousse', carmine, darker at the centre and often with a silvery edge to the ruffled petals; 'Festiva Maxima', white with irregular dark crimson flecking; and 'Sarah Bernhardt', large and very full, a confection of silvery and darker pinks. 'Bowl of Cream', with clustered heads of white flowers showing yellow stamens

Paeonia 'Bowl of Beauty'

in the muddled centres represents a range of stiff-stemmed American hybrids described by their raisers as 'estate' peonies because of their value in landscaping large gardens. Imperial peonies include: **'Cheddar Gold'**, white with yellow petaloids; and **'Bowl of Beauty'**, the mass of twisted and tapered petaloids bursting at the centre of a bright pink cup. Some superb American hybrids owe nothing to *P. lactiflora* and of these *P.* **'Late Windflower'**, with white nodding flowers over finely cut leaves, is a lovely example. The flowers are sweetly scented, an inheritance from one of its parents, the Himalayan peony (*P. emodi*).

Paeonia mlokosewitschii

P. mlokosewitschii *Caucasus*
Caucasian peony
Flowers: late spring to early summer. H and S 2–3ft (60–90cm). FH.
The opening of the single lemon-yellow flowers filled with golden stamens is one of the supreme moments in the gardening calendar but you must not blink, for the ethereal trembling beauty of the bowls is quickly dashed. Fortunately this peony has other attributes. The emerging foliage makes a cluster of arresting forms in rich copper pink, softening to grey-green divided leaves that accompany the flowers and persist throughout the summer. A surprise in autumn is the combination of scarlet and glossy black when the seed pods split open. Mollie-the-witch, to those defeated by the pronunciation of the specific

name, has a ravishing peer in another Caucasian species, **P. wittmanniana**. This grows to 3ft (90cm), has glossy, dark green leaves, tinted pink as they emerge, and the single pale yellow flowers cup yellow anthers and deep pink filaments.

P. officinalis *Europe*
Common peony
Flowers: early to mid-summer. H and S 20–30in (50–75cm). FH.
The wild plant is a single with deep red or pink cup-shaped flowers over dark green, divided leaves. Much more familiar in cultivation are doubles such as **'Rubra Plena'**, with sheeny full flowers in vivid crimson. Although living in the shadow of opulent plants of eastern origin, this is still an impressive and astonishingly long-lived perennial. Another but slightly smaller European species, **P. peregrina**, has single flowers with deep red satiny petals cupping yellow stamens; in **'Otto Froebel'** the colour is orange-red.

PAPAVER

PAPAVERACEAE Poppy

The Oriental poppies, with crumpled petals opening to large satiny flowers, are the most spectacular of about 70 species and their magnificent prime makes up for the untidy wreckage of their sprawling leaves and the awkward gap they leave in summer. Representatives of the genus are found in a wide range of habitats in much of the temperate world. Some of the perennials are short-lived but in gardens self-seed freely. The Spanish **P. rupifragum**, for instance, with fluttering silky, soft orange flowers on stems about 20in (50cm) tall, can be a nuisance if it strays into an inappropriate colour scheme. Self-seeding in gritty free-draining ground is the easiest way of maintaining populations of the small alpine species. The Iceland poppy (**P. nudicaule**) is best treated as a biennial. Annual species include the field poppy (**P. rhoeas**), a widely naturalized weed of arable land from which the exquisite single to double **Shirley Series** have been developed, and the opium poppy (**P. somniferum**). *CULTIVATION* Require full sun and well-drained soil.
PROPAGATION By division, in spring. From root cuttings, taken in early winter. From seed, sown in spring.
POTENTIAL PROBLEMS Aphids; fungal wilts, downy mildew and pedicel necrosis.

P. alpinum *Europe*
Alpine poppy
Flowers: summer. H 6–8in (15–20cm), S 4–10in (10–25cm). FH.
The name is often used to cover short-growing alpine species with charming tissue-paper flowers in yellow, orange, red or white. The pale yellow **P. miyabeanum** from Japan is similar in character.

Papaver orientale 'Black and White'

P. orientale *Caucasus, N.E. Turkey, N. Iran*
Oriental poppy
Flowers: late spring to mid-summer. H 18–36in (45–90cm), S 2–3ft (60–90cm). FH.
The species makes clumps of bristly foliage, the leaves 1ft (30cm) or more long with numerous segments cut almost to the central rib. The stems, which often sprawl if not supported, carry orange-red flowers that are up to 6in (15cm) across, with near-black central blotches and stamens around the central knob. A more upright plant **var. bracteatum** from northern Iran, reaches a height of 4ft (1.2m), and has bracts beneath the large, deep red flowers. The numerous Oriental poppies in a colour range from white and pink to red and orange that are usually listed under *P. orientale* are probably of hybrid origin. All of the following are single and have black or purplish basal blotches: **'Allegro'**, orange-red; **Goliath Group 'Beauty of Livermere'**, crimson; **'Black and White'**, white; and **'Mrs Perry'**, soft pink. **'Türkenlouis'** is pale salmon pink and has no basal marks.

Papaver orientale 'Mrs Perry'

PELARGONIUM

GERANIACEAE

In the garden the most widely planted pelargoniums are hybrids that are valued as long-flowering bedding and container plants. There are however, about 230 species, most of which are evergreen perennials, subshrubs or shrubs. Many of these are native to southern Africa, where they are found in a range of habitats, including periods of desert. A number have succulent stems and other adaptations that help them to survive drought. The relatively few species in cultivation are mainly grown for their scented foliage: *P. odoratissimum*, for example, smells of apples, while *P. tomentosum*, with large, velvety, grey-green leaves, is mint scented. The members of the genus are often referred to as "geraniums" but this is confusing as the pelargoniums are distinct from the mainly hardy perennials of the genus *Geranium*. The main hybrid groups are described below but others of great charm include the angel and the unique pelargoniums. The angels are small-leaved and bushy, growing to about 20in (50cm). In shape the single flowers are like the regals but smaller and they are usually in 2 colours, the combinations including shades of pink, mauve and purple or white. The uniques also have small single flowers like the regals but their colour range is wider than that of the angels and the plants are shrubby and some can be trained to a height of well over 4ft (120cm).

CULTIVATION Most require full sun but regal pelargoniums should be lightly shaded from the strongest sun. All require well-drained soil (JI No. 2). If not treating as annuals, rooted cuttings or mature plants that have been cut back by about one-third should be overwintered under glass in frost-prone areas.

PROPAGATION Sow seed in late winter. Take cuttings from late winter to early spring or from late summer to early autumn.

POTENTIAL PROBLEMS Aphids, root mealy-bugs, vine weevil; black leg, grey mould (*Botrytis*), rust.

WARNING In rare instances contact with the foliage may aggravate skin allergies.

HYBRIDS

Ivy-leaved

Flowers: late spring to mid-autumn. Foliage: spring to autumn. H 10–20in (25–50cm). S 1–4ft (30–120cm). FT.

Pelargonium 'Tavira'

Tall pots and wall-mounted or hanging containers are ideal for the numerous hybrids derived from *P. peltatum* that have trailing stems, fleshy leaves and showy heads of single to double flowers over a long season. The following are examples from a colour range that extends from white and mauve to bright pink, purple and vivid red: 'Amethyst', semi-double purple flowers; 'L'Elégante', single white flowers marked purple and cream-edged leaves, tinted purplish pink if kept dry; 'Rote Mini-cascade', single starry flowers of pinkish red; and 'Tavira', compact, with double flowers of bright red.

Regal

Flowers: late spring to mid-autumn. H 14–24in (35–60cm). S 10–18in (25–45cm). FT.

Richly coloured large flowers, usually single (as are those described) and often ruffled and strikingly veined or blotched, are borne on erect shrubby plants that in general do better under glass than in the open garden. 'Aztec' has large white flowers, each petal bearing a scarlet and bronze blotch. 'Grand Slam' is reddish pink and 'Lord Bute' has purplish black petals that are outlined in wine red.

Scented-leaved

Foliage: spring to autumn. Flowers: late spring to mid-autumn. H 10–40in (25–100cm). S 8–30in (20–75cm). FT.

In some the flowers have a pretty delicacy but it is the foliage of

Pelargonium 'Lady Plymouth'

these hybrids that counts. The leaves, usually pleasing in their texture and outline, readily release aromatic oils and the surprising range of evocative scents makes collecting an innocent addiction. Four of note are: 'Fragrans', with pine scented sage-green leaves and neat white flowers; 'Graveolens', vigorous, with handsomely cut leaves smelling strongly of lemon-rose and small mauve flowers; 'Lady Plymouth', in effect a variegated 'Graveolens'; and 'Prince of Orange', with small leaves of intense orange scent and freely borne mauve flowers.

Zonal

Flowers late spring to mid-autumn. H 8–24in (20–60cm), S 4–12in (10–30cm). FT.

These evergreen bushy hybrids have stiff, succulent stems, rounded pungently aromatic leaves, in many cases boldly marked, and clusters of single, semi-double or double flowers that are usually borne well above the foliage. The dwarf hybrids grow to 5-8in (13-20cm) while the miniatures to 5cm (13cm). The colour range includes white and shades of pink, magenta, scarlet and orange. Singles include: 'Dryden', with white-centred flowers shading to scarlet; 'Mr Wren', orange-red flowers with white edging; and 'Paul Crampel', bright scarlet. The Century Series and the Multibloom Series are examples of F1 hybrid seed strains with simple flowers. Double and semi-double zonals include the following: 'Ashfield Monarch', bright red; 'Beatrix', magenta with a white eye; 'Genie', coral-red; 'Irene', crimson; 'Memories', delicate mauve pink; and 'Santa Maria', salmon pink. In doubles that are described as "rosebud" pelargoniums, the central petals do not open, an example of these being 'Apple Blossom Rosebud', which has pink and white flowers. The stellar pelargoniums are another distinctive group. Their starry flowers can be single or double and their pointed lobes gives the leaves a zigzag outline. 'Bird Dancer' is a dwarf example with pale pink and light coral spidery flowers. 'The Boar', which has lax stems and deep green leaves with a near-black central mark and long-stalked clusters of single soft orange flowers, is not strictly a zonal but is often listed with them. Fancy-leaved zonal perlagoniums, notable for the markings of their foliage, include: 'Dolly Varden', with single scarlet flowers over leaves that are white, red and green; **'Mrs Quilter'**, the gold leaves marked bronze and the single flowers salmon pink; and **'Sophie Dumaresque'**, with leaves zoned green, bronze, red and cream and red single flowers.

PENSTEMON

SCROPHULARIACEAE

The foxglove-like flowers of the taller penstemons, most of them hybrids, can be used to brighten up beds and borders from mid-summer to autumn. The flowers are tubular and 2-lipped, with 5 lobes at the mouth and hairs (beard) in the throat. Although the border penstemons are generally the most widely grown in gardens, this is a large genus of about 250 species that are distributed in a wide range of habitats, mainly in North and Central America. It includes many dwarf species that originate from subalpine and alpine zones, among them some fine subshrubs for rock gardens. Border penstemons are often treated as bedding plants, either raised from seed annually or planted out in spring from cuttings taken in late summer and over-wintered under glass. In the selection below, the alpine penstemons are described before the taller border plants.
CULTIVATION Alpine and border penstemons both require full sun and well-drained soil, sharply drained in the case of the alpines.
PROPAGATION By division, in spring. From softwood cuttings, in early summer, or semi-ripe cuttings, in mid-summer. From seed (border penstemons), sown in late winter or spring at 55–64°F (13–18°C).
POTENTIAL PROBLEMS Slugs and snails, chrysanthemum eelworm; powdery mildew.

ALPINE PENSTEMONS

P. davidsonii var. menziesii
N.W. USA, W. Canada
Flowers: summer. H 6–10in (15–25cm), S 8–12in (20–30cm). FH.
The purplish violet, tubular flowers appear above the mat of dark green leathery leaves in summer.

P. fruticosus var. scouleri
N.W. USA, W. Canada
Flowers: summer. H and S 12–18in (30–45cm). FH.
This subspecies of the shrubby penstemon has narrow leathery leaves that are almost lost beneath a profusion of narrow purple flowers. In **f. albus** the creamy buds open to pure white flowers.

P. newberryi *USA (California, Nevada)*
Flowers: early summer. H 6–10in (15–25cm), S 8–12in (20–30cm). FH.
Similar to **P. davidsonii var. menziesii**, this plant produces many spikes of vibrant red-pink tubular flowers which hide the mat of dark green leathery leaves.

Penstemon pinifolius

P. pinifolius *Mexico, S. USA*
Flowers: summer. H 8–16in (20–40cm), S 8–12in (20–30cm). FH.
Loose spikes of bright scarlet tubular flowers – bright yellow in **'Mersea Yellow'** – rise above the needle-like foliage.

Penstemon pinifolius **'Mersea Yellow'**

P. rupicola *W. USA*
Rock penstemon
Flowers: late spring to early summer. H 3–4in (8–10cm), S 12–18in (30–45cm). FH.
This penstemon forms a ground-hugging mat of leathery grey-green leaves that produce many clusters of red-pink flowers.

BORDER PENSTEMONS

P. barbatus *Mexico, W. USA,*
Beardlip penstemon
Flowers: early summer to early autumn. H 3–4ft (90–120cm), S 18–24in (45–60cm). FH.
The semi-evergreen clump of basal leaves produces lax branching stems that carry drooping narrow flowers of bright vermilion. This penstemon gets its common and specific name from the yellow beards on the lower lips of the flowers.

Penstemon **'Apple Blossom'**

P. hybrids
Flowers: mid-summer to mid-autumn. H 18–30in (45–75cm), S 1–2ft (30–60cm). FrH to FH.
The hardiness of the tall-growing hybrids, mainly derived from the Mexican species **P. hartwegii**, varies considerably but, in general, plants with narrow leaves and small flowers, such as those listed below, are the most frost-resistant: **'Andenken an Friedrich Hahn'**, deep wine-red and almost bell-shaped flowers; **'Apple Blossom'**, pale pink with white throat; **'Evelyn'**, bright pink with pale striped throat; **'Hidcote Pink'**, salmon-pink, veined crimson in the throat; **'Stapleford Gem'**, larger in leaf and flower than the others listed here but as hardy; the flowers are a softly opalescent blend of pink and mauve.

PERSICARIA

POLYGONACEAE Knotweed

The Japanese knotweed (**P. cuspidata**) has invasive roots that produce thickets of nightmarish density. There are, however, better-behaved perennials in this genus of about 75 species, which are widely distributed in both hemispheres. Although they also have spreading roots, they are valuable for their ground-covering abilities, especially in moist soil and, in many cases, for the decorative flower spikes produced over a very long period. The main appeal of **P. virginiana 'Painter's Palette'** is its foliage: the mounds, which are about 2ft (60cm) high, are composed of leaves that combine green, cream, pink and V-shaped brown marks.
CULTIVATION Tolerate full sun or partial shade and require moist soil.
PROPAGATION By division, in spring or autumn. From seed, sown in spring.
POTENTIAL PROBLEMS Blackfly (*P. bistorta*), slugs and snails (*P. virginiana* 'Painter's Palette').
WARNING Contact with any part may irritate the skin. Swallowing the sap may cause stomach upset.

P. affinis *Himalayas*

Foliage: autumn. Flowers: mid-summer to mid-autumn. H 8-10in (20-25cm), S 1-2ft (30-60cm). FH. Dense mats of lance-shaped leaves are punctuated with spikes of tiny cup-shaped flowers, pink at first, but then darkening to red, before turning brown. The foliage bronzes in autumn and is russet throughout the winter. '**Darjeeling Red**' and '**Donald Lowndes**' are compact. '**Superba**' is a more luxuriant clone.

P. amplexicaulis *Himalayas*

Bistort

Flowers: mid-summer to early autumn. H and S 3-4ft (90-120cm). FH.
For weeks wiry stems thickened with a slender terminal red spike – crimson in '**Firetail**' – criss-cross above dense and expanding clumps of dock-like leaves.

Persicaria bistorta 'Superba'

P. bistorta *Europe, N. and W. Asia*

Bistort

Flowers: early summer to mid-autumn. H 24-30in (60-75cm), S 2-3ft (60-90cm). FH.
The species, a vigorous colonizer of moist soils, makes dense clumps of large dock-like leaves. In '**Superba**', numerous stiff stems carry soft pink bottlebrushes for many weeks.

PHLOMIS

LAMIACEAE

In a genus of about 100 widely distributed species, most of which grow in stony, free-draining ground, the best-known perennial is a rough but bold plant which has a substantial base of evergreen leaves.
CULTIVATION Requires full sun and well-drained soil.
PROPAGATION By division, in spring or autumn. From seed, sown in spring.
POTENTIAL PROBLEM Leafhoppers.

P. russeliana *Syria, Turkey*

Foliage: year-round. Flowers: late spring to early autumn. H 3-4ft (90-120cm), S 24-30in (60-75cm). FH.
The heart-shaped leaves, which grow up to 8in (20cm) long, are hairy, like the foliage of many other species in this genus. From the dense clumps rise stiff stems that are ringed at intervals with whorls of hooded pale yellow flowers and, later, attractive seedheads.

Phlomis russeliana

PHLOX

POLEMONIACEAE

As showy garden plants, the taller perennial species, which in the wild are found in river valleys in wooded regions of eastern North America, are commonly known as border phloxes. This almost exclusively North American genus of 67 species also includes the very popular annual *P. drummondii* and a number of dwarf perennial or subshrubby species that make rock gardens vivid with their generous flowering in spring and early summer. Some are low plants of cool moist woodland or its margins. Although they have such diverse habitats and characters, the phloxes are frank about their family connections: the flower in most cases consists of a narrow tube opening to 5 flat petal lobes. The dwarf phloxes precede the border phloxes in this selection.
CULTIVATION Some dwarf phloxes, such as *P. douglasii* and *P. subulata*, require full sun and well-drained soil. Others, including *P. adsurgens*, *P. divaricata* and *P. stolonifera*, require partial shade and moist soil containing plenty of organic matter. *P. paniculata* and the many border phloxes tolerate full sun or partial shade and require a well-drained but moist and fertile soil.
PROPAGATION Dwarf phloxes: from basal cuttings, taken in mid-summer; from seed, sown in spring. *P. paniculata* and the many border cultivars: from stem cuttings, in early spring; from root cuttings, in late winter or early spring; by division of healthy plants, in autumn or spring; from seed in spring.
POTENTIAL PROBLEMS Stem eelworms; leafy gall, powdery mildew, leaf spot.

DWARF PHLOXES

P. adsurgens *N.W. USA*

Flowers: late spring to early summer. H and S 10-12in (25-30cm). FH.
This semi-evergreen species, with creeping stems that root as they go, is one of several alpine phloxes preferring cool, moist conditions. It is best known for '**Wagon Wheel**', with salmon-pink petal lobes that are narrow and spoke-like. Another plant requiring similar conditions and flowering at the same time is **P. divaricata** subsp. **laphamii** '**Chattahoochee**'. Sprays of mauve-blue flowers with a staring purplish red eye arch out on an open, lightly hairy plant about 10in (25cm) high. The creeping phlox (**P. stolonifera**) needs a soil rich in organic matter in order to spread. The flowers, on erect stems up to 6in (15cm) high, are usually in shades of purple. '**Blue Ridge**' is mauve-blue.

Phlox douglasii 'Red Admiral'

P. douglasii *USA (S. Washington to California)*

Flowers: late spring to early summer. H 4-8in (10-20cm), S 12-18in (30-45cm). FH.
Even sink gardens can house the evergreen tufts of needle-like leaves, studded for several weeks with short-stemmed, rounded flowers. In the wild, the colour is mauve, pink or white. Selections include '**Boothman's Variety**', a cool mauve-blue with an irregular circle of dark purple at the centre and '**Red Admiral**', a rich crimson.

P. subulata *E. to C. USA*

Moss phlox

Flowers: late spring to early summer. H 2-6in (5-15cm), S 18-24in (45-60cm). FH.
When in flower, a tide of colour sweeps over the dull evergreen mats of spiky leaves. There is a wonderful choice of cultivars, all with more or less starry flowers, usually darker at the centre and with notched lobes. '**G.F. Wilson**' is soft mauve-blue, '**McDaniel's Cushion**' deep pink, and '**Temis-kaming**' dark red.

BORDER PHLOXES

P. paniculata E. USA
Perennial phlox
Flowers: late summer to early
autumn. H 2–4ft (60–120cm),
S 2–3ft (60–90cm). FH.
The border phloxes derived from
this species are the most important
perennials of the genus for general
garden use. Their fragrant flowers
are grouped in dense pyramidal
trusses on upright plants, making
colourful displays in late summer
and even into autumn. The colour
range goes well beyond that of the
plant in the wild, which is restricted
to pink, mauve, purple and white.
A contrasting dark eye is an
attractive feature of many of the
cultivars. Staking is usually not
necessary except in exposed
gardens. Breeding and selection of
border phloxes began in the early
19th century and there are now
many cultivars to choose from. The
following is a very small selection:
'**Amethyst**', violet-blue; '**Bright
Eyes**', pale pink with red eyes;
'**Eventide**', mauve-blue; '**Fujiyama**',
white, and late flowering; '**Norah
Leigh**', mauve, with white-variegated
foliage; '**Prince of Orange**', orange-
red; '**Starfire**', bright red; and the
pure white '**White Admiral**'. The
cluttered density of the flowers
and the susceptibility to eelworm
attack are drawbacks of the
perennial phlox. However, these
are not such serious problems
with the more slender meadow
phlox (*P. maculata*). Growing to
about 3ft (90cm), it carries its
fragrant small mauve-pink flowers
in cylindrical heads. '**Omega**' is
white with a purplish red eye.

Phlox paniculata 'White Admiral'

PHORMIUM

AGAVACEAE

Although the flower stems are a
curious addition, even without
them the 2 evergreen species in
this genus are impressive foliage
plants, making large clumps of
broad strap-like leaves, ranging
from yellow-green to dark green.
The New Zealand flax (*P. tenax*) is
found wild in a remarkably wide
range of habitats, from coastal sand
dunes to mountain gullies.
However, in cultivation it is worth
giving *P. tenax* and the hybrids
between it as well as the mountain
flax (*P. cookianum*), which also
originates from New Zealand, the
moist conditions in which they
do best.
CULTIVATION Require full sun and
moist well-drained soil.
PROPAGATION By division, in spring.
From seed, sown in spring at
55–64°F (13–18°C).
POTENTIAL PROBLEM Mealybugs.

P. cookianum New Zealand
Mountain flax
Foliage: year-round. Flowers: mid-
to late summer. H 4–6ft (1.2– 1.8m),
S 3–4ft (90–120cm). FrH.
Its smaller size and lax arching
leaves distinguish the mountain flax
from the New Zealand flax. The
cream banding of **subsp. bookeri
'Cream Delight**' and the pale yellow
and red margins of **subsp. bookeri
'Tricolor**' add to the vivacity of
these plants. Many hybrids show
the lax growth of *P. cookianum*.
P. '**Bronze Baby**' makes a clump
up to 30in (75cm) of purplish
brown leaves. *P.* '**Dazzler**' has
bronze-red leaves with purple,
orange and pink longitudinal
stripes. *P.* '**Sundowner**' has
bronze-green leaves with deep
pink margins, which can reach a
height of 5ft (1.5m) high.

Phormium tenax Purpureum Group

P. tenax New Zealand
New Zealand flax
Foliage: year-round. Flowers: mid-
to late summer. H 6–12ft (1.8–
3.7m), S 4–6ft (1.2–1.8m). FrH.
The clump of stiff sword-like
leaves, which are grey-green and of
leathery texture, has a dramatic
bomb-burst outline. The woody
purple flower stems rise well
above the foliage and side brackets
carry short rows of erect, dull red
flowers, about 2in (5cm) long.
Flaxes in the **Purpureum Group**
have bronze-purple or coppery
leaves; in '**Variegatum**' the leaves
are striped yellow at the margins.

PHYSOSTEGIA

LAMIACEAE

There are about 12 species of
Physostegia in North America but
only the surprisingly compliant
P. virginiana, a plant of moist soils,
is in general cultivation. Push an
individual flower in any direction
and it will hold its position.
CULTIVATION Tolerate full sun or
partial shade and require well-
drained but moist and fertile soil.
PROPAGATION From seed, sown in
autumn. By division, in autumn or
spring.
POTENTIAL PROBLEMS Slugs; fungal
and bacterial rots.

Physostegia virginiana

P. virginiana E. North America
False dragonhead, obedient plant
Flowers: mid-summer to early
autumn. H 3–4ft (90–120cm),
S 18–24in (45–60cm). FH.
The running roots make large
clumps of irregularly toothed
leaves. Above the leaves, stems,
which are square in section, carry
spikes of tubular 2-lipped flowers.
In the wild the almost stalkless
flowers are usually mauve-pink or
purple. '**Summer Snow**' is a lovely
white with green bracts; '**Vivid**', a
bright purplish pink. The pale
mauve-pink of **subsp. speciosa
'Bouquet Rose**' is less assertive in
the autumn garden.

PLATYCODON

CAMPANULACEAE Balloon flower

Once the flowers have opened, it is
easy to see the *Campanula*
connection of the single species in
this genus, but it is the ballooning
buds that are so riveting as they
seem to threaten a sequence of
minor explosions. In the wild it is a
plant of high meadows where
there is plenty of moisture but also
good drainage.
CULTIVATION Require full sun and
well-drained soil, rich in organic
matter.
PROPAGATION From seed, sown in
spring. By division, in spring.
POTENTIAL PROBLEMS Slugs and
snails.

P. grandiflorus *Japan, Korea, N. China*
Flowers: late summer. H 18–24in (45–60cm), S 12–18in (30–45cm). FH.
The fleshy roots are easily damaged by careless digging early in the season because growth is not made until late spring. The clean-cut flowers, borne above blue-green leaves, are a spreading bell shape, up to 2in (5cm) across. Veining intensifies their shade of blue or violet and adds an exquisite shadow to '**Albus**'. The dwarf *mariesii*, which rarely exceeds 1ft (30cm), flowers early and freely.

Platycodon grandiflorus

POLEMONIUM

POLEMONIACEAE

The common name of Jacob's ladder (*P. caeruleum*), grown in Europe since at least the 16th century, alludes to the foliage and its rung-like arrangement of leaflets. Like others in a genus of about 25 species found in Europe, Asia and Central and North America, this is a perennial of moist meadows and woodland margins. Others, such as *P. eximium* from western North America, are alpines. In gardens, they prefer an open position with sharp drainage. *P. caeruleum*, like most of the species in cultivation, deteriorates unless divided every 2 to 3 years. Cutting back early-flowering species after flowering can bring a second, smaller display.
CULTIVATION Tolerate full sun or partial shade and require well-drained but moist soil.
PROPAGATION By division, in spring. From seed, sown in autumn or spring.
POTENTIAL PROBLEMS Powdery mildew.

P. caeruleum *N. Asia, N. and C. Europe, W. North America*
Greek valerian, Jacob's ladder
Flowers: early summer. H 18–36in (45–90cm), S 1–2ft (30–60cm). FH.
Above the laddered foliage are sprays of bell-shaped, mauve-blue flowers with orange-yellow stamens. *P.* '**Hopleys**' has dark

buds, opening to blue flowers that fade to near-white, all stages being present at the same time. The North American species *P. archibaldae* is like a sturdy version of Jacob's ladder.

Polemonium caeruleum

P. 'Lambrook Mauve'
Flowers: late spring to early summer. H and S 16–20in (40–50cm). FH.
Sprays of soft mauve-blue flowers arch languidly over a relaxed clump of foliage with the characteristic arrangement of paired leaflets.

POLYGONATUM

CONVALLARIACEAE Solomon's seal

The graceful arching stems and small bell flowers of the familiar Solomon's seal are characteristic of a number of species in a genus comprising about 50 woodland perennials, widely distributed in temperate regions of the Northern Hemisphere. They are rhizomatous, and the taller species are best seen in colonies as companions to ferns and other shade-lovers. A few dwarf species, including the diminutive pink-flowered *P. hookeri*, are ideal for a raised bed.
CULTIVATION Require full or partial shade and a well-drained but moist soil, rich in organic matter.
PROPAGATION By division, in spring. From seed, sown in autumn.
POTENTIAL PROBLEMS Slugs and sawfly larvae.
WARNING Swallowing any part may cause stomach upset.

P. × hybridum
Common Solomon's seal
Flowers: late spring. H 2–4ft (60–120cm), S 12–18in (30–45cm). FH.
This vigorous hybrid between **P. multiflorum** and **P. odoratum** has outclassed its parents, as well as many showier plants, with its arching stems, alternate leaves and ivory, green-tipped bells. The strongly veined leaves lie horizontally and the clusters of 2 to 4 faintly scented flowers hang lightly from the leaf axils. '**Striatum**' is a choice variegated plant. The

Polygonatum × hybridum

North American **P. biflorum** is similar to the commonly grown Solomon's seal, but as much as twice its size in ideal conditions.

PONTEDERIA

PONTEDERIACEAE

The single widely grown species from this small New World genus of 5 species is an impressive foliage plant of water margins.
CULTIVATION Requires full sun. Plant in loamy soil in water 4–6in (10–15cm) deep.
PROPAGATION By division, in late spring. From seed, sown as soon as ripe.
POTENTIAL PROBLEMS Usually none.

P. cordata *E. North America*
Pickerel weed
Flowers: late summer. H 3–4ft (90–120cm), S 24–30in (60–75cm). FH.
Thick rootstocks steadily ease themselves out into shallow water, sending up stiff crowded stems bearing spear-shaped glossy leaves with irregular light shadowing in purplish brown. During late summer spikes of small blue flowers thrust through the foliage.

Pontederia cordata

POTENTILLA

ROSACEAE Cinquefoil

The sun-loving perennials in this very large genus of about 500 species, which also contains numerous shrubs of great garden value, include many that produce dazzling flowers in early summer. The species are found in a wide range of habitats in the Northern

Hemisphere – many of them are plants of open sites and well-drained ground. The larger species and their hybrids make bright accents at the front of borders; the dwarf species, mainly plants of rocky mountainous areas where the drainage is sharp, are good for rock gardens. See also SHRUBS.
CULTIVATION Require full sun and well-drained soil. Rock garden species require very well-drained, gritty soil.
PROPAGATION From seed, sown in autumn or spring. By division, in spring or autumn.
POTENTIAL PROBLEMS Usually none.

Potentilla 'Yellow Queen'

P. hybrids

Flowers: early to late summer. H 1–2ft (30–60cm), S 18–24in (45–60cm). FH.
One parent of a range of brilliant hybrids is the Himalayan cinquefoil (*P. atrosanguinea*) with startling blood-red flowers or, in the silver-leaved **var. argyrophylla**, yellow with an orange centre. The following hybrids fling out loose sprays of colourful flowers over foliage, which in most cases is green, with strawberry-like leaflets: **'Gibson's Scarlet'**, single, dashing scarlet; **'Gloire de Nancy'**, double, vermilion; **'William Rollison'**, semi-double, orange-red with yellow touches and reverse; and **'Yellow Queen'**, semi-double, bright yellow and silvery foliage.

P. nepalensis *W. Himalayas*

Flowers: summer. H 1–3ft (30–90cm), S 18–24in (45–60cm). FH.
Reddish wiry stems carry hairy palmate leaves and many sprays of saucer-shaped flowers in shades of purplish pink or crimson. **'Miss Willmott'**, 12–18in (30–45cm) high, has rich pink flowers with a darker centre.

P. × tonguei

Flowers: summer. H 4–8in (10–20cm), S 10–14in (25–35cm). FH.
Although not as compact as other cinquefoils for rock gardens, this hybrid has a profusion of apricot blooms with a dark red eye.

PRIMULA

PRIMULACEAE

Primula vulgaris

Representatives of this varied plant group have had a long history in cultivation. There are about 400 species, the majority from the Northern Hemisphere with nearly half concentrated in the Himalayas. A very high proportion have flat primrose-like flowers and some have a mealy powdering (farina) that whitens leaves, stems and calyces. They grow in a wide range of habitats, from moist woodland, open grassy banks and alpine meadows to bogs and rugged mountain faces, many on acidic soils but others on lime, among them several European species for alpine houses, such as *P. allionii*. A few primulas – including *P. kewensis* and *P. obconica* – are grown as short-lived greenhouse or house plants and the spring-flowering polyanthus hybrids are usually treated as biennials (the **Barnhaven Gold-laced Group** are of great charm). The groupings used below for the remainder reflect how they are used in gardens and their history in cultivation. The alpine primulas described represent a tiny proportion of the large number that are appealing to the specialist grower. Many of them are Asiatic but others are from Europe eastward to the Caucasus and North America. Although the auriculas owe much to the alpine *P. auricula*, these hybrids are a group on their own. They have been much meddled with to give

Primula allionii

rounded, often curiously coloured or subtly enamelled flowers, with a hold on the affections because of their association with generations of artisan gardeners. The border, bog and woodland primulas include the European primrose (*P. vulgaris*) as well as larger species of Asiatic origin and their hybrids, which demand a reliably moist soil.
CULTIVATION Primulas have varying requirements. Most alpine primulas and auriculas tolerate full sun or partial shade and require a gritty but moist soil, rich in organic matter (JI No.1 with added leafmould and grit). In general, the Asiatic species require moister conditions than the European alpine species. Some, including *P. frondosa*, require lime-free soil. Other primulas tolerate full sun or partial shade and require a moisture-retentive soil containing generous quantities of organic matter. The candelabra primulas, such as *P. florindae*, require permanently moist conditions and flourish in bogs.
PROPAGATION By division, between autumn and early spring. From basal or offset cuttings, in autumn or early spring. From root cuttings, in winter. From seed, sown in early spring.
POTENTIAL PROBLEMS Aphids, red spider mites, leafhoppers, vine weevil, slugs; primula brown core, grey mould (*Botrytis*), viruses.

Primula farinosa

ALPINE PRIMULAS

P. frondosa *Central Bulgaria*

Flowers: late spring to early summer. H 4–6in (10–15cm), S 6–10in (15–25cm). FH.
The underside of the spoon-shaped leaves, the stems and the buds are powdered white. Up to 30 mauve-pink flowers with prettily notched petal lobes radiate from the top of each stem.
P. farinosa, which is widely distributed in Europe and northern Asia, is a similar but short-lived plant that is also dusted with meal. The lilac-pink flowers have a yellow eye.

P. marginata *European Alps*
Flowers: early to mid-spring.
H 4–6in (10–15cm), S 6–10in
(15–25cm). FH.
Farina whitens the margins of the
leathery leaves and the stems, and
the residue in the eye of the
mauve-blue flowers gives them a
charming bleariness. There are
many named clones, some
probably of hybrid origin. The
combination of dusty whiteness
and soft mauve-blue is particularly
tender in **'Linda Pope'**.

P. × pubescens
Flowers: spring. H 4–6in (10–
15cm), S 6–10in (15–25cm). FH.
Many cultivars are listed under
this name which covers hybrids
between *P. auricula* and
P. hirsuta. They are partially
evergreen, with strong stems
carrying crowded heads of flowers
above rosettes of slightly leathery
leaves, in some cases powdered
with meal. The colour range
includes white and numerous
shades of pink, purple and red.
'Christine' is reddish purple, and
the old favourite **'Faldonside'** is
crimson with a white eye.

AURICULAS

P. auricula *Europe (Alps,
Apennines, Carpathians)*
Flowers: spring. H 4–8in (10–
20cm), S 4–10in (10–25cm). FH.
Under the name of a fragrant,
yellow-flowered species which is
widely distributed in the
mountains of Europe are listed
numerous hybrids that have had a
long history in cultivation. They
reached their peak of popularity in
the 18th and 19th centuries, when
they were particularly associated
in Britain with the weavers of
Lancashire. There are three main
categories. The show auriculas,
which are characterized by a
mealy white ring at the centre of
the flower, have many
subdivisions, among the most
distinctive being those with
flowers edged green or grey. In
'Orb', for instance, the white ring is
surrounded by black and then by a
green margin. The selfs, such as the
very dark **'Neat and Tidy'**, have a
single colour extending from the
white ring to the margins. Easily
spoilt by wet and rough weather,
the show auriculas are grown
under glass. The alpine auriculas
have no meal on the flowers or
leaves and can be grown outdoors.
There is a strong contrast between
the yellow or light centre and the
colour of the petal lobes. **'Mark'**,
for example, is pink with a white

centre; **'Bookham Firefly'**, red
with a gold centre. The hearty
border auriculas, in some cases
with a powdering of meal, are
suitable for the open garden. **'Old
Red Dusty Miller'** and **'Old Yellow
Dusty Miller'** both have meal on
the leaves and in the eye of the
flowers. Specialist nurseries have
many tempting treasures in all
three categories.

BORDER, BOG AND WOODLAND
PRIMULAS

Primula denticulata

P. denticulata *Afghanistan to
S.E. Tibet, Burma, China*
Drumstick primula
Flowers: mid-spring to summer.
H and S 12–18in (30–45cm). FH.
The rosette of long leaves, fine-
toothed and mealy, reaches its full
development after sturdy stems
have pushed up a spherical head,
as much as 3in (8cm) across and
packed with flowers. These are
yellow-eyed and in shades of
mauve or purple; in **var. alba** they
are white.

P. florindae *S.E. Tibet*
Giant cowslip
Flowers: mid- to late summer.
H 2–4ft (60–120cm), S 2–3ft
(60–90cm). FH.
Where the soil is fertile and
unfailingly moist, this is a giant
among primroses, making large
rosettes of long-stalked leaves and
sending up tall stems, with a ring
of numerous lemon-yellow flowers
dangling from the tip. They are
powdered with meal and fragrant.
The Himalayan cowslip
(**P. sikkimensis**) is a plant of
similar character but usually less
than 3ft (90cm) in height.

P. japonica *Japan*
Japanese primrose
Flowers: late spring to early summer.
H 24–30in (60–75cm),
S 9–12in (23–30cm). FH.
In this plant, the tiered whorls of
flowers typical of the candelabra
primulas rise above rosettes of
pale green leaves. The flowers are

Primula japonica 'Miller's Crimson'

usually a shade of red. **'Miller's
Crimson'** is richly coloured and
'Postford White' is pale pink in
bud, opening white with a reddish
pink eye. The Chinese species
P. beesiana, which is of similar size
and blooming at the same time, is a
piercing magenta. A taller and
more elegant candelabra primula
for the same season is another
Chinese species, *P. pulverulenta*.
It grows to 3ft (90cm) in height
and has mealy stems and flowers
of reddish purple. The **Bartley
Hybrids**, derived from it, have pale
pink flowers with red eyes.

Primula japonica 'Postford White'

P. prolifera *Himalayas, east to
mountains of Indonesia*
Flowers: early summer. H 2–3ft (60–
90cm), S 9–10in (23–25cm). FH.
A white-powdered stout stem
makes a candelabra with up to 7
whorls of fragrant flowers in
shades of yellow. The rosette of
leaves lasts through the winter.
P. bulleyana, of similar size, has
orange-tinted flowers. The orange-
red *P. aurantiaca* is rarely more
than 1ft (30cm) tall.

Primula prolifera

P. vialii *China (Sichuan, Yunnan)*
Flowers: summer. H 6–18in
(15–45cm), S 9–12 (23–30cm). FH.
Erect stems, rising from a rosette of
upright, softly hairy leaves, carry
single, rocket-like heads of tightly
packed flowers. At the pointed tips
the unopened buds are a vivid red;
the open flowers below are a
mauve-blue.

Primula 'Miss Indigo'

P. vulgaris *Europe, W. Turkey*
Primrose
Flowers: early to late spring.
H 6–8in (15–20cm), S 10–14in
(25–35cm). FH.
The common primrose, one of the
most beautiful of European wild
flowers, was brought into gardens
centuries ago. In spite of their
familiarity, it is hard to improve on
the pale yellow flowers that
emerge in profusion from bright
green corrugated leaves. However,
variations in colour and doubling
have long been valued. The
flowers of **subsp.** *sibthorpii*, from
the Balkans and further east, are
usually pale pink. A white double
similar to **'Alba Plena'** was known
in the 16th century. Another
double, *P.* **'Miss Indigo'**, has storm-
dark, violet-blue flowers with a
white edge to the petals.

PULMONARIA

Boraginaceae Lungwort

As low-growing groundcover in
shade, many of the lungworts,
especially the evergreens with
spotted or silvered leaves, are hard
to beat and their flowers – in a
number of cases making a magical
transition from pink to blue – are
among the first of the year borne
by perennials. The genus, which is
made up of about 14 species,
contains a large number of named
clones from selected seedlings. The
species are found in a wide range
of habitats in Europe and Asia,
usually in partial shade where the
soil is reliably moist but not
waterlogged. Similar conditions
suit these plants in the garden,
either under trees and shrubs or in
the shade of walls.

CULTIVATION Require full or partial
shade and well-drained but moist
soil that is rich in organic matter.
PROPAGATION By division, after
flowering or in autumn. From root
cuttings, in mid-winter. From seed,
sown as soon as ripe.
POTENTIAL PROBLEMS Slugs and
snails; powdery mildew.

P. angustifolia *C., E. and N.E.
Europe*
Blue cowslip
Foliage: spring to autumn. Flowers:
early to late spring. H 9–12in (23–
30cm), S 12–18in (30–45cm). FH.
This species is deciduous, its
unspotted, lance-shaped, hairy
leaves, up to 16in (40cm) long,
developing as the pink buds open
to blue. The short-growing
'Munstead Blue' is very early
flowering. Among named clones
that are deciduous and similar in
character to this species is
P. **'Mawson's Blue'**, with flowers
of gentian intensity.

Pulmonaria 'Mawson's Blue'

P. officinalis *Europe*
Jerusalem cowslip, soldiers and
sailors, spotted dog
Foliage: year-round. Flowers: early
to late spring. H 10–12in
(25–30cm), S 12–18in (30–45cm).
FH.
The bristly heart-shaped leaves of
this evergreen species are spotted
and its flowers change from pink,
through violet to blue. The
selection **'Sissinghurst White'** is
less coarse, the white flowers
opening from pale pink buds over
thickly spotted leaves.

**Pulmonaria officinalis
'Sissinghurst White'**

P. rubra *S.E. Europe*
Foliage: year-round. Flowers: late
winter to mid-spring. H 12–15in
(30–38cm), S 2–3ft (60–90cm). FH.
The foliage of this species is velvety
and unspotted and the red flowers
are borne over a long period from
mid-winter. In **'Bowles' Red'**, the
leaves are lightly spotted and the
flowers coral.

**Pulmonaria saccharata
'Frühlingshimmel'**

P. saccharata *C. and N. Italy,
S.E. France*
Jerusalem sage
Foliage: year-round. Flowers: late
winter to late spring. H 12–18in
(30–45cm), S 18–24in (45–60cm).
FH.
The silver or pewter marbling and
splashing of the leaves, which are
up to 1ft (30cm) long, is
outstanding in this evergreen
species. The flowers, which have
purple calyces, open pink but
become blue. In the **Argentea
Group**, the leaves have an almost
completely metallic finish.
'Frühlingshimmel' has sky-blue
flowers with a darker centre over
lightly spotted leaves.

PULSATILLA

Ranunculaceae

The silky hairiness of the pasque
flower (*P. vulgaris*) and many of
its close relatives gives them a
winningly tactile quality. The
genus comprises approximately 30
species, widely distributed in the
Northern Hemisphere but usually
in alpine or subalpine zones. They
are often found growing in short
turf where there is plenty of
moisture but also sharp drainage.
Alpine enthusiasts treasure the
white-flowered **P. vernalis**, the
yellow-flowered **P. alpina subsp.
apiifolia** and a number of other
species that need protection from
winter wet as well as gritty, free-
draining soil. Beautiful though
these species undoubtedly are, the
common pasque flower, which has
been grown in gardens since at
least the 16th century, is certainly
their equal.

CULTIVATION Require full sun and very well-drained soil (equal parts JI No.1 and grit).
PROPAGATION From seed, sown as soon as ripe.
POTENTIAL PROBLEMS Slugs and snails.
WARNING Contact with the sap may irritate the skin. Swallowing any part may cause stomach upset.

P. vulgaris *Europe east to Ukraine*
Pasque flower
Flowers: mid-spring. H and S 8–12in (20–30cm). FH.
Silken buds push through a ferny tuft of hairy leaves, opening to nodding flowers with rich yellow anthers. In the wild the colour ranges from pale mauve to deep purple; in cultivation it extends to white and shades of pink and red. The tactile fascination of the plant is later sustained by the feathery seedheads.

Pulsatilla vulgaris

RAMONDA

GESNERIACEAE

Although it shows an astonishing ability to revive after enduring a period of drought, the Pyrenean *R. myconi* and the less familiar plants of this small genus of only 3 species are, in fact, moisture-lovers. In the wild, these evergreen perennials lodge tightly in the shady crevices of rock faces. In the garden, moisture around the rosettes during the winter may cause them to rot, a problem that can be overcome by setting plants on their sides in a rock wall, such as the shady side of a raised bed. They look more at home in such a position than on the bench of an alpine house, where they need shade from hot sun.
CULTIVATION Requires partial shade and well-drained but moist soil, rich in organic matter (equal parts loam, leafmould and grit).
PROPAGATION From seed, sown as soon as ripe. From rosette cuttings, in early summer. From leaf cuttings, in early autumn.
POTENTIAL PROBLEMS Slugs and snails.

Ramonda myconi

R. myconi *N.E. Spain, Pyrenees*
Flowers: late spring to early summer. H 4–6in (10–15cm), S 6–8in (15–20cm). FH.
The dark green crinkly leaves, which are hairy and have a purplish red fringe, form a flat rosette. From this stems emerge usually bearing several, almost flat-faced, purple-blue flowers, each lit at the centre by a cluster of yellow anthers. Some seedlings produce white or pink flowers.

RANUNCULUS

RANUNCULACEAE Buttercup

For several centuries the horticultural reputation of this genus, better known for beautiful weeds than garden flowers, was made by the half-hardy tuberous Persian buttercup (**R. asiaticus**), the gorgeous doubles of which are now usually raised commercially under glass. The genus, however, comprises about 400 species, some of which are annuals, found in a wide range of habitats, including bogs and watery places, damp meadows, dry grassland, woodland and mountain slopes. Several species excite alpine specialists, including **R. calandrinioides** from the Atlas Mountains, a frail-flowered beauty for the alpine house, and the magnificent but testing giant buttercup (**R. lyallii**), from the New Zealand Alps. The lustre of the flowers and fascinating doubling are appealing, even in such weedy species as the lesser celandine (**R. ficaria**) and the creeping buttercup (**R. repens**).

Ranunculus calandrinioides

R. ficaria has staged a comeback with the darkly glossy '**Brazen Hussy**', with chocolate-brown leaves, and such curious doubles as the anemone-flowered '**Collarette**'.
CULTIVATION The species have varying requirements but those described tolerate full sun or partial shade and require a well-drained but moist soil, rich in organic matter.
PROPAGATION By division, in spring or autumn. From seed, sown as soon as ripe.
POTENTIAL PROBLEMS Slugs and snails, aphids; powdery mildew.
WARNING Contact with the sap may cause allergic skin reactions.

Ranunculus aconitifolius 'Flore Pleno'

R. aconitifolius '**Flore Pleno**'
Fair maids of France, fair maids of Kent, white bachelor's buttons
Flowers: late spring to early summer. H 18–24in (45–60cm), S 12–18in (30–45cm). FH.
Even the plant with single white buttercups over glossy, jaggedly lobed leaves is attractive in an open woodland garden, but since at least the 16th century it has been outclassed by the double.

R. constantinopolitanus '**Plenus**'
Flowers: mid-spring to mid-summer. H 10–12in (25–30cm), S 6–10in (15–25cm). FH.
Green centres add zest to neat and sheeny double flowers borne over a handsome clump of leaves with fanned and toothed lobes.

R. montanus '**Molten Gold**'
Flowers: early summer. H 4–6in (10–15cm), S 8–12in (20–30cm). FH.
In a rock garden this makes a deep green mat of glossy leaves, above which shine cup-shaped yellow flowers.

RAOULIA

ASTERACEAE

Several of the larger plants of this genus of about 20 species, including **R. eximia**, which can form dense cushions over 3ft

(90cm) across and 1ft (30cm) or more thick, are known as vegetable sheep: from a distance their grey shapes look like animals grazing on sparse vegetation at the edge of mountain screes. They are difficult plants in cultivation, needing controlled conditions in an alpine house, but in this almost exclusively New Zealand genus there are other species – some alpines, some plants of shingly river flats – that make attractive evergreen mats in rock gardens, raised beds or scree beds. The starry flowers are tiny.
CULTIVATION Require full sun and well-drained soil (equal parts loam, leafmould and sharp sand with grit top-dressing).
PROPAGATION By division of mat-forming species, in spring. From rosette cuttings of cushion-forming species, in early summer and in partial shade.
POTENTIAL PROBLEMS Aphids and red spider mites under glass.

Raoulia australis

R. australis *New Zealand*
Flowers: summer. H ½in (1cm), S 12–18in (30–45cm). FrH.
Silvery mats of close overlapping leaves, tiny in the **Lutescens Group**, flow among and over rocks, the minute flowers creating a velvety yellow pile.

Raoulia hookeri

R. hookeri *New Zealand*
Flowers: mid- to late spring. H ½in (1cm), S 8–12in (20–30cm). FrH.
Silky hairs give the packed rosettes of leaves a silvery lustre. The small straw-coloured or greenish flowers are not long-lasting.

RHEUM

POLYGONACEAE Rhubarb

The culinary rhubarb
(**R. × hybridum**) gives some idea of the ornamental potential of several large-leaved species with plume-like flower spikes that thrive in moist fertile soils. The chief interest of a few species, including **R. alexandrae** from swampy ground in western China and Tibet, are the conspicuous bracts that hide the flowers. This unusual species, which carries its creamy bracts on stems up to 3ft (90cm) high, has a reputation for being difficult, succeeding only where the soil is permanently wet. There are about 50 species in the genus.
CULTIVATION Tolerate full sun or partial shade and require deep moist soil, rich in organic matter. *R. alexandrae* requires permanently wet soil.
PROPAGATION By division, in early spring. From seed, sown in autumn.
POTENTIAL PROBLEMS Slugs; crown rot and viruses.
WARNING Swallowing the leaves may cause severe stomach upset.

R. palmatum *N.E. Tibet, N.W. China*
Chinese rhubarb
Foliage: late spring to mid-summer. Flowers: early summer. H 5–8ft (1.5–2.5m), S 4–6ft (1.2–1.8m). FH.
The relentless eruption of this plant in spring and early summer is splendid: the jagged leaves, eventually growing up to 3ft (90cm) long, reveal their purple-red undersides as they thrust out, and the tall stems shoot up well above the leaves which are plumed cream or red. The volcanic tints of **'Atrosanguineum'** are particularly fine, the young leaves purplish red, the tiny flowers bright crimson; even the seed cases have a rosy flush. The hybrid **R. 'Ace of Hearts'**, which grows to 4ft (1.2m), has heart-shaped leaves that are purplish red on the reverse and its thin plumes are pale pink or cream.

Rheum 'Ace of Hearts'

RODGERSIA

SAXIFRAGACEAE

The 6 species in this genus are rhizomatous perennials of forest glades, woodland margins and streamsides in mountainous country from Burma eastward to Japan. They include several fine foliage plants which, in cultivation, as in the wild, will grow in full sun or light shade, provided there is plenty of moisture in the soil. They are most commonly seen as bog and waterside plants but also make magnificent stands in damp borders. Although the reputation of the genus is founded on splendid foliage, some species have very ornamental plume-like flowers followed by distinctive seedheads.
CULTIVATION Tolerate full sun or partial shade and require moist soil, rich in organic matter, in a sheltered position.
PROPAGATION From seed, sown in spring. By division, in early spring.
POTENTIAL PROBLEM Slugs.

R. aesculifolia *N. China*
Foliage: late spring to autumn. Flowers: mid-summer. H 4–6ft (1.2–1.8m), S 2–3ft (60–90cm). FH.
The impressive stack of foliage, the leaves fingered like those of a giant horse chestnut and with red-brown furring to the stalks and veins, is topped by pyramidal plumes of tiny, star-shaped, white or pink flowers.

Rodgersia pinnata 'Superba'

R. pinnata *China (Sichuan, Yunnan)*
Foliage: late spring to autumn. Flowers: mid- to late summer. H 3–4ft (90–120cm), S 24–30in (60–75cm). FH.
The plumes of cream or pink flowers stand well above the dark green foliage base, made up of large overlapping leaves, each composed of 5 to 9 heavily veined and crinkled leaflets up to 8in (20cm) long. In **'Superba'**, which has bright pink flowers and red-brown seedheads, the leaves are bronze-tinted when young and usually colour richly in autumn.

263

Rodgersia podophylla

R. podophylla *Japan, Korea*
Foliage: late spring to autumn.
Flowers: mid- to late summer.
H 3–5ft (90–150cm), S 3–6ft
(90–180cm). FH.
In comparison with the other
widely grown species, this makes
a poor show in flower. However,
the foliage is dramatic, the leaves
usually consisting of 5 wedge-
shaped and jagged leaflets splayed
out like a rosette. They are bronzed
when young and their copper
tones are particularly rich later in
the year, provided plants are grown
in full sun.

ROMNEYA

PAPAVERACEAE Californian poppy,
matilija poppy, tree poppy

The wilfulness of the tree poppy
(there are only 2 species in the
genus) is a fact that has to be
accepted, the wandering roots of
the subshrubs throwing up shoots
in unexpected and not necessarily
convenient places. In the chaparral
of southern California it is quick to
colonize areas that have been
burnt or cleared. In sunny warm
gardens a colony fluttering with
large white poppies is a glorious
sight, even though disconcertingly
ill-defined in its extent. Plants are
easily battered by winds and need
a sheltered position, in frost-prone
areas at the foot of a warm wall. A
dry mulch, say of straw, will help to
protect plants in winter.
CULTIVATION Require full sun and
well-drained soil.
PROPAGATION From seed, sown in
spring at 55–61°F (13–16°C). From
basal cuttings, in spring. From root
cuttings, in winter.
POTENTIAL PROBLEMS Caterpillars;
verticillium wilt.

R. coulteri *North America
(N. Mexico, S. California)*
Flowers: mid-summer to early
autumn. H and S 4–8ft (1.2–
2.5m). FrH.
Crumpled white petals unfold
around a knob of bright yellow
stamens, and the fragrant flowers,
which can be over 4in (10cm)

across, seem to float randomly in
and above the slashed blue-green
foliage. **'White Cloud'** is vigorous
and noted for its very large flowers
and glaucous leaves.

Romneya coulteri

ROSCOEA

ZINGIBERACEAE

At a quick glance, the curious
hooded flowers of these fleshy
rooted perennials seem very
orchid-like. There are nearly 20
species, all of them found in the
Himalayas and China, most of them
growing in cool, moist conditions.
These are the ideal conditions for
them in cultivation as well. Suitable
positions include shady corners of
rock gardens, raised beds, or, in
combination with other choice
woodland plants, in glades among
shrubs or trees. In frost-prone
areas, a deep mulch of leafmould
will help protect plants in winter.
CULTIVATION Require partial shade
and moist, well-drained soil, rich in
organic matter.
PROPAGATION By division, in spring.
From seed, sown as soon as ripe.
POTENTIAL PROBLEMS Slugs, vine
weevils.

R. cautleyoides *China (Sichuan,
Yunnan)*
Flowers: mid-summer. H 16–20in
(40–50cm), S 6–12in (15–30cm).
FH to FrH.
Plants in cultivation usually have
pale yellow flowers of ghost-like
outline quivering above the mid-
green leaves. However, the colour
range also includes shades of
purple and white.

Roscoea cautleyoides

R. humeana *China (Sichuan,
Yunnan)*
Flowers: early summer. H and S
6–12in (15–30cm). FrH to FH.
This is one of the first of the
species to flower and when it does
come into bloom the leaves are
usually not yet fully developed. In
addition to the rich reddish purple
most commonly seen in
cultivation, the colour range
includes white, mauve and yellow.
R. purpurea, a taller plant, usually
1ft (30cm) or more high and
coming into flower a few weeks
later, has purple flowers.
Occasionally it is bicoloured, with
white and purple flowers.

RUDBECKIA

ASTERACEAE Coneflower

Rudbeckia 'Goldquelle'

The yellow daisy flowerheads of
the perennials in this North
American genus of around 20
species have drooping ray-florets
around a dark-coloured or green
central cone. In the wild they are
mainly plants of open moist
ground, often near water. They
tolerate somewhat drier conditions
in well-cultivated borders, giving a
long display in summer and early
autumn. The singles have a cleaner
look than the bright yellow
R. 'Goldquelle' and other doubles.
A short-lived, bristly perennial
species, **R. hirta**, is usually grown as
an annual. The yellow flowerheads
have purplish brown cones.
CULTIVATION Tolerate full sun or
partial shade and require heavy,
moist, well-drained soil.
PROPAGATION From seed, sown in
early spring. By division, in autumn
or spring.
POTENTIAL PROBLEM Slugs.

R. fulgida *E. USA*
Black-eyed Susan
Flowers: late summer to mid-
autumn. H 2–3ft (60–90cm),
S 18–24in (45–60cm). FH.
The pick of these dark-eyed yellow
daisies, widely distributed in
eastern North America, is **var.
sullivantii 'Goldsturm'**. The erect

stems rise above the dark green basal leaves, carrying flowers, up to 5in (13cm) across, that are rich yellow and have narrow ray florets.

Rudbeckia fulgida var. sullivantii 'Goldsturm'

R. 'Herbstsonne'

Flowers: mid-summer to early autumn. H 5–7ft (1.5–2.2m), S 30–36in (75–90cm). FH.
The stature of *R. nitida*, one of the parents, shows in this tall coneflower. Above clumps of lobed or toothed glossy leaves branching stems carry large bright yellow but world-weary flowerheads, the ray florets sagging below the green central knob.

Rudbeckia 'Herbstsonne'

SALVIA

LAMIACEAE

The shrubby culinary sage (*S. officinalis*) and a few other European representatives of this very large genus – which includes about 900 species of annuals, biennials, perennials and shrubs – have a long history in cultivation. Sages have culinary, medicinal and cosmetic uses, the volatile oils they contain being used in perfumery. The species have an enormous spread in temperate and tropical areas of the world. Many plants from a wide range of habitats, especially the tender species, came into cultivation in the 19th century. These tender introductions are, in many instances, true perennials or subshrubs and are grown as such, provided the climate is mild enough. They are also frequently grown as annuals, new stock being raised each year, usually from cuttings taken in autumn or spring. (Some are treated as such in this book.) Several of the plants described have aromatic foliage and all have flowers with an upper lip that is hooded and a lower lip that is more spreading. Even when flowers are small, their impact is often enhanced by colourful, long-lasting bracts. The perennial salvias are useful plants for sunny borders and provide some outstanding blues. See also ANNUALS AND BIENNIALS and SHRUBS.
CULTIVATION Salvias have varying requirements but all of those described need full sun and well-drained soil, preferably containing generous quantities of organic matter (JI No.2).
PROPAGATION From seed, especially of *S. patens* and *S. pratensis* Haematodes Group, sown in spring. By division, in spring (not subshrubs).
POTENTIAL PROBLEMS Slugs and snails; aphids, red spider mites, whiteflies (under glass); foot and root rots.

S. fulgens *Mexico*
Cardinal sage
Flowers: mid- to late summer. H and S 18in (45cm). HH.
Vivid red flowers, downy on the lower lip, rise in numerous spikes above a leafy bush. Where the climate is mild enough this may be an evergreen subshrub.

S. guaranitica *Argentina, Brazil, Uruguay*
Flowers: late summer to late autumn. H 4–5ft (1.2–1.5m), S 24–30in (60–75cm). HH.
This lax subshrubby perennial produces branching stems loaded with deep blue sage flowers in autumn. The flowers of **'Blue Enigma'** are fragrant and richly coloured, with bright green calyces.

S. nemorosa *Europe to C. Asia*
Flowers: summer. H 2–3ft (60–90cm), S 18–24in (45–60cm). FH.
The species and several hybrids are bushy plants that branch freely to produce many erect spikes; the effect of the flowers is long lasting because of the bracts that remain even after the flowers have faded. The compact **'Ostfriesland'**, about 18in (45cm) high, has deep violet-blue flowers and red-purple bracts. Closer to the species in size but with similar colouring to 'Ostfriesland' is *S. × superba*. Cultivars of the hybrid *S. × sylvestris* range in height from 18–30in (45–75cm). **'Mainacht'** is one of the taller examples, with large, deep blue flowers and purple bracts.

Salvia nemorosa 'Ostfriesland'

S. patens *Mexico*
Flowers: mid-summer to mid-autumn. H 18–24in (45–60cm). S 12–18in (30–45cm). FrH.
Where the climate is mild enough, this makes a superb perennial, for many weeks bearing large paired flowers that gape at the mouth. A contrast between the familiar deep blue species and the pale **'Cambridge Blue'** is very pleasing. The fleshy roots are tuberous and plants can be lifted and stored in a frost-free place over winter. This species is also grown as an annual.

Salvia patens 'Cambridge Blue'

S. pratensis Haematodes Group *Greece*
Flowers: summer. H 2–3ft (60–90cm), S 12–18in (30–45cm). FH.
The basal rosette consists of large, grey-green, crinkled leaves with purple veins. Branched stems carry sprays of mauve-blue flowers. Plants are easily raised from seed.

Salvia pratensis Haematodes Group

S. uliginosa *Argentina, Brazil, Uruguay*
Bog sage
Flowers: late summer to mid-autumn. H 5–6ft (1.5–1.8m), S 2–3ft (60–90cm). FrH.
In its carefree grace this tall species defies the approach of winter, its freely branching stems carrying small spikes of sky-blue flowers well into autumn.

SANGUINARIA

PAPAVERACEAE Bloodroot, red puccoon

The red sap that the plant exudes when damaged has given the one species in this North American genus its generic and common name. A plant of cool, moist woodland, it is suited to a raised bed or shady area in a rock garden.
CULTIVATION Require deep or partial shade and well-drained but moist soil that is rich in organic matter.
PROPAGATION By division, immediately after flowering. From seed, sown in autumn.
POTENTIAL PROBLEMS Usually none.

Sanguinaria canadensis 'Plena'

S. canadensis *E. North America*
Flowers: late spring. H 4–6in (10–15cm), S 8–12in (20–30cm). FH.
The single-flowered form is a pleasing plant, especially in the way the buds are enclosed by the scalloped grey-green leaves, but it is eclipsed by the white purity of the double **'Plena'**.

SANGUISORBA

ROSACEAE Burnet

Salad burnet (**S. minor**), long cultivated as a herb, is a plant of dry grassland. However, the most ornamental of the burnets are moisture-lovers, found wild in damp meadows. In late summer or autumn, the pinnate foliage is topped by bottlebrush-like spikes of flowers. There are about 18 species, all from temperate or cool areas of the Northern Hemisphere. Those most commonly grown benefit from light twiggy support.

CULTIVATION Tolerate full sun or partial shade and require moist well-drained soil.
PROPAGATION By division, in spring or autumn. From seed, sown in spring or autumn.
POTENTIAL PROBLEM Slugs.

S. canadensis *N.E. North America*
Canadian burnet
Flowers: mid-summer to mid-autumn. H 4–6ft (1.2–1.8m), S 2–3ft (60–90cm). FH.
The leaves are pale green and the slender white, occasionally pink-tinted, bottlebrushes are carried on erect stems.

Sanguisorba obtusa

S. obtusa *Japan*
Flowers: mid-summer to early autumn. H 3–4ft (90–120cm), S 2–3ft (60–90cm). FH.
Lax stems carry soft arching spikes, their pink a pleasing match for the grey-green foliage.

SAPONARIA

CARYOPHYLLACEAE

Its pretty flowers and easy-going ways made the common soapwort or bouncing bet (**S. officinalis**) popular as a cottage garden plant, especially in its double pink or white forms; it was also valued for its cleansing properties. An untidy and invasive plant, it is now found naturalized beyond its European homeland. There are about 20 species in the genus. A few compact sun-loving species from mountainous regions in Europe are plants for rock gardens and raised beds. The Pyrenean **S. caespitosa**, a small congested mat of leaves brightened by pink flowers, is one of these. The plant described becomes loose and untidy unless cut back hard after flowering.
CULTIVATION Require full sun and well-drained soil that is neutral to alkaline.
PROPAGATION From seed, sown in autumn or spring. By division, in spring or autumn. From cuttings, in early summer.
POTENTIAL PROBLEMS Slugs and snails.

Saponaria officinalis

S. ocymoides *Mountains from Spain to former Yugoslavia*
Tumbling Ted
Flowers: all summer. H 3–4in (8–10cm), S 12–18in (30–45cm). FH.
Tumbling Ted, as this species is sometimes known, rides roughshod over less assertive alpines but its vigour allows it to plunge recklessly over the edge of retaining walls, trailing dark green drapery which is almost obscured by bright pink flowers. It has its own compact form, **'Rubra Compacta'**, and there are several hybrids also of restrained dense growth. *S.* **'Bressingham'** makes a low mat with a spread of about 1ft (30cm), covered by almost stemless bright pink flowers in mid-summer. The dense cushion of *S.* × *olivana*, usually less than half this in size, is covered with pale pink flowers in early summer.

Saponaria ocymoides

SAXIFRAGA

SAXIFRAGACEAE Saxifrage

For the alpine specialist this is undoubtedly one of the key genera. It comprises about 440 species, a large proportion of which are from mountainous habitats in the Northern Hemisphere. Despite their small scale, the species and the large number of hybrids derived from them show a wonderful variety in habit, foliage and flower. The selection described can only hint at the range but includes representatives of the most widely grown groups. Among the most spectacular are the silver or encrusted saxifrages, a few of which are mentioned under the entry *S. longifolia*. These are evergreens, forming large rosettes which are silvered with a liberal encrustation of lime. Plants may take several years before they flower and after flowering the central rosette usually dies. The mossy saxifrages, which derive this general name from the moss-like growth of their small rounded hummocks or dense mats, are mainly represented in cultivation by hybrids, such as *S.* 'Peter Pan'. Two other groups rich in alpine treasures are the Kabschia and Engleria sections. In both, the silver rosettes, encrusted with lime, are densely packed. These saxifrages are often prized plants for an alpine house but those described can be grown outdoors, ideally in tufa, especially if protected from excessive wet in winter. The purple saxifrage (*S. oppositifolia*) does not fit into any of the above categories but is one of the most widely distributed of all the alpine species.

Such is the quality and number of the alpine saxifages that the larger species, mainly woodland plants although some of them are well suited to borders, are easily overlooked. In the descriptions that follow, border and woodland saxifrages appear after the alpines. *CULTIVATION* Saxifrages have varying requirements. Many alpine species are best in light shade and require well-drained soil that is neutral to alkaline (JI No.1 with added limestone chippings). *S. longifolia* and the plants described with it thrive in full sun and need very sharp drainage, but *S. cotyledon* and its progeny are best on lime-free soil. The mossy saxifrages such as *S.* 'Peter Pan' require shade and a reasonably moist but well-drained soil that is neutral to slightly acid (JI No.2 with added grit). The border and woodland saxifrages require partial or full shade and well-drained but moist soil that is rich in organic matter.
PROPAGATION By division, in spring. From rosette cuttings, in late spring or early summer. From seed, sown in autumn.
POTENTIAL PROBLEMS Slugs, aphids, vine weevil grubs, red spider mites.

ALPINE SAXIFRAGES

S. × anglica 'Cranbourne'
Flowers: early summer. H 1–1½in (2.5–4cm), S 6–8in (15–20cm). FH. Even the purists cannot fail to see

the winning qualities of this hybrid Kabschia saxifrage. The almost stemless flowers, scattered thickly over huddled grey-green rosettes, are at first a deep and vivid pink, but then turn paler as they age.

S. × apiculata 'Gregor Mendel'
Flowers: early spring. H 3–4in (8–10cm), S 6–10in (15–25cm). FH. Few of the Kabschia saxifrages perform better in the rock garden. In their season, the pale yellow flowers almost obscure the cushion of tight glossy leaves. They also do well planted in walls.

Saxifraga × apiculata 'Gregor Mendel'

S. × irvingii 'Jenkinsiae'
Flowers: early spring. H 1–2in (2.5–5cm), S 8–12in (20–30cm). FH. Although the rosettes do not have the exquisite tightness of some Kabschias, the vigour of this hybrid counts when it is grown in the rock garden. Quantities of dark-centred pale pink flowers cover the low grey-green cushion in spring.

Saxifraga × irvingii 'Jenkinsiae'

S. longifolia *Pyrenees*
Pyrenean saxifrage
Flowers: summer. H 18–24in (45–60cm), S 8–12in (20–30cm). FH. In the wild the species establishes a foothold in a cliff-face niche and eventually extends arching sprays that are dense and dazzling with innumerable cup-shaped white flowers. *S.* 'Tumbling Waters', said to be a natural hybrid with *S. longifolia* as one of its parents, is, if it is possible, an even more

magnificent plant. Another of the silver or encrusted saxifrages is *S. cotyledon*, a white-flowered species that is widely distributed in mountainous areas of Europe. *S.* 'Southside Seedling', a cultivar or hybrid of it, produces sprays up to 1ft (30cm) high of white flowers with heavy red markings.

S. oppositifolia *Arctic, mountains of Europe, North America, W. Asia*
Purple saxifrage
Flowers: early summer. H 1in (2.5cm), S 8–12in (20–30cm). FH. The astonishingly wide distribution of this alpine species accounts for its varied appearance. As it is usually seen, the cup-shaped, almost stemless, purplish pink flowers stand shoulder to shoulder above an evergreen mat of hoary leaves.

S. 'Peter Pan'
Flowers: late spring. H 2–3in (5–8cm), S 10–12in (25–30cm). FH. Like most of the mossy saxifrages in gardens, this is a hybrid. In spring wiry stems make a miniature crimson forest which supports a canopy composed of pink cups. *S.* 'Triumph', which has bright red flowers, is one of many on a larger scale, with stems up to 6in (15cm) high.

Saxifraga 'Peter Pan'

BORDER AND WOODLAND SAXIFRAGES

S. fortunei *Japan*
Foliage: early summer to mid-autumn. Flowers: late summer to early autumn. H 12–18in (30–45cm), S 12–15in (30–38cm). FH. The semi-evergreen foliage is of long-lasting beauty, the scalloped edge echoed in overlapping leaves, which are kidney-shaped or rounded and purplish red on the underside. In some cultivars, such as *S.* 'Rubrifolia', the upper surface is bronze-red. The showers of small white flowers make a dramatic late appearance, the unequal size of the petals creating the effect of a hovering cloud of insects.

Saxifraga × *urbium*

S. × urbium

London pride
Foliage: year-round. Flowers: early
summer. H 12–18ft (30–45cm),
S 18–24in (45–60cm). FH.
In gardens London pride has
largely displaced **S. umbrosa**, one
of its parents. Even on poor soils
the interloper makes respectable
groundcover. Leathery rosettes of
spoon-shaped, toothed leaves
spread freely and in spring tall
stems support a haze of tiny white
flowers that are pink at the centre.

SCABIOSA

DIPSACACEAE Pincushion flower,
scabious

The pincushion of the scabious
flower, so attractive to bees and
butterflies, is formed by a dome of
central florets with protruding
styles, and is surrounded by ray
florets, which in the showiest
species are wavy and overlapping.
The 75 or so annual and perennial
species are found mostly in the
Mediterranean region, but also in
the rest of Europe, Africa, Asia and
Japan. They are plants of open
grassland or rocky slopes, usually
on alkaline soils. The star of the
perennials is *S. caucasica*, formerly
widely grown for the cut-flower
trade and a long-flowering border
plant if dead-headed regularly. It
needs to be divided every 3 to 4
years. A few shorter growing
species, including **S. graminifolia**,
are suitable for rock gardens. Sweet
scabious (**S. atropurpurea**), with
fragrant flowers in shades of pink,
purple or white, is an annual which

Scabiosa caucasica 'Stäfa'

originates in southern Europe.
CULTIVATION Require full sun and
well-drained neutral or slightly
alkaline soil.
PROPAGATION From seed, sown as
soon as ripe or in spring. By
division, in spring. From basal
cuttings, in spring.
POTENTIAL PROBLEMS Usually none.

Scabiosa 'Butterfly Blue'

S. 'Butterfly Blue'

Flowers: mid- to late summer.
H and S 14–18in (35–45cm). FH.
The small scabious (**S. columbaria**),
which is a plant of chalk grassland
in Europe, is said to be a parent of
this hybrid. During the summer,
the hybrid provides a long display
of mauve-blue flowers over divided
grey-green leaves.

Scabiosa caucasica 'Miss Willmott'

S. caucasica Caucasus,
N.E. Turkey, N. Iran

Flowers: early summer to early
autumn. H 18–24in (45–60cm),
S 16–20in (40–50cm). FH.
A basal clump of grey-green leaves
produces numerous, almost
leafless, stems carrying solitary
pale blue or mauve-blue flowers
up to 3in (8cm) across. Named
clones include the soft mauve
'Clive Greaves', the white **'Miss
Willmott'** and dark blue **'Stäfa'**.

SCHIZOSTYLIS

IRIDACEAE Kaffir lily

The single species is found wild in
the Drakensberg Mountains of
Natal and Lesotho, usually growing
near streams. In the garden, it will
produce long-lasting spikes of
lustrous, cup-shaped flowers in the

autumn, provided it is kept well
supplied with moisture through
the summer months. The flowers
are as good for cutting as they are
for garden display.
CULTIVATION Require full sun and
moist, well-drained soil.
PROPAGATION By division, in spring.
From seed, sown in spring at
55–61°F (13–16°C).
POTENTIAL PROBLEMS Usually none.

Schizostylis coccinea 'Major'

S. coccinea Lesotho, South Africa,
Swaziland

Flowers: early autumn. H 24–30in
(60–75cm), S 9–12in (23–30cm).
Fr.H.
In moisture-retentive soil the
rhizomatous roots form large,
nearly evergreen clumps of
narrow, blade-like leaves; in early
autumn they are thick with spikes
of up to 10 cup-shaped, scarlet
flowers that are starry when fully
open. Cultivars include the pink
and rather small-flowered **'Mrs
Hegarty'** and **'Viscountess Byng'**.
Hearty plants with large flowers
include **'Major'**, which is sheeny
red, and **'Sunrise'**, with silky
salmon-pink flowers.

Schizostylis coccinea 'Sunrise'

SEDUM

CRASSULACEAE Stonecrop

The 400 or so species of succulents
that comprise this large genus are
of very varied character and widely
distributed. The majority are from
mountainous regions in the
Northern Hemisphere, while some
originate in arid parts of South
America. The more tender, such as
the Mexican **S. morganianum**,

with its tress-like trailing stems and starry, pale pink to deep scarlet-purple flowers produced in spring and summer, are often grown as greenhouse or conservatory plants. A few sedums, such as the common stonecrop or wallpepper (*S. acre*), can become tiresome weeds. There are, however, many hardy species and hybrids that are suitable for borders and rock gardens, where their foliage is as valuable as their flowers. Another good reason for growing them is that they are mobbed by butterflies and bees. Tall sedums such as S. 'Herbstfreude' should be divided every 4 to 5 years.
CULTIVATION Require full sun and well-drained soil, preferably neutral or slightly alkaline (JI No.2 with added leafmould and grit).
PROPAGATION By division, in spring. From cuttings, in early summer. From seed, sown in autumn or spring.
POTENTIAL PROBLEMS Slugs and snails; fungal, bacterial crown and root rots.
WARNING Contact with the sap may irritate the skin. Swallowing any part may cause stomach upset.

S. spathulifolium *W. North America*
Foliage: year-round. Flowers: early summer. H 2–4in (5–10cm), S 10–20in (25–50cm). FH.
The tightly packed rosettes of fleshy purple-red leaves, unevenly coated with a waxy bloom, form low mats topped by star-shaped, bright yellow flowers. In '**Cape Blanco**' the bloom is heavy; in '**Purpureum**' the purple-red is rich and vivid. Another mat-forming species, *S. spurium*, which comes from the Caucasus but is widely naturalized elsewhere, has star-shaped, pinkish purple or white flowers and makes useful groundcover in poor dry soils. Forms with foliage that is strongly tinted red or purple, such as '**Schorbuser Blut**', are especially suitable. The star-shaped flowers are a deep pink.

Sedum spathulifolium '**Purpureum**'

Sedum spectabile '**Brilliant**'

S. spectabile *China, Korea*
Ice plant
Foliage: summer. Flowers: late summer. H 12–18in (30–45cm), S 18–24in (45–60cm). FH.
The clump of fleshy grey-green leaves, which makes a pleasing presence throughout summer, is transformed in early autumn when every stem produces a flat head, as much as 6in (15cm) across, packed with starry flowers. Its mauve-pink is wishy-washy but '**Brilliant**' and '**Septemberglut**' are strong pinks. The hybrid *S.* '**Herbstfreude**', of which this species is probably a parent, is a larger plant, up to 2ft (60cm) high and across, the flowers opening deep pink and then changing to a warmer salmon-pink before turning copper red. The brown seedheads are superb when rimmed with frost.

Sedum '**Vera Jameson**'

S. 'Vera Jameson'
Foliage: early summer to autumn. Flowers: late summer to early autumn. H 8–12in (20–30cm), S 12–18in (30–45cm). FH.
The fleshy dark purple leaves that clothe the arching stems are completely obscured in late summer by heads of star-shaped purple-pink flowers. A likely parent of this fine hybrid and twice its size is *S. telephium* subsp. *maximum* '**Atropurpureum**'. A striking brown-purple foliage plant, it is perfect for the front of a border. The flowerheads in autumn are pink, the seedheads that follow a rich brown. The other parent may have been the hybrid *S.* '**Ruby Glow**', which makes a

spreading purplish green clump about 10in (25cm) high, vibrant with claret flowerheads from mid-summer to early autumn.

Sedum '**Ruby Glow**'

SEMPERVIVUM

CRASSULACEAE Houseleek

The rosettes of fleshy leaves have a flower-like quality that is more ornamental than the starry true flowers. The stalk bearing the flowers is, however, dramatic in its eruption. In the genus there are approximately 40 species which are distributed in the mountain regions of Europe and Asia. In gardens this number is augmented by numerous hybrids and selected clones. The naming of these is confused, so making your own choice from a specialist nursery is the best guarantee of satisfaction. Sun and sharp drainage in a rock garden or dry stone wall suit these plants well but they are also attractive grown in pans. Protection in an alpine house from winter wet will benefit those that are softly hairy. The genus *Jovibarba* is very closely related.
CULTIVATION Require full sun and very well-drained soil with added grit (equal parts JI No.2 and grit).
PROPAGATION From offset cuttings, in spring or early summer. From seed, sown in spring.
POTENTIAL PROBLEM Rust.

S. arachnoideum *Europe (Alps, Apennines, Carpathians)*
Cobweb houseleek
Foliage: year-round. Flowers: mid-summer. H 1–3in (2.5–8cm), S 8–12in (20–30cm). FH.
Busy spiders seem to have worked feverishly among the red-green rosettes to net them with a fine web of white hairs. The flowers, which are produced on leafy stems, are reddish pink. Another species with quite small but very tightly incurved rosettes is *S. giuseppii*, from Spain. The bright green leaves are dark at the tip and those at the centre of the rosette are hairy. The flowers are reddish pink.

S. tectorum *Mountains of S. Europe*

Common houseleek
Foliage: year-round. Flowers: mid-summer. H 3–6in (8–15cm), S 12–20in (30–50cm). FH.
Lodged among roof tiles, where it survives on meagre fare, this plant charms lightning to strike elsewhere, or so it was believed. The blue-green leaves, bristly at the tip, usually turn red-purple as summer advances. The flowers are purplish pink. Two other species with medium to large rosettes are **S. calcareum**, from the French Alps, and **S. marmoreum**, from the Balkans. Hybrids include **S. 'Commander Hay'**, with green-tipped purple-red leaves, and **S. 'Othello'**, which is dark purple.

Sempervivum 'Commander Hay'

SIDALCEA

MALVACEAE False mallow, prairie mallow

In gardens, this North American genus of about 20 to 25 species is usually represented by hybrids between **S. candida** and **S. malviflora**, the latter species sometimes known by the common name of checkerbloom. Like their parents, the hybrids produce spires of silky hollyhock-like flowers in summer, followed by a lesser display, provided the stems of faded blooms are cut back. The basal clump of leaves makes good cover. A drawback of the tall cultivars is that they usually need staking. In other respects they are easy-going border plants for lime-free soils in full sun.
CULTIVATION Require full sun and well-drained soil, preferably neutral to slightly acid.
PROPAGATION From seed, sown in autumn or spring. By division, in spring or autumn.
POTENTIAL PROBLEMS Slugs; rust.

S. 'Rose Queen'

Flowers: early to mid-summer.
H 2–3ft (60–90cm), S 16–20in (40–50cm). FH.
Lightly branched stems, rising from a base of lobed leaves, carry bright

Sidalcea 'Rose Queen'

pink flowers that are 2in (5cm) or more across. Other hybrids of similar character and size include: **'Elsie Heugh'**, with fringed, purplish pink flowers, and **'William Smith'**, which is salmon-pink. **'Puck'**, a smaller plant about 16in (40cm) high, has deep pink flowers.

SILENE

CARYOPHYLLACEAE Campion, catchfly

Although a large genus, with about 500 species, strongly concentrated in the Mediterranean area, *Silene* provides relatively few perennials for the garden. In the past the European red campion (**S. dioica**) was more widely grown than it is today, double forms being particularly popular in cottage gardens. Of the other perennials, the most useful are several low-growing species that are suitable for a rock garden. These include true alpines as well as plants of other harsh rocky habitats, such as the sea campion (**S. uniflora**), most favoured in its double form. Rose of heaven (**S. coeli-rosa**), a pretty and easy annual with notched petals is a triumphant success with children.
CULTIVATION Tolerate full sun or partial shade and require well-drained soil that is neutral to slightly alkaline.
PROPAGATION From seed, sown in autumn. From basal cuttings, taken in spring.
POTENTIAL PROBLEMS Slugs and snails. Under glass: aphids, whiteflies, red spider mites.

Silene schafta

S. schafta *W. Asia*

Flowers: late summer to autumn.
H 4–6in (10–15cm), S 9–12in (23–30cm). FH.
Its late flowering gives this species a special value in the rock garden. Sprays of magenta flowers, which are long-tubed and have prettily notched petals, brighten low tufts of small green leaves.

SISYRINCHIUM

IRIDACEAE

The reputation of some in a genus of nearly 100 species, of which the perennials are the most important ornamentally, has been tarnished because of their free-seeding tendencies; a few have become naturalized well beyond their home territories in North and South America. This is so with the blue-eyed grass (**S. angustifolium**), but it is undeniably pretty when its grassy tufts are topped by flowers of rich blue satin. The perennials, which are rhizomatous and in a number of cases semi-evergreen, are from a range of habitats, but those in cultivation do well in sunny, well-drained rock gardens, at the front of borders or in gravel. They should be given protection from winter wet.
CULTIVATION Require full sun and poor, well-drained soil that is neutral to slightly alkaline.
PROPAGATION By division, in spring. From seed, sown in autumn or early spring.
POTENTIAL PROBLEMS Under glass: aphids, red spider mites; root rot.

Sisyrinchium 'Californian Skies'

S. idahoense var. bellum *W. USA*

Flowers: summer. H 5–10in (13–25cm), S 4–6in (10–15cm). FH.
The yellow throat contrasts with the deep violet-blue of the starry flowers, which are as much as 1in (2.5cm) across. The linear leaves are semi-evergreen. Hybrids in the blue colour range include **S. 'Californian Skies'**, with sky-blue flowers, and **S. 'E.K. Balls'**, with flowers of rich mauve-blue. These are both about 10in (25cm) high.

S. striatum *Argentina, Chile*
Flowers: early to mid-summer.
H 12–18in (30–45cm), S 6–12in
(15–30cm). FH.
The plain-leaved form of this
evergreen is no match ornamentally
for '**Aunt May**', with its vertical
creamy stripes on iris-like leaves.
Stiff stems zigzag above the foliage
from one small cluster of pale
yellow flowers to another. The
frost-hardy **S. californicum**, about
18in (45cm) tall, has brighter
yellow flowers with dark veining.

Sisyrinchium striatum

SMILACINA

CONVALLARIACEAE False Solomon's
seal

The foliage of the most frequently
grown species shows clearly the
link between this genus and true
Solomon's seals. Most of the 25 or
so rhizomatous perennials in the
genus are woodland plants of
central and eastern Asia as well as
North and Central America.
CULTIVATION Requires partial or
deep shade and moist, well-drained
soil, rich in organic matter, that is
lime-free.
PROPAGATION By division, in spring.
From seed, sown in autumn.
POTENTIAL PROBLEMS Usually none.

S. racemosa *Mexico, North
America*
False spikenard
Foliage: early to late spring.
Flowers: mid- to late spring.
H 30–36in (75–90cm), S 18–24in
(45–60cm). FH.
The arching stems, clothed with
strongly veined leaves that are

Smilacina racemosa

alternate but closely arranged, are
tipped with fluffy tapering heads
of creamy fragrant flowers.

SOLDANELLA

PRIMULACEAE Snowbell

In lowland gardens soldanellas do
not take kindly to winter wet but
where they do succeed these
European alpines speak modestly
but eloquently of high mountains
being freed from frost and snow.
Panes of glass and cloches look
unsightly but can be used to keep
plants dry. There are about 10
species in the genus.
CULTIVATION Tolerate full sun or
partial shade and require moist,
very well-drained soil, rich in
organic matter (equal parts lime-
free compost, leafmould and grit).
PROPAGATION By division, in early
spring. From seed, sown as soon as
ripe and subjected to cold.
POTENTIAL PROBLEMS Slugs and
snails.

Soldanella carpatica

S. alpina *Mountains of C. and
S. Europe*
Alpine snowbell
Flowers: early spring. H 3–6in
(8–15cm), S 6–9in (15–23cm). FH.
Blue-purple flowers with fringed
petals, 2 to 5 to a stem, nod above
kidney-shaped, evergreen and
fleshy leaves. The similar
S. carpatica, originating from the
western Carpathians, is said to
flower more freely.

SOLIDAGO

ASTERACEAE Aaron's rod, golden
rod

The coarse naturalized plants that
yellow waste ground in many parts
of the temperate world in late
summer and autumn with their
plume-like heads of fluffy flowers
give an idea of the pushy character
of some of the 100 or so species
in this mainly North American
genus. These are vigorous
colonizers and self-seed freely. The
best of the taller kinds of Aaron's
rod, such as the hybrid '**Golden
Wings**', which grows to 6ft (1.8m),

have their place in wild gardens
where the soil is poor. More
suitable for borders are several
smaller hybrids.
CULTIVATION Require full sun and
light, well-drained soil.
PROPAGATION By division, in
autumn or spring.
POTENTIAL PROBLEM Powdery
mildew.

Solidago 'Goldenmosa'

S. hybrids
Flowers: late summer to early
autumn. H 24–30in (60–75cm),
S 16–20in (40–50cm). FH.
'**Goldenmosa**' is widely used as a
mid-border plant, its yellow froth
reaching a height of 30in (75cm).
'**Queenie**' is only about 10in
(25cm) high and its dense heads
make a bright yellow front-of-
border plant. '**Luteus**' is often
listed under *Solidago* but belongs
to a bigeneric cross (× **Solidaster
luteus**) between a *Solidago* and an
Aster. It has larger daisy flowers
than a true Aaron's rod, and their
lemon-yellow plumes, up to 30in
(75cm) high, are attractive in the
garden over many weeks and
provide good material for cutting.

STACHYS

LAMIACEAE

Relatively few of the 300 or so
species of this genus find a place
in gardens. The species are found
in a wide range of habitats but
those in cultivation are perennials
or subshrubs that need plenty of
sun and good drainage. The
2 species described make dense
mats and are valuable ground-
covering plants. The soft hairy
lambs' ears (*S. byzantina*) is widely
used as a grey foliage plant and is
particularly valuable in frontal
positions but may not survive cold
wet winters.
CULTIVATION Require full sun and
well-drained soil (JI No.2 with
added grit).
PROPAGATION By division, in early
spring. From seed, sown in autumn
or spring.
POTENTIAL PROBLEMS Slugs;
powdery mildew.

S. byzantina *Caucasus to Iran*
Lambs' ears, lambs' lugs, lambs'
tails, lambs' tongues
Foliage: year-round. Flowers: early
summer to early autumn.
H 12–18in (30–45cm), S 1–2ft
(30–60cm). FH.
The thick grey leaves owe their
woolly texture and appearance to
a dense covering of silvery hairs.
'Silver Carpet' is non-flowering and
particularly effective in making
close ground-covering mats. Other
cultivars produce woolly square
stems with small magenta flowers,
which are less impressive than the
spike itself. **'Cotton Boll'** produces
the flower stems but dispenses
with the flowers, contenting itself
with a string of curious bobbles.

Stachys byzantina 'Silver Carpet'

S. macrantha *Caucasus,*
N.E. Turkey, N.W. Iran
Flowers: early summer to early
autumn. H 18–30in (45–75cm),
S 12–18in (30–45cm). FH.
Branching stems that emerge from
dark green clumps of wrinkled and
scalloped leaves carry whorls of
purplish-pink funnel-shaped
flowers. **'Robusta'** and **'Superba'**
are superior forms.

STOKESIA

ASTERACEAE Stokes' aster

Fringed ray florets surround the
central disk so that the
flowerheads of the single species
in this genus from south-eastern
USA have a cornflower-like
appearance. Stokes' aster, which is
found wild on moist acid soils, is a
sprawling plant that is easily
stiffened by twiggy supports and
best positioned at the front of a
moist border. The rosette of strap-
shaped leaves is evergreen. The
colourful flowers are particularly
good for cutting. A deep, dry mulch
should be provided in areas with
severe winters.
CULTIVATION Require full sun and
moist well-drained soil that is acid.
PROPAGATION From seed, sown in
autumn. By division, in spring.
From root cuttings, in late winter.
POTENTIAL PROBLEMS Usually none.

S. laevis *S.E. USA*
Flowers: mid-summer to early
autumn. H 12–18in (30–45cm),
S 16–20in (40–50cm). FH.
Regular dead-heading will help to
ensure a long succession of
flowerheads over the evergreen
foliage. The long-lasting flowerheads
are purplish blue with a creamy
centre. The white **'Alba'** is equally
appealing.

Stokesia laevis

SYMPHYTUM

BORAGINACEAE Comfrey

The watch-spring uncurling of the
buds, which open to tubular
flowers, is fascinating but most of
the 25 or so species from Europe,
North Africa and western Asia are
aggressively colonizing woodland
perennials with rhizomatous roots
that form large patches of rather
coarse foliage. They should be
confined to the wildest parts of
the garden, where they belong.
One of the best for such a position
is **S. 'Rubrum'**, which makes good
groundcover about 18in (45cm)
high with deep red flowers in
spring. The pick are those with
variegated foliage, all the better if
flower stems are cut down.
CULTIVATION Tolerate full sun or
partial shade and require moist,
fertile soil.
PROPAGATION By division, in spring.
From root cuttings, in early winter.
POTENTIAL PROBLEM Slugs when
establishing.
WARNING Contact with the foliage
may cause allergic skin reactions.
Swallowing any part of the root or
leaves may cause stomach upset.

S. × uplandicum **'Variegatum'**
Foliage: mid-spring to autumn.
Flowers: late spring to late
summer. H 30–36in (75–90cm),
S 24–30in (60–75cm). FH.
The tendency of this comfrey to
revert, which is more likely if the
roots are damaged or the plant is
grown in poor soil, is a drawback,
but the irregular cream margins of
the grey-green leaves make this a
very striking plant in shade. Its
flowers are mauve-pink. A shorter-

Symphytum × *uplandicum*
'Variegatum'

growing variegated comfrey is
the hybrid **S. 'Goldsmith'**, which
makes a mound about 1ft (30cm)
high with yellow and cream
markings on dark green. The
flowers are blue, pink or, less
frequently, cream.

Symphytum 'Goldsmith'

TANACETUM

ASTERACEAE

Two herbs belonging to this genus
of about 70 species, which are
mostly found in dry open sites in
the Northern Hemisphere, give a
misleading idea of the range the
genus encompasses. Feverfew
(**T. parthenium**) is a short-lived
but prodigal self-seeder, which in
the ornamental garden is best
represented by doubles such as
'White Bonnet' or the yellow-
leaved **'Aureum'**. More acridly
aromatic is tansy (**T. vulgare**), fast
spreading but with attractively
dissected leaves, especially in the
curly-leaved **var. crispum**, and
yellow button flowerheads.
Pyrethrums (**T. coccineum**) are
attractive and colourful daisies for
borders and cutting and several
grey-leaved plants are suitable for
rock gardens or edging. They give a
second display if cut back after the
first flush.
CULTIVATION Require full sun and
very well-drained soil.
PROPAGATION By division, in spring
or after flowering. From seed, sown
in early spring at 50–55°F
(10–13°C).
POTENTIAL PROBLEMS Aphids, leaf
miners, chrysanthemum eelworm.

WARNING Contact with the foliage may aggravate skin allergies.

T. coccineum *Caucasus, S.W. Asia*
Painted daisy, pyrethrum
Flowers: early summer. H 18–36in (45–90cm), S 16–20in (40–50cm). FH.
Feathery bright green foliage is topped by yellow-centred daisy flowerheads. These are up to 3in (8cm) across in the single and double cultivars, which range in colour from white to pink and crimson. The single **'Brenda'** is a vivid cerise pink.

Tanacetum coccineum 'Brenda'

T. densum subsp. *amani*
Turkey
Foliage: spring to mid-winter.
Flowers: late summer. H 6–8in (15–20cm), S 10–16in (25–40cm). FH.
Felted, deeply cut leaves make low silvery mounds, which some gardeners find more appealing without the clusters of yellow flowers. *T. haradjanii* is similar but slightly larger in leaf and the flowerheads do not have ray florets.

TELLIMA

SAXIFRAGACEAE Fringe cups

The saxifrage family provides in the single species of the genus yet another good plant for groundcover. In the wild this evergreen is found in moist forest and woodland over a large area of western North America. As a garden plant it is at its best in light shade where the soil is moist. Nevertheless, it is remarkably drought-tolerant.
CULTIVATION Tolerate full sun and dry soil, but best in moist soil, rich in organic matter, and partial shade.
PROPAGATION By division, in spring. From seed, sown as soon as ripe.
POTENTIAL PROBLEM Slugs.

T. grandiflora *E. North America (Alaska to California)*
Flowers: late spring to mid-summer. H 18–24in (45–60cm), S 12–18in (30–45cm). FH.
The hairy leaves, which are round and scalloped, take on crimson

Tellima grandiflora **Rubra Group**

tints in autumn. The numerous tiny bells, carried on erect spikes, open greenish yellow but develop a pink tinge as they age. The leaves of the **Rubra Group** are reddish purple on the underside and colour richly in autumn and winter.

THALICTRUM

RANUNCULACEAE Meadow rue

The best of the thalictrums manage to be stately in their general effect but dainty in their detail, with delicate foliage and fluffy or airy heads of small flowers. There are more than 120 species, most of them plants of the temperate Northern Hemisphere found wild in meadows and woodland, usually in moist soil and often in light shade. The species described are distinguished border plants but the more fine-boned are best among sheltering shrubs that give them some support. Staking is almost fatal to their charm.
CULTIVATION Tolerate full sun or partial shade and a wide range of soils but best in well-drained but moist soil, preferably neutral to acid, with plenty of organic matter.
PROPAGATION By division, in early spring. From seed, sown as soon as ripe or in early spring.
POTENTIAL PROBLEMS Slugs; powdery mildew.

T. aquilegiifolium *Europe to temperate Asia*
Foliage: late spring to late summer.
Flowers: early summer. H 2–3ft (60–90cm), S 18–24in (45–60cm). FH.

Thalictrum aquilegiifolium

The specific name draws attention to the fans of columbine-like foliage, which are carried on purple stems. These are topped by sprays of tiny purplish buds that open to misty clusters of mauve-pink stamens. In **'Thundercloud'** the stamens are dark purple.

T. delavayi *E. Tibet to W. China*
Flowers: mid-summer to early autumn. H 4–5ft (1.2–1.5m), S 18–24in (45–60cm). FH.
The refined foliage is matched by the swaying grace of large open heads of tiny pendent flowers, their purple sepals opening to show creamy stamens. There is a lovely white, **'Album'**, and in **'Hewitt's Double'** an explosion of tiny mauve-blue pompons is magically suspended in mid-air.

Thalictrum delavayi

T. flavum *Europe to Caucasus and Siberia*
Yellow meadow rue
Flowers: summer. H 4–5ft (1.2–1.5m), S 16–20in (40–50cm). FH.
This species, with fragrant yellow flowers, is coarser than the others described, but subsp. *glaucum* is impressive in stature and in the combination of blue-grey foliage and pale yellow, fluffy flowers.

TIARELLA

SAXIFRAGACEAE Foam flower

The common name suggests that the flowers are the principal feature of the half dozen or so woodland plants that make up this genus. The airy sprays of small flowers are delightful in spring and early summer but the foliage is of more enduring appeal and, in this respect, the genus is similar to the closely related *Heuchera*. The best-known species are North American but the genus is also represented in eastern Asia.
CULTIVATION Require deep or partial shade and moist, cool soil that is rich in organic matter.
PROPAGATION From seed, as soon as ripe or in spring. By division, in spring.
POTENTIAL PROBLEM Slugs.

T. cordifolia *North America*
Foam flower
Foliage: autumn. Flowers: late spring to early summer. H 6–12in (15–30cm), S 10–14in (25–35cm). FH. Creeping rhizomes ensure a good, even excessive, cover of greenish yellow, hairy leaves, which are gently lobed, have a serrated outline and are deeply veined. Erect stems carry the foaming floral display of tiny, creamy white stars.

T. wherryi *USA (Appalachians)*
Foliage: autumn. Flowers: late spring to early summer. H 8–12in (20–30cm), S 8–14in (20–35cm). FH. This species, which does not have the wandering root system of **T. cordifolia**, slowly builds up a clump of maple-like leaves. Variations of foliage colouring in the wild are reflected in several named clones, '**Bronze Beauty**' showing a mixture of green and purplish brown. Flower colour ranges from white to pale pink.

Tiarella wherryi

TOLMIEA

SAXIFRAGACEAE Pick-a-back plant, youth-on-age

The common names of the single species in this genus refer to the way young plants are produced on the leaves. In the wild it is found spreading freely on the floor of coniferous woodland. Although it is widely grown as a house plant, it makes effective groundcover under shrubs and trees, protected from strong sun, which will scorch the leaves.
CULTIVATION Require partial or deep shade and cool moist soil that is rich in organic matter (JI No.2).
PROPAGATION By division, in spring. By removal of leaf plantlets, in mid- to late summer. From seed, sown in autumn.
POTENTIAL PROBLEMS Usually none.

T. menziesii *W. North America*
Pick-a-back plant, thousand mothers, youth-on-age
Flowers: late spring to early summer. H 12–20in (30–50cm), S 18–24in (45–60cm). FH.

The hairy leaves, lobed and toothed so that they strongly resemble those of *Tiarella cordifolia*, are more important ornamentally than the spires of small, slightly fragrant, purplish brown flowers. '**Taff's Gold**' has pale green leaves irregularly speckled with pale yellow.

Tolmiea menziesii '**Taff's Gold**'

TRADESCANTIA

COMMELINACEAE Spiderwort

The very varied species in this genus, totalling about 65 and coming from a range of habitats in North, Central and South America, include several, like the wandering Jew (**T. fluminensis**), that are best known as house or conservatory plants. A foliage, mat-forming species, it is most suitable for hanging baskets. The most familiar of the spiderworts seen in temperate gardens are hybrids derived in part from **T. virginiana**. These all show a preference for moist conditions, although they are prone to making leafy growth at the expense of flowers if they are grown in a highly fertile soil.
CULTIVATION Tolerate full sun or partial shade and require moist soil.
PROPAGATION By division of hardy species and cultivars, in spring or autumn.
POTENTIAL PROBLEMS Grubs, aphids, vine weevil.
WARNING Contact with the foliage may irritate the skin.

T. × andersoniana
Flowers: early summer to early autumn. H and S 18–24in (45–60cm). FH.
Although individual blooms are short-lived, they come in a long succession, small clusters of 3-petalled flowers, which have a fluff of stamen filaments in the centre, spilling from between grooved leaves at the top of the flower stems. The foliage somewhat mars the effect, the amount of coarse untidy leaves being disproportionate to the flowers. The colour range includes white, blue-purple, pink and red-purple.

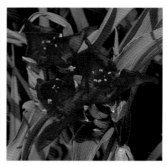

Tradescantia × *andersoniana* '**Isis**'

'**Isis**' has large dark blue flowers, while '**J.C. Weguelin**' has large mauve-blue blooms with blue fluff in the centre. Cutting back flowered stems prevents seeding and encourages the production of further flowers.

Tradescantia × *andersoniana* '**J.C. Weguelin**'

TRICYRTIS

CONVALLARIACEAE Toad lily

The waxy speckled flowers of the toad lilies hold a unique fascination that makes these perennials worth planting wherever their detail can be enjoyed. The strap-shaped segments open to form a dished star with a sturdy arrangement of stamens and styles in the centre. There are about 16 species, all found in Asia, mainly in rugged and wooded habitats where the soil is moist. When they are grown at the margins of their hardiness, they should be protected in winter with a deep mulch.
CULTIVATION Require deep or partial shade and moist, well-drained soil that is rich in organic matter.
PROPAGATION By division, in early spring. From seed, sown as soon as ripe.
POTENTIAL PROBLEMS Slugs and snails.

T. formosana *Taiwan*
Flowers: early autumn. H and S 2–3ft (60–90cm). FH.
Gently zigzagging stems clothed in glossy oval leaves, which are deeply veined, carry branched heads of upward-facing pale mauve flowers, heavily spotted with purple.

T. hirta *Japan*
Flowers: late summer to mid-autumn. H and S 24–30in (60–75cm). FH.
The pale green leaves of this clump-forming species are hairy and the purple-spotted white flowers are borne in the leaf axils. '**Miyazaki**' has large flowers and a yellow edge to the leaves.

Tricyrtis hirta 'Miyazaki'

TRILLIUM

TRILLIACEAE Trinity flower, wood lily

The arrangement of leaves, petals and calyces in threes is the hallmark of this mainly North American genus of 30 or so woodland species. Their numerical obsession is not the only factor contributing to their homogeneous character, for they are all plants preferring cool moist conditions and fertile soil well laced with leafmould. Most are, at the least, fascinating and several are plants of sublime radiance and poise, justifying a prime position in a woodland garden. The dwarf species, such as *T. rivale*, with white or pale pink flowers lightly spotted purple, are prize plants for raised beds on acid soils.
CULTIVATION Require partial or deep shade and well-drained but moist soil, preferably neutral to acid, that contains plenty of organic matter.
PROPAGATION By rhizome division, in late summer or autumn. From seed, sown as soon as ripe.
POTENTIAL PROBLEMS Slugs and snails.

T. chloropetalum *USA (California)*
Flowers: early spring. H and S 12–18in (30–45cm). FH.
The fragrant flowers, which are usually greenish white but also yellow or purplish brown, stand erect above foliage that is mottled with grey-green and maroon. The smaller toad-shade (**T. sessile**), usually less than 1ft (30cm) high, which also has marbled and blotched leaves, has maroon

flowers with narrow petals standing erect above spread-out sepals. Both sepals and petals are usually a shade of deep maroon.

Trillium chloropetalum

T. grandiflorum *E. North America*
Wake robin
Flowers: late spring to early summer. H and S 12–18in (30–45cm). FH.
This is the unrivalled queen of the genus, carrying its veined but pristine white flowers, backed by green sepals, above a low mound of dark green leaves. When fully open, the flowers are almost triangular in outline, despite the wavy margin of the petals and their recurved tips. The double '**Flore Pleno**' defies all reservations that purists might have about double flowers.

Trillium grandiflorum

TROLLIUS

RANUNCULACEAE Globeflower

A liking for moisture characterizes the 20 or so species of the buttercup-like, clump-forming globeflower, which are found throughout the temperate regions of the Northern Hemisphere. In gardens they are generally represented by a range of hybrids but one of the parents, the common European globeflower (**T. europaeus**), which is found in north-eastern North America as well as Europe, is not to be overlooked. The cool radiance of its exquisite, pale yellow orbs is as telling in the garden as it is in the subalpine meadows where it is most commonly found in the wild.

Globeflowers naturalized near water brighten a wild or semi-wild garden in late spring and early summer, but their early flowering season also makes them valuable for borders where the soil does not dry out.
CULTIVATION Tolerate full sun or partial shade but best in sun where the soil is permanently moist, as in a bog garden.
PROPAGATION By division, in early spring. From seed, sown as soon as ripe or in spring.
POTENTIAL PROBLEM Powdery mildew.

Trollius europaeus

T. × cultorum
Flowers: mid-spring to mid-summer. H 2–3ft (60–90cm), S 18–24in (45–60cm). FH.
The hybrids that go under this name make strong clumps of lobed and jaggedly toothed leaves, the globular flowers held well clear of this attractive glossy green base by erect stems. All have flowers in the yellow to orange range. '**Feuertroll**' and '**Orange Princess**' are in shades of orange, while '**Goldquelle**' is yellow. '**Alabaster**' is a less vigorous hybrid, growing to 2ft (60cm) in height, but the yellowed ivory of its flowers is unique.

Trollius × cultorum 'Alabaster'

UVULARIA

CONVALLARIACEAE Merrybells

The woodland plants in this North American genus of 5 species are shy and easily overlooked if not positioned prominently in a shady border or raised bed.

CULTIVATION Require deep or partial shade and moist, well-drained soil that is rich in organic matter.
PROPAGATION By division, in early spring. From seed, sown as soon as ripe.
POTENTIAL PROBLEMS Slugs and snails.

U. grandiflora *E. North America*
Large merrybells
Flowers: mid- to late spring.
H 24–30in (60–75cm), 9–12in (23–30cm). FH.
The drooping foliage and the dangling yellow flowers with their curiously twisted yellow segments convey the impression that the plant is just pulling itself out of a heavy torpor. The shorter
U. perfoliata, about 18in (45cm) high, is slightly later flowering and the flowers are paler.

Uvularia grandiflora

VERATRUM

MELANTHIACEAE

The genus comprises nearly 50 species, of which only a handful is in general cultivation. Even these are somewhat neglected, perhaps because they are so slow to reach flowering size from seed. Plants of moist ground in woodland or meadows in the Northern Hemisphere, they achieve their full splendour in rich, well-watered soil, preferably lightly shaded, and where a *cordon sanitaire* keeps drooling slugs at bay.
CULTIVATION Tolerate sun or partial shade and require moist, well-drained soil, rich in organic matter.
PROPAGATION By division, in autumn. From seed, sown as soon as ripe.
POTENTIAL PROBLEMS Slugs and snails.
WARNING Contact with the foliage may irritate the skin. All parts are very toxic if swallowed.

V. nigrum *Europe to China, Korea, Siberia*
Foliage: spring to late summer.
Flowers: mid- to late summer.
H 2–5ft (60–150cm), S 18–24in (45–60cm). FH.

Deeply veined and pleated leaves, up to 1ft (30cm) long, mound to form an impressive base from which rises a tall stem, its short branches densely set with small starry flowers of purple-black or maroon. In its funereal distinction, this species outclasses the false or white hellebore (*V. album*), with greenish white flowers.

Veratrum nigrum

VERBASCUM

SCROPHULARIACEAE Mullein

The genus of more than 350 species from Europe, North Africa and west and central Asia, includes many biennials, among them *V. bombyciferum*, which is silvered with fine hairs. Even most of the perennials, such as the purple mullein (*V. phoeniceum*), tend to be short-lived. Numerous species survive in very dry, stony landscapes and most need an open position. They are ideal for growing in gravel or sunny borders. Shorter mulleins, such as *V. 'Letitia'*, up to 1ft (30cm) with bright yellow flowers, are suitable for sunny rock gardens or raised beds.
CULTIVATION Require full sun and poor well-drained soil that is alkaline (JI No. 2).
PROPAGATION From seed, sown in late spring or early summer. By division, in spring. From root cuttings, in winter.
POTENTIAL PROBLEMS Figwort weevils, moth caterpillars; powdery mildew.

V. chaixii *C., E. and S. Europe*
Nettle-leaved mullein
Flowers: mid- to late summer.
H 3–4ft (90–120cm), S 18–24in (45–60cm). FH.
The plant is anchored by a semi-evergreen rosette of hairy basal leaves, from which rises a felted stem densely set with pale yellow flowers with a bruised purple eye.

V. 'Helen Johnson'
Flowers: early to late summer.
H 30–36in (75–90cm), S 12–16in (30–40cm). FH.
Purple-tinted copper and buff, soft-textured flowers combined with grey foliage, felted stems and woolly buds is a designer success.

Verbascum 'Helen Johnson'

VERBENA

VERBENACEAE

The colourful hybrid verbenas that are popular as bedding and container plants have stolen the limelight from the 250 or so species, most of which come from warm temperate or tropical areas of North, Central or South America. Although the hybrids are perennials, they are half-hardy and almost invariably grown as annuals. This option is usually followed for the few species that are grown in gardens, such as the tuberous *V. rigida,* with its fragrant bright purple flowers. The wiry *V. bonariensis*, at first sight so unlike the hybrid verbenas, makes a tall and airy addition to dry sunny borders and is excellent planted in gravel. It is most attractive when allowed to self-seed and form irregular colonies with outliers nosing their way into other plants. See also ANNUALS AND BIENNIALS.
CULTIVATION Require full sun and well-drained moist soil.
PROPAGATION From seed, sown in autumn or spring. By division, in spring.
POTENTIAL PROBLEMS Aphids, thrips, leafhoppers, slugs; powdery mildew.

Verbena rigida

Verbena bonariensis

V. bonariensis *South America (Brazil to Argentina)*
Flowers: mid-summer to early autumn. H 4–6ft (1.2–1.8m), S 18–24in (45–60cm). FrH.
An angular framework of rigid branching stems rising from a base of rough leaves supports numerous tight clusters of small purplish pink flowers over a long season. The flowers are fragrant and attractive to butterflies.

VERONICA

SCROPHULARIACEAE Speedwell

Although the colour range of the speedwells includes white and pink, it is their blues that stand out in the garden and even make of the irrepressible white-eyed *V. filiformis* a very beautiful weed. There are about 250 species of annuals, perennials and subshrubs, most of which are natives of Europe. They are found in a wide range of habitats, including swampy ground, dappled shade under trees, grasslands and rocky slopes. A number of low-growing species, including several alpines, are plants of open sites where the ground drains freely; they are suitable for rock gardens, the front of borders, and for planting among paving or in gravel. The taller species tend to be plants of richer, moister soils.
CULTIVATION Tolerate full sun or partial shade and require well-drained, loamy, moist soil (equal parts loam, leafmould and grit).
PROPAGATION From seed, sown in autumn. By division, in spring or autumn.
POTENTIAL PROBLEMS Powdery mildew, downy mildew, leaf spot.

V. austriaca subsp. **teucrium**
Europe
Flowers: summer. H and S 1–2ft (30–60cm). FH.
This low-growing plant is usually represented in gardens by named clones that are outstanding for the intensity of their blue spikes. The gentian brilliance of '**Crater Lake Blue**', 1ft (30cm) high, is almost

matched by the blue of the slightly taller '**Kapitän**'. The short spikes of a similar species, *V. prostrata*, are also upright but the stems lie close to the ground. In '**Trehane**' the deep blue flowers are set against yellow-tinged foliage.

Veronica austriaca subsp. teucrium
'Crater Lake Blue'

V. cinerea *E. Mediterranean, Turkey*
Flowers: early summer. H 4–6in (10–15cm), S 9–12in (23–30cm). FH.
The flowers are tiny but their blue strikes a piercing note against the dense silvery mat of felted leaves.

V. gentianoides *Caucasus, N. and C. Turkey, Ukraine (Crimea)*
Flowers: early summer. H and S 9–18in (23–45cm). FH.
Spikes of pale blue flowers rising from mats of fleshy dark green leaves make cool short verticals for the front of borders or large rock gardens.

V. peduncularis *Caucasus, Turkey, Ukraine*
Flowers: early spring to early summer. H 3–4in (8–10cm), S 24–30in (60–75cm). FH.
A low mat or cushion of purple-tinged leaves is swamped in mid-summer by white-eyed blue flowers of saucer shape. '**Georgia Blue**' is a free-flowering cultivar.

Veronica spicata subsp. incana
'Nana'

V. spicata *Europe, C. and E. Asia*
Flowers: early to late summer. H 1–2ft (30–60cm), S 6–12in (15–30cm). FH.

The cone-shaped flower spikes stand up from a mat of grey-green leaves, pink in '**Heidekind**' and white in '**Icicle**', variations on the bright blue, star-shaped flowers of the species. The hairy foliage of **subsp.** *incana*, the silver speedwell, is very grey and a pleasing base for the spikes of blue-purple flowers. '**Nana**' has violet-blue flowers.

VIOLA

VIOLACEAE

Generations of gardeners have felt a strong attachment to this genus, so striking in its contrasts of reserve and pertness. There are about 500 species, annuals and biennials in the genus, as well as perennials, which are found in a wide range of habitats in temperate regions of the world. Relatively few of these are seen outside specialist collections; complex hybrids resulting from crosses between a small group of species account for the important role of the genus in gardens. The garden pansies (*V. × wittrockiana*) – and the European heartsease (*V. tricolor*) which is one of the parents of this large group – are short-lived perennials that are usually grown as biennials. The hybrid violas (and the smaller violettas, which are similar to violas but even more compact, sweetly fragrant and with no lines radiating from the central eye) are longer-lived. However, their heavy flowering takes its toll and these plants need to be propagated on a regular basis. The plants that are described here have many uses but they are particularly effective as a skirt to larger perennials and shrubs, at the front of borders and in the rock garden. Regular dead-heading prolongs the flowering season. Straggly plants of *V. cornuta* and hybrid violas that are cut back in mid-summer will make fresh growth and flower again during late summer and autumn. See also ANNUALS AND BIENNIALS.
CULTIVATION Tolerate full sun or partial shade and require well-drained soil that is moist and fertile (JI No.2 with added leafmould and grit).
PROPAGATION From basal cuttings, taken in the second half of summer. From seed, sown as soon as ripe or in spring.
POTENTIAL PROBLEMS Slugs and snails, aphids, red spider mites, violet leaf midges; powdery mildew, leaf spot, rust, mosaic viruses.

Viola cornuta **Alba Group**

V. cornuta *Spain (Pyrenees)*

Horned violet, viola
Flowers: late spring to late
summer. H 6-12in (15-30cm),
S 15-24in (38-60cm). FH.
The horned violet has played an
important role in the development
of hybrid violas. It is, though, a
generous and endearing viola in its
own right, filling in the leggy bases
of other plants, even climbing
among them and showing off over
a long season with a prodigious
display of mauve-blue flowers. The
white of the **Alba Group** is
unbeatable in shade and all the
gradations of blue and purple are
worth a place in the garden.

Viola 'Jackanapes'

V. hybrids

Tufted pansy, viola
Flowers: spring to autumn. H 4-8in
(10-20cm), S 6-12in (15-30cm).
FH.
Spreading stems clothed in
toothed leaves carry masses of
flowers over a long season. Some
cultivars spread freely by
underground shoots. Most are
lightly scented, some are very
fragrant and all, as the following,
have a lively charm: '**Huntercombe
Purple**', deep violet-purple with a
tiny white eye; '**Irish Molly**', velvety
and an unusual mixture of bronze
and lime-green; '**Jackanapes**',
small-flowered, with red-brown top
petals and rays on the rich yellow
lower petals; '**Maggie Mott**', pale
mauve with a cream centre and
well scented; '**Molly Sanderson**',
matt black with a tiny yellow eye;
and '**Vita**', small-flowered, pale pink
with a yellow eye.

V. odorata *S. and W. Europe*

English violet, garden violet, sweet
violet
Flowers: late winter to early
spring. H 4-6in (10-15cm),
S 12-18in (30-45cm). FH.
The species, with sweetly scented
blue or white flowers, spreads by
stolons and self-seeds freely in
shady, moist places. Some of the
hybrids derived from it, which
were once grown commercially on
a vast scale, are still available.
V. '**Czar**' is long-stemmed and the
large flowers are a rich purple.

V. riviniana *Europe, N. Africa*

Common dog violet, wood violet
Flowers: late spring to early
summer. H 4-8in (10-20cm),
S 10-16in (25-40cm). FH.
Although its running growth soon
makes it a nuisance elsewhere, in
the wild garden the blue-purple,
scentless flowers of the common
dog violet set among heart-shaped
leaves are a lovely discovery. The
dark purple leaves and light purple
flowers of the **Purpurea Group** are
seen at their best contrasted with
light colours.

V. sororia *E. North America*

Sister violet, woolly blue violet
Flowers: late spring to summer.
H 4-6in (10-15cm), S 6-8in
(15-20cm). FH.
The species is unremarkable, with
leaves that are hairy on the
underside and flowers that are
violet-blue or white with streaking
and speckling, but '**Freckles**', its
cultivar, has caught the imagination
of gardeners with its spray-gunned
spotting of purplish blue.

ZANTEDESCHIA

ARACEAE

All 6 species in this genus of aroids
are moisture-lovers and in their
home territory of southern and
East Africa they are found near
open water or in swampy ground.
The hardiest species is *Z. aethiopica*
but in frost-prone areas the fleshy
rhizomes need to be set deeply in
mud and protected with a mulch
in winter. It can also be grown as a
marginal aquatic in water no
deeper than 1ft (30cm).
CULTIVATION Require full sun and
moist soil, rich in organic matter
(JI No.2).
PROPAGATION By division, in spring.
From seed, sown as soon as ripe at
70-81°F (21-27°C).
POTENTIAL PROBLEMS Aphids; fungal
diseases, various viruses.
WARNING Contact with the sap
may irritate the skin. Swallowing
any part may cause stomach upset.

Z. aethiopica *Lesotho, South Africa*

Arum lily
Foliage: spring to autumn. Flowers:
late spring to mid-summer. H 3-4ft
(90-120cm), S 20-30in (50-75cm).
FrH.
Dense clumps of glossy, arrow-
shaped leaves make a lovely
contrast to the lines of grasses and
reeds near water. The flower-like
white spathe swirls with a couturier
flourish around the yellow spadix,
on which the tiny true flowers are
clustered. '**Crowborough**' is said to
be a particularly hardy clone. In
'**Green Goddess**' the flowers are
large and green except for a white
throat.

Zantedeschia aethiopica

ZAUSCHNERIA

ONAGRACEAE Californian fuchsia

The 4 species in this genus are from
dry stony habitats in western North
America. Their tubular bright red
flowers, borne profusely from late
summer to autumn, make a bright
shower on a stepped rock garden.
CULTIVATION Require full sun and
light well-drained soil.
PROPAGATION From basal cuttings,
in spring. By division, in spring.
POTENTIAL PROBLEM Slugs.

Z. californica *USA (California)*

Flowers: late summer to early
autumn. H 12-18in (30-45cm),
S 18-24in (45-60cm). FH.
The woody based species is
variable; **subsp.** *cana* has scarlet
flowers and hairy, narrow, usually
evergreen leaves. '**Dublin**', brilliant
in flower, is deciduous.

Zauschneria californica **subsp.** *cana*

bulbs, corms and tubers

Bulbs are the making of the temperate garden in spring, when there are still few perennials and shrubs that can rival them for brilliance. Using a strict definition of a bulb, this section should cover only plants, typified by daffodils (*Narcissus*), with an underground storage organ consisting of fleshy scales attached to a basal plate. However, in general use the term bulb covers a range of storage organs. Crocuses and gladioli have swollen stem bases known as corms while the swollen rootstocks of cyclamen are tubers. Although several bulbs have interesting foliage, it is the flowers, often deliciously fragrant, that make them winning ornamentals. They achieve perfection in a woodland garden or meadow (see p. 73 and pp. 64–65 respectively) but are equally valuable in beds or borders and containers. The lilies provide a summer wave of superlative plants, their greatest fault as a group being a susceptibility to viruses.

The entries give advice on the best time for planting and suitable planting depths. Many bulbs are long-lived and can be left in the ground to flower from year to year. It is important, however, to let the foliage die down naturally. In many cases bulbs multiply very freely from offsets as well as from seed.

Top **Crocus chrysanthus** 'Zwanenburg Bronze'
Centre **Colchicum agrippinum**
Bottom **Crocosmia** × **crocosmiiflora** 'Emily McKenzie'

ALLIUM

ALLIACEAE Onion

Among approximately 700 species in this large genus of mainly bulbous plants several are of inestimable culinary value. These include chives, garlic, leeks and onions. The onion or garlic smell haunts even the most ornamental species but is rarely obtrusive except when leaves are bruised. The predominance of purplish mauve in the flower colour is a limitation and, in the case of many species, the dying back of foliage before or just as the flowers develop calls for skilful masking of the base. Some species can be bothersome weeds. Even yellow-flowered *A. moly* is best kept in the wild garden. The real strength of the genus lies in the number of bulbs it contains that thrive in sunny dry gardens, even those that endure long parching summers. Some graceful small species, like the blue-flowered *A. beesianum* W.W. Smith and *A. cyaneum* from China, are suitable for rock gardens. Others, including most of those described here, are impressive in scale and ideal for planting among shrubs and perennials that thrive in Mediterranean conditions. In some species the umbels dry to make attractive winter decorations.
CULTIVATION Require full sun and well-drained soil. Plant in autumn, with bulbs covered to a depth 3 to 4 times the height of the bulb.
PROPAGATION From offsets of bulbous species, in autumn. By division of rhizomatous species, in spring. From seed, sown as soon as ripe.
POTENTIAL PROBLEMS Onion fly; fungal diseases, such as white rot.
WARNING Contact with the bulbs may cause an allergic reaction.

A. atropurpureum E. Europe
Flowers: late spring to early summer. H 2–3ft (60–90cm), S 8–10in (20–25cm). FH.
The purplish black depths of the wine-red flowers make this plant one of the most richly coloured in the onion family. The small starry flowers, 2in (5cm) across, are borne in a hemispherical head.

A. caeruleum N. and C. Asia
Flowers: early summer. H 1–2ft (30–60cm), S 2–3in (5–8cm). FrH.
The linear, mid-green, stem-clasping leaves die back by the time stiff stems carry tight heads, up to 1⅜in (4cm) across, of star-shaped, sky-blue flowers. This species sometimes produces bulbils in the flowerhead.

Allium cristophii

A. cristophii C. Asia, Turkey
Flowers: early summer. H 10–20in (25–50cm), S 6–8in (15–20cm). FrH.
The size of the spherical heads, up to 8in (20cm) across, and the metallic glint of the purple flowers, of which there may be up to 80 in a head, make this eye-catching. The dried heads are highly ornamental.

A. flavum S. and E. Europe
Flowers: mid- to late summer. H 4–12in (10–30cm), S 2–3in (5–8cm). FH.
There are dwarf forms of this variable species that make attractive plants for rock gardens and raised beds. The pale yellow, bell-shaped flowers are usually produced in a loose head. The flowers droop but the seedheads are carried erect.

A. giganteum C. Asia
Flowers: early summer. H 3–5ft (90–150cm), S 6–8in (15–20cm). FH.
To be seen to best effect this impressive species should be planted so that the basal leaves, which die back before flowering, are obscured. The ball-like heads, about 4in (10cm) across, are packed with purplish pink flowers.

Allium hollandicum 'Purple Sensation'

A. hollandicum C. Asia
Flowers: early summer. H 24–30in (60–75cm), S 4–6in (10–15cm). FH.
The spherical heads are as much as 4in (10cm) across and are tightly packed with starry, purplish-pink flowers. The strawy seedheads are also an asset. In '**Purple Sensation**' the flowers are of a richer purple.

A. karataviense C. Asia
Flowers: late spring to early summer. H 6–10in (15–25cm), S 4–6in (10–15cm). FH.
Unlike many alliums, the leaves, broad and purplish grey, are attractive in the flowering season. The pale-pink flowers, 50 or more in a head that is up to 4in (10cm) across, dry attractively.

Allium karataviense

A. oreophilum C. Asia
Flowers: early to mid-summer. H 4–8in (10–20cm), S 2–3in (5–8cm). FH.
The rich purplish pink flowers are larger than in most species and carried in a loose head about 1½in (4cm) in diameter. When dry, they are pale beige. '**Zwanenburg**' has flowers of exceptionally rich pink.

A. rosenbachianum C. Asia
Flowers: late spring to early summer. H 20–36in (50–90cm), S 4–6in (10–15cm). FrH.
This is a handsome bulb to plant in drifts. The tall naked stems support spherical heads, 4in (10cm) across, densely packed with small purple flowers, from which protrude violet stamens.

AMARYLLIS

AMARYLLIDACEAE

In warm climates the single species in this genus makes a spectacular appearance in open ground at the onset of the autumn rains. In cooler climates it needs a warm and sheltered position outdoors so that it gets a good summer baking. Under glass it needs a position in full light.
CULTIVATION Requires full sun and fertile, well-drained soil (JI No. 2 with additional sharp sand). Plant in mid-summer, with the top of the bulb just covered.
PROPAGATION From seed, sown as soon as ripe and kept at a temperature of 16°C (61°F); plants raised this way are likely to take 8 years to flower. By division, as soon as leaves die back in summer.
POTENTIAL PROBLEMS Slugs, narcissus bulb fly.

Amaryllis belladonna

A. belladonna *South Africa*
Belladonna lily
Flowers: early to mid-autumn.
H 24-30in (60-75cm), S 4-6in
(10-15cm). FrH.
Purplish stems emerge in autumn
before the leaves and bear an
impressive head of 3 to 4 trumpet
flowers, sometimes more, each
4-6in (10-15cm) across and sweetly
scented. They are commonly
bright pink; the strap-shaped
leaves that emerge after the
flowers last until mid-summer.

ANEMONE

RANUNCULACEAE Windflower

The spring-flowering anemones,
which grow from tubers and
rhizomes can either be modest
woodlanders, ideal for naturalizing
under deciduous trees and among
shrubs, or bright plants suitable for
growing in sunny rock gardens. In
all of the 120 species the petal-like
segments of the flowers surround
a conspicuous boss of stamens.
See also PERENNIALS.
CULTIVATION A. coronaria and
A. × fulgens require full sun and
well-drained soil (JI No. 2 with
added grit). Others listed do well
in dappled shade. *A. nemorosa*
needs moist soil (JI No. 2 with
added organic matter). Plant in
early to mid-autumn; cover with
1½-2in (4-5cm) of soil or compost.
PROPAGATION By division, in late
summer. From offsets, in late
summer.
POTENTIAL PROBLEMS The hybrids
of *A. coronaria* are susceptible to
viral and fungal diseases.

Anemone blanda

A. blanda *S. to E. Europe, Turkey*
Flowers: early to mid-spring.
H 4-6in (10-15cm), S 4-6in
(10-15cm). FH.
One of the loveliest of early spring
flowers, this species, which grows
from a rounded tuber, is most
beguiling when naturalized in
short turf, in the open or under a
light deciduous canopy. It does
particularly well on chalk. The
finely divided leaves emerge before
the yellow-centred flowers, which
have 10-20 segments in shades of
blue, pink and mauve or in white.
Cultivars include: **'Ingramii'**, deep
blue; **'Radar'**, purplish pink with a
white centre; **var. rosea**, pink; and
'White Splendour', brilliant white.

Anemone coronaria

A. coronaria *Mediterranean*
Flowers: early to mid-spring.
H 6-18in (15-45cm), S 4-6in
(10-15cm). FH.
The knobbly tubers give no hint of
the charm of the flowers, in the
wild studding open ground with
blooms in red, purple, blue or
white, 5 to 8 segments surrounding
the central knob. The species has
been displaced in gardens by
single- and double-flowered hybrids
between *A. coronaria* and closely
related species. By manipulation of
the planting time and forcing these
can be brought into flower at
almost any season. The **De Caen
Group** is a race of giant single
anemones producing many
flowers over a long season. **'Die
Braut'** is semi-double, a hint of
green at the centre setting off the
white segments. The **Saint Brigid
Group** includes giant doubles and
semi-doubles in a good colour
range but these flower less
prolifically than the singles.

A. × fulgens
Flowers: spring. H 10-12in (25-
30cm), S 4-6in (10-15cm). FH.
The Mediterranean peacock
anemone (**A. pavonia**), usually red,
blue or pink in flower, is a parent
of this hybrid. It can be planted to
create a drift of brilliant scarlet.
The flowers, up to 2in (5cm)
across, have narrow segments.

Anemone × fulgens

A. nemorosa *Europe*
Flowers: early to mid-spring.
H 4-8in (10-20cm), S 6-8in
(15-20cm). FH.
The creeping rhizomes of this
species spread freely in woodland
where the soil is moist, creating
sheets of nodding white flowers,
often suffused with pink or mauve
on the outside, over finely cut
leaves. Few plants so artlessly
establish a feeling of naturalness in
a woodland garden. Most of the
selections available have larger
flowers and stronger colouring
than the type. In **'Allenii'** the
flowers, stained mauve on the
outside, surround yellow stamens
with pale blue. **'Robinsoniana'** has
flowers of exquisite mauve-blue.

Anemone nemorosa 'Robinsoniana'

ARISAEMA

ARACEAE

In addition to the large number of
tropical aroids, there are several
from temperate zones which have
flowers of fascinating, even
sinister, appeal and attractive
foliage. In the case of aroids the
term "flower" is used loosely for
the funnel-like bract or spathe,
often hooded, that surrounds the
spadix. Here at its base cluster the
insignificant true flowers. In some
species, including jack-in-the-pulpit
(**A. triphyllum**), the berries are a
conspicuous feature during the
autumn. There are well over 100
species in this genus of tuberous
and rhizomatous perennials. Often
they do not make growth above
ground before early summer so
care must be taken when working

around other plantings in spring. Those described below and other reasonably hardy species do well when planted under a light deciduous canopy, in cool raised beds or in a cool greenhouse.

CULTIVATION Require light shade and neutral to acid soil that is moist and rich in organic matter (JI No. 2 with added leafmould and grit). Plant the tubers in mid-autumn; cover with 3–6in (8–15cm) of soil or compost.

PROPAGATION From offsets, taken in summer, when the leaves have died down.

POTENTIAL PROBLEMS Slugs, vine weevils.

Arisaema candidissimum

A. candidissimum *W. China*
Flowers: early summer. H 10–12in (25–30cm), S 4–6in (10–15cm). FrH.

The spathe, which appears before the leaves, consists of a tube opening out into a hood that terminates in a short tail. It is white with vertical stripes, usually of green at the base shading into pale pink, and surrounds a white or greenish yellow spadix. The large leaves have 3 lobes. This species will grow in boggy ground and in a relatively open position.

Arisaema sikokianum

A. sikokianum *Japan*
Flowers: spring. H 16–20in (40–50cm), S 4–6in (10–15cm). FrH.
In flower this is a very eyecatching species. A purplish brown spathe, with paler striations in the hood, has a white interior around a white club-shaped spadix. The dark leaves have 3 to 5 large leaflets.

ARUM

ARACEAE

In flower this genus of aroids (see *Arisaema*) is generally more curious than beautiful but some of the 26 species have attractive foliage. The plants described are Mediterranean in origin and do best in a fairly sheltered position in full sun or partial shade.

CULTIVATION Tolerate full sun or partial shade and require soil rich in organic matter. Plant in autumn or spring with the tubers covered by 4–6in (10–15cm) of soil.

PROPAGATION From offsets, taken during the second half of summer.

POTENTIAL PROBLEMS Slugs, snails.

WARNING Sap may cause an allergic skin reaction. Toxic if eaten.

Arum italicum subsp. *italicum* 'Marmoratum'

A. italicum *North Africa, S. Europe, Turkey*
Foliage: autumn to spring. Flowers: spring. Berries: autumn and winter. H 10–12in (25–30cm), S 6–8in (15–20cm). FH.
Glossy white-veined leaves, resembling a cluster of wavy-edged spearheads, are ornamental in winter, especially in **subsp.** *italicum* 'Marmoratum'. The pale green spathe appears in early summer and is followed by a spike of bright orange-red berries, which is usually still startlingly vivid when the new leaves are making growth.

BEGONIA

BEGONIACEAE

This large genus has about 900 species, which are found in tropical, subtropical and warm temperate regions. Among the best known are those with tuberous rootstocks, especially the hybrids, with their often sensationally large and showy flowers. These tender winter-dormant plants are widely grown in containers and in summer bedding schemes. Male and female flowers are borne on the same plant but the former are the most eye-catching.

CULTIVATION Require good light but protection from direct sun, and fertile, neutral to slightly acid soil that is rich in organic matter and drains freely (JI No. 2). Start tubers into growth, hollow-side uppermost, in early to mid-spring but in frost-prone areas do not plant outdoors until early summer.

PROPAGATION From basal cuttings, taken in mid-spring. From seed, sown in late winter or early spring.

POTENTIAL PROBLEMS vine weevils; fungal diseases such as grey mould (*Botrytis*) and powdery mildew.

B. hybrids (Tuberhybrida)
Flowers: summer. H 12–24in (30–60cm), S 12–18in (30–45cm). FT.

These bushy plants have succulent, brittle stems and glossy, toothed leaves, approximately heart-shaped and with a pointed tip. The attention-seeking double male flowers, which overshadow the few single female flowers, are 6in (15cm) or more in diameter, their colour range extending from white, yellow and pink to orange and red, with subtler intermediate shades and eye-catching picotee bicolours. Breeders have concentrated on perfection of flower form, the flowers of many hybrids resembling a double camellia in the neat layering of segments that open almost flat, others having a rosebud conical centre. Examples of upright begonias include: '**Anniversary**', yellow and lightly ruffled; '**Bernat Klein**', pure white; '**Fairylight**', ivory flowers touched with salmon-pink at the edges; '**Herzog van Sagan**', yellow with notched, red margins; '**Jean Blair**', frilly yellow flowers with scarlet edges; '**Marmorata**', white outlined in red; and '**Roy Hartley**', soft pink. A few hybrids are distinguished from erect begonias by trailing stems, up to 3ft (90 cm) long, and the small double flowers, usually 2–3in (5–8cm) across. Ideal for hanging baskets. '**Gold Cascade**' is bright yellow; '**Lou Anne**', pale pink; and '**Orange Cascade**', apricot-orange.

Begonia sutherlandii

B. sutherlandii *South Africa, Tanzania*
Flowers: summer. H 10–20in (25–50cm), S 30–40in (75–100cm). HH.
This offers no competition to the fireworks of the hybrids, but is a fine plant for tall containers and hanging baskets. The generous trailing growth, thickly furnished with slightly toothed bright green leaves, gives a long cascading display of small apricot-orange flowers.

CALOCHORTUS

LILIACEAE

Although the 60 or so species, natives of open woodland in western North America and Mexico, are rather flimsy plants, with thin stems and linear leaves, the refined beauty of their flowers puts them in the first rank of bulbs. Common names such as cat's ears, fairy lantern, globe lily and mariposa tulip applied to various species hint at their charm. The flowers have 6 segments, the 3 outer ones usually small, the 3 showier inner petals, sometimes fringed and lined with hairs. They also have a gland at the base, often blotched and surrounded by exquisite markings. Most species have proved difficult in cultivation outside their native territory, needing dry conditions during their dormancy.
CULTIVATION Require full sun and well-drained soil (JI No. 2 with added grit) that is dry during dormancy. Plant in autumn, covering the bulbs with 4–6in (10–15cm) of soil or compost.
PROPAGATION From seed, sown as soon as ripe. From offsets, taken in autumn. From bulbils (in the case of species that produce these in the leaf axils), planted in late spring.
POTENTIAL PROBLEMS Usually none.

C. barbatus *Mexico*
Flowers: late summer. H 6–12in (15–30cm), S 3–4in (8–10cm). FrH.
The nodding, bell-like flowers, which are fringed and hairy, are usually mustard-yellow but sometimes a purple flush suffuses the outside of the flower.

C. uniflorus *W. USA*
Flowers: late spring to early summer. H 4–8in (10–20cm), S 2–4in (5–10cm). FrH.
In the wild this plant thrives in damp, even heavy soils; in cultivation it will tolerate some moisture during the dormant period. At the end of the stem several long stalks carry erect

mauve flowers, up to 2in (5cm) across with a purple spot at the centre of the inner petals.

Calochortus venustus

C. venustus *USA (California)*
Flowers: late spring to summer. H 8–24in (20–60cm), S 3–4in (8–10cm). FrH.
The cup-shaped flowers, up to 3 per stem, vary in colour from white or yellow to shades of purplish red. A dark red blotch at the base of each inner petal is ringed with yellow.

CAMASSIA

HYACINTHACEAE Quamash

The 6 species all make basal clumps of strap-shaped leaves above which rise spikes of starry flowers that are pale blue to dark violet or white. In the wild the species occur in damp grassland. They are not so showy as to be out of place when naturalized in similar conditions. They are useful additions to moist borders, especially those on heavy soils. The bulbs are usually large and weighty.
CULTIVATION Tolerate full sun or partial shade and require fertile moist soil. Plant in autumn, covering the bulbs with about 4in (10cm) of soil.
PROPAGATION From offsets, taken in early autumn. From seed, sown as soon as ripe in summer.
POTENTIAL PROBLEMS Usually none.

Camassia cusickii

C. cusickii *USA (Oregon)*
Flowers: early to mid-summer. H 2–3ft (60–90cm), S 4–6in (10–15cm). FH.

In this species, a stem of pale to deep blue flowers tops a clump of rather fleshy leaves, which have wavy margins. The large bulbs mutiply quickly.

C. leichtlinii *W. North America*
Flowers: late spring to early summer. H 30–55in (75–140cm), S 4–6in (10–15cm). FH.
The strong, straight stems carry flowers that are very variable in colour, ranging from creamy white through shades of blue to violet. There are double and semi-double flowers in **subsp. *leichtlinii***; in **subsp. *suksdorfii* Caerulea Group** there are blues of great intensity.

Camassia quamash

C. quamash *W. Canada and USA*
Camass, Quamash
Flowers: early to mid-summer. H 10–36in (25–90cm), S 4–6in (10–15cm). FH.
This is a widespread and variable species and a number of subspecies have been recognized. It quickly forms large clumps when naturalized in meadow-like conditions. The flowers, up to 2in (5cm) across, are usually bright blue but they can be darker and also white.

CARDIOCRINUM

LILIACEAE Giant lily

The 3 Asiatic species in this genus are all monocarpic, the bulb dying after flowering while leaving numerous offsets. The bulbs, which have trumpet-shaped flowers, rarely take less than 7 years to reach flowering size from seed and 4 to 5 years from offsets. The species described is hardy and looks spectacular when sited in a dappled glade.
CULTIVATION Requires partial shade, shelter, and moist soil, rich in organic matter but not stagnant, and preferably lime-free. Plant in autumn, just covering the bulbs.
PROPAGATION From offsets, taken in autumn. From seed, sown as soon as ripe.
POTENTIAL PROBLEMS Slugs; lily viruses.

Cardiocrinum giganteum

C. giganteum *Himalayas*
Flowers: mid- to late summer.
H 6–10ft (1.8–3m), S 16–20in
(40–50cm). FH.
The stout stem, which is better left
unstaked, develops from a rosette
of large green leaves and bears 10
to 20 downward-facing trumpets,
about 6in (15cm) long and strongly
scented. The flowers are white on
the outside, sometimes tinged
green, while the inside usually has
reddish-purple markings.

CHIONODOXA

HYACINTHACEAE Glory of the snow

In their alpine habitats in the
eastern Mediterranean and in
western Turkey these are among
the first bulbs to flower. There are
6 species, those described being
fully hardy. Their short lax stems of
early starry flowers, usually blue,
look delightful in rock gardens,
raised beds and containers. They
can also compete with grass in a
wild garden. There is confusion in
the naming of cultivated plants.
CULTIVATION Require full sun and
well-drained soil (JI No. 2 with
added grit). Plant in early autumn,
covering bulbs with 3in (8cm) of
soil or compost.
PROPAGATION From offsets, in late
summer. From seed, sown as soon
as ripe.
POTENTIAL PROBLEMS Usually none.

Chionodoxa forbesii 'Pink Giant'

C. forbesii *W. Turkey*
Flowers: late winter to early spring.
H 6–8in (15–20cm), S 2–3in
(5–8cm). FH.
The lax stem carries 4 to 10
flowers, rich blue with a white eye
and up to ¾in (2cm) across. There
are also white and pink variants.
'Pink Giant' has large flowers
tinted pink around white centres.

Chionodoxa luciliae Gigantea Group

C. luciliae **Gigantea Group**
W. Turkey
Flowers: late winter to early spring.
H 4–8in (10–20cm), S 2–3in
(5–8cm). FH.
The stem usually carries 3 blue
starry flowers with white eyes.

C. sardensis *W. Turkey*
Flowers: late winter to early spring.
H 4in (10cm), S 1½in (4cm). FH.
The stems carry up to 12 slightly
down-turned deep blue flowers.

COLCHICUM

COLCHICACEAE Autumn crocus

Most of the 45 or so species found
in Europe, N. Africa and parts of
Asia are autumn flowering.
Irregularly shaped corms thrust
large crocus-like flowers through
bare earth to teeter elegantly on
long stems, in fact the tubes of the
flowers, before collapsing in
autumn rain and gales. The double-
flowered **'Waterlily'** quickly
becomes a mauve-pink muddle in
rough weather. Purplish pink is the
predominant flower colour and
chequered patterns on the petal-
like segments are a distinctive
feature of some colchicums. It is a
fault in some eyes that the leaves
of most of these species do not
appear with the flowers and that
when they do develop in winter or
spring they are large, as much as 3
times the height of the flowers
given below, and then untidy
when dying down. Grass should
not be cut until the leaves have
withered, a week or two before
mid-summer. The spring-flowering
species, including the yellow
C. luteum, are on the whole more
difficult garden plants.

CULTIVATION Tolerate full sun or
partial shade and require well-
drained soil (JI No. 2 with added
grit). Plant in summer or early
autumn, covering the corms with
4in (10cm) of soil or compost.
PROPAGATION From offsets, taken
in summer. From seed, sown in
summer as soon as ripe.
POTENTIAL PROBLEM Slugs.
WARNING Contact with any part
may irritate the skin. All parts of
the plant are toxic if eaten.

C. agrippinum *Origin unknown*
Flowers: late summer to mid-
autumn. H 3–4in (8–10cm),
S 3–4in (8–10cm). FH.
Each corm produces several starry
flowers with narrow, rather
pointed segments, strongly
patterned with a reddish purple
chequering. The green-tinted tube
is often rather weak and the flowers
are easily toppled by rough
weather.

C. autumnale *Europe*
Meadow saffron
Flowers: late summer to mid-
autumn. H 4–6in (10–15cm),
S 3–4in (8–10cm). FH.
The common name is misleading:
the source of saffron is *Crocus
sativus*. The corms of this robust
species, which is suitable for
naturalizing, produce a jostling
cluster of soft purplish pink
flowers with narrow segments.

C. byzantinum *probably Turkey*
Flowers: late summer to early
autumn. H 6–8in (15–20cm),
S 4–6in (10–15cm). FH.
A corm of this large and free-
flowering species can produce up
to 20 flowers in succession in a
soft purplish pink. The broad
leaves appear in spring.

Colchicum 'Lilac Wonder'

C. 'Lilac Wonder'
Flowers: late summer to mid-
autumn. H 6–8in (15–20cm),
S 4–6in (10–15cm). FH.
Mauve-pink flowers on short white
stems, up to 10 per corm, have
pointed segments and are lightly
chequered.

Colchicum speciosum

C. speciosum *Caucasus, Iran, N.E. Turkey*

Flowers: early to mid-autumn.
H 8–12in (20–30cm), S 4–6in
(10–15cm). FH.
Its vigour and the beauty of its
goblet-shaped flowers on sturdy
stems put this species in the first
rank. The flowers vary in colour
from pale to deep purplish pink,
often with a white centre. '**Album**'
has pure white goblets carried on
green stems. In '**Atrorubens**' the
flowers, white-throated and
purplish crimson, are carried on
purple stems.

COSMOS

ASTERACEAE

This tuberous perennial in a genus
of 25 species of plants originates
in Mexico. Where mulching is not
enough to keep it going through
winter out of doors, it can be lifted
annually and replanted in spring.
See also ANNUALS AND BIENNIALS.
CULTIVATION Requires full sun and
moist well-drained soil.
PROPAGATION From basal cuttings,
taken in early spring.
POTENTIAL PROBLEMS Aphids, slugs;
Botrytis (grey mould).

Cosmos atrosanguineus

C. atrosanguineus *Mexico*

Black cosmos, chocolate cosmos
Flowers: mid-summer to autumn.
H 24–30in (60–75cm), S 12–18in
(30–45cm). FrH.
From a base of dark green divided
leaves, wiry purplish stems carry
cup-shaped reddish chocolate
flowerheads, which are amazingly
matched by a chocolate scent.

CRINUM

AMARYLLIDACEAE

There are more than 100 species
in this genus of mainly tropical and
subtropical bulbs, the most
ornamental carrying clusters
(correctly umbels) of showy,
funnel-shaped flowers at the head
of stout stems. Among the hardiest
are two from South Africa,
C. bulbispermum and *C. moorei*,
both plants of soils that are moist
in the growing season; in cool
temperate gardens these require
warm, sheltered positions and
protection from frost. They are
much less widely grown than the
slightly hardier hybrid between
them described below.
CULTIVATION Require full sun and
fertile well-drained soil (JI No. 2).
Plant in mid- to late spring,
covering the bulbs with 6–10in
(15–25cm) of soil or compost.
PROPAGATION From offsets,
removed in early spring. From
seed, sown as soon as ripe.
POTENTIAL PROBLEMS Usually none.
WARNING Contact with the sap may
irritate the skin. Eating the bulbs
may cause nausea.

Crinum × powellii 'Album'

C. × powellii

Flowers: late summer to early
autumn. H 2–3ft (60–90cm),
S 10–12 (25–30cm). FH.
Elegantly curved tubes springing
from the head of a stout stem open
out to slightly drooping, flared
trumpets about 4in (10cm) across
at the mouth. There may be as many
as 10 and they open in succession.
'**Album**', with pure white flowers,
is a cut above the more familiar
pink forms. The strap-shaped leaves
can often look the worse for wear.
Congested clumps may flower freely.

CROCOSMIA

IRIDACEAE Montbretia

The montbretias come into their
own in the second half of summer,
their elegant sprays of funnel-
shaped flowers, 6 segments
opening at the mouth of a long
tube, providing borders with an airy

dash of warm colours, from yellow
to intense and fiery red. They
make fans of grassy leaves. The 7
species, including *C. masoniorum*,
are from fairly moist South African
grasslands but much more common
in cultivation are the slightly hardier
hybrids, often covered by the
umbrella name *C. × crocosmiiflora*,
as are some of the cultivars
described below.
CULTIVATION Tolerate full sun or
partial shade and require fertile
well-drained soil. Plant in early
spring, covering with 3–4in
(8–10cm) of soil.
PROPAGATION By division, in early
spring. From seed, sown as soon
as ripe.
POTENTIAL PROBLEMS Usually none.

**Crocosmia × crocosmiiflora
'Solfaterre'**

C. × crocosmiiflora

Flowers: late summer to early
autumn. H 20–24in (50–60cm),
S 6–8in (15–20cm). FrH.
Among the many hybrids '**Emily
McKenzie**' has large flowers, with
chocolate splashes on orange and
paler throats. '**Solfaterre**' has soft
apricot flowers, enhanced by the
soft bronze tint of the foliage. The
taller '**Gerbe d'Or**', which grows to
30in (75cm), has lemon-yellow
flowers. Use these to cool down
red and orange summer schemes.

C. 'Lucifer'

Flowers: mid- to late summer.
H 3–4ft (90–120cm), S 6–8in
(15–20cm). FrH.
Clumps of stiff, sword-like leaves
are topped by sprays of furnace-
red flowers.

Crocosmia 'Lucifer'

285

CROCUS

IRIDACEAE

Crocuses are best known for their sudden bursts of brilliant or subtle colours (red excluded) in late winter and early spring but there are also autumn-flowering species and the Dutch crocuses (listed here under *C. vernus*) are sometimes still flowering in mid-spring. In many cases, sweet scent adds to the sheeny perfection of the flowers, made vivid by stamens and styles of contrasting colour. The 80 or so species are distributed in Asia, Europe and N. Africa. The plants grow from corms, the character of the tunic being a distinguishing feature. In the case of many species the linear leaves appear with or just after the flowers, sometimes growing taller than the flowering heights given below. Crocuses that need a dry spell in summer are best grown in an alpine house. Those described generally thrive outdoors in sunny rock gardens and raised beds and several are easily naturalized.
CULTIVATION Most require full sun and well-drained soil (JI No. 1), see entries. Plant autumn-flowering crocuses in late summer, winter- and spring-flowering crocuses in early autumn, covering corms with 2–3in (5–8cm) of soil or compost.
PROPAGATION From offsets, separated in summer. From seed, sown as soon as ripe in summer.
POTENTIAL PROBLEMS Rodents, birds; fungal diseases.

C. ancyrensis *Turkey*
Flowers: mid- to late winter. H 2–3in (5–8cm), S 1–2in (2.5–5cm). The orange-yellow flowers, almost uniform in intensity, are among the first of the yellow crocuses.

C. angustifolius *Armenia, S. Ukraine*
Cloth of gold
Flowers: late winter to early spring. H 2–3in (5–8cm), S 1–2in (2.5–5cm). FH.
The exteriors of the orange-yellow flowers are marked with bronze.

Crocus angustifolius

C. chrysanthus *E. Europe*
Flowers: late winter to early spring. H 2–3in (5–8cm), S 1–2in (2.5–5cm). FH.
In wild plants the flowers, globular in outline and honey-scented, are usually yellow with darker markings outside. However the variability of the species and some hybridizing have resulted in numerous free-flowering cultivars in a wide colour range that are among the pick of the dwarf crocuses. The opalescent 'Blue Pearl' is silvery blue, the outside mauve and bronze at the base, and the throat yellow. The very free-flowering 'Cream Beauty' has an orange style and rich yellow throat surrounded by a pale cream cup. The creamy-yellow flowers of 'E.A. Bowles' are marked bronze and purple at the base. One of the smallest is var. *fuscotinctus*, with gold flowers striped and feathered with bronzy purple on the outside. 'Ladykiller' is sheeny white with bold purple over most of the outer segments. More dazzling in its whiteness is 'Snow Bunting', with only light purple feathering on the outside and a yellow throat. The flowers of 'Zwanenburg Bronze' have a deep red-brown exterior and a vivid orange-yellow interior.

C. goulimyi *S. Greece*
Flowers: early to mid-autumn. H 3–4in (8–10cm), S 1–2in (2.5–5cm). FH.
The tube of the flower forms a slender stem expanding to a mauve globe surrounding the yellow style and stamens. This sweetly scented species increases rapidly. Leaves appear with the flowers.

C. imperati *S. Italy*
Flowers: mid-winter to early spring. H 3–4in (8–10cm), S 1–2in (2.5–5cm). FH.
The corms that are commonly available are of subsp. *imperati* 'De Jager' in which the violet inner segments of the flowers contrast exquisitely with the outer ones, which are buff streaked with deep purple. The throat and anthers are yellow, while the style is orange. The fully open flowers are up to 3in (8cm) across.

C. kotschyanus *Lebanon, N.W. Syria, Turkey*
Flowers: early to mid-autumn. H 2–3in (5–8cm), S 1–2in (2.5–5cm). FH.
This is the earliest of the autumn-flowering crocuses: the large and curiously irregular corms produce flowers before the leaves appear. The stock usually available is subsp. *kotschyanus*. The pale

tube opens to mauve segments with dark purple veining; bright orange spots ring the yellow throat.

C. × luteus 'Golden Yellow'
Flowers: late winter to early spring. H 3–4in (8–10cm), S1–2in (2.5–5cm). FH.
This free-flowering crocus, ideal for naturalizing, has bright, clear yellow flowers with a few maroon stripes on the outer segments.

Crocus sieberi 'Hubert Edelsten'

C. sieberi *Greece*
Flowers: late winter to early spring. H 2–3in (5–8cm), S 1–2in (2.5–5cm). FH.
Gold-throated rather globular flowers have segments in shades of mauve or purple. Its outstanding cultivars include a brilliant white 'Albus', pristine except for the throat and orange style. 'Firefly' is deep mauve. In 'Hubert Edelsten' the pale mauve inner segments are cupped by deep purple segments, across each of which is an arc of fine white markings. 'Violet Queen' has numerous flowers, more purple than violet.

Crocus speciosus

C. speciosus *C. Asia, Caucasus, Iran, S. Ukraine, Turkey*
Flowers: early to mid-autumn. H 4–6in (10–15cm), S 1–2in (2.5–5cm). FH.
The elegant, fine-stemmed goblet-like flowers, in shades of mauve or violet-purple, often conspicuously veined, cup a much-dissected, orange-red style. This crocus naturalizes readily in sun or partial shade. Named cultivars include a ravishing white, 'Albus'. A good

crocus to follow it is the shorter-growing *C. medius*, with scarlet style and yellow stamens showing off rich purple flowers.

Crocus tommasinianus

C. tommasinianus W. former Yugoslavia

Flowers: late winter to early spring. H 3–4in (8–10cm), S 1–2in (2.5–5cm).FH.

Although this crocus multiplies profligately in both full sun and partial shade, such a charming plant could hardly be thought a weed. Its shades of mauve and purple are often variable, even within a single colony. The outer segments are pale, the inner richer in colour about a frilled orange style. Cultivars include '**Ruby Giant**', with large reddish purple flowers (sterile but clumps build up by division), '**Whitewell Purple**', purple flowers with silver-mauve lining, and the white **f. albus**.

Crocus vernus 'Pickwick'

C. vernus S. and E. Europe

Dutch crocus

Flowers: early spring. H 3–4in (8–10cm), S 2–3in (5–8cm). FH.
The name covers a range of plants, often regarded as several species, found in mountainous country. It is also under this name that the large-flowered Dutch crocuses are commonly listed. They are vigorous enough to be naturalized in grass in full sun or light shade, and are excellent container plants but they are too beefy for the rock garden. Taller than the species, their goblet-shaped flowers can be up to 15cm (6in) high. The following are widely available:

'**Jeanne d'Arc**' has large flowers of startling white, violet at the base with light feathering, cupping an orange style. In '**Pickwick**', the very pale mauve ground colour is dramatically streaked with deep purple to contrast with the yellow stamens and style. The sheeny goblets of '**Purpureus Grandiflorus**' are a deep purple with yellow stamens and style. '**Remembrance**' is striking in the contrast of its violet-purple flowers, streaked with dark purple, and the bright orange style and stamens. '**Vanguard**', the earliest to flower, can produce its slender, silvery-mauve flowers in late winter.

CYCLAMEN

PRIMULACEAE Sowbread

The numerous and often subtle variations on a simple theme make the 19 or so members of this genus delightful plants. The charm of the flowers lies more in their shape and poise than in their limited colour range (pink, magenta and white, but often with attractive dark stains at the mouth). Some are sweetly scented. The petals, sometimes elegantly twisted, are sharply reflexed so that the flowers look like miniature shuttlecocks hovering in mid-air. In some species they appear before the leaves, in others with them, which are in many cases an outstanding feature on account of the silvering and marbling of their surfaces and variability of size and shape. The more tender species are attractive plants for a cool greenhouse or alpine house.
CULTIVATION Most like partial shade and well-drained soil, rich in organic matter (JI No. 2 with added leafmould and grit) where they dry out in summer, but see entries. Plant in late summer or early autumn, covering tubers with 1in (2.5cm) of soil or compost.
PROPAGATION From seed, sown as soon as ripe.
POTENTIAL PROBLEMS Mice and other rodents, under glass red spider mite; fungal diseases.

Cyclamen cilicium

C. cilicium S. Turkey

Flowers: mid- to late autumn; H 2–4in (5–10cm), S 4–6in (10–15cm). FrH.
Pink or white flowers, which have conspicuous carmine spots at the mouth, appear at the same time as the rounded or heart-shaped leaves, usually marked with silver.

Cyclamen coum

C. coum Bulgaria, Caucasus, Lebanon, Turkey

Flowers: early winter to early spring. Foliage: winter and spring. H 2–3in (5–8cm), S 3–4in (8–10cm). FH.
The rounded leaves, sometimes patterned with silver, are purplish red on the underside, and appear either before or at the same time as the short-petalled flowers. These can be magenta, pink or white with a carmine flush near the white mouth. White and carmine contrast pleasingly in **subsp. coum f. album**. The cool metallic finish of the leaves is a striking feature of **subsp. coum Pewter Group**.

Cyclamen hederifolium f. *album*

C. hederifolium Greece, Italy, W. Turkey

Flowers: late summer to late autumn. Foliage: autumn to spring. H 3–5in (8–13cm), S 6–10in (15–25cm). FH.
This star among dwarf plants tolerates heavy shade, producing well-proportioned, sometimes fragrant, flowers. Colours include magenta, shades of pink and white (**f. album**). The leaves are purplish underneath and develop while the plant is in flower. They vary in shape and in their silvery markings.

C. purpurascens *C. and E. Europe, N. Italy*
Flowers: mid-summer to autumn. H 3–5in (8–13cm), S 4–8in (10–20cm). FH.
This fragrant species with pink, carmine and, rarely, white flowers, has more or less evergreen heart- or kidney-shaped leaves, faintly patterned with silver or plain green. It is important that it does not completely dry out in summer.

C. repandum *S. France eastward to Greek islands*
Flowers: mid- to late spring. H 4–6in (10–15cm), S 4–8in (10–20cm). FrH.
The scented flowers have twisted petals, usually rich pink and darker at the mouth, but carmine and white forms are known. The heart-shaped or triangular leaves are dark green with silvery flecking or patterning above, purple-red on the underside.

DAHLIA

ASTERACEAE

In the sixteenth century Europeans in Mexico found that the Aztecs were already growing doubles derived from tuberous-rooted species. The thousands of dahlia hybrids that have been produced since, with flowerheads available in an astonishing range of form, colour and size, demonstrate the mutability of plants as the result of hybridization. One relatively hardy species among the 30 or so is included here. The remainder are hybrid border dahlias that in frost-prone areas are usually planted out in spring and lifted in autumn, once the leaves have been blackened by the first frosts. Border dahlias, like bedding dahlias, are very often planted out in beds specially prepared for them. They are sometimes simply lined out if they are being grown for cutting or exhibition, for which they remain very popular, but they are also valued for plugging gaps in borders after mid-summer as well as for growing in containers. They are usefully categorized according to the form of their flowerheads, which have the appearance of single flowers but in fact consist of many. For the purposes of exhibition some categories of dahlia hybrids are subdivided by size of flowerhead into 5 groups: giant, over 10in (25cm); large, 8–10in (20–25cm); medium, 6–8in (15–20cm); small, 4–6in (10–15cm); miniature, less than 4in (10cm). Dahlias with giant, large and medium flowerheads are

40–60in (1–1.5m) in height; miniature and small dahlias are 3–4ft (90–120cm) high.
CULTIVATION Require full sun and fertile well-drained soil, rich in organic matter (JI No. 2 with added humus) that is well-watered throughout the growing season. Plant unsprouted tubers in mid-spring, covering with about 4in (10cm) of soil or compost. Delay planting sprouted tubers until there is minimal risk of frost.
PROPAGATION By division of tubers, in early to mid-spring. From basal shoot cuttings, in early spring.
POTENTIAL PROBLEMS Aphids, capsid bugs, earwigs, slugs and snails; virus and fungal diseases, including powdery mildew.

SPECIES

D. merckii *Mexico*
Flowers: mid-summer to mid-autumn. H 3–5ft (90–150cm), S 2–3ft (60–90cm). FrH.
Even in areas that are prone to frost, many gardeners successfully grow this slender species without lifting it every year and value it for the longevity of its flower display. The mauve-pink single flower-heads, with a maroon centre showing yellow stamens, are carried on long arching stalks and have a refinement that is lacking in most of the hybrids.

HYBRIDS

Flowers: mid-summer to mid-autumn. H 2–5ft (90–150cm), S 18–48in (45–120cm), but see notes on dimensions below. HH.
In the following descriptions the aim has been to show the character of the main categories (as recognized by The National Dahlia Society of Great Britain) and, where helpful, to give a few representative or outstanding hybrids from a range that is constantly changing.

Dahlia 'Yellow Hammer'

Single
These dahlias are up to 2ft (60cm) in height. The flowerheads, up to 4in (10cm) across, have only 1 or 2

rows of ray-florets, frequently overlapping, surrounding the central cluster of disc-florets. 'Yellow Hammer' has rich yellow flowerheads with an orange disc and dark purple leaves.

Anemone-flowered
The flattened ray florets surround a packed cluster of tubular, initially erect florets, which are often of contrasting colour. Plants are usually less than 4ft (1.2m) in height and the flowerheads usually 4–6in (10–15cm) in diameter. This category is no longer widely represented in cultivation.

Dahlia 'Clair de Lune'

Collerette
The distinctive feature is a collar of short florets surrounding the central disc and set against the single row of ray florets. Most hybrids are 30–48in (75–120cm) in height with flowerheads 4–6in (10–15cm) across. 'Clair de Lune' has a deep yellow centre and pale yellow ray-florets and a cream collar. In 'Easter Sunday' the ray florets and collar surrounding the yellow centre are creamy white. 'La Cierva' has a banded effect with a white collar surrounded by white-tipped purple ray-florets.

Dahlia 'John Street'

Waterlily
The flowerheads, much less densely packed than most of the other doubles, have broad ray-florets that are flat or slightly incurved. There are 5 subdivisions according to size of bloom. The most popular are the small-flowered, which include 'Glorie

van Heemstede', noted for its generous display of yellow blooms; **'John Street'**, a bright scarlet; and **'Porcelain'**, white with a delicate mauve tinge.

Decorative

The double flowerheads, which have no central disc, consist of layers of broad ray-florets that are usually blunt-tipped. There are 5 subdivisions according to size of flowerhead. **'Arabian Night'** (small), is outstanding for the depth of its dark red. **'David Howard'** (miniature) is pale orange with a darker centre and bronzed foliage, **'Duet'** (medium) has startling flowerheads in which the ray-florets are purplish red with white tips and **'Eveline'** (small) is pearly white tinted with mauve. Giant-flowered examples that are popular for exhibition include: **'Hamari Gold'**, bronzed yellow-orange; **'Kidd's Climax'**, pink with yellow shading; and **'Zorro'**, which is deep red.

Dahlia 'Hamari Gold'

Ball

The spherical flowerheads of dahlias in this group have blunt or rounded ray-florets that are arranged in a spiral. There are two sizes of flowerhead, small and miniature, but all hybrids are about 3–4ft (90–120cm) tall. Good miniatures are **'Kathryn's Cupid'** and **'Peach Cupid'**.

Dahlia 'Moor Place'

Pompon

These are in the same mould as the Ball hybrids and of a similar height but the flowerheads are 2in (5cm)

or less in diameter and the ray-florets curve in elegantly over the whole of their length. **'Mi Wong'** is pale pink with darker touches at the margins of the florets; **'Moor Place'** is rich purplish red in colour.

Cactus

The narrow, pointed ray-florets are quilled for more than half their length, giving the double flowerheads a spiky appearance. There are 5 subdivisions according to size of flowerhead. **'Athalie'** (small) has bronze-tinted pink flowerheads; **'Hillcrest Royal'** (medium) is purplish red; and in **'Lady Kerkrade'** (small) the pink flowerheads fade to cream near the centre.

Dahlia 'Hillcrest Royal'

Semi-cactus

There are 5 subdivisions according to size of flowerhead. The ray florets are broader than those of cactus dahlias and quilled for less than half their length. Good examples include: **'Conway'** (small), purplish-pink flowers with gleams of pale yellow; **'Daleko Jupiter'** (giant), a popular exhibition hybrid in a mixture of red and yellowish pink; **'Dana Iris'** (small), vibrant red; **'Pink Pastelle'** (medium), rich pink; and **'Salmon Keene'** (large), shaggy soft orange with yellow tips and yellow near the flower centre.

Miscellaneous

All dahlias not included in the main groups belong here and are classified in informal subgroups, such as Orchid-flowering and Lilliput dahlias. There are considerable differences in size between the groups, the Lilliput dahlias being only 12–18in (30–45 cm) tall with flowerheads up to 1¼in (3cm) across. The peony-flowered **'Bishop of Llandaff'**, however, is 40–48in (1–1.2m) in height and has flowerheads which reach up to 2½in (6cm) across. It is much admired for the combination of its bronze-purple foliage and open, semi-double bright red flowerheads.

Dahlia 'Bishop of Llandaff'

DIERAMA

IRIDACEAE Angel's fishing rod, wandflower

The common names of this South African genus of 44 species allude to the gracefully arching flower stems, which are weighed down at the tips by the bell-like flowers. A waterside planting meets their requirements while making the most of their languid beauty. In cold areas annual lifting of the corms allows the plants to be grown outdoors.

CULTIVATION Require full sun and well-drained soil, rich in organic matter, with a plentiful supply of moisture during the growing season. Plant in early autumn, covering the corms with 4in (10cm) of soil or, in areas that have cold winters, in mid-spring. Lift the corms in mid-autumn and store them in conditions that are frost-free.

PROPAGATION From offsets, separated in autumn. From seed, sown in early to mid-spring.

POTENTIAL PROBLEMS Usually none.

D. pulcherrimum *S. Africa*
Flowers: late summer to mid-autumn. H 4–5ft (1.2–1.5m), S 18–24 (45–60cm). FrH.
Wiry flower stems emerge from a sheaf of narrow leaves and arch over gracefully, loaded towards the tip with violet-purple bells that open from silvered papery bracts. A smaller version of this, **D. pendulum**, grows to about 3ft (90cm) in height.

Dierama pulcherrimum

ERANTHIS

RANUNCULACEAE Winter aconite

The small bulbs, among them the tuberous winter aconites, that flourish under the canopy of deciduous trees are among the chief delights of temperate gardens in late winter and early spring. There are about 7 species from Europe and Asia in the genus, which is mainly represented in gardens by the fully hardy *E. hyemalis*. This species naturalizes readily. It can also form extensive colonies, especially when it is planted in alkaline soils.
CULTIVATION Tolerate a wide range of conditions, including full sun or partial shade around trees or deciduous shrubs and well-drained alkaline soils or heavy loams. If possible, plant tubers immediately after flowering in winter or, alternatively, in late summer, covering dry tubers with 1in (2.5cm) of soil.
PROPAGATION By division of tubers, in spring after flowering. From seed, sown as soon as ripe in late spring.
POTENTIAL PROBLEM Smuts, with swellings on stalks bursting to release black spores.
WARNING Contact with the sap may irritate the skin. All parts of the plant are mildly toxic if eaten.

E. hyemalis *Europe*
Flowers: late winter to early spring.
H 2–4in (5–10cm), S 2–3in (5–8cm). FH.
The jaunty flower is a lustrous cup of lemon yellow, about 1in (2.5cm) across, set off by a bract that forms a ruff of bright green. The plant dies down by early summer. Other *Eranthis* with distinctive characteristics, but now included with this species, are generally less vigorous plants and are free-flowering. The **Cilicica Group**, from Turkey, has slightly larger flowers of a richer yellow colour. The globular yellow flowers of **'Guinea Gold'**, a selection of the **Tubergenii Group**, are also large and the leaves are bronze-green.

Eranthis hyemalis

ERYTHRONIUM

LILIACEAE Dog's-tooth violet, trout lily

The poise of their flowers, like scaled down Turk's-cap lilies, gives these woodland plants a distinctive character. There are about 22 species and an attractive feature of many, including *E. citrinum* and *E. oregonum* as well as *E. revolutum*, which is described below, is the purplish brown mottling of the leaves. Most can be grown with successful results provided they are given moist conditions under a deciduous canopy, which is open in spring but cool and shady in summer. Erythroniums are not tailor-made for mass marketing, the fleshy corms deteriorating if allowed to dry out. They are, however, well worth seeking out from specialist nurseries.
CULTIVATION Require dappled or light shade and moist but not stagnant soil, rich in organic matter. Plant in late summer or early autumn, covering the corms with 4–6in (10–15cm) of soil.
PROPAGATION From offsets, taken in summer. From seed, sown when ripe (slow to germinate; plants may take 5 years to reach maturity).
POTENTIAL PROBLEMS Slugs, snails.

Erythronium californicum **'White Beauty'**

E. californicum *USA (California)*
Flowers: mid- to late spring.
H 6–18in (15–45cm), S 4–6in (10–15 cm). FH.
Above glossy, dark green leaves, which are heavily mottled, float cream flowers that have orange-brown markings at the centre. In **'White Beauty'** the leaves are marbled and the ring at the throat of the creamy flowers is rust-red.

E. dens-canis *Asia, Europe*
Dog's-tooth violet
Flowers: early to mid-spring.
H 4–6in (10–15cm), S 3–4in (8–10cm). FH.
This species is more tolerant than most of dryness in summer. In shape the corm is similar to a dog's canine tooth, hence the common

name. The blue-green leaves are strongly mottled. Nodding flowers are variable in colour, ranging from purplish pink, through pale pink to white, and the centre, usually yellowish, is surrounded by a band of orange-brown marks. Named selections include **'Pink Perfection'**, **'Rose Queen'** and **'Snowflake'**; the many variants are equally delectable.

E. 'Kondo'
Flowers: mid- to late spring.
H 8–16in (20–40cm) S 4–6in (10–15cm). FH.
This vigorous hybrid, of which *E. tuolumnense* is probably a parent, produces several scented flowers per stem. The greenish yellow flowers are red-brown at the centre.

E. 'Pagoda'
Flowers: mid- to late spring.
H 10–18in (25–45cm), S 4–6in (10–15cm). FH.
E. tuolumnense is probably one of the parents of this vigorous hybrid, which has bronze mottling on the leaves and several creamy yellow flowers per stem.

E. revolutum *Canada and USA (British Columbia to N. California)*
American trout lily
Flowers: mid- to late spring.
H 8–14in (20–35cm), S 4–6in (10–15cm). FH.
Above a brown-mottled clump of leaves, which are wavy at the margins, the upright stems carry several purplish pink flowers with yellow centres and anthers.

Erythronium tuolumnense

E. tuolumnense *USA (California)*
Flowers: mid- to late spring.
H 8–14in (20–35cm), S 4–6in (10–15cm). FH.
Although it is smaller in flower size than many of the others in the genus, this species does well in cultivation. The very large corms, often over 3in (8cm) in length, produce bright green leaves which have no mottling. The stems of the plant can carry up to 4 yellow flowers, which have attractive green centres.

FREESIA

IRIDACEAE

This South African genus of about 6 species is best known for the numerous hybrids derived from plants such as **F. lactea**. Their fragrance, wide colour range and responsiveness to forcing have made them a standby of the florist trade. An appealing feature of species and hybrids is the way the stems, rising above fanned tufts of grassy leaves, angle the flower spike so that the funnel-shaped flowers are more or less erect and open in succession towards the tip. The species and hybrids, which are half-hardy, can be container-grown in a cool greenhouse. Treated corms that flower in summer can be planted outdoors after the frosts. In areas where the climate is mild enough, untreated corms multiply freely when planted outdoors.
CULTIVATION Require full sun or well-lit conditions and fertile, well-drained soil (JI No. 2), with a plentiful supply of moisture in the growing season. Plant in late summer or early autumn for winter and spring flowering, with corms covered by 2–3in (5–8cm) of soil or compost; plant prepared bulbs for summer flowering in mid-spring.
PROPAGATION From offsets, removed in late summer. From seed, sown from early spring to early summer and grown on without check during the summer.
POTENTIAL PROBLEMS Particularly when grown under glass, aphids and red spider mite; fungal diseases, like *Fusarium* wilt, viruses.

Freesia hybrids

F. hybrids
Flowers: under glass, mid-winter to mid-spring; untreated bulbs outdoors, mid- to late spring; treated bulbs outdoors, early to late summer. H 18–24in (45–60cm), S 4–6in (10–15cm). HH.
The funnel-shaped flowers, which are up to 2in (5cm) long, include some doubles, although most are singles, opening out to 6 lobes. In most cases they are fragrant with a colour range extending from white and soft pastels to strong oranges, reds and purples. The throat is usually white or yellow, often streaked with a stronger colour.

FRITILLARIA

LILIACEAE Fritillary

The fritillaries have a strong following among specialist growers. Although rarely showy, they are intriguing for their subtle combinations of colour, sometimes in chequered patterns, and for the way the hanging bells hide the nectaries at the base of each of the segments. The genus, of about 100 species, is widely distributed in the Northern Hemisphere and representatives are found in a wide range of habitats, including mountain screes, open woodland and damp meadows. The bulbs should be handled carefully and, if lifted, not allowed to dry out. They consist of 2 or more fleshy scales and some produce large numbers of "rice-grain" bulblets.
CULTIVATION Most of the species described require full sun and well-drained soil (JI No. 2 with added grit) but for exceptions see individual entries. Plant in early to mid-autumn, covering the bulbs with a depth of soil or compost equal to 4 times the height of the bulb, the large bulbs of *F. imperialis*, for example, being covered by about 8in (20cm) of soil. In heavy soils plant on a bed of coarse sand.
PROPAGATION From offsets or bulbils, in late summer. From seed, sown when ripe in mid- to late summer.
POTENTIAL PROBLEMS Attack by lily beetles and slugs.

Fritillaria acmopetala

F. acmopetala *Cyprus, Syria, S. Turkey*
Flowers: late spring. H 12–18in (30–45cm), S 4–6in (10–15cm). FH.
This example of the subtle colour combinations found in fritillaries does well in a fairly wide range of conditions. From a slender stem, with a few linear leaves, hang 1 to 3 pale green bells, the inner segments with maroon stains and veining and the rim curved back.

Fritillaria camschatcensis

F. camschatcensis *Alaska to N.W. USA, N.E. Asia*
Black sarana
Flowers: late spring to early summer. H 10–16in (25–40cm), S 4–6in (10–15cm). FH.
Stems with glossy, narrow leaves, arranged in whorls, are topped by one or, more often, several bell-shaped, near-black purple flowers. This mysterious species, which is unusual in straddling Asia and America, tolerates light shade and is ideal for a raised bed with moist soil rich in organic matter.

Fritillaria imperialis

F. imperialis *S.E. Turkey to W. Himalayas*
Crown imperial
Flowers: mid- to late spring. H 2–4ft (60–120cm), S 8–12in (20–30cm). FH.
For many centuries the crown imperial has been admired as a spring bulb of stately grandeur. A stout stem, surrounded by whorls of glossy twisted leaves to about half its height, is crowned by a tight ring of up to 8 nodding flowers, which can be as much as 2in (5cm) long and as wide at the mouth. A green tuft makes a curious topknot. The colour range extends from lemon-yellow to deep brownish red. Recommended cultivars include: '**Aurora**', orange-red; '**Maxima Lutea**', deep lemon-yellow; and '**Rubra Maxima**', brick red with darker shading. The crown imperial does well on heavy soils.

F. meleagris *C. Europe, W. to Great Britain and N. to Scandinavia*
Snake's head fritillary
Flowers: mid- to late spring.
H 12–18in (30–45cm), S 4–6in (10–15cm). FH.
Wild and naturalized colonies of this fritillary flourish in damp meadows. However, this chequered species will grow in any reasonably moist soil, producing 1 or 2 square-shouldered bells above grassy, grey-green leaves. The pattern is usually in dark purple on a paler shade. Particularly bewitching when dotted among darker forms are flowers with pale green patterning on white ('**Alba**').

Fritillaria meleagris

F. michailovskyi *N. E. Turkey*
Flowers: early to mid-spring.
H 4–6in (10–15cm), S 2–3in (5–8cm). FH.
The broad yellow rim of the deep plum, nodding bells is a particularly eye-catching feature. Each stem carries up to 5 flowers which are about 1in (2.5cm) in length and as much across. The foliage is sparse. In order to prosper, this species requires dry conditions during the dormant summer season.

Fritillaria michailovskyi

F. pallidiflora *N.W. China, Siberia*
Flowers: mid-spring. H 12–18in (30–45cm), S 4–6in (10–15cm). FH.
The stems of this attractive fritillary bear up to 4 square-shouldered, cream bells, which are suffused with green and spotted with red on the inside. Their scent is rank. The leaves are glaucous.

Fritillaria pyrenaica

F. pyrenaica *Pyrenees*
Flowers: mid-spring. H 10–18in (24–45cm), S 6–8in (15–20cm). FH.
In the wild this species is found in the light shade of open woodland as well as in open rocky terrain, showing a versatility that is useful in the garden. Slender stems carry 1, occasionally 2, bells of very variable colouring. Often purple-crimson patterning is super-imposed on dark purple-brown on the outside, while the interior is tinged greenish yellow.

GALANTHUS

AMARYLLIDACEAE Snowdrop

The snowdrops, of which there are about 19 species, are a remarkably homogeneous group of bulbs, usually producing foliage and flowers in late winter, the single bloom dangling lightly from a slender stalk beneath the arching tip of the stem or scape. However, the snowdrop season begins in autumn with **G. reginae-olgae Winter-flowering Group**. The 3 outer flower segments of snowdrops are typically pure white and the 3 inner ones, which are shorter and notched, are marked with green. The variations of this appealing formula excite passionate enthusiasm. There are doubles and singles, differences in vigour as well as in the proportions of the segments and in poise. The distribution of green on the inner segments is a major distinguishing feature. There are even a few cases of green on the outer segments and of pale yellow being substituted for green. Also important is the arrangement of the leaves (2 pressed flat against each other as they emerge or one wrapped round the other), their colour, width and the extent to which the margins are turned back. The common snowdrop is one of the most rewarding bulbs to naturalize under deciduous trees or shrubs.
CULTIVATION Tolerate a wide range of conditions (including chalk) but most do best in light shade and moist heavy soil (JI No. 2). Plant

dry bulbs (usually slow to become established) in early autumn, covering with 1–2in (2.5–5cm) of soil; preferably "in the green", that is after, even during, flowering but before leaves die back.
PROPAGATION By division of clumps, at or immediately after flowering but while leaves are still green. From seed, sown as soon as ripe.
POTENTIAL PROBLEMS Narcissus bulb fly; grey mould (*Botrytis*).

G. 'Atkinsii'
Flowers: late winter. H 6–10in (15–25cm), S2–3in (5–8cm). FH.
Although setting no seed, this snowdrop increases freely. It shows its *G. nivalis* lineage in its foliage and flower. The outer segments are long, sometimes deformed.

Galanthus 'Atkinsii'

G. caucasicus *Probably Caucasia, Transcaucasia and Turkey*
Flowers: mid- to late winter.
H 6–8in (15–20cm), S 2–3in (5–8cm). FH.
The broad, grey-green leaves, one wrapped round the other at the base and curving back as they grow, are a distinctive feature. There are green marks at the tips of the inner segments but not the base.

G. elwesii *W. Turkey and adjacent islands*
Flowers: late winter to early spring. H 6–10in (15–25cm), S 2–3in (5–8cm). FH.
The broad, grey-green leaves are wrapped round one another at the base. The inner segments of the large flowers have green markings at the tip and base.

Galanthus elwesii

G. ikariae *Aegean islands*
Flowers: late winter to early spring. H 4–6in (10–15cm), S 2–3in (5–8cm). FH.
The glossy, bright-green leaves, one wrapped round the other at the base, are up to 1in (2.5cm) across and turn back at the tips. Green marks at the tips of the inner segments show between the claw-like outer segments. The very similar **Latifolius Group** from the Caucasus, N.E. Turkey and N.W. Iran, does well on relatively dry soils.

G. nivalis *Europe, from Spain to the Ukraine*
Common snowdrop
Flowers: mid- to late winter. H 4–6in (10–15cm), S 2–3in (5–8cm). FH.
The strap-shaped leaves, rather narrow and with a light-grey bloom, are flat against each other at the base and the inner segments of the flowers are marked green at the apex. There are numerous selections, some of which are frankly very difficult to tell apart, as well as numerous hybrids, some of which are listed separately. There are also several named doubles, including '**Flore Pleno**', with its irregular dumpy flowers, the outer segments stretched over numerous green-edged underskirts. This is sterile but colonies build up quickly from offsets to form very dense white carpets. The forms in which the green of the flowers is replaced by a pale yellow, such as the single '**Sandersii**', are rather weak-growing curiosities. Other more vigorous variants include the **Scharlockii Group**, in which two long spathes stand erect above the flowers, the outer segments of which are touched with green, and '**Viridapicis**', a hearty plant with green spots at the tips of the outer segments.

Galanthus nivalis 'Flore Pleno'

G. plicatus *Crimea, N. Turkey, Romania*
Flowers: late winter to early spring. H 6–8in (15–20cm), S 2–3in (5–8cm). FH.
The grey-green leaves of this large-flowered snowdrop are pressed flat against each other on emerging and the margins fold back. There is a conspicuous green mark around the notch of the inner flower segments. **Subsp. byzantinus**, from N.W. Turkey, formerly considered a separate species, has green marks at the base of the inner segments as well as at the apex.

Galanthus plicatus

G. 'S. Arnott'
Flowers: mid- to late winter. H 6–8in (15–20cm), S 2–3in (5–8cm). FH.
This hybrid follows the common snowdrop in the arrangement of its leaves and in the green markings of the inner flower segments. It is very pleasing in its proportions and is one of the best to plant in small groups in prominent positions.

Galanthus 'S. Arnott'

GALTONIA

HYACINTHACEAE

The tall, hyacinth-like stems of pendent bells, which spring from clumps of strap-shaped leaves, are elegant verticals for sunny gardens in late summer and autumn. There are 4 species. The 2 described look best in sheltered borders where the subtle beauty of their white or green-tinted flowers is not overwhelmed by brilliant colours. In areas subject to hard frosts they are worth growing in pots and keeping under glass in winter.
CULTIVATION Require full sun and well-drained soil (JI No. 2) with a good supply of moisture in spring and summer. Plant in early to mid-spring, or, where there is little risk of outdoor frost or under glass, in mid-autumn, covering bulbs with about 6in (15cm) of soil or compost.
PROPAGATION From offsets, although these are not abundant, removed in autumn or spring. From seed, sown in early spring.
POTENTIAL PROBLEMS Usually none.

G. candicans *Lesotho, South Africa*
Flowers: late summer to early autumn. H 3–4ft (90–120cm), S 6–8in (15–20cm). FH.
The most widely grown species has grey-green leaves and up to 30 waxy bells, widely spaced on the stem, that are white, tinted green at the base, and lightly scented.

Galtonia candicans

G. viridiflora *Lesotho, South Africa*
Flowers: late summer to mid-autumn. H 2–3ft (60–90cm), S 4–6in (10–15cm). FH.
The pale green of the wide-spreading bell-shaped flowers has made this a favourite among flower-arrangers. The leaves narrow abruptly at their tip from a width of about 4in (10cm).

Galtonia viridiflora

GLADIOLUS

IRIDACEAE

It is by their large-flowered hybrids that gladioli are best known but there are over 150 species and these, as well as some of the small-flowered hybrids, include some plants of exceptional refinement. There is a concentration of species in southern Africa but gladioli are also found in other parts of Africa, the Arabian peninsula, west Asia and Europe, especially the Mediterranean. Their corms produce fans of linear or sword-shaped leaves and spikes of more or less trumpet-like flowers, the tube opening out to 6 lobes that often differ in shape and size. This selection includes several species and examples of the Nanus Group hybrids. There are only general entries for the other hybrid categories (Grandiflorus Group, Primulinus Group and Butterfly hybrids) because new hybrids are constantly taking the place of older ones. Hybrids with large spikes, ideal for cutting, are difficult to integrate in planting schemes.

CULTIVATION Require full sun and well-drained soil (JI No. 2 with added sharp sand), most needing a plentiful supply of moisture in the growing season. In frost-prone areas delay planting the summer-flowering gladioli (indicated by A after the flowering season in the entries) including the large-flowered hybrids, until mid- to late spring. Lift the corms once the foliage begins to die down after flowering in order to store them in frost-free conditions. Plant gladioli that flower in late spring or early summer (marked B) in autumn, where the climate is mild enough outdoors, but otherwise cultivate under glass. Cover all the corms with 4–6in (10–15cm) of soil or compost and in heavy soils place them on a bed of coarse sand.

PROPAGATION From cormlets, removed in the dormant season and planted at the same time as the adult corms. From seed, sown in late winter or early spring.

POTENTIAL PROBLEMS Aphids and thrips; fungal diseases, including gladiolus corm rot.

Gladiolus **'Amanda Mahy'**

G. 'Amanda Mahy'
Flowers: early summer (B). H 20–30in (50–75cm), S 2–4in (10–20cm). HH.
Upward-tilted flowers, 5 to 7 to a stem and about 2in (5cm) across, are soft pink to apricot, with mauve marks on 3 segments.

G. Butterfly hybrids
Flowers: early to late summer (A). H 2–3ft (60–90cm), S 4–6in (10–15cm). HH.
The flowers, slightly smaller than those of the Primulinus hybrids, are ruffled or frilled and usually strikingly blotched.

G. callianthus *E. Africa (Eritrea to Mozambique)*
Flowers: late summer to early autumn (A). H 20–40in (50–100cm), S 4–6in (10–15cm). HH.
The unpromising linear leaves are topped by stems carrying 6 to 10 deliciously scented flowers. They arch out on long slender tubes, the pointed segments making an unequal white star 2–3in (5–8cm) across, with a deep purple throat. **'Murieliae'** is a vigorous selection.

Gladiolus communis **subsp. byzantinus**

G. communis subsp. byzantinus *North Africa, Sicily, Spain*
Flowers: early summer (B). H 20–30in (50–75cm), S 3–4in (8–10cm). FH.
The intense magenta of the flowers, up to 20 per stem and arranged in 2 alternating ranks, is scarcely relieved by creamy-white stripes on the lower segments. It strikes a piercing note among grey foliage.

G. Grandiflorus Group hybrids
Flowers: early to late summer (A). H 3–4ft (90–120cm), S 4–6in (10–15cm). HH.
The stiff, one-sided spikes with up to 24 flowers tightly packed one above the other, 8 to 10 often being open at the same time, make these large-flowered hybrids popular in exhibitions. Many have ruffled flowers, some as much as 7in (17cm) across, and the colour range, although weak in blue, is exceptional, the lip and throat often contrasting with the main colour of the flower. In exhibition, they are divided into 5 categories (Miniature, Small, Medium, Large and Giant) based on the size of the bottom and largest flower.

G. Nanus Group hybrids
See the separate entries for 'Amanda Mahy', 'Prins Claus' and 'The Bride'.

Gladiolus papilio

G. papilio *South Africa*
Flowers: late summer to early autumn (A). H 2–3ft (60–90cm), S 3–4in (8–10cm). FrH.
Although it does not flaunt bright colours, this is one of the most alluring of the gladioli. Spikes of 5 to 10 flowers are carried above a thin clump of narrow, grey-green leaves. The flowers, very variable in colouring, are almost bell-shaped and droop slightly. The foundation colour ranges from creamy yellow to green, usually with bruise-like purple markings on the reverse and with a conspicuous eye on the lower segments. In the **Purpureoauratus Group** the cream, green-tinted body of the flower is suffused with purple and the eye is purplish red edged with yellow.

G. Primulinus Group hybrids
Flowers: early to late summer (A). H 2–3ft (60–90cm), S 4–6in (10–15cm). HH.
These are like less vigorous versions of the Grandiflorus hybrids, the alternate arrangement of the flowers making an obvious zigzag up the stem. The flowers, up to 3in (8cm) across, come in a wide colour range. The central top segments project forward like a hood over the stigma and anthers.

G. 'Prins Claus'
Flowers: early summer (B). H 20–30in (50–75cm), S 2–4in (5–10cm). HH.
Tongue-like marks of deep pink on the 3 lower segments of this Nanus hybrid stand out against the whiteness of the flowers.

G. 'The Bride'
Flowers: mid-spring to early summer (B). H 18–24in (45–60cm), S 2–4in (5–10cm). HH.
The starry flowers, which are about 2in (5cm) across and number 3 to 6 per stem, have white pointed

segments around a greenish yellow throat. This gladiolus is one of the original small-flowered hybrids in the style of, but predating, the Nanus Group hybrids.

G. tristis *South Africa (W. Cape)*
Flowers: late winter to late spring (B). H 18–48in (45–120cm), S 3–6in (8–15cm). HH.
Slender refinement and sweet night scent are all of a piece in this gladiolus. The blooms, usually about 10 per stem, but up to 20 in number, are trumpet-shaped, flaring to a width of 2in (5cm), and pale yellow or cream lightly tinged with purplish bronze.

Gladiolus tristis

GLORIOSA

COLCHICACEAE

The botanical name makes great claims but the single tropical species is not a disappointment. *G. superba* produces vivid, lily-like flowers in summer. The tapering leaves of this slender climber are usually tipped with small hooks that allow the plant to haul itself up into shrubs or artifical supports. In frost-prone areas it is best grown under glass. Whether plants are grown outdoors or under glass, store tubers dry over winter.
CULTIVATION Require full sun and fertile well-drained soil (JI No. 2) with a plentiful supply of moisture in the growing season. Plant in late winter or early spring, covering the tubers with about 4in (10cm) of soil or compost.
PROPAGATION From offsets, detached and planted in late winter. From seed, sown in late winter or early spring and germinated at a temperature of 21–24°C (70–75°F).
POTENTIAL PROBLEMS Aphids.
WARNING Contact with the tubers may irritate the skin. All parts of the plant are toxic if eaten.

G. superba *Africa, India*
Flowers: mid- to late summer.
H 4–6ft (1.2–1.8m), S 12–18in (30–45cm). FT.
The long stalks that carry flowers spring from the upper leaf axils at an angle of about 45°. The nodding flowers, like air-borne bursts of flame, have wavy-edged, reflexed segments that change as they age from yellow to orange and red. The stamens form a conspicuous circle beneath the segments and the style, instead of protruding vertically, extends abruptly at a right angle. '**Lutea**' has yellow flowers and in '**Rothschildiana**', which can grow to 8ft (2.5m), the red segments are yellow at the base and on the very crimped margins.

Gloriosa superba 'Rothschildiana'

HERMODACTYLUS

IRIDACEAE

A peculiarity of the ovary puts a single darkly beautiful *Iris* relative in a genus of its own. It needs a warm position, such as the base of a sunny wall where there is room for the creeping tubers to develop.
CULTIVATION Requires full sun and free-draining, preferably alkaline soil (JI No. 2 with added grit). Plant in autumn, covering tubers with 3–4in (8–10cm) of soil or compost.
PROPAGATION By division, as soon as leaves die down.
POTENTIAL PROBLEMS Slugs, snails.

Hermodactylus tuberosus

H. tuberosus *E. Mediterranean, N. Africa, S. Europe*
Flowers: mid- to late spring.
H 6–12in (15–30cm), S 2–3in (5–8cm). FH.
The scented flowers, which are sombre for spring but appealing in their subtle colour combination and texture, are borne on rather weak stems. The flowers are about 2in (5cm) across and a shadowed yellowish green with sharply recurved outer segments (known as the falls) of velvety purplish black. The leaves can grow to 20in (50cm).

HIPPEASTRUM

AMARYLLIDACEAE

About 80 Central and South American species make up the genus but it is the large-flowered hybrids that are best known. They are usually grown in containers and are popular for winter display indoors and under glass. They are often incorrectly known as amaryllis.
CULTIVATION Require a well-lit position and well-drained fertile soil (JI No. 2) with good supplies of moisture and liquid fertilizer when in active growth. Plant in autumn, only half-covering the bulbs with soil or compost.
PROPAGATION From offsets, removed in autumn. From seed, sown as soon as ripe.
POTENTIAL PROBLEMS Bulb scale mite, large narcissus bulb fly; fungal diseases.
WARNING Swallowing any part may cause stomach upset.

Hippeastrum 'Apple Blossom'

H. hybrids
Flowers: winter to spring
H 12–18in (30–45cm), S 6–10in (15–25cm). FT.
The 4 to 6 funnel-shaped flowers, which are up to 6in (15cm) across, radiate from the top of a stout stem on short stalks. This umbel arrangement, like a cluster of floral megaphones, often looks crowded. The vigour and brilliance of these giant blooms, however, have appeal during the winter. The colour range available includes white, pink, red and orange. Many of the plants sold are simply identified by their colour. Named selections include: '**Apple Blossom**', pink-tipped white flowers; '**Picotee**', white with segments outlined in red; '**Red Lion**', brilliant scarlet, and '**Star of Holland**', red with a white mark in the throat.

HYACINTHOIDES

HYACINTHACEAE Bluebell

Two of the 3 species of bluebell are well-known and superb plants for the wild garden. The blue haze of massed English bluebells under trees is a platitude of spring but unfailingly refreshing to the eye. They are, however, brawny, increasing quickly from offsets and seed to make spreading clumps of rather coarse strap-shaped leaves. They should be kept out of beds, borders and rock gardens. The two species described hybridize freely.
CULTIVATION Tolerate full sun or partial shade and a wide range of soils, preferably moist. Plant in autumn, covering bulbs with about 3in (8cm) of soil (the bulbs deteriorate quickly in storage).
PROPAGATION From offsets, removed in summer. From seed, sown as soon as ripe.
POTENTIAL PROBLEMS Usually none.

H. hispanica *N. Africa, Portugal, Spain*
Spanish bluebell
Flowers: mid-spring to early summer. H 12–16in (30–40cm), S 4–6in (10–15cm). FH.
An erect stem forms a sturdy campanile carrying up to 15 broad bells. The flowers are unscented and usually pale blue with blue anthers. Yet the colour range of cultivars and hybrids includes dark blue, pink and white.

Hyacinthoides hybrid

H. non-scripta *W. Europe*
English bluebell
Flowers: mid-spring to early summer. H 10–14in (25–35cm), S 4–6in (10–15cm). FH.
The bells, 6 to 12 in number, are rather tube-like in shape but the segments curl back prettily at the mouth. Their somewhat one-sided arrangement on the stem causes the slender tip to bend slightly.

Pink and white forms exist but the lightly scented flowers are usually purplish blue in colour with cream-coloured anthers.

HYACINTHUS

HYACINTHACEAE Hyacinth

The modern hyacinths, sometimes known as florists' or Dutch hyacinths, with columns of densely packed fragrant flowers, are almost the only representatives of the genus in gardens; having displaced the species, *H. orientalis*, from which they are derived. The "improvement" of the species over centuries has produced plants of a rather plastic perfection. They are popular because of their heavy scent, the uniform growth of individual cultivars, and their predictable performance when forced and as container and garden plants. Prepared bulbs (heat treated for forcing) should not be put in a warm room until the flower spike is showing.
CULTIVATION Tolerate full sun or light shade and require well-drained soil (JI No. 2 or, for forced bulbs, bulb fibre). Plant unprepared bulbs in autumn, covering the bulbs with 3–6in (8–15cm) of soil or compost; prepared bulbs in late summer or early autumn with the tops of the bulbs just showing.
PROPAGATION From offsets, removed in summer. By specialist techniques, involving scooping or scoring the base of bulbs.
POTENTIAL PROBLEMS Several fungal diseases, including grey bulb rot.
WARNING Contact with the bulbs may cause an allergic skin reaction. All parts of the plant are toxic to some degree if eaten.

Hyacinthus orientalis 'City of Haarlem'

H. orientalis *E. Mediterranean, S. Turkey*
Flowers: late winter to late spring; prepared bulbs, mid-winter to early spring. H 8–12in (20–30cm), S 3–4in (8–10cm). FH.
The species, a rather lax-stemmed plant, is barely recognizable in its progeny, except for the powerful

fragrance of the bell-like flowers. The modern cultivars, to which the dimensions given above apply, have stout stems carrying 40 or more waxy bells with recurved tips to the lobes and glossy, strap-shaped leaves. The colour range extends from white and soft shades of pink, blue and yellow to red, violet and orange. Unless stated otherwise, unprepared bulbs of the following cultivars flower from early to mid-spring; those described as late flower between mid- and late spring: **'Anna Marie'**, single, pale pink, suitable for forcing; **'Blue Jacket'**, single, large deep blue, paler at the edges; **'Carnegie'**, single, white, late; **'City of Haarlem'**, single, soft yellow, late; **'Delft Blue'**, single, soft blue with metallic lustre; **'Hollyhock'**, double, carmine-red, late; **'Jan Bos'**, single, reddish pink; **'L'Innocence'**, single, less congested than many modern cultivars, pure white; **'Oranje Boven'**, single, salmon pink; **'Ostara'**, single, strong blue with violet band down the centre of each segment; and **'Pink Pearl'**, single, glistening deep pink with paler edges, popular for forcing.

Hyacinthus orientalis 'Jan Bos'

IPHEION

ALLIACEAE

There are 10 species in this South American genus. The few representatives in gardens do not make dramatic entrances but their clumps of leaves are topped by beautifully formed, scented flowers for many weeks in spring. Their foliage, which smells of onions when bruised, makes growth in late autumn and dies down in summer. It usually recovers if lightly frost damaged but in areas prone to prolonged frosts, these are plants for a cold greenhouse.

CULTIVATION Require full sun and well-drained soil. Plant in early autumn, covering bulbs with about 3in (8cm) of soil (JI No.2).
PROPAGATION By division of clumps during dormancy, in summer. From seed, sown as soon as ripe.
POTENTIAL PROBLEMS Slugs, snails.

I. 'Rolf Fiedler'

Flowers: early to mid-spring.
H 4–6in (10–15cm), S 4–6in (10–15cm). FrH.
Vivid blue intensified by the yellow tips of the stamens gives the flowers an enamelled beauty.

Ipheion uniflorum

I. uniflorum *Argentina, Uruguay*

Flowers: early to mid-spring.
II 6–8in (15–20cm), S 4–6in (10–15cm). FrH.
The narrow tubular flower opens to an upward-facing star, about 1½in (4cm) across, usually of silvery blue but varying in colour intensity. In '**Album**', brown centre lines to the segments and green shadows add a sombre note to the white flowers. '**Froyle Mill**' has violet flowers. '**Wisley Blue**', with dark central veins, shades from a near-white centre, through mauve to violet at the tips.

Ipheion uniflorum 'Froyle Mill'

IRIS

IRIDACEAE

The horticultural riches of this genus of about 300 species are shared between those that are bulbous and an even larger number that are rhizomatous. The popularity of irises throughout their long history in cultivation owes much to the distinctive make-up of the flower and the numerous variations on the basic formula, usually underlined by rich or subtle colouring. In all irises the flower is made up of 6 segments. The outer 3, the falls, extend on a horizontal or upward-tilted haft with a downturned, often sharply recurved, blade. The beard that is such a conspicuous feature on the falls of a large group of rhizomatous irises is not present in bulbous irises but there is sometimes a clearly marked crest. The 3 inner segments, the standards, are usually more or less erect but can arch outwards or even droop and are smaller than the falls. Petal-like style branches or arms arch over the falls, each protecting a stamen.

The bulbous irises fall into three sections, two of which are described. The Juno irises, such as *I. magnifica* and *I. orchioides*, are not represented because of the difficulties they present in cultivation. See also PERENNIALS.

RETICULATA IRISES

These jewel-like and astonishingly hardy dwarf bulbs, which flower in late winter or early spring, are mainly from Turkey, the Caucasus and further east. Distinctive features include the net-like (reticulate) tunic of the bulb and the fact that the roots die away in the dormant period. In most species the rather narrow leaves, which have 4 or 8 ribs, are short at flowering but later grow much longer. In the wild the species experience a long, hot and dry summer and are often most successful in a bulb frame or alpine house. Most hybrids tolerate moister conditions in free-draining soil.
CULTIVATION Require full sun and well-drained soil, preferably neutral to slightly alkaline (JI No. 2 with added grit). Plant in early to mid-autumn, covering with 3–6in (8–15cm) of soil or compost.
PROPAGATION From offsets, separated in the dormant season. From seed, sown as soon as ripe.
POTENTIAL PROBLEMS Slugs and snails; ink spot fungus.

I. danfordiae *Turkey*

Flowers: mid- to late winter.
H 3–4in (8–10cm), S 2–3in (5–8cm). FH.
This is one of the first Reticulata irises to flower and its intense lemon-yellow, with small dark spots on the falls, makes it very conspicuous for its size. The standards are insignificant, so that the flower looks squat and stocky. The honeyed scent is a rarely appreciated feature. The square-sectioned leaves eventually reach a height of about 8in (20cm).

Iris danfordiae

I. histrioides *Turkey*

Flowers: mid- to late winter.
H 4–6in (10–15cm), S 3–4in (8–10cm). FH.
The royal blue of the clone sold under the name '**Major**' is a dazzling discovery in winter. The flowers, which open before the leaves develop, are up to 3in (8cm) across, with falls, extending on nearly horizontal hafts, which have an orange ridge edged by white streaking. The relatively short and broad standards add to the impression of a compact flower. The hybrid *I.* '**Joyce**' has a similar outline. Its broad falls, a deeper blue than the sky-blue of the standards, have a bright yellow ridge with white flecking.

Iris 'Katharine Hodgkin'

I. 'Katharine Hodgkin'

Flowers: late winter to early spring. H 4–6in (10–15cm), S 3–4in (8–10cm). FH.
In general outline this sturdy hybrid resembles its parents, *I. histrioides* and *I. winogradowii*, the latter having lemon-yellow flowers with green spots on the falls around a pale orange high-light. The hybrid is white suffused with pale sea green and lightly veined with blue. There are yellow ridges to the falls, which seem to be casually spotted with dark blue.

I. reticulata *E. from central Turkey to Caucasus, N.E. Iraq, N. Iran*
Flowers: late winter to early spring. H 4–8in (10–20cm), S 2–3in (5–8cm). FH.
The upward-tilted haft of the falls gives a characteristic shape to the classic Reticulata iris. The solitary scented flower, up to 3in (8cm) across, has rather slender segments but proves much less flimsy than it seems. The stock usually sold under the species name has deep violet-blue flowers with an orange-yellow crest on the falls. The leaves, which have 4 ribs, are normally short at flowering but subsequently extend to about 14in (35cm). There is said to be considerable colour variation in the wild, through shades of blue, violet and purple, which is reflected in the range of cultivars and hybrids, all of them desirable. They include: *I.* **'Cantab'**, pale blue lit on the slightly darker falls by an orange crest edged by white streaking; *I.* **'Clairette'**, with pale blue and a white blaze on the deep violet falls; and *I.* **'J.S. Dijt'**, reddish purple in colour, the orange ridge, edged by white markings, which extend over a very deep purple blotch.

Iris **'J.S. Dijt'**

XIPHIUM IRISES

This section comprises several species from south-west Europe and north-west Africa, including *I. xiphium* itself, and the hybrids, known as English, Dutch and Spanish irises, derived from them. They are summer flowering; the bulbs have a smooth tunic and there are no fleshy roots that persist throughout the year. The hybrids are popular as cut flowers but they are also useful in borders between spring and full summer.
CULTIVATION Require full sun and well-drained (but moist rather than dry for *I. latifolia* and *I.* English hybrids) neutral to slightly alkaline soil (JI No. 2). Plant in early to mid-autumn; cover bulbs with 4–6in (10–15cm) of soil.

PROPAGATION From offsets, in late summer or autumn. From seed (species only), sown in spring.
POTENTIAL PROBLEMS Usually none.

I. Dutch hybrids
Dutch iris
Flowers: early summer. H 18–30in (45–75cm), S 3–4in (8–10cm).FH.
The Dutch irises, which are the first of the Xyphium hybrids to flower, are commonly sold as colour mixtures, which include white, yellow, bronze, blue and purple, the flowers often pleasingly bicoloured. Some fine named selections are also available. These include: **'Blue Magic'**, contrasting pale violet standards and deep violet falls; **'Golden Harvest'**, rich yellow; and **'Wedgwood'**, pale blue.

I. English hybrids
English iris
Flowers: early to mid-summer. H 16–24in (40–60cm), S 3–4in (8–10cm). FH.
The forms and hybrids of *I. latifolia* are more commonly seen than the species itself and are widely sold as mixtures, rarely as named selections. Yellow does not feature in the colour range but there are wonderful shades of blue, purple and violet as well as pale tints and pure whites. These Xiphium irises follow the species in their general character, having more substantial flowers than the Dutch hybrids, which flower before them.

Spanish (*xiphium*) iris

I. Spanish hybrids
Spanish iris
Flowers: early to mid-summer. H 12–18in (30–45cm), S 3–4in (8–10cm). FH.
Although smaller in all their parts, the Spanish irises resemble the Dutch irises, but flower 2 to 3 weeks later. They are usually sold as mixed colours, including white, cream, yellow, bronze, blue, violet and purple with a yellow or orange mark. Bicolours have purple standards and bronze falls with an orange blotch.

LEUCOJUM

AMARYLLIDACEAE Snowflake

The snowflakes, of which there are about 10 species, do not have the ardent following of their relatives the snowdrops, but like them include plants of quiet charm that flower in winter, spring and autumn. The flowers have 6 segments of equal length. The spring and summer snowflakes do well in heavy soils. The slender *L. autumnale*, which produces small white bells tinged with pink in late summer or early autumn, needs sun and good drainage.
CULTIVATION The species described below tolerate full sun or partial shade and thrive in moisture-retentive soils. Plant *L. autumnale* in mid- to late summer, covering the bulbs with 2in (5cm) of soil and spring-flowering species in autumn, covering bulbs with 3–4in (8–10cm) of soil.
PROPAGATION From offsets, separated during dormancy. From seed, sown in autumn.
POTENTIAL PROBLEMS Slugs, narcissus bulb fly.

Leucojum aestivum **'Gravetye Giant'**

L. aestivum *From British Isles to C. and E. Europe, Caucasus and Turkey*
Summer snowflake
Flowers: mid- to late spring. H 18–24in (45–60cm), S 4–6in (10–15cm). FH.
This bulb defies its name and flowers in spring. A sturdy leafless stem, above a clump of strap-shaped leaves, terminates in several white bells with green markings just above the tips of the segments. **'Gravetye Giant'** is a well-proportioned selection that can grow up to 3ft (90cm).

L. vernum *S. and E. Europe*
Spring snowflake
Flowers: late winter to early spring. H 8–12in (20–30cm), S 2–3in (5–8cm). FH.
The spring snowflake is like an early, shorter-growing summer snowflake but with larger flowers,

usually 1 or 2 per stem, and thrives in the same moist conditions. The robust **var. *vagneri*** has green markings on the segments but **var. *carpathicum*** has yellow tips.

Leucojum vernum

LILIUM

LILIACEAE Lily

No other genus of summer-flowering bulbs can match lilies as garden and container plants and there are few genera of any kind that include such a high proportion of outstanding ornamentals. There are about 100 species distributed throughout Europe, Asia and North America, and the hybrids raised from these are legion. The bulbs of lilies consist of fleshy scales, from which the basal roots develop, and some produce stolons or rhizomes that allow them to spread laterally. Several produce bulbils in the leaf axils or low on the stem as a means of propagation. A large number of lilies, described as stem-rooting (as distinct from the basal-rooting lilies that produce only basal roots), also produce roots on the stem above the bulb. In the descriptions below stem-rooting lilies are indicated as such after the dimensions. There is a very wide colour range, not including blue, and the segments may be spotted and partly covered with warty protuberances known as papillae. The flowers, all arranged in 6 parts, may be upward- or outward-facing, nodding or down-turned, and carried 1 to a stem, in tiered profusion or in tight clusters. The trumpet, as in *L. regale*, is the classic shape but equally distinctive is the turk's-cap flower of the martagon lily (*L. martagon*), in which the segments are sharply recurved. Other lilies are said to have flowers of funnel or bowl shape but many are intermediate in character. Although far from all lilies are scented, some are exceptionally fragrant while a few are rank smelling; its unpleasant scent counts against the easily grown **L. pyrenaicum**, with yellow

turk's cap flowers. Many of the species are woodland plants from mountainous areas, where there is a plentiful supply of moisture but also good drainage and where the base of plants is often shaded. Some lilies, including the American turk's-cap lily (**L. superbum**), are plants of marshy ground and a few species like a warm, sunny position. Most lilies do well in containers and several that are not fully hardy, including **L. formosanum var. pricei** and **L. longiflorum**, make magnificent plants for cool greenhouses or conservatories.

A major shortcoming of many lilies, including the spectacular golden-rayed lily (**L. auratum**) from Japan, is susceptibility to virus diseases. Control of pests such as aphids will help prevent these diseases becoming established.

A classification of lilies into 9 divisions is widely used, all the true species being placed together while the other divisions reflect to some extent the often complex parentage of the hybrids. In the lily selection that follows the species are given first, followed by the hybrids with the relevant division. *CULTIVATION* Most tolerate partial shade but prefer the flower stem in full sun and the base in shade, and require well-drained soil that is rich in organic matter and neutral to slightly acid (JI No. 2 with additional leafmould and grit), but see entries. Plant between mid-autumn and early spring, basal-rooting lilies preferably in autumn. Cover the bulbs of basal-rooting lilies with 3–6in (8–15cm) of soil or compost and stem-rooting lilies with 6–8in (15–20cm). Keep well-watered in the growing season. *PROPAGATION* From offsets, scales, bulblets and bulbils, in dormancy (using virus-free stock). From seed, sown in early to mid-autumn. *POTENTIAL PROBLEMS* Pests in and above the soil, including aphids, leatherjackets, lily beetles and slugs; viruses and fungal diseases, including grey mould (*Botrytis*).

SPECIES

L. canadense *E. North America* Meadow lily
Flowers: mid-summer. H 3–6ft (90–180cm), S 10–12in (25–30cm). FH.
The meadow lily, which requires moist, lime-free soil or compost, is exceptionally graceful, the long flower stalks, arched like violin bows, carrying the flowers up and out from the stem before turning over so that the bells hang vertically. There can be up to 20

lightly scented flowers, but often less than half this number, varying in colour from yellow or pale orange to red, usually marked internally with dark spots. The flowers, which are 2–3in (5–8cm) long, have segments that turn up gently at the tips.

L. candidum *E. Mediterranean* Madonna lily
Flowers: H 3–6ft (90–180cm), S 8–10in (20–25cm). FH.
Despite its capriciousness and susceptibility to grey mould (*Botrytis*), this lily is in the first rank of flowers. It does best in full sun and well-drained, slightly alkaline soil, planted with the tips just below the soil surface. The stiff stem carries up to 15 outward-facing, pure white trumpets, 3–4in (8–10cm) in length, which flare widely at the mouth. They are heavily scented and lit by the vivid yellow of the anthers. A rosette of overwintering basal leaves appears in early autumn.

L. henryi *C. China*
Flowers: late summer to early autumn. H 3–8ft (90–250cm), S 10–12in (25–30cm). Stem-rooting. FH.
The tall arching stems of this graceful lily need staking. The 10 to 20 lightly fragrant turk's-cap flowers, suspended on horizontal stalks, are orange with black spotting among warty protuberances. Neutral to slightly alkaline soils suit this species.

Lilium lancifolium var. splendens

L. lancifolium *China, Japan, Korea*
Tiger lily
Flowers: late summer to early autumn. H 3–6ft (90–180cm), S 8–10in (20–25cm). Stem-rooting. FH.
Susceptibility to virus is a drawback of this species, which prefers lime-free soil or compost. It does not usually set seed but produces bulblets in the leaf axils. The turk's-cap flowers are reddish orange, heavily spotted on downy stems. There can be as many as 25 to a stem in the vigorous **var. *splendens***.

Lilium martagon

L. martagon *Widespread in Asia and Europe*
Turk's-cap lily
Flowers: early to mid-summer.
H 3–5ft (90–150cm), S 6–10in
(15–25cm). Stem-rooting. FH.
In the wild this species, the most widely distributed of the lilies, is found in woodland and open meadows. As a garden plant it does well on alkaline soils and is most appealing when naturalized in dappled shade. The purplish stem can carry up to 50 nodding flowers, usually about 2in (5cm) across, with the segments so tightly rolled back that the tips touch the flower stalk. The flowers, which have a rank scent, are usually purplish pink with darker spotting but the depth of colouring varies considerably in wild populations. The white **var. album**, with yellow anthers, is exceptionally beautiful. **Var. cattaniae** is tall-growing and has unspotted flowers of inky purple.

L. monadelphum *Caucasus, N.E. Turkey*
Flowers: early to mid-summer.
H 3–5ft (90–150cm), S 8–10in
(20–25cm). Stem-rooting. FH.
In a well-grown specimen the stout stem can carry more than 20 nodding scented flowers, up to 4in (10cm) across, of pale or rich yellow. The base and the turned back tips of the segments are tinged purple and there is often purple spotting inside the flower.

L. pardalinum *W. USA*
Leopard or panther lily
Flowers: mid-summer. H 5–7ft (1.5–2.2m), S 10–12in (25–30cm). FH.
The orange-red turk's-cap flowers are spotted with purplish brown. Normally about 10 per stem, their lively colouring makes this an ideal species to naturalize in dappled shade, clusters of bulbs building up in the lime-free soil it requires.

L. pumilum *N. China, N. Korea, Mongolia, Siberia*
Flowers: early summer. H 10–24in
(25–60cm), S 6–8in (15–20cm).
Stem-rooting. FH.
Unlike some of the short-growing hybrid lilies, this species, which is intolerant of lime, is well-proportioned, carrying up to 30 nodding turk's-cap flowers of vivid scarlet. They are scented and some have black spots at the centres.

Lilium regale

L. regale *W. China*
Regal lily
Flowers: mid-summer. H 3–6ft
(90–180cm), S 6–8in (15–20cm).
Stem-rooting. FH.
Popularity cannot spoil the distinction of this lily, which is one of the easiest to grow. A wiry stem carries several richly scented trumpets, often more than 10, that are up to 5in (13cm) long. They are glistening white with purple staining on the outside, the golden anthers protruding from a yellow throat. Flowering plants of this lime-tolerant species can be raised from seed within two years.
'Album' has trumpets of dazzling whiteness warmed by a golden radiance in the throat. **'Royal Gold'** is a surprising variation; the flowers are bright yellow but have a sobering purplish brown exterior.

Lilium regale 'Album'

L. speciosum *Japan*
Flowers: late summer to early autumn. H 4–6ft (1.2–1.8m), S 10–12in (25–30cm). Stem-rooting. FrH.
Although this species and its varieties only do well outdoors in areas where the climate is mild,

they are well known as greenhouse plants and as cut flowers. They all require lime-free soil. There are usually about 12 strongly scented blooms to a stem, carried on long stalks and outward-facing or nodding. They are white or pink, stained pink to crimson at the centre. The waxy segments have wavy edges and the tips turn back revealing a surface warty with dark-coloured papillae. **Var. roseum** has pink flowers on green stems but in **var. album**, with white flowers, and the rich carmine-red **var. rubrum** the stems are purplish brown.

Lilium speciosum var. rubrum

L. × testaceum
Nankeen lily
Flowers: mid- to late summer.
H 4–6ft (1.2–1.8m), S 8–10in
(20–25cm). FH.
The unique buff colour of the flowers is warmed by the orange-red of the anthers and faint spotting in the centre. This old garden hybrid has up to 12 flowers per stem, the long buds held vertically before opening to nodding turk's-caps about 3in (8cm) across.

HYBRIDS

L. African Queen Group
(Trumpet and Aurelian hybrid)
Flowers: mid- to late summer.
H 4–6ft (1.2–1.8m), S 10–12in
(25–30cm). Stem-rooting. FrH.
The richly scented, funnel-shaped flowers in a blend of purplish maroon, tawny peach and radiant apricot form a compact pyramid at the head of a stout stem.

L. 'Bright Star' (Trumpet and Aurelian hybrid)
Flowers: mid-summer. H 30–36in
(74–90cm), S 6–8in (15–20cm).
Stem-rooting. FH.
The flowers of this lime-tolerant hybrid, usually 5 or more to a stem, hang from nearly horizontal stalks, their ivory white segments curling back at the tips to reveal a star formed by central, orange-yellow bands, bordered by papillae, on each segment.

Lilium 'Casa Blanca'

L. 'Casa Blanca' (Oriental hybrid)
Flowers: mid- to late summer.
H 3–4ft (90–120cm), S 8–10in
(20–25cm). Stem-rooting. FH.
The stiff stem terminates in a
cluster of fragrant bowl-shaped
flowers of splendid whiteness.
Even the papillae are white but the
anthers are a bold orange red.

L. 'Côte d'Azur' (Asiatic hybrid)
Flowers: early to mid-summer.
H 16–30 (40–75cm), S 6–8in
(15–20cm). Stem-rooting. FH.
Greenish buff upright buds make
an attractive contrast of colour and
form among the bowl-shaped,
deep pink flowers clustered at the
end of a short stem. **L. 'Red Carpet'**,
an even more compact Asiatic
hybrid, 14–16in (35–40cm) tall,
with upward-facing flowers of fiery
red, is good for bedding schemes.

L. 'Fire King' (Asiatic hybrid)
Flowers: mid-summer. H 3–4ft
(90–120cm), S 8–10in (20–25cm).
Stem-rooting. FH.
The intense orange-red colour in a
well-formed head of 5 or more
outward-facing flowers makes this
an arresting lily.

L. 'Journey's End' (Oriental
hybrid)
Flowers: late summer. H 3–5ft
(90–150cm), S 8–10in (20–25cm).
Stem-rooting. FH.
The erect buds become more
outward-facing as they open to star-
shaped, fragrant flowers. These are
up to 8in (20cm) across, with wavy
segments that recurve elegantly.
There is maroon spotting on the

Lilium 'Journey's End'

vivid crimson flowers, which pale
to near white at the margins and
tips of the segments. **L. 'Star
Gazer'**, another Oriental hybrid of
similar size with recurved flowers,
is familiar as a cut flower because
it responds well to forcing. The
fragrant blooms have broad, rich
crimson segments, pale at the tip
and margins and liberally spotted
with maroon dots.

L. 'Mont Blanc' (Asiatic hybrid)
Flowers: early to mid-summer.
H 2–3ft (60–90cm), S 6–8in
(15–20cm). Stem-rooting. FH.
Erect pale pink buds, usually 5 to 8
in number, open to upward-facing
creamy flowers, which are
peppered maroon at the centre
and have dark orange anthers.
L. 'Enchantment' is another short
Asiatic hybrid with upward-facing
flowers. They are bowl-shaped,
brilliant orange, spotted black in
the centre, and there can be as
many as 16 to a stem.

Lilium 'Enchantment'

L. Pink Perfection Group
(Trumpet and Aurelian hybrid)
Flowers: mid- to late summer.
H 4–6ft (1.2–1.8m), S 10–12in
(25–30cm). Stem-rooting. FH.
Stout stems carry several slightly
nodding and strongly scented
trumpet flowers. The pale to
purplish-pink segments curl back
from dark orange anthers.

Lilium Pink Perfection Group

L. 'Sterling Star' (Asiatic hybrid)
Flowers: early to mid-summer.
H 3–4ft (90–120cm), S 8–10in
(20–25cm). Stem-rooting. FH.
Buff-tinted white starry flowers,

usually 6 to 10 per stem, open
nearly flat from pale greenish pink
buds. The anthers are dark orange
and dark brown dots speckle the
centre. Another Asiatic hybrid of
similar size with upward-facing
flowers is **L. 'Connecticut King'**.
Flowers are star-shaped and a rich
greenish yellow with warmer
shading. **L. 'Montreux'** is slightly
shorter, with greenish buds
opening to nearly flat pink flowers
that have minute brown dots
speckling the centre.

Lilium 'Montreux'

MUSCARI

HYACINTHACEAE Grape hyacinth

The commonly grown grape
hyacinths represent a relatively
small proportion of the 30 or so
species distributed in Europe and
south-west Asia. The bulbs are
fleshy and the leaves, basal and
usually grass-like but channelled
on the inside surface, begin to
appear in autumn. A few species
are autumn-flowering but most
produce their spikes of densely
packed bells in spring. The flowers,
in most cases blue and less than
½in (1cm) in length, are constricted
at the mouth. The topmost
flowers, which are generally
sterile, are often paler than those
lower on the spike. Some species
are sweetly scented. In general
grape hyacinths thrive on well-
drained soil in partial shade as well
as in open positions but produce
leaves rather than flower spikes
when deprived of sunlight. Some,
especially **M. neglectum**, spread so
freely that they should be
introduced only with caution. The
less vigorous are attractive in rock
gardens and raised beds. The
strong family resemblance among
Muscari extends to the pick of a
closely related genus, **Bellevalia
paradoxa**, although its flowers
are not constricted at the mouth.
This species requires similar
conditions to the *Muscari*
described here.
CULTIVATION Tolerate full sun or
partial shade and require well-
drained soil (JI No. 2). Plant in

301

early autumn, covering bulbs with about 4in (10cm) of soil or compost.
PROPAGATION From offsets, removed in summer. From seed, sown in late summer or early autumn.
POTENTIAL PROBLEM Viruses.

M. armeniacum *Caucasus to S. E. Europe and Turkey*
Flowers: mid- to late spring. H 8–10in (20–25cm), S 2–3in (5–8cm). FH.
The narrow leaves, which appear in autumn, are rather lax and untidy but the spike of tightly packed, scented flowers is sturdy. The flowers are bell-like and bright blue, with hints of purple and violet. The constricted mouth has a thin white rim. This is the best grape hyacinth for general planting. **'Blue Spike'** has a heavy head of large, double flowers with strong purple and violet shading. **'Heavenly Blue'** is a misleading name for a selection with single flowers of dark blue.

Muscari aucheri

M. aucheri *N.W. Iran*
Flowers: early to mid-spring. H 6–8in (15–20cm), S 2–3in (5–8cm). FH.
The contrast between the deep blue fertile flowers and the pale blue sterile ones above them is remarkable in this species, sometimes known as the Oxford and Cambridge grape hyacinth.

M. azureum *Caucasus, E. Turkey*
Flowers: early to mid-spring. H 4–6in (10–15cm), S 2–4in (5–10cm). FH.
The short spike, surrounded by broad leaves, is packed with pale blue bells with a darker stripe down the centre of each lobe. This species often self-seeds freely.

M. botryoides *C. and S.E. Europe*
Flowers: mid-spring. H 6–8in (15–20cm), S 2–3in (5–8cm). FH.
The dense spikes of this species have globular blue flowers with a white rim. It and the pearly white **'Album'** are refined plants suitable for rock gardens.

Muscari botryoides 'Album'

M. comosum *Iran, S. Europe, Turkey*
Tassel grape hyacinth
Flowers: late spring to early summer. H 10–20in (25–50cm), S 2–3in (5–8cm). FH.
The species, which is common in the wild in cultivated and rough ground, is easy to grow but its lax spike of fertile olive-green flowers topped by a tuft of purplish blue sterile flowers is not of great ornamental value. **'Plumosum'** is, however, an interesting curiosity. All the flowers are sterile, the long-lasting mauve plumes that make it so distinctive and give it the name feather hyacinth consisting of elongated filaments.

NARCISSUS

AMARYLLIDACEAE Daffodil

Daffodils and other narcissi have been very popular spring bulbs for hundreds of years. Thousands of cultivars have been developed from the 50 or so species found in Europe, north Africa and Asia, the strongest concentration being in W. Europe, particularly in the Iberian peninsula. In the wild the species occupy a range of habitats from sea level to the sub-alpine zone, often growing in open meadows or short turf, sometimes on the fringes of woodland. The bulbs produce strap-shaped or rush-like basal leaves and erect leafless stems bearing a solitary flower or umbels with up to 20 flowers breaking out of the sheath at the head of the stem.
What has always fascinated gardeners is that sitting at the centre of the 6 petal-like segments is a cup or trumpet, a structure known as a corona. Gold, greenish yellow, soft yellow, cream and white are the predominant colours but among the numerous bicoloured cultivars many have orange and a few have pink coronas. Most of the species and cultivars are fragrant and some, especially the jonquils (*N. jonquilla* and hybrids of which it is a parent) have sweet scent of superlative

quality. The species and hybrids are a versatile group of garden plants, the more robust being unbeatable for the bold effects they create when naturalized. Colonies are usually very long-lived, provided the leaves are allowed to die down naturally. The really beefy hybrids are best naturalized in park-like settings, the species and the smaller, well-proportioned hybrids being more suitable for beds and borders and for naturalizing in a wilder setting. There is a wide choice of plants for rock gardens and containers.
All the divisions in the standard categorization of the genus are represented in the following selection (the name of the division is given in the head of the hybrid entries) but it is unapologetically weighted in favour of the species, which are described first, and the more lightly built hybrids. The swept back segments of the cyclamineus hybrids, a trait derived from *N. cyclamineus*, give these well-proportioned daffodils a breezy character. They are among the most versatile of all the narcissi, many naturalizing well and all suitable for beds, borders, rock gardens and containers.
CULTIVATION Most tolerate full sun or partial shade and require well-drained soil (JI No. 2, with added grit for dwarf species) and a good supply of moisture in spring, but see under headings and individual entries. Plant in early autumn, covering bulbs with 2–6in (5–15cm) of soil or compost, at a depth about 3 times the height of the bulb, deeper in dry soil and in grass.
PROPAGATION From offsets, removed in the dormant season. From seed, sown as soon as ripe.
POTENTIAL PROBLEMS Narcissus bulb fly, narcissus eelworm, slugs; viruses and fungal diseases.

SPECIES

N. bulbocodium *N.W. Africa, Portugal, Spain, S.W. France*
Hoop-petticoat daffodil
Flowers: late winter to early spring. H 4–10in (10–25cm), S 2–4in (5–10cm). FH.
In the wild this highly distinctive but very variable dwarf species is mainly found in alpine turf. The flowers, produced singly among dark green narrow leaves, are dominated by a funnel-shaped corona 1–2in (2.5–5cm) across, in which can be seen the curved stamens and style. The narrow, short segments, hardly more than vestiges, are the same rich yellow

as the petticoat. The numerous variations on this theme are all remarkable plants, two superlative examples being the free-flowering deep yellow **subsp**. *bulbocodium* **var**. *conspicuus* and **subsp**. *bulbocodium* **var**. *citrinus*, which has large, lemon-yellow flowers.

Narcissus cyclamineus

N. cyclamineus *Portugal, Spain*
Flowers: late winter to early spring. H 4–8in (10–20cm), S 2–4in (5–10cm). FH.
In damp acid soils that match conditions in its native mountain pasture habitat this dwarf species, a parent of some of the finest daffodil hybrids, will spread freely to form low drifts even in light shade. The bright yellow flowers have segments swept back from the narrow frilled trumpet.

N. jonquilla *Portugal, Spain*
Wild jonquil
Flowers: mid-spring. H 10–12in (25–30cm), S 2–4in (5–10cm). FH.
The strong sweet scent is an outstanding feature. The jonquil, which has semi-cylindrical leaves, produces 3 to 6 deep yellow flowers per stem, the pointed segments radiating from a tiny cup. It does best in full sun on neutral to slightly alkaline soil that is moist in spring.

N. poeticus **var**. *recurvus*
Switzerland
Old pheasant's eye
Flowers: late spring. H 14–16in (35–40cm), S 3–4in (8–10cm). FH.
Swept-back segments of glistening white give this variety of the pheasant's eye narcissus a fresh, wind-tossed look when thriving on moist soils. The small cup is green and yellow with a red rim.

N. pseudonarcissus *Europe*
Wild daffodil, Lent lily
Flowers: early spring. H 6–14in (15–35cm), S 2–4in (5–10cm). FH.
The fragrant flowers, usually solitary, are carried above a tuft of strap-shaped, grey-green or bluish green leaves. The trumpet, which is slightly flared at the mouth, is

pale to deep yellow and the creamy yellow segments are usually slightly twisted. The species, subspecies and cultivars are among the best daffodils for naturalizing, shaming the heavy-weight hybrids by their graceful proportions. 'Lobularis' is a short-growing bicoloured selection, rarely more than 8in (20cm) high, with slightly drooping flowers. The flowers of the Tenby daffodil, **subsp**. *obvallaris*, are a uniform rich yellow and the trumpet, sometimes more than 5cm (2in) long. The flower stems are about 1ft (30cm) high.

Narcissus pseudonarcissus **subsp**. *obvallaris*

N. triandrus **var**. *triandrus*
Portugal, Spain
Angel's tears
Flowers: early to mid-spring. H 4–10in (10–25cm), S 2–4in (5–10cm). FH.
The pendulous creamy white flowers, 1 to 6 to a stem, with segments swept back and the anthers protruding from the cup, have a balletic charm that invites close inspection. This makes it a superb plant for the alpine house. It can be naturalized in short turf, especially on neutral to acid soils.

HYBRIDS

N. 'Actaea' (Poeticus)
Flowers: late spring. H 18–20in (45–50cm), S 4–6in (10–15cm). FH.
The fragrant flowers are about 3in (8cm) across. Crisp white, broad segments surround a small yellow cup with a conspicuous red rim.

Narcissus '**Actaea**'

N. '**Cantabile**', a shorter-growing Poeticus daffodil, to 14in (35cm) high, has brilliant white segments forming a nearly circular outline and a small flattened cup, which has bands of green and yellow and an orange-red rim.

Narcissus '**Ice Follies**'

N. 'Carlton' (Large-cupped)
Flowers: early to mid-spring. H 18–20in (45–50cm), S 3–5in (8–13cm). FH.
The flowers are large but the corona is almost trumpet-like, giving this soft yellow hybrid pleasing proportions. Among daffodils in this division that have 'pink' flowers *N.* '**Satin Pink**' is one of the truest in colour and has a long corona. The overlapping segments are pure white. *N.* '**Ice Follies**' is a coarser but sturdy hybrid in this division. The overlapping segments are creamy white and the short gaping cup, frilled at the edge, fades from lemon-yellow to near white.

Narcissus '**Rip van Winkle**'

N. 'Cheerfulness' (Double)
Flowers: mid-spring. H 16–18in (40–45cm), S 3–4in (8–10cm). FH.
A soft orange glow emanates from the muddled centres of the creamy double flowers, usually 3 to a stem. The scent is very sweet. *N.* '**Yellow Cheerfulness**' has soft yellow flowers. The small scale of *N.* '**Rip van Winkle**', only 6–8in (15–20cm) high, makes it a more appealing curiosity than larger double daffodils with single flowers. Its green-tinted sunburst is composed of numerous narrow yellow segments.

Narcissus 'February Gold'

N. 'February Gold'
(Cyclamineus)
Flowers: early spring. H 10–12in
(25–30cm), S 3–4in (8–10cm). FH.
Although rarely as precocious as
the name suggests, this stalwart
flowers early and is long lasting.
The flowers are up to 3in (8cm)
across with deep yellow trumpets
and slightly paler segments.
N. 'February Silver' is a crisper
version, with a lemon-yellow
trumpet, slightly ragged at the
mouth, surrounded by creamy
white segments. A slightly taller
companion for these from the
same division is N. 'Peeping Tom',
with a strikingly long narrow
trumpet, flaring at the mouth, and
of an almost uniform rich yellow.

N. 'Golden Harvest' (Trumpet)
Flowers: mid-spring. H 16–18in
(40–45cm), S 3–5in (8–13cm). FH.
Rich yellow flowers, the trumpet
flaring widely and the segments
slightly twisted, and its way of
increasing freely have made this a
favourite among the many large
trumpet daffodils. Other yellow
heavyweights include N. 'Arctic
Gold' and N. 'Dutch Master'.
Among whites are the glacial
N. 'Empress of Ireland' and
N. 'Mount Hood'.

N. 'Hawera' (Triandrus)
Flowers: mid-spring. H 8–10in
(20–25cm), S 2–3in (5–8cm). FH.
This slender N. triandrus and
N. jonquilla hybrid produces several
stems per bulb, each with 3 to 5
canary yellow flowers up to 2in
(5cm) across, with segments that
are swept back. N. 'Petrel', is similar
but white, with rounded segments.
N. 'Thalia', with several milk-white
flowers to a stem, is 12–14in
(30–35cm) high. The elegant
N. 'Rippling Waters', is short-
cupped, creamy white, and taller.

N. 'Jenny' (Cyclamineus)
Flowers: early to mid-spring.
H 10–12in (25–30cm), S 2–3in
(5–8cm). FH.
The poise and neat proportions of
this hybrid are outstanding. The

creamy white, pointed segments
are swept back from a waisted
trumpet that is lemon-yellow on
opening but soon fades to palest
cream. N. 'Dove Wings' is similar
but with more rounded segments.
More pronounced bicoloured
effects in this division are found in
N. 'Jack Snipe', with creamy white
segments swept back from a short
golden trumpet, and N. 'Itzim',
which has strongly reflexed yellow
segments and a short orange
trumpet, pale at first but
intensifying in colour. These 2
hybrids are 8–10in (20–25cm) high.

Narcissus 'Jack Snipe'

N. 'Merlin' (Small-cupped)
Flowers: mid-spring. H 16–18in
(40–45cm), S 3–4in (8–10cm). FH.
The broad, overlapping segments
make a nearly circular surround of
pure white for the yellow corona,
which has a wobbling orange rim.
N. 'Birma' has a small, orange cup
with ruffled rim flaring at the
centre of soft yellow segments.

Narcissus 'Birma'

N. 'Orangery' (Split corona)
Flowers: mid-spring. H 16–18in
(40–45cm), S 3–4in (8–10cm). FH.
The split corona that gives this
daffodil its unusual form consists
of a ruffled orange collar with only
the margins of the creamy
segments showing.

N. 'Rijnveld's Early Sensation'
(Trumpet)
Flowers: late winter. H 10–12in
(25–30cm), S 2–3in (5–8cm). FH.
This bright yellow hybrid with
long-lasting blooms is one of the
first trumpet daffodils to flower.

Short-growing, but well-
proportioned, trumpet hybrids of
early spring include N. 'Topolino',
6–8in (15–20cm) high, with
creamy yellow segments and a
lemon-yellow trumpet, and the
taller, creamier N. 'W.P. Milner'.

Narcissus 'Rijnveld's Early
Sensation'

N. 'Silver Chimes' (Tazetta)
Flowers: mid-spring. H 12–14in
(30–35cm), S 3–4in (8–10cm). FH.
Each stem of this vigorous and
fragrant hybrid produces a shower
of up to 10 nodding white flowers
with tiny cups of palest yellow. A
slightly taller Tazetta, N. 'Geranium',
has a cluttered head of 5 to 6
sweetly scented flowers with
orange-red cups standing out
against pure white.

Narcissus 'Sweetness'

N. 'Sweetness' (Jonquilla)
Flowers: mid-spring. H 14–16in
(35–40cm), S 3–4in (8–10cm). FH.
This hybrid bears only one
nodding flower per stem but it is
superbly scented, beautifully
proportioned and a lovely clear
yellow throughout.

N. 'Tête-à-Tête' (Miscellaneous)
Flowers: late winter to early spring.
H 6–8in (15–20cm), S 2–3in
(5–8cm). FH.
This dwarf daffodil shows its
Cyclamineus parentage in the
yellow segments swept back from
a more richly coloured cup. It
deserves its popularity as a
container plant, giving an early and
long-lasting display. N. 'Jumblie'
has 2 or 3 short orange-yellow
trumpets to a stem.

Narcissus 'Tête-à-Tête'

N. 'Trevithian' (Jonquilla)
Flowers: mid-spring. H 16–20in
(40–50cm), S 3–4in (8–10cm). FH.
The elegance of the flowers, 2 or 3
to a stem, small cupped and a
uniform soft yellow, make this a
distinctive jonquil, and the purity
of the sweet scent is unimpaired.
The shorter *N.* 'Pipit', about 10in
(25cm) high, has 2 to 3 fragrant
lemon-yellow flowers to a stem,
their small cups quickly fading to
cream. The dwarf, rich yellow
N. 'Sundial', 6–8in (15–20cm)
high, has tiny disc-like central cups.

Narcissus 'Trevithian'

NECTAROSCORDUM

Alliaceae

Three species make up a small
genus closely related to the onions
(*Allium*). The species described is
a tall, intriguing, summer-flowering
bulb. The basal leaves, linear and
with a sharp keel, smell strongly of
garlic but the dried seedheads are
both decorative and scentless.
Plants may self-seed freely.
Cultivation Tolerate full sun or
partial shade and require well-
drained soil. Plant in autumn,
under 4–6in (10–15cm) of soil.
Propagation From offsets,
removed in late summer. From
seed, sown as soon as ripe.
Potential problems Usually none.

N. siculum *France, Italy*
Flowers: late spring to early
summer. H 2–4ft (60–120cm),
S 4–6in (10–15cm). FH.
The numerous bell-shaped flowers
spraying out on downward-arching
stalks from the head of a stout

stem are creamy white with green
tints and reddish purple markings.
The plant is also attractive when
carrying seeds, the stalks turning
to hold the pods erect. The colour
combination of straw, green and
maroon in **subsp.** *bulgaricum*,
from S.E. Europe, Turkey and the
Crimea, is even more unusual.

Nectaroscordum siculum subsp.
bulgaricum

NERINE

Amaryllidaceae

This genus from southern Africa
comprises about 30 species,
usually found in dry rocky terrain,
many species flowering
particularly freely in autumn after
summer fires. The flowers, borne
in umbels before the leaves, are
like small lilies, with 6 strap-shaped
segments. These are often wavy at
the margins, curling back from the
thrusting cluster of stamens and
style. Species such as *N. sarniensis*
and the hybrids do well in pots,
preferring some crowding to
frequent repotting. The crystalline
sparkle of the long-lasting flowers
makes nerines good for cutting.
Cultivation Require full sun and
well-drained soil (JI No. 2 with
added grit), dry during dormancy.
Plant in late summer, under glass
setting the bulbs with their tips
showing, outdoors covering bulbs
with 3–4in (8–10cm) of soil.
Propagation By division of
clumps, after flowering. From
seed, sown as soon as ripe.
Potential problem Slugs.
Warning Swallowing any part may
cause stomach upset.

Nerine bowdenii

N. bowdenii *South Africa
(Eastern Cape, KwaZulu/Natal,
Orange Free State)*
Flowers: early to late autumn.
H 18–24in (45–60cm), S 3–4in
(8–10cm). FH.
In cool climates this useful garden
plant needs a favoured position,
such as the base of a warm wall,
and it is worth covering the bulbs
with a mulch during winter where
frosts are heavy. The 3 to 9 flowers
at the head of a stiff stem have
glistening pink rather narrow
segments with crimped edges. In
the vigorous selection *N.* 'Mark
Fenwick' has a stem that is
purplish green.

ORNITHOGALUM

Hyacinthaceae Star of Bethlehem

A cool beauty distinguishes a few
among the 80 mainly unglamorous
species in this genus. The fleshy
bulbs produce basal leaves that are
generally linear or strap-shaped
and a stem carrying numerous
starry or cup-shaped flowers, in
many cases white, with a green
stripe on the reverse of the 6
segments. The untidy leaves,
which sometimes have a silver
stripe, die back just before or just
as plants start flowering and need
masking in beds and borders. The
half-hardy chincherinchee
(*O. thyrsoides*), familiar as a cut
flower, can be grown in frost-
prone areas but requires similar
cultivation to hybrid gladioli.
Cultivation O. arabicum needs full
sun and well-drained soil (JI No. 2).
Others tolerate full sun or partial
shade and require well-drained
soil. Plant in mid-autumn (half-
hardy species outdoors in mid-
spring), covering the bulbs with
3–4in (8–10cm) of soil or compost.
Propagation From offsets,
removed in the dormant season.
From seed, sown in autumn or
spring.
Potential problems Usually none.
Warning Contact with the sap may
irritate the skin. Swallowing any
part may cause stomach upset.

O. arabicum *Mediterranean*
Flowers: late spring to early
summer. H 16–30in (40–75cm),
S 3–4in (8–10cm). HH.
A stout stem carries 6 to 12,
occasionally more, cup-shaped,
scented flowers that are 2in (5cm)
or more across. Their pearly
whiteness is accentuated by the
conspicuous black ovary that is
situated right at the flower's
centre. The dark green, semi-erect
leaves can be up to 60cm (24in)
in length.

Ornithogalum nutans

O. nutans *Europe, S.W Asia*
Flowers: mid- to late spring.
H 12–18in (30–45cm), S 2–3in
(5–8cm). FH.
This true woodlander has widely
distributed naturalized populations
beyond the Balkans, to which it is
thought to be native. The one-
sided spikes usually carry 10 to 12
flaring bells that are silvery white
on the inside and have a broad,
jade-green stripe on the outside.
The leaves are marked with a
central grey line.

Ornithogalum umbellatum

O. umbellatum *E. Mediterranean,
Europe, N. Africa, Turkey*
Star of Bethlehem
Flowers: mid- to late spring.
H 6–12in (15–30cm), S 3–4in (8–
10cm). FH.
Although its rapid increase and the
untidiness of its leaves, which have
a central silver stripe, makes this
species a nuisance in beds and
borders, in the wild garden it is an
asset. It has stout stems which
carry numerous starry white
flowers that are tinted green at
the centre and striped green on
the reverse.

OXALIS

OXALIDACEAE

Among more than 500 species
some are tiresome weeds.
However, there are dwarf species
with swollen rootstocks that are
well-behaved and have clover-like
leaves (in some species these fold
at night) and 5-petalled flowers
that are exquisitely furled in bud
and open to wide funnels in sun.

CULTIVATION Require full sun and
well-drained soil (JI No. 2 with added
grit). Plant in early autumn or early
to mid-spring (*O. tetraphylla*),
covering the rootstock with about
2in (5cm) of soil or compost.
PROPAGATION From bulblets or
division of the rootstock, in the
dormant season. From seed, sown
in early spring.
POTENTIAL PROBLEMS Usually none.

Oxalis adenophylla

O. adenophylla *Argentina, Chile*
Flowers: early to mid-summer.
H 3–4in (8–10cm), S 4–6in
(10–15cm). FH.
Once it captures the eye, this
Andean species is beguiling in its
detail. The small bulb, padded
with the fibrous bases of old
leaves, produces a cushion of grey-
green leaves, consisting of
numerous neatly pleated heart-
shaped leaflets. These are studded
with buds that unfurl to spreading
flowers that are purple in the
throat and have pink veining and
shading on white.

O. enneaphylla *Falkland Islands,
Patagonia*
Flowers: late spring to early
summer. H 3–4in (8–10cm), S 4–6in
(10–15cm). FH.
The blue-green, hairy, fleshy leaves
of this plant are umbrella shaped,
with 9 or more pleated segments.
There are numerous solitary
flowers that are white or pink and
darkly veined. '**Rosea**' has white-
throated pink flowers that are
tinged with mauve.

O. tetraphylla *Mexico*
Good luck plant, lucky clover
Flowers: early to late summer.
H 6–8in (15–20cm), S 6–10in
(15–25cm). FrH.
The funnel-shaped pink flowers,
4 to 12 to a stem, that are borne
throughout summer are less
interesting than the leaves. These
consist of 4 triangular leaflets that
meet at their apex and fold in as
light fails. In '**Iron Cross**' there is a
chocolate band at the centre of the
leaf that creates a bold cross when
the leaflets are open.

PUSCHKINIA

HYACINTHACEAE

The single species in this genus is
an early-flowering dwarf bulb that
is closely related to **Scilla** and
glory of the snow (**Chionodoxa**).
In its mountainous native habitat it
is found growing in short turf and
flowers as the snow melts. Its
silvery beauty is seen to good
effect in an alpine house. In the
open garden it looks at home in
front of shrubs or mixed with
other dwarf plants in rock gardens
or raised beds.
CULTIVATION Tolerate full sun or
partial shade and require well-
drained soil with a plentiful supply
of moisture in the growing season
(JI No. 2 with added grit). Plant in
autumn, covering the bulbs with
2–3in (5–8cm) of soil or compost.
PROPAGATION From offsets,
removed during the dormant season.
From seed, sown as soon as ripe.
POTENTIAL PROBLEM Viruses.

Puschkinia scilloides var.
libanotica

P. scilloides *Caucasus, Lebanon,
N. Iran, N. Iraq, Turkey*
Flowers: early to mid-spring.
H 6–8in (15–20cm), S 2–3in
(5–8cm).FH.
A pair of strap-shaped leaves flanks
the lax stem, which bears
numerous bell-shaped flowers.
Although the depth of colour
varies, they are usually a very pale
blue and each segment is marked
with a darker blue central stripe.
In **var. libanotica** the flowers are
smaller and the blue striping less
conspicuous.

RHODOHYPOXIS

HYPOXIDACEAE

The flat flowers of these bright
miniatures are puzzling, the 6
segments being arranged in such a
way that the style and stamens at
the centre are obscured. There are
6 species, all from southern Africa.
The species described and its
cultivars or hybrids, here all listed
under *R. baurii*, make a colourful
display, despite their diminutive

size, in the alpine house or in rock gardens and raised beds. The corm-like rootstocks need protection from excessive wet in winter.
CULTIVATION Require full sun and lime-free, well-drained soil with plenty of moisture in the growing season (ericaceous compost with added grit). Plant in early autumn, covering the rootstock with about 1in (2.5cm) of soil or compost.
PROPAGATION From offsets, removed in early autumn. From seed, sown in autumn or spring.
POTENTIAL PROBLEMS Usually none.

Rhodohypoxis baurii 'Alba'

R. baurii *South Africa*
Flowers: late spring to early autumn. H 2–4in (5–10cm), S 2–4in (5–10cm). FrH.
A long succession of pale to dark pink flowers, no more than ¾in (2cm) across, are produced among a tuft of hairy, linear leaves. The cultivars, some of which may be of hybrid origin, similar in general character to the species, include: 'Alba', white; *R.* 'Appleblossom', a soft combination of pink and green; *R.* 'Harlequin', small white flowers with a pink suffusion and pink margins; *R.* 'Helen', pure white flowers nearly twice as large as those of the species; *R.* 'Tetra Pink', large pink flowers; and *R.* 'Tetra Red', like a much darker version of *R.* 'Tetra Pink'.

Rhodohypoxis 'Tetra Red'

SCILLA

HYACINTHACEAE

The small species from temperate Europe and S.W. Asia are among the great delights of spring, their blues in some cases startlingly vivid. The genus contains about 90 species, with representatives in tropical and southern Africa and E. Asia. Naturalized colonies of the spring-flowering species from mountainous country make blue eddies in short grass or among deciduous shrubs and are suitable for rock gardens and alpine houses.
CULTIVATION *S. peruviana* requires full sun and fertile well-drained soil. Other species tolerate full sun or partial shade and require well-drained soil (JI No. 2 with added leafmould and grit) and plentiful moisture in spring. Plant in autumn, covering bulbs of spring-flowering species with 3–4in (8–10cm) of soil or compost; set bulbs of *S. peruviana* just below the surface.
PROPAGATION From seed, sown as soon as ripe. From offsets (produced sparingly), removed during the dormant season.
POTENTIAL PROBLEM Viruses.

S. bifolia *S. Europe to Turkey*
Flowers: late winter to early spring. H 3–6in (8–15cm), S 2–3in (5–8cm). FH.
Lax reddish stems seem to teeter among the fleshy leaves, leaning with the one-sided arrangement of up to 10 starry flowers. The flowers face outwards or upwards and the colour is usually a strong mauve-blue, although there is considerable variation. 'Rosea' is pink.

Scilla mischtschenkoana

S. mischtschenkoana *From Georgia to N.W. Iran*
Flowers: late winter to early spring. H 4–6in (10–15cm), S 2–3in (5–8cm). FH.
The precocious silvery blue flowers, with a darker reverse and stripe down each segment, seem to emerge from below ground already open. There are several stems to a bulb, each with 2 to 6 rather flat flowers that face outwards.

S. peruviana *Italy, N. Africa, Portugal, Spain*
Flowers: late spring to early summer. H 8–12 in (20–30cm), S 6–8in (15–20cm). FrH.
The stout stem terminates in a cone-like arrangement of up to 100 flowers, which are a metallic blue or white. This species does not have a dormant season, the new linear leaves starting into growth in autumn as the older leaves die.

Scilla peruviana

S. siberica *Russia and Ukraine to N. Iran and Turkey*
Siberian squill
Flowers: early spring. H 4–8in (10–20cm), S 2–3in (5–8cm). FH.
The piercing blue of the flowers provides one of the most intense colour sensations of early spring. There are usually several stems to a bulb, each bearing about 4 down-turned flowers, in some paler forms with a dark stripe down the centre of the segments. 'Spring Beauty' is a robust, early-flowering selection of very deep colouring.

Scilla siberica

STERNBERGIA

AMARYLLIDACEAE

The best-known species in this small genus of only 8 species produces crocus-like flowers in autumn. Like others in the genus, whether autumn- or spring-flowering, in the wild it is usually found in stony ground, often on chalk, that is baked for several months by an implacable sun. In cooler climates it does best at the base of a sunny wall.
CULTIVATION Requires full sun and well-drained soil (JI No. 2 with added grit) with a dry period in summer. Plant in late summer or early autumn, covering bulbs with 4–6in (10–15cm) of soil or compost.

PROPAGATION From offsets, removed in late summer. From seed, sown as soon as ripe.
POTENTIAL PROBLEMS Narcissus bulb flies and eelworms; narcissus viruses.

Sternbergia lutea

S. lutea *S. Europe east to C. Asia*
Flowers: early to mid-autumn.
H 4–6in (10–15cm), S 4–6in (10–15cm). FH.
Linear, deep green leaves show off the sheeny gold of the flowers, which are about 2in (5cm) long. The leaves reach their full length of about 12in (30cm) in spring.

TECOPHILAEA

TECOPHILAEACEAE

There are only 2 species in this South American genus and the one described, a very great beauty, is now extremely rare or extinct in its native habitat in the high Andean meadows of Chile. As a garden plant, it evokes rapturous responses but success cannot be taken for granted and, as corms are scarce, the half-hearted are better admiring the achievement of others. Because of its rarity it is usually treated as a treasure for the alpine house.
CULTIVATION Require full sun and sandy well-drained soil that dries out in summer (JI No. 2 with added grit). Plant in mid-autumn, covering the corms with about 2in (5cm) of soil or compost.
PROPAGATION From offsets, removed in late summer. From seed, sown as soon as ripe.
POTENTIAL PROBLEMS Usually none.

Tecophilaea cyanocrocus 'Leichtlinii'

T. cyanocrocus *South America*
Chilean blue crocus
Flowers: early to mid-spring.
H 3–6in (8–15cm), S 2–3in (5–8cm). FrH.
The stems that rise among the linear basal leaves bear 1 to 3 scented flowers that seem to have been drenched in blue pigment except for a small white centre. When the 6 segments open nearly flat the flowers are about 2in (5cm) across. **'Leichtlinii'** is paler and has more white in the throat.

TIGRIDIA

IRIDACEAE Peacock flower, tiger flower

Of the 20 or so species in this mainly Central American genus only the gorgeous peacock flower, which is naturalized in many tropical and subtropical countries, is widely known. The exotic blooms only last a day but each stem bears up to 6 in succession and a fairly long display in late summer can be achieved by planting batches of corms over a period of 5 or 6 weeks.
CULTIVATION Requires full sun and well-drained fertile soil with plentiful moisture in the growing season (JI No. 2 with added humus and grit). Plant from mid-spring, covering the bulbs with 3–4in (8–10cm) of soil or compost.
PROPAGATION From seed, sown in spring.
POTENTIAL PROBLEM Virus diseases.

Tigridia pavonia

T. pavonia *Guatemala, Mexico*
Peacock flower, tiger flower
Flowers: mid-summer to early autumn. H 16–24in (40–60cm), S 4–6in (10–15cm). FT.
The vivid flowers, which float above a fan of basal leaves, have 3 large outer segments and when fully open are up to 4in (10cm) across. The colour range includes red, orange, yellow, white and purple. Often their dramatic effect is enhanced by bold spotting or splashing of the central cup and small inner segments, usually in a shade of red on white or yellow.

TULIPA

LILIACEAE Tulip

The tulip is so strongly associated with Holland that its early status as a garden flower in Turkey is often neglected. There are about 100 species, growing mainly in areas with hot, dry summers, many being native to Central Asia. Many species are suitable for sunny well-drained positions in rock gardens and raised beds and the numerous hybrids are popular for bedding schemes and container gardening.

A standard classification of tulips in 15 divisions is based on flower characteristics, season of flowering and parentage. The most familiar tulips, with single globular or cup-shaped flowers on stems roughly 12–24in (30–60cm) tall are found in the Single Early, Triumph, Darwin Hybrid and Single Late groups. Distinguished from these by their numerous segments are the Double Early and Double Late groups. Another flower shape is provided by the Lily-flowered tulips, their goblet-shaped blooms having long pointed segments that recurve sharply. Other groups with distinctive characteristics include the Fringed tulips, the Viridiflora Group, with green suffusions and streaks, and the Parrot Group, flamboyant confections usually with twisted segments that are irregularly striped and cut. Another once greatly prized group, the Rembrandt or "broken" tulips have the main colour interrupted by streaks or "feathers" of a darker colour. They are not represented as they are no longer readily available, virus being the cause of the colour breaking. The Kaufmanniana, Fosteriana and Greigii Groups each takes its name from a species and includes hybrids in which the character of the species dominates. The waterlily tulip (**T. kaufmanniana**) is a parent of an important group of showy dwarf hybrids with flowers that open wide to form a 6-pointed star. Some reveal the influence of the taller growing **T. greigii** in the purplish mottling and streaking of grey-green leaves. The sheeny brilliance of the scarlet **T. fosteriana** has been passed on to other tulips in its group. The Miscellaneous Group contains many characterful species, a counterbalance to the hybrids of stolid virtue. In the following descriptions, the species precede the hybrids and the division to which hybrids belong is given with each entry.

CULTIVATION All require full sun and well-drained soil, the species and hybrids close to them usually needing sharper drainage than other hybrids (JI No. 2, with added grit). Plant in mid- to late autumn, covering the bulbs with 4–6in (10–15cm) of soil or compost. Most species as well as Greigii and Kaufmanniana hybrids can be left in the ground from year to year, but lift hybrids when the foliage has died down, ripen under glass and replant in autumn.
PROPAGATION From offsets, when lifting. From seed, sown when ripe.
POTENTIAL PROBLEMS Aphids, stem and bulb eelworms; viruses, tulip fire.

SPECIES

Tulipa clusiana var. chrysantha

T. clusiana *Iran to W. Himalayas*
Lady tulip
Flowers: mid-spring. H 10–12in (25–30cm), S 3–4in (8–10cm). FH.
This slender beauty has white flowers with broad red bands on the 3 outer segments. As a fully open star it shows a purple-red blotch at the centre. It has grey-green, hairless leaves. **Var. *chrysantha*** is similar but the flower is yellow with yellow anthers, but with the 3 outer segments flushed red.

Tulipa linifolia

T. linifolia
Afghanistan, N. Iran, Uzbekistan
Flowers: early to mid-spring. H 6–8in (15–20cm), S 3–4in (8–10cm). FH.
Red flowers with pointed segments and purplish black at the base

stand above narrow grey-green leaves with a wavy red margin. The **Batalinii Group** has soft yellow flowers. **'Bright Gem'** with yellow flowers warmed with orange, is one of several cultivars from this group in shades of apricot and bronze.

Tulipa linifolia Batalinii Group

T. marjolletii *S.W. Europe*
Flowers: early to mid-spring. H 10–20in (25–50cm), S 3–4in (8–10cm). FH.
This lightly built tulip, which may be of garden origin, has elegantly cup-shaped flowers that are yellow with delicate shading in dark pink at the segment edges.

T. praestans *C. Asia*
Flowers: mid-spring. H 12–18in (30–45cm), S 4–6in (10–15cm) FH.
There are up to 5 red flowers to a stem on this downy plant. **'Fusilier'** makes a strong statement in vermilion. **'Unicum'** has variegated foliage with creamy white leaves.

Tulipa saxatilis

T. saxatilis *Crete, W. Turkey*
Flowers: mid- to late-spring. H 12–18in (30–45cm), S 3–4in (8–10cm) FH.
In a sunny warm position this tulip spreads by stolons to form sizeable clumps. The yellow-centred, pinkish purple flowers, which are 1 to 3 per stem, are up to 3in (8cm) across. In the **Bakeri Group** the flowers are more deeply coloured.

T. sprengeri *Turkey*
Flowers: late spring to early summer. H 18–24in (45–60cm), S 4–6in (10–15cm). FH.
Few tulips are more satisfactory for

naturalizing and this does well in the dappled shade of an orchard or open woodland as well as in full sun. The globular flowers are red and have pointed segments.

T. tarda *C. Asia*
Flowers: early spring. H 4–6in (10–15cm), S 3–4in (8–10cm). FH.
When the bunch of starry flowers, 4 to 6 to a stem, are fully open they appear yellow with white tips. In fact the outside of the flowers is also white, but tinged green or red. It normally flowers well without annual lifting.

Tulipa tarda

T. urumiensis *N.W. Iran*
Flowers: early spring. H 5–8in (13–20cm), S 4–6in (10–15cm). FH.
The yellow flowers are tinged lilac on the outside and appear 1 or 2 to a stem above mid-green leaves.

HYBRIDS

T. 'Angélique' (Double late)
Flowers: late spring. H 14–16in (35–40cm), S 4–6in (10–15cm). FH.
The double pink flowers have hints of cream and yellow in their choked centres. *T.* **'Carnaval de Nice'**, white streaked with dark red, and *T.* **'Mount Tacoma'**, white with some green, are both variegated and slightly larger.

T. 'Apeldoorn' (Darwin hybrid)
Flowers: mid- to late spring. H 24–26in (60–65cm), S 4–6in (10–15cm). FH.
Sturdy tulips of regimented scarlet-orange suit a massed display. *T.* **'Golden Apeldoorn'** has yellow goblets shaded greenish bronze.

T. 'Artist' (Viridiflora)
Flowers: late spring. H 12–16in (30–40cm) S 4–6in (10–15cm). FH.
A central green stripe runs to the tip of each segment, the margins of which are like wavy flanges of purple and salmon-pink. The inside of these arresting flowers has a strong green flush.
T. **'Groenland'**, a taller Viridiflora tulip, has pale lemon and bright pink edges to green stripes.

Tulipa 'Couleur Cardinal'

T. 'Bellona' (Triumph)
Flowers: mid-late spring. H 14–16in
(35–40cm) S 4–6in (10–15cm). FH.
The glowing yellow flowers are
well-scented. *T.* '**Couleur Cardinal**'
is crimson red with a grey bloom.
T. '**Prinses Irene**' has orange cups
licked by purple tongues.

T. 'Estella Rijnveld' (Parrot)
Flowers: late spring. H 20–22in
(50–55cm) S 4–6in (10–15cm). FH.
White and red stripes swirl in an
extravagant mixture.

Tulipa 'Estella Rijnveld'

T. 'Generaal de Wet' (Single
early)
Flowers: mid-spring. H 14–16in
(35–40cm) S 4–6in (10–15cm). FH.
Few hybrid tulips are better scented
and the cup-shaped flowers are a
radiant yellow warmed by rich
orange. *T.* '**Keizerskroon**', an old
cultivar, has scarlet segments with
some broad yellow margins.

Tulipa 'Keizerskroon'

T. 'Hamilton' (Fringed)
Flowers: late spring. H 20–22in
(50–55cm), S 4–6in (10–15cm). FH.
A heavy fringe, thistly to the eye,

but soft to the touch, trims a deep
yellow cup.

T. 'Heart's Delight'
(Kaufmanniana)
Flowers: early to mid spring.
H 8–10in (20–25cm), S 6–8in
(15–20cm). FH.
The flower of this tulip is bright
carmine-red with a pale pink edge.
This contrasts markedly with the
white inside, which has a yellow
base. The leaves are streaked and
mottled with purple-brown.
T. '**Stresa**', another waterlily tulip,
has yellow flowers with red
markings, including triangular
shapes on the 3 outer segments
and blotches of red at the base.

Tulipa 'Madame Lefeber'

T. 'Madame Lefeber'
(Fosteriana)
Flowers: mid-spring. H 14–16in
(35–40cm), S 4–6in (10–15cm). FH.
This vivid scarlet tulip has large
well-shaped flowers that have a
yellow base. They are touched
with a luxurious satin finish.

T. 'New Design' (Triumph)
Flowers: mid- to late spring.
H 18–22in (45–55cm), S 4–6in
(10–15cm). FH.
On the outside the flowers are
pale yellow with reddish pink
margins; inside there is a strong
yellow base and apricot flames.
The margin of the leaves is silvery
with pink staining. *T.* '**Douglas
Bader**' is soft pink with darker
shading. The flowers of the taller
T. '**Shirley**', which grows 24in
(60cm) high, are white, edged
with a purple stain.

T. 'Purissima' (Fosteriana)
Flowers: mid-spring. H 14–16in
(35–40cm), S 4–6in (10–15cm). FH.
The milky white flowers provide a
useful contrast to more brightly
coloured spring flowers.

T. 'Queen of Night' (Single late)
Flowers: late spring. H 24–26in
(60–65cm) S 4–6in (10–15cm). FH.
Not the legendary black tulip but
the velvety maroon is of wonderful
depth. Others in this division

include: *T.* '**Bleu Aimable**', mauve-
pink darkening to a purple bruise
near the stem, and *T.* '**Maureen**',
with a pure white flower.

Tulipa 'Queen of Night'

T. 'Red Riding Hood' (Greigii)
Flowers: early to mid-spring.
H 8–10in (20–25cm) S 6–8in
(15–20cm). FH.
Compact plants, the foliage strongly
mottled, bear waisted flowers of
dashing scarlet with black bases.

T. 'Schoonoord' (Double early)
Flowers: mid-spring. H 10–12in
(25–30cm) S 4–6in (10–15cm). FH.
The pure white flowers are frothy
with generous doubling. Another
stocky double, *T.* '**Peach Blossom**',
has rosy pink flowers that often
show greenish white at the base.

T. 'Toronto' (Greigii)
Flowers: early to mid-spring.
H 10–12in (25–30cm) S 6–8in
(15–20cm). FH.
Several flowers to a stem make a
reddish pink bouquet above
foliage that is lightly mottled.

T. 'White Triumphator'
(Lily-flowered)
Flowers: late spring. H 24–26in
(60–65cm) S 4–6in (10–15cm). FH.
The beauty of this tulip depends
on its whiteness, the generosity of
the cup and the curve of the
pointed segments. In *T.* '**Marilyn**'
red flames flicker to the pointed
tips of the ivory-white segments.
Other shorter lily-flowered tulips
include: *T.* '**Aladdin**', scarlet with
yellow edging; and *T.* '**West Point**',
yellow, with narrow pointed tips.

Tulipa 'West Point'

annuals and biennials

True annuals carry out their life cycle from germination to setting seed within one year. In the wild the life cycle may be completed with great rapidity, dormancy as seed being the safest state for some plants during unfavourable conditions. In addition to true annuals there are perennials, usually tender, such as hybrid verbenas, that flower in the first year and are normally grown as annuals. Biennials make leaf growth in the first year but do not flower until the second. A few biennials, including wallflowers (*Erysimum*), may be half-heartedly perennial but in gardens are usually discarded after the first flowering. Plant breeders maintain a constant supply of new introductions, many of which are F1 hybrids. These crosses of 2 pure-bred lines give vigorous, uniform, first-generation offspring.

There is labour in preparing ground and regularly sowing annuals and biennials, which counts against them in a mature garden. However, they make ideal fillers and rewarding plants for containers, most thriving in a standard compost such as John Innes No.2. The seed can be sown directly in the garden or, for an early start, germinated under glass. The usual temperature range for germination is 59–64°F (15–18°C) but for certain plants higher temperatures, which are given in the entries, are appropriate.

Top *Bracteantha bracteata* **Bright Bikinis Series**
Centre *Eschscholzia californica*
Bottom *Tagetes* **Afro-French Group**

AGROSTEMMA

CARYOPHYLLACEAE

Corn cockle (*A. githago*), once common on arable land, is the only widely grown species in this genus of 2 to 4 annuals from the Mediterranean and west Asia. The flowers are good for cutting.
CULTIVATION Require full sun and poor, well-drained soil.
PROPAGATION From seed, sown where plants are to flower in autumn or early spring.
POTENTIAL PROBLEMS Usually none.
WARNING The seeds can be toxic.

A. githago *Mediterranean*
Corn cockle
Flowers: summer. H 2–3ft (60–90cm), S 8–12in (20–30cm). FH.
Branching downy stems with grey-green leaves carry 5-petalled flowers in purplish pink with a white eye or, rarely, fully white. Those of **'Milas'** are deep plum-pink and up to 2in (5cm) across.

Agrostemma githago

ALCEA

MALVACEAE Hollyhock

The genus comprises about 60 species of biennials and short-lived perennials from temperate parts of Europe and Asia. The long-cultivated hollyhock (*A. rosea*), which is troubled by rust, is best grown as a usefully tall and striking biennial.
CULTIVATION Require full sun and reasonably fertile, well-drained soil.
PROPAGATION From seed, sown under glass in late winter or where plants are to flower in mid-summer.
POTENTIAL PROBLEMS Cutworms, slugs, mallow flea beetles, aphids, capsid bugs; hollyhock rust.

A. rosea *W. Asia*
Hollyhock
Flowers: summer. H 5–8ft (1.5–2.5m), S 18–24in (45–60cm). FH.
Tall cultivars may need support and have bare shins but they make their point by streaking up to carry impressive spikes of single to fully double flowers. **'Nigra'** is a

dark maroon single with a yellow throat to the funnel-shaped flowers. The colour range of **Chater's Double Group** includes red, apricot, white, yellow and purple. The loss of the well-defined flower shape in the doubles is a shortcoming.

Alcea rosea **'Nigra'**

AMARANTHUS

AMARANTHACEAE

Several tropical species in a genus comprising about 60 annuals and short-lived perennials have long fascinated gardeners with their catkin-like arrangements of densely clustered flowers and, in the case of Chinese spinach or tampala (cultivars of *A. tricolor*), brightly variegated red, yellow and green leaves.
CULTIVATION Require full sun in a sheltered site and moist soil, rich in organic matter.
PROPAGATION From seed, sown under glass (at a minimum of 64°F/18°C) from early to mid-spring.
POTENTIAL PROBLEMS Aphids; various virus diseases.

Amaranthus caudatus

A. caudatus *Africa, India, Peru*
Love-lies-bleeding, tassel flower
Flowers: summer to autumn.
H 3–5ft (90–150cm), S 18–30in (45–75cm). HH.
Light green leaves on an upright bushy plant make a good background to the tassels of tiny crimson-purple flowers. These can grow up to a length of 18in (45cm) or more. The tassels of **'Viridis'** are initially vivid green, fading to cream.

ANTIRRHINUM

SCROPHULARIACEAE Snapdragon

The 30 to 40 species of annuals, perennials and subshrubs, widely distributed in Europe, north Africa and North America, produce tubular 2-lipped flowers. Most are plants of open rough ground, the widely naturalized snapdragon (*A. majus*), a short-lived perennial, being as much at home on old walls as on rocky outcrops. Named selections of this species were formerly propagated by cuttings; the modern cultivars are, however, grown as annuals from seed. Snapdragons are favourite plants for including in a cottage garden, where they will flower from summer into autumn.
CULTIVATION Require full sun and fertile, well-drained soil.
PROPAGATION From seed, sown thinly under glass from late winter to early spring. Light is necessary for germination.
POTENTIAL PROBLEMS Aphids; antirrhinum rust, powdery mildew.

Antirrhinum majus **'Coronette Cherry'**

A. majus *Mediterranean, S.W. Europe*
Flowers: mid-summer to autumn.
H 2–3ft (60–90cm), S 12–18in (30–45cm). FH to HH.
The glossy-leaved wild plant produces spikes of flowers that are purplish pink but its cultivars cover a wide colour range and include bicolours. There are doubles and cultivars selected according to height, weighted in favour of rather congested dwarf kinds with a height of 8–12in (20–30cm). Some cultivars show a degree of resistance to rust such as the **Monarch Series**, which is intermediate at 1–2ft (30–60cm), and available in a range of simple colours. The intermediate **Madame Butterfly Series** has variously coloured double flowers, described as azalea-like. The tall **Coronette Series** which grows to the same height as the species comes in various colours as well as in single colours.

BELLIS

ASTERACEAE Daisy

The 15 species in the genus, all of them originating from Europe and east to Turkey, are rosette-forming perennials that grow in grass. The common daisy (*B. perennis*) is highly successful as a lawn weed but since the Middle Ages numerous variants have been grown, usually as biennials, for the undoubted attraction of their charming spring flowers.

CULTIVATION Tolerate full sun or partial shade and require well-drained, reasonably fertile soil. *PROPAGATION* From seed, sown thinly in a seedbed in early summer. By division, in spring after flowering (*B. perennis* 'Dresden China' and 'Rob Roy'). *POTENTIAL PROBLEMS* Usually none.

Bellis perennis Pomponette Series

B. perennis *Europe*
Common daisy
Flowers: late winter to summer. H and S 2–8in (5–20cm). FH. The short-stemmed flowerheads standing above fresh green leaf rosettes have yellow centres surrounded by white ray-florets that are often tinged pink or red. Cultivars available as seed, such as the **Carpet Series**, have fully double flowerheads in white, pink or red. The tight flowerheads of the **Pomponette Series** have quilled ray-florets. Cultivars not available from seed include **'Dresden China'**, with very neat pink flowerheads, and **'Rob Roy'**, a rich red.

BIDENS

ASTERACEAE

A few perennials from this diverse genus of about 200 very widely distributed species are grown as annuals, usually in containers. *CULTIVATION* Requires full sun and fertile, moist but well-drained soil. *PROPAGATION* From seed, sown under glass in early to mid-spring. From stem cuttings, taken in spring or late summer. *POTENTIAL PROBLEMS* Usually none.

Bidens ferulifolia

B. ferulifolia *Mexico, S. USA*
Flowers: summer to autumn. H 9–12in (20–30cm), S indefinite. FrH.
The plant flings out slender stems with finely dissected leaves, bearing sprays of starry rich yellow flowerheads over a long season.

BRACHYSCOME

ASTERACEAE

Of the 60 to 70 species, from New Guinea or Australasia, the best-known is the Swan river daisy (*B. iberidifolia*), a free-flowering dwarf annual. There are dwarf perennials such as the frost-hardy *B. rigidula*. *CULTIVATION* Require full sun in a sheltered site and fertile, well drained soil. *PROPAGATION* From seed, sown under glass (at a minimum of 64°F/18°C) in early spring. *POTENTIAL PROBLEMS* Slugs, snails.

B. iberidifolia *Australia*
Swan river daisy
Flowers: summer. H 8–16in (20–40cm), S 10–18in (25–45cm). FT. Small flimsy bushes with finely divided leaves bear lightly fragrant, yellow-centred daisies, in shades of mauve, blue, purple or pink, and in white. The **Splendour Series** provides a representative range.

Brachyscome iberidifolia
Splendour Series

BRACTEANTHA

ASTERACEAE

There are about 7 species of annuals and perennials in this Australian genus and all are plants of open scrubland or grassland. The flowerheads are daisy-like, with papery bracts around a central corolla (whorl of petals). *CULTIVATION* Require full sun and a poor, light soil (for good flower colour) or a more moist, fertile soil (for more numerous flowers). *PROPAGATION* From seed, sown under glass (at a minimum of 64°F/18°C) from late winter to early spring. *POTENTIAL PROBLEM* Downy mildew.

B. bracteata *Australia*
Golden everlasting, strawflower
Flowers: spring to autumn. H 12in–4ft (30–120cm), S 8-12in (20–30cm). FrH to HH.
This is unreliably perennial but as an annual is one of the most widely grown of the 'everlasting' flowers with bright daisy-like flowerheads. The colour range covers yellow, orange, pink, red and white. In the dwarf **Bright Bikinis Series**, 12–18in (30–45 cm) tall, the double flowerheads are as much as 3in (8cm) across. The frost-hardy **'Dargan Hill Monarch'** is a vivid yellow single.

Bracteantha bracteata
Bright Bikinis Series

BRASSICA

BRASSICACEAE

The genus comprises 30 species, mainly annuals and biennials found on rocky slopes and waste ground from the Mediterranean to Asia. Its value lies in the number of vegetables developed from a few species, especially *B. oleracea*. A vegetable patch with broccoli, cabbages, cauliflowers and sprouts is beautiful but ornamental kales and cabbages are more striking. *CULTIVATION* Require full sun and fertile, well-drained soil, preferably rich in lime. *PROPAGATION* From seed, sown under glass in early spring or where plants are to grow from mid- to late spring. *POTENTIAL PROBLEMS* Aphids, whitefly, root flies, flea beetles, caterpillars; black leg, downy mildew, clubroot.

B. oleracea W. Europe
Ornamental cabbage and kale
Foliage: autumn to winter. H and S
10–18in (25–45cm). FH.
Ornamental kinds are inedible but
are strikingly coloured, mostly in
shades of red, pink, green and
white. Ornamental cabbages
(*B. oleracea* var. *capitata*), such
as the frilled **Osaka Series** and the
smooth-edged '**Tokyo**', tend to
form rounded compact heads of
foliage, while ornamental kale
(*B. oleracea* var. *acephala*) such
as '**Nagoya**' have a more open
habit and deeply cut leaves. Plants
prefer cool conditions, and colours
intensify as night temperatures fall
below 50°F (10°C).

Brassica oleracea var. **capitata**
'Osaka Red'

CALENDULA

ASTERACEAE Marigold

The genus comprises 20 to 30
species of annuals and biennials
that are found in rough open
ground or as weeds of cultivated
ground in the Mediterranean region
and north Africa. The pot marigold
(*C. officinalis*), one of the easiest
and most satisfying ornamentals to
grow and long cultivated as a
medicinal herb, as a flavouring, a
food colorant and an ornamental,
is widely naturalized.
CULTIVATION Tolerate full sun or
partial shade and poor soil provided
it is well-drained.
PROPAGATION From seed, sown
where plants are to flower in
early autumn or spring. In cold
areas autumn-sown seedlings need
cloche protection.
POTENTIAL PROBLEMS Aphids;
powdery mildew, cucumber
mosaic virus.

C. officinalis N. Africa to
S. Europe.
Pot marigold
Flowers: summer to autumn.
H 12–28in (30–70cm), S 12–18in
(30–45cm). FH to FrH.
Fast-growing bushy plants with
aromatic spoon-shaped leaves
produce many daisy-like single to
double flowerheads, up to 4in

(10cm) across, in shades of yellow
and orange. The semi-double **Art
Shades Mixed**, up to 2ft (60cm)
tall, include subtle tones of apricot
and cream, and the dwarf **Fiesta
Gitana Mixed**, up to 1ft (30cm)
high, produce mostly double
flowerheads in pastel shades of
orange and yellow.

**Calendula officinalis Art
Shades Mixed**

CALLISTEPHUS

ASTERACEAE China aster

The single species in this genus is
a Chinese annual of rough open
ground and cultivated fields. The
modern cultivars produce
single to double chrysanthemum-
like flowerheads that are good
for cutting.
CULTIVATION Require full sun and a
fertile, moist but well-drained soil,
preferably alkaline to neutral.
PROPAGATION From seed, sown
under glass in early spring or
where plants are to flower from
late spring to early summer.
POTENTIAL PROBLEMS Aphids,
cutworms; aster wilt, cucumber
wilt, tomato spotted wilt.

C. chinensis cultivars
Flowers: summer to autumn.
H 8–24in (20–60cm), S 4–8in
(10–20cm). HH.
These fast-growing bushy plants
with coarsely toothed leaves bear
showy flowerheads. The petal-like
ray-florets are predominantly
violet-blue and purple in colour
but also include white and shades
of pink, crimson and yellow. Tall

**Callistephus chinensis
Duchesse Series**

cultivars, about 2ft (60cm) high,
include the **Duchesse Series**, with
double incurved flowerheads, the
Ostrich Plume Series, also double,
with wide-spreading narrow ray-
florets, and the **Princess Series**,
semi-double, with incurved quill-
like ray-florets. The compact
Milady Series, which grows to
about 1ft (30cm) tall, has double
flowerheads.

CENTAUREA

ASTERACEAE

Modern farming methods have
almost eliminated cornflower
(*C. cyanus*) from arable land so that
this, the best-known annual of a
genus of 450 species, mainly from
Europe and the Mediterranean,
now takes refuge in the garden.
The more variously coloured and
scented sweet sultan (*Amberboa
moschata*), which resembles a large
cornflower, was formerly included
in this genus. See also PERENNIALS.
CULTIVATION Require full sun and
well-drained soil.
PROPAGATION From seed, sown
where plants are to flower in early
autumn or early spring.
POTENTIAL PROBLEMS Usually none.

Centaurea cyanus

C. cyanus Northern temperate
regions
Blue-bottle, cornflower
Flowers: summer. H 10–36in (25–
90cm), S 12–18in (30–45cm). FH.
The flower colour of the species is
a very intense violet-tinted blue.
Cultivars with pink, purple, red or
white flowerheads are available,
but they seem to miss the point.
'**Blue Diadem**' is a tall double of
piercing blue. Short-growing
mixtures include the **Florence
Series**, up to 14in (35cm) tall.

CLARKIA

ONAGRACEAE

The genus comprises about 36
species of annuals, which are
widely distributed in dry open
habitats, sometimes in mountainous
country, in W. North America and
South America.

CULTIVATION Require full sun and moderately fertile, moist but well-drained soil, preferably slightly acid.

PROPAGATION From seed, sown where plants are to flower in early autumn or early spring. In cold areas autumn-sown seedlings need cloche protection.

POTENTIAL PROBLEMS Foot, root and stem rot.

C. amoena USA (California)
Satin flower

Flowers: summer. H 20–30in (50–75cm), S 8–12in (20–30cm). FH. The sheeny flowers, borne at the tips of stems, are spreading and funnel-shaped, each with 4 petals. Many cultivars, sometimes described as "azalea-flowered", have semi-double or double flowers, the petals often prettily frilled. Shades of pink and red predominate, often with contrasting colours in the centre or at the margin of the same flower, as in plants in the **Grace Series** and the dwarf **Satin Series**, up to 8–12in (20–30cm) tall. Both of these have single flowers.

Clarkia amoena **Satin Series**

C. unguiculata USA (California)
Flowers: summer. H 1–3ft (30–90cm), S 6–8in (15–20cm). FH. Slender reddish stems carry single spidery flowers in the upper leaf axils. Many of the cultivars have more dense double flowers. Their colour range covers shades of pink, red and purple and, less commonly, white. **Royal Bouquet Series** has double frilly flowers.

CLEOME

CAPPARIDACEAE

This tropical and subtropical genus contains about 150 species, most of them annuals. The only one widely grown is described here and is a useful filler in a border.

CULTIVATION Require full sun and fertile, free-draining soil.

PROPAGATION From seed, sown under glass (at a minimum of 64°F/18°C) in spring.

POTENTIAL PROBLEM Aphids.

C. hassleriana South America
Spider flower

Flowers: summer. H 4–5ft (1.2–1.5m), S 16–20in (40–50cm). FT. The plant is erect and bushy, with palmate leaves, the long leaf stalks having spines at the base. The fragrant white and pink flowers, which form rounded clusters at the ends of stems, have prominent stamens that justify the common name. The flowers of the **Queen Series** are carmine and violet-pink.

Cleome hassleriana **'Pink Queen'**

CONSOLIDA

RANUNCULACEAE

The genus, closely related to *Delphinium,* comprises about 40 species of annuals. These are erect, slender-stemmed plants usually found on rough open ground, including fields and steppes, from southern Europe and the Mediterranean to central Asia. The species described has dense spikes of spurred flowers, ideal for cutting and drying.

CULTIVATION Require full sun and light, fertile, well-drained soil. Tall cultivars benefit from support.

PROPAGATION From seed, sown where plants are to flower in early autumn or from spring to early summer. In cold areas autumn-sown seedlings need cloche protection.

POTENTIAL PROBLEMS Slugs, snails; powdery mildew.

WARNING The seeds can be toxic if eaten.

C. ajacis Mediterranean
Larkspur

Flowers: summer. H 2–3ft (60–90cm), S 9–12in (23–30cm). FH. Upright well-branched plants carry finely dissected leaves and densely packed spikes of single or double flowers in shades of pink, blue and purple or in white. There are dumpy short-growing cultivars, such as the **Dwarf Rocket Series**, which grow to 12–20in (30–50cm) high, but they are poor alternatives to the tall kinds, such as the **Giant Imperial Series**.

Consolida ajacis **Dwarf Rocket Series**

COSMOS

ASTERACEAE

There are annuals and perennials, some bulbous, in this genus of about 25 species, most of them growing in grass or scrubland in southern USA or Central America. The species described is renowned for its airy grace. While it produces its long-stemmed flowers in pinks and reds, as well as white, the equally elegant *C. sulphureus* provides blooms in rich shades of orange and yellow. See also BULBS, CORMS AND TUBERS.

CULTIVATION Require full sun and moderately fertile, moist but well-drained soil.

PROPAGATION From seed, sown under glass from early to mid-spring or where plants are to flower in late spring.

POTENTIAL PROBLEMS Aphids, slugs; grey mould (*Botrytis*).

Cosmos bipinnatus **Sensation Series**

C. bipinnatus Mexico
Flowers: summer. H 2–4ft (60–120cm), S 10–18in (25–45cm). FT. Saucer-shaped yellow-centred flowerheads that are white, pink or crimson are carried freely above feathery foliage on a slender but wiry and erect plant. Cultivars in the **Sensation Series** grow to about 3ft (90cm) high and the flowers are over 3in (8cm) across. **'Sea Shells'**, also tall, has flowers with tubular ray-florets. The **Sonata Series** is compact, with a spread of 12–18in (30–45cm), but at the expense of gracefulness.

DIGITALIS

SCROPHULARIACEAE Foxglove

The 22 or so species are biennials and short-lived perennials, most from woodland in Europe and east to central Asia. The genus is noted for its spires of tubular to bell-shaped flowers, making vertical accents among freer shapes. **D. × mertonensis**, which is reasonably perennial, has spires up to 3ft (90 cm) high with large flowers of an unusual bruised pink. The biennial rusty foxglove (**D. ferruginea**) only has small flowers but their tawny gold makes the spikes, up to 4ft (1.2m) high, very arresting.
CULTIVATION Tolerate full sun or shade and any soil except those that are very wet or dry.
PROPAGATION From seed, sown where plants are to flower from late spring to early summer.
POTENTIAL PROBLEMS Powdery mildew, leaf spot.
WARNING All parts can be toxic if eaten.

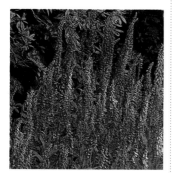

Digitalis purpurea

D. purpurea *Europe*
Common foxglove
Flowers: summer. H 3–6ft (90–180cm), S 18–24in (45–60cm). FH. Tall one-sided spikes carry steeply angled, purple, pink or white flowers, spotted maroon or purple inside. This variable biennial or short-lived perennial seeds itself too freely for ordered gardens. The white of **f. albiflora** gives woodland a spectral beauty. The **Excelsior Group** are hefty, the flowers, in pastel shades of creamy yellow, white, purple or pink, evenly spaced around the stem and held horizontally.

DOROTHEANTHUS

AIZOACEAE

This South African genus contains 10 species of low-growing succulent annuals of open ground and stony or sandy soils. They have glistening leaves and numerous daisy-like flowerheads that are sensitive to light, closing in dull weather.
CULTIVATION Require full sun and well-drained, preferably poor, sandy soil.
PROPAGATION From seed, sown under glass from late winter to early spring.
POTENTIAL PROBLEMS Slugs, snails, greenfly; foot rot.

**Dorotheanthus bellidiformis
Magic Carpet Series**

D. bellidiformis *South Africa (Western Cape)*
Livingstone daisy
Flowers: summer. H 4–6in (10–15cm), S 10–12in (25–30cm). HH. Dazzling flowerheads in shades of pink, red, orange and yellow, usually with a paler zone around the dark central disc, beam from a mat of fleshy leaves. Livingstone daisies are usually available only as mixtures such as '**Magic Carpet**'. '**Lunette**', with red-centred yellow flowers, is a happy exception.

ERYSIMUM

BRASSICACEAE Wallflower

Among the 80 species in this genus, there are annuals, biennials and also a number of woody-based evergreen perennials, although these are sometimes not long lived. Wherever they are found – in Europe, north Africa, North America and west Asia – they are usually plants that prefer sunny positions where the ground is free-draining and often calcareous. The flowers, consisting of 4 petals arranged in a cross, are usually carried in dense spikes. Those described below are grown as biennials but the fully hardy
E. 'Bowles' Mauve' is a bushy, short-lived perennial, which gives a long but unscented display of dark mauve flowers.
CULTIVATION Require full sun and poor to moderately fertile, well-drained soil, preferably neutral to alkaline. Pinch out growing tips when plants are 6in (15cm) high.
PROPAGATION From seed, sown in a seedbed from late spring to early summer.
POTENTIAL PROBLEMS Clubroot, mildew.

E. × allionii
Siberian wallflower
Flowers: spring. H 20–24in (50–60cm), S 10–12in (25–30cm). FH. The mound of deep green lance-shaped, often toothed, leaves is topped by erect spikes of spice-scented flowers. Their bold orange hue contributes vibrancy to a spring border.

E. cheiri *S. Europe*
Wallflower
Flowers: spring. H 10–30in (25–75cm), S 12–16in (30–40cm). FH. Wallflowers that seed themselves in old walls often prove reasonably perennial, but as bedding plants they are grown as biennials. The velvety sweetly scented flowers are predominantly orange and yellow but the colour range also includes pastel tones of pink and cream as well as deep reds and bronze. The deep green leaves are lance-shaped. Cultivars include those of the **Bedder Series**, which are sturdy compact plants producing flowers in orange, scarlet, primrose and rich yellow, and '**Fire King**', which carries orange-red flowers.

Erysimum cheiri 'Golden Bedder'

ESCHSCHOLZIA

PAPAVERACEAE California poppy

The 8 to 10 species, from western North America, are annuals and perennials of dry, sunny places. The poppy-like flowers, carried above finely cut leaves, tend to close in dull weather.
CULTIVATION Require full sun and poor, well-drained soil.
PROPAGATION From seed, sown where plants are to flower in early autumn or mid-spring.
POTENTIAL PROBLEMS Usually none.

E. californica *USA (western coastal regions)*
California poppy
Flowers: summer. H 8–12in (20–30cm), S 6–8in (15–20cm). FH. Silky saucer-shaped flowers up to 3in (8cm) across, produced prolifically over ferny blue-green leaves, are predominantly orange,

but the colour range includes cream, yellow and scarlet. Long cylindrical seedpods follow. Several selections, including '**Ballerina**' and the frilly '**Monarch Art Shades**', have semi-double or double flowers.

Eschscholzia californica

IBERIS

BRASSICACEAE Candytuft

There about 40 species of annuals, perennials and evergreen sub-shrubs in this genus, most of them found in open and usually rocky habitats, predominantly on lime-rich soils. The flowers, typically white, with 2 long and 2 short petals, are borne in dense clusters. The evergreen *I. sempervirens* is a spreading bushy plant that is grown in rock gardens for its dazzling, fragrant, white flowers, occasionally flushed lilac, from spring to early summer.
CULTIVATION Require full sun and fertile, moist but well-drained soil, preferably neutral to alkaline.
PROPAGATION From seed, sown where plants are to flower in early autumn or from early to mid-spring.
POTENTIAL PROBLEMS Clubroot.

Iberis umbellata **Fairy Series**

I. umbellata *S. Europe*
Common candytuft
Flowers: spring to summer.
H 6–12in (15–30cm), S 8–10in (20–25cm). FH.
The leaves of the common candytuft are almost hidden by dense clusters, up to 4in (10cm) across, of small scented flowers in a colour range that includes

mauve, purple, crimson, white and some bicolours, the full range being available in the **Fairy Series**. Another annual species, the summer-flowering *I. amara*, is a taller plant with stems growing to a height of 12–18in (30–45cm) and supporting cones of predominantly white flowers.

IMPATIENS

BALSAMINACEAE

The plants in this genus of about 850 annuals, evergreen perennials and subshrubs have brittle, fleshy stems and lush foliage. The 5-petalled flowers are borne singly or in clusters. Most species and cultivars are excellent for summer bedding and as houseplants. *Impatiens* thrive even in shady conditions, making them particularly useful plants for brightening up dull corners that receive little or no sun.
CULTIVATION Require partial shade with shelter from wind and fertile, moist but well-drained soil. Under glass, require good light and moderate to high humidity.
PROPAGATION From seed, sown under glass in early spring.
POTENTIAL PROBLEMS Aphids; grey mould (*Botrytis*).

I. balsamina *China, India*
Balsam
Flowers: summer to autumn.
H 24–30in (60–75cm), S 14–18in (35–45cm). FT.
This sparsely branched annual produces cup-shaped, hooded flowers, 1–2in (2.5–5cm) across, in shades of pink, red, purple or white. Cultivars include **Camellia-flowered Series** with large, double, pink or red flowers that are mottled with white.

I. New Guinea Group hybrids
Flowers: summer to autumn.
H and S 12–20in (30–50cm). FT.
These hybrid perennials, derived from *I. hawkeri* and other species, are usually grown as annuals. They are excellent in mixed container plantings and as individual pot plants. The foliage is ornamental, often attractively bronzed or a dark, glossy green. The striking flowers are mostly available in vibrant shades of red, pink and purple.

I. walleriana *E. Africa*
Busy Lizzie
Flowers: summer. H and S 18–24in (45–60cm). FT.
This subshrub-like perennial is usually represented in gardens by dwarf hybrids that are grown as

annuals. They grow to just 6–12in (15–30cm) tall and bear flattened, spurred flowers in a wealth of colours. The **Accent Series**, the **Impulse Series**, the **Super Elfin Series** and the **Tempo Series** are among those offering blooms in a range of bright and sometimes pastel colours, some bicoloured or with a conspicuous eye.

Impatiens walleriana **Accent Series**

LAVATERA

MALVACEAE Mallow

The 25 species in this widely distributed genus are annuals, biennials, perennials and shrubs. The leaves of mallows are rather coarse but the flowers are nicely formed, especially in the commonly grown annual, *L. trimestris*. See also SHRUBS.
CULTIVATION Require full sun in a sheltered site and well-drained soil.
PROPAGATION From seed, sown where plants are to flower in early autumn or from mid- to late spring.
POTENTIAL PROBLEMS Stem rot, rust, soil-borne fungal diseases.

Lavatera trimestris '**Mont Blanc**'

L. trimestris *Mediterranean*
Flowers: summer. H 2–3ft (60–90cm), S 14–18in (35–45cm). FH.
Upright bushy plants with lobed mid-green leaves bear open funnel-shaped flowers, 3–4in (8–10cm) across, in shades of pink, reddish pink or white. Cultivars include the compact '**Mont Blanc**', with dark green foliage and white flowers, and '**Silver Cup**', which has bright pink flowers, with darker veining. Both grow to a height of 20in (50cm).

LIMNANTHES

LIMNANTHACEAE

This genus comprises about 17 species of annuals from western North America. Most are plants of moist soils but the poached egg plant (*L. douglasii*), the only species commonly grown, self-seeds successfully wherever it can get a cool root run, doing well in chinks between paving.
CULTIVATION Requires full sun and fertile, moist but well-drained soil.
PROPAGATION From seed, sown where plants are to flower in early autumn or early spring.
POTENTIAL PROBLEMS Usually none.

L. douglasii USA (California, Oregon)
Poached egg plant
Flowers: summer to autumn.
H and S 6–8in (15–20cm). FH.
Sprawling plants with slightly fleshy, light green leaves bear a profusion of broadly funnel-shaped flowers, which are white with a yellow 'yolk'. They are lightly scented and a nectar-rich enticement to bees.

Limnanthes douglasii

LIMONIUM

PLUMBAGINACEAE Sea lavender, statice

About 150 species of annuals, biennials and perennials are distributed worldwide, many of them adapted to extreme desert and salt-marsh conditions. The small flowers are papery and long lasting, making statice one of the most popular flowers for drying. The annual *Psylliostachys suworowii*, which grows to 18in (45cm) and produces narrow branching spikes packed with small, deep pink flowers, was formerly placed in this genus.
CULTIVATION Require full sun and well-drained, preferably sandy soil.
PROPAGATION From seed, sown under glass from late winter to early spring or where plants are to flower from mid- to late spring.
POTENTIAL PROBLEM Powdery mildew.

L. sinuatum Mediterranean
Statice
Flowers: summer to autumn.
H 16–24in (40–60cm), S 10–12in (25–30cm). FrH.
A perennial grown as an annual, statice has stiff, winged stems that branch to carry clusters of tiny flowers surrounded by long-lasting papery calyces. In the cultivars the white and mauve-blue colour range has been extended; the **California Series** includes 9 different strong colours, among them blue, purplish pink and yellow. The **Fortress Series** has both strong and pastel shades.

Limonium sinuatum Fortress Series

LINARIA

SCROPHULARIACEAE Toadflax

The genus comprises about 100 species of annuals, biennials and perennials. These sun-loving plants are found in open habitats on free-draining soils in the temperate Northern Hemisphere. The small flowers are spurred and have 2 lips. Many species are lightweight and only one annual is widely grown. See also PERENNIALS.
CULTIVATION Require full sun and light, well-drained, preferably sandy soil.
PROPAGATION From seed, sown in a seedbed from early to mid-spring.
POTENTIAL PROBLEMS Aphids; powdery mildew.

Linaria maroccana 'Fairy Bouquet'

L. maroccana N. Africa (Morocco)
Flowers: summer. H 9–18in (23–45cm), S 4–6in (10–15cm). FH.
Erect bushy plants with linear

leaves produce slender stems carrying numerous miniature snapdragons with a white or yellow blotch on the lower lip. **'Fairy Bouquet'** and the longer-flowering **'Northern Lights'** both have flowers in white, yellow, orange, mauve and carmine and in shades of pink.

LOBULARIA

BRASSICACEAE

There are 5 species in this genus, but only one is commonly grown. In the past sweet alyssum (*L. maritima*) has been used to excess in bedding schemes but it is an adaptable plant for containers and the open garden and tolerant of coastal conditions.
CULTIVATION Require full sun and light, well-drained soil.
PROPAGATION From seed, sown where plants are to flower from early to mid-spring.
POTENTIAL PROBLEMS Slugs, flea beetles; downy mildew, clubroot, white blister.

Lobularia maritima 'Carpet of Snow'

L. maritima Mediterranean
Sweet alyssum
Flowers: summer to autumn.
H 3–6in (8–15cm), S 8–12in (20–30cm). FH.
Freely branching, bushy plants bear tiny fragrant flowers clustered densely at the ends of stems. The flowers have 4 petals arranged in a cross shape and the colour range in the cultivars includes white, pink and purple. **'Carpet of Snow'** is a low spreading plant with white flowers. The **Easter Bonnet Series**, compact and early flowering, covers the whole colour range.

LUNARIA

BRASSICACEAE Honesty

The 3 species in this genus are adaptable plants, readily colonizing disturbed or open ground in a range of habitats in Europe and west Asia. The familiar annual or biennial honesty (*L. annua*) self-seeds with great success in shrubberies and wild gardens.

Both it and the hardy perennial *L. rediviva*, from Europe and west Siberia, flower in spring, and bear translucent seedpods, those of *L. rediviva* being more elliptical. *CULTIVATION* Tolerate full sun or partial shade and require fertile, moist but well-drained soil. *PROPAGATION* From seed, sown in a seedbed from late spring to early summer. *POTENTIAL PROBLEMS* Clubroot, white blister, viruses.

Lunaria annua var. albiflora

L. annua *Europe*
Honesty, satin flower
Flowers: spring and summer.
H 30–36in (75–90cm), S 10–12in (25–30cm). FH.
Upright stems, well-clothed with heart-shaped to triangular, coarsely toothed leaves, bear numerous 4-petalled flowers that are purple or white. The shimmering moon discs that follow are highly ornamental in the garden or in dried arrangements. The flowers of **var. albiflora** are white.

MALOPE

MALVACEAE

The 4 species of annuals and perennials are found in open scrubland and arable fields on lime-rich soils in western Asia and the Mediterranean. The species described, which does well near the sea, is grown for its showy trumpet-shaped flowers. These are ideal at the front of a border as well as for cutting.
CULTIVATION Require full sun and moist but well-drained soil.
PROPAGATION From seed, sown where plants are to flower from early to mid-spring.
POTENTIAL PROBLEMS Aphids; rust.

M. trifida *W. Mediterranean*
Flowers: summer to autumn.
H 30–36in (75–90cm), S 8–10in (20–25cm). FH.
Upright plants carry the purplish pink mallow flowers singly in the leaf axils. The flowers are as much as 3in (8cm) across and dark purple veining adds to their glamour. '**Vulcan**' bears an abundance of large magenta flowers, those of '**White Queen**' are pure white.

Malope trifida

MATTHIOLA

BRASSICACEAE Gillyflower, stock

Only a few of the 50 or so species are grown but these have long been valued for their rich fragrance. Night-scented stock (**M. longipetala** subsp. **bicornis**), a hardy annual from Greece and eastward into Asia, seems inconsequential, but a scattering among other plants exhales a seductive perfume as dusk falls.
CULTIVATION Require full sun in a sheltered site and fertile, moist but well-drained soil, preferably neutral to slightly alkaline.
PROPAGATION From seed, sown under glass from late winter to early spring or where plants are to flower from mid- to late spring.
POTENTIAL PROBLEMS Aphids, flea beetles, cabbage root flies; fungal diseases, including clubroot, downy mildew and grey mould (*Botrytis*).

Matthiola incana East Lothian Mixed

M. incana *Europe (S. and W. coastal regions)*
Gillyflower, stock
Flowers: spring to summer.
H 12–30in (30–75cm), S 10–12in (25–30cm). FH to FrH.
In the wild this woody-based perennial bears fragrant cross-shaped single flowers that are purple, pink or white. Doubles and a more varied colour range, including mauve-blue violet, crimson and yellow, have been in cultivation for centuries, the stiff plants usually being grown as annuals or biennials. The cultivars, often a mixture of single and double flowers, fall into a number of categories. **Brompton** stocks, bushy upright plants about 18in (45cm) high, are grown as biennials. The similar but more compact and smaller-flowered **East Lothian** stocks, about 1ft (30cm) high, can be grown as biennials or spring-sown. **Ten Week** stocks, with dwarf and tall cultivars, and the even faster maturing **Trisomic Seven Week** stocks, about 18in (45cm) high, are grown as annuals.

MIMULUS

SCROPHULARIACEAE Monkey flower

Several of the monkey flowers are plants of dry habitats, but of some 150 species most are annuals, perennials and evergreen shrubs of moist, often boggy conditions. The yellow-flowered Chilean *M. luteus* and the North American *M. guttatus*, also yellow but often heavily spotted, have played an important role in hybridizing.
CULTIVATION Tolerate full sun or light shade and require very moist soil that is rich in organic matter.
PROPAGATION From seed, sown under glass from late winter to early spring.
POTENTIAL PROBLEMS Slugs, snails; powdery mildew.

Mimulus × hybridus Calypso Mixed

M. × hybridus
Flowers: summer. H 5–12in (13–30cm), S 10–14in (25–35cm). FrH.
These bushy perennials are usually grown as annuals. The solitary flowers, borne in the leaf axils, are tubular then flaring open, with lobed lips. The flowers are usually spotted in a contrasting colour, the colour range in cultivars such as **Calypso Mixed** and the low and spreading **Malibu Series** including yellow, orange and red. The early-flowering **Magic Series** has small blooms and includes pastel shades and bicolours.

MYOSOTIS

BORAGINACEAE Forget-me-not

Despite having small flowers, many forget-me-nots make a strong impression with their sprays of dainty, mainly blue, flowers. There are about 50 species, including annuals, biennials and perennials, which are widely distributed throughout the world in habitats ranging from woodland and meadows to swampy ground and the water's edge.
CULTIVATION Tolerate full sun or partial shade and a range of soils but do best in moist well-drained conditions that are not too rich.
PROPAGATION From seed, sown in a seedbed from late spring to early summer.
POTENTIAL PROBLEMS Powdery and downy mildew.

Myosotis sylvatica 'Blue Ball'

M. sylvatica *Europe*
Flowers: spring to summer. H 6–14in (15–35cm), S 6–8in (15–20cm). FH.
The familiar forget-me-not is a pleasing biennial self-seeder in woodland, among shrubs and in the wild garden, but it is also often used in a more disciplined way in bedding schemes, its flowering coinciding with that of tulips. Colours other than blue seem a curious lapse but there are white and pink cultivars. The emphasis in seed catalogues is on compact cultivars such as the **Ball Series**, about 6–8in (15–20cm) high, but fortunately there are taller cultivars, such as '**Royal Blue**'.

NEMESIA

SCROPHULARIACEAE

This South African genus comprises about 50 species of annuals, perennials and subshrubs, many of them plants of scrubland or more open ground where the soil is free-draining but seasonally moist. The flowers are 2-lipped, the upper lip with 4 lobes the lower lip with 2, and are borne singly in the leaf axils or in short racemes at the stem tips. A perennial, sometimes woody-based species, **N. caerulea** is less showy than the well-known annual species but gives a long display from mid-spring to autumn, its flowers sometimes white but usually ranging from pale mauve or pink to violet-purple with a yellow mark in the centre. It is frost hardy and cultivars like deep violet '**Joan Wilder**' are best treated as short-lived and annually propagated from cuttings in late summer.
CULTIVATION Require full sun and moderately fertile, moist but well-drained soil, preferably slightly acid.
PROPAGATION From seed, sown under glass from early to mid-spring.
POTENTIAL PROBLEMS Foot rot, root rot.

Nemesia caerulea 'Joan Wilder'

N. strumosa *South Africa*
Flowers: summer. H 6–12in (15–30cm), S 4–6in (10–15cm). HH.
The small but distinctive flowers, with a broad lower lip and a fanned upper lip, are carried in profusion on erect bushy plants. The colour range in the cultivars is very wide, some being bicoloured and almost all having yellow throats. '**Blue Gem**' has bright blue flowers, the **Carnival Series** is compact with a mixture of jolly colours, and '**Mello Red and White**' is boldly bicoloured. '**Mello White**' has a deep yellow centre.

Nemesia strumosa 'Mello White'

NEMOPHILA

HYDROPHYLLACEAE

Saucer- or bell-shaped, blue or white flowers are borne by the 11 species of annuals in this genus. They are all natives of western North America but they are found in a wide range of habitats.
CULTIVATION Tolerate full sun or partial shade and require fertile, moist but well-drained soil.
PROPAGATION From seed, sown where plants are to flower in early autumn or early spring.
POTENTIAL PROBLEM Aphids.

Nemophila maculata

N. maculata *USA (California)*
Five-spot
Flowers: summer. H and S 6–12in (15–30cm). FH.
Low plants carry profuse long-stalked, saucer-shaped flowers, each with 5 white petals, sometimes veined or tinted mauve, and tipped with violet-blue. Baby blue-eyes (**N. menziesii**), a slightly larger species, has bright blue flowers with lighter centres.

NICOTIANA

SOLANACEAE Tobacco plant

Hybrids derived from the South American **N. alata** are the most commonly grown of the tobacco plants, but a few of the 67 species are unusual short-lived garden plants. **N. langsdorffii**, a scentless Brazilian annual up to 5ft (1.5m) high, has green tubular flowers that open to a 5-lobed mouth. The equally tall **N. sylvestris** from Argentina, usually grown as a biennial, bears long-tubed slender white trumpets that are sweetly fragrant. These half-hardy species do well in moist dappled shade.
CULTIVATION Tolerate full sun or partial shade and require fertile, moist but well-drained soil.
PROPAGATION From seed, surface-sown under glass (at a minimum of 64°/18°C) from late winter to early spring.
POTENTIAL PROBLEM Aphids.
WARNING Contact with the foliage may irritate the skin.

Nicotiana sylvestris

N. hybrids

Flowers: summer. H 10–24in (25–60cm), S 9–12in (23–30cm). FT.
N. alata is a short-lived perennial that is sticky to the touch. It has white flowers that are usually closed during the day but are strongly scented when open at night. The hybrids of which it is a parent are grown as annuals and come in a colour range that includes white, pink, red and lime-green; their flowers are open during the day but, except for some whites, are almost unscented. The **Domino Series**, about 18in (45cm) high, has upward-facing flowers in a wide colour range. The **Havana Series** is more compact and the dwarf **Merlin Series** is usually under 1ft (30cm) in height. '**Lime Green**', about 2ft (60cm) tall, has yellow-green flowers.

Nicotiana '**Lime Green**'

NIGELLA

RANUNCULACEAE

There are about 20 species in the genus, all annuals of open stony ground, including fields and wasteland, in the Mediterranean region, north Africa and eastward into Asia. A few other species are sometimes seen, but love-in-a-mist (*N. damascena*) is by far the most commonly grown, ensuring its place by self-seeding freely.

CULTIVATION Require full sun and well-drained soil.
PROPAGATION From seed, sown where plants are to flower in early autumn or early spring.
POTENTIAL PROBLEMS Usually none.

N. damascena N. Africa, S. Europe.

Devil-in-a-bush, love-in-a-mist
Flowers: summer. H 16–24in (40–60cm), S 8–10in (20–25cm). FH.
This upright bushy annual has feathery foliage and sky-blue flowers that sit within a ruff-like surround of wispy leaves. These are followed by inflated seed capsules that dry well. The blooms also make good cut flowers. There are dwarf cultivars under 16in (40cm) in height, but the tall '**Miss Jekyll**', with semi-double bright blue flowers, and the intermediate **Persian Jewel Series**, which is semi-double and available in shades of blue, pink or in white, are better poised.

Nigella damascena '**Miss Jekyll**'

PETUNIA

SOLANACEAE

It is hard to believe that the fashion for petunias ever waned. The long-flowering plants that are so popular now in bedding and container gardening, like the petunias that were all the rage in the 19th century, are perennial hybrids that are grown as annuals. The genus originates from South America and comprises about 40 species which are found in a range of habitats, but mostly on open and stony ground.
CULTIVATION Require full sun in a sheltered site and light, well-drained soil.
PROPAGATION From seed, sown under glass in early spring.
POTENTIAL PROBLEMS Aphids, slugs; virus diseases.

P. hybrids

Flowers: spring to autumn. H 8–16in (20–40cm), S 10–36in (25–90cm). FT.
These are bushy or trailing plants bearing single or double trumpet-shaped flowers with a broad 5-lobed mouth. The colour range in the numerous seed selections includes blue and yellow as well as white, pink, purple and red. Deep veining and contrasting colours in the mouth, at the edges or in the form of a superimposed star add to the variety in the mixtures, but the range of single colours is limited. Compact cultivars have a spread of 10–16in (25–40cm), trailing kinds of 18–36in (45–90cm). There are 2 main groups, although some hybrids are of intermediate character. The **Grandiflora** petunias have large flowers up to 4in (10cm) across, often rather floppy and vulnerable to weather damage. They include the early-flowering **Daddy Series**, with heavily veined and ruffled single flowers; the **Picotee Series**, with single ruffled flowers outlined in white; and the **Surfinia Series**, freely branching and trailing, with many flowers that stand up well to rough weather. The **Multiflora** petunias bear many weatherproof flowers that are about 2in (5cm) across. They include compact hybrids such as the **Carpet Series**, usually less than 10in (25cm) high; the **Duo Series**, with double flowers, and the **Primetime Series**, with a wide colour range.

Petunia '**Daddy Blue**'

RESEDA

RESEDACEAE

About 55 to 60 species of annuals and perennials in this genus are found in the wild in the Mediterranean region, Africa and Asia, mainly on stony hillsides, in scrubland, and at the edges of cultivated fields. Few are grown other than mignonette (*R. odorata*) which has long been valued for its scented flowers.
CULTIVATION Tolerates full sun or partial shade and requires moderately fertile, well-drained soil, preferably alkaline.
PROPAGATION From seed, sown where plants are to flower in early autumn or from early to mid-spring.
POTENTIAL PROBLEMS Usually none.

R. odorata *N. Africa*
Mignonette
Flowers: summer to autumn.
H 1–2ft (30–60cm), S 8–10in
(20–25cm). FH.
Upright branching plants bear
loose, conical heads of starry
flowers. These are tiny and usually
buff or greenish white, the central
tuft of orange stamens being the
most conspicuous feature. They
are grown for their scent, which
lingers strongly even in dried plants.

Reseda odorata

SALPIGLOSSIS

SOLANACEAE

The 2 species of this genus are
from the southern Andes and are
annuals or short-lived perennials of
rough, open, often dry, terrain.
Cultivars of the single species in
general cultivation have long-
lasting richly coloured flowers.
CULTIVATION Require full sun in a
sheltered site and moist well-
drained soil, rich in organic matter.
PROPAGATION From seed, sown
under glass (at a minimum of 64°F/
18°C) from late winter to mid-
spring.
POTENTIAL PROBLEMS Foot rot,
root rot.

***Salpiglossis sinuata* Casino Series**

S. sinuata *Argentina, Peru*
Flowers: summer to autumn.
H 18–24in (45–60cm), S 10–12in
(25–30cm). HH.
Lightly branched, erect and sticky
plants bear funnel-shaped flowers,
about 2in (5cm) across, each with
5 notched lobes. The flowers,
often burnished with an overlay of
gold, come in shades of yellow,

orange, red, purple or blue with
darker or contrasting veining. The
cultivars in the **Casino** and
Festival Series are compact, about
18in (45cm) high.

SALVIA

LAMIACEAE

This large genus of 900 species is
represented in several categories.
In frost-prone areas tender
perennials and subshrubs are
usually grown as annuals. See also
PERENNIALS and SHRUBS.
CULTIVATION Require full sun and
well-drained soil.
PROPAGATION From seed, sown
under glass from late winter to
early spring (frost-tender plants)
or where plants are to flower from
early to mid-spring or in summer
(fully hardy plants).
POTENTIAL PROBLEMS Slugs, snails.

***Salvia farinacea* 'Victoria'**

S. farinacea *Mexico, USA (Texas)*
Mealy sage
Flowers: summer to autumn.
H 20–24in (50–60cm), S 10–12in
(25–30cm). FT.
In mild climates this is perennial
but it is commonly grown as an
annual. Mealy white stems carry
slender spikes of purplish blue
flowers clear of the glossy foliage.
'**Alba**' bears white flowers, while
'**Victoria**' has intense purple-blue
flowers and stems.

S. sclarea var. **turkestanica**
C. Asia, Europe
Flowers: spring to summer.
H 30–36in (75–90cm), S 12–16in
(30–40cm). FH.
The leaves of this biennial clary are
large, hairy and coarsely aromatic
and the branching flower spikes
create a long-lasting haze of pink
and mauve, the purplish bracts
persisting when the flowers have
finished. The plant seeds itself
freely in dry gardens.

S. splendens *Brazil*
Scarlet sage
Flowers: summer to autumn.
H 10–16in (25–40cm), S 10–14in
(25–35cm). FT.
This upright, bushy perennial,
usually grown as an annual, looks
shocking with its dense spikes of
long-tubed, bright red flowers,
which are surrounded by scarlet
bracts. There are some less
strident colours in the **Cleopatra
Series**, including salmon-pink,
purple and white.

S. viridis *Mediterranean*
Annual clary
Flowers: summer. H 18–20in (45–
50cm), S 8–10in (20–25cm). FH.
The flowers are insignificant but
they are surrounded by bracts up
to 1½in (4cm) long that are pink,
purple or white with darker veins.
There is a comprehensive colour
range in the **Claryssa Series**,
plants being well branched and
growing to a height of about 16in
(40cm).

SCHIZANTHUS

SOLANACEAE Butterfly flower

This South American genus
comprises about 12 to 15 species
of annuals and biennials, which are
mainly found in dry rocky habitats.
S. pinnatus has superficially orchid-
like flowers; its showy cultivars,
which can be grown under glass or
as bedding plants, are the most
commonly seen representatives of
the genus.
CULTIVATION Require full sun and
fertile, moist but well-drained soil.
PROPAGATION From seed, sown
under glass from early to mid-
spring.
POTENTIAL PROBLEM Aphids.

S. pinnatus *Chile*
Butterfly flower, poor man's orchid
Flowers: spring to autumn.
H 10–24in (25–60cm), S 8–12in
(20–30cm). HH.
The ferny, light green leaves are
overlooked when the plants are in
bloom because the effect of their
dense clusters of flared bright

***Schizanthus pinnatus* 'Hit Parade'**

flowers is dazzling. The main colours are pink, red, purple, yellow or white and usually there is a striking yellow flash in the throat that is splashed with dark markings. Contrasting colours add zest to the compact '**Hit Parade**', with plants about 1ft (30cm) high.

SOLENOPSIS

CAMPANULACEAE

In this genus of about 25 annuals and perennials, one species, *L. axillaris*, is a long-flowering and pretty edging and container plant. In the wild, this Australian species, like others in the genus from Central and South America, is a plant of dry open habitats.
CULTIVATION Requires full sun and moderately fertile well-drained soil.
PROPAGATION From seed, sown under glass from late winter to early spring.
POTENTIAL PROBLEM Aphids.

S. axillaris *Australia*
Flowers: spring to autumn. H and S 10-12in (25-30cm). FT.
Long tubular buds that burst open into starry flowers with 5 narrow lobes stand proud above a dome of feathery green leaves. The flowers, lightly scented in the evening, are mainly blue, and sometimes white or pink. This is perennial but usually raised annually from seed.

Solenopsis axillaris

TAGETES

ASTERACEAE Marigold

There are in all about 50 species of annuals and perennials in the genus, most of them occupying hot and often dry habitats from southern USA to Argentina. The well-known bedding and container marigolds of gardens are hybrids of 3 Mexican species, *T. erecta*, *T. patula* and *T. tenuifolia*. They have vividly coloured flowerheads, mostly in shades of yellow and orange, and are borne on neat upright plants above divided green leaves that emit a pungent smell when bruised. They fall into 4 main groups and it is under these

that the cultivars and hybrids are described below.
CULTIVATION Require full sun and moderately fertile well-drained soil. Water all varieties freely in dry seasons and deadhead regularly to prolong flowering.
PROPAGATION From seed, sown under glass (at a minimum of 64°F/ 18°C) from early to mid-spring or where plants are to flower in late spring.
POTENTIAL PROBLEMS Usually none.

T. African Group
African marigold
Flowers: spring to autumn.
H 8-18in (20-45cm), S 12-18in (30-45cm). FT.
Derived from *T. erecta*, these are compact bushy plants topped by large, densely double, pompon-like flowerheads, up to 5in (13cm) across. Plants in the **Antigua Series** and the **Excel Series** grow to about 1ft (30cm) and are in a range of yellow and orange shades.

T. Afro-French Group
Afro-French marigold
Flowers: spring to autumn.
H 8-18in (20-45cm), S 12-16in (30-40cm). FT.
These bushy annuals, derived from *T. erecta* and *T. patula* crosses, bear many small, single or double flowerheads, 1-2½in (2.5-6cm) across, usually in orange or yellow and sometimes marked with red-brown. The **Beaux Series** has double flowerheads in shades of rich yellow, orange splashed with red, or copper-red. In the **Zenith Series** the flowerheads are red, orange and shades of yellow. In both of these series, plants grow to about 1ft (30cm).

T. French Group
French marigold
Flowers: spring to autumn.
H 8-18in (20-45cm), S 6-12in (15-30cm). FT.
The plants, derived from *T. patula*, are usually compact with single or double flowerheads about 2in (5cm) across, their colour range including yellow and orange, often with red-brown markings. Plants in the robust **Boy Series**, which reach a height of about 6in (15cm), have dense crested flowerheads in a range of orange, yellow and reddish brown shades, the crest sometimes contrasting with the rest of the flowerhead. The **Disco Series**, which reaches a height of 8-10in (20-25cm), is a selection with single flowerheads in yellow, orange and orange-red, some of them also with reddish brown markings. The pert

'**Naughty Marietta**' produces single deep yellow flowerheads which have mahogany markings at the centre.

Tagetes '**Disco Golden Yellow**'

T. Signet Group
Signet marigold
Flowers: spring to autumn. H 8-18in (20-45cm), S 10-16in (25-40cm). FT.
These plants derived from *T. tenuifolia* are upright and branch freely to carry numerous single flowerheads, about 1in (2.5cm) across, in shades of yellow and orange. Plants in the **Gem Series** grow to a height of approximately 10in (25cm). The starry clear lemon-yellow flowers of '**Lemon Gem**', carried above the bright green ferny foliage, correct the rather common impression that marigold flowers are simply blobs of crude colour.

VERBENA

VERBENACEAE

Out of a total of about 250 species in this genus, most of them from the Americas, only a small number of tropical and subtropical perennials, including the scarlet-flowered *V. peruviana*, has been involved in the crosses that have produced the long-flowering hybrid verbenas. At the height of their popularity as bedding plants in the 19th century enormous numbers were propagated annually from cuttings, but most of the modern hybrids are raised from seed. The small, sometimes scented flowers, clustered in a domed or flattish head at the end of slender stems, have 5 lobes, 2 upper and 3 lower ones. Some make good container plants. See also PERENNIALS.
CULTIVATION Require full sun and moderately fertile, moist but well-drained soil.
PROPAGATION From seed, sown under glass (at a minimum of 64°F/ 18°C) from mid-winter to early spring.
POTENTIAL PROBLEMS Slugs; powdery mildew.

Verbena × *hybrida*
'Peaches and Cream'

V. hybrids

Flowers: summer to autumn.
H 6–18in (15–45cm), S 10–36in
(25–90cm). HH to FT.
The many colourful hybrids raised
from seed include bushy upright
plants, with a spread of 10–14in
(25–35cm), and others that are
low and sprawling, with a spread
of 18–36in (45–90cm). The bushy
plants in the **Novalis Series** cover
a broad range of colours, some
plants having a conspicuous white
eye. '**Imagination**', with small
flowers of intense violet-blue,
makes a spreading mound about
1ft (30cm) high. '**Peaches and
Cream**', also spreading but with
stiffer stems and larger flowers,
combines shades of cream, yellow,
orange and salmon pink. The
Romance Series is bushy but
compact with bright-eyed flowers
or single colours. Cultivars that do
not come true from seed and are
raised from cuttings include:
'**Silver Anne**', a sprawling plant
with lightly scented flowers that
are bright pink when first open
but fade to near white and the low,
mat-forming '**Sissinghurst**', with
bright pink flowers.

VIOLA

VIOLACEAE

About 500 species, mainly annuals,
biennials and perennials, are found
in the temperate regions of the
world, in a variety of habitats.
Heartsease (*V. tricolor*), a small-
flowered short-lived species
widely distributed in Europe and
Asia, has played a major role in
the complex breeding that has
produced the garden pansy
(*V.* × *wittrockiana*). The hybrids,
too, can be short-lived perennials
but they are most commonly
grown as annuals and biennials. In
the heartsease flower, the 5 petals
are clearly defined: the spurred
lower petal is flanked by 2 laterals
and topped by another 2. In
breeding the garden pansy, trouble
was taken to defy this distinctive
shape and create a rounded flower

to satisfy a notion of floral
perfection. Heartsease retains the
affection of gardeners with self-
seeding colonies giving a spring or
summer display of flowers in
purple, blue, yellow and white.
There are many equally pretty
hybrids or cultivars such as
V. '**Bowles' Black**', yellow-eyed but
of the deepest black-purple and
V. '**Prince Henry**', with dark purple
flowers. See also PERENNIALS.
CULTIVATION Tolerate full sun or
partial shade and require fertile,
moist but well-drained soil.
PROPAGATION From seed, sown
under glass from late winter to early
spring (for summer flowering) or in
a seedbed from mid- to late summer
(for winter flowering).
POTENTIAL PROBLEMS Slugs, snails,
aphids, red spider mites, violet leaf
midge; leaf spot, mosaic viruses,
rust, powdery mildew.

Viola × *wittrockiana* Universal
Series 'True Blue'

V. × wittrockiana

Pansy
Flowers: spring to summer.
H 6–9in (15–23cm), S 9–12in (23–
30cm). FH.
The garden pansies are usually
spreading plants producing a
profusion of flowers, in some cases
as much as 4in (10cm) across, and
continuing in flower over a long
season provided they are regularly
dead-headed and fed generously.
Some are grown exclusively for
their summer display, but there are
in addition winter-flowering
pansies that in mild weather bloom
from autumn to spring. The colour
range is exceptional; there are
single colours and bold bicolours,
some with central masks and
numerous combinations of colours.
Summer-flowering pansies include
the following: '**Bambini**', which
has small flowers in many colours,
usually with a white or yellow face
and whiskered; the **Clear Crystal
Series**, with medium-sized flowers
in a wide range of clear, single
colours; the **Joker Series**, having
medium-sized bicoloured flowers
with strongly marked faces; the
Princess Series, with small

flowers, mainly in shades of yellow
and blue; and the **Super Chalon
Giants**, with large, ruffled,
bicoloured flowers. The best-
known winter-flowering pansies
are those of the **Universal Series**,
with medium-sized flowers in
single colours or bicolours, many
with a dark central blotch. The
Ultima Series also has medium-
sized flowers in a wide colour
range, from early winter to spring.

ZINNIA

ASTERACEAE

Most of the annuals, perennials
and subshrubs in this genus are
plants of dry scrubland or more
open habitats. Many of the 20
species are from Mexico but
representatives are found from
southern USA to South America.
Those in cultivation are among the
most successful annuals in areas
that have dry hot summers.
CULTIVATION Require full sun and
fertile, well-drained soil that is rich
in organic matter.
PROPAGATION From seed, sown
under glass in early spring or
where plants are to flower in late
spring.
POTENTIAL PROBLEMS Usually none.

Z. elegans *North America*

Flowers: summer. H 18–30in (45–
75cm), S 6–12in (15–30cm). HH.
The flowerheads of the wild
species are purplish red but those
topping the stiffly upright
cultivars come in a variety of
bright colours and are single to
fully double. Tall zinnias include
the **Cactus-flowered Group**,
carrying semi-double flowerheads
up to 5in (13cm) across,
composed of quilled florets; '**State
Fair**', a mixture with fully double
flower-heads; and '**Envy**', a semi-
double of unusual lime-green
colouring. There are also
numerous short-growing and
dwarf cultivars, among them the
Peter Pan Series and the
Thumbelina Series. These grow to
a height of 4–12in (10–30cm).

Zinnia elegans Peter Pan Series
'Peter Pan Orange'

bamboos, grasses, grass-like plants, and ferns

Until recently the main ornamental use of grasses was in lawn turf. The bamboos, shrubby grasses with woody, usually hollow, canes or culms, are an important exception. They have long been cultivated in the East and there have also been vogues for them in Western gardens. The bamboos are included here with other true grasses, annuals as well as perennials, and sedges, rushes and cat's tails, three groups of plants that superficially resemble grasses. The chief feature of many of these plants is the foliage. The flowers are not immediately showy but the plumes, spikes and spray-like arrangements can be very graceful. In the garden, they introduce a light airy note and, if gathered before ripening, can be dried to make long-lasting indoor decorations. The scale, deportment and texture of grasses varies so much that an exciting, year-round garden can be made entirely of grasses and grass-like plants.

Ferns (pp. 333–36) are pure foliage plants, their fronds (either deciduous or evergreen) adding to the cool depths of moist shady places, although a surprising number tolerate full sun and fairly dry conditions. These primitive plants are propagated by spores, the sori (clusters of spore-producing organs) usually visible as rusty patches on the back of fertile fronds.

Top Pleioblastus variegatus
Centre Imperata cylindrica 'Rubra'
Bottom Matteuccia struthiopteris

BAMBOOS, GRASSES AND GRASS-LIKE PLANTS

ALOPECURUS

Poaceae Foxtail grass

The foxtail grasses owe their generic and common name to their bushy cylindrical flower spikes. There are about 35 annual and perennial species found in a wide range of habitats in the Northern Hemisphere, including subarctic tundra, moist fertile meadows and dry screes. The woolly foxtail grass (*A. lanatus*), with blue-green leaves covered in soft white hairs, demands a very free-draining gritty soil and protection from excessive wet.
Cultivation Tolerate full sun or partial shade and require fertile moist but well-drained soil.
Propagation By division, in late spring or early summer.
Potential problems Usually none.

A. pratensis 'Aureovariegatus'
Foliage: spring and summer.
Flowers: mid-spring to mid-summer. H 8-12in (20-30cm), S 10-14in (25-35cm). FH.
Rich yellow variegation makes this a bright plant for a frontal position. The clumps are topped by green or purplish flower spikes but these are sacrificed if the plants are clipped to achieve a dense, radiant foliage effect. The leaves of *A. pratensis* '**Aureus**' are rich yellow.

Alopecurus pratensis '**Aureus**'

ARUNDO

Poaceae

The 2 or 3 species are evergreen rhizomatous perennials which are native to warm temperate regions of the Northern Hemisphere. In the wild the best-known, the giant reed (*A. donax*), often forms large stands at the edge of rivers and in other watery places but, in cultivation, it also adapts to drier conditions.
Cultivation Requires full sun and prefers moist conditions. Cut stems back annually for the best foliage effect.

Propagation From stem cuttings, taken in summer. By division of the rootstock, in late spring. From seed, sown in spring.
Potential problems Usually none.

A. donax *S. Europe*
Giant reed
Foliage: year-round. H 12-15ft (3.7-4.5m), S 4-6ft (1.2-1.8m). FH.
This is one of the most impressive grasses of the temperate world. Clumps of stout stems carry broad, drooping, blue-grey leaves, about 2ft (60cm) long. The feathery plumes, purple at first but later nearly white, are produced on second-year stems where the climate is mild enough.

Arundo donax

BRIZA

Poaceae Quaking grass

Several of the approximately 20 annual and perennial species have sprays of pretty spikelets that tremble in the lightest breeze and rattle when strongly shaken. These are widely distributed grasses of temperate regions; the annuals, which naturalize in dry open ground beyond their original homeland, often self-seed freely.
Cultivation Annual species require full sun. Perennial species tolerate full sun or partial shade. All need well-drained soil.
Propagation From seed, in spring or autumn. *B. media* by division, in late spring or early summer.
Potential problems Usually none.

Briza maxima

B. maxima *Mediterranean*
Greater quaking grass, puffed wheat
Flowers: late spring to mid-summer. H 16-24in (40-60cm), S 6-10in (15-25cm). FH.
The elongated heart-shaped spikelets of this annual are pale green tinged with red-brown or purple. They dangle on fine stalks above loose tufts of narrow leaves and, like the foliage, become straw-coloured in late summer.

B. media *Europe, W. Asia*
Common quaking grass, trembling grass
Flowers: late spring to late summer. H 1-2ft (30-60cm), S 8-12in (20-30cm). FH.
This perennial species, which spreads slowly by creeping rhizomes, has blue-green leaves and sprays of heart-shaped shiny spikelets. These are purplish green at first, later fading to beige.

CALAMAGROSTIS

Poaceae

The most commonly grown reed grass is a hybrid between *C. arundinacea* and *C. epigejos*, 2 of some 250 species of rhizomatous perennials found on moist soils in woodland and open heathland in temperate regions. Its cultivars remain attractive in autumn and winter when the clumps turn shades of soft brown and parchment.
Cultivation Tolerate full sun or partial shade and a wide range of soils provided they are fairly moist.
Propagation By division, in mid- to late spring.
Potential problems Usually none.

Calamagrostis × *acutiflora* '**Overdam**'

C. × acutiflora '**Karl Foerster**'
Feather reed grass
Foliage: year-round. Flowers: mid- to late summer. H 5-6ft (1.5-1.8m), S 18-24in (45-60cm). FH.
The narrow column of grey-green leaves is topped by soft pink-

326

bronze plumes, which fade to buff. **'Overdam'**, up to 4ft (1.2m) tall, has purplish plumes that age to silvery pink and makes a loose clump of arching leaves with yellow margins.

CAREX

CYPERACEAE Sedge

Although sedges are common to bog and moorland in temperate and arctic regions, members of this large genus, with more than 1500 perennial species, are found in a range of moist, rather than dry, habitats, extending to high elevations in the tropics. The main feature of the few grown in gardens is the grass-like foliage.
CULTIVATION Tolerate full sun or partial shade and require moist soil (but see also individual entries).
PROPAGATION By division, in late spring or early summer. From seed, sown in spring. (The seed of Northern Hemisphere species generally needs a period of winter cold to germinate.)
POTENTIAL PROBLEMS Usually none.

C. buchananii New Zealand
Leatherleaf sedge
Foliage: year-round. Flowers: mid- to late summer. H 20–30in (50–75cm), S 2–3ft (60–90cm). FrH.
The very narrow cylindrical-looking leaves are in fact 3-angled, and taper to a fine curled point, forming an orange-brown tussock. The flower spikes are brown.

C. conica **'Snowline'**
Foliage: year-round. Flowers: early summer. H 6–12in (15–30cm), S 10–14in (25–35cm). FrH.
The silver tufts of arching leaves have white margins. The flower spikes are purplish brown.

C. elata **'Aurea'**
Bowles' golden sedge
Foliage: spring to summer. Flowers: late spring to early summer. H 20–28in (50–70cm), S 16–20in (40–50cm). FH.
In early summer this variant of the tufted sedge, a European fenland

Carex elata 'Aurea'

plant that will grow in shallow water, has arching bright yellow leaves with narrow green margins. As summer advances, the overall effect becomes greener. The brown male flower spikes are borne above the stalkless green female spikes.

C. **'Frosted Curls'**
Foliage: year-round. H and S 12–18in (30–45cm). FrH.
The silvery green tuft is dense but softened by the curling tips of the arching leaves.

C. hachijoensis **'Evergold'**
Foliage: year-round. Flowers: mid- to late spring. H 10–18in (25–45cm), S 12–18in (30–45cm). FH.
This outstanding variegated form of an evergreen Japanese species is best grown in light shade. The dark green in the leaves brightens the central yellow stripe which ages to a creamy yellow. The flower spikes are brown. The variegated *C. morrowii* **'Fisher's Form'** makes a larger clump, 18–20in (45–50cm) high, with leaves edged and striped with yellow that fades to creamy white.

C. pendula Europe, N. Africa
Drooping sedge, pendulous sedge, weeping sedge
Foliage: year-round. Flowers: late spring to early summer. H and S 4–5ft (1.2–1.5m). FH.
Arching stems rising through dense evergreen clumps of shiny leaves bear green-brown flower spikes, which are erect at first but then hang like catkins. This shade-tolerant woodland sedge also looks graceful by the water's edge.

CORTADERIA

POACEAE

The 20 or so species, mainly from South America and New Zealand, include several distinctive grasses that make large mounds of narrow leaves topped by magnificent plumes. The best-known is the South American pampas grass (*C. selloana*) but the New Zealand toe toe (*C. richardii*) is useful in a large planting of grasses as it flowers in early to mid-summer. Although plants of long-lasting beauty, they can be difficult to place in small gardens, reflecting, perhaps rather unfairly, suburban arcadia at its most dispiriting.
CULTIVATION Require full sun and fertile well-drained soil. With gloves on, remove dead leaves in spring.
PROPAGATION By division, in spring. From seed, sown in spring.
POTENTIAL PROBLEMS Usually none.

Cortaderia richardii

C. selloana Temperate South America
Pampas grass
Foliage: year-round. Flowers: late summer to mid-autumn. H 7–10ft (2.2–3m), S 4–5ft (1.2–1.5m). FH.
The grey-green tussock of narrow arching leaves is impressive but the plant is transformed by the tall stems of glistening plumes, usually creamy white or silver, sometimes tinged purple or red. The gold variegated **'Aureolineata'** is shorter and the free-flowering **'Pumila'** reaches a height of only 4–6ft (1.2–1.8m). The long-lasting plumes of **'Sunningdale Silver'** are silvery white.

Cortaderia selloana 'Sunningdale Silver'

DESCHAMPSIA

POACEAE

Among the 40 to 50 species in this genus of mainly perennial grasses, widely distributed in temperate regions, are several highly ornamental species. Those described are plants of moist acid soils, often found in poorly drained moorland.
CULTIVATION Tolerate full sun or light shade and require moist neutral to acid soil.
PROPAGATION By division, in late spring. From seed, sown in autumn or spring.
POTENTIAL PROBLEMS Usually none.

Deschampsia cespitosa 'Goldschleier'

D. cespitosa *Temperate and arctic Eurasia, mountains of Africa*
Tufted hair grass, tussock grass
Foliage: year-round. Flowers: early to late summer. H 4–6ft (1.2–1.8m), S 4–5ft (1.2–1.5m). FH.
Narrow dark green leaves, often inrolled, form a dense tussock but this base, attractive enough in winter and spring, is overwhelmed by airy plumes from early summer. Their colour, usually starting green or purplish, changes as the season advances. In **'Bronzeschleier'** the plumes progress from silvery green to bronzy yellow, in **'Goldschleier'** to pale sheeny gold.

D. flexuosa *Europe, N. Asia, N.E. USA, temperate South America*
Wavy hair grass
Foliage: year-round. Flowers: early to mid-summer. H and S 20–30in (50–75cm). FH.
The evergreen clump of thread-like leaves is topped by light flower plumes that are silvery, brown or purple. The leaves of **'Tatra Gold'** are bright yellow-green throughout most of the year and stiff stems carry bronzed flowerheads.

FARGESIA

POACEAE

Fargesia murieliae

Two outstanding bamboos that have endured several changes of name now rest in this genus of about 4 species. In the wild they are clump-forming plants of moist forest margins. In the garden the clumps expand slowly but never

get out of hand. Their fountain-like shape makes them effective when they are grown as isolated clumps but they are also appealing planted as a small grove. *F. murieliae*, more wind-tolerant than *F. nitida*, provides an elegant hedge; both make impressive container plants.
CULTIVATION Require moisture-retentive soil (JI No. 3 with added organic matter). *F. murieliae* tolerates sun or shade and *F. nitida* requires partial shade and shelter from cold winds.
PROPAGATION By division, in mid- to late spring.
POTENTIAL PROBLEMS Usually none.

F. murieliae *China*
Umbrella bamboo
Foliage: year-round. H 10–12ft (3–3.7m), S 4–6ft (1.2–1.8m). FH.
Slender yellow-green canes, which have a white bloom when young, surge up as a column before arching out under the cumulative weight of numerous narrow leaves.

F. nitida *China*
Fountain bamboo
Foliage: year-round. H 12–15ft (3.7–4.5m), S 4–6ft (1.2–1.8m). FH.
This thin-leaved bamboo needs shade and shelter from cold winds in order to make an upright column of purplish grey canes that arch lightly with an elegant burden of narrow leaves.

FESTUCA

POACEAE Fescue

The fescues, a large genus of over 300 species, are among the most important pasture grasses in the temperate world (they are also found in mountains of the tropics). Some, such as *F. rubra*, look good in ornamental turf. Several evergreen perennial fescues, mainly plants of dry rough terrain, have a more sophisticated ornamental value, their short bluish tufts providing contrasts of colour and texture and making stubby edgings.
CULTIVATION Require full sun and well-drained soil.
PROPAGATION By division, in autumn or spring. From seed, sown in mid-spring.
POTENTIAL PROBLEMS Usually none.

F. glauca *Temperate regions*
Blue or grey fescue
Foliage: year-round. Flowers: early to mid-summer. H 6–12in (15–30cm), S 8–10in (20–25cm). FH.
Dense tufts bristling with narrow blue-green leaves send up stiff stems with blue-green flower plumes tinged violet. The steel-

blue foliage is particularly striking in the compact **'Blaufuchs'** and in the taller **'Elijah Blue'**. The compact *F. valesiaca* **'Silbersee'** has pale silvery blue foliage. The large blue fescue (*F. amethystina*), which grows to 18in (45cm), has a hint of mauve in its blue-grey foliage.

Festuca glauca

HAKONECHLOA

POACEAE

The genus comprises a single deciduous perennial, *H. macra*, a woodland grass of Japan, found mainly in mountainous areas. The plain-leaved plant, which has yellow-green foliage, is outshone by its variegated forms.
CULTIVATION Tolerate full sun or partial shade and require moist, organic-rich soil (JI No. 2 with added organic matter).
PROPAGATION By division, in mid- to late spring.
POTENTIAL PROBLEMS Usually none.

Hakonechloa macra 'Aureola'

H. macra 'Aureola'
Foliage: spring to autumn. Flowers: late summer to early autumn. H 8–14in (20–35cm), S 14–18in (35–45cm). FH.
Tapering ribbon-like leaves, piled on top of one another to form a soft mound, are bright yellow with fine green stripes. In late summer and autumn, when sprays of pale green flowers are produced, the foliage often takes on a pink or red tint. The leaves of **'Alboaurea'** are slightly broader and the narrow white, yellow and green stripes are often flushed bronze.

HELICTOTRICHON

POACEAE

The grass described, one of about 50 deciduous and evergreen species found in the temperate Northern Hemisphere, is a plant of stony ground on calcareous soils. It is suitable for sunny borders and for planting in gravel.
CULTIVATION Requires full sun and well-drained soil, preferably alkaline.
PROPAGATION By division, in spring. From seed, sown in spring.
POTENTIAL PROBLEMS Usually none.

Helictotrichon sempervirens

H. sempervirens *Europe*
Blue oat grass
Foliage: year-round. Flowers: early to mid-summer. H 3–4ft (90–120cm), S 18–24in (45–60cm). FH.
Narrow blue-green leaves, which are erect in the centre but surrounded by others arching out, form a spiky clump. Slender erect stems, which change from blue-green to buff, carry small sheeny plumes well clear of the foliage.

HORDEUM

POACEAE

Barley (**H. vulgare**), one of the first cultivated cereal crops, is among the 20 or so annual and perennial grasses in this genus, most of which are found on rather dry soils in temperate regions, often where the ground has been disturbed. The flowers of the annual species described are remarkable for their long awns (bristles).
CULTIVATION Require full sun and well-drained soil.

Hordeum jubatum

PROPAGATION From seed, sown where plants are to grow in autumn or spring.
POTENTIAL PROBLEMS Usually none.

H. jubatum *N. America, N.E. Asia*
Squirrel tail grass
Flowers: early to mid-summer. H 20–24in (50–60cm), S 10–12in (25–30cm). FH.
Erect stems rising from short tufts of mid-green leaves arch over to form a silky head with long soft hairs. The spikelets, pale green at first, often have a red or purple flush before the colour bleaches.

IMPERATA

POACEAE

This small genus of 6 rhizomatous perennials from tropical or warm temperate regions contains a species, *I. cylindrica*, which is grown for the red staining of its foliage. In a warm climate it can spread with weed-like abandon, but in cool temperate regions it is suitable for the open garden and also attractive in a container.
CULTIVATION Tolerate full sun or dappled shade and require moist, soil rich in organic matter (JI No. 2 with added organic matter).
PROPAGATION By division, in late spring.
POTENTIAL PROBLEMS Usually none.

Imperata cylindrica 'Rubra'

I. cylindrica *S. Europe to Japan and Australia*
Foliage: spring to autumn. Flowers: late summer to early autumn. H 16–24in (40–60cm), S 10–12in (25–30cm). FrH.
The plant usually seen is **'Rubra'** from Japan, remarkable for the strong red staining of the flat upright leaves, which becomes more bloodied as summer advances. The flowers are silvery.

JUNCUS

JUNCACEAE Rush

The rushes, a large genus of about 300 grass-like evergreen or deciduous plants, are found in many parts of the world in marshy

conditions, particularly on acid soils. Rushes are a common feature of boggy ground in cool temperate regions. The relatively few species that are cultivated are useful marginals for ponds.
CULTIVATION Requires full sun and wet soil, tolerating water to a depth of about 4in (10cm).
PROPAGATION By division, in mid- to late spring.
POTENTIAL PROBLEMS Usually none.

Juncus effusus 'Spiralis'

J. effusus 'Spiralis'
Corkscrew rush
Foliage: spring to autumn. Flowers: early to late summer. H 16–20in (40–50cm), S 12–18in (30–45cm). FH.
The corkscrew variant of the soft rush is a curiosity for the margin of a small pool. The glossy dark green stems seem to spiral randomly, some lying coiled on the ground in the tangle. The cluster of brownish flowers emerges well below the stem tip.

LAGURUS

POACEAE Hare's tail

The bobbing flowerheads of the annual hare's tail (*L. ovatus*), the single species in this genus, are a familiar sight in sandy coastal areas of the Mediterranean. This easily grown garden plant can be dried.
CULTIVATION Requires full sun and well-drained soil.
PROPAGATION From seed, sown where plants are to grow in spring or autumn, or in autumn under glass in containers.
POTENTIAL PROBLEMS Usually none.

Lagurus ovatus

L. ovatus *Mediterranean*
Hare's tail
Flowers: early to late summer.
H 12–18in (30–45cm), S 6–10in
(15–25cm). FH.
The slender erect stems rising from
tufts of downy grey-green leaves
carry fluffy, silky, egg-shaped heads
that are greenish white at first,
usually with a purplish tinge, and
eventually turn beige.

LUZULA

JUNCACEAE Woodrush

The woodrushes are mainly plants
of moist woodlands, with about 80
species, the majority perennials,
widely distributed in temperate
regions of the world. These grass-
like plants, which are closely
related to the true rushes (*Juncus*),
have rather broad leaves and
produce clusters of very small
flowers. They make unspectacular
but useful groundcover in shade.
CULTIVATION Tolerate full sun or
partial shade and require moist
soil, rich in organic matter, that
does not dry out. *L. nivea* needs
full sun.
PROPAGATION By division, in late
spring or early summer. From seed,
sown in containers in autumn or
spring.
POTENTIAL PROBLEMS Usually none.

L. nivea *S. and C. Europe*
Snowy woodrush
Foliage: year-round. Flowers: early
to late summer. H 18–24in (45–
60cm), S 14–18in (35–45cm). FH.
This evergreen perennial forms
slowly spreading tufts of deep
green leaves topped by tightly
clustered heads of tiny, lustrous,
pale buff flowers, which dry well.

Luzula sylvatica 'Aurea'

L. sylvatica *S., W. and C. Europe,
S.W. Asia*
Greater woodrush
Foliage: year-round. Flowers: mid-
spring to early summer. H 28–32in
(70–80cm), S 18–20in (45–50cm).
FH.
Dense evergreen tussocks provide
groundcover under trees and
shrubs. Airy heads of tiny brown

flowers appear above glossy dark
green leaves. 'Aurea' has yellow-
green leaves that turn bright
yellow in winter and the leaves of
'Marginata' have a cream edge.

MILIUM

POACEAE

This small genus of 6 annual and
perennial woodland grasses
includes the semi-evergreen wood
millet (**M. effusum**), which is
widely distributed in Europe and
North America. The plain-leaved
plant is rarely grown, although the
light green of its foliage shows up
well in semi-shade.
CULTIVATION Require partial shade
and moist soil, rich in organic
matter.
PROPAGATION By division, in
spring. From seed, sown in spring.
POTENTIAL PROBLEMS Usually none.

Milium effusum 'Aureum'

M. effusum 'Aureum'
Bowles' golden grass, golden wood
millet
Foliage: spring to late summer.
Flowers: late spring to mid-
summer. H 16–24in (40–60cm),
S 10–12in (25–30in). FH.
Even on a dull day in spring the
rich yellow, ribbon-like leaves of
this perennial catch the light. Tiny
golden flowers shimmer on slender
stems. The limp foliage becomes
more green as the season advances.

MISCANTHUS

POACEAE

There are about 20 species of
these elegant perennial grasses
and, although widely distributed, a
high proportion come from Japan
and China, where they are usually
found in moist, even marshy soils
with other grasses and herbaceous
plants. Those plants described,
which increase steadily without
being invasive, remain beautiful
when reduced to bleached
parchment in winter but should be
cut down before new growth is
made in spring.
CULTIVATION Require full sun and
fertile moist but well-drained soil.

PROPAGATION By division, in mid-
to late spring. From seed, sown in
spring.
POTENTIAL PROBLEMS Usually none.

Miscanthus sacchariflorus

M. sacchariflorus *S.E. Asia*
Silver banner grass
Foliage: year-round. Flowers: late
summer to early autumn. H 6–10ft
(1.8–3m), S 3–5ft (90–150cm). FrH.
In a large-scale waterside planting
this is a match for giants such as
Gunnera manicata. The silky
purple-brown flowerheads are
rarely produced in cool temperate
regions but the bamboo-like
clumps, with their long rustling
leaves, arch gracefully.

M. sinensis *S.E. Asia*
Foliage: year-round. Flowers: early
to mid-autumn. H 4–10ft (1.2–3m),
S 3–5ft (90–150cm). FH.
The wild form has been displaced
in gardens by a range of beautiful
cultivars, the leaves making an
arching counterpoint to the
vigorous upward thrust of the
stems. The silky buff-pink sprays of
M. 'Silberfeder', up to 8ft (2.5m)
tall, and less dependent than most
on a warm summer to flower, is in
a class of its own. Other fine
cultivars include: **'Gracillimus'**, up
to 5ft (1.5m) high and gracefully
slender; **'Grosse Fontäne'**, a
vigorous grower up to 6½ft (2m)
with purple stems and cascading
leaves, with distinctive white midribs, and red-tinted plumes;
'Malepartus', up to 8ft (2.5m)
high, with silver-veined leaves that
turn purplish in autumn and large
mahogany plumes ageing to silver;

Miscanthus sinensis 'Zebrinus'

and '**Zebrinus**', the zebra grass, which grows to 6ft (1.8m), with irregular horizontal banding in shades of cream or yellow.

MOLINIA

POACEAE

The genus comprises only 2 species, both of them perennial grasses of moist acidic moorland. In cultivation, however, the purple moor grass (*M. caerulea*) and its variegated cultivars succeed in a fairly wide range of conditions. They are suitable for borders and woodland gardens, while the dwarfer kinds are ideal for outcrops in rock gardens.
CULTIVATION Tolerate full sun or partial shade and require moist soil, preferably neutral to acid.
PROPAGATION By division, in late spring. From seed, sown in spring.
POTENTIAL PROBLEMS Usually none.

Molinia caerulea **subsp.** *caerulea* **'Moorhexe'**

M. caerulea *Europe, N. and S.W. Asia*
Purple moor grass
Foliage: spring to autumn. Flowers: mid-summer to early autumn. H 2–4ft (60–120cm), S 18–24in (45–60cm). FH.
The dense tussocks from which stiff stems rise bear purplish flowers. The tall flower stems of **subsp. arundinacea**, about 4ft (1.2m) high, even up to 7ft (2.2m) in '**Windspiel**', turn amber yellow in autumn. The narrow upright growth of **subsp. caerulea** '**Moorhexe**', only 18in (45cm) high and topped by dark flowers, contrasts well with rambling plants. The pick of these grasses is **subsp. caerulea 'Variegata'**, which has arching leaves, with cream stripes, and feathery purplish buff plumes. It reaches 18–24in (45–60cm) high.

PENNISETUM

POACEAE

Over 100 species are distributed from warm temperate to tropical regions of the world. The Kikuyu

grass (*P. clandestinum*), grown for pasture, is of economic importance. The appealing flowerheads of those grown ornamentally resemble hairy caterpillars. The species described are plants of open grassland and tolerant of dry conditions.
CULTIVATION Require full sun and well-drained soil.
PROPAGATION By division, in late spring. From seed, sown in spring.
POTENTIAL PROBLEMS Usually none.

P. alopecuroides *E. Asia to W. Australia*
Fountain grass
Foliage: year-round. Flowers: early to mid-autumn. H and S 2–4ft (60–120cm). FrH.
This evergreen species makes a dark green mound of narrow leaves, its arching growth emphasized in autumn when fuzzy purplish flowerheads weigh down the stem tips. '**Hameln**' is compact and flowers in late summer.

P. orientale *C. and S.W. Asia, N. India*
Foliage: spring to autumn. Flowers: mid-summer to early autumn. H and S 18–24in (45–60cm). FrH.
In cool temperate regions this deciduous perennial can be grown as an annual, started under glass in early spring. Large caterpillar-like flowerheads, at first mauve pink, later buff to near white, sway above clumps of narrow leaves.

Pennisetum villosum

P. villosum *Mountains of N.E. tropical Africa*
Feathertop
Foliage: spring to autumn. Flowers: late summer to early autumn. H and S 20–24in (50–60cm). FrH.
Where the climate suits it, as in parts of Australia, this deciduous perennial grass is a weed. Like *P. orientale*, it can be grown as an annual. Beige flowerheads, made tactile and feathery with long hairs, bob in the breeze above a clump of arching grey-green leaves.

PHALARIS

POACEAE

The genus contains about 15 species of annual and perennial grasses from a wide range of habitats but the representatives usually seen in gardens are variegated forms of a moisture-loving evergreen perennial, reed canary grass (*P. arundinacea*).
CULTIVATION Tolerate full sun or partial shade and wet to moderately moist soil.
PROPAGATION By division, from mid-spring to early summer.
POTENTIAL PROBLEMS Usually none.

Phalaris arundinacea **var.** *picta* **'Feesey'**

P. arundinacea var. picta 'Feesey'
Gardeners' garters
Foliage: year-round. Flowers: early to mid-summer. H and S 2–3ft (60–90cm). FH.
This is a sport of the vigorous **var. picta**, one of the first variegated grasses for gardens. Half-and-half longitudinal green and white striping on ribbon-like leaves make it tempting although it is invasive. '**Feesey**' is whiter and paler green and spreads slowly to form dense clumps. The pale green to buff spikelets stand clear of the leaves.

PHYLLOSTACHYS

POACEAE

Several graceful bamboos belong to this genus of about 80 species, most of them woodland plants from the Himalayas and further east. As well as an elegant form and beautiful foliage, several have distinctive canes, including the fishpole or golden bamboo (*P. aurea*). The young shoots of many, including *P. edulis*, are edible. The giant timber bamboo (*P. bambusoides*), has much commercial value.
CULTIVATION Tolerate full sun or partial shade and require moist well-drained soil (JI No. 3).
PROPAGATION By division, in mid- to late spring.
POTENTIAL PROBLEM Slugs.

331

Phyllostachys nigra

P. nigra *E. and C. China*
Black bamboo
Foliage and canes: year-round.
H 5–10ft (1.5–3m), S 6–10ft
(1.8–3m). FH.
The rich foliage is a feature of this
clump-forming bamboo as are the
arching canes which turn from
green in the first year to mottled
brown and then nearly black in
the second or third year. **'Boryana'**
produces yellowish green canes
with purple-brown marks. The
canes of **var. henonis** are bright
green at first, turning yellow-
brown as they mature. The leaves
are dark green.

PLEIOBLASTUS

POACEAE

This Asiatic genus of about 20
bamboos includes several
characterful low-growing species.
In the wild these bamboos, most
of which have running roots,
form thickets in glades and on
woodland margins. The low-
growing invasive species,
P. humilis and **P. pygmaeus**,
make attractive container plants.
CULTIVATION Tolerate full sun or
partial shade (variegation is best
in full sun). Require moist soil (JI
No. 3) and shelter from cold winds.
PROPAGATION By division, in mid-
to late spring.
POTENTIAL PROBLEMS Usually none.

Pleioblastus auricomus

P. auricomus *Japan*
Foliage: year-round. H and S 2–5ft
(60–150cm). FH.
In shade the leaves of this bamboo
look sickly green but make a bright
yellow splash in full sun, which
brings out the rich yellow striping.

P. variegatus *Japan*
Foliage: year-round. H and S 2–4ft
(60–120cm). FH.
The pale green canes carry spiky
tufts of narrow downy leaves with
bold dark green and white stripes.
The roots run but this charmingly
bright bamboo is easily controlled.

SEMIARUNDINARIA

POACEAE

The 10 or so tall bamboos that
make up this genus are from China
and Japan. In the wild they usually
form large thickets in or at the
margins of woodland in rough
mountainous country. In a cool
temperate climate the species
described forms a dense clump
from which rhizomes establish
neighbouring clumps.
CULTIVATION Tolerates full sun or
light shade and requires moist, well-
drained soil, rich in organic matter.
PROPAGATION By division of young
rhizomes, in spring.
POTENTIAL PROBLEM Slugs.

Semiarundinaria fastuosa

S. fastuosa *Japan*
Narihira bamboo
Foliage and canes: year-round.
H 15–25ft (4.5–7.5m), S 5–8ft
(1.5–2.5m). FH.
The shiny green leaves are carried
high up on tall stiff canes, which
eventually turn yellow-brown, but
when young are glossy green with
purple stains at the nodes. It
makes a good hedge or screen.

STIPA

POACEAE Feather grass

Many of the species in this large
genus of several hundred
temperate and tropical grasses,
most of them perennial, are highly
ornamental as well as remarkably
tolerant of dry conditions. The

leaves are usually quill-like with
rolled-in margins.
CULTIVATION Require full sun
and well-drained soil. Tolerate
dry conditions except for
S. arundinacea.
PROPAGATION By division, in mid-
to late spring. From seed, sown
in spring.
POTENTIAL PROBLEMS Usually none.

S. arundinacea *New Zealand*
Pheasant's tail grass
Flowers: mid-summer to early
autumn. H 18–24in (45–60cm),
S 3–4ft (90–120cm). FH.
The orange and russet tones that
develop in the arching clumps
throughout summer make a
striking feature in winter. The
flower stems are light and weighed
down by a haze of soft brown
flowers.

S. calamagrostis *S. Europe*
Flowers: summer to early autumn.
H and S 3–4ft (90–120cm). FH.
This free-flowering deciduous
grass makes a lax clump that is
improved by light support. The
feathery green plumes eventually
turn warm buff and last through
the winter.

S. gigantea *Portugal, Spain*
Giant feather grass, golden oats
Flowers: early to mid-summer.
H 6–8ft (1.8–2.5m), S 3–4ft
(90–120cm). FH.
The lax evergreen or semi-
evergreen clump of narrow leaves
is undistinguished but the tall
flowering stems that spring from it
carry heads of oat-like, pinkish
purple flowers. These turn to gold
and spangle beautifully in the
lightest breeze.

Stipa tenuissima

S. tenuissima *USA (Texas, New
Mexico), Mexico, Argentina*
Flowers: mid-summer to autumn.
H 18–24in (45–60cm), S 10–12in
(25–30cm). FH.
The fine bright green leaves make
a soft-textured vase-like clump
with a billowing silky head of
silver-green flowers that turn
buff as they age.

FERNS

ADIANTUM

ADIANTACEAE Maidenhair fern

This genus consists of over 200 species of evergreen, semi-evergreen and deciduous ferns. Many occur in tropical and sub-tropical forest in North and South America, while others are found in temperate woodland or woodland margins in Europe, Asia, Australasia and North America. The variable fronds are divided, with oval or rounded segments carried on long, thin, shiny purple-black leaf stalks. True maidenhair fern (*A. capillus-veneris*), often grown as a pot plant, is notable for its light green triangular fronds.
CULTIVATION Prefer full or partial shade and moist well-drained soil. Do not allow to dry out or become waterlogged.
PROPAGATION By division, in spring. From spores, sown as soon as ripe.
POTENTIAL PROBLEMS Usually none.

A. pedatum *North America*
H 6–8in (15–20cm), S 12–24in (30–60cm). FH.
Light green, lance-shaped, deciduous fronds with toothed margins are borne on thin, glossy, purple stalks. The Aleutian maidenhair fern (**A. pedatum var. subpumilum**), which is also fully hardy, is considerably larger than the species, with a height and spread of 30in (75cm). Blackish purple stems support finely divided, fingered fronds that are tinged pink when young, later turning pale to mid-green.

Adiantum pedatum

A. venustum *China, Tibet*
Himalayan maidenhair fern
Foliage: year-round. H and S 6–9in (15–23cm). FH.
Vivid bronze-pink fronds emerge in late winter and early spring. As the fronds develop, they turn mid-green and open out into a triangular shape, with narrowly fan-shaped segments.

ASPLENIUM

ASPLENIACEAE Spleenwort

The plants in this large genus of over 700 semi-evergreen and evergreen ferns are found in most parts of the world in a wide range of habitats. The fronds grow in tufts on short, erect or creeping rhizomes, and are deeply divided or entire. The bird's nest fern (**A. nidus**), which is a tropical epiphyte, has bright green glossy fronds, rather like long tongues, arranged in a rosette. This fern is, however, susceptible to attacks from scale insects. In contrast, the terrestial rusty-backed fern (**A. ceterach**) has fronds made up of small, rounded dark green leaflets, with felt-like brown scales beneath.
CULTIVATION Prefer partial shade. Require a sheltered site and well-drained soil rich in organic matter.
PROPAGATION From spores, sown as soon as ripe. By division, in spring.
POTENTIAL PROBLEMS Usually none.

Asplenium scolopendrium Crispum Group

A. scolopendrium *Asia, Europe, North America*
Hart's tongue fern
Foliage: year-round. H 12–24in (30–60cm), S 10–20in (25–50cm). FH.
The clusters of tufty fronds are light green with a leathery texture, and resemble shuttlecocks. Its variations include the **Crispum Group**, with fronds that have a pronouned wavy margin; the **Cristatum Group**, with crested and ruffled fronds; and the **Undulatum Group**, with fronds that have irregular wavy margins.

A. trichomanes *Most temperate regions*
Maidenhair spleenwort
Foliage: year-round. H and S 3–9in (8–23cm). FH.
Attractive fronds of dark green leaflets with rounded tips are produced on thin, glossy dark brown to black stems. The fronds grow in dense tufts on short, erect, occasionally creeping rhizomes.

ATHYRIUM

ATHYRIACEAE Lady fern

Over 180 species of deciduous lady ferns occur throughout the world in moist temperate and tropical woodland, yet very few have been cultivated for garden use. The common lady fern (*A. filix-femina*), much-loved by Victorian gardeners, is highly variable, with numerous cultivars.
CULTIVATION Require partial or full shade and fertile, moist, neutral to slightly acid soil.
PROPAGATION By division, in spring. From spores, sown as soon as ripe.
POTENTIAL PROBLEMS Usually none.

Athyrium filix-femina 'Frizelliae'

A. filix-femina *Temperate N. hemisphere*
Lady fern
H and S 18–36in (45–90cm). FH.
The arching outline of this fern is one of its chief assets. The fronds, rising from erect rhizomes, are usually finely divided into long, pointed leaflets. '**Frizelliae**' (Mrs. Frizell's lady fern, tatting fern) has small, rounded segments on the fronds, 8in (20cm) long, which resemble "tatting" (knotted lace-like trimming).

A. niponicum var. **pictum**
Japanese painted fern
H and S 12–18in (30–45cm). FH.
This slow-spreading Japanese fern, with individual fronds produced from a creeping rhizome, will cover small areas with a carpet of silver-green fronds. The midribs are flushed maroon-purple.

Athyrium niponicum var. **pictum**

BLECHNUM

BLECHNACEAE Hard fern

Between 150 and 200 species of
hard ferns, the majority of which
are evergreen, occur mostly in
moist, acid, sheltered sites in
temperate and tropical regions.
The hardiest and most garden-
worthy of these ferns make useful
evergreen groundcover plants for
moist, acid soils. The drooping or
nearly prostrate infertile fronds
and the erect, spore-bearing
fronds, developed in the centre of
the foliage rosettes, provide a
striking contrast in form.
CULTIVATION Require partial or full
shade and moist acid soil rich in
organic matter.
PROPAGATION By division, in
spring. From spores, sown in late
summer.
POTENTIAL PROBLEMS Usually none.

Blechnum penna-marina

B. penna-marina *Australasia,
South America*
Foliage: year-round. H 4–8in
(10–20cm), S indefinite. FH.
Creeping rhizomes produce dense
tufts of evergreen fronds. The
fertile fronds have more widely
spaced segments than those of the
sterile fronds.

B. spicant *Europe, N. Asia,
W. North America*
Hard fern
Foliage: year-round. H 12–18in (30–
45cm), S 18–24in (45–60cm). FH.
Fertile fronds, standing bolt
upright, are frequently produced
in the centre of large, mature, flat
rosettes of sterile fronds. Variations
in frond shape include crested and
serrated segments.

CYSTOPTERIS

ATHYRIACEAE Bladder fern

The 10 to 20 deciduous ferns in
this genus occur in temperate and
subtropical regions, where they
grow on rocky mountainsides, in
woodland and in damp valleys,
usually in alkaline soil. The sori of
their delicately bowed, soft, very
finely divided fronds have a

bladder-like covering which gives
the group its common name. Some
species, such as *C. bulbifera*,
produce small bulbils on the frond
stalk; the bulbils drop when ripe
and sprout new ferns.
CULTIVATION Require partial shade,
shelter from cold, drying winds
and fertile moist but well-drained
soil with stone chippings added.
PROPAGATION From bulbils, in late
summer (*C. bulbifera*). By division,
in spring. From spores, sown in
late summer.
POTENTIAL PROBLEMS Usually none.

C. bulbifera *E. North America*
H 12–18in (30–45cm), S 8–12in
(20–30cm). FH.
This lime-tolerant fern has
graceful, swirling rosettes of light
green, slender, divided fronds with
curving tips. Bulbils develop
beneath the midribs, which are
lightly tinged with red.

C. fragilis *E. North America*
Brittle bladder fern
H and S 8–10in (20–25cm). FH.
Widely distributed in northern
temperate regions, and also found
in Chile, this clump-forming fern
produces lacy tufts of grey-green,
divided fronds.

Cystopteris fragilis

DICKSONIA

DICKSONIACEAE

There are about 25 species of
evergreen and semi-evergreen
ferns in this genus, occurring in
sheltered forest in temperate and
tropical regions of Australasia, S.E.
Asia and South America. The
rhizomes are often thick, trunk-like
and upright, but occasionally
creeping. Dark glossy green,
leathery, divided fronds form
terminal clusters. Man fern
(*D. antarctica*) grows successfully
in coastal regions.
CULTIVATION Prefers full or partial
shade, but tolerates full sun.
Prefers moist acid soil rich in
organic matter.
PROPAGATION From spores, sown
as soon as ripe.
POTENTIAL PROBLEMS Usually none.

Dicksonia antarctica

D. antarctica *E. Australia
(including Tasmania)*
Man fern, soft tree fern, woolly
tree fern
Foliage: year-round. H and S 6–12ft
(1.8–3.7m). FH.
This statuesque, slow-growing fern
gradually develops into a single
furry trunk made up of the fibrous
remains of old leaf stalks. The
large, finely divided fronds, up to
6ft (2m) long, are glossy mid-green
on the upper side and matt green
on the underside.

DRYOPTERIS

ASPIDIACEAE Buckler fern

There are about 200 species of
ferns in this genus. They are found
in the temperate Northern
Hemisphere, often in woodland or
on mountainsides and near water.
Most are deciduous, but a few stay
green in winter if grown in
favourable conditions.
CULTIVATION Require partial or full
shade, a sheltered site and moist
soil rich in organic matter. Golden
male fern (*D. affinis*) tolerates a
less sheltered site.
PROPAGATION By division, in spring
or autumn. From spores, sown as
soon as ripe.
POTENTIAL PROBLEMS Usually none.

Dryopteris affinis

D. affinis *Mediterranean to
Himalayas, W. Europe*
Golden male fern
Foliage: year-round in mild winters.
H and S 2–4ft (60– 120cm). FH.
Golden brown scales on each
frond midrib show to best effect as
the young growth unfurls in

spring. The leathery fronds are dark green and rise from erect rhizomes. Among cultivars **'Cristata The King'** has the brightest golden scales and is notable for the heavily crested tip to each frond.

D. dilatata *C. and N.W. Europe*
Broad buckler fern
H and S 2–4ft (60–120cm). FH.
Arching, triangular, divided fronds rise from erect rhizomes to create an elegant shuttlecock form. The fronds are pale green in spring, maturing to dark green. The midribs are covered with brown scales with buff-brown margins.

Dryopteris erythrosora

D. erythrosora *China, Japan, Korea*
Foliage: year-round in mild winters. H and S 18–24in (45–60cm). FH. Slowly creeping rhizomes make loose tufts of spreading, triangular, divided fronds, showy copper-red while young, fading to dark green. Bright red young sori often show well against the summer foliage.

D. filix-mas *Europe, North America*
Male fern
H and S 2–4ft (60–120cm). FH.
Spear-shaped, deep glossy green, finely divided fronds arch so that the tips almost touch the ground. This fern spores prolifically. Slower-growing **'Crispa Cristata'** has crested fronds and crested, wavy-edged leaflets. Less vigorous **'Cristata'** (crested buckler fern) is more spreading; the fronds are yellowy green with finely divided, crinkled edges. **'Linearis'** has delicate-looking fronds.

D. wallichiana *Himalayas to S.E. Asia*
Wallich's wood fern
Foliage: spring to autumn. H 3–5ft (90–150cm), S 30–36in (75–90cm). FH.
A massive shuttlecock of lance-shaped, divided, dark green fronds form a bold feature. The brownish black midrib scales contrast dramatically with the yellow-green spring foliage.

MATTEUCCIA

ASPIDIACEAE

This genus comprises 3 or 4 species of deciduous ferns, widely distributed in deciduous woodland in the Northern Hemisphere. The large, finely divided fronds appear in spring, and are followed by fertile, spore-bearing fronds in mid-summer, which persist into winter.
CULTIVATION Prefers partial or dappled shade, but tolerates sun. Requires moist well-drained soil rich in organic matter.
PROPAGATION From spores, sown as soon as ripe. By division, in early spring.
POTENTIAL PROBLEMS Usually none.

M. struthiopteris *Asia, Europe, North America*
Shuttlecock fern
H 3–5ft (90–150cm), S 2–3ft (60–90cm). FH.
This deciduous fern has an outer rim of gently arching, yellow-green sterile fronds, up to 3ft (90cm) long. The shorter greenish brown inner fronds are fertile. Both inner and outer fronds are broadly spear-shaped, very thin and deeply cut, with blackish brown midribs.

Matteuccia struthiopteris

ONOCLEA

ASPIDIACEAE

Genus of a single species of deciduous fern occuring in damp sites. It is ideal for a damp shady border or beside water.
CULTIVATION Prefers partial shade (the fronds may burn in full sun) and moist, preferably acid, soil.
PROPAGATION By division, in autumn or early spring. From spores, sown as soon as ripe.
POTENTIAL PROBLEMS Usually none.

O. sensibilis *E. Asia, E. USA*
Foliage: autumn. H 12–24in (30–60cm), S indefinite. FH.
Bright green sterile fronds, often bronze-pink in spring, turn butter-yellow in autumn. Shorter spore-bearing fronds, which are stiffly upright, turn dark brown.

Onoclea sensibilis

OSMUNDA

OSMUNDACEAE

The 12 or so deciduous moisture-loving ferns in this genus are found in damp places in all continents except Australasia. The mid-green, broadly spear-shaped, very finely divided fronds arch gently from the base. The undersides of the inner fronds are covered with spore capsules which turn brown when ripe, usually in mid-summer.
CULTIVATION Prefers partial shade and requires moist fertile soil. Tolerates full sun in a damp site.
PROPAGATION From spores, sown as soon as ripe. By division, in spring.
POTENTIAL PROBLEMS Usually none.

O. regalis *Temperate and subtropical regions*
Flowering fern, royal fern
H and S 4–5ft (1.2–1.5m). FH.
The broadly triangular, bright green sterile fronds are followed by fertile fronds with long, tassel-like tips. This fern gradually builds up a mass of crowns and matted black roots 2–3ft (60–90cm) above the ground.

Osmunda regalis

POLYPODIUM

POLYPODIACEAE

Most of the 75 or more species are evergreen, epiphytic ferns from tropical regions in the Americas. Some species tolerate drought more than most other ferns.
CULTIVATION Require dappled or full shade and moderately fertile, acid, gritty, well-drained soil.

FERNS

PROPAGATION By division, in spring
or early summer. From spores,
sown when ripe.
POTENTIAL PROBLEMS Usually none.

P. vulgare *Africa, E. Asia, Europe*
Common polypody
Foliage: year-round. H 6–15in
(15–38cm), S indefinite. FH.
This fern is grown for its lance-
shaped, leathery, dark green
fronds, which rise from tough,
creeping rhizomes. Growing either
epiphytically or terrestrially, it
grows in dry-stone walls, on mossy
boulders and tree stumps, or on
banks or dunes. **'Cornubiense
Grandiceps'** has finely divided
fronds, crested or branched in
quite a pronounced manner at
each frond tip.

Polypodium vulgare

POLYSTICHUM

ASPIDIACEAE Shield fern

There are nearly 200 species of
these ferns, most of which are
evergreen. They occur in a wide
range of habitats, from alpine cliffs
to tropical forests worldwide, and
are resilient and tolerant of dry
conditions. Many have intricately
divided dark green fronds, which
spiral in shuttlecocks around erect
central rhizomes. Characteristic of
many species are the toothed
segments, terminating in a sharp
point or bristle and giving the
fronds sharp definition.
CULTIVATION Tolerate full sun or
dappled to deep shade and require
moderately fertile, gritty soil.
PROPAGATION By division, in
spring. From spores, sown when
ripe. From bulbils (cultivars of
P. setiferum), in autumn.
POTENTIAL PROBLEMS Usually none.

P. aculeatum *C. and N.W.
Europe*
Hard shield fern, prickly shield fern
Foliage: year-round. H 2–3ft (60–
90cm), S 12–30in (30–75cm). FH.
Broad, arching, vase-shaped
shuttlecocks are formed by the
narrow, lance-shaped, divided
fronds. These are leathery in
texture and dark green in colour.

Polystichum aculeatum

P. munitum *N.W. North America*
Sword fern
Foliage: year-round. H 2–4ft (60–
120cm), S 3–4ft (90–120cm). FH.
The leathery, lance-shaped fronds
are matt dark green, slightly hairy
on the underside and form
shuttlecocks. The leaflets are
spiny-toothed.

P. setiferum *Europe*
Soft shield fern
Foliage: year-round in mild
winters. H 2–4ft (60–120cm),
S 30–36in (75–90cm). FH.
The divided, soft-textured, dark
green fronds make a drooping and
ornamental, vase-shaped
shuttlecock. Each frond stem is
covered in soft brown scales. Ferns
in the **Acutilobum Group** have
pronounced long, pointed fronds,
spiralling elegantly around the
crown. They are drought-tolerant –
even thriving in full sun on fertile,
moist soils – and producing bulbils
on frond midribs. **Divisilobum
Group** contains ferns with
intricately divided fronds and long,
narrow, leathery leaflets earning
them the name filigree fern.
Bulbils often form along the frond
midribs. **'Herrenhausen'** has
broad fronds, spreading to
flattened shuttlecocks as much as
20in (50cm) across.

THELYPTERIS

THELYPTERIDACEAE

The 2 ferns in this genus are
deciduous and are found in bogs
and swamps in temperate regions
throughout the world. They are
often mat-forming, producing a
roving mass of rhizomatous roots
from which emerge lance-shaped
fronds with deeply divided leaflets.
They are ideal plants for a moist
border or beside a pond.
CULTIVATION Tolerates full sun or
partial shade and requires
perpetually moist, moderately
fertile soil.
PROPAGATION By division, in spring
or summer. From spores, sown as
soon as ripe.
POTENTIAL PROBLEMS Usually none.

T. palustris *Europe, Asia*
Marsh fern
H and S 2–3ft (60–90cm). FH.
This fern spreads to provide a
dainty, grey-green, soft-fronded
edging and thrives in bogs or by
water. The long-stalked, lance-
shaped, divided fronds rise from
amidst the creeping rhizomes.

Thelypteris palustris

WOODWARDIA

BLECHNACEAE Chain fern

Of the 10 species of evergreen and
deciduous ferns in this genus, only
2 are commonly cultivated in
temperate gardens. Their natural
habitats are moist, shady banks
near water or acid bogs, in warm
temperate and tropical zones.
Where winters are mild, they are
among the largest and grandest of
ferns, with broad, arching fronds.
The sori are arranged in chains,
hence the common name.
CULTIVATION Requires partial shade
in a sheltered position and
moderately fertile, moist soil.
PROPAGATION By division, in
spring. From spores, sown in late
summer or early autumn. From
bulbils, in autumn.
POTENTIAL PROBLEMS Usually none.

W. radicans *Atlantic Islands,
S.W. Europe*
European chain fern
Foliage: year-round. H 3–4ft (90–
120cm), S 4–8ft (1.2–2.5m). FrH.
Broad, lance-shaped, divided
fronds, with finely toothed leaflets,
form bold, spreading arches. A
single bulbil is produced near the
tip of each frond.

Woodwardia radicans

PLANTS FOR SPECIAL CONDITIONS

The following plant lists are intended as starting points for gardeners who are choosing plants for specific growing conditions. The lists should be used in conjunction with the entries in the "Plant Directory", in which the information on cultivation will give an indication of any other requirements for satisfactory growth. These lists do not attempt to be comprehensive. For example, all the rhododendrons described in the book are not listed under "Plants Requiring or Tolerating Acid Soils". However, an asterisk after a plant name indicates that the genus contains other ornamentals that will grow in the conditions suitable for the plant listed.

PLANTS FOR SUNNY DRY CONDITIONS

The plants in the following listings vary in their tolerance of drought but all require well-drained conditions and as mature plants are to some degree capable of withstanding dry periods. However, as young plants all are much more dependent on regular supplies of water and, even when established, need moisture during their peak period of growth. However, given the scarcity of water resources at the present time The Royal Horticultural Society recommends avoiding excessive irrigation whenever possible.

TREES
Acer negundo
Ailanthus altissima
Betula pendula*
Cercis siliquatrum
Genista aetnensis
Gleditsia
   triacanthos
Ilex aquifolium
Populus alba*
Robinia
   pseudoacacia

SHRUBS
Ballota pseudo-
   dictamnus*
Berberis darwinii*
Brachyglottis
   Dunedin Group
   'Sunshine'*
Buddleja davidii*
Calluna vulgaris
Caryopteris ×
   clandonensis*
Ceanothus
   impressus*
Choisya ternata*
Cistus laurifolius*
Convolvulus
   cneorum*
Coronilla
   valentina
Cotinus 'Flame'*
Cotoneaster
   frigidus*
Cytisus × praecox*
Elaeagnus
   angustifolia*
Erica carnea*
Fremontodendron
   'California
   Glory'*
Genista lydia*

Helianthemum
   hybrids*
Hibiscus
Hypericum
   olympicum*
Laurus nobilis
Lavandula
   angustifolia*
Lavatera
   'Barnsley'*
Philadelphus
   'Beauclerk'*
Potentilla
   fruticosa*
Pyracantha
   hybrids*
Rosmarinus
   officinalis
Ruta graveolens
Salvia officinalis*
Santolina
   chamaecyparissus
Tamarix
   ramosissima*
Thymus serpyllum*
Yucca filamentosa*

CONIFERS
Cedrus libani
   subsp. atlantica*
Juniperus
   communis*
Pinus sylvestris*
Taxus baccata*

CLIMBERS
Bougainvillea ×
   buttiana*
Hedera helix*
Lathyrus latifolius
Solanum crispum
   'Glasnevin'
Vitis vinifera

ROSES
Rosa rugosa*

PERENNIALS
Acaena
   microphylla*
Acanthus mollis
Acanthus spinosus
Achillea
   'Taygetea'*
Alstroemeria Ligtu
   hybrids
Alyssum
   montanum
Anthemis tinctoria*
Armeria
   maritima*
Artemisia
   ludoviciniana*
Asphodeline lutea
Asphodelus albus
Aubrieta hybrids
Aurinia saxatilis
Centaurea
   dealbata*
Centranthus ruber
Convolvulus
   cneorum*
Crambe maritima*
Cynara
   cardunculus
Dianthus
   superbus*
Diascia rigescens*
Dictamnus albus
Echinops ritro*
Eryngium ×
   tripartitum*
Euphorbia
   characias*
Gaura lindheimeri
Gypsophila repens*
Iris unguicularis*
Linum narbonense

Lychnis coronaria
Oenothera
   macrocarpa*
Origanum
   laevigatum*
Osteospermum
   ecklonis*
Penstemon
   barbatus*
Phlomis
   russeliana*
Phlox douglasii*
Salvia patens*
Saponaria
   ocymoides*
Sedum
   spathulifolium*
Sempervivum
   arachnoideum*
Stachys
   byzantina*
Verbascum chaixii*
Zauschneria
   californica

**BULBS, CORMS
AND TUBERS**
Allium giganteum*
Calochortus
   barbatus*
Colchicum
   autumnale*
Crocosmia ×
   crocosmiiflora*
Crocus
   ancyrensis*
Cyclamen
   hederifolium*
Eranthis hyemalis*
Fritillaria
   michailovskyi*
Gladiolus
   communis subsp.
   byzantinus*

Hermodactylus
   tuberosus
Iris danfordiae*
Lilium candidum
Nectaroscordum
   siculum
Nerine bowdenii*
Oxalis
   adenophylla*
Sternbergia lutea*
Tecophylaea
   cyanocrocus
Tulipa linifolia*

**ANNUALS
AND BIENNIALS**
Calendula
   officinalis
Centaurea cyanus
Erysimum
Eschscholzia
   californica
Lavatera trimestris
Limnanthes
   douglasii
Limonium
   sinuatum
Linaria maroccana
Lobularia
   maritima
Salvia viridis*

GRASSES
Festuca glauca*
Helictotrichon
   sempervirens
Hordeum jubatum
Lagurus ovatus
Pennisetum
   alopecuroides*
Stipa gigantea*

WATERSIDE AND BOG PLANTS

Even with a generous selection from the plants listed below, a garden pool would not be complete without submerged oxygenating plants and plants of the pond floor such as water lilies (Nymphaea) that produce long stems and floating leaves. Plants marked M are marginals that thrive with their feet in water.

TREES
Alnus glutinosa*
Populus tremula
   'Pendula'*
Quercus palustris*

Salix × sepucralis
   var. chrysocoma*

SHRUBS
Amelanchier
   lamarckii*
Cornus alba*
Salix hastata

'Wehrhahnii'*
Spiraea ×
   vanhouttei
Symphoricarpos ×
   doorenbosii*

CONIFERS
Metasequoia
   glyptostroboides
Taxodium
   distichum

PERENNIALS
Acorus calamus
  'Variegatus' M
Aruncus dioicus
Astilbe hybrids*
Astilboides
  tabularis
Caltha palustrus M
Darmera peltata
Doronicum
  'Miss Mason' *
Eupatorium
  purpureum*
Filipendula
  ulmaria 'Aurea' *

Gunnera
  manicata*
Hemerocallis
  hybrids*
H. sieboldiana var.
  elegans*
Houttuynia
  cordata
Inula magnifica
Iris ensata
I. laevigata M*
Ligularia
  przewalskii*
Lobelia
  cardinalis*

Lysichiton
  camtschatcensis*
Lysimachia
  nummularia
  'Aurea'
Lythrum salicaria
Mimulus
  cardinalis*
Persicaria
  amplexicaulis*
Pontederia
  cordata M
Primula
  florindae *
Rheum palmatum

R. podophylla*
Trollius ×
  cultorum*
Zantedeschia
  aethiopica M

**BULBS, CORMS
AND TUBERS**
Leucojum
  aestivum*

**GRASSES, GRASS-
LIKE PLANTS AND
BAMBOOS**
Carex elata

'Aurea' M*
Fargesia mureiliae*
Juncus effusus
  'Spiralis' M
Arundo donax
Phalaris
  arundinacea var.
  picta 'Feesey'

FERNS
Onoclea sensibilis
Osmunda regalis
Thelypteris palustris
Woodwardia
  radicans

PLANTS TOLERANT OF DRY SHADE

Areas of dry shade are among the most difficult to plant. Most of the plants suggested here will do better where the ground is reasonably moist but are tenacious even where there is little moisture.

SHRUBS
Aucuba japonica
Daphne laureola
Euonymus
  fortunei
Pachysandra
  terminalis

CLIMBERS
Hedera helix

PERENNIALS
Acanthus mollis
Cornus canadensis
Epimedium
  alpinum*
Euphorbia
  amygdaloides*
Geranium
  phaeum*

Helleborus
  foetidus*
Iris foetidissima
Saxifraga ×
  urbium*
Tellima grandiflora

**BULBS, CORMS
AND TUBERS**
Arum italicum
Cyclamen
  hederifolium*
Hyacinthoides
  non-scriptus*

**ANNUALS AND
BIENNIALS**
Digitalis purpurea

FERNS
Polypodium
  vulgare
Polystichum
  setiferum

PLANTS FOR HEAVY CLAY SOILS

Roses have not been listed separately, almost all roses doing well on reasonably moist clay soils.

TREES
Alnus glutinosa*
Carpinus betulus*
Crataegus
  laevigata*
Cercis canadensis
Eucalyptus gunnii*
Fraxinus ornus*
Ilex × altaclarensis*
Malus × zumi
  'Golden Hornet' *
Populus tremula
  'Pendula' *
Prunus 'Shirotae' *
Quercus robur*
Salix alba*
Sorbus aria*
Tilia × euchlora*

SHRUBS
Abelia ×
  grandiflora*
Aralia elata
Aucuba japonica
Berberis ×
  stenophylla*
Brachyglottis
  Dunedin Group*
Chaenomeles ×
  superba*
Choisya ternata
Cornus alba*
Corylus avellana*
Cotinus coggyria*
Cotoneaster
  frigidus*
Cytisus × praecox*
Deutzia ×
  elegantissima*
Euonymus fortunei
Forsythia ×

intermedia*
Hamamelis ×
  intermedia*
Hibiscus syriacus
Hypericum
  'Rowallane' *
Lonicera nitida*
Mahonia japonica*
Magnolia ×
  soulangeana*
Osmanthus
  delavayi*
Philadelphus
  hybrids*
Potentilla
  fruticosa*
Pyracantha
  hybrids*
Ribes sanguineum*
Salix hastata
  'Wehrhahnii' *
Sambucus
  racemosa*
Skimmia japonica
Spiraea × arguta*
Symphoricarpos ×
  doorenbosii*
Viburnum
  plicatum*
Weigela
  hybrids*

CONIFERS
Abies koreana*
Chamaecyparis
  pisifera*
Juniperus sabina*
Taxodium
  distichum
Taxus baccata*
Thuja plicata*

CLIMBERS
Campsis ×
  tagliabuana*
Celastrus scandens
Clematis
  montana*
Hedera colchica*
Humulus lupulus
Hydrangea
  anomala subsp.
  petiolaris
Lathyrus latifolius
Parthenocissus
  tricuspidata*
Passiflora
  caerulea*
Vitis coignetiae*
Wisteria sinensis*

PERENNIALS
Aconitum 'Newry
  Blue' *
Acanthus mollis*
Achillea ptarmica
  'Boule de Neige' *
Ajuga reptans*
Alchemilla mollis*
Anemone ×
  hybrida*
Aruncus dioicus*
Aster novi-belgii*
Astilbe hybrids*
Bergenia
  purpurascens*
Brunnera
  macrophylla
Caltha palustris*
Darmera peltata
Dodecatheon
  meadia*
Doronicum 'Miss

Mason' *
Epimedium
  grandiflorum*
Eupatorium
  purpureum*
Euphorbia
  amygdaloides
  var. robbiae*
Filipendula
  ulmaria*
Gunnera
  manicata*
Helenium hybrids*
Helleborus
  orientalis*
Hemerocallis
  hybrids*
Hosta fortunei*
Houttuynia
  cordata
Inula magnifica*
Iris sibirica*
Lamium
  maculatum*
Lobelia
  cardinalis*
Lysichiton
  camtschatcensis*
Lysimachia
  clethroides*
Lythrum salicaria*
Mentha suaveolens
  'Variegata' *
Monarda hybrids*
Persicaria
  bistorta*
Phormium tenax*
Polemonium
  caeruleum*
Polygonatum ×
  hybridum*

Pontederia cordata
Primula japonica*
Pulmonaria
  angustifolia*
Ranunculus
  aconitifolius*
Rheum
  palmatum*
Rodgersia
  podophylla*
Rudbeckia fulgida*
Saxifraga ×
  urbium*
Solidago hybrids*
Symphytum ×
  uplandicum
  'Variegatum' *
Trollius ×
  cultorum*
Zantedeschia
  aethiopica

**BULBS, CORMS
AND TUBERS**
Anemone
  nemorosa
Camassia cusickii*
Crocsmia 'Lucifer' *
Eranthis hyemalis
Fritillaria
  meleagris
Galanthus nivalis*
Hyacinthoides
  non-scripta*
Leucojum vernum*
Narcissus
  pseudonarcissus*

**ANNUALS AND
BIENNIALS**
Bellis perennis

Digitalis purpurea*
Mimulus ×
    hybridus
Myosotis sylvatica
Nicotiana hybrids*

GRASSES, GRASS-LIKE PLANTS AND BAMBOOS
Alopecurus
    pratensis
    'Aureovariegatus'*

Carex pendula*
Deschampsia
    caespitosa*
Fargesia nitida*
Miscanthus
    sinensis*

Molinia caerulea
Pleioblastus
    auricomus*

FERNS
Dryopteris

filix-mas*
Matteucia
    struthiopteris
Onoclea sensibilis
Osmunda regalis*
Thelypteris palustris

PLANTS FOR ALKALINE SOILS

The range of plants that can be grown in alkaline conditions varies greatly according to the depth of the soil and its moisture content, the most difficult conditions being shallow soils over chalk.

TREES
Acer negundo*
Aesculus × carnea*
Betula pendula
Carpinus betulus
Cercis siliquastrum
Cornus mas
Crataegus
    laevigata*
Eucryphia ×
    nymansensis
Fagus sylvatica
Fraxinus ornus*
Ilex aquifolium
Magnolia kobus
Malus 'John
    Downie'*
Morus nigra
Populus alba*
Prunus 'Shirofugen'*
Sorbus aria*

SHRUBS
Aucuba japonica
Berberis darwinii*
Brachyglottis
    Dunedin Group*
Buddleja davidii
Buxus
    sempervirens
Ceanothus
    impressus*
Ceratostigma
    willmottianum
Choisya ternata
Cistus ladanifer*
Cotoneaster
    horizontalis*
Cytisus
    battandieri*
Daphne cneorum*
Deutzia longifolia*
Elaeagnus
    angustifolia*
Escallonia 'Iveyi'*
Euonymus
    europaeus*
Forsythia
    suspensa*
Fuchsia
    magellanica*
Hebe cupressoides*
Hibiscus syriacus
Hydrangea aspera
    Villosa Group
Hypericum
    'Rowallane'
Kolkwitzia
    amabilis
Laurus nobilis
Ligustrum
    ovalifolium*
Lonicera ×
    purpusii*
Mahonia
    aquifolium
Osmanthus

delavayi*
Paeonia
    suffruticosa*
Philadelphus
    'Belle Etoile'*
Photinia × fraseri
Pittosporum
    tenuifolium*
Potentilla
    fruticosa*
Pyracantha
    'Teton'*
Rhus typhina*
Rosmarinus
    officinalis
Sambucus
    racemosa*
Sarcococca
    confusa*
Spartium junceum
Spiraea japonica
Stachyurus
    chinensis*
Symphoricarpos ×
    doorenbosii*
Syringa vulgaris*
Viburnum tinus
Weigela florida*

CONIFERS
× Cupressocyparis
    lawsoniana
Cedrus libani*
Cupressus
    sempervirens*
Gingko biloba
Juniperus
    communis*
Pinus mugo*
Thuja
    occidentalis*

CLIMBERS
Actinidia
    kolomikta
Akebia quinata
Ampelopsis
    glandulosa var.
    brevipedunculata*
Campsis ×
    tagliabuana
    'Madame Galen'*
Celastrus scandens
Clematis montana*
Eccremocarpus
    scaber
Fallopia
    baldschuanica
Hedera helix*
Hydrangea
    anomala subsp.
    petiolaris
Jasminum
    officinale*
Lathyrus latifolius*
Lonicera
    periclymenum*

Parthenocissus
    tricuspidata
Passiflora caerulea
Trachelospermum
    jasminoides
Vitis coignetiae*
Wisteria sinensis*

ROSES
Rosa 'Frau Dagmar
    Hastrup'
R. Fruhlingsgold
R. 'Fruhlingsmorgen'
R. pimpinellifolia
R. 'Roseraie de l'Haÿ'
R. rugosa

PERENNIALS
Acanthus mollis*
Achillea
    filipendulina*
Alchemilla mollis*
Alyssum
    montanum*
Anchusa
    caespitosa*
Anemone ×
    hybrida*
Anthemis tinctoria*
Aquilegia vulgaris*
Armeria maritima*
Artemisia
    ludoviciana*
Aubrieta hybrids
Aurinia saxatilis
Baptisia australis
Bergenia
    cordifolia*
Brunnera
    macrophylla
Campanula
    lactiflora*
Catananche
    caerulea
Centaurea
    dealbata*
Centranthus ruber
Convallaria
    majalis
Coreopsis
    verticillata*
Delphinium
    elatum*
Dianthus alpinus*
Doronicum
    'Miss Mason'*
Echinops ritro*
Eremurus
    robustus*
Eryngium
    alpinum*
Euphorbia
    griffithii*
Galega officinalis*
Geranium
    pratense*
Gypsophyla

paniculata*
Helenium
    'Moerheim
    Beauty'*
Helleborus
    orientalis*
Hemerocallis
    hybrids*
Hepatica nobilis*
Heuchera
    cylindrica*
Knautia
    macedonica
Kniphofia 'Royal
    Standard'*
Iris 'Florentina'*
Linum
    narbonense*
Liriope muscari
Lychnis
    chalcedonica*
Paeonia lactiflora*
Papaver orientale*
Phlox douglasii*
Primula florindae*
Pulsatilla vulgaris*
Ramonda myconii
Raoulia australis*
Salvia nemorosa*
Saponaria
    ocymoides*
Saxifraga
    longifolia*
Scabiosa
    caucasica*
Verbascum chaixii*
Veronica spicata*

BULBS, CORMS AND TUBERS
Anemone blanda*
Chionodoxa luciliae
    Gigantea Group*
Colchicum
    speciosum*
Crocosmia 'Lucifer'*
Crocus speciosus*
Cyclamen
    hederifolium*
Eranthis hyemalis
Fritillaria imperialis
Galanthus nivalis*
Gladiolus communis
    subsp. byzantinus*
Hermodactylus
    tuberosus
Iris histrioides*
Leucojum
    aestivum*
Lilium candidum*
Muscari
    armeniacum*
Narcissus
    pseudonarcissus*
Scilla siberica*
Tulipa clusiana*

ANNUALS AND BIENNIALS
Alcea rosea
Antirrhinum
    majus
Calendula
    officinalis
Callistephus
    chinensis
Centaurea cyanus*
Clarkia amoena*
Cosmos bipinnatus
Dianthus
    barbatus*
Erysimum cheiri*
Helianthus annuus
Iberis umbellata*
Lathyrus odoratus*
Lavatera trimestris
Limonium
    sinuatum
Linaria
    maroccana*
Lobelia erinus*
Lobularia
    maritima
Lunaria annua
Malope trifida
Matthiola incana*
Myosotis sylvatica*
Nemesia strumosa*
Nemophila
    maculata*
Nigella damascena*
Papaver rhoeas*
Petunia hybrids
Verbascum
    bombyciferum*
Verbena hybrids*
Salvia viridis*
Tagetes hybrids*
Zinnia elegans

GRASSES
Briza maxima*
Festuca glauca*
Helictotrichon
    sempervirens
Stipa gigantea*

FERNS
Asplenium
    trichomanes
Polypodium
    vulgare
Polystichum
    setiferum*

PLANTS FOR MOIST ACID CONDITIONS

The plants listed below require or thrive in moist acid soils, many of them being woodland plants. Roses have not been listed individually, most thriving in neutral to acid soils that are well-drained but reasonably moist.

TREES
Betula utilis
Magnolia campbellii
Nyssa sylvatica
Stewartia
  pseudocamellia

SHRUBS
Acer palmatum*
Amelanchier
  lamarckii*
Callistemon
  citrinus*
Calluna vulgaris
Camellia ×
  williamsii*
Cassiope
  'Edinburgh'*
Cornus kousa*
Corylopsis
  pauciflora*
Daboecia
  cantabrica
Enkianthus
  campanulatus*
Erica carnea*
Eucryphia

glutinosa*
Fothergilla major*
Gaultheria
  mucronata*
Hamamelis ×
  intermedia*
Hydrangea
  macrophylla*
Kalmia latifolia*
Lithodora diffusa
Lupinus arboreus
Magnolia stellata*
Pachysandra
  terminalis
Pieris formosa*
R. yakushimanum*

CONIFERS
Chamaecyparis
  obtusa*
× Cupressocyparis
  leyandii
Juniperus
  horizontalis*
Larix kaempferi*
Metasequoia
  glyptostroboides

Picea abies*
Pinus parviflora
Taxodium
  distichum
Tsuga heterophylla*

CLIMBERS
Berberidopsis
  corallina
Lapageria rosea
Tropaeolum
  speciosum

PERENNIALS
Baptisia australis
Cornus canadensis
Corydalis
  cashmeriana*
Gentiana sino-
  ornata*
Iris innominata*
Kirengeshoma
  palmata
Lewisia cotyledon*
Liriope muscari
Lupinus hybrids
Meconopsis

betonicifolia*
Phlox divaricata
  subsp. laphamii
  'Chattahoochee'*
Polygonatum
  hookeri*
Primula frondosa*
Roscoea humeana*
Sanguinaria
  canadensis
Saxifraga 'Peter Pan'*
Smilacina racemosa
Soldanella alpina*
Tricyrtis
  formosana *
Trillium
  grandiflorum *
Uvularia
  grandiflora *

**BULBS, CORMS
AND TUBERS**
Arisaema
  camdidissimum*
Begonia hybrids
  (Tuberhybrida)*
Cardiocrinum

giganteum
Erythronium
  revolutum*
Fritillaria
  camschatcensis*
Lilium canadense*
Narcissus
  cylcamineus*
Rhodohypoxis
  baurii*

**GRASSES AND
GRASS-LIKE
PLANTS**
Carex elata 'Aurea'*
Descahmpsia
  caespitosa*
Luzula nivea*
Molinea caerulea*

FERNS
Blechnum penna-
  marina*
Osmunda regalis
Polypodium
  vulgare

PLANTS FOR COASTAL GARDENS

The plants in the following selection to some extent tolerate strong winds and salt. However, all of these benefit from shelter until they are established.

TREES
Arbutus unedo*
Cordyline australis
Crataegus
  monogyna*
Eucalyptus
  pauciflora subsp.
  niphophila
Genista aetnensis
Ilex × altaclarensis*
Populus alba*
Quercus ilex*
Salix alba*
Sorbus aria*

CONIFERS
× Cupressocyparis
  leylandii
Cupressus
  macrocarpa*
Juniperus
  communis*
Pinus mugo*

SHRUBS
Aucuba japonica
Brachyglottis
  Dunedin Group
  'Sunshine'
Buddleja davidia
Calluna vulgaris
Ceanothus hybrids*
Choisya ternata
Cistus hybrids*
Cotoneaster
  conspicuus*
Cytisus scoparius*
Daboecia
  cantabrica

Elaeagnus ×
  ebbingei*
Escallonia
  hybrids*
Euonymus
  japonicus*
Fuchsia
  magellanica*
Garrya elliptica
Genista lydia*
Hebe hybrids*
Helianthemum
  hybrids*
Hydrangea
  macrophylla
Laurus nobilis
Lavandula ×
  intermedia*
Lavatera
  'Barnsley' *
Leycesteria
  formosa
Lonicera pileata
Lupinus arboreus
Pittosporum
  tenuifolium*
Potentilla
  fruticosa*
Pyracantha
  hybrids*
Rhamnus
  alaternus
Rosmarinus
  officinalis
Ruta graveolens
Sambucus
  racemosa
Santolina chamae-
  cyparissus*

Spartium junceum
Tamarix tetandra*
Thymus vulgaris*
Viburnum tinus
Yucca filamentosa*

ROSES
Rosa 'Blanche
  Double de
  Coubert'
R. 'Roseraie de l'Haÿ'
R. rugosa

CLIMBERS
Bougainvillea ×
  buttiana*
Fallopia
  baldschuanica
Lathyrus latifolius
Solanum crispum*

PERENNIALS
Achillea hybrids*
Agave americana*
Anthemis punctata
  subsp. cupaniana*
Armeria maritima*
Asphodeline lutea
Aubrieta hybrids
Artemisia
  absinthium*
Bergenia cordifolia*
Campanula
  portenschlagiana*
Catananche
  caerulea
Centaurea
  hypoleuca*
Centranthus ruber

Crambe maritima
Echinops ritro*
Erodium corsicum*
Euphorbia
  characias*
Geranium
  cinereum*
Gypsophila repens
Kniphofia
  triangularis*
Linaria purpurea
Lychnis flos-jovis
Morina longifolia
Origanum
  laevigatum*
Osteospermum
  jucundum*
Phlomis russeliana
Phormium tenax*
Salvia officinalis*
Scabiosa caucasica
Sedum
  'Herbstfreude' *
Sempervivum
  tectorum*
Stachys byzantina
Veronica spicata*

**BULBS, CORMS
AND TUBERS**
Allium cristophii*
Anemone
  coronaria*
Colchicum
  agrippinum*
Crocus meadius*
Cyclamen
  hederifolium
Hyacinthoides

non-scripta
Nerine bowdenii*
Sternbergia lutea

**ANNUALS AND
BIENNIALS**
Antirrhinum majus
Brachyscome
  iberidifolia
Bracteantha
  bracteata
Calendula
  officinalis
Dorotheanthus
  bellidiformis
Eryngium
  maritimum
Eschscholzia
  californica
Iberis umbellata
Limonium
  sinuatum
Linaria maroccana
Linum
  grandiflorum
Lobularia maritima
Malope trifida
Matthiola incana
Salvia viridis
Tagetes French
  Group

GRASSES
Briza maxima*
Festuca glauca
Helictotrichon
  sempervirens
Hordeum jubatum
Lagurus ovatus

GENERAL INDEX

A
acid soil 20, 71, 78, 80-1
algae 84, 87
alkaline soil 18, 20, 78-9
alpines 40-1, 77, 92-5
  see also mountains; rocky landscapes
annuals 58, 62, 311-24
  wildflowers 64
architectural features 68-9, 74
associations 8, 11
atolls 47
Austin, David 61
autumn, herbaceous borders 53-5

B
bamboos 325-32
beds
  see also borders
  raised 81, 94-5
  scree 93-4
berries 61
biennials 62, 311-24
Bloom, Alan 55
bog gardens 38, 86-7
borders
  herbaceous 52-5
  in shade 74-5
  perennials 63
  sunny mixed 58-63
boreal forest 24
bromeliads 29
bulbs 279-310
  alpine 41, 42
  borders 54, 62
  grasslands 65
  scrubland 31
  woodland 65, 72-3

C
cacti 45, 91
calcicoles 78
calcifuges 78
canopy 18-19, 28-9, 66-7
Cape heaths 36
carnivorous plants 39
carr 38-9
chalk, wildflowers 65, 78
chalk downland 35
chaparral 30-1
chernozem 20, 34
clay 19, 82
climate 11, 16-21
climbers 29, 68-9, 175-88
coastal areas 46-7, 77
coastal gardens 96-7
common names 7
communities 12, 16, 18, 21
conifers 22, 24-5, 165-74
coppicing 19, 23, 62
cordillera 25

D
deciduous trees 22-3, 67
desert 44-5
desert gardens 90-1

drainage 11, 82-3, 93-5
drought 18, 20
dry gardens 88-90
dry stone walls 94-5

E
Edwardian borders 58
emergents 28, 38
ephemerals 44
epiphytes 29
evaporation 88
evolution 46
  flowering plants 24

F
fens 38
ferns 325-32
fire
  conifers 24
  heath 36
  scrubland 31
flowers
  borders 52
  evolution 24
  herbaceous 52-5
  meadows 64-5
  perennials 56-7
  shrubs 60-1
  trees 67
Foerster, Karl 56
foliage
  shade 74-5
  shrubs 59
  trees 67
forest 16, 22-5
  light 18-19, 22-3
  tropical 26-9
formal planting, trees 66-7
frost 16-17, 70
fynbos 30-1

G
garrigue 30-1
germination 17-18
gley 19
grasses 32-5, 325-32
grasslands 32-5
grazing 35
growing conditions 7-9, 11-12

H
hardiness 50
hardpan 33
heathland 36-7
heather gardens 80-1
herbaceous borders 52-5
Highdown 78
humidity 17-18
hybrids 12
hydrangeas 71
hypertufa 95

I
irrigation 88
island beds 55
isotherms 16

J
Jekyll, Gertrude 52, 53
June gap 54

L
land clearance 22
lawns
  flowered 65
  trees 66
lianas 29
lichen 36
light 18-19, 50
  see also shade; sun
  epiphytes 29
  woodland management 23
lime 76, 78-9
llanos 33

M
mallee scrub 30
mangroves 46-7
marginals 39, 85
matorral 30-1
meadows 35
  wildflowers 64-5
minerals 20
mixed forest 25
moisture 17-18, 76-7, 88
montane forest 40
moorland 36
mountain fynbos 36
mountains 40-3
mowing 35, 65
mulch 51, 88

N
Nicolson, Sir Harold 53
nutrients 17, 19, 20, 33

O
orchids 29, 100-1
orientation 11

P
pampas 34
paths 95
peat 19, 36, 38-9
perennials 56-7, 63, 197-278
  wildflowers 64
  woodland 73
pH 20, 51, 78-9
photosynthesis 17, 18, 19
phrygana 30-1
pioneer plants 18, 24, 36
pneumatophores 39, 46
podzols 19
pollarding 23
ponds 38, 84-7
prairies 33-4
precipitation 17-18

R
rainfall 17-18
rainforests 16, 19, 21, 25-9
ramblers see climbers
reedmaces 35
reeds 35
rhododendrons 70-1, 78-9
Robinson, William 64
rock gardens 93-4
rock plants 42, 92-5

see also alpines
rocky landscapes 40-3
root hairs 17
roses 61, 189-96
  lime tolerance 79
  shade 74-5
rushes 35

S
Sackville-West, Vita 53
salinity 20, 46
salt marshes 46
sand dunes 47
savanna 33
scree beds 93-4
scrubland 30-1
sedges 35
selection 7-8, 12
self-seeding 57
shade 18-19, 51
  borders 74-5
  trees 23, 67, 98-9
  shrubs 121-64
    desert 44-5
    flowering 60-1
    foliage 59
    roses 61
    scrubland 30-1
    shade 74-5
    waterside 87
    woodland 70-1
Sissinghurst 53
snow 17-18
soil 19-20
  chemistry 12
  moisture 17-18
  moisture-retentive 82-3
  pH 20, 51, 78-9
  sandy 96-7
staking 55, 63, 74
stems 61-2
steppes 34
stilt roots 46
stomata 17, 33
subtropical gardens 98-101
succulents 45
summer, dry gardens 90
sun 18-19, 50-1
sun-loving plants 52-69
supports, climbers 68-9
synonyms 8, 104

T
taiga 24
temperature 16-17
terracing 95
tomillares 30-1
transpiration 16-17
tree line 19-20, 40
trees 66-7, 107-20
  see also forest; woodland
  dry ground 89
  seaside 97
  waterside 87
  wet ground 39
trellis 69
tropical forests 26-9
tropical gardens 98-101
tufa 95

tundra 21, 36-7
  alpine 40
  soil 19

U
understorey 18

V
variegation 75
von Humboldt, Alexander 16

W
wallflowers, borders 54
walls
  climbers 68-9
  dry stone 94-5
water 38-9
  soil 17-18
water gardens 84-7
water lilies 84
weather 20
wildflower meadows 64-5
wind 16, 20-1
woodland 16, 22-5
  floor 72-3
  shrubs 70-1
  trees 66
woodland gardens 66
Wright, Frank Lloyd 90

X
xeriscaping 90

Z
zonation, mountains 16, 40

PLANT INDEX

Page numbers in *italics* refer to illustrations. Plants in **bold** represent 250 of David Joyce's favourite plants. There are cross-references for genus synonyms as well as for common names. Those plants with an AGM (Award of Garden Merit) are marked with an asterisk.

Picture Credits

Key	a = above	b = bottom	c = centre	l = left
	m = middle	r = right	t = top	

All photographs taken by Jerry Harpur unless stated otherwise.

PRELIMINARY PAGES AND INTRODUCTION
Photographer's credits: 1 RHS Wisley; Surrey; 2 RHS Rosemoor, Great Torrington, Devon; 3 Park Farm, Great Waltham; 4-5 designers: Oehme & van Sweden Associates, Washington DC; 6 Beth Chatto, Elmstead Market, Essex; 8 t Beth Chatto as before; 8 b RHS Wisely; 9 Rita & Samuel Robert, Nantucket Island, Mass. Architect Edward Knowles; 10 The Garden House, Buckland Monachorum, Devon; 11 t Bellevue Botanic Garden, Seattle; 11 b Savill Garden, Englefield Green, Surrey; 12 t Tresco Abbey Gardens, Isles of Scilly; 12 b Beth Chatto as before; 13 t Tresco Abbey Gardens, Isles of Scilly; 13 b Beth Chatto; 14-15 "Les Quatres Vents", La Malbaie, Quebec, Canada.

PLANT COMMUNITIES IN NATURE

Bruce Coleman Ltd
Stephen Bond 20-21 b; Fred Bruemmer 46 tr; Bob and Clara Calhoun 18 rm; Mr P Clement 36 abr; Alain Compost 28 abr; Derek Croucher 43 tr; Gerald Cubitt 30-31c; 33 rm; Adrian Davies 47 t; Geoff Dore 34 bl; 41 tr 42 tr; MPL Fogden 16 rm, 17 rm, 28-29 b; Jeff Foott Productions 19 b, 44-45 b; Christer Frederiksson 28 l; Sir Jeremy Grayson 36 tr, 37 tr; 39 tl; Peter A Hinchliffe 46 tl; Janos Jurka 22-23b; CC Lockwood 45 tc, 46 bl; Luiz Claudio Marigo 28 btr & br; George McCarthy 42 tl; Dr Eckart Pott 38 br; Marie Read 22 bl; Hans Reinhard 18 tr 19 t; 35 tr, 40 t; Dr Frieder Sauer 34-35 t; Dr Sabine M Schmidt 34 ml; John Shaw 23 ar, 30-31 b, 34 tl, 40 rm; 45 br; Kim Taylor 44 bl, 45 tr; G Ziesler 24 t, 38 t, 43 tl.

Robert Harding Picture Library Ltd
36 btr; Norma Joseph 32 t; John Miller 47 br.

Images Colour Library Ltd
16 t, 17 t, btl, br, 18 tl, 21 c, 22-23 c, 23 br, 30 tl, 40-41 b, 42-43 b, 44 cb, 44-45 t, 45 cr.

Impact Photos
Colin Jones 21 br; David Palmer 27 c.

NHPA
L Campbell 39 tr; Paal Hermansen 36-37 b; Helio and Van Ingen 35 br; Alberto Nardi 46-47 b; Rod Planck 33 tl; Christophe Ratier 32 c; David Woodfall 39 bl.

Jerry Pavia
20 t; 24-25 c; 41 ml.

Wildlight Photo Agency Ltd
Mark Lang 24-25 b; 26 c; Milton Wordley 31 tr.

PLANT ASSOCIATIONS IN THE GARDEN
Photographers credits: 48-49 Dr J R Smart "Marwood Hill", Nr Barnstaple, Devon; 50 t Beth Chatto's woodland; 50-51 b RHS Wisely, Surrey; 51 t Garden in the Woods, Framingham, Mass.; 51 m Great Dixter, Northiam, Sussex; 51 b The Old Rectory, Kirby Bedon, Norfolk; 52 t House of Pitmuies, Guthrie-by-Forfar, Tayside; 52 b Carl Niels, Dallas, Texas; 53 l Xa Tollemache's design for The Evening Standard at RHS Chelsea 1997; 53 tr Beth Chatto as before; 53 br Manor House, Heslington, York; 54 t Springfields Garden, Spalding, Lincs.; 54 bl Peter Wooster, Roxbury, Connecticut; 54 br Linda Teague, Del Mar, Ca.; 55 t Manor House, Heslington, York; 55 b Rita & Sam Robert, Nantucket, Mass.; 56 t The Garden House as before; 56 bl Beth Chatto as before; 56-57 Beth Chatto; 57 t The Garden House; 58 t Rita & Sam Robert as before; 58-59 Eastgrove Cottage Garden, Sankyns Green, Nr Worcs.; 59 tc Designers: Charles Price & Glen Whitty, Seattle, Wa.; 59tr Eastgrove Cottage as before; 59 b RHS Rosemoor as before; 60 tl Tessa King-Farlow, Edgbaston, Birmingham; 60 m Savill Garden as before; 60 b RHS Wisely; 61 tl Stone House Cottage, Stone, Worcs.; 61 tr Designer: Tessa Hobbs, The Red House, Kirby Cane, Suffolk; 61 b Saling Hall, Great Saling, Essex; 62 l The Manor House, Bledlow, Bucks; 62 tr Great Dixter as before; 62-63 "The Dingle", Welshpool, Powys; 64-65 t Writtle Horticultural College, Essex; 64 m Designer: Sylvia Oxenford, Patagonia; 64-65 b Great Dixter as before; 65 m Great Dixter; 66 t "Dolwen", Llanrhaeadr-ym-Mochnant, Powys; 66 b Westonbirt Arboretum, Glos.; 67 t House of Pitmuies as before; 67 m Blandy Gardens, Madeira; 67 b Highdown, Goring-by-Sea, West Sussex; 68 tl Burford House, Tenbury Wells, Worcs.; 68-69 Helmingham Hall, Stowmarket, Suffolk; 68 br Designer: Tessa Hobbs as before; 69 tr Tessa King-Farlow as before; 69 bl Shelia McQueen, Leverstock Green, Herts.; 70 tl Barnsley House, Barnsley, Glos.; 70 bl Valley Garden, Englefield, Surrey, 70-71 Exbury Gardens, Nr Southampton, Hants; 71 tmr Designer: Margaret Locket, Seattle; 71 br Beth Chatto as before; 72 l Designer: Dan Hinkley, "Heronswood", Seattle, Wa.; 72 tr Mr & Mrs Lucas, Castle Hedingham, Ex.; 72-73 Exbury Gardens as before; 73 Winterhur, Wilmington, Delaware; 74 Foxgrove Plants, Enborne, Berks.; 74 ml Eastgrove Cottage as before; 74 mr Mr & Mrs Lucas as before; 74-75 b Dr. Chris Grey Wilson, Suffolk; 75 r Savill Garden, Englefield Green, Surrey; 76t Dr & Mrs Stalbow, Stanmore; 76 b "Inverewe", Poolewe, Ross & Cromarty; 77 t Joe Eck & Wayne Winterrowd, Readsboro, Vermont; 77 mr RHS Wisely as before; 77 b Beth Chatto gravel garden as before; 78 tl Park Farm, Chelmsford, Essex; 78b Ebrington Village, Glos.; 78-79 t Highdown, Goring-by-Sea, Sussex; 79 tr Valley Garden, Englefield Green; 79 b Stone House Cottage as before; 80 t,m,b all Valley Garden; 81 lb & rb Savill Garden as before; 82-83 t "Dolwen" as before; 82-83 m Wollerton Old Hall, Wollerton, Shropshire; 83 t Peter Wooster as before; 83 b Beth Chatto; 84 tl "Dolwen" as before; 84-85 Beth Chatto; 84 br Burnby Hall Gardens, Pocklington, Yorks.; 85 b Designer: Ken Ruzicka, Patchogue, NY; 86 m Beth Chatto; 86 b Wave Hill, The Bronx, New York; 86-87 "Marwood Hill" as before; 87 t Beth Chatto as before; 87 b Burnby Gardens as before; 88 t Beth Chatto; 88 m Sun House, Long Melford, Suffolk; 88-89 b Moat House, Cockfield, Suffolk; 89 t Beth Chatto's gravel garden as before; 89 br Beth Chatto; 90 t Tresco Abbey Gardens as before; 90 r Domaine Rayol, Rayol, South of France , designer: Gilles Clement; 91 t Gardenworld, Keysborough, Victoria, Australia; 91 m&b Huntington Botanic Garden, Ca.; 92 l Eastgrove Cottage Garden; 92 tr & 92-93 m The Garden House as before; 92-93 b Dr & Mrs Rivers, Balscote, Oxon.; 93 t Foxgrove Plants, Enborne, Berks.; 94 l Sylvia Oxenford, Patagonia; 94 r Highdown as before; 95 t Shepherd House, Inveresk, Midlothian; 95 m Burnby Hall as before; 95 b Shepherd House as before; 96 tl Domaine Rayol as before; 96 bl Tresco as before; 97 t Mme Ferrari, Hyères, South of France; 97 b Inverewe, Poolewe, Ross & Cromarty; 98 t Orchid Garden, Singapore Botanic; 98 bl Mrs Ileana de Teran, Costa Rica; 98-99 Orchid Garden, Singapore as before; 99 tr Fern Valley, The Domain, Auckland, New Zealand; 99 mr Fairchild Tropical Garden, Miami, Fla; 99 br on a house wall in Funchal, Madeira; 100 tl Wally Berg's Garden, Miami; 100 bl Bok Tower Gardens, Lake Wales, Fla.; 100 br Longwood Gardens, Kennett Square, Pennsylvania; 101 tl Mrs McLemare, Miami; 101 tr &101 b Orchid Garden, Singapore Botanic.

DIRECTORY

Andrew Lawson Photography
104; Trees: 106 c; 107 r; 108 lb; 109 cb & r; 110 rb; 111 lt & rt; 113 lt; 115 l; 116 l; 118 r; Shrubs: 125 c; 130 lb; 132 l & cb; 135 r; 137 c; 146 l; 150 l & cb; 157 l & r; 158 lb; 161 c & r; 162 rt & rb Conifers: 166 ct; 169 c; 171 l; 173 c; 174 lt & c; Roses: 192 lt & lb; Perennials: 199 cb; 200 c; 201 cb; 203 c; 205 l; 214 rb; 217 lt; 221 l & c; 245 r; 247 lt; 251 r; 258 l; 272 c & r; 276 c; Bulbs, Corms, and Tubers: 298 c; Annuals and Biennials: 312 ct; 313 cb; 314 r; 324 l; Bamboos, Grasses, and Grasslike Plants: 326 cb; 328 lt; 329 rb.

Photos Horticultural
Trees: 107 ct; 114 r; 117 c & rt; Shrubs: 124 c; 129 cb & rt; 144 c; Conifers: 167 rt; 168 cb; 171 rb; 173 lt; Climbers: 176 l; 177 c; 178 l; 181 l; 186 l & r; 188 c; Perennials: 202 r; 210 l; 216 l; 219 ct; 223 rb; 228 lb; 232 r; 236 cb; 243 l; 245 ct; 254 cb; 262 ct & r; 268 ct; 270 ct & cb; 271 c; 273 l; 275 cb; 276 l; Bulbs, Corms, and Tubers: 291 l; 294 l; 295 cb; 306 c; 308 c; Annuals and Biennials: 313 l; 314 l & ct & cb; 315 rt; 316 c; 317 rb; 318 cb & r; 319 cb & r; 320 cb; 321 c & r; 322 lb & rb; 323 r; Bamboos, Grasses, and Grasslike Plants: 328 lb; 329 lb & rt; 332 c; Ferns: 334 c; 336 l.

Clive Nichols Garden Pictures
Perennials: 250 ct.

John Glover Photography
Perennials: 216 rb; 217 r; 220 r; 224 cb; 247 ct; 263 r.

Bruce Coleman Ltd
Perennials: 207 lt: Sir Jeremy Grayson.

The Garden Picture Library
Ferns: 336 rb.

Author's Acknowledgments

I regret the lack of space to record the influence of individual gardeners and their gardens in this book, not to mention countless landscapes where plants grow in the wild. But it is a pleasure to acknowledge here the enormous debt I owe to others for information and to recognize humbly the many influences that have helped to form my opinions.

Many people have played a role in the making of this book, some of whom I cannot adequately thank. First among these is Caroline Davison, the project editor, who has shown extraordinary commitment, great ability as an organizer, and keen judgement during a testing production schedule. I also gratefully acknowledge the enormous amount of work put in by the editors Jane Chapman and Stella Vayne, and by the art editor, Paul Tilby. The work of Jerry and Marcus Harpur and the other photographers speaks for itself.

I join the publishers in thanking the following individuals for their help in compiling this book: Steven Bradley, Cathy Buchanan, Liz Dobbs, Sue Fisher, Jenny Hendy, and John Swithinbank.

Photographer's Acknowledgments

Jerry Harpur would like to thank Susan Rowley for her conscientious help in the editing of his transparencies, liaising with the publisher, and keeping delivery to schedule. Without her, and his son Marcus, who photographed many of the plants and some of the gardens in Great Britain, this book would not have been possible.

He would also like to thank the following garden owners, nurseries, and designers for their generous cooperation:

Jacques Amand Ltd., Stanmore, Middlx; Ruth Bancroft Garden, Walnut Creek, Ca.; D. Barker, NCCPG Epimediums Collection, Danbury, Essex; Bellevue Botanical Garden, Seattle; Blandy Gardens, Madeira; Botanic Gardens, Funchal, Madeira; Rupert Bowlby, Reigate, Surrey; Broadleigh Gardens, Bishops Hull, Somerset; Burnby Hall, Pocklington, Yorks.; Sheila Chapman, Chelmsford, Essex; Molly Chappellet, Napa Valley, Ca.; Beth Chatto, Elmstead Market, Essex; Bradenham Hall, Norfolk; Simone de Chazal, Funchal, Madeira; "Chiffchaffs", Bourton, Dorset; Mr & Mrs N Coote, Oxford, Oxon.; Copford Bulbs, Colchester, Essex; The Dingle Nursery, Welshpool, Wales; "Dolwen", Llarhaeadr-ym-Mochnant, Powys; The Domain, Auckland, New Zealand; Domaine Rayol, Rayol, France; Eastgrove Cottage Garden, nr. Worcester; Joe Eck and Wayne Winterrowd, Readsboro, Vt.; Exbury Gardens, Hants; Foxgrove Plants, Enborne, Berks.; Sonny Garcia, San Francisco, Ca.; Gardenworld, Keysborough, Vic., Australia; Garden House, Buckland Monachorum, Devon; "Glen Chantry", Wickambishops, Essex; Great Dixter, Northiam, Sussex, "Heronswood", Kingston, Seattle; "Heronswood", Dromona, Vic., Australia; Hillier Arboretum, Hants; "Highdown", Goring-by-Sea, Sussex; Hoecroft Plants, nr Dereham, Norfolk; V. H. Humphrey, Dorking, Surrey; Huntington Botanic, LA, Ca.; W.E Th. Ingwersen, East Grinstead, Sussex; La Casella, Opio, South of France; Langthorns Plantery, Dunmow, Essex; Rod & Jane Leeds, nr Lavenham, Norfolk; Philippe Levrat, Hyères, France; Lincluden Nursery, Bisley, Surrey; Margaret Locket, Seattle, Wa.; Longwood Gardens, Kennett Square, Pa.; Manor House, Heslington, York; "Marwood Hill", nr Barnstaple, Devon; New York Botanical Garden; Paradise Centre, Bures, Suffolk; Parc Bagatelle, Paris, France; Park Farm, Chelmsford, Essex; Plantsman Nursery, Okehampton, Devon; Potterton & Martin, Nr Caistor, Lincs.; RHS Hyde Hall, Rettendon, Essex; RHS Rosemoor, Great Torrington, Devon; Rougham Hall Nurseries, Bury St. Edmunds, Suffolk; Royal Botanic Garden, Kirstenbosch, RSA; Royal Botanic Garden, Melbourne, Australia; Royal Botanic Garden, Kew, Surrey; Royal National Rose Society, St Albans, Herts.; Susan Ryley, Victoria, BC, Canada; Saling Hall, Essex; Savill Garden, Englefield Green, Surrey; Scott Arboretum, Swarthmore, Pa.; Secrett's Nursery, Milford, Surrey; Shepherd House, Inveresk, Midlothian; Singapore Botanic Garden, Springfields Gardens, Spalding, Lincs.; Stone House Cottage, Stone, Worcs.; Sun House, Long Melford, Suffolk; Linda Teague, Del Mar, Ca.; Ileana de Teran, Costa Rica; Tresco Abbey Gardens, Isles of Scilly; Villa Roquebrune, Cannes; J. Walkers Bulbs, nr. Spalding, Lincs.; Wave Hill, The Bronx, New York; Westonbirt Arboretum, Glos.; Wildflower Research Centre, Austin, Texas; Winterthur; RHS Wisely, Surrey; Wollerton Old Hall, Shropshire; Peter Wooster, Roxbury, Connecticut; Writtle Horticultural College, Essex.